To Noreen,

Happy Christmas
Happy New Year
&
Happy Reading

Love,
John

A TREASURY OF
NEW ENGLAND
FOLKLORE

A TREASURY OF
NEW ENGLAND
FOLKLORE

STORIES, BALLADS, AND TRADITIONS
OF YANKEE FOLK

Revised Edition

Edited by B. A. BOTKIN

*There is more than humor in the saying that New England is a state
of mind. There is New England, wherever New Englanders go.*
　　　　　　　　　　　　　　　—William Chauncy Langdon

BONANZA BOOKS · NEW YORK

CONTENTS

Introduction   xviii

PART ONE: FABULOUS YANKEES
I. THE YANKEE'S REPUTATION

Introduction   2
     The Fabulous Yankee—The Yankee Clown—Yankee Wits and Sages—
     Sharp Yankees—Village Store and Tavern Humor—Practical Jokers
Yankees and Englishmen   7
     Corn Cobs Twist Your Hair   7
     Captain Basil Hall and the Countryman   9
     Fanny Kemble and the Yankee Farmer   10
     The Road to Walpole   10
     Provincial Phraseology and Hospitality   11
     Comic Yankee Servants   11
     A Yankee in London: Buying Gape-Seed   12
     The Yorkshireman of America   13
     Yorkshire Stories   14
         I'm Yorkshire   14
         My Dog Is Yorkshire, Too   15
         Yorkshire   15
Tricks of the Trade   16
     Peddler Humor   16
     A Watch Trade   16
     Razor-Strop Trade   17
     Wooden Clocks and Wooden Oats   18
     Grandma Willey's Chair   20
     A Deal in Timberland   21
Horse Jockeys   22
     From Nags to Riches   22
     The Chestnut Mare   23
     Playing the Game   25
     A Dependable Horse   25
     His Father's Horse   27
     A First-Rate Setter   28
Smart Merchants and Customers   29
     Sam Temple's Store: A Rhyming Advertisement   29
     Cordwood   30
     Deaconing   32
     As Good as His Word   33
     Turning Water into Grog   33
     Paying for the Cider   34
     The Egg, the Darning-Needle, and the Treat   35
     Paying for the Stolen Butter   35
     The Soap Cure   38
     The Stolen Cheese   38
     Who Stole the Pork?   39
     Hazing New Clerks   39
     No Store for Him   39
     The Lazy Shopkeeper   40
     Grindstone Out of Cheese   40
Yankee Workmen and Businessmen   41
     The Clever Blacksmith   41
     Too Good to Spoil   41
     Boots and Shoes   42
     For Knowing How   43
     A Day's Pay   44
     "Make a Job or Take a Job": A Yankee Work Saga   44
         Working on the Farm   44
         Railroading   45

Irishman Stories 46
Getting Rid of the Deadwood 47
Chicopee Dam 47
Depression Jobs 48
Road Work 49
Joe Dago, Logging Boss 49
George Van Dyke 50
Jams and Stunts 50
Beans 51
The Loggers and the Circus Fellows 51
Save the Peavies 51
The Drummer and the Stagecoach 53
Yankee Drummer Stories 54

II. LOCAL CHARACTERS

Introduction 58
"Characters"—Droll Yankees—Yankee Wit
Country People and Storytellers 61
Ghosts 61
The Ghost in the Attic 61
Halloween Prank 62
Kicking the Pig 62
Sorting the Pigs 63
Breaking Steers 64
The Off Ox 64
A Deal in Oxen 64
The Shower 65
Wild Blueberries 66
A Byword 67
Shutting the Old Man Up 67
Coming of Age 67
Jack and Hudson 68
A Calm Man 68
Apple Cider 69
The Sheriff and the Shoes 69
Model T 70
The Critic 71
Why Ansel Rawson Never Joined the Grange 71
Oren Wilder and the White Stones 72
Martin Richardson Stayed 72
The Electric Fence 73
The Fire 73
Marrying Late 74
Vermont Summer 74
Stubborn Yankees 74
Our Town 74
Franklin Forestalling Inquiry 75
He Might as Well Have Stayed 75
A Yankee in Georgia 76
The Return of the Native 77
"Real Characters" 78
Country Squire 79
Independent Vermonters 80
The Snows of Yesteryear 81
God and the New Hampshire Farmer 82
Rock Farm 82
Building Wall 82
Answering One Question by Asking Another 82
The Man from Monkton 83
Taunton's Seasons 83
Jim Eldridge's Old Mill 84

Contents

Characters   84
Migratory Birds   85
Exhuming the Remains   85
Bringing in the Log   86
Salt Water Yankees   87
Ma'am Hackett's Garden   87
Following the Wrong Gulls   87
The Captain's Hat   88
How Long from Port?   88
Counting the Children   89
Whalers' Bastards   89
Captain Peleg's Letter   89
Captain Eleazer's *Bulldog*   90
The Captain's Prescription   90
Thar She Blows!   91
The Stammering Sailor   92
The Seagoing Coffin   92
She Sleeps Six   93
Cap'n Tibbett and the Body   93
A Wreck's a Wreck   94
A Long Wreck Hook for the Preacher   94
Anecdote Characteristic of Sailors   95
Yankee Preachers   96
Fisherman's Reward   96
Prayer for Rain   97
Prayer for Wind   99
Schooner Ashore   100
Minister and Fish   100
The World, the Flesh, and the Devil   101
A Timely Text   101
The Rev. Mr. Bulkley's Advice   102
Johnny-Cake under the Stove   103
The Dominie and the Horse   103
Yankees and Indians   104
Wickhegan   104
When the Powder Grows   104
Head Work   104
A New Way to Make People Happy   105
Indian Justice   105
The Englishman with Two Heads   106
Justice Waban   107
Yankee Husbands and Wives   107
Abraham Underhill's Wife   107
The Reformed Wife   107
The Will of the Lord   108
Thomas Hatch's Courtship   109
Pulling the Rope   109
Don't Hit That Post Again   110
Breaking the Pitcher   110
Rat or Mouse   111
The Old Couple and the Bear   111
Yankee Diligence   112
The Parsimonious Widower   112
The Clever and the Foolish   113
The Secret of True Economy   113
The Poor Butter   113
Selling the Dog   113
Misfits   114
Getting More for His Money   114
Recognizing the Broom   115
The Double Hitch   115
Spelling His Name   116

The Thief's Defense	116
Not Bright	116
An Honest Man	117
Uncle Jed	117
A Shovel for "Uncle Ed"	117
The Laziest Man in Vermont	118
Wife Sitter	118
Two Round Trips	119
Sylvester and John	119
How the Old Lady Beat John	120
A Careless Cuss	122
Salmon or Cod?	122
Eggs Is Eggs	123
Answering the Reproof	123
Painting the Meeting-House	124
The Order of their Going	124
Whittling without a Purpose	124
A Couple of Reasons Too Many	125
The Ungallant Suitor	125
The Captain's Pudding	125
Diploma Digging	126
Damaging the Engine	126
He Might as Well Have Et	126
Quite a Storm	126
Saving a Fuss	127
Timothy Crumb's Courtship	127

III. STOUT FELLOWS AND HARD LIARS

Introduction	129
"Overplus of Expression"—"I Came to New England Seeking Wonders"— Local Pride and Prejudice	
Monstrosities of Mirth	132
Hard Lying	132
The Man Who Bottled Up the Thunder	133
The Man that Cut Bread So Fast with the Shoe-Knife	134
Nantucket "Sleigh Ride"	135
Strong Men	135
John Strong and the Bear	135
Stout Jeffrey	136
Jonas Lord	137
Jigger Johnson, River Boss	138
Old Sam Hewes, River Man	140
Remarkable Hunting and Shooting	141
Jonathan's Hunting Excursion	141
Slow Powder	142
Captain Paddock's Whale Iron	142
Sharp Shooting	143
A Gone Coon	143
The Double-Barreled Shotgun	144
Old Town Tall Tales	145
The Cat with the Wooden Leg	145
Bringing in the Bear	145
Tying a Knot in a Painter's Tail	146
Duck Hunting Yarn	147
The Green Duck Hunter and the Live Decoy	148
Jotham Stories	149
Fisherman's Luck	152
Grant's Tame Trout	152
Catching Trout by Tickling	154
A Creel of Big Ones	155
Easy Fishing	155

The Hoopajuba   155
Truthful Jake   155
Simple Explanation   156
Saturation Point   156
Expert Advice   156
The Law   156
Outboard Motor   157
That Man That Liked to Fish   157
Remarkable Animal Behavior   158
  A Gone Fish   158
  The Mink Story   159
  Why I Never Shoot Bears   160
  The Hawk Feather That Ate the Chicken Feathers   161
  Tall Tales from the Maine Woods   162
    The Tree Bears   162
    The Stove Pipe   162
    Big Eating   163
    The Lost Shoat   163
    Legal Tender   163
Local Wonders   164
  The Mosquitoes with the Canvas Britches   164
  Frozen Death   164
  Human Hibernation: The Mystery Solved   166
  Fog Yarn   168
  Shingling Out onto the Fog   169
  Maine's Woodland Terrors   169
  The Tote-Road Shagamaw   171
  Gazerium and Snydae   172
  Gyascutus   172
  The Come-at-a-Body   173

PART TWO: MYTHS, LEGENDS, AND TRADITIONS

I. WONDERS OF THE INVISIBLE WORLD

Introduction   176
  Providences and Prodigies—History *versus* Myth—Nature Myths—
  Ghost-Ridden and Devil-Doomed
Singular Occurrences   179
  The New Haven Specter Ship   179
  The Moodus Noises   180
    Contemporary Accounts   180
    An Interview   183
  The Windham Frogs   183
  The Great Ipswich Fright   185
  The Palatine Light   188
Mysterious Creatures   190
  The Reverend Samuel Peters' Contribution to the Natural History of Connecticut   190
    Caterpillars and Wild Pigeons   190
    The Whapperknocker   190
    The Cuba   191
    The Dew-Mink   191
    The Humility   191
    The Whippoorwill   192
    Belled Snakes   192
    Tree-Frogs   193
  Cotton Mather's Snake Stories   193
  The New England Sea-Serpent   194
  Caldera Dick   199
Haunts and Specters   202
  Ocean-Born Mary   202
  The Ghosts of Georges Bank   205

II. THE POWERS OF DARKNESS

Introduction 213
  Monster or Gentleman?—Dancing to the Devil's Fiddle
The Devil Is in It 215
  Old Trickey, the Devil-Doomed Sandman 215
  Jonathan Moulton and the Devil 216
  The Devil and the Card-Players 220
  Cheating the Devil 220
  The Loup-Garou 221
  The Devil and the Loups-Garous 222
  Why Purgatory Was Made 224
The Witch Is in It 225
  How Old Betty Booker Rode Skipper Perkins Down to York 225
  Old Deb and Other Old Colony Witches 227
  The Man Who Could Send Rats 230
  The Man Who Made Weather 231

III. PLACE LORE

Introduction 233
  "A Local Habitation and a Name"—"More Patient Almost of
  Anything than of Flatness"
The Art of Naming Places 235
  There Are No Peruvians in Peru 235
  Yankee Flavor 236
  Names of the New England States 239
  Nicknames of the New England States 240
  The Naming of Cape Cod 241
  Why the White Mountains Are Called "White" 241
  Names in the White Mountains 242
  The Christening of Vermont 243
  The Naming of Auburn 245
  These Haddams 246
  Which Dover? 247
  Lake Charcogg-Etc.-Maugg 247
  The Origin of "Hoosic"—A Satire 248
  Point Judith 249
  Lemon Fair River 250
  Bride Brook 250
  Mingo Beach 251
  Sea-Gull Cliffs 251
  The Devil's Ash Heap 252
Local Color and Local Rivalry 253
  "Proper Bostonians" 253
  The Devil and the Wind in Boston 255
  Damnation Alley 255
  The S.S. Pierce Pung 255
  Why Boston Streets Are Crooked 256
  Cape Cod Rivalries 256
  How the Cranberry Came to Cape Cod 257
  Provincetown and the Devil 257
  Fishhouse Stories 258
  Fishermen's Races 258
  A Town Divided 259
  The Woman Who Sold Winds 260
  Moving a Town down a Hill 261
  Ephraim Wright and the Underground Railroad 261
  The Lost Child 262

IV. HISTORICAL TRADITIONS

Introduction 264
  Tradition and History—The Bardic Tradition—The Yankee as Hero:
  Legend and Myth
Fables and Symbols 267
  Priscilla and John Alden 267
  The Tinker and the Fencing-Master 268
  The Angel of Hadley 268
  Lovel and the Indians 269
  Captain Putnam and the British Major 270
  Old Put's Wolf 271
  Yankee Doodle 273
  The Young Rebels 273
  The Original Brother Jonathan 274
  A Loyal Tory of Hancock 274
  The Satisfied Redemptioner 276
  The Yarn-Beam Cannon 277
  Skipper Ireson's Ride 277
  Mrs. Bailey's Petticoat 279
Rogues, Eccentrics, and Heroes 280
  Captain Kidd Legends in New England 280
    Kidd's Tomb 280
    Kidd's Ghost 281
  Tom Cook, the Leveler 281
  George White, Horse Thief 282
  Dexter's Profitable Blunders 284
  Sam Hyde, Proverbial Liar 286
  The Old Darnman 287
  Crazy Lorenzo Dow 291
  Exploits of Ethan Allen 294
    His Legend 294
    What He Said at Ticonderoga: A Variant 297
    Hunting Exploits 297
    Chastising Yorkers 298
    He Eats Iron 299
    A Conjurer by Passion 300
    Ethan and Fanny Wall 300
    Drunk or Sober 302
    My Name Is Allen 302
  "Ave" Henry, Lumber Baron 302
  The Enigma of Silent Cal 307
    "You Got to Be Mighty Careful" 307
    His Apparent Irrelevance 309
    His Silence 309
    His Laconic Style 309

PART THREE: BELIEFS AND CUSTOMS
I. THE POWER OF FAITH

Introduction 316
  Evanescent Clues—The Power of Sympathy
Signs and Warnings 318
  St. Elmo's Fire 318
  St. Elmo Sees Them Through 319
  The Wraith in the Storm 320
  The Cradle Will Rock 322
  The Girl in the Fog 323
  The Black Newfoundland Dog 323
  The Telltale Seaweed 324
  Esau and the Gorbey 326

Rooster Talk 330
Luck, Divination, and Conjuration 331
  The Dream Line 331
  Flower Oracles 331
  Apple Divinations 332
  A Fortune in a Stick 333
  Sailors' Superstitions 333
  Lucky and Unlucky Ships' Names 334
  Ship Figureheads 335
  Say "Minister" 336
  Why the Flounder Has a Wry Mouth and Two Colors 336
  Snake Lore 337
  A Letter to the Rats 339
    Conjuring Rats 339
    Aunt Weed's Rat Letter 340
  Driving a Witch Out of the Soap 342
  The Fairies Who Didn't Stay 343
Weather Lore 344
  Signs and Seasons 344
  Prognostics of the Weather 346
  Signs in the Sea's Rote 350
Cures 351
  Simples and Benefits 351
  Roots and Herbs 351
  Tonics and Family Rights 352
  Meetin' Seed 353
  Plantain 354
  Snake Ball 355
  Skunk Oil and Other Remedies 355

II. THE FORCE OF CUSTOM

Introduction 357
  The Good Old Days—Co-operation and Ritual
Old New England Dishes 359
  Narragansett Johnny-Cake 359
  Corn Dishes 361
  Narragansett Fried Smelts and Broiled Eels 364
  Nantucket Quahaugs 365
  New England *versus* Manhattan Clam Chowder 367
  Daniel Webster's Fish Chowder 369
  Herring Sticks 369
  Lobster Stew 370
  Scootin'-'long-the-Shore 371
  New England Boiled Dinner 372
  Muslin Toast 372
  Nantucket Wonders 372
  Skully-Jo 373
  "Biled Cider Apple Sass" 373
  Salt Horse 374
  Whaleship's Menu 375
Lost Arts and Passing Institutions 376
  Barnum Recalls the Good Old Days 376
  Some Public Land Record Lore of Vermont and New Hampshire 379
  Bees, Change-Work, and Whangs 381
  Raisings 382
  Country Auctions 384
  Sugaring Science 385
  Building a Stone Wall 389
  Samplers 390
  Quilting 393
  Coast Traders 396

Ride and Tie 398
Chebobbins 398
Stanger's Fire 399
Pillow Bears and Feather Voyages 399
Filling Boots with Flaxseed 400
Powder-Horns 400
Jagger-Knives 401
Noggin and Piggin 402
Cat Holes 402
Boarding Around 403
Letter Writing 404
Visiting and Advertising Cards 405
Deaconing the Psalm 406
The Meetinghouse Bell 406
Stove and Anti-Stove Factions 407
Bundling 411
Tarrying 413
Courting-Sticks 414
Courting with Stones 414
Bride Stealing 414
The Devil's Fiddle 415
Shift Marriages 416
Calendar Customs 418
Thanksgiving 418
Its History 418
Its Customs 421
Christmas Eve on Beacon Hill 422
Menin Jesu in Provincetown 422
Hallowe'en 423
The Fourth of July 423
Guy Fawkes' Day 425
Nantucket Sheep Shearing 425
Town Meeting Day 427
Muster or Training Day 427
Pastimes and Games 428
Chimney-Corner Story-Telling 428
The Debating Society 429
Sleigh Riding 430
Husking Bees or Frolics 431
Cattle Show 432
County Fair 432
Cockroach and Bedbug Match 434
The Gam 435
A Childish Pastime 436
Horse Chestnut Men 437
Fly Away, Jack 437
Smell Brimstone 437
I Languish 438
Hailey Over 438
Violet Fights 438
Statues 439
Old Witch 440
Tiddledewinks 442
Games of Boston Boys 443
Punk 443
The Locust 443
Coasting 443
Marbles 445
Kite-Flying 445
Tops 446
Stilting 446
Tip-Cat 446

    Choosing Sides   446
  Games of Nantucket Boys   447
    Cracks and Squares   447
    Pitching Penny Shells and Leadies   447
    Kick Poke   448
  Round Ball   449

PART FOUR: WORD LORE
I. YANKEEISMS

Introduction   452
  Regionalism in Yankee Speech—Folk Speech and Speech Folklore
Provincial Speech   455
  Vermont Dialect Areas   455
  The Yankee Twang   456
    The Nasal Tone   456
    An Odd Mixture   457
  Ancient Pronunciation   458
  Kentish Provincialisms in New England   458
  Nantucket Pronunciation of the Points of the Compass   459
  Contributions to the New England Vocabulary and Idiom   459
    From Lowell's Lexicon   459
    Chiefly from Portsmouth   460
    From Maine and New Hampshire   461
Stories in Words   465
  The Baldwin Apple   465
  The Bofat   465
  The Cape Cod Cat   466
  Cape Cod Turkey   466
  "Cat" Words   467
  Comfort Powders   467
  A Dead Horse   468
  Drail   468
  Ear-Timers   468
  Gallbuster   470
  Heave and Haul   470
  Herb Tea   471
  Hubbub   471
  Interval(e)   472
  Johnny-Cake   473
  Kennebec Turkey   473
  Killcor   474
  The Minister's Rib Factory   474
  Mooncussin'   474
  Mud Time   475
  Munching Drawer   476
  The Pilgrims   476
  P. I.'s and Frenchmen   478
  Pot Luck   478
  Pumpkin-Heads   478
  The Sacred Cow   479
  Schooner   479
  Shun-Pikes   480
  Thank'ee Ma'ams   480
  Towner   480
  Twitches   481
  Twizzles   481
  Wangan   481
  Yankee   482
    According to Reverend Gordon   482
    According to Mencken   482

Names and Nicknames 484
  Old Testament Names in New England 484
  Providential Names 486
  Girls' Names 486
  Double Christian Names 487
  Portuguese American Names and Nicknames 487
  Ships' Names 488
  Ships' Names on Old Barns 489
  'Sconset House Names 489
  Names of Apples 490
  Poor Old Country Railroad 491
  The Hub 491
  Back Side and Bay Side 492

II. FOLK-SAY

Introduction 493
  Mythology in Folk Speech—Local Bywords and Proverbs
Salt of the Sea 496
  Nantucket Nauticalisms 496
  Varieties of Nantucket Wind and Weather 499
  Nantucketisms 499
  Nantucket Similes and Sayings 503
    "As Mad as Tucker" 504
    "As Weak as Annie Burrill's Tea" 504
    "As Bad as Old Skitzy" 504
    "As Handy as Caleb's Cheese" 504
    "A Poor Gamaliel" 504
    "You Haven't Got Dinah Paddock to Deal with" 504
    "Keeping Still like Uncle Jimmy" 505
    "No More Use for Them than Meader Had for His Teeth" 505
Yankee Eloquence 505
  Wit in Yankee Speech 505
  Humor in Yankee Speech 507
  Miscellany 508
  A Vermont "Idioticon" 510
  Seamen's Sermon 511
  A 'Sconseter's Will 513
Proverbs and Sayings 515
  Old English Proverbs 515
  The Sayings of Poor Ned 516
  Aphorisms of Manners 516
  Hi's Got Some Great Sayings 517
  Famous Sayings and Allusions 517
  Cold Roast Boston 518
Stories in Bywords 519
  Better Have Paid Your Washwoman 519
  Boston Folks Are Full of Notions 519
  Ethan Allen's Saying 520
  Kilroy Was Here 521
  Mind Your Orts 521
  Oh, Rinehart! 522
  Pick Up Your Feet 522
  "Sock Saunders" Sayings 523

PART FIVE: SONGS AND RHYMES

I. BALLADS AND SONGS

Introduction 526
  Yankee Songs and Singers—Songs of the Sea and the Woods
Old and New England 529

Cape Ann 529
Old Colony Times 531
Over There 532
Away Down East 533
Yankee Manufactures 535
Hymns of Faith and Freedom 536
Chester 536
Free America 537
Ballad of the Tea Party 538
The Boston Tea Tax 539
The Ballad of Bunker Hill 541
Rifflemen's Song at Bennington 543
The *Constitution* and the *Guerrière* 544
Ballads 546
The Miller's Three Sons 546
Mary of the Wild Moor 548
The Shining Dagger 549
Jim Fisk 550
The Brookfield Murder 552
The Pesky Sarpent 554
Michigania 555
No, Never, No 556
Sea Songs and Chanteys 557
The Boston Come-All-Ye 557
Blow, Boys, Blow 558
Reuben Renzo 560
Cape Cod Shanty 561
The Mermaid 562
Lumberjack Songs and Ballads 564
The Lumberman's Alphabet 564
Jack Haggerty, or the Flat River Girl 566
The Lumberman's Life 567
Canada I O 569
Nursery and Humorous Songs 571
Nantucket Lullaby 571
The Frog in the Spring 571
Birds' Courting Song 573
The Little Pig 574
Johnny Sands 575
Old Grimes 576
Derby Ram 577
The Herring Song 578
The Old Man Who Lived in the Wood 579
The Lone Fish-Ball 580
The College Version 580
The History of the Song 581
Game and Dance Songs 585
Pompey 585
Old Woman All Skin and Bone 586
Quaker's Courtship 587
Hey, Betty Martin! 587
Devil's Dream 588
The Merry Dance 589
Wild Goose Chase 590

II. RHYMES AND JINGLES

Introduction 591
Children's Rhymes—Local Rhymes
Play Rhymes 595
Counting-Out Rhymes 595

Contents

Ball-Bouncing Rhymes   596
Rope-Skipping Rhymes   596
Tickling Rhymes   597
Children's Taunts   598
Rhymes for Occasions   598
Incantations and Formulæ   598
The Weather   599
The Winds   600
Campaign Rhymes   601
Sailors' Rhymes   602
For Occasions   602
Rules of the Road, at Sea   603
Index of Authors, Collectors, Informants, Titles, and First Lines of Songs 605
Index of Subjects and Names   613
Geographical Index   617

INTRODUCTION

As a folklore country, New England has an advantage over other regions in that it possesses a large, well-defined, well-documented body of tradition which is part local history and part folklore. A tradition derives its strength from a sense of group identity, on the one hand, and a sense of historical continuity, on the other. Continuity and identity New England has in great plenty. As a "finished place," in Bernard De-Voto's words, New England was the "first American section . . . to achieve stability in the conditions of its life." At the same time, New England has a strong oral tradition which links it with the past. "All through my life," writes Wilbur Cross, "I learned of the past not from books but from the lips of men and women."

The Yankee's sense of identity links him also with the present. His iden-tification is based on the indigenous environment of the small farm, the small factory, the village, the local church, and the family circle (all char-acteristic of the small-scale, closely-knit topography, economy, and social life of the region). To one who has entrée to the local reminiscers and story-tellers, the lives and legends of local characters are an open book.

Identification and continuity also proceed from conservatism—a con-servatism amounting almost to a religion. As Clifton Johnson has written of Northampton folk, "Conditions made them conservative; and it be-came almost proverbial among them that if a man owned a strip of meadow land, belonged to the First Church, bought his clothes of Deacon Daniel Kingsley, and was a subscriber to the Hampton *Gazette,* he surely would go to heaven when he died."

Such conservative provincialism taken together with the Yankee's "re-luctant eloquence" makes for an implicit regionalism as compared with the explicit regionalism of the South and West with their "expansive eloquence." At least this was true until New England, taking advantage of the new curiosity about America's past and the renewed nostalgia for the good old days, began to build its vacation and tourist industry in competi-tion with other regions.

In the late nineteen-twenties and thirties, in the wake of the First World War and in the midst of the Depression, Americans in every corner of the country were exploring and mustering their native cultural resources. This new regionalism resulted in a decentralization in literature paralleling the local-color movement of the 1870's and after. Regionalism as social science was promulgated by sociologists like Howard W. Odum, on the premise that folk society is basic to regional society and that folk-regional society is basic to social studies and social engineering. It was as a transplanted New Englander in Oklahoma that I first became interested in regional folklore via the Southwest renascence. Writing in *Folk-Say,* 1929, I pointed out that there is "not one folk group but many folk groups—as many as there are regions and racial [ethnic] and occupational groups within a region."

In the preparation and revision of this book (first published in 1947), I have come home again to my native New England. For returning natives homesick for New England and for outsiders discovering it, this "Yankee homecoming" is a return to more than a region of America. To the rest of the country, New England has always stood in much the same relation as England has to America—that of spiritual homeland and mother country. The "homecoming" completes the process begun with the "Yankee exodus." Wherever Yankees went, they carried with them their traditional culture and their social institutions, with which they New Englandized their new-found land. In coming home to the region, prodigals and tourists alike have been drawn by the lure of landscape, villages, architecture, local foods, recreation, and everything that spells Yankee—the sea and the hills, seasons and weather, mindskills and handskills, proverbs and speech, the New England state of mind, and above all the Yankee people. And outsiders settling in New England have enriched it with their own lore.

In a sense, New England's physical amenities and folk culture are one. They are both part of the at-homeness with one's environment and with one's neighbors that makes for the good life. This, I trust, is the feeling that emerges from the songs and stories, the folksay and folkways in this book. "We treasure our remembered people and doings after repeated hearings" wrote the late Dorothy Canfield Fisher in *Memories of Arlington, Vermont,* "because they are comments on human life, drawn from somebody's first-hand experience in living."

One of the richest veins of New England folk story and folksay is the body of local anecdotes kept alive in the oral tradition of every community. Bring a group of oldtimers together and ask them for old stories or stories of old times and an apparently inexhaustible flow of reminiscence and anecdote is released. One item suggests another and a single name recalls an entire cycle of stories built around a person who has become legendary. Typical story openings are: "There was a man by the name of —— that lived in ——." "Years ago there was a man in —— who ——." "It was back in the days when ——." "When I was a youngster ——." "When my grandfather was a young man ——." "It seems that my father ——."

Such references to time and place are part of the actual or supposed historicity of the anecdote, since the local anecdote, unlike the folktale proper, is a story told as true and to be believed. Its larger truth, however, is its truth to human nature and, at the same time, to local color, flavor, folkways, and idiom. But like all stories, the local anecdote is told primarily because it is a good story well told. In addition, it takes on a folk quality from the oral and vernacular style and a traditional quality from the fact that it is told over and over by more than one person and sometimes the same story is related about more than one person (as it becomes attached to different individuals possessing the same trait).

The good folk story teller is not simply a transmitter. He is also a creator with a native story sense and a feeling for the authentic, expressive detail, the right phrase, and the lively image, plus a good memory and an insight born of identification with the people who are his neighbors, his kinfolk, and his forebears.

In its combination of expressive utterance and spontaneous flow of language with native imagery and idiom, the local folk story is part of "the oral, linguistic, and story-telling aspects of folklore" and the "own story" for which I coined the word "folksay" in 1928. Ultimately what makes folk story living story and folklore living lore is what makes folksay folksay—the point of view of the participant or eyewitness, as expressed in the words "I did or saw and heard these things myself."

"In our modern bookish world," I wrote in *The English Journal* for February, 1940, "things begin to take on the nature of words—abstractions and labels as against actualities. But in the bookless world, where things have a superior vividness and persistence, things have an effect on words so that words come to resemble things. The result is a concreteness and directness of language which is close to gesture and action as well as objects, and a plasticity of phrase and construction."

Some of this folksay quality is captured in the use of folk-conversation as rural recreation to which Marion Nicholl Rawson in *Forever the Farm* (1939) applies the name "tell." For example:

"Mornin', Sally. Hear about Ella's nephew being took sick to Bennington? She had a big turkey dinner all ready with stuffin' and all, and then they couldn't come and eat it."

"Yes, she was real good, she brought me over some, me living alone so."

"My lands, you was lucky! I wish'd I'd been living neighbor to her."

"She come in and says: 'Since poor nephew was took sick and couldn't come for the turkey dinner I thought you ought to have some of the turkey with us. So Pa and me ate the legs. Then I didn't know whether you liked white meat or dark meat better, so I brought some of the stuffing and some beans.' "

While storytelling is the heart of folklore, it is not the whole of it. The stories—and the song-stories—cannot be separated from the rest of folklore any more than the lore can be separated from the folk and the folklife. Without attempting to relate specific items to their specific community setting, a general background in folkways and folk speech is provided in the sections of "Beliefs and Customs" and "Word Lore." Many beliefs and customs are also found in "Myths, Legends, and Traditions," where Yankee faith and credulity, mysticism and symbolism have been stimulated by places, place names, natural phenomena, spirits, strange creatures, and famous men.

Of such stuff is New England folklore made. In it are the materials of a homely epic—the epic of Yankee toil, ingenuity, and enterprise building "against sore-pressing Need"; of a human comedy—the comedy of Yankee tricks, idiosyncrasies, and expedients, full of pithy and salty humor; and of a local mythology whose heroes, eccentrics, monsters, sprites, witches, and demons remind us of the wild rout of antic mummers in "The Maypole of Merry Mount." Out of this mingled fantasy and tradition, retention and invention, folksay and booksay emerges a portrait of a down-to-earth, staunch, if notionate people, whose collective lineaments resemble the Great Stone Face—the typical American face of Uncle Sam, who began as Brother Jonathan.

It was on seeing the Great Stone Face that Daniel Webster paid New Hampshire an eloquent tribute that might well apply to Yankee excellence as a whole and to the human quality of New England folklore: "Men hang out signs indicative of their respective trades. Shoemakers hang out a gigantic shoe, a jeweler a monstrous watch and the dentist hangs out a gold tooth. But in the Mountains of New Hampshire God Almighty has hung out a sign to show that there he makes men." [1]

In the present edition I have omitted what seems to me less essential material in favor of important new material that has come to hand since the book's first appearance.

B. A. Botkin

Croton-on-Hudson, N.Y.

---

[1] Ernest Poole, *The Great White Hills of New Hampshire* (Garden City, New York: Doubleday & Company, 1946), p. 343.

A NOTE OF THANKS

A MONG THE many institutions and individuals who helped make the original edition of this book possible and feasible I am especially indebted, for courteous service, to the Library of Congress, the New York Public Library, the Boston Public Library, the Harvard University Library, the Massachusetts Historical Society, the American Antiquarian Society, the Croton Free Library, the Ossining Public Library, and the Field Library of Peekskill; to the Pageant Book Store and other antiquarian booksellers; to Mrs. Frances Kurland, who transcribed and edited a number of tunes; to the many friends who have furnished suggestions and assistance of one kind or another; and to Bertha Krantz and Edmund Fuller of Crown Publishers for seeing the manuscript through production.

To my former colleagues and the field workers of the Federal Writers' Project (whose surplus folklore manuscripts are on deposit in the Archive of Folksong in the Library of Congress), I owe special thanks for the contributions acknowledged in the source notes.

For special assistance in locating field informants and for their own contributions to the revised edition, I am grateful to Mr. and Mrs. Heman Chase of Alstead, New Hampshire. For interviews and recorded material I also want to thank the following: Mr. and Mrs. Walter Burroughs and Fred Mills of Alstead; Elsie Goodenow and Clarence Miller of South Acworth, New Hampshire; Chester C. Mason of Langdon, New Hampshire; and Herbert Tucker and William W. Kingsbury of Walpole, New Hampshire. Carl Withers also made valuable suggestions for the revision.

Thanks are due to Millen Brand of Crown Publishers for editorial assistance in the revision.

Finally, I am grateful as always to my wife, Gertrude F. Botkin, for her collaboration and her unstinting effort in the preparation of this book at every step of the original work and its revision.

B. A. B.

ACKNOWLEDGMENTS

The editor and publishers wish to thank the following authors or their representatives, publishers, historical societies and committees, for their kind permission to use the material in this book. Full copyright notices are given on the pages on which the material appears.

The Abingdon-Cokesbury Press; Joseph C. Allen; John Allison; The Altrurian Club of Springfield, Vt.; D. Appleton-Century Co., Inc.; A. S. Barnes & Co., Inc.; Mrs. Phillips Barry; The Bobbs-Merrill Co.; *The Boston Traveler;* Brandt & Brandt; Thomas and Joseph Butterworth; Chicago *Tribune;* Cornell Maritime Press; Coward-McCann, Inc.; F. A. Davis Co.; The Dial Press, Inc.; Dodd, Mead & Co.; Doubleday, Doran & Co., Inc.; Duell, Sloan & Pearce, Inc.; E. P. Dutton & Co., Inc.; Flanders Ballad Collection in Middlebury College; Wilfred Funk, Inc.; *Gourmet* Magazine; Harcourt, Brace & Co., Inc.; Walter and Margaret Hard; Harper & Bros.; Harvard University Press; Henry Holt & Co., Inc.; Houghton Mifflin Co.; Idlewild Press; Mrs. Clifton Johnson; Marshall Jones Co.; *Journal of American Folklore;* Keynote Recordings, Inc.; Alfred A. Knopf, Inc.; Freeman Lincoln; Mrs. J. Freeman Lincoln; J. B. Lippincott Co.; Little, Brown & Co.; McGraw-Hill Book Co.; The Macmillan Co.; The Marine Research Society; Marshfield Tercentenary Committee; Musicraft Records, Inc.; *The New Yorker; The New York Times;* Northampton Historical Society; W. W. Norton & Co.; Haydn S. Pearson; G. P. Putnam's Sons; Random House, Inc.; Reynal & Hitchcock; Rinehart & Co., Inc.; Russell & Volkening, Inc.; G. Schirmer, Inc.; Charles Scribner's Sons; M. S. Snowman; Sigmund Spaeth; Mrs. Guy E. Speare; Stephen Daye Press; Donald G. Trayser; University of California Press; The University of Michigan Press; The Vanguard Press; Vermont Historical Society; The Viking Press, Inc.; Ives Washburn, Inc.; Waverly House; Wehman Bros.; Weymouth Historical Society; The Williams & Wilkins Co.; The World Publishing Co.; Yale University Press; Yankee, Inc.

A TREASURY OF
NEW ENGLAND
FOLKLORE

PART ONE

FABULOUS YANKEES

If one of the main products of the region was the New England conscience, another, at least according to the popular belief in other districts, was the wooden nutmeg.

—ODELL SHEPARD

Even Cotton Mather could not avoid a tone of pious boastfulness when he narrated the doings of New England. Everything was remarkable. New England had the most remarkable providences, the most remarkable painful preachers, the most remarkable heresies, the most remarkable witches. Even the local devils were in his judgment more enterprising than those of the old country. They had to be in order to be a match for the New England saints.

—SAMUEL MCCHORD CROTHERS

But what I chiefly lament is the disappearance of the Yankee—not the conventional Yankee of the theatre, for he had never an existence elsewhere; but the hearty yet suspicious, "cute" though green, drawling, whittling, unadulterated Yankee, with his broad humor, delicious patois, *and large-hearted patriotism. . . . Railway and telegraph, factory and work-shop, penetrating into the most secluded hamlets, have rubbed off all the crust of an originality so pronounced as to have become the type, and often the caricature too, of American nationality the world over.*

—SAMUEL ADAMS DRAKE

I predict that on the last day of this planet, when the sun hangs cold in the sky, only two men will be left to face it. One will be a Chinaman, and if you ask the other he will say, "O yes, I was born at Cohasset."

—VAN WYCK BROOKS

1. THE YANKEE'S REPUTATION

"Yankee" has become almost a synonym for ingeniousness, thrift, and "cuteness." . . . He is a born arguer, and a born peddler, and a born whittler, a Jack-at-all-trades and good at them all.
—CLIFTON JOHNSON

. . . trading and swapping was more than a livelihood there. It was an emotional safety valve, perhaps—maybe the Yankee Puritan's substitute for gambling.—R. E. GOULD

Mankind luv to be cheated, but they want to hav it dun bi an artist.—JOSH BILLINGS

1. THE FABULOUS YANKEE

IN THE fabulous country of Yankeeland, Yankeedom, or Down East lives a fabulous creature known as the Yankee. The oldest and best known of American traditional types, this generic folk hero of New England is not to be confused with actual New Englanders any more than the legendary Backwoodsman, Hoosier, etc., are to be mistaken for the original. Type or stereotype, the fabulous Yankee has a basis in reality and humanity.

Perhaps no regional type has attracted to itself more myths and libels than the sensible, self-dependent, God-fearing, freedom-loving conservative, stubborn, practical, thrifty, industrious, inventive, and acquisitive Yankee. One reason for this is the fact that "The individual whom they call Yankee is very difficult to find, because you hardly know what to accept for a definition of him." [1] Another reason is to be sought in the sectional pride and prejudice, the local solidarities and loyalties, which have helped to shape popular conceptions of the Yankee. These conflicts and changes are reflected in the origin and growth of the word "Yankee" itself, through its varying connotations, favorable and unfavorable.

As a result, the history of the fabulous Yankee is the history not of a single type but of many sub-types—the Connecticut Yankee, the Vermont Yankee, the Yankee countryman, the Yankee peddler, the Yankee storekeeper, the comic Yankee, the sage Yankee, etc.—in which history and tradition are inextricably mixed. Many Yankee types, necessarily vanished or vanishing, survive largely in folklore.

---

[1] Mark Miles, "The Yankee," *The Mirror of the Philomathean Society*, Phillips Academy, Andover, Vol. 5 (July, 1859), No. 3, p. 17.

2. THE YANKEE CLOWN

The fabulous Yankee is first of all the comic countryman—the Yorkshire clown [1] and the English Hodge of the jest books transplanted to American soil. With them he belongs to the tradition of the "countryman in the great world" or the "rustic set in a complicated environment." Under the guise of Jonathan—the simple, awkward rustic, agape and agog at the world—the comic Yankee makes his bow in "Yankee Doodle." This song of uncertain origin and authorship, half British satire and half American self-burlesque, gave rise to many folk versions and parodies, such as "The Yankee's Return from Camp" and "Corn Cobs Twist Your Hair," and is said to have begun and ended the Revolution.

> "Yankee Doodle" is the tune
> Americans delight in;
> 'Twill do to whistle, sing, or play
> And just the thing for fightin'.

Thereafter, the character of Jonathan, like the song, was identified with the homespun pose of the provincial American—raw, bumptious, inquisitive—and associated with the development of national and regional consciousness.

After the Revolution, the comic Yankee became a stock figure on the stage, beginning with Jonathan, in the first American comedy, *The Contrast* (1787) by Royall Tyler (a Boston-born Harvard lawyer, later chief justice of the Vermont Supreme Court) and continuing down to the Civil War through such characters as Jonathan Ploughboy, Hiram Dodge, Solomon Swop, and Sam Patch, acted by George Handel ("Yankee") Hill, James H. Hackett, and Dan Marble. For the vogue of the stage Yankee, these and other comedians' Yankee impersonations and monologues, drawing upon oral tradition, were even more directly responsible.

The history of the comic Yankee is thus the history of a folk legend and a literary stereotype, in which oral yarns and popular songs rub shoulders with jest books, almanacs, newspaper sketches, travel books, local color stories, poems, and plays, and professional humorous writings.

3. YANKEE WITS AND SAGES

Like the Yorkshire clown the comic Yankee was not all fool but more rogue than fool. Although his brash greenness made him the natural butt of jokes and practical jokes, his deceptive simplicity (as in Royall Tyler's Jonathan) concealed a heart of gold and native wit and sagacity, which served as a convenient vehicle for social and political satire.

---

[1] The name Yorkshire has become a synonym for acuteness, not unmixed with a touch of unscrupulousness. In Lincolnshire, for example, when anything is done which is very clever, sharp, or unscrupulous, they say: That's real Yerksheer. To put Yorkshire on a person means in Lancashire to cheat, trick or overreach him; in Lancashire and Lincolnshire, a sharp overreaching person is called a Yorkshire bitc. Even in his own country the Yorkshireman has this reputation.—Elizabeth Mary Wright, *Rustic Speech and Folklore* (London, 1913), pp. 2–3.

The possibilities of the comic Yankee as a homely critic were first fully realized in the 1830's, when the homespun Yankee, originally the spokesman of American democracy, became the mouthpiece of conservative politics. As the original cracker-box philosopher, the Yankee has always stood for sound common sense and the good old days as against radical and newfangled notions. In January, 1830, Seba Smith inaugurated in the Portland *Daily Courier* (the first Maine daily) his thirty-year series of Jack Downing letters. These were written in Down East language to the folks back home in Downingville by a "green, unsophisticated lad from the country," who blundered into the halls of the Maine legislature (then the scene of intense party rivalry) and so into national politics as the friend and critic of President Andrew Jackson.

In creating a new comic type, the cracker-box or rustic philosopher, Smith remained true to Down East character, background, and vernacular, and gave us the first real Yankee in American humor, in contrast to the more artificial stage Yankee. Jack Downing had many imitators of the same and other names, including Davy Crockett of anti-Jackson, anti-Federalist propaganda, and became a popular figure in political cartoons— the prototype of Uncle Sam, with his beaver hat, swallow-tailed coat, and striped trousers. As political hanger-on and commentator, he continued the tradition of the "countryman in the great world"—a "talkative, prying, speculative jimcrack of a fellow."

Like many another successful Yankee, Jack Downing, characteristically, began as a peddler, coming to Portland with a wagonload of ax handles, hoop poles, and other notions to sell. He thus foreshadows the droll, glib figure of the Yankee peddler, picaresque and pawky, who was destined to become the masterpiece of the comic Yankee—the beatinest fellow on earth.

4. SHARP YANKEES

The Yankee peddler, hawking first his own handiwork and then other "notions," originated in the household and jackknife industries and small manufactures of New England. Here a hard land and climate, coupled with a middle-class, mercantile heritage and ingrained habits of thrift, diligence, and handiness, produced an industrious and restless race of jobbing, tinkering, whittling, contriving, swapping Yankees. Beginning as a neighborhood trader, the Yankee spilled over into the roads and sea-lanes of commerce (just as the home craftsman spilled over into the factories) to become roving merchant to the country and the world.

As Marjorie Barstow Greenbie points out, the Yankee (perpetual motion incarnate) had a genius not only for making things but also for placing them. "Moving about, setting things to rights, actively using his hands, the New Englander constantly observed that the great trouble with the world is that things are not in the right place. By simple locomotion you can turn a deficit into an asset, and turn misfortune into a gift from the gods. Take ice, for example. There is altogether too much of it in winter. . . . But move the ice to the tropics. . . ."[1]

It remained for a Nova Scotia judge, Thomas Chandler Haliburton, to immortalize the Yankee peddler in literature by combining the picaresque pattern of the peddler's travels with the character of the crackerbox philosopher, thus making him a peddler of intellectual as well as wooden wares. Although *The Clockmaker; or The Sayings and Doings of Sam Slick, of Slickville* (1836), originated in the author's desire to promote the development of Nova Scotia's natural resources and to preach provincial Toryism and Imperialism, it is remembered chiefly for the character of Sam Slick and the latter's wise saws and droll anecdotes.

Sam Slick (whom James Russell Lowell declared to be a "libel on the Yankee character, and a complete falsification of Yankee modes of speech") was half Yankee and half backwoodsman. In thus making him a composite of Jack Downing and Davy Crockett, Haliburton revealed, consciously or unconsciously, the close connection that existed between the peddler and the frontier. For, like the Indian trader and fur trader before him, the peddler followed the shifting fringe of settlement in pursuit of a livelihood and was an active force in the extension of the frontier. To the folks back home he brought valuable information about the new country. And many a peddler gladly exchanged his pack for land and a home in the South or the West.

As a picaresque character, combining rascality with humor, the peddler was at home on the frontier, where, in Simon Suggs's words, "It is good for a man to be shifty in a new country," and where it was said that "You might as well try to hold a greased eel as a live Yankee!" As the comic Yankee became a hero-legend, so the "scheming Yankee" became a myth of the Confederate South.

The peddler's proverbial unscrupulousness in taking advantage of a situation and even creating a situation to sharpen his wits on was reflected in the language of the time. A "Yankee trick" became a "common name for anything very smart, done in the way of trade, no matter in which of the States the doer was born." [1] To *yankee* and *out-Yankee* meant to cheat and outcheat. The peddler also carried over the folklore motif of the comic contest of wits between the merchant and his customer, with the tables frequently turned on the former. And just as the peddler's audience enjoyed the spectacle of good-natured roguery, of a trap being set and the victim walking into it, so the New Englander, however much he may have deplored the peddler's shady reputation, began to enjoy the joke on himself and joined in the laughter at the countless stories of "cute" Yankee tricksters and "biters bit," told in village stores and taverns and circulated in newspapers, almanacs, and jokebooks.

5. Village Store and Tavern Humor

With the passing of the Yankee peddler, by the time of the Civil War, his mantle fell on the Yankee storekeeper. Since in many cases the latter started as a peddler, he retained many of the peddler's characteristics and tricks and perpetuated much of the lore of peddling. Stationary trade, however, made it necessary for the storekeeper to steer a middle course between the peddler's *caveat emptor* and the merchant's ingratiating motto,

---

[1] Cornelius Mathews, *Writings* (1846), II, 308, cited by Thornton in *An American Glossary* (Philadelphia, 1912), II, 961.

"The customer is always right." At the same time the calculating ethics of "Honesty is the best policy" permitted a wide margin of haggling, chiseling, and hoodwinking on the part of both merchant and customer; and stories of Yankee storekeepers, tavernkeepers, and other tradesmen stress the petty, legalistic side of small business in contrast to the freebooting, swindling methods of the footloose peddler and the "merchant adventurer." There is still a comic contest of wits between buyer and seller, but the chief contestants are the storekeeper who is a "little nigh on a trade" and the snug customer, who tries to get something for nothing. The storekeeper also had to keep his weather eye open and his sails trimmed for the lazy or dishonest clerk and the high-pressure drummer.

The nature of the general store as a social center put the storekeeper further on his mettle and on his guard. Along with the tavern the store served as a resort for village loafers, gossips, jesters, story-tellers, and pundits. In the atmosphere of easy sociability and fun-making thus created, customers and hangers-on indulged in petty pilfering, shop-lifting, sophistries, and ruses, which put a strain on the storekeeper's pocketbook and bookkeeping as well as on his vigilance and good humor. Favorite themes of store and tavern humor are "skunking" and "skinning" hoaxes; the detection and punishment of petty thieves; the hypocritical greed and ice-water charity of deacons; the pranks, forfeits, kangaroo courts, and boasting and lying contests of the store and tavern "clubs"; and the chicanery of horse-jockeys.

In the folkways of village humor the tavern occupied a special place. Here the native and the stranger, the countryman and the great world, met on the jousting ground of wit and story-telling. Here the commercial traveler followed in the peddler's footsteps; local politicians brought the affairs of the state and nation closer to home; and the city slicker and the farmer come to town matched wits with each other and with the landlord and the tavern-haunters.

6. Practical Jokers

In village store and tavern humor we find Yankee tricks of the trade generalized into Yankee tricks, and sharpness and greenness interchangeable, with tricksters tricked and the tricked turning trickster. And when the comic contest of wits is transferred to the realm of practical jokes, "sharp practice spiced with good humor" becomes good humor spiced with sharp practice. But, more than mere fun-making or mischief-making, Yankee pranks and sells were thought to serve a useful purpose by affording the victim a "surplus fund of experience."

The greatest and most practical "practical wag" that ever came out of a country store was the Connecticut Yankee, P. T. Barnum. As a clerk in his father's store in Bethel, he learned that "sharp trades, tricks, dishonesty, and deception are by no means confined to the city." [1] And as the world's greatest showman, he capitalized on the "perfect good nature with which the American public submit to a clever humbug," [2] while indulging the "jocose element" in his character, for any excess of which, he says, part of

---

[1] *Struggles and Triumphs* (Buffalo, 1873), p. 33.
[2] *Ibid.*, p. 148.

the blame must attach to his early surroundings of the store—the "theatre of village talk, and the scene of many practical jokes."

B. A. B.

YANKEES AND ENGLISHMEN

Corn Cobs Twist Your Hair

There was a man in our town,
    I'll tell you his condition.
He sold his oxen and his plough,
    To buy him a commission.

Chorus:
    Corn Cobs twist your hair,
        Cart wheel run round you,
    Fiery dragons take you off,
        And mortar pestal pound you.

When this man a commission got,
    He prov'd to be a coward,
He wouldn't go to Canada,
    For fear he'd get devour'd.

But he and I we went to town,
    Along with Captain Goodin,
And there we saw the Yankee boys,
    As thick as hasty puddin.

Now there was General Washington,
    With all the folks about him,
He swore they got so tarnal proud,
    They couldn't do without him.

And there they had a great big thing,
    Big as a log of maple,
And ev'ry time they wheel'd it round,
    It took two yoke of cattle.

And when they went to fire it off,
    It took a horn of powder,
It made a noise like Daddy's gun,
    Only a nation louder.

And there they had a little thing,
    All bound round with leather,
With little sticks to beat upon,
    To call the men together.

And there we saw a hollow stick,
    With six holes bor'd right in it,
And ev'ry time they blow'd upon,
    We thought the devil was in it.

And there we saw them with
    big knives,
    Stuck in a piece of leather,
And when the Captain he cri'd draw,
    They all draw'd out together.

From "Corn Cobs Twist Your Hair," A Favorite National Melody, Arranged to a Comic Song and Chorus and Sung by Little Yankee Hill, Written, Selected, and Arranged for the Pianoforte. Entered according to the Act of Congress, in the Year 1836, by George Endicot, in the Clerk's Office of the District Court, of the Southern District of New York. In *Series of Old American Songs*, Reproduced in Facsimile from Original or Early Editions in the Harris Collection of American Poetry and Plays, With Brief Annotations, by S. Foster Damon, Curator, No. 19. Providence, Rhode Island: Brown University Library. 1936.
This song is a folk development of the earliest version of "Yankee Doodle," with a Tom o' Bedlam refrain.—S. F. D.

8

Facsimile of the Original Sheet Music, 1836.

take you off. And mortal pes tal pound you.

take you off. And mortal pes . tal pound you.

take you off, And mortar pes . tal pound you.

take you off, And mortar pes . tal pound you.

ff

Now brother Ike was very bold,
  As bold as Captain Crocket,
For he sneak'd round on t'other side,
  And held on Daddy's pocket.

Now I and brother Ike goes hum,
  We wasn't fraid of powder,
For Daddy said he'd learn us both,
  To scream a little louder.

Our cousin Jim he went to town,
  With a pair of striped trowses,
He swore the town he couldn't see,
  There was so many houses.

Our Aunt Jemima climb'd a tree,
  She had a stick to boost her,
And there she sat a throwing corn,
  At our old bob tail rooster.

Now cousin Sal she went to town,
  And got upon a steeple,
She took a frying pan of grog,
  And pour'd it on the people.

Our Uncle Ben he lost his cow,
  And didn't know where to find her,
And when the cow she did cum hum,
  She had her tail behind her.

Now Sister Sue grows very thin,
  And no one knows what ails her,
She us'd to eat nine pound of pork,
  But now her stomach fails her.

And now I've sung you all my song,
  I've told you all the causes,
And all that I do want of you,
  Is all your kind applauses.

Captain Basil Hall and the Countryman

[CAPTAIN HALL] was walking up and down the veranda of a country tavern in Massachusetts, while the coach changed horses. A thunder-storm was going on, and, with that pleasant European air of indirect self-compliment in condescending to be surprised by American merit, which we find so conciliating, he said to a countryman lounging against the door, "Pretty heavy thunder you have here." The other, who had divined at a glance his feeling of generous concession to a new country, drawled gravely, "Waal, we *du,* considerin' the number of inhabitants."

From Introduction to "The Biglow Papers, Second Series," in *The Poetical Works of James Russell Lowell,* p. 225. Copyright, 1848, 1857, 1866, 1868, 1869, 1876, and 1885, by James Russell Lowell. Boston and New York: Houghton, Mifflin and Company.

Fanny Kemble and the Yankee Farmer

WHEN Boston was Fanny Kemble's home, and her summers were spent here and there in rural .Massachusetts, she engaged a worthy neighbor to be her charioteer during the season of one of her country sojournings. With kind-hearted loquacity he was beginning to expatiate on the country, the crops and the history of the people roundabout, when Fanny remarked, in her imperious dogmatic fashion, "Sir, I have engaged you to drive for me, not to talk to me." The farmer ceased, pursed up his lips, and ever after kept his peace.

When the vacation weeks were over, and Miss Kemble was about to return to town, she sent for her Jehu and his bill. Running her eyes down its awkward columns, she paused. "What is this item, sir?" said she. "I cannot understand it." And with equal gravity he rejoined, "Sass, five dollars. I don't often take it, but when I do I charge."

The Road to Walpole

THE next town we wished to reach was Walpole, but the roads offered by no means easy travelling. The inhabitants of Vermont, noted for their industry, their honesty, and their stationary character, are also distinguished for a peculiar turn of humor in their remarks and some oddities of manner, being in the latter respect even more primitive than the Pennsylvanians. Their neighbors of Massachusetts (by some termed the Scotch of North America), in passing continually through this state on their way to and from Canada and the back countries, are frequently exposed to the ridicule of the inhabitants. One of the many stories in circulation bearing on this subject was that of a Bostonian travelling through Vermont, and overtaken by night on a lonely road, who at length saw a youngster some distance ahead, and apprehensive that he had mistaken his way, called out to the lad:

"Jack! Jack! I want to know which is the way to Chesterfield?"

"How did you know my name was Jack?" responded the youth.

"Why, I guessed it," replied the traveller.

"Oh, then you may guess your way to Chesterfield!"

Fearful of being nonplussed in a similar way myself, I was very particular each morning before I quitted the tavern to learn all I could of the road we were to pursue throughout the day, as there were few oppor-

From *Modern Eloquence*, edited by Thomas Reed and others, Vol. X, p. 189. Copyright, 1900, by the University Society. Philadelphia: John D. Morris and Company.

From *Retrospections of America, 1797–1811,* by John Bernard, Edited from the Manuscript by Mrs. Bayle Bernard, With an Introduction, Notes, and Index, by Laurence Hutton and Brander Matthews, pp. 319–320. Copyright, 1886, by Harper & Brothers. New York. 1887.

tunities afterwards of ascertaining anything on the subject. Notwithstanding this caution, I lost my track one day, and was actually retracing my steps to Boston. I learned this in a characteristic manner when I pulled up to inquire of a countryman who was felling a tree by the roadside—

"My good friend," said I, "am I on the right road to Walpole?"

"Yes," replied the man; "you are on the right road; but I reckon you must turn your horse's head or you'll never get there!"

Provincial Phraseology and Hospitality

THE inn most esteemed in Providence is kept by one Amidon, and there I was accordingly advised to go. Arriving about the hour of nine in the forenoon, I asked for breakfast. Mr. Amidon replied by saying, "Breakfast is almost through"; and on my pressing the question, he added, that "He did not know how it would operate." Both these answers were given with a slow utterance and even tone of voice, such as greatly increased what I thought their ridicule. Reduced into English, they meant, first, that breakfast was almost over; and secondly, that he did not know whether the house could or could not conveniently afford me a breakfast.

I had already acquired so much acquaintance with this provincial phraseology, and provincial manner of answering questions, as to be at no loss for the meaning of my host; and passing into the house, where I found a large table, with the wreck of the breakfast that was *through*, I was at length courteously indulged with a breakfast for myself.

My wants were equally ill-timed on the morning of my departure. It was about six o'clock when I prepared to leave Mr. Amidon's; and I confess that I had not promised myself (what nevertheless is most agreeable to me) to breakfast before setting out. Discovering, however, in the kitchen, while I was paying Mrs. Amidon her bill, that two or three kettles were already boiling, I became unreasonable enough to ask, whether or not I could have some tea? but I received for answer the words, "Not at *this* time of the day!"

Comic Yankee Servants

MANY anecdotes are current about the manners of the young people who come down from the retired parts of the country to domestic service in

From *Travels through the Northern Parts of the United States, in the Years 1807 and 1808*, by Edward Augustus Kendall, Esq., Vol. II, pp. 2–3. New York: Printed and published by I. Riley. 1809.

From *Society in America*, by Harriet Martineau, Vol. II, pp. 253–254. New York and London: Saunders and Otley. 1837.

Boston. A simple country girl obeyed her instructions exactly about putting the dinner upon the table, and then summoning the family. But they
delayed a few minutes, from some cause; and when they entered the dining-
room, found the domestic seated and eating. She had helped herself from
a fowl, thinking that "the folk were so long a-coming, the things would get
cold." A young man from Vermont was hired by a family who were in
extreme want of a footman. He was a most friendly personage, as willing
as he was free and easy; but he knew nothing of life out of a small farmhouse. An evening or two after his arrival, there was a large party at the
house. His mistress strove to impress upon him that all he had to do at
tea-time was to follow, with the sugar and cream, the waiter who carried
the tea; to see that every one had cream and sugar; and to hold his
tongue. He did his part with an earnest face, stepping industriously from
guest to guest. When he had made the circuit, and reached the door, a
doubt struck him whether a group in the furthest part of the room had
had the benefit of his attentions. He raised himself on his toes with, "I'll
ask"; and shouted over the heads of the company, "I say, how are ye off
for sweetenin' in that ere corner?"

A Yankee in London: Buying Gape-Seed

A YANKEE, walking the streets of London, looked through a window upon
a group of men writing very rapidly; and one of them said to him in an
insulting manner, "Do you wish to buy some gape-seed?" Passing on a
short distance the Yankee met a man, and asked him what the business of
those men was in the office he had just passed. He was told that they wrote
letters dictated by others, and transcribed all sorts of documents; in short,
they were writers. The Yankee returned to the office and inquired if one
of the men would write a letter for him, and was answered in the affirmative.
He asked the price, and was told one dollar. After considerable talk, the
bargain was made; one of the conditions of which was that the scribe should
write just what the Yankee told him to, or he should receive no pay. The
scribe told the Yankee he was ready to begin; and the latter said,—
    "Dear marm:" and then asked, "Have you got that deown?"
    "Yes," was the reply, *"go on."*
    "I went to ride t'other day: have you got that deown?"
    "Yes; go on, go on."
    "And I harnessed up the old mare into the wagon: have you got that
deown?"
    "Yes, yes, long ago; *go on."*

By John B. Gough. From *Brilliant Diamonds of Poetry and Prose,* Comprising the
Most Unique, Touching, Pithy, and Beautiful Literary Treasures. . . , edited by Rev.
O. H. Tiffany, pp. 57–58. Copyright, 1883, by O. H. Tiffany. Union Publishing Com-
pany. 1893.

"Why, how fast you write! And I got into the wagon, and sat deown, and drew up the reins, and took the whip in my right hand: have you got that deown?"

"Yes, long ago; *go on.*"

"Dear me, how fast you write! I never saw your equal. And I said to the old mare, *'Go 'long,'* and jerked the reins pretty hard: have you got that deown?"

"Yes; and I am impatiently waiting for more. I wish you wouldn't bother me with so many foolish questions. Go on with your letter."

"Well, the old mare wouldn't stir out of her tracks, and I hollered, *'Go 'long, you old jade! go 'long.'* Have you got that deown?"

"Yes, indeed, *you pestersome fellow; go on.*"

"And I licked her, and licked her, and licked her [continuing to repeat these words as rapidly as possible].

"Hold on there! I have written two pages of 'licked her,' and I want the rest of the letter."

"Well, and she kicked, and she kicked, and she kicked—[continuing to repeat these words with great rapidity].

"Do go on with your letter; I have several pages of *'she kicked.'*"

[The Yankee clucks as in urging horses to move, and continues the clucking noise with rapid repetition for some time.]

The scribe throws down his pen.

"Write it deown! write it deown!"

"I can't!"

"Well, then, I won't pay you."

[The scribe, gathering up his papers.] "What shall I do with all these sheets upon which I have written your nonsense?"

"You may use them in doing up your *gape-seed.* Good-by!"

The Yorkshireman of America

THIS is, perhaps, the most appropriate place for some observations on him who plays the "title-rôle" in this part of the States; though the prevalent absurdity in England of calling an American of whatever state by the general title of Yankee is not greater than the misapplication of the title in America to all classes of New-Englanders. The origin of the name, indeed, as stated by Heck Welder,[1] is the Indian pronunciation of "English"—"Yengeese"—by which appellation they distinguished the New-Englanders from the Virginians, or Southern people, whom they called the

From *Retrospections of America, 1797–1811*, by John Bernard, Edited from the Manuscript by Mrs. Bayle Bernard, With an Introduction, Notes, and Index by Laurence Hutton and Brander Matthews, pp. 36–37. Copyright, 1886, by Harper & Brothers. New York. 1887.

[1] Rev. John Gottlieb Ernestus Heckewelder. See "Yankee" below.

"Long-knives." Yankee, however, is really now a term denoting character rather than locality, and represents a certain set of qualities in a particular grade of society. The Yankee is a man of the lower orders, sometimes a farmer, more often a mechanic (the very spirit of mechanism embodied), and yet more usually a travelling trader. The Yankee is the Yorkshireman of America; the same cunning, calculating, persevering personage, with an infusion of Scotch hardiness and love of wandering. Like him, he goes upon the principle that all men are rogues, and like him he is instanced by his customers as the best illustration of the doctrine. He has the same talent for expedients; the same keen eye to character and to expedite a sale; the same want of nicety in regard to means, so long as they are not legally offensive (going to jail he considers not so much a disgrace as a waste of time), so that it would be just as appropriate to call the refined gentry and enlightened manufacturers of the County of York "regular Yorkshiremen," as to cite any man who moves in the respectable circle of Boston as "a regular Yankee."

Yorkshire Stories

I'M YORKSHIRE [1]

THE Rev. Robert Collyer tells a good story about a Yorkshireman. He says they are much like the Yankees in some respects; for instance, they are always sharp at bargaining, and also full of curiosity, and, like Yankees, are given to asking questions on every occasion where information can be gained thereby, on any subject however trivial. But sharp as they are at bargains, when they once agree to make a trade and shake hands on it, they stick to it, although subsequently one of the parties may discover that he has been overreached by the other. He said that on one occasion a Yorkshire farmer was ploughing with his horse, and the animal suddenly dropped dead in the furrow. The farmer let him lie there, and instantly drove over to the house of another farmer about five miles away. He dismounted and walked into the house on the invitation of his farmer friend, and they talked on various subjects. At last the visitor said:—

"You know my white horse?"

"Oh, yes, very well," was the reply.

"How will you trade your bay horse for him?"

"Even," said his friend.

"Shake hands on it," and they shook hands.

Whereupon the visitor remarked:—

[1] From *Funny Stories*, Told by Phineas T. Barnum, pp. 123–124. Copyright, 1890, by Phineas T. Barnum. New York, London, Glasgow and Manchester: George Routledge and Sons, Limited.

"My horse lies dead in the furrow, where he fell while ploughing this afternoon."

"All right," said the other, "mine died last Thursday, and his skin is hanging in the barn."

MY DOG IS YORKSHIRE, TOO[2]

A Yorkshire boy visited Liverpool one day, taking his dog along with him. He never had been in so large a city before, and consequently stared into all the store-windows and gazed around, as nearly every object was new to him, keeping up a run of questions to passers-by.

"What be that?" was his question continually repeated. Entering the large fish-market, whenever he saw a fish that was new and strange to him the question was immediately put, "What be that?" He came to a barrel full of live lobsters. "What be they?" he asked in astonishment, pointing his finger to the barrel.

"Lobsters," was the reply; "and you may take hold of them if you like."

"Nay, nay, I be Yorkshire, I be."

"Well, put your dog's tail in the barrel."

"Ay, I will do that"; upon which he lifted up his dog and let his tail drop in among the lobsters. One large-sized one caught his tail, upon which the dog jumped from its master and ran yelping down the street, the lobster holding on firmly. The fishermen all screamed with delight, and ran to the door to hear the dog yelp and see him run.

The young Yorkshireman looked on with astonishment and open mouth. Presently the dog turned the corner of the street and was out of sight.

"Hold on!" cried the fisherman; "your dog has run away with my lobster; call him back."

"Nay," said the boy, "my dog is Yorkshire, too; call back your lobster!"

YORKSHIRE [8]

A Yorkshire boy asked a gentleman for some salt, who gave it [to] him, and asked why he wanted it. "Perhaps," said the boy, "you may give me an egg, and I wish to be ready to eat it." "Then take an egg," replied the gentleman. "Are there not many horse stealers in Yorkshire?" "My father," quoth the boy, "is a Yorkshireman, and is thought to be an honest man, but would no more mind stealing a horse, than I would drinking your ale" (turning the gentleman's ale down his throat at the same time). "That will do: I see you are Yorkshire."

---

[2] *Ibid.*, pp. 124–125.

[9] From *The Laughing Philosopher:* or Fun, Humour, and Wit; Being a Collection of Choice Anecdotes, Many of Which, Never Before in Print, Originated in or about "The Literary Emporium," p. 92. Pittsburgh, Pennsylvania: Published by Cook and Schoyer. Louisville, Kentucky: Maxwell, Cook and Company. 1834.

TRICKS OF THE TRADE

Peddler Humor

THE reputation the early peddler won was enjoyed by chapmen of even so late a date as the Civil War. In fact, it was shrewdly turned to account as a bit of humour in the introductory remarks that preceded the bargaining. A peddler would drive up to a house and blithely address his prospective customer in some such patter as this: "Madam, are you in need of any pocket saw-mills? Horn gun flints? Basswood hams? Wooden nutmegs? White oak cheeses? Tin bungholes? Or calico hog troughs?" And having gained the smile of the lady of the house, he proceeded to recite what he actually did have in his wagon—tinware, mats, glassware, brooms, washboards, clothes pins, rolling pins, matches, paddy irons, kettles, and pots.

The yarns about Yankee clock peddlers are legion. Perhaps the most amusing is the one about the peddler who always sold a clock on the understanding that he would return in a few weeks, and, if the clock did not run satisfactorily, would replace it with another. It was also his rule to sell all the clocks in his stock but one. When he reached the end of his route he turned back with his one remaining clock. At the first house, the clock he had sold did not run, so he replaced it with the one that remained. At the second house, he replaced the unsatisfactory clock with the one he had taken from the first house. And so on, he went, selling and replacing clocks that never would work, and waxing fat on the proceeds!

One of the Yankee maritime peddling tricks was this: The New England crew would buy corn of the plantation owners. The grain was measured on the quarter deck near the centre. When the measuring commenced, one of the crew began playing a jig on a violin, and all the spare hands started dancing vehemently. As the deck was springy, some of the corn would spill into the scuppers. The percentage of corn gained by this operation was considerable.

A Watch Trade

AFTER seeing your letter to Ephraim, as I said before, I concluded it wouldn't be a bad scheme to tackle up and take a load of turkeys, some

From *Hawkers & Walkers in Early America*, Strolling Peddlers, Preachers, Lawyers, Doctors, Players, and Others, from the Beginning to the Civil War, by Richardson Wright, pp. 22, 84, 254. Copyright, 1927, by J. B. Lippincott Company. Philadelphia.

From *My Thirty Years Out of the Senate*, by Major Jack Downing, pp. 46–49. Entered, according to Act of Congress, in the Clerk's Office of the District Court of the Southern District of New York, by Seba Smith. New York: Oaksmith & Company. 1859.

apple-sass, and other notions that the neighbors wanted to get to market, and as your Uncle Nat would be in Boston with the ax-handles, we all thought best to try our luck there. Nothing happened worth mentioning on the road, nor till next morning after I got here and put up in Elm street. I then got off my watch pretty curiously, as you shall be informed. I was down in the bar-room, and thought it well enough to look pretty considerable smart, and now and then compared my watch with the clock in the bar, and found it as near right as ever it was, when a feller stept up to me and ask'd how I'd trade? and says I, for what? and says he, for your watch, and says I, any way that will be a fair shake; upon that says he, I'll give you *my* watch and five dollars; says I, it's done! He gave me the five dollars, and I gave him my watch. Now, says I, give me *your* watch; and, says he, with a loud laugh, I han't got none, and that kind a turned the laugh on me. Thinks I, let them laugh that lose. Soon as the laugh was well over the feller thought he'd try the watch to his ear; why, says he, it don't go; no, says I, not without it's carried; then I began to laugh. He tried to open it and couldn't start it a hair, and broke his thumb nail into the bargain. Won't she open, says he? Not's I know on, says I, and then the laugh seemed to take another turn.

Razor-Strop Trade

"I RECKON I couldn't drive a trade with you to-day, Square," said a "ginooine" specimen of a Yankee peddler, as he stood at the door of a merchant in St. Louis.

"I reckon you calculate about right, for you *can't*," was the sneering reply.

"Well, I guess you needn't git huffy 'beout it. Now here's a dozen ginooine razor-strops—worth $2.50; you may have 'em for $2.00."

"I tell you I don't want any of your traps—so you may as well be going along."

"Wal, now look here, Square, I'll bet you five dollars, that if you make me an offer for them 'ere strops, we'll have a trade yet."

"Done!" replied the merchant, placing the money in the hands of a bystander. The Yankee deposited a like sum.

"Now," said the merchant, "I'll give you a picayune [sixpence] for the strops."

"They're your'n!" said the Yankee as he quietly pocketed the stakes.

"But," said he, after a little reflection, and with great apparent honesty, "I calculate a joke's a joke; and if you don't *want* them strops, I'll trade back."

The merchant's countenance brightened.

From *Cyclopaedia of Commercial and Business Anecdotes* . . . by Frazar Kirkland, Vol. II, p. 555. Entered, according to Act of Congress, in the year 1864, by D. Appleton and Company, in the Clerk's Office of the District Court of the United States for the Southern District of New York. New York and London.

"You are not so bad a chap, after all," said he; "here are your strops, give me the money."

"There it is," said the Yankee, as he received the strops and passed over the sixpence. "A trade is a trade; and, now you are wide awake, the next time you trade with that 'ere sixpence, you'll do a little better than to buy razor strops."

And away walked the peddler with his strops and his wager, amidst the shouts of the laughing crowd.

Wooden Clocks and Wooden Oats

... "Ye sees, [said the "poor white" Tennessee native to me] dad hed nary clock, an' couldn't tell when the sun riz—he hed a great reespect fur the sun, nuver got up afore it in all his life—so, when a peddler come 'long with a whole waginload uv clocks, he war drefful put ter't ter hev one. They wus the eight-day kine, all painted up slick, an' worronted to gwo till the eend uv time. The peddler axed ten dollar fur 'um, an' dad hedn't but three. I hed two thet I'd bin a savin' up, an' dad wanted ter borre 'um, but I wouldn't a lent 'um ter him ter save his soul, fur I know'd he'd nuver pay in nuthin' but promises, an' fur his age, dad war the most promizin' man ye uver know'd on. Wall, I buttoned up my pocket, and dad eyed the clocks; an' sez he ter the peddler: 'Stranger, I'd loike 'un uv them mightily, but rocks is sca'ce, jest now; I hain't got on'y three dollars in the wurle.'

" 'Hain't ye!' said the peddler; 'wall, thet's a all-fired pity; but bein's ye's a monstrous nice sort o' man, an' bein's I allers kind o' took ter sech folks as ye is, ye kin hev a clock fur yer three dollars. But I wouldn't sell 'un ter nary uther man for thet money, nohow.'

"Wall, dad tuck the clock, and the peddler tuck the money and mosey'd off.

"Dad sot druffel high on thet clock. He took on over it fur all the wurle, jest like a chile over a new playthin'. He got up airlier, an' sot up later then I uver know'd him afore, jest ter yere it strike, but arter a few days it stopped strikin', an' nuver struck agin! Dad wus sold—an' sold, too, by a rantankerous Yankee; an' dad allers 'counted (but mind, stranger, I doan't guv this as my 'pinion) thet a Yankee ar a leetle the measliest critter in all creation. Wall, not more'n a month arter thet, as dad an' I wus a wuckin' in the corn patch 'un day, who shud come 'long the road but the Yankee peddler. As soon as dad seed him he sez ter me, sez he 'Bullets an' blisters, Tom! but thar's thet outdacious Yankee! Now, ef I doan't strike better time on his noggin then his dingnation clocks uver

From *Down in Tennessee, and Back By Way of Richmond*, by Edmund Kirke, pp. 113–117. Entered according to Act of Congress, in the year 1864, by J. R. Gilmore, in the Clerk's Office of the District Court of the United States for the Southern District of New York. New York: Carleton, Publisher.

struck in all thar lives, I'll pike stret fur kingdom-come, ef I hes ter gwo afoot.' Bilin' with wrath, dad moseyed fur the peddler; but he hedn't more'n got inside o' hearin', 'fore the Yankee bawled out: 'I say, Mister, ye's got a clock as b'longs ter me. It woan't gwo, an' I want's ter get it, an' guv ye 'un as wull gwo. I hed jest 'un bad one in the lot, an' I'se bin a sarchin' fur it 'mong nigh onter a hun'red folks I'se sold clocks ter, an' hain't found it yit, so ye mus' hev tucken it; I knows ye did, case I sees it in yer eye.'

"That mellored dad ter onst, an' ter own the truth, it guv *me* a sort o' good 'pinion uv the Yankee. Wall, dad and he swopped clocks, an' the peddler stayed ter dinner—an' the old man 'udnt take a red fur't, he war so taken with him. As he wus a gwine ter leave, the peddler ope'd the hind eend uv his wagin, an' takin' out a peck measure, heapin' full of what 'peared the tallest oats thet uver grow'd, he sez ter me, sez he: 'Tom, ye an' yer farder hes bein 'mazin clever ter me, an' I nuver loikes ter be obligated ter no body, so yere's some o' the finest plantin' oats ye uver know'd on; take 'um; they'll grow ye a monstrous tall crop, as big as oak trees.'

"Now ye sees, I hed a four-year-old mar I'd a raised up with my own han's. I sot drefful high on har, an' she got drefful high on oats, an' I'd bin a savin' up them two dollars s'pressly ter buy seed ter make a crap fur her privat' eatin'. So, when I seed them oats o' the peddler's they filled my eye, loike the camel filled the eye of the needle in Scriptur'. He hedn't guv'n me 'nuff ter gwo no distance in plantin', but bein' he war so gen'rous loike, I couldn't ax him ter guv me more, so I sez ter him: 'Stranger, wouldn't ye sell a bushel o' them oats?'

" 'Wall, Tom,' he sez; 'bein's it's ye, an' ye an' yer farder is sech monstrous clever folk, I doan't know but I'd sell ye the *whole* on 'um, fur the fact ar' they's too hearty loike fur my hoss; ye see the feller's got a sort o' weak stomach, an' can't 'gest 'um. I guess thar's nigh on ter five bushel, an' bein's they hain't uv no use ter me, ye shill have the whole on 'um fur them ar' two dollars o' yourn.' Now, I figger'd on my fingers, an' foun' thet warn't more'n forty cents a bushel; an' oats, sech as war raised in our diggins, an' they warn't no way nigh so nice as them—went fur sixty, so ye kin reckon I tuck 'um, an' ye mought b'lieve it rained big blessin's on thet peddler 'bout the time he druv off. He'd altered my 'pinion o' the Yanks 'pletely, an' I tole him he orter make hisself inter a wild munag'ree, an' travil the whole southin kentry, jest ter show folk what the Yankees raaly is; fur I know'd ef he done it they'd swap thar 'pinions jest as I hed, an' thet ye know would do a mighty heap to'ards perpertratin' the Union. Wall, arter he was gone, I tuck the five bushel inter the house, an' kivered 'um up keerful in the cockloft; but, feelin' mighty gen'rous loike, on 'count uv my big bargin', I thor't I'd guv the mar a sort o' Christmas dinner o' the peck measure full. So I put 'um afore her, an' she smelled on 'um ravernous mad fur a minnet, but then she turned up har nose, an' wouldn't luck at 'um agin.

"She found them too hearty loike; I suppose," I said, restraining a strong inclination to laugh.

"I 'spose she did, an' I reckon they *would* hev bin raather hard o' 'gestion, fur they WUS SHOE PEGS!'"

"Shoe pegs?"

"Yas, shoe pegs! The durnation Yankee hed a scowrn the hull deestrict, an' found no 'un green 'nuff ter buy 'um, but me."

Amid the general laugh which ensued, I asked:

"And how about the clock: how did that turn out?"

"Twus wuss nur 'tother—it nuver struck onst."

"Well that Yankee was smart," said the captin. "It takes a smart one to get ahead of you, Tom."

"He didn't git ahead uv me," replied Tom, with comic indignation. "I wus three dollars inter him when I got shut o' them oats. Ye sees, I toted 'um ter Pikeville, an' sold 'um fur whot they raaly wus—shoe pegs—an' got five dollars fur the lot. The peddler mought hev done it, ef he could onyhow hev brought his mind to act honest, but he'd ruther cheat fur half price, nur trade fa'r fur full pay. An' thet's the sort o' Yankee ye's sent 'mongst us, Stranger. They's done a heap to'ards guvin us a bad 'pinion on ye, an' brungin' on this war."

Grandma Willey's Chair

I TOOK a party once from Black Mountain House over to Crawford Notch. They wanted to visit the old Willey House. I remember it was kept at the time by Azariah Moore. You've heard about the Willey Slide, how the whole family was destroyed by rushing out doors when the slide came, and how if they'd stayed in the house they'd have been saved. The slide split behind up the house and went both sides of it—never touched the house. Lots of legends clustered about the old house. One was that there was a crippled old Grandma Willey who couldn't run out when the rest did and sat in her wooden rocking chair while the slide went by on her both sides.

At the time my crowd was up there they were very curious about an old wooden rocking chair which stood in the middle of the room. It was pretty dilapidated, chopped up, pieces hacked out of it. "What's that chair?" one of them asked. "Why," said Azariah Moore, "that's old Grandma Willey's rocking chair. One she sat in time of the slide, and was saved. Ain't you never heard about it?" They never had, so he told 'em. Nothing will do with these summer people but they must have a souvenir from every place they visit, and as Azariah explained that the condition of the chair was due to the hunger of visitors for souvenirs, my people asked if they might have a chip. "Oh, certainly," he consented. "Everybody teased me so for chips along back—they even whittled 'em out of the chair

---

As told by Mr. Willis to Mr. Pratt. Manuscripts of the Federal Writers' Project of the Works Progress Administration for the State of New Hampshire.

when I wa'n't looking. Go ahead. And I even furnish the hatchet to cut out the chips with. Here 'tis, if you want to use it."

They did, and as they were busy using it, Azariah slyly crooked his finger at me from the door to come out into the kitchen toward the bar room. "You see, Willie," he told me in a low voice, "when I found the summer folks was so possessed to lug away souvenirs of every curiosity in the mountains I got to providing 'em. I provide 'em old Grandma Willey's chair in there. I buy 'em new, scratch and bang 'em up, hack 'em up, till they look pretty old, for a starter, and then turn 'em over to the summer folks, and they do the rest. That's the third old Grandma Willey chair they've had this season. Oh, of course, they give me a little something—a quarter a chip—standard price."

A Deal in Timberland

I MADE my money from lumber and real estate mostly. I got started young and I worked hard. First I used my hands and muscles; then I started using my brain and letting other men work with their hands. A lot more strong backs in this country than there are sharp minds. Didn't take me long to figger it out neither. I was a young feller, in my twenties, and doing pretty well. I owned a sawmill and a store and a lot of land. I had some good timberlands, some of the best around. I always knew my lumber. I took to lumber like a redheaded woodpecker.

This big New York company wanted to buy some of my timberland. They sent men up here to look it all over, and they liked the looks of it first-rate. I made sure they saw the best stuff standing. Well, after fussing and fooling around they went back to New York to report. Had some correspondence with the company. I was supposed to go to New York to close the deal. I knew them fellers thought I was pretty green, so I thought I'd have some fun with 'em.

I bought a whole new outfit for the trip down to New York. I bought some overalls, a jumper, boots, sheepskin, leggings, and I dressed up in 'em and wore 'em down. Them city fellers liked to died when they see me come in the office!

I says to 'em: "Had a tarnation of a time finding this place. So many big high buildings and so many people. You're way up in the air here, ain't you? How fur you s'posed it is down to the ground? I ain't used to all this commotion. Almost wish I had stayed to home!"

I says to 'em: "This is my best outfit I got on here. Only wear it to dress up for something special. Couple of years I'll buy me a new one, and I'll put this right on for everyday. Up home we have to be sparing of our clothes."

As told by "Hank" Davis to Roaldus Richmond. Manuscripts of the Federal Writers' Project of the Works Progress Administration for the State of Vermont.

I says: "What be them cars that run up on top of them tall poles and make such an awful racket. I wouldn't dare to walk under 'em, let alone ride in 'em. I never see such contraptions as you got here in the city."

Well, by God, them city fellers was having more fun with me, you know —but not half so much fun as I was having with them. Finally we got round to talking business. They wanted to give me three thousand dollars, down payment. I held out for five thousand. They begin to sweat and squirm a little then. After quite a spell they got ready to write me off a check for five thousand. I stalled 'em off some more, said I'd promised my wife not to close the deal till I talked with her. They wanted me to use the office phone, but I said I had to have a private telephone booth when I talked to my wife on account she had such a loud voice it might rupture folks's eardrums that wa'n't used to listening to it. So they let me go out. I stopped in a place I knew before and got a couple of drinks. I gave the bartender some more of that farmer lingo, and the fellers in there liked to died laughing at me. What I really went out for was to go to a bank and see if their check was any good. I found out it was and I went back to the office and picked it up. Them fellers didn't appear none too happy!

Then I asks 'em how I'm going to get back to the depot.

I told 'em I was pretty apt to get lost in all the crowds and traffic and noise. I said I couldn't keep from looking up at the high buildings and it made me dizzy and I was apt to fall down and get run over. Well, by God, you know what they did? They sent a man right along with me clear up as far as White River Junction!

Well, in the spring them city fellers came up to take over, you know, and I collected the rest on the land. After they talked to some of the local lumbermen, they begun to think maybe they hadn't made such a good deal as they thought. They found out they hadn't stung Hank Davis a whole hell of a lot. And here's the best part of it all now. That company went *bankrupt* trying to get the lumber out of there!

HORSE JOCKEYS

From Nags to Riches

A CLASSIC story of New England horse trading is one told about the Vermont Yankee who set out from his home in the northern part of the state driving a sorry nag hitched to a decrepit buggy. At the first opportunity he swapped the horse and buggy and then traded again and again as he proceeded southward through his native state. When he reached Brattle-

From *The Horse & Buggy Age in New England,* by Edwin Valentine Mitchell, p. 193. Copyright, 1937, by Coward-McCann, Inc. New York.

boro he was driving a fine span of horses hitched to a splendid new carriage.

The Chestnut Mare

THE country storekeeper, if he is to be a successful merchant, must be able to deal with any and all, must buy a great many things—must know what to say and must sift a small amount of truth out of a vast pile of lies and must know values of nearly everything. One morning in early summer when business wasn't very rushing, I was hoeing in my garden and thinking how nicely things were growing and what a beautiful world we lived in and was wishing I could do someone a kindness, when a man drove up with a chestnut mare with a new harness on, in a new top buggy, all looking like something out of a Sears & Roebuck catalog. He said, "Gould, I want to sell you this horse. My wife is in the hospital and I have got to have some money. She is a nice young horse just seven years old. I know because I raised her myself. She is all sound and kind and right in every way and I will take $75 for her and she is worth $150 of any man's money."

Now I found out later that the only true thing about this whole statement was that he wanted to sell me that horse. I took a look at the lady and kept on hoeing. I noted that her ears were laid back at a peculiar slant and that she had eyes like a stinking fish, nearly all white, and that scattered over her hide were numerous stripes of white hair that looked to me as if someone had remonstrated with her with a club. I said, "She looks a lot more like $5 than $75," and he hit her a crack with the whip and vanished in a cloud of dust.

I thought I had looked my last upon the chestnut mare, but it was not to be. About a month later the telephone rang and I answered and a voice asked, "Did you tell Harold that you would give $5 for his chestnut mare?" I said, "No, but I guess I would." He said, "I'll bring her over," and I had a horse. The owner had put her out to pasture and she proved to be breachy. The pasturer demanded that she be removed and because he couldn't do any better, I got her. I couldn't imagine a sound horse that wasn't worth $5, but she was it. Of all the detestable beasts I ever owned she was the undoubted queen. She refused to work single or double. I could drive her at a very slow pace if I didn't feed her any grain, but if she was fed four quarts of oats for a week, no one could drive her. I had had balky horses before and had always found ways to make them useful, but not this lady.

One balky horse that I had owned was cured as far as I was concerned, but he could not be trusted with hired men. I had a neighbor who was disliked by everyone, named S.K. Neversole. One of my hired men went up to a neighbor's one evening and said, "I believe Gould is crazy. He talks to his horses just as if they were men. That horse he calls Josh balked up with me today; he wouldn't work nor let the other one work. I went down and told Gould and he said, 'That is funny, he don't do that with me.' And he went up and took the horse by the head and turned him around and lifted up his collar and patted his neck, and then he took him by the head and said, 'Now Josh, if you don't go to work I shall change your name and call you S.K. Neversole,' and I'll be damned if the horse didn't go to work."

But changing her name made no impression. I found then that a balky mare is a poor bet. When winter came and I had a man hauling wood, I had quite a quantity of wood that had to be yarded to the road to top out the load. I got a one-horse sled and took the old mare into the woods, resolved to make her haul or know the reason. On my way into the woods I stopped and cut a thorn bush about ten feet long and about two inches in diameter. I trimmed off enough brush to give me a handle and threw it on the sled and drove up to a pile of wood and threw on six sticks. The old pirate turned her head and watched me and I hung the reins on a stake and said, "Get up." She humped herself up like the dromedary on a package of dates and grunted and rolled those dead-white eyes at me, saying in the horse language, "What are you going to do about it?" She soon learned.

I gave an awful yell and picked up my persuader and swung it over my head and brought it down with a crash. There must have been a thousand thorns on it. She grunted once, but the second one followed the first and the third was on its way when she quit. I had a wild ride out to the road. I halted her and threw off the wood and went back. This time I put on twelve sticks. She humped up and grunted again, but another yell and a second application started her. By noon I had her so she was hauling a fair load and would start when I yelled. After dinner I had to use the bush once more, but soon she was working like anyone's horse.

Near my woodpile lived a man with nothing to do except worry about other people's business. He used to come out and talk to me while I was unloading, and he often spoke of what a fine work horse she was. I didn't like to dispute him, but one day I came home and found a horse dealer who told me he wanted a young cheap horse. I told him I had one and led her out. He asked, "What is the story?" and I said, "The man I bought her of said she was seven years old and smooth and sound and a good driver and kind so women could handle her and my wife drives." He asked, "What kind of a worker is she?" and I said, "I wouldn't recommend her as a worker. She isn't built for it. She is a better driver than a worker, still I yarded out that pile of wood with her." He asked the price and I told him $50. He went up and asked my neighbor and got a red-hot recommendation for a work horse. He came back and said, "You have got to shave that price—I am a dealer and I have got to make something." I finally took off ten percent and we traded.

When he drove off with the old mare leading behind he said, "I'll have her looking different in three weeks." The next time I saw him he said, "Gould, you lied to me about that mare." I said, "If I have lied to you in the least degree, I will refund your money and take her back. Now what did I say that wasn't the truth?" He said, "You said she was a good worker." I said, "No, I said I wouldn't recommend her as a worker as she was a much better driver than a worker." He said, "She is no driver at all." I ended, "Have you tried to work her?" He said, "No." I said, "You try that and you will find that I was right." He said, "She balks in a buggy in the stable floor." I said, "You mustn't feed her grain as she can't bear prosperity." Finally he said, "Your neighbor said she was a fine worker." I said, "If I was in your place I would sue him for damages as she never was and I don't think ever will be, but to show that my heart is right, I will give you the thorn bush that I used to stimulate her with before she came out of the woods."

He invited me to go to hell but I was always glad that I told him the truth and if you are going to deal with hard-headed, hard-hearted Yankees, I advise you to go no farther.

Playing the Game

HORSETRADING . . . was not supposed to be honest; it was a game of skill played by two professionals set to do each other down. Women said that horsetrading was wrong but men who liked to dicker about horses paid no attention. A smart trader was said to have swapped horses seven times at Camp Meeting, going home with the horse he started with and $100 to boot. If the buyer were cheated, the procedure was to say nothing, defend the animal to all comers and get rid of him as soon as possible and then do the cheater down on some subsequent trade, much later. Two really confirmed traders would spend two hours arguing, "If you will agree that the horse is worth $100, I will let you have him for $85 cash." . . . "Iffen you will let him go for $85, stands to reason he ain't worth $65. . . ."

A Dependable Horse

FOGG'S General Store—Grain, Coal, Groceries, Notions, Tobacco, and Candy [Hancock, New Hampshire]. It was an important institution, circa 1910. . . . Fogg's was more than a place of business, however. It was

From *A Maine Hamlet*, by Lura Beam, p. 171. Copyright, 1957, by Lura Beam. New York: Wilfred Funk, Inc.

From *New England Flavor, Memories of a Country Boyhood*, by Haydn S. Pearson, pp. 58, 60–63. Copyright, 1961, by W. W. Norton & Company, Inc. New York. Reprinted by permission of the publisher.

a focal point for part of the town's social and civic life. Around that old stove, men discussed local, state, and national politics. While they waited around for their women-folk to make up their minds what they were going to buy, the men often cooked up a smart trade.

"Heard you was thinking of selling your old mare, Jim."

"No, I wasn't thinking of selling. Just happened to mention the other day at mail time that I didn't need three horses. Besides, Bessie isn't old, Amos. She's a mighty dependable mare. Can't be over eight or ten, maybe eleven."

"I'm not really thinking of buying, Jim. Just heard you wanted to sell. Did you hear about the new school teacher and how she went riding with that slick city drummer the other night? Heard she didn't get home until way after ten o'clock. Kinder risky, don't you think?"

"Could be. Though I don't think the drummers today are what they used to be. Now you take back about 1890, those drummer fellows were real actors. The last twenty years things have been going downhill. Look at these newfangled smelly contraptions they call automobiles. Go twenty miles an hour, I hear. Human beings weren't meant to go through life that fast. You thinking of getting another horse, Amos?"

"No, just heard you wanted to sell Bessie, Jim."

"Don't really want to sell. Bessie's a good-looking mare. Dependable too. 'Course if you needed another horse and the price was right I might trade. But I'd hate to see Bessie go. Got her last year from Bill Adams over in Hilltown. Bill said she was dependable. And she is. Say, Amos, has the road agent fixed up that mud hole over on your road? Heard tell you was a little stirred up over it."

"No, that dad-lazy rascal's been fixing up all the roads around town except mine. Over two weeks I couldn't get to town last April. We raised twelve hundred dollars at town meeting for roads and Seth's been spending money everywhere except over our way. I'm a taxpayer and I'm entitled to a good road like everyone else. How old did you say Bessie was?"

"She's probably going on ten or eleven, Amos. Might be twelve, but it's kinder hard to tell. Teeth are good and she's fat as a butterball. Good mare, Bessie, and dependable. Hate to see her go. She's a regular member of the family. Every morning she whinnies when I open the barn door, and she'll nuzzle me until I give her a lump of sugar or a piece of cookie. Has a sweet tooth, Bessie does. You need another horse?"

"No, don't really need one. But I sold one of mine last week and I like to keep three horses. When work is rushing it's good to have a spare. Heard you was over to Centerville to see your wife's folks last Sunday. They all well?"

"Yes, pretty good. Her folks are getting along but they keep tolerable. Her father's rheumatism kicks up in stormy weather. What sort of a horse you looking for, Amos?"

"Wasn't really looking, Jim. Just ·inquiring round. You put a price on Bessie yet?"

"No. I like Bessie. Don't know whether I ought to sell her or not. Harvest season coming on and a man needs a spare horse, like you say. Bessie's dependable. Hate to see her go."

"What price did you say, Jim?"

"Well, if you're anxious to buy, Jim, I'd let her go for $75.00."

"Guess you don't care much whether you sell or not, Jim."

"Might shade it a little. But Bessie's worth $60.00."

"Don't think I'd want to pay over $45.00 for just a spare horse."

"Bessie's more than a $45.00 horse, Amos. She's dependable. How's the corn and oats this season?"

"Got a good crop, Jim. Never saw corn come along any better than it has this year. You want to consider $50.00 for Bessie?"

"Well, I might. I don't need a third horse right now, and besides I'm thinking of trading with Alvin Stevens. Says he might swap his young gelding for a couple of my Jersey heifers. Could you make it $55.00? Bessie's dependable, Amos."

"No. I don't think she's worth $55.00. But if you'll throw in a horse collar, a whiffletree, and a pitchfork, I'll give you $52.50 and I'll take her along home right now."

And that's how the trade went. Maybe two weeks later, Jim and Amos would see each other again at Fogg's.

"Afternoon, Jim."

"Afternoon, Amos."

"Thought you said Bessie was dependable. She balks every time she's asked to pull a load."

"That's what I said. She's dependable. She balks, Amos, if she's asked to work. You can depend on it every time. By the way, I heard Jethro Seldon over in Antrim is looking for a good dependable horse. You might drop around and see him. Crops growing well, Amos?"

His Father's Horse

It is said to be a peculiarity of the Yankees that when they are buying a thing they have a habit of depreciating its worth by criticizing and finding faults with it in order to cheapen the cost. On one occasion one of this kind wanted to buy a horse from a dealer. A fine-looking animal was led out of the stable for him to examine. He looked him over and saw that apparently there was no defect and no room for complaint.

"Oh," said he, "that horse has a fine head—I won't run him down with so fine a head; it is astonishing how much that head reminds me of a horse my father owned twenty years ago. Well, that is a good shoulder too; forelegs well formed. How much they do remind me of a horse my father owned twenty years ago."

From *Funny Stories,* Told by Phineas T. Barnum, pp. 161–162. Copyright, 1890, by Phineas T. Barnum. New York, London, Glasgow, and Manchester: George Routledge and Sons, Limited.

Passing along the animal he continued:

"And those hind quarters are good; and what a beautiful fine tail! It is really wonderful how they remind me of a horse my father owned twenty years ago."

Turning round on the other side of the horse, he said:

"Fine mane, nice ears, splendid eyes. I declare it is marvelous how much they remind me of a horse my father owned twenty years ago."

And then opening the mouth to look at the teeth, he quietly said, "I guess it's the same horse."

A First-Rate Setter

THE story about the mule I think I have seen in print; it was about a farmer who wanted to buy a mule for his own use on his farm, which was several miles outside of the village in which he lived. A neighbour in the village owned a mule, and offered him for sale. The two men talked the matter over, the owner of the mule assuring the other that the animal was perfectly sound and good in every respect. The farmer purchased the animal, and while riding him out to his farm the next day, after going a mile or two, the mule suddenly stopped, sat down on his haunches, and would not budge. The usual mode of pulling, kicking and coaxing was resorted to, and at last the animal got on his feet again and went on. At night the farmer took the mule to his former owner, and said:—

"I have had enough of that animal. You said he was gentle and well-broken in every way; but to-day, while riding him toward my farm, he suddenly stopped, sat down, and would not budge an inch."

"Did you see a rabbit?" the mule-seller asked.

"Rabbit? No! What has that got to do with it?"

"Well, were you near any woods?"

"Let me see—yes, there were some woods close by; but what has that got to do with the mule?"

"I forgot to mention to you that he is a setter, and he must have seen a rabbit somewhere, and sat down, as he always does."

"I never heard of such a thing," exclaimed the purchaser.

"Well, I can't help that. He is a first-rate setter, and in all other respects is an excellent mule."

"Then I shall not often go where there are rabbits; so if this is all that ails him, I will keep him."

The next day, while riding the mule in the country, he attempted to cross a stream, and in the middle of the river the mule sat down as before, half-drowning the farmer. During the struggle to get him on his feet again, the farmer grew very indignant, and used some emphatic language not often heard in those parts. On his return to the village, he took the mule again to his former owner, and said:—

Ibid., pp. 103–105.

"There, you can take this animal back; I have had enough of him in the last two days."

"What is the matter now?"

"Why, I was nearly drowned to-day; the confounded beast sat down with me on his back in the middle of the stream!"

"Oh, that is all right; he is just as good on fish as he is on rabbits."

SMART MERCHANTS AND CUSTOMERS

Sam Temple's Store: A Rhyming Advertisement

Salt Pork and Powder, Shot and Flints,
Cheese, Sugar, Rum and Peppermints,

Tobacco, Raisins, Flour and Spice,
Flax, Wool, Cotton and sometimes
   Rice,

Old Holland Gin and Gingerbread,
Brandy and Wine, all sorts of Thread,

Segars I keep, sometimes on bunch;
Materials all for making Punch,

Biscuit and Butter, Eggs and Fishes.
Molasses, Beer and Earthen Dishes.

Books on such subjects as you'll find
A proper food to feast the mind.

Hard Soap and Candles, Tea and
   Snuff,
Tobacco Pipes—perhaps enough,

Shells, Chocolate, Stetson's Hoes
As good as can be (I suppose),

Straw Hats, Oats, Baskets, Oxen
   Muzzles,
A thing which many people puzzles,

Knives, Forks, Spoons, Plates, Mugs,
   Pitchers, Platters,
A Gun with shot wild geese bespatters,

Spades, Shovels, Whetstone, Scythes
   and Rakes,
As good as any person makes,

Shirts, Frocks, Shoes, Mittens, also
   Hose,
And many other kinds of Clothes,

Shears, Scissors, Awls, Wire, Bonnet
   Paper,
Old Violin and Cat Gut Scraper,

Tubs, Buckets, Pails and Pudding
   Pans,
Bandana Handkerchiefs and Fans,

Shagbarks and Almonds, Wooden
   Boxes,
Steel Traps (not stout enought for
   Foxes,

But excellent for holding Rats
When they elude the Paws of Cats),

From *Norfolk Repository*, Dedham, 1805. In *Grandfather Was Queer*, Early American Wags and Eccentrics from Colonial Times to the Civil War, by Richardson Wright, pp. 36–37. Copyright, 1939, by Richardson Wright. Philadelphia, New York, Toronto and London: J. B. Lippincott Company.

Samuel Temple, who harried the youth of his day by writing "Temple's Arithmetic," was also a rhymester of sorts. When he went into storekeeping, at Dedham, Mass., he set forth his stock in verse—and saw that it was printed in the local paper. —R. W.

I've more than Forty kinds of Drugs,
Some good for Worms and some for
    Bugs,

Lee's, Anderson's and Dexter's Pills,
Which cure at least a hundred ills,

Astringents, Laxatives, Emetics,
Cathartics, Cordials, Diuretics,

Narcotics, Stimulants and Pungents,
With half a dozen kinds of Unguents.

Perfume most grateful to the Nose
When mixed with Snuff or dropped on
    clothes,

One Medicine more (not much in
    fame),
Prevention is its real name,

An ounce of which, an author says
Outweighs a Ton of Remedies.

The many things I shall not mention
To sell them cheap is my intention.

Lay out a dollar when you come
And you shall have a glass of Rum.

N.B. Since man to man is so unjust,
'Tis hard to say whom I can trust.

I've trusted many to my sorrow:
Pay me today: I'll trust tomorrow.

Cordwood

. . . SKIN JUBB landed a load of cordwood at Jim's store a few weeks ago, small stuff, and half of it crookeder'n a dog's hind leg. Skin took his pay and started to hurry off as Jim went out to look it over. But 'fore Skin got out of hearin' Jim called him back—then handed him a quarter extry and a fi'-cent cigar. "Wut's all this for?" says Skin.

"Waal," says Jim, "the quarter is for the extry time you must-a spent huntin' up the smallest, crookedest sticks you could find—and the cigar's a prize for stackin' 'em up into a cord o' wood you could chase a cat through from any p'int of the compass!"[1]

Back in the days when bartering was more common, a man agreed to deliver a load of cordwood for a new pair of boots. He brought a load of poplar wood, which is very poor firewood. He received his pair of boots, but after he had worn them a couple of weeks the stitches began to come out and the eyelets to rip out and tear. He hurried into the shoemaker's and started to complain. The shoemaker silenced him with, "Wal, what do you expect of popple boots."[2]

---

[1] From *Village Down East*, Sketches of Village Life on the Northeast Coast of New England before "Gas-Buggies" Came, from Conversations with Zackary Adams, Duck Trap Cove, Maine, by John Wallace, p. 42. Copyright, 1943, by Stephen Daye Press, Inc. Brattleboro, Vermont.

[2] From "Whitefield" by Ola G. Veazie. Manuscripts of the Federal Writers' Project of the Works Progress Administration for the State of New Hampshire.

There's Odds in Deacons

TALES have been handed down of an elder who was a "leetle nigh" on a trade. To a would-be purchaser said he, "Waal, I'll allow that you'll be pleased to see that horse go up hill." The man bought the horse, soon returning. "The pesky critter balked at the first rise; tho't you sed she was a prime goer!" "Not jes so," answered the elder, "I said you'd be pleased to see her go up hill: naow wouldn't you?"

Expecting a customer for a cow, and wishing to keep the bargain on his side, Elder C. selected the most undesirable cow and placed her in his best stall; the farmer was affably told that he might choose any from the herd except Mammy's pet butter cow. "Couldn't part with her no ways." The customer got the pet cow. There is a saying in New England, "All deacons are good, but there's odds in deacons." [1]

The customers of a certain Deacon ——, who sold milk, complained after a while that the article furnished was blue and poor; to which he replied, "Do you think I would cheat you? I say upon my honor that I never put a drop of water in my milk in all my life." This answer satisfied his customers, till a certain hired man of his got mad, and left his service, when he let out the secret. He said, "The Deacon told you the truth when he said he never put a drop of water in his milk in all his life; but I'll tell you what he did do. He put water in his milk pail, and then milked into it." [2]

It reminded me of the good old deacon in Connecticut who was in the habit of selling milk to his neighbors on all days in the week. One Sunday, however, his parson came home with him to tea, and while they were at the table a little girl came in for a quart of milk. The deacon was afraid of being scandalized in the presence of the parson, and so he told the girl he did not sell milk on Sunday. The girl, who had been accustomed to buy on that day as on other days, was much surprised and turned to go away, when the sixpence in her hand was too much of a temptation for the deacon, who called out:

---

[1] From *Old Paths and Legends of the New England Border:* Connecticut, Deerfield, Berkshire, by Katharine M. Abbott, pp. 265–266. Copyright, 1907, by Katharine M. Abbott. New York and London: G. P. Putnam's Sons.

[2] From *Legends of Woburn,* Now First Written and Preserved in Collected Form . . . by Parker Lindall Converse, p. 129. Copyright, 1892, by Parker L. Converse. Woburn, Mass.: Printed for Subscribers Only.

"Here, little girl! you can leave the money now, and call and get the milk to-morrow!" [3]

The tobacco had to be kept from drying and this furnished the occasion of the wicked slander on the deacon, who was supposed to have said to his clerk, "John, have you wet down the tobacco?" "Yes, sir." "Have you sanded the sugar?" "Yes, sir." "Then come in to prayers!" [4]

One season had been very dry and the mill yard of Deacon Joel's saw mill was full of logs. The water to saw them was exhausted. The day before Fast Day, observed by the Orthodox as Sunday, there came a big rain. The pond began to run over into the spillway. This was too much for the Deacon. He lifted the gate and sawed away all day. Meeting Parson Leonard a few days later, he was surprised to be upbraided for what he had done. He answered with some acrimony: "Now, Parson, which is the more sinful, for me to work on Fast Day and give the money to the poor, or for you and Parson Sewall to swap horses at Little's Bridge twice every Sunday when you exchange pulpits and defraud the Bridge Company of its tolls?" [5]

Deaconing

IN PREPARING and packing fruit for the market, the practice of "deaconing," as it is called, is very extensively followed—that is, topping off a barrel of apples with the best specimens; the rather irreverent term "deaconing" having its origin, probably, from some one holding that office having been unfortunately distinguished for his frequent adoption of the

---

[3] From *Struggles and Triumphs: or, Forty Years' Recollections of P. T. Barnum, Written by Himself*, pp. 731–732. Entered according to Act of Congress, in the year 1871, by P. T. Barnum, in the Office of the Librarian of Congress, at Washington. Entered also at Stationer's Hall, London, England. Buffalo, New York: Warren, Johnson & Co. 1873.

[4] From *Black Tavern Tales, Stories of Old New England*, by Charles L. Goodell, p. 102. Copyright, 1932, by Charles L. Goodell. Brooklyn: Willis McDonald & Co.
Other versions refer to watering the rum, dusting the pepper, chicorying the coffee, larding the butter, and flouring the ginger.

[5] From *Marshfield, 70°–40' W: 42°–5' N, The Autobiography of a Pilgrim Town*, Being an Account of Three Hundred Years of a New England Town; Founded by the Pilgrims; Lived in and Developed by the Royalists; Adopted by Daniel Webster & Beloved by Many of the Ancestors of Those Who Today Make It Their Home, 1640–1940, p. 167. Copyright, 1940, by Marshfield Tercentenary Committee. Marshfield, Massachusetts.

From *Cyclopaedia of Commercial and Business Anecdotes* . . . , by Frazar Kirkland, Vol. I, p. 206. Entered, according to Act of Congress, in the year 1864, by D. Appleton and Company, in the Clerk's Office of the District Court of the United States for the Southern District of New York. New York and London.

plan, so as to put an inviting show on his fruit. A dealer down East, who happened to be "posted," sold a barrel of apples to a customer, at the same time recommending them as the choicest apples that had been raised in the town. In due time the barrel was opened, and found to contain a very inferior quality; whereupon the customer, feeling that he had been imposed upon, made complaint to the seller, who in turn very coolly made answer, that he guessed he must have opened the barrel at the wrong end! The only change this little episode was known to produce in the seller's practice was to make him careful afterward to "deacon" *both* ends.

As Good as His Word

IN AN interior town in old Connecticut lives a shaky character, named Ben Hayden. Ben has some good points, but he will run his face when and where he can, and never pay. In the same town lives Mr. Jacob Bond, who keeps the store at the corners. Ben had a "score" there, but to get his pay was more than Mr. Bond was equal to, as yet. One day Ben made his appearance with a bag and wheelbarrow, and said, "Mr. Bond, I want to buy two bushels of corn, and *I want to pay cash for it*." "Very well," replied Mr. Bond, "all right"; and so they both ascended the loft, and when the necessary operations were gone through with, they respectively returned. But by the time the trader had got down and looked around him, old Ben had got some distance from the door, and was rapidly making for home. "Halloo, halloo, Ben!" cried out the trader lustily; "you said you wanted to pay cash for that corn." Old Ben deliberately sat down on one handle of his barrow, and cocking his head on one side, said, "That's all true, Mr. Bond. I *do* want to pay you the cash for the corn, but I can't!"

Turning Water into Grog

A WELL known old sea captain of Searport, when about sixty years of age, nearly lost his shipping business and five schooners as a result of his taste for liquor. His eldest son was appointed conservator of his estate, and allowed the old captain to take a voyage now and then. The captain of the schooner on which he sailed was always instructed never to let the old gentleman have any money when on shore.

On the occasion of one of his trips, while anchored at T Wharf in Boston, the captain sat on deck looking the length of Atlantic Avenue, viewing the many saloon signs with a parched throat. After speculating

---

Ibid., 262.

By Mrs. Elva Kimball Walker, Mascoma, New Hampshire. Contributed by Mrs. Grace Partridge Smith, Carbondale, Illinois.

for hours as to how he could obtain a drink, he became inspired. Going to the cabin he filled a gallon demijohn half full of water, and hurried to the nearest saloon. Entering, he informed the bartender that he wanted the demijohn filled with rum, and said he thought that it would take about two quarts as it was already half full. When the bartender had filled the demijohn and demanded his pay the captain told him to charge it. Whereupon the bartender reclaimed his two quarts of rum. Repeating this at the next five saloons along the avenue, the captain returned to his ship with two quarts of excellent rum.

Paying for the Cider

AFTER I had walked about three or four hours I come along towards the upper end of the town where I found there were stores and shops of all sorts and sizes. And I met a feller, and says I, what place is this? Why this, says he, is Huckler's Row. What, says I, are these the stores where the traders in Huckler's Row keep? And says he, yes. Well then, thinks I to myself, I have a pesky good mind to go in and have a try with one of these chaps, and see if they can twist my eye teeth out. If they can get the best end of a bargain out of me, they can do what there aint a man in Downingville can do, and I should jest like to know what sort of stuff these ere Portland chaps are made of. So in I goes into the best looking store among 'em. And I see some biscuit lying on the shelf, and says I, Mister, how much do you ax apiece for them are biscuit? A cent apiece, says he. Well, says I, I shant give you that, but if you 've a mind to, I 'll give you two cents for three of 'em, for I begin to feel a little as though I should like to take a bite. Well, says he, I would n't sell 'em to any body else so, but seeing it's you I don't care if you take 'em. I knew he lied, for he never see me before in his life. Well he handed down the biscuits and I took 'em, and walked round the store awhile to see what else he had to sell. At last, says I, Mister, have you got any good new cider? Says he, yes, as good as ever you see. Well, says I, what do you ax a glass for it? Two cents, says he. Well, says I, seems to me I feel more dry than I do hungry now. Aint you a mind to take these ere biscuit again and give me a glass of cider? And says he, I dont care if I do; so he took and laid 'em on the shelf again, and poured out a glass of cider. I took the cider and drinkt it down, and to tell the truth it was capital good cider. Then, says I, I guess it 's time for me to be a going, and I stept along towards the door. But, says he, stop Mister. I believe you have n't paid me for the cider. Not paid you for the cider, says I, what do you mean by that? Did n't the biscuit that I give you jest come to the cider? Oh, ah, right, says he. So I started to go again; and says he, but stop, Mister, you did n't pay me for

From *The (Old) Farmer's Almanack,* Calculated on a New and Improved Plan for the Year of Our Lord 1934, No. 142, by Robert B. Thomas, p. 49. Copyright, 1933, by Carroll J. Swan. Boston, Massachusetts.

the biscuit. What, says I, do you mean to impose upon me? do you think I am going to pay you for the biscuit and let you keep 'em tu? Aint they there now on your· shelf, what more do you want? I guess sir, you dont whittle me in that way. So I turned about and marched off, and left the feller staring and thinking and scratching his head, as though he was struck with a dunderment. Howsomever, I did n't want to cheat him, only jest to show 'em it wan't so easy a matter to pull my eye teeth out, so I called in next day and paid him his two cents.

The Egg, the Darning-Needle, and the Treat

. . . A TRADE at a store was an occasion for drinking; and I have an anecdote at command which illustrates how strong the obligation of the custom was upon the merchant to treat his customer after trading with him. (The occurrence is said to have taken place on the New York side of the lake; though, if the story is true, I think one of the parties must certainly have been a Yankee.) According to the account, the patronizing customer took an egg, and went to the store to buy a darning-needle. The purchase was made, and the egg taken in payment. The purchaser remained some time as if waiting for something; but the merchant seemed rather disposed to take no notice of the common rule, in such case made and provided. At length the customer seemed to suspect a design to dodge, and getting somewhat out of patience, he turned and popped the momentous question: "An't ye goin' to treat?" "O certainly," said the merchant, and the decanter of brandy, a bowl of sugar, a pitcher of water and a tumbler were set on. The mixture was made, when the customer again looked up and said, "I guess I'll take an egg to put into it." The same egg that had just been bought was accordingly handed on. But, on breaking it the customer exclaimed: "Here, see! the egg I let ye have had *two yelks*, and I guess you ought to let me have two darning-needles." And the darning-needle was accordingly handed over, and thus the trade was closed.

Paying for the Stolen Butter

No OTHER class of men in any country possess that facetious aptness of inflicting a good-humored revenge which seems to be innate with a Green

From Gov. Eaton's Temperance Address—an Extract, Delivered before the Young Men's Temperance Association, at Enosburgh in 1855, in *The Vermont Historical Gazetteer: A Magazine Embracing a History of Each Town, Civil, Ecclesiastical, Biographical and Military*, edited by Abby Maria Hemenway, Vol. II, p. 161. Entered according to Act of Congress, in the year 1871, by Abby Maria Hemenway, in the Office of the Librarian of Congress, at Washington. Burlington, Vermont.

From *Wehman's Idle Hours with the Humorists*, Brimful of Fun about Yankee Yarns, Western Sports, Boarding-House Hash, Rich College Scrapes, Wild Widows' Wit, and Tall Tales of Sailors and Marines, pp. 28–30. New York: Published by Henry J. Wehman. [n. d.]

Mountain boy. Impose upon or injure a Vermonter, and he will seem the drollest and best-natured fellow you ever knew in all your life, until suddenly he pounces upon you with some cunningly devised offset for your duplicity; and even while he makes his victim smart to the core, there is that manly open-heartedness about him which infuses balm even while the wound is opening, and renders it quite impossible that you should hate him, however severe may have been the punishment he dealt out to you. These boys of the Green Mountains seem to possess a natural faculty of extracting fun from every vicissitude and accident that the changing hours can bring; even what are bitter vexations to others, these happy fellows treat in a manner so peculiar as to completely alter their former character and make them seem to us agreeable, or at least endurable, which was before in the highest degree offensive. Another man will repay an aggravation or an insult by instantly returning injury, cutting the acquaintance and shutting his heart for ever against the offender; but a Vermonter, with a smile upon his face, will *amuse* himself while obtaining a far *keener* revenge, cracking a joke in conclusion, and making his former enemy forgive him and even love him after chastisement.

One winter evening, a country store-keeper in the Green Mountain State was about closing his doors for the night, and while standing in the snow outside putting up his window shutters, he saw through the glass, a lounging worthless fellow within grab a pound of fresh butter from the shelf and hastily conceal it in his hat.

The act was no sooner detected than the revenge was hit upon, and a very few moments found the Green Mountain store-keeper at once indulging his appetite for fun to the fullest extent, and paying off the thief with a facetious sort of torture for which he might have gained a premium from the old inquisition.

"I say, Seth!" said the store-keeper, coming in and closing the door after him, slapping his hands over his shoulders and stamping the snow off his shoes.

Seth had his hand upon the door, his hat upon his head, and the roll of new butter in his hat, anxious to make his exit as soon as possible.

"I say, Seth, sit down; I reckon, now, on such an *e-tar*-nal night as this a little something warm wouldn't hurt a fellow; come and sit down."

Seth felt very uncertain; he had the butter, and was exceedingly anxious to be off, but the temptation of "something warm" sadly interfered with his resolution to go. This hesitation, however, was soon settled by the right owner of the butter taking Seth by the shoulders and planting him in a seat close to the stove, where he was in such a manner cornered in by barrels and boxes and while the country grocer sat before him there was no possibility of his getting out, and right in this very place sure enough the store-keeper sat down.

"Seth, we'll have a little warm Santa Cruz," said the Green Mountain grocer, as he opened the stove door, and stuffed in as many sticks as the space would admit. "Without it you'd freeze going home such a night as this."

Seth already felt the butter settling down closer to his hair, and jumped up, declaring he must go.

"Not till you have something warm, Seth; come, I've got a story to tell you, too; sit down, now"; and Seth was again pushed into his seat by his cunning tormentor.

"Oh! It's too darn'd hot here," said the petty thief, again attempting to rise.

"Set down—don't be in such a plaguey hurry," retorted the grocer, pushing him back in his chair.

"But I've got the cows to fodder, and some wood to split, and I *must* be agoin'," continued the persecuted chap.

"But you mustn't tear yourself away, Seth, in this manner. Set down; let the cows take care of themselves, and keep yourself *cool*, you appear to be fidgetty," said the roguish grocer, with a wicked leer.

The next thing was the production of two smoking glasses of hot rum toddy, the very sight of which, in Seth's present situation, would have made the hair stand erect upon his head, had it not been well oiled and kept down by the butter.

"Seth, I'll give you a *toast* now, and you can *butter* it yourself," said the grocer, yet with an air of such consummate simplicity that poor Seth still believed himself unsuspected. "Seth, here's—here's a Christmas goose— [it was about Christmas time]—here's a Christmas *goose*, well *roasted* and *basted* eh? I tell you, Seth, it's the greatest eatin' in creation. And, Seth, don't you never use hog's fat or common cooking butter to baste with; fresh pound butter, just the same as you see on that shelf yonder, is the only proper thing in natur to baste a goose with—come take your *butter* —I mean, take your toddy."

Poor Seth now began to *smoke*, as well as to *melt*, and his mouth was as hermetically sealed up as though he had been born dumb. Streak after streak of the butter came pouring from under his hat, and his handkerchief was already soaked with the greasy overflow. Talking away, as if nothing was the matter, the grocer kept stuffing the wood into the stove, while poor Seth sat bolt upright, with his back against the counter, and his knees almost touching the red-hot furnace before him.

"Darnation cold night this," said the grocer. "Why, Seth, you seem to perspire as if you was warm! Why don't you take your hat off? Here, let me put your hat away!"

"*No!*" exclaimed poor Seth at last, with a spasmodic effort to get his tongue loose, and clapping both hands upon his hat, "No! I must go; let me out; I ain't well; let me go!" A greasy cataract was now pouring down the poor fellow's face and neck, and soaking into his clothes, and trickling down his body into his very boots, so that he was literally in a perfect bath of oil.

"Well, good night, Seth," said the humorous Vermonter, "if you *will* go"; adding, as Seth got out into the road, "Neighbor, I reckon the fun I've had out of you is worth a shilling, so I shan't charge for that *pound of butter!*"

The Soap Cure

AN OLD lady who used to come to town to sell butter and eggs was a pest
and a sort of a thief. She'd hit my store about noon and make some small
purchase such as a pound of tea. Then she would grab a couple of pilot
biscuits and run for the cheese case. She'd grab a knife and jab it into
the cheese and cut out at least a half pound, and this made her lunch.
When she got through we'd have to trim away another half pound to
satisfy the next customer—who couldn't be blamed for disliking twice the
amount of rind he should have had.

I studied the case of the cheese-swiping old woman for a long time, and
then one day my heart lit up and radiated joy all over. We had a very
firm cheese of light yellow color. We also had some Goodwill soap about
the same color. The next time I saw the old lady on her way to my place,
I took a bar of Goodwill soap and cut out a wedge of it. I also cut a wedge
out of the cheese, and inserted the soap wedge daintily. I cleaned up all
the scraps and hid the knife. In she came, and she fell for it. She gagged
and sputtered and coughed and hid behind a pile of canned goods until
the spasm passed. She finally came out, paid for her pound of tea, and I
never saw her in my store again.

The Stolen Cheese

. . . ONE day, after selling a customer a few pounds of wool and putting
it into the bag, he went into his counting room, and looking into a glass
which reflected the counter, he saw the man slip in a small skim cheese.
Mr. S. on returning said, he thought he had by mistake put in more wool
than was ordered, and would just place the bag in the scale again. The
man objected, as he said the weight was all right—but Mr. S. threw it in,
and finding it some eight pounds heavier, offered to take back a part of
the contents. The customer however concluded that he would take the
whole, and so to save exposure paid between two and three dollars for a
cheese which might have been bought for twenty-five cents.

From *Yankee Storekeeper,* by R. E. Gould, p. 124. Copyright, 1946, by Curtis
Publishing Co. and R. E. Gould. New York and London: Whittlesey House, McGraw-
Hill Book Company, Inc.

From *Rambles about Portsmouth,* Second Series. Sketches of Persons, Localities
and Incidents of Two Centuries: Principally from Tradition and Unpublished Documents, by Charles W. Brewster, p. 131, with a Biographical Sketch of the Author,
by Wm. H. Y. Hackett. Entered according to Act of Congress, in the year 1869, by
Lewis W. Brewster, in the Clerk's Office of the District Court of the District of New
Hampshire. Portsmouth, New Hampshire.

Who Stole the Pork?

ON ANOTHER occasion, after missing a barrel of pork some months, a man said to him one day, Mr. Sheafe, did you ever find out who stole that pork? O yes, said Mr. S. Indeed, who was it? Nobody but you and I ever knew it was stolen: so pay for it at once, if you wish nobody else to know about it. The man paid for the pork.

Hazing New Clerks

THERE was fun in the old store, though. The old man never remonstrated so long as customers were not inconvenienced. One gag was to give a new clerk a hammer and nail, and point out a post where he was to drive the nail to hang his coat on. One swat with the hammer revealed that the post was iron, and it would ring about fifteen minutes. I'd been there about four days when I came back and found my frock pockets full of lard, a discovery that amused the older clerks more than it did me. I improved on the trick, and got revenge, by varying with some molasses.

A favorite trick was to let a new clerk take an order from a good-looking girl customer. He would be writing down the order, putting his best foot forward after the manner of his kind, and she would often be coyly assisting his maneuvers. It would look like a romance for sure, when one of the older clerks would walk by and say, in passing, "Your wife wants you to bring home a pound of butter when you come to supper." . . .

No Store for Him

NEXT north of the "brick store," was a wooden store, formerly owned by the late Bohan King, the father of Henry, William and Seth King. He was a hatter, and died many years ago. The store was once occupied by Richard Falley, who was an inveterate fisherman. He would leave the key in the door, and with his fishing rod, would take to the streams, as if fishing was the main business of his life. One of his friends remonstrated with him,

---

Ibid., p. 132.

From *Yankee Storekeeper*, by R. E. Gould, pp. 34-35. Copyright, 1946, by Curtis Publishing Co. and R. E. Gould, New York and London: Whittlesey House, McGraw-Hill Book Company, Inc.

From *The Westfield Jubilee:* A Report of the Celebration at Westfield, Mass., on the Two Hundredth Anniversary of the Incorporation of the Town, October 6, 1869, with the Historical Address of the Hon. William G. Bates, and Other Speeches and Poems of the Occasion, with an Appendix, Containing Historical Documents of Local Interest, p. 188. Westfield, Mass.: Clark & Story. 1870.

alleging that his absences incommoded his friends who wished to buy goods. "Why," said Falley, "I always leave the key in the door!" "Yes, but they may omit to leave the money, or to charge for the goods taken, and so you will fail." "Well," said he, "that may be so; but if a store can't support itself, it's no store for me!"

The Lazy Shopkeeper

A STORY is told of a lazy Nantucket shopkeeper who was not inclined to give up his personal comfort or ease. Whenever he saw a customer enter the front door he would call out from his chair: "Well, what is it? What is it? Because perhaps I haven't got it." On one occasion a customer wished to buy a pail and inquired the prices of the different sizes hanging in a line from the ceiling. The shopkeeper, without getting out of his chair, designated each pail with his foot, saying: "That is 50 cents; that is 62½ cents." "Well," said the customer, "I will take that one," pointing to the pail he wished to buy. The shopkeeper did not stir, and a wave of distress seemed to be passing over him. Presently, with an air of great perplexity, he said: "No, I won't sell it, for I shall only have to buy another."

Grindstone Out of Cheese

LOT [Crummit] told me about his boyhood [in the hinterlands of New Brunswick] and about an illiterate trader who kept store in the back settlement where Lot was "riz."

"This storekeeper couldn't read ner write anythin' 'cept figgers. Benson— Ike Benson was his name—kep' track of things after a fashion by drawrin' pitchers of things he bought, sold er swapped. . . . Feller came inta the store one day 'long twerds spring t' settle up. 'Well,' Benson says, after studyin' his book awhile, 'you owe me jest twenty-four dollars.'

" 'Twenty-four *dollars*!' the feller says, bristlin' up considerable. 'How do you make *that* out?'

" 'Well,' Benson says, 'ye've hed two bags o' flour, and a grindstone, hain't ye?'

From *The Nantucket Scrap Basket,* Being a Collection of Characteristic Stories and Sayings of the People of the Town and Island of Nantucket, Massachusetts, Compiled, Edited and Arranged by William F. Macy and Roland B. Hussey, and published for the benefit of "The Sons and Daughters of Nantucket," pp. 60–61. Copyright, 1916, by William F. Macy and Roland B. Hussey. Nantucket: The Inquirer and Mirror Press.

From *Maine Stories,* by John William Stolle, aided and abetted by M. S. (Boob) Snowman, p. 40. Copyright, 1953, by John William Stolle. Bangor, Maine: H. P. Snowman, printer.

" 'Grindstone be blowed!' the feller says. 'I hed two bags o' flour and a round *cheese. That's* what I hed charged.'

"Benson took another look at his book and scratched his head. 'Shore 'nuff—my mistake!' he says. 'I drawred a *square* hole into yer cheese, enstid of a *round* one! Now what you s'pose made me do that?' "

YANKEE WORKMEN AND BUSINESSMEN

The Clever Blacksmith

. . . NAILER TOM served his seven years' apprenticeship at blacksmithing, in Newport, with a man named Dodge, I think, who did a good deal of ship work, sometimes by the job, at others by the pound. Dodge's shop was near Gravelly Point. When he was engaged in job work, the question would be sometimes asked, "Mr. Dodge, ain't you making that work rather light?" The reply would be: "Nobody can tell the strength of iron." When, on the other hand, he would be doing the ship work by the pound, the question would be asked, "Mr. Dodge, ain't you making that work very heavy?" The reply would be: "Nobody can tell the power of the wind and the waves." . . .

Too Good to Spoil

AT THAT time [1811] every vessel placed upon the stocks was wholly completed and equipped for sea before it sailed over the bar. This brought a multiplicity of business to the town. Along the wharves stretched lofty warehouses crowded with merchandise. Carts and drays rattled up and down, incoming and outgoing vessels came and went, the merry songs and "heave ho's" of the sailors, blended with the cheery tones and hearty jests of the stevedores, carts from the interior unloaded and loaded—at every turn was bustle, industry and activity. Here were the spacious sail and rigging lofts, pump and block makers' shops, and ship chandlers' stores, everything that pertained to maritime trade. Mr. Joshua Norton, Joseph Stanwood and the Messrs. Davis and Haynes had large sail lofts; Thomas Prichard a rigging loft on Ferry wharf; Enoch Toppan a block maker's shop on Carter's wharf. Maj. Joshua Greenleaf did most of the ship iron work at his large smithy on Liberty street. Mr. Gordon had a similar estab-

From *The Jonny-Cake Papers of "Shepherd Tom,"* Together with Reminiscences of Narragansett Schools of Former Days, by Thomas Robinson Hazard, With a Biographical Sketch and Notes by Rowland Gibson Hazard, p. 326. Copyright, 1915, by Rowland G. Hazard. Boston: Printed for the Subscribers.

From *Reminiscences of a Nonagenarian,* Edited and Illustrated by Sarah Anna Emery, pp. 226–227. Newburyport: William H. Huse & Co., Printers. 1879.

lishment at Bellevilleport. This gentleman was somewhat economical in his household. At that period cheese was a customary appendage of the dinner table, being considered an accessory to digestion. Mr. Gordon employed several workmen. One day a large cheese was placed on the table; after the meat had been disposed of, Mr. Gordon took a knife to cut the cheese; turning it over, he exclaimed, "This is a good cheese, a pretty cheese, too good to spoil!" and laying down the knife, he rose and called his men to their work. That afternoon, a large anchor was to be forged, the fire was kindled, the iron heated.

"That is a good heat!" exultantly exclaimed the master.

"A good heat," with one voice responded the men.

"A grand heat," reiterated the master.

"A grand heat," again responded the men.

"Then why don't you strike?" impatiently demanded the master.

"It is a good heat?" queried the foreman.

"Yes, yes, strike, strike, I tell ye," hurriedly ordered the master in a quick authoritative tone. "Strike, strike."

"Don't you think it is too good a heat to spoil?" quietly returned the foreman, while not an arm was uplifted.

The hint was taken; the cheese brought with a loaf of brown bread. The luncheon eaten and well washed down with grog, the anchor was forged with a will. . . .

Boots and Shoes

CALEB HAWES, when he took from the factory a case of boots (to be "made" at home as the custom was), if they ran in sizes from 6 to 10 he would always make up the 6's first. His explanation was this: "Wall, ef I wuz to die, the other fellow would hev to make the larger sizes."

The daily stent would be two to three pairs, but if Caleb was in a carefree mood he would decide upon "Two pairs and a fox hunt to-day, and four pairs to-morrow."

One day this manufacturer criticized one of his oldest hands, a man who had spent most of his life treeing boots and shoes. After some fault-finding the "boss" said, "Now I will show you how to tree a shoe," and he did so and passed it up with the remark, "There, that's the way I want a shoe treed." The workman waited until the boss had passed along, and placed the shoe in a conspicuous place, resuming his work. After dinner the boss walked into the room—and also into the trap. Picking up the same shoe, "Do you call that shoe treed?" "No," was the reply, "I don't, but that is the shoe *you* treed this forenoon."

From *History of Weymouth, Massachusetts,* Vol. 2, pp. 789, 803, 806–807, 810. Published by the Weymouth Historical Society, Howard H. Joy, President, Under Direction of the Town. 1923.

Nathaniel Shaw, a sincere publicist, was a shoe manufacturer who always had the interests of his workmen at heart, and paid them as liberally as he could for their services. On one occasion, when he told one of his men who was getting 25 cents per case for his work that he would be increased to 26 cents, much to his astonishment the workman said, "No, Nat., leave it at twenty-five; it is easier to reckon."

One of the shop's crew on leaving his employ was asked by a friend why he left. The reply was, "Oh, Nat. kept hinting and so I quit." "Hinting?" commented the friend, "what do you mean—what did he say?" "Why, he said he didn't want me any more."

In the pioneer days of the boot and shoe industry many of the manufacturers kept a "general store" and paid their workmen in part with goods out of the store. Col. Ebenezer Humphrey of North Weymouth had an employee named Athanasius Stoddard, and times were so hard that when Mr. Stoddard brought in some shoes and wanted his pay the Colonel said, "I can't pay you in money, but have in the store some very nice satinet to make clothes for yourself or family." "No, Colonel," was the response, "my family can't eat satinet all the time."

For Knowing How

"WHAT is the price of the work? he (Coolidge) asks, looking at the shoe carefully. . . . Well, Mr. Lucey, there is one thing about shoes you'll never learn!"

"And what is that?" I asked. And I wasn't so pleased—'cause I know how to make shoes. An' he told me a story. A long one, it was. About a plumber that charged twenty-five dollars for fixin' a drain, for which he said five dollars was for the drain and twenty dollars was for knowin' how.

"That's your trouble, Mr. Lucey," he said. "You don't charge enough. You don't charge for knowin' how." [1]

ONE time a man got stranded beside the road with his car, which was a large one. Along came a man with an old dilapidated Ford and offered to help. He fixed the car, and when the man offered to pay him, he said that he would accept $1.10. Curiosity prompted the man to ask why such an odd amount. The reply was, "Ten cents for the labor and a dollar for the knowledge." [2]

---

[1] From *The Life of Calvin Coolidge*, by Horace Green, pp. 52-53. Copyright, 1924, by Duffield & Company. New York.

[2] From "Littleton," by Ola G. Veazie. Manuscripts of the Federal Writers' Project of the Works Progress Administration for the State of New Hampshire.

A Day's Pay

HARRY CRAIG worked for us when we first started to build our house. He got to talking about old times and how he had often worked for Mrs. Williams.* She had said one day to him, "Harry, the brush is growing up in our view, and it's getting so we can't see the lake. Harry, will you work for us a few days and cut the brush?" And Harry said, "Why, yes, Mrs. Williams. Sure, I'll do it." And then she said, "Well, Harry, how much are you going to charge?" And he said, "Well, I'll charge you $3.60 a day." Then she said, "Oh, Harry, I can't pay you that much. I'll pay you $3.00 a day." And Harry said to her, "Oh, yes, I'll work for you for $3.00 a day." And then turning to me, he said, "I didn't go to school for nothing. I know how to figure a three-dollar day."

   * This name has been changed.

"Make a Job or Take a Job": A Yankee Work Saga

WORKING ON THE FARM

I STARTED out as a kid. At fourteen years old I went to work for a farmer —eight months. I bound out for eight months. That was in Wilbraham, Mass. Sixteen Acres, they called it there. I did farming—driving team and milking cows and one thing another.

That pretty well educated me, in the first place I worked. The woman was a small woman and she had a husband that used to be a traveling salesman, a salesman on the road, and a son. He never done much, only puttered around the farm. He had a heavy beard and he always carried a little stick around in his pocket to tamp down his tobacco in his pipe. Oh, he was a kind of—I'd call him a kind of sissy in a way. And he always liked to boss around him. I was down with a team harrowing some ground there and of course these old A-harrows—they had teeth, you know, and once in a while one of them teeth would get loose and you'd take a piece of leather and drive the tooth back in. And I was doing that and he hollered down at me to keep the team going. But instead of keeping the team going I unhitched it and took it up to the barn. But the old man come out and wanted to know what the matter was and I says, I ain't taking that from nobody. And he says, Well, he says, don't pay no attention to him. You're working for me. So I went back to work again.

Then there was the woman—she was so nice. She patched all my overalls and washed them. She put patch on top of patch just to keep you

As told by Heman Chase, Alstead, New Hampshire, February 11, 1964. Recorded by B. A. Botkin.

As told by Fred ("Uncle Freddie") Mills, Alstead, New Hampshire, February 12, 1964. Recorded by B. A. Botkin.

going. Well, I got some new overalls one day and I put 'em on and come down, big as life. Well, she says, so you put on your new overalls. And I says, Yeh, and she says, You go right up and put the old ones on. They're just as good to work in around here.

Well, she was an awful happy old lady. She used to sing a song. I remember it just as well as today. She'd sing—what was it now? "I never say die, say I." That was the song. I forget the words of it. That was a little song she used to sing: "I'm happy-go-lucky. Never say die, say I." I don't know the whole song. She'd turn out more work than one twice her size, I was gonna say. No, I don't remember the tune. I'm not much of a musician. I couldn't sing myself, anyhow.

I worked there about eight months, I guess. During that time we had an awful thunder shower, and it struck right across from us. Really it was two thunder showers meeting. And after the shower was all over it was a nice moonlight night, and you could see the prettiest aluminum borealis they call it—a rainbow from the moon—that I ever see in my life—the only one I ever see. That was way back in—I was fourteen years old. My people had ten in the family. Somebody had to get out and do something.

RAILROADING

When I worked on the railroad I had a contract job too, which was putting in underground passages between Springfield and Albany. They put in twenty-three underground roads and calverts [culverts] and one thing another. And one time we were up in West Pittsfield and evidently they had a copper mine there at some time other and it filled up but the old swamp was kind of damp and we were pulling up a guy on the derrick and the guy hit the electric wires and we all got a shock from it, and we couldn't either let go of the guy or pull it off. And after a while the boss come around and seen the situation. There were about four of us tied up on it. And he hit the guy with a stick and it bounced off the wires so we let go of it. But that was an awful experience to be holding the big heavy guy on the derrick and not have to let go of it or pull it up or anything.

And we had quite a time on that job anyway. One way another I was working mostly on the derrick. And we went from one place to another on the road and set up derricks. But it would take them about two days to take down the derrick and get it loaded and get it where we were. So we'd go ahead and we'd wait for the derrick and after we'd get it set up we'd go somewhere else and set up a derrick. It was quite interesting.

So we'd get up there one day and that boss that was over us he'd have to get a boarding place for us to stay overnight. So we got up there one night and he'd got a place for us and we set up a derrick. And I happened to meet up with a pretty nice looking girl so she wanted me to go to church with her. I put on my old stiff shirt. At that time we wore white bosom shirts. Well, we was in the church there and pretty soon I happened to look down and a big bedbug was making tracks across the front of my shirt. I was quite embarrassed, but I guess nobody saw it but myself. But I got rid of it.

Well, I was gonna tell you what happened when I was working on that job. They were quite a few Irishmen—most of them were Irishmen. This fellow was—oh—a great big fellow about six foot tall and he'd just come over. So at night we used to jump a freight and go down to Pittsfield from West Pittsfield and have a few beers and one thing another and entertain ourselves. So we had to get off before we got in the depot. We'd jump off in a place that was kinda sandy and nice to jump off of the train, you know. So we'd all let ourselves down the way brakemen do, you know. We seen them do it. And this fellow he was last—he had to get off. He jumped straight out and turned three somersaults and landed at the bottom of the heap. So that was quite an experience for him.

Oh, the Irish were a jealous kind of a lot. They wanted the boss kind of jobs. I had a job at that time going up and hitching up the falls on the derrick and the boom, you know, hitching the falls to the mast and one thing another and oiling it and one thing another. So this fellow thought I had it pretty easy so he wanted to get the job. And of course, they favored their own quite a little so they told me that he wanted the job. Well, I says, give it to him. But when they got him on the stick and the rope pulling him up the mast, I motioned to the other fellows to give it to him quick. Well, he went about fifteen feet and hung on to the mast and called to let him down. He couldn't go up there. Oh, the masts were probably forty-five feet high and he went up only about a third of the way and he got enough of the climbing.

IRISHMAN STORIES

Do I remember any of the Irishmen's stories?

I remember the stories about the bull and the strawberry patch. Well, on one place I worked they had two–three bulls in the pasture, you know, and they got kind of sick of being in the pasture. So the big bull he pushes the fence over and gets outside. Well, the fence being down, a second bull he thought he'd go out. Well, he went quite a little ways away from the fence. But then there comes the little bull. Well, he went off about a half mile, so you see that a little bull goes a long ways.

This happened down at Waterbury, Vermont. They have an insane asylum there and quite a lot of inmates that aren't bad, they leave work around the yard. And so a neighbor lived above them, and he had to go down by the place to another neighbor's to get him some horse manure to put on his strawberry patch. So he went down there and got loaded up and come on along back and this fellow working out in the yard there he says, "What you got there?" He says, "I got some horse manure to put on my strawberry patch." And the fellow began to laugh and have a great time on it and he says, "Well, I wanted to put some sugar on my strawberries the other day and they thought I was crazy."

GETTING RID OF THE DEADWOOD

Well, I got a job there in Bellows Falls on the transfer. That's for transferring freight, you know, from one car to another and putting it in station order so they can get at it. But the railroad at that time—the Brotherhood was thinking the railroad was making enough so they could afford to pay 'em a little more wages. So they ask for more wages and they win. But the railroad, to get back at 'em, why, they'd lay off so many men. Supposing you had five men working, they'd make four men do the work that the five men had been doing.

Oh, they were cutting down men to beat the band there, so you didn't know who'd be next, you know, who'd get fired. And one day the boss, the superintendent said, Well, he wasn't worried about his job. He was joint man; he was working for the railroad there on the Boston and Maine and the Rutland too. So he thought they'd probably keep him. He was all set.

The next day or so the janitor didn't show up. So they told me I'd have to do the janitor work. And then I got down in the office where the superintendent was and he wanted I should polish all the brassworks on the sink and one thing another. Well, I got the polish and worked pretty good and got a pretty good shine on 'em. Well, he says after a while, you don't need to spend all day at it. Well, I told him, he wanted them polished, didn't he, and if I was going to polish them, then I'd spend a little time on them. Well, he says, we're going to get rid of some of this drywood, deadwood, around here pretty soon. And I says, Yes, you bet they are. Just joking, you know, I was. And he didn't know what to say about that. But next morning he got his notice that he was all done. And he swore that I knew that he was going to get fired. But I didn't know a thing about it. I just happened to hit the nail on the head, that's all. He said we're going to get rid of the deadwood around here and I says, Yes, you're right, they are. Hah! And he got fired.

CHICOPEE DAM

Well, you ask me how I happened to get all these jobs. Well, sometimes I done it kind of in a funny way. I know one time I wanted very much to work on the Chicopee dam. I thought it would be interesting to work on that and so I went down and asked for a job and told them I was pretty good at giving signals to the engineer to hoist things up and lower them down and pretty good on the derrick. So he said they couldn't use any more—right now, anyway. So I says to him, Oh, all right, I'll be down in the morning. So I went home and I went down in the morning and put up a bluff. I went to work. And the timekeeper came around and got my name, and pretty soon the boss came around that I asked for the job. And he says, Who put you to work? Why, I says, you asked me to come in the morning, didn't you? Well, he says, that's pretty good. Well, go ahead, he says. So that's the way I got that job. I just simply went to work and they kept me. That's all. And I finished the job. And at the end of the job they filled up the old canal there with water and forgot about a half a dozen picks and crowbars and so I had to go down and get them. It was quite dirty and quite nasty a job to do, but I got them all out.

DEPRESSION JOBS

During the depression I had to make jobs for myself in a way. Somebody'd have a load of wood out in front of their place or something and I'd go and ask them if they wanted to get somebody to saw it up, to split it up. And some people there in Morgans had fifteen cord of wood and wanted it split, thrown in the shed and piled up. So I said I'd do it for a dollar and a quarter a cord. And I see that I wasn't going to make much on it. So I used to get up jest as soon as I could get started in the morning and work as long as I could see at night. So it being long days I'd work probably fourteen hours a day. Well, it worked out all right. I got it done in a week. So I got pretty good pay. I got over fifteen dollars.

And the boss, over at the scythe snaths, Mr. Ryder, come down and he says, You're an awful [good] worker. We'd like to hire a man like that. Well, I says, I am at liberty. I could take a job all right. Well, he says, come on over to the shop, he says. I'll introduce you to the superintendent and see what he thinks of it. So the next morning I goes over. But the superintendent didn't think I was heavy enough for that job. He thought that I wouldn't be able to do it. So I told him that I guessed if he'd try me a week or two weeks and if I didn't fill the bill, I could then get out and get me another job. But if he was satisfied, I'd like to work there. So I worked for two weeks and he couldn't find no fault on my work. And so I was kept there for eight years. After that I worked at the same place making scythe snaths. They had quite a time there. The old fellow had a lot of chin whiskers and a big watch that he used to cover up with them whiskers. Behind his back they used to make fun of him, you know. But he was a pretty good old superintendent. So that one time my father was sick, and I had to go home and so I asked him if they could give me my pay in advance. And he says, No need of that. So he put his hand in his pocket and pulled out fifty dollars. And he says, How much do you want? Oh, fifteen dollars, I says. Any time you want any money he says, ask me.

I always keep forty or fifty dollars in my pocket. So I thought that from a man that didn't want to hire me and that I had worked for him so many years, that I'd done pretty well.

ROAD WORK

Yes, I could always get a job because I'd either make a job or take a job or do something. And in depression time it was pretty hard to get work. One time I couldn't get very much work and I went to the town manager and asked him for a job. And he said I owned a house, so there's a lot of people on the town and he'd have to give them preference to me. And I told him I couldn't live on the shingles. But anyway I got a fellow who was pretty good at writing to write me a letter into headquarters and they told him to put me to work. So I got the job that way.

They worked us five hours a day and the other gang five hours a day. We worked upon the road, putting in a new road. He'd have to use so much manpower before he could put his machinery in there. So I guess probably we worked there three months or so. And then they cut down the gang. And at the time I was working for the boss of grading in grading the banks alongside the road after they finished them. So my name was amongst the rest of them. But the old fellow said, No, he said, don't let him go. He's one of my best graders. Well, they let me go just the same. And I got a job building a camp over here for Mr. Brown over here at Warren's Pond and worked a couple of weeks and they called me back again. And this time, why, they were putting in the posts beside the road. My job was to paint the posts, the black and the white. And things like that beside the road. And we had to dig some of the postholes too. But I got a job there after everybody else left the job. And still they had to let me go there for a couple of weeks. They found out they had a good man, I guess. They hired me back anyway.

JOE DAGO, LOGGING BOSS

Well, I was telling you about Mr. Dago. He was a boss on the job and he was an awful good man on logs. At that time they would leave a lot of logs at Bellows Falls and then put the rest on to Holyoke. Well, in the middle of the river they had what they called piers. They'd put logs down and fill them with stone and make piers, and they'd have a boom run from one pier to another, you know, to hold the Bellows Falls logs in, and then the other logs would go by. But when we wanted to get any logs we'd open up one of the places and push out quite a few. We had a log from the pier to the bank while we pulled them out. And then we'd pull the boom around and hold them in there. Well—I don't know what they called a sheepshank or what they call it—they had a lot of logs hitched together, you know, and they'd come up there with a boat and pull them around and fasten it and then we'd walk on that boom and push the logs in so they could chain them and take them out.

Well, the old fellow couldn't swim any. The boss couldn't swim any. And so for some reason he was pulling on the rope and the rope must have slipped off the log or something. It let loose, anyway, and he went over backwards—he went down into the water. And he went hand over hand on the rope. And pretty soon somebody sees the rope sliding over the boom, so they stepped on it. Pretty soon the boss came up. Of course when he got a hold of the log he could get himself back on again all right. Instead of trying to swim around he went hand over hand on the rope and pulled himself out of the water. And that's probably the only way he knew probably.

George Van Dyke

Well, I don't know too much about that myself. But I know Van Dyke backed down there and they were losing a lot of peavies and one thing another and he wanted to know where the losses and things were going. He was more interested in his tools and his gear and hosses and things than he was in the men themselves, I guess. Well, anyway, he backed down there on the edge of the bank there and watched them and after a while he'd get what he wanted to get and see what he wanted to and he told the driver to go ahead and without reversing and without thinking anything about it he started up the engine and they went backwards into the river. That's about all I know about him.

I know he was quite an old tyrant. He'd come down with the logs and they'd have to shut the mills down so as to raise the water over the dam so the logs could go over them. And sometimes the mills was very busy and they wanted to finish out some orders they had. Well, he said he'd give them twenty-four hours or he'd blow up the dam. And they claimed he would do it too, because he had the right of way down through. These other logs went down to Holyoke.

But in the end it got so they floated down a lot of pulpwood that they chopped, oh, four feet long or so. And a good deal of it was done in freight cars. They'd freight in and then they'd have a pair of horses and jerk the car down to where you was unloading it. The old long logs that they used to have, they done away with. They used short logs after that.

Jams and Stunts

You ask about the log jams. They had several of them. Sometimes they'd have to dynamite them to get them loose. A pretty dangerous job, that was. Sometimes a logger was left on a log all by himself. But logdrivers they knew how to ride logs. They'd jam up and get tangled up and get a jam there and you'd have to bust them up some way.

Oh, yes, a lot of the young fellows would have fun on logs. They'd get on there and roll 'em. And end them up over end, if it was a short log. Oh, they'd do all kinds of stunts on them. Oh, they even had some of them were so good that they had them in fairs and things around in Keene and Bellows Falls and around. They'd have them for an exhibition and see who'd do the best. And they had choppers would have a bee, then see who could chop a log in two fastest. Things like that. They had a little entertainment along with their hard work. But they used to have to work anywhere from daylight to dark. Sometimes sixteen hours a day. No, they didn't do much singing.

BEANS

They had to live mostly on beans—and them beans was cooked in the ground. They'd heat up a lot of hot stones and then put the beans in them and bake them and they were delicious. Sometimes we used to take the old cook there over a half a pint and he'd give us a dish of beans. That is before I had anything to do working for the railroad. Beanhole beans—they were baked in the ground. I lived on beans when I was a kid. My father wasn't rich and we used to raise bushels of beans. And we had beans and plenty of corn, so we had beans and Johnnycake quite a lot. Well, maybe four days a week. And I got kinda fed up on beans.

THE LOGGERS AND THE CIRCUS FELLOWS

That was in North Walpole. The Ringling Brothers had a circus over in there, and they had quite a crowd there. Oh, they had, like all circuses, some gum games—gambling games. And some of the logging fellows went up there and you either get a box of cigars or two dollars. And they took the two dollars, but the circus fellow wouldn't give them the two dollars. So they got in an argument about it. Of course, the circus fellows brought out their gang and was going to put them right off. And one of the logging fellows went down a short distance and got his gang back, and they come back and well, they had quite a fight. And I guess probably the circus fellows got a little jammed up because these logdrivers wear spiked shoes, you know, calked shoes. And I think Mr. Burroughs can tell you that they didn't look so good when you see them next day down in Keene.

Save the Peavies

I WORKED on the drives from Connecticut Lake to Mt. Tom. But I generally stopped at Turner's Falls. I'd go up in the fall and spend the winter

By Robert Wilder. Manuscripts of the Federal Writers' Project of the Works Progress Administration for the State of Massachusetts.

According to Mr. Wilder, who knew Van Dyke and who has heard the circumstances of the story many times, this version was written from memory after hearing it told by an old riverman named "Hop."

in the woods. We'd cut the logs and pile 'em on the bank of a little stream somewheres, if it warn't handy to get them to the river. We had to mark each one with the company mark, kind of a brand, I guess, cut in the end of each log. And they were piled in such a way that when the freshet came in the spring, we could yank out a couple of props, and the whole caboodle of logs would go rolling into the water.

We'd send a small gang on ahead—maybe a couple of boats—to break up the jams, and keep the drive going. Then the bunch of us would come with the horses. And last would come another small gang with maybe a team or two, to haul in the logs the farmers had stole offen us. And I guess maybe the gang changed the marking on a log once in a while, if they thought it would pay.

The idea was for the first bunch to ride the freshet. And not let the drive get held up. Of course, the water would take the logs over meadows, and when the river went down, we'd have to haul them out with horses. But we knew where it was liable to happen, so we'd have a man at the right place to keep them in the current. And sometimes two, or three. And sometimes we'd string a boom—hitch logs end to end. And hitch the ends to trees, maybe—so the boom would steer the logs for us. For the quicker we got the drive through, the cheaper it was for old Van Dyke. He didn't have so big a payroll. And that old devil was everywhere. Last part of it he had a car and chauffeur, so's he didn't have to drive, but could keep his mind on swearing.

Such sleep as we got, we got on the ground. And then be waked up by a kick from Van Dyke's boot, if he caught you at it. Guess he never slept at all. And to save time in cooking, the cook of the first gang would bury beans in bean pots in holes dug in the sand and filled with hot coals, so that the next bunch didn't need to waste any time.

I got sick of being wet and cold all the time, so I got a job cooking. Van Dyke told me that if I'd let rum alone I could stand on a log. And what the hell was I cold for? That work would keep me warm. But I told him I thought I could save him money on the grub. So I got the job.

We used to buy our supplies from little stores in the towns along the river that stood in with Van Dyke. And they used to give me a little book with what I'd bought written in it. I bought anything they had that I thought the boys would like. But I made the storekeeper write in beans so much, and codfish so much. But nothing else. I let the storekeeper charge up a pound or so extra for doing this.

One day Van Dyke came running. He'd seen some egg shells in the ashes of one of my campfires up river. "Show me your books!" he yelled. I showed 'em. He couldn't read much. But he knew beans and codfish when he seen it. He looked surprised. But he said. "That's the stuff, Hop, beans and codfish is good enough for peasoups.[1] Sock it to 'em!" But after that I buried my egg shells.

He said codfish helped a man to swim. And that beans was better than

[1] French Canadians.—R. W.

dynamite for blowing up a jam. What he meant was he liked them because they was cheap. And that men had to be well fed on something or they couldn't do their work.

One time, in the French King Rapids, the logs jammed. And when a couple of the gang went out to hunt the key log, the jam broke. The men ran for it, but it was no use. Both got knocked into the water. Of course, we ran out on the logs to help. But old Van Dyke yelled, "Never mind the men, save the peavies!" That was him. Never mind the men, he could get more. But the peavies—the hooks on a wooden handle, that we rolled logs with—was property. And property cost money.[1]

So maybe we didn't cheer that day at Turner's Falls, when Van Dyke had his chauffeur back his touring car to the edge of that cliff that overlooks the Falls, so's he could stand up in back and wave his arms and swear at us. I was standing on a boom out in the middle of the river, pushing logs that was branded for down the river so's they'd go over the Falls, and steering those we wanted inside the boom, and keeping one eye on Van Dyke, like everyone else. Guess the Falls was making too much noise to suit him, and he wanted to get nearer so's we wouldn't miss anything he was saying. He waved the chauffeur to back more. The chauffeur acted scared and only backed a couple of feet, and stopped so's Van Dyke almost lost his balance—he was standing in back. He turned around and said something to the chauffeur, then stood watching him fumbling with the handles. The man was badly rattled, I guess, with Van Dyke right there on his neck, almost. The car coughed once or twice, and then shot back over the cliff. And, my, didn't we cheer! "Never mind the man, save his matches!" yelled somebody. And we all cheered again.

We were awful sorry for the chauffeur, though. We'd forgotten all about him. And both of 'em were killed deader'n the codfish old Van Dyke used to make us eat.

The Drummer and the Stagecoach

IT WAS BACK in the days when the stages was driven by stagecoach. This

---

[1] "Never mind the man! Grab his cant dog! That cost the company money!" That was the old river-hogs' battle cry.—Louise Dickinson Rich, *We Took to the Woods*. (Philadelphia, 1942), p. 213.

As told by Clarence Miller, South Acworth, New Hampshire, February 12, 1964. Recorded by B. A. Botkin.

"Stages" [the old word for mail routes] covers the fact that the mail carriers not only carried the mail but also any passengers or express or supplies people might want on the route. Sometimes the mail was carried almost for nothing and the driver made his living from passengers and merchandise. The stage has now been replaced by bakers' carts, express trucking companies, and private cars, but in this region, anyway, the mail car is still often spoken of as the "stage."—Elsie Goodenow, letter to the Editor, March 9, 1964.

particular stage went from Alstead to Hancock, New Hampshire. And
what was called drummers in those days would be known as salesmen now.
And they'd come in on the train to Bellows Falls and then get on to the
stages to go through these small towns to see what business they could
pick up.

And this one he was quite a big fat man. And it was in Marlow. And
when the stagecoach was getting ready to leave and the driver was up on
his seat, up on top, and he was the last one in, and when he stepped on
the step to get into the stagecoach, it couldn't stand his weight and it let
him down on to the ground. And he was kind of ruffled. It didn't hurt
him any—only his dignity. And he got out and looked the thing over—
you know how these coaches were shaped—and says, "When does this old
beanpot start?" The driver says, "Just as soon as we can get the pork in."

Yankee Drummer Stories

ONE OF the whist players, a drummer who was selling crackers and fancy
biscuits, tried to cheer us by telling us that in this French-Canadian
country the people were the kindest in the world. . . .

*   *   *   *   *

"Have you ever dealt with them?" the drummer asked me, and I acknowledged that this was to be my first experience, but we had some French-
Canadian agents and I hoped to get others.

"Just because they haven't any education and mostly have to sign their
names with a cross, don't make any mistake about their brains," he said.
"For native shrewdness and a highly developed trading instinct, I'd back
them against the Yankees any day."

He told me of a friend of his who stopped to look at a horse that a
Frenchman had to sell. Her coat was a little unkempt but she seemed to
be a good sound animal. The Frenchman assured him that she was.

"She's a damn' good horse," he insisted, "only she don't look very
good." The drummer's friend bought the horse, but he hadn't got her
home before he discovered that it was quite true that she didn't "look very
good." She was stone blind.

Whenever we traveling men got together of a Sunday in a little village
hotel in this [French] section of the Maine woods and had nothing better
to do, we would punctuate our games of pitch with stories about these
Frenchies. On one such occasion a young man who represented the Oliver

From *Yankee Drummer,* by R. E. Gould, pp. 55–56, 66–67, 86–87, 99–100, 137, 221–
222. Copyright, 1947, by R. E. Gould. New York and London: McGraw-Hill Book
Company, Inc. Reprinted by permission of Russell & Volkening, Inc.

Plow Company showed me a letter that was sent him from his firm. The writer was a smart old Frenchman whose son was not quite so shrewd. When the boy arrived at the age of twenty-one, the father felt that he couldn't afford to lose the services of the son and didn't want to pay him a man's wages, so he hit on the plan of a partnership and had a sign painted on the barn, "Louis Michaud and Son."

The Oliver Plow man, who was out looking for an agent, found the son at home and sold him six sulky plows that retailed at about $50 each and got a contract signed by the son as "Louis Michaud and Son, by Henry Michaud." Evidently the son did not take his father into his confidence, for on the evil day that the plows arrived at the railroad station, the knowledge of his son's contract burst on the old man as a complete surprise. He sat down in his wrath and wrote this letter:

Dear Mr. Holiver Plow:

I am surprise like hell when I go by the Rollrode an see what come by Louis Michaud an Son. He is dam fool an I ain't gone take him, so, Mr. Holiver Plow, you come to get him. She's come to most $300, an Mr. Holiver Plow she ain't worth 300 cents.

Louis Michaud.

I'm goin' tell you right now there ain't no more Louis Michaud an Son.

. . . Once I was rescued by one of my stories that happened to go very well with the proprietor of a little general store in Franklin County. It was a bitter cold morning and there was a crowd around the fire in the pot-bellied stove. The proprietor was telling a story about the village bum, who had come in the day before and bought a quart of vinegar, a quart of linseed oil, and the same amount of turpentine, which he mixed in a gallon jug. When the storekeeper went home that night, he found that his wife had bought from the bum a pint bottle of furniture polish for which she had paid fifty cents. It was the same mixture that the bum had made in her husband's store. It works well, too; I made it and sold it afterward.

A lot of the customers were swapping stories, so I told a simple little one about Joe Gordon, an old employee of the Portsmouth Navy Yard. One time the yard shut down, and Joe had to go to Newburyport looking for work. Knowing that no private yard would employ a man who had worked in the Navy Yard, where the employees had a record for killing time, he said "No" when the foreman of the shipyard at which he applied asked him if he had ever worked in the Yard. He was hired, and as he was a good workman, he was doing well when one day another Portsmouth man came along. Seeing Joe, he inquired how one got a job.

"I just went in and asked," Joe replied.

The man went to the hiring office and when he was asked, "Did you ever work in the Navy Yard?" answered, "Yes."

"We never hire Navy Yard men," he was told.

He answered, "Like hell you don't. You have Joe Gordon working for you, and he never worked anywhere else."

The foreman called in Joe and accused him of lying, but Joe insisted that he had told the truth.

"I *was* there for a long time," he admitted, "but I never done a lick of work. You can ask anyone who was there."

Why the adventures of Joe should have seemed so funny to the proprietor I shall never understand, but he liked them so well that he went to the phone and began to call up his friends.

"Come over, Bill. Here's a fellow that's got a story for you."

Until noon I sat there repeating the story. When the proprietor couldn't think of another friend who hadn't heard it, he asked me, "What in hell do you sell, anyhow?"

"The Buckeye mower," I told him. He gave me an order for half a dozen.

I sometimes got my fingers burned while getting used to Vermonters. One agent with whom I was trying to settle an old account and to make a new contract was an innocent-looking old farmer. If you shook him you would have expected to see hayseed drop out of his beard. He told me he didn't think he would handle the line any more, as the mowers didn't stand up. He showed me a mower with the crankshaft almost worn through the frame and said, "I had to take this back." His expression as he looked at it would have touched the heart of Pharaoh. It touched me and made me feel so sorry for him that I promised I'd see him through. I said I'd write the company and make them give him a new frame and on the first holiday I'd come back and put it on for him so he wouldn't be out a cent. The look of what I took to be gratitude in his eyes made me feel proud of my warmheartedness for several days.

On Memorial Day I returned at my own expense, knowing that the company would not look with favor on such a long trip for one call, and put in the new frame. The old farmer beamed with pleasure.

Soon afterward I met the salesman whose territory I had taken, and when I told him about the old fellow, he exploded.

"Why, the old so-and-so," he exclaimed. "He sold that mower to a New Yorker who didn't put any oil on it and burned out the bearing. He admitted it, and we finally took back the mower and allowed him $10 on it toward a new mower. Now the old so-and-so has worked on you so he has a new mower that cost him only $10."

In a little hotel in one of these [New York] villages [on the Canadian line] I found a crowd of drummers all having a hard time getting business. As we sat at a big table for supper we told our experiences. One man said, "I got two orders today. One customer told me to get out and another told me to stay out."

After we had all made the best story we could out of our hard luck, someone asked an old man who had been sitting there and saying nothing, "How are things with you, Pop?"

The old man answered cheerfully, "Why, not too bad, but that isn't strange, because they arrest men who don't buy my goods."

After a moment's silence someone asked, "What do you sell?" and he solemnly answered, "Men's pants."

In White River Junction one might be driven to do anything, but usually there were two or three of us stranded together, so we found some way of entertaining ourselves even if we were reduced to exchanging stories about the ways we managed to get ahead of the home office. Personally, I never did pad my expense account unless I was driven to it; but however scrupulous I was, the treasurer always found some item of expense to complain about. Once I was goaded into telling him that if it was his idea that my job was to save money for the firm, the best way he could do it was to take me off the road. That kept him quiet for a while.

One traveler I met told how he had charged an item for taking a customer to a show, and the treasurer made a great howl about it. The next week when the drummer was given his money, the treasurer said, "I didn't see any item this week for entertainment." As the drummer put his money in his pocket, he answered, "No, you didn't see it, but it was there just the same."

Our favorite story at that time was about the new man that a company sent to Maine to make one trip for their old salesman, who was sick. When he came back to the office, the treasurer said the young fellow had forgotten to charge for a team to Vinalhaven and he should have included it, as the old man always did. The salesman was on the spot. He didn't like to point out that Vinalhaven is an island about ten miles offshore.

II. LOCAL CHARACTERS

The running of the first train over the Eastern Road from Boston to Portsmouth . . . was attended by a serious accident . . . this initial train . . . ran over and killed—LOCAL CHARACTER.
—THOMAS BAILEY ALDRICH

Ice and granite, it is said, are the chief products of New England; and they fitly symbolize the hardy character of her sons.
—GEORGE R. RUSSELL, in *The (Old) Farmer's Almanack*, 1855

A strange hybrid, indeed, did circumstance beget, here in the New World, upon the old Puritan stock, and the earth never

*before saw such mystic-practicalism, such niggard-geniality, such
calculating-fanaticism, such cast-iron-enthusiasm, such sour-
faced-humor, such close-fisted-generosity.*
                                        —JAMES RUSSELL LOWELL

*The people of the region think of themselves as reticent, and as
given to dry humor and understatement; as having a strong sense
of lineage and of'relationship to their past; as being unusually
aware of their past and influenced by it; as keeping a tenacious
grip on possessions, either land or heirlooms; as having a certain
suspicion of the outsider; as being ingenious and inventive in
dealing with physical problems; as having a strong sense of individual responsibility and an almost complete inability to play or
to take things lightly; as having their emotions constantly sup-
pressed but expressed for all in an assumed belief in the little
white church, the public school, and the savings bank. Now people scarcely hold to these beliefs. The traits they ascribe to themselves are not real but accredited characteristics fostered by literary treatments of the region.*
—Conference on the Eastern Maritime Region, August 29–31,
            1942, Rockland, Maine, Summary of the Discussion

1. "CHARACTERS"

"WHAT is a 'character'?" asks Joseph C. Lincoln, and answers: "Why,
he or she is, apparently, an individual who speaks and acts and,
perhaps, thinks in a manner different from that in which you, yourself,
speak and act and think. And it is just possible that he, because of that
difference, may consider you a character; he has that privilege, of course.
. . . It depends on the point of view, doesn't it? And there is another
point to be considered. A 'character' may not be a character at all in his
own environment and become one when he steps outside of it." [1]

Thomas Bailey Aldrich emphasized the localism of local characters. To
him a local character was an indigenous "individual built on plans and
specifications of its [the community's] own, without regard to the prejudices and conventionalities of outlying districts." With the coming of the
railroad, he adds, local character "was not instantly killed," but "died a
lingering death." And by a process of attrition it gradually disintegrated,
dissolving into "certain bits of color, certain half obsolete customs and
scraps of the past." [2]

Continuing the Puritan emphasis on character, New England localism
bred "characters" and a distinct feeling for "characters." New England
provincialism (in the best sense of the word) rests on the twin pillars of
family tradition and the tradition of the New England town or village and
self-government (symbolized by the town meeting). Both traditions, espe-

---

[1] *Cape Cod Yesterdays* (Boston, 1935), pp. 258–259.
[2] *An Old Town by the Sea* (Boston, 1894), pp. 105–106, 108–109.

cially in rural communities, foster respect for strong characters and distinctive traits and talents, which become part of the social heritage. Thus the Yankee ideal of a hard-working, efficient, upright, democratic citizenry includes the tough and hardy builders of pioneer New England; the stern, self-sufficient patriarchs of the farm; and the charmingly crotchety villagers that inhabit places like Harriet Beecher Stowe's "Oldtown" (Natick, Massachusetts).

New England also had its rebels and non-conformists who carried the Yankee spirit of self-dependence—the right to be one's self—to extremes. Violating the sense of order inherent in the neat, tight pattern of New England farm and village life, their revolt broke through the surface of New England constraint to give us erratic geniuses like Margaret Fuller, Thoreau, and Melville, as well as a host of minor recluses, cranks, self-constituted prophets, reprobates, vagrants, and ne'er-do-wells. The very ideals of hard work, thrift, and duty produced a reaction in the form of the village-do-nothing, typified by Mrs. Stowe's Sam Lawson, who nevertheless possessed the virtue of handiness or "faculty," while complete inability or unwillingness to make adjustment to social norms or personal tragedy resulted in pathetic schizophrenics and vagrants like the Old Darnman and the Leatherman.

2. Droll Yankees

The discovery of the comic Yankee—half clown, half rogue—came about, as we have seen, as part of the discovery of national and regional traits and showed the forces of local patriotism and sectional rivalry at work—another instance of localism in New England character. In the course of this discovery, the Yankee, from the laughable "countryman in the great world," became a homely critic of the outside world and a sharp trader engaged in a comic contest of wits with the world at large. And in the composite portrait of the fabulous Yankee that grew up in oral and written tradition, we find the comic (green), sage, and "cute" Yankee gradually fusing into the droll Yankee—the indigenous countryman (a truly local character), at home in his own little world.

The droll Yankee, whose lineaments may first be traced in James Russell Lowell's Hosea Biglow (1848) is chiefly distinguished by his matter-of-fact or "reluctant" wit and eloquence, superimposed upon moral earnestness and down-to-earth common sense. He is a man of few words and many notions, of strong principles and decided opinions, expressed in odd behavior, observations, and speech. Farmer, old salt, workman, the droll Yankee is closer to New England than the simple yokel or slick peddler—a "character" in his idiosyncrasies and a "local character" in the sense of being strongly colored and flavored by locality and localisms of speech.

3. Yankee Wit

The hallmark of the droll Yankee is wit. Dry, homely, sharp, shrewd, salty, quaint, crabbed, sly, pithy, enigmatic, Yankee wit is essential wit—saying much in little—"enlivened with many curious twists and turns and out-of-the-way notions." These qualities are externalized by the Yankee's habit of slow speaking, of turning a question "over in his mind once or twice before he gives answer, often improving the interval to spit seriously and meditatively."

Such tricks of expression have become familiar as the stock-in-trade of the humorist and humorous lecturer of the crackerbox philosopher variety. As devices for telling a humorous story, it will be remembered, Mark Twain recommended the grave manner, the studied silences, and the casually dropped, absent-minded, often irrelevant and incongruous remarks dealt in by Artemus Ward.[1] What Mark Twain calls the story-teller's "soliloquizing way" is simply the Yankee's habit of talking as if he were thinking aloud or talking to himself; and what he calls the "pause" is the Yankee's habit or trick of slow timing. According to Charles Edward Crane, the Yankee "loves to bait his listener" and "He lights a slow fuse and with a poker face he watches that fuse burn to the setting off of a little bomb of the unexpected."[2]

Thus the droll Yankee's apparently unconscious humor, slow speech, twangy drawl, and eloquent silence involve a considerable element of artifice. "Silent Cal" Coolidge's public silence was both deliberate and natural, for "in private Coolidge was garrulity itself."[3] Crane testifies that he knows many Vermonters "who have little in common with 'Silent Cal' and who can talk the 'handle off the pump,' or the 'tin ear off an iron dog.'"[4] If this seems like a paradox, it is related to and borne out by that other Yankee paradox of inquisitiveness and curiosity with respect to strangers in contrast to suspicious distrust of outsiders.

Finally, Yankee wit is characterized by understatement—"triple-X in dryness," according to Crane, or underemphasis, according to Joseph C. Lincoln, appropriate to the "reluctant or rustic philosophic style" of eloquence which George Philip Krapp contrasts with the "expansive" eloquence of the hyperbolical orator and the exuberant eloquence of the back-

---

[1] In the character of the itinerant showman, which Charles Farrar Browne added to the gallery of American folk types, Jennette Tandy sees him aiming "at the presentation of a national, not a local type." Yet in his rôle as lecturer, Browne, like that other Yankee humorist and lecturer, Henry Wheeler Shaw (Josh Billings), retained many Yankee traits. And the following description of Artemus Ward, the genial showman, clearly relates him to the tradition of the droll Yankee: "The shrewdness of a Barnum was to be united with the stupidity of an uneducated itinerant exhibitor. . . . The old showman was to have the smartness of a Yankee, combined with the slowness of one whose time had been chiefly spent among the backwoods; he was to blend humorous stupidity with unscrupulous mendacity, to have very little of the reverential about him, a modicum of the philosophical, and a large amount of the broadly comic."—E. P. Hingston, *The Genial Showman* (1870), Vol. I, pp. 136, 137. Cited by Jennette Tandy, *Crackerbox Philosophers in American Humor and Satire* (New York, 1925), p. 136.

[2] *Let Me Show You Vermont* (New York, 1937), p. 29.

[3] Stewart H. Holbrook. See "The Enigma of Silent Cal" below. Cf. Horace Green, *The Life of Calvin Coolidge* (New York, 1924), p. 20: "But particularly in the habit of reticence, broken by salty epigrams, does he reveal traits of the soil; for the smaller the community, the less is small talk honored."

[4] *Op. cit.,* p. 29.

woods Southerner and Westerner.[1] Lowell also notes a love of incongruity, which he defines as "that humorous quality of the mind which delights in finding an element of identity in things seemingly the most incongruous, and then again in forcing an incongruity upon things identical."[2] There is further incongruity between the "sober treatment of comic things and comic treatment of sober matters" (such as death)—a source of quaintness traced by John Camden Hotten to the Puritans.[3] The result is that dry utterance of funny things in an unfunny, commonsensical fashion and what Lincoln calls the "unsmiling gravity with which the point of the joke is delivered," combining the right proportions of greenness, sageness, and "cuteness" in the droll Yankee.

B. A. B.

COUNTRY PEOPLE
AND YANKEE STORYTELLERS

Ghosts

No, I don't believe in ghosts. I never saw one. But a man in our neighborhood he claimed he believed in ghosts. And on being pressed for proofs in the matter, couldn't seem to come up with any. So his neighbor asked him, "Did you ever see a ghost?" And the man answered, "No, I never saw one, Ches, but my dog did."

The Ghost in the Attic

WE GOT a chance to board with a farmer there. They had a couple of rooms and beds up in the attic, so that made it good. So me and this old Irishman lived up there. We went up through the shed and in the shed they had a horse. He had a halter on and a chain and we'd go through the open attic into the room that we had up there. And we wouldn't much more than get quieted down before that old horse would start to shake his head and the chains would rattle and they had all the looms and everything

---

[1] *The English Language in America* (New York, 1925), Vol. I, pp. 324 ff.

[2] Introduction to *The Biglow Papers: Second Series, The Poetical Works of James Russell Lowell* (Boston, 1885), p. 225.

[3] Introduction to *The Complete Works of Charles F. Browne* (London, 1865), p. 27.

As told by Chester C. Mason, Langdon, New Hampshire, February 12, 1964. Recorded at South Acworth by B. A. Botkin.

As told by Fred ("Uncle Freddie") Mills, Alstead, New Hampshire, February 12, 1964. Recorded by B. A. Botkin.

else out in the attic. So this Irishman he'd get kinda spooky anyway.
Well, he swore that there'd been some murder or something done in that
house and he'd say he would hear them walking round in the house, hear
chains rattling. He really worked himself up, especially if he'd-a been out
and had a few little beers or something to drink, and come home. I told
him that as long as they left us alone we didn't care. I pretty nearly knew
what was happening anyway because I knew it was the old horse come
there shaking his head and the chain would rattle. But he'd say they'd
drag the chain across the floor and looms were droning and he got himself
all worked up that there was a ghost there. And he finally—he left there.
He said he couldn't stand it any longer. But really I told him that was a
horse and I almost talked him out of it. But he couldn't really believe it
then. He thought sure that such a place was haunted.

Halloween Prank

THIS WAS down in Ludlow, Massachusetts. We picked up Wilbur Funk,
Fred Fuller, Charlie, and—I dunno—there was four or five of 'em around
there, and we got a big rail, and it being Halloween night we felt like raising the dickens. So we'd go along the farmhouses, you know, and put the
rail in front of one of the outhouses and push and over she'd go! Well, I
guess we'd pushed over about four or five of them and the last one we'd
pushed over we heard an awful screaming and hollering, and this fellow
come out with a lantern and it seems there was an old lady in the place.
There was no light there, we didn't know there was anybody in there, but
we tipped her over too with the outhouse. We were pretty quiet about
that. I never told that till after I grew up and got away from the place and
I guess they were all probably passed away before I told the story to anybody. Well, we were pretty shaky there for a while.

Kicking the Pig

WHEN MY grandfather was a young man he lived in the town of Saugus,
Massachusetts. This was back in—well, it would be back in the 1830's.
And that section of Massachusetts at that time would bear little resemblance
to that section of Massachusetts as you move through there today. In
fact, when I was a youngster there was a lot of things there that's different
than it is now. And this morning he was roused by a noise out in his wood-

---

As told by Fred ("Uncle Freddie") Mills, Alstead, New Hampshire, February 11,
1964. Recorded by B. A. Botkin.

As told by Chester C. Mason, Langdon, New Hampshire, February 12, 1964,
Recorded at South Acworth by B. A. Botkin.

shed. And he scrambled out in his nightshirt, being warm time of year, and went out into the woodshed to see what was going on. Well, there was a rooting around there in the shed. So he figured that the pig had got out of the pen and was rummaging around, and the best thing was to either drive or catch the pig and get him back in the pen. So he grabbed down a fork that was laying there beside the shed and stepped around the pig, and the pig started out of the shed ahead of him. And he stepped along briskly after the pig and kicked the pig two or three times, first with one foot and then with the other. And the pig went right out of the shed, and instead of going around toward the pen, where they'd naturally go, he started right out across the field in front of the buildings. And he chased right along after the pig, the pig just keeping out of reach, and across the field to a little drop-off to a brook, where there was some brush growing, and right straight down into the brook, and started out the other side into the woods.

At that time he begun to come to and begun to wonder a little bit. And when it came daylight he went back to look the situation over. He thought it peculiar—a pig to be taking to the woods that way. And in the daylight the tracks leading down into the brook and up to the other side were not split hooves like a pig's; they were the tracks of a bear.

Sorting the Pigs

I HAD ONE neighbor here that now has been dead for quite a number of years and he was about my father's age. He was quite insistent that he have his own way in anything that was done. And it seemed that he had at that time about a dozen pigs running in under the barn on the manure and he had sold three of them—three of the biggest ones. He had the butcher there that was going to do the butchering for him, and they were under the barn trying to pick out the three big pigs that they wanted. And anybody that knows pigs knows that it's quite a little contract to sort out three pigs out of a dozen.

And they weren't getting along as well as he thought they ought to. And finally he picked up a door that was there—probably five feet long and maybe three feet wide, and he held it right in front of him and walked right up into the corner pushing the pigs along in front of him. And he said he'd show 'em the proper way to catch pigs and get them sorted out. He'd got them very nearly into the corner, and as the door wasn't clear down to the manure, one or two of them stuck their nose under the bottom of it and started out through. And the door went on top of the pig's back and he went on top of the door, and he rode that door from the back end of the manure pit clear out into the barnyard.

As told by William W. Kingsbury, Walpole, New Hampshire, February 12, 1964. Recorded by B. A. Botkin.

Breaking Steers

THERE WAS a man by the name of Edmund Johnson that lived in the town [of Acworth] that was very good in breaking steers and handling oxen. And there was another man that was trying to break a pair of steers. This Edmund Johnson come along—was watching him a while. The man who was trying to break them without any luck said, "You can do anything with steers. How do you do it?"

He says, "Well, to break a pair of steers you have to know a little more than the steers do."

The Off Ox

YEARS AGO there was a man in the neighborhood that had a pair of oxen he wanted to sell. There was another one come along and was looking at them. And the first man was describing them to him and he says, "This near ox is as good an ox as ever lived, and I don't know why the other one isn't."

And the other man looked them over and liked 'em and bought 'em. He came back in a few days and told him, "That off ox is no good." He says, "Well, I told you the near ox was just as good an ox as ever lived and I didn't know why the other one wasn't. And I don't."

A Deal in Oxen

ON THIS same mountain referred to there used to be living on the south side of the mountain a man by the name of Charles Cummings—lived about a mile down. On the north side there was a man by the name of Levi Spalding—lived just about a mile down on the north side. Well, this was before prohibition times and Spalding had been to the South Village and he'd had a little cheer and he was making his way back home up over the mountain and had to pass by Cummings' place. Going home, he stopped in. Cummings had a nice pair of oxen in the barn and Spalding was taken with these oxen and thought they looked pretty nice. They talked and chewed a while and finally he broached the subject: "What would you take for this pair of oxen?"

As told by Clarence Miller, South Acworth, New Hampshire, February 12, 1964. Recorded by B. A. Botkin.

As told by Clarence Miller, South Acworth, New Hampshire, February 12, 1964. Recorded by B. A. Botkin.

As told by Chester C. Mason, Langdon, New Hampshire, February 12, 1964. Recorded at South Acworth by B. A. Botkin.

Well, they hemmed and hawed and traded a while and finally a price was set on the oxen and Levi started up on over the mountain towards home.

Well, after he left, Cummings kept thinking things over to himself. He says, "He liked those oxen pretty well. Gosh, I could have got another ten dollars for those oxen just as well as not. He really thought those oxen were pretty good."

Well, as Levi worked on up over the mountain the effects of his cheer begun to wear off and he begun to wonder just a little bit. "What did I want with those oxen?" He says, "I didn't need those oxen. I needn't have bought those oxen."

And he went on over to his home not feeling too good about his trade.

Well, the next morning, Cummings was to drive the oxen over and get his pay. And as he went up by, he thought over a bit, "Gosh, I still could have got a little more money out of him. I'll have to see what I can do about it. So on arriving at Spalding's place he said, "After you left the other day there was a man came along, and he offered me ten dollars more than you did for those oxen."

Old Levi fished in his pocket. "I vummy," he says, "here's a dollar. You drive those oxen right back and you let the other fellow have 'em."

The Shower

WHEN I was a youngster we lived on top of a mountain, and down on the south side, in quite a sizable reach, there was a man considered considerable of a farmer. In those days it was the horse and buggy days, the days of the one-room schoolhouse they used to call the little red schoolhouse—when we wanted to go anywhere and git there quick we went on foot. This man —Moses Fuller, by name—he had a gang on. They were mowing the hay, mowing with scythes. And at the time, in the morning he and his men were in the shed, some of 'em turning the grindstone, the rest of 'em by the scythes sharpening up, getting ready for the day's work.

Further up the mountain there were quite large blueberry pastures—considerable commercial business in blueberries got carried on at the time. And a neighbor by the name of John Chenery come up through to start his work picking berries for the day, and stopped in to pass the time of day with Mr. Fuller. Moses says, "It's a nice day, isn't it, Mr. Chenery?"

John said, "Yes, it's a nice day. But along about 3 o'clock or half past you're going to see a real thunder shower. It's really coming down."

And a few more words, and Mr. Chenery passed on up the mountain about his business. After he left, Moses said, "Well, any man that thinks it'll rain on a day like this isn't much short of a fool."

As told by Chester C. Mason, Langdon, New Hampshire, February 12, 1964. Recorded at South Acworth by B. A. Botkin.

Well, along in the middle of the afternoon, when they were busy mowing, the shower walked right over the top of the mountain and Mr. Fuller and his men they hustled for the shed and got in under cover.

A few minutes later Mr. Chenery come right down the mountain and he come in and got under cover too. And they just about got settled when Mr. Chenery he started in. He says, "Mr. Fuller, I heard you say when I got out of hearin' that any man that said it would rain on a day like this was a fool. Now, Mr. Fuller, what do you think?"

Wild Blueberries

IN THE EARLY 1900's, when the wild blueberry business was carried on at considerable extent, the practice in getting these berries picked was to allow the picker two thirds of the amount of berries picked, and the owner of the pasture had the other third for his bother in burning pasture, taxes, and whatever other expense he went to. There were some little misunderstandings that come up when this was first put into practice. Originally, no one paid much attention to these. Every one went and picked as they had a mind to.

There was a man by the name of Nathan Cummings that owned the top of the mountain where these pastures were. He was one of the first ones to put this practice to work. And he used to be at the gates to the pasture when the pickers come down at night, and take account. And the previously mentioned John Chenery was picking in this pasture. He came down with two big red pulp pails full of blueberries. And Nathan says to him, "Mr. Chenery, it's our practice now that the owner has a third of the berries." "Eek," says Chenery, "left your third on the bushes."

Amongst the earlier pickers was a man by the name of John Lover. Used to follow lumber camps—chop wood and various things. He wouldn't be considered one of the shining lights as of today. Liked John Barleycorn pretty well. While he could turn in a good day's work, he wasn't altogether particular about it. Well, he used to work in these berry pastures. And at this time there was no very great supervision. The pickers went in and picked wherever they had a mind to. And this man Lover he was picking for Moses Fuller in his pasture. And it was getting to the point where the berries weren't too thick in some of the places. So this day my father, working in my grandfather's pasture, come down through and he finds John right over in that pasture in some very good berries filling up his pails just as fast as he could pick. And John climbed right back over the wall into Fuller's and went right along with his pails.

This type of mentality may seem peculiar: That a man would go over the wall and steal berries and give another man a third of 'em when if he's going to steal berries he could just as well have had 'em all.

As told by Chester Mason, Langdon, New Hampshire, February 12, 1964. Recorded at South Acworth by B. A. Botkin.

A Byword

IT SEEMS that my father went to school at the district school, and when he got out of school one night and started to walk home this man came along with an old pung sleigh. And there were several boys there about Dad's age, and he stopped the colt—he was breaking a colt—and he stopped the colt and asked them to get in and have a ride—that he'd take them home. And they hadn't any more than started afterwards before the colt run away. The boys were beginning to be a little bit scared, and they worked their way along back in the sleigh, thinking that they probably would jump out into the snow. It would be the safest. They didn't want to get smashed up. And the man saw what was going on, and so he just looked over his shoulder as calm as could be, and he said, "Just set right still, boys. Uncle Eb's driving." And after years I can remember when Dad always said that. When things didn't go just right he'd say, "Well, set right still, boys. Uncle Eb's driving."

Shutting the Old Man Up

MY FATHER used to tell this one. It seems that there was this man living here in town [Walpole] that had a young son who was going to school, and during the summer time he worked on the farm with him. It was quite a custom of the father to always be giving the boy some problems to figure out when they were out in the field working. And the boy got more or less fed up with that sort of program, thinking he went to school about enough. And the hired man also got wise to what was going on and he got the boy to one side and told him that the next time his father gave him a problem he'd have one that he could hand back that might shut the old man up.

And so the next time the old man offered a problem the boy said, "Well, now, I've got one for you to figure out. If one little apple costs all hell and damnation, how much will a barrel of cider cost?"

Coming of Age

ANOTHER anecdote that my dad used to tell was that this man that lived here in this town [of Walpole] had a son that worked for him and they

---

As told by William W. Kingsbury, Walpole, New Hampshire, February 12, 1964. Recorded by B. A. Botkin.

As told by William W. Kingsbury, Walpole, New Hampshire, February 12, 1964. Recorded by B. A. Botkin.

As told by William W. Kingsbury, Walpole, New Hampshire, February 12, 1964. Recorded by B. A. Botkin.

didn't apparently get along very well. They were always in some argument. And it came time when the boy was going to be twenty-one and the father knew that he was going to leave home.

So the morning that he was twenty-one he came down to breakfast, and the father said, "Well, I expect you will be leaving us today." And he said, "Yes, sir. I will be going."

The father's reply was that he could take the oxen and harrow till noon. He wasn't born till after dinner.

Jack and Hudson

THERE LIVED in Walpole a man named Jack Harty. Jack worked for a well-to-do farmer named Hudson Bridge. They were very friendly and it was always Jack and Hudson between them. Jack had a habit of getting pretty drunk, but the liquor always went to his legs and not to his head.

One day Jack came up the sidewalk toward the stores, Mr. Bridge saw him coming and saw that he was drunk and knew that Jack would have some remark. As there were several people there at the time Mr. Bridge thought it best to keep out of sight, so he stepped behind a large elm tree that was handy. Jack came on up the sidewalk, grabbed hold of the tree, swung around where Mr. Bridge was, and said, "I'm not so drunk that I can't tell you from a cord of wood, Hudson."

A Calm Man

THIS MAN that lived in Alton, New Hampshire, he was very easy-going and a very nice man but nothing ever disturbed him. No matter what was going on, he never was excited and always very calm. And one night he'd gone to bed and his wife was getting ready for bed, and when she looked out the window the barn was afire. And she says, "For heaven's sake, Fred! The barn's on fire!" And he got up on the elbow in the bed and looked out the window and he says, "Damned if it ain't!" And she rushed around and out in the other room and finally come back and says, "Aren't you going to get up, Fred?" And he says, "Well, have you called the fire department?" She says, "Of course, I have." "Well, hell!" he says, "they'll take care of it then," and laid right back down.

Contributed by William W. Kingsbury, Walpole, New Hampshire, February 29, 1964.

As told by William W. Kingsbury, Walpole, New Hampshire, February 12, 1964. Recorded by B. A. Botkin.

Apple Cider

BACK IN the days when the snow in the roads was rolled down with a large wooden roller drawn by six or eight horses, there lived in Walpole a man named Ed Kidder. Ed was the salt of the earth but didn't talk a whole lot. One day the roller reached Ed's house about noon so the men fed the horses and went into Ed's kitchen to eat their dinner. One of the young drivers (Charlie Ramsay) had bragged that he could get some cider at Ed's house and the other men said, no. As they ate dinner the conversation went something like this:

Charlie—Have a good crop of apples this year, Ed?
Ed—Pretty good.
Charlie—Pretty good quality?
Ed—Fair.
Charlie—Had some cider apples, didn't you?
Ed—A few.
Charlie—Made a little cider, didn't you?
Ed—Just enough for my own use.

The Sheriff and the Shoes

I CAN THINK of another incident that happened in Walpole quite a number of years ago. There was this man named Horace Ferry who was sheriff in Walpole. A very, very nice man and everyone liked him. But he was one of these men that everybody liked to pick on, and his temper was a little bit short.

In those days there were no automobiles and the train run from Walpole to Bellows Falls. One went up about twelve o'clock and another one came back down about one-thirty. It was the custom of a lot of people in the village—ladies especially—to go up on one train, do a little shopping, and come back on the next one. And one day Horace took the twelve o'clock train and went to Bellows Falls and bought himself a pair of shoes and came back. And after he got home he found that the shoes were too tight and he couldn't wear them. So the next day he took the twelve o'clock train again. But before he went down to the train he went into the barber shop and visited with the boys in there. In the meantime they got his attention some other place and they got hold of the shoe box and of course by the time he was ready to go to meet the train the shoe box was back in place. And he took the train as usual—the one at twelve o'clock.

Contributed by William W. Kingsbury, Walpole, New Hampshire, February 13, 1964.

As told by William W. Kingsbury, Walpole, New Hampshire, February 12, 1964. Recorded by B. A. Botkin.

And when he got back at the shoestore they undid the package and he was quite disgusted because the shoes were too tight. And when the package was unwrapped instead of having the new pair of shoes he had an old worn-out pair of overshoes. And he'd made the trip to Bellows Falls and back again for nothing.

As soon as he got back into Walpole he made it known right away in the barber shop that unless somebody produced those shoes before four o'clock somebody was going to get arrested and he'd shut them up where they'd have time to think over their funny jokes. And they all knew that he had a nap every afternoon. So as soon as they thought he was having his nap one of them went over and told his son-in-law the story. So when Horace woke up from his nap his shoes were on the foot of the bed and nobody got arrested.

Model T

THERE'S ANOTHER one that I can tell you on the same man, Horace Ferry. It seems that he was one of the first ones to buy an automobile here in town. Had a Model T. And one of his jobs was to meet the trains and take the mail bag down and bring up whatever express there was. And after he'd practiced with his automobile quite a little while he thought he was capable of meeting the train with that instead of the old horse. So he started for the depot with the mail bag and made it all right. And the train came in and he got the incoming mail and what little express there was, and started back.

Well, just out of the depot there's quite a hill coming up, and he got so excited coming up the hill that he'd forgotten how to shift the Model T. And it chugged and chugged and chugged—a little slower and a little slower—but it finally made the hill without any shifting. And by the time he got up the top of the hill he was really getting excited and he'd forgot how to let the gas off. And he came through Walpole Village a little faster and faster and faster and, as the druggist explained afterward, he made the corner to go up Main Street "by the grace of God and three inches," and headed for the steep hill that he knew would stop him. And he went up that hill as far as the Model T would go without shifting gears and it finally died. And he let it back into the ditch and got out and took the mail bag and walked back to the post office. I never did know how he got his car.

As told by William W. Kingsbury, Walpole, New Hampshire, February 12, 1964. Recorded by B. A. Botkin.

The Critic

THERE WAS a man down to Walpole by the name of Bellows—the same family of Bellows for whom Bellows Falls was named. He was working in his field with oxen and a plow and having quite a lot of trouble with the stones and his plow not staying in the furrows.

A neighbor came along with his horse and buggy and stopped to jeer at him and complain about the way he was doing things. Mr. Bellows stood it as long as he could, and turned to the man in the road and said, "*Some* people make a good living minding their *own* business."

Why Ansel Rawson Never Joined the Grange

GENE AND Sarah Wilder lived up at the end of the road above where Edith and I built our house at the foot of Prentice Hill. They earned their living entirely by farming, as far as I know, and a little bit of work out, in the years that I knew them.

There was a young man, Jack Dougherty, who spent every summer at the old Caldwell place, about a mile beyond the Wilder farm, and they always got their milk from Wilders. And one day when Jack was getting the milk he and Gene got to talking about old times. And somehow the Rawson family got into the conversation. He happened to mention that Ansel Rawson had never been a member of the Grange. I think it was Ansel. And Jack thought there seemed to be some reason why Ansel hadn't joined the Grange. So he asked Gene, "Why didn't Ansel join the Grange?" And Gene said, "I guess he did think of doing so once. Yes, he came to one meeting. Just once. He started to go into the hall and just as he put his foot on the doorstep, somebody leaned out a window upstairs and spit right down on him. It run right down his coat front. Oh, it made him awful mad." And Jack, thinking about this, said, "Oh, I suppose probably it was dirty old tobacco juice, wasn't it?" Gene said, "Oh, no! no! No, it wasn't! It was just as nice clean white spit as you could want."

As told by Elsie Goodenow, South Acworth, New Hampshire, February 12, 1964. Recorded by B. A. Botkin.

As told by Heman Chase, Alstead, New Hampshire, February 11, 1964. Recorded by B. A. Botkin.

Oren Wilder and the White Stones

ONE OF the few times I ever visited with Oren Wilder was on the occasion of my going over to see if he would let me pick up some of the white stones beside the road adjoining his land in Alstead Center. I went over on a Sunday afternoon with my car and my trailer, expecting to get some stones. I went to his house and told him what I wanted, and he said, "Well, let's go down and look at them." So we walked down the road and we looked at the stones and then as we walked back—nothing was said about whether I could have them—he happened to mention, across the road, his twenty-acre mowing. And I said to him, "Is that really twenty acres?" And he said, "Well, I've always called it twenty acres. I think it is." And then he said, "By the way, you're a surveyor. I wonder if you'd pace it off and see whether it is twenty acres." And I, thinking, "Now here's a wonderful chance to put Mr. Wilder in a good mood," I said, "Yes, I'll be glad to do that." But unfortunately, after pacing it off for the length and the width and figuring the acreage, it turned out a disappointment to him. I only found eleven acres. I supposed this didn't sit very well with him. Anyhow, when we got back to the house we exchanged several pleasant remarks and then I came to the point. I said, "Well, Mr. Wilder, what about the stones?" And he said, "Oh! oh! the stones! We'll—leave 'em—right where they are."

Martin Richardson Stayed

HARTLEY Dennett, my stepfather, and my mother thought a great deal of Martin Richardson. He even taught my mother how to make dandelion wine. Toward the end of his life, I believe, he was living alone in the brick house above East Alstead. His wife had died quite a while before, I believe. Mr. Richardson had, I believe, a niece named Miss Daggett, in Keene, and she came up one day and talked a long time with Martin telling him how he was getting old and wasn't very well. And what would happen to him, she asked, if he got sick and nobody could take care of him? He might die right there and nobody would know about it. Wouldn't that be awful? She said, "Why don't you come down to Keene and live with us?" They had a house or apartment in West Keene.

Martin had lived on his farm all these years and naturally it was home to him; he didn't want to leave. He wanted to stay where he was. But

As told Heman Chase, Alstead, New Hampshire, February 11, 1964. Recorded by B. A. Botkin.

As told by Heman Chase, Alstead, New Hampshire, February 11, 1964. Recorded by B. A. Botkin.

she talked to him so long she got him quite upset. Finally, I believe, perhaps the next day, he came down and visited Hartley and my mother and told them how upset he was and asked them what they thought he'd better do. And they agreed with him. He'd better live where he was, where he'd be happy. And I remember my mother ended the argument by saying, "Why, Martin, as for me, I'd rather die in East Alstead than live in Keene."

The Electric Fence

MY FRIEND Al Wilcox of Weston said that he was once driving along a country road in Vermont and had to stop for a few minutes because an old couple were getting a bunch of cattle back into a pasture from which they had strayed out into the road. There was an electric fence across the barway, but they were driving the cattle right over the fence anyhow. When they finally got the cattle all through and signaled to him to come along, he did so, but he stopped and said, "Well, I see you're having quite a lot of trouble with your cattle." And the old lady said, "Wal, you know, the electricity you get nowadays ain't no good."

The Fire

A MAN in Langdon who had a farm that he thought a great deal of was taken sick and was in the rest home. And he figured, I guess, it was about the end. He was afraid his son-in-law was going to get possession of his farm. And he didn't want him to have it. And he said he'd burn the place before he'd let him have it. And if he died before he had a chance to, he'd come back and do it. And the night before his son-in-law did get possession of it—the night before he was gonna move into the place, there come up some violent thunder showers, and lightning struck the place and burned it.

From where I live, we could see the brightness of the flames, and we started out to find out where the fire was and got there in time to see the house burning. And a kind of rather spooky burning. One end of the house, the opposite from where the fire had started in it, was burning, and the end where it started wasn't burning much. One dark room that we was watching, the curtains disappeared, but we could see no flame there. And afterwards we were at the place and some of the kitchen wallpaper wasn't even smoked.

As told by Heman Chase, Alstead, New Hampshire, February 11, 1964. Recorded by B. A. Botkin.

As told by Clarence Miller, South Acworth, New Hampshire, February 12, 1964. Recorded by B. A. Botkin.

Marrying Late

THIS MAN from Vermont didn't get around to marrying till quite late in life, and some of his friends was kidding him about it. "Well," he says, "if you get the right one, she's worth waiting for, and if you don't, you ain't got so long to live with her."

Vermont Summer

A MAN come in from outside and was talking to a Vermonter. "I hear you have short summers here." "Last year it came on Thursday." And we was telling that story to our grain man that's a Vermonter while he was making out the bill. And he says, "Morning or afternoon?"

STUBBORN YANKEES

Our Town

I SPENT a summer in the Eastern States, for the purpose of studying Yankee character, and picking up such peculiarities of dialect and expression as I could, from constant communication with the "critters" themselves. In Boston, I was thus invited by a countryman to visit the town in which he lived.

"Wal, stranger, can't you come down our way, and give us a show?"

"Where do you live?" inquired I.

"Oh, abeout halfway between this 'ere and sunrise."

"Oh, yes," said I, adopting at once the style of the countryman, "I know; where the trees grow underground, and galls weigh two hundred pounds. Where some on 'em are so fat, they grease the cart-wheels with their shadow, and some on 'em so thin, you're obliged to look at 'em twice afore you can see 'em at all."

"Wal, I guess you've been there," says he, saying which, the countryman departed.

As told by Clarence Miller, South Acworth, New Hampshire, February 12, 1964. Recorded by B. A. Botkin.

As told by Clarence Miller, South Acworth, New Hampshire, February 12, 1964. Recorded by B. A. Botkin.

From *Traits of American Humor,* by Native Authors [edited by Thomas C. Haliburton], Vol. II, pp. 111–112. London: Colburn and Company. 1852.

Franklin Forestalling Inquiry

THE late Dr. Franklin, in the early part of his life, followed the business of a printer, and had occasion to travel from Philadelphia to Boston. In his journey he stopped at one of their inns, the landlord of which possessed the true disposition of his countrymen, which is, to be inquisitive, even to impertinence, into the business of every stranger. The Doctor, after the fatigue of the day's travel, had set himself down to supper, when his landlord began to torment him with questions. The Doctor well knew the disposition of those people; he apprehended, that, after having answered his questions, others would come in, and go over the same ground, so he determined to stop him. Have you a wife, landlord? Yes, Sir. Pray let me see her. Madam was introduced with much form. How many children have you? Four, Sir. I should be happy to see them. The children were sought and introduced. How many servants have you? Two, Sir, a man and woman. Pray fetch them. When they came the Doctor asked if there were any other persons in the house; and being answered in the negative addressed them with much solemnity: My good friends, I sent for you here to give you an account of myself. My name is BENJAMIN FRANKLIN; I am a printer, of —— years of age, reside at Philadelphia, and am going from thence to Boston. I sent for you all, that if you wish for any further particulars, you may ask, and I will inform you, which done, *I flatter myself you will permit me to eat my supper in peace.*

He Might as Well Have Stayed

"I SUPPOSE it was a perfectly natural feeling I had when I returned from Europe," said the Boston drummer, "and that feeling, of course, was to let everybody know I had made the trip. No doubt I made a good many folks tired, but I got the knock-out when I least expected it. I was down Cape Cod way to visit a brother, and one day entered a village store where half a dozen farmers were sitting around. I managed to get the conversation around to 'Yurup,' and as they were all good listeners I had the floor to myself for half an hour. I told them of London, Paris, Rome, Venice, and all that, and not one of them asked a single question. I hadn't got tired out yet, but had paused to get a better hold when an old gray-head with the soberest face you ever saw looked up and queried:

" 'So, stranger, ye've crossed the ocean?'

From *Weatherwise's Almanack,* for the Year of Our Lord 1797. Printed at Boston, and Sold by J. Boyle, C. Bingham, B. Larkin, Wm. Pelham, E. Larkin, J. Nancrede, J. West, J. Bumstead, and other Booksellers in Town and Country.

From *The (Old) Farmer's Almanack . . . 1900,* by Robert B. Thomas, No. 108, p. 45. Boston: William Ware & Company.

" 'Yes, sir.'

" 'And seen all them places in Yurup?'

" 'Yes.'

" 'And got back as slick as grease?'

" 'As you see.'

" 'Well, that's powerful smart of ye,' he continued, 'but I'd like to ask ye a question or two. How high is a six-rail fence?'

"I had to reply that I didn't know.

" 'How much does a bushel of wheat weigh?'

"I wasn't sure within five pounds.

" 'When does a baby get its first tooth?'

"I was stumped on that and said so.

" 'Then I'll ask ye some easy ones,' he said. 'How many 'taters does a farmer plant in a hill?'

" 'I can't say.'

" 'What's the object in having the front wheels of a wagon the smallest?'

" 'I give it up.'

" 'How long does it take chickens to hatch?'

" 'I never knew.'

" 'Which end does a horse get up on first?'

" 'I—I never watched.'

"The old man and the crowd turned from me in contempt," said the drummer, "and feeling at least a foot shorter than when I went in I edged for the door. My questioner had something in reserve, however. As I reached the door, he called—

" 'Wall, stranger, mebbe you wasn't so much to blame for goin' to Yurup, bein' ye had the time and money, but for the next year or two I'll be wonderin' why on airth you didn't stay over there the rest o' yer days?' "

A Yankee in Georgia

SOME YEARS ago a man from our town was traveling through the South. He stopped in a small town in Georgia, and put up at a little hotel. He asked for a good room. The landlord said, "I'll give you the best one in the hotel." So he put up for the night, and in the night he was visited by a number of these little fellows called legion. And he wasn't very well pleased with his accommodations.

So when he come down from his room in the morning, he complained to the landlord. He says that all these little fellows here in the night—he wasn't accustomed to any such kind of performance as that. They kept their rooms and their beds, etc., better in his section of the country.

As told by Chester C. Mason, Langdon, New Hampshire, February 12, 1964. Recorded at South Acworth by B. A. Botkin.

The landlord said, "Well, I don't know why there should be anything particularly bad about this room. And that is the same bed that William Jennings Bryan slept in when he stopped here."

"Well," our man says, "I don't know as I've any objections to sleeping with William Jennings Bryan. But I don't care to sleep with the whole Democratic party."

The Return of the Native

... A YOUNG man who had gone away from a New England village with his family at an early age returned after an absence of many years for the purpose of measuring the family wood-lot. On his arrival he went to the post-office to make certain inquiries of the postmaster, and on emerging from the post-office he paused to pass the time of day with four or five old residents who were sitting on the post-office steps, apparently allowing their minds to turn over silently in neutral, as one might say.

"Looks a little like rain," he remarked by way of an opening wedge.

His words were greeted with a rich silence on the part of the old residents.

"I say," he repeated, after something of a wait, "it looks as though it might rain."

After another long and eloquent silence, one of the natives removed his pipe from his mouth, neatly deluged an adjacent fly, turned his head slowly, gazed blankly at the young man, and finally asked:

"What you say yuh name wuz?"

"Why," said the young man, "my name's Eldridge. My family used to live over at Baxter's Dam Corners. Looks a little like rain, doesn't it?"

At this the silence again settled down over the post-office steps, but eventually the same inquisitive native once more turned his head and looked coldly at the stranger. "Any relation to Eben Eldridge?" he asked carelessly.

"Yes, indeed," said the young man. "Eben Eldridge was my uncle. We'll probably get a little rain, don't you think so?"

"Then your father wuz Herb Eldridge, wa'n't he?" asked the native.

"Yes, Herbert Eldridge was my father," the young man replied.

"Oh, that so!" said the native, deftly favoring another fly with a shower bath. "Eben Eldridge's nephew and Herb Eldridge's boy, hey? Hm! Well, well!"

He and his companions studied the toes of their shoes intently for a few moments, and finally the native looked up at the sky dubiously. "Well," he admitted with some reluctance, "it *may* rain."

From *Concentrated New England. A Sketch of Calvin Coolidge,* by Kenneth L. Roberts, pp. 8–10. Copyright, 1924, by the Bobbs-Merrill Company. Indianapolis.

"Real Characters"

OUR NATIVE-BORN Ethan Frome types are about all dead now, their mores and tenets, their very accent all but forgotten. Nor are their ways especially mourned by the handful of us, their descendants, who still live on the Old Place. It is the newcomers from Boston and New York and Indianapolis who keep their memory green. And these people are always insisting they see in us all the homely and quaint traits of our forebears. "Real characters, these neighbors of ours—lived right on the same spot for generations. . . ."

* * * * *

Fortunately, the native-born in our town long ago became quite well integrated with the summer people. For had we not begun to practice intermarriage we would now be almost extinct. Today we can mingle freely in any gathering and an outsider would never spot us.

A Hungarian psychiatrist, looking for a vacation spot, lost his way and stopped at our house to ask directions. After some conversation, he inquired: "And how you peoples get along wiz natives in zis remote place? You find them friendly?"

My answer was automatic. "They're a damned tough lot," I told him. "Suspicious and unpredictable. You never know where you stand. We're beginning to make some progress with them, but it takes a lot of patience."

"So? You have been here for some time?"

"We've been right here since about seventeen-sixty," I said. He looked at me a little strangely, bade us good-by, and drove away.

* * * * *

For a long time Ed Wilson was our town road agent. A New York lawyer who summered up beyond the village used to interrogate Ed frequently about the road work—when was he going to draw some more gravel, fill a mudhole, things of that sort. Ed was the kind who would not have cultivated the lawyer's favor even without the questioning.

One day the lawyer went for a walk and encountered the road agent and his crew. Ed was sitting down, holding drill, while one of the boys swung a sledge. When they stopped to rest, the lawyer greeted them pleasantly, and approaching Ed, went on, "And just what are you good men planning to do here, if I may inquire?"

"Well, I'll tell ye," Ed said promptly. "We're drillin' this here ledge that's blockin' the ditch. When we get deep enough, I'm goin' to fill the hole with dynamite. Then we'll touch her off, and anybody standin' around with nothin' better to do than ask damn fool questions will get blown straight to hell!"

From *North of Monadnock,* by Newton F. Tolman, pp. 22, 183–185. Copyright, 1961, by Newton F. Tolman. Boston and Toronto: By permission of Little, Brown and Company, Atlantic Monthly Press.

Such independence of spirit on the part of town officials has in recent years almost disappeared. Now when the road agent wants to dig out a culvert or cut a little brush, he consults with the selectmen, who discuss it with the planning committee, who decide we had better hold an open meeting.

* * * * *

Nobody could have been more surprised than Old Frank, our neighbor to the south, when we voted to remove the rock from the dead-end road just beyond his house. He had complained at every town meeting for forty years. True, it was a big cobblestone and you had to dodge around it, but the road didn't go much farther anyway, and no road agent ever paid it the slightest attention.

Sometime after the stone had been exhumed, I was visiting with Old Frank, and spoke about the improvement. "Well, I don't know," he mused. "Many a time, Sunday night, I'd be settin' here by the kitchen window, and a car would go by. Somebody hadn't seen the turnoff and think they was headed back to Boston. They would go roarin' up past and then bang! After awhile, they'd come creepin' back down, and next morning I'd see a little trail of oil in the middle of the road . . . I kind of miss that old rock."

Country Squire

SOMETIME around 1880, one Louis Cabot bought up large holdings in the townships of Dublin, Harrisville, Nelson, Antrim, and Hancock. Farms of one hundred to five hundred acres with buildings more or less intact could be bought for a pittance in those days. The railroads had isolated the hill country, and farming had moved westward. The Cabot estate, most of it never accurately surveyed, at a conservative guess may have run to more than a hundred thousand acres. For a time we were pretty well surrounded by Cabot land, my grandfather having been one of the few natives silly enough to refuse all offers of the estate agents.

One day Mr. Cabot was touring the back roads, as was his wont on summer days, behind a fast team driven by his coachman. He passed a large open slope growing up to poplar whips, a promising situation for woodcock. Cabot was an upland game enthusiast and bought land with an eye for bird cover. On coming to a farmhouse, he stopped to inquire of an old man who was outside splitting wood.

"Looks like good woodcock country along here. Are there many birds around?"

"Plenty of 'em," the old man told him.

"Is that land across the road for sale, by any chance?"

Ibid., pp. 175–176.

"Dunno."

"Don't you own it?"

"Nope."

"Well, then, who does?"

"Rich old cuss from Boston, name o' Cabot."

Independent Vermonters

A VERMONTER seldom hurries and he never wastes a motion. Vermont humor is like that—it ambles along, takes its time, and never wastes a word.

* * * * *

A theme of clannishness and rejection of the outsider runs through a lot of Vermont stories. One couple bought an old house and started down the road to find a man named Olin Warren who, they had been told, not only lived in the neighborhood but would be willing to make some basic repairs on the house. After walking about a half mile they saw a man cutting the roadside brush with a scythe.

"Do you know where Olin Warren lives?" asked the wife.

Without looking up the man said, "Yup."

They waited for further information. None came.

"Will you tell us where he lives?" the husband asked.

The man put down his scythe and pointed to a small house a mile up on the mountain.

"It's quite a walk," the husband continued. "You don't happen to know if he's home or not, do you?"

"Nope," said the man. "He ain't home." Then he looked at the couple for the first time. "What did you want with him."

"Well," said the wife, "we bought the old Gokey place down the road and somebody told us Olin Warren might be willing to do some repairing for us."

The man rested his scythe for a moment. "I be he," he said.

* * * * *

As is true in most states, there are really two Vermonts. One is the new Vermont that has grown up along the tourist routes and makes its living supplying consumer goods to travelers. I include ski slopes in this category. The other is the old rural Vermont that hasn't changed much for more than two hundred years. The line dividing the two is indistinct, however, for it is still possible to ask for an advertised item in a store and be told it is not kept in stock because it sells too fast.

The matter of scenery comes in for a good deal of comment for, of

---

By Keith W. Jennison. *Chicago Tribune Magazine,* May 20, 1956, p. 25.

course, it looks different to the tourist than it does to the native. One visitor exclaimed over the beauty of a certain vista, only to get the following response:

"Well, maybe, but if you had to fence that view, plow it, plant it, hoe it, mow it, and pay taxes on it—it would look pretty durned ugly."

The ornery quality of Vermont humor is not always directed toward strangers. One man came back to his home town after what he considered an illustrious career in New York. To his surprise, there was nobody at the station to meet him. Finally he found the station master asleep on a baggage truck on the shady side of the station. Upon being awakened, the station master looked up, rubbed his eyes, and said:

"Why, hello, Johnny, going some place?"

Another Vermonter took a trip of a completely different nature. He lived in Vermont close to the New Hampshire border. The survey for a new road, however, disclosed that his farm actually had always been on the New Hampshire side of the line. When he was told this, he said,

"Well, thank the good God almighty, I couldn't have stood another of them Vermont winters."

Some of the old trades aren't practiced anymore. Blacksmiths, for example, are hard to find. But one out-of-state motorist managed to find one within a mile of the place where his car had broken down. He explained his trouble and asked the blacksmith if he thought he could fix it.

"Sure," said the blacksmith. "I do everything from shoeing horses—on down."

With Vermont's new look as one of America's favorite summer and winter playgrounds, you don't hear as much of the biting humor as you used to. It never really dies out, though. . . .

Although you couldn't get one to admit it, the answer most Vermonters feel is the truest was made in response to a question asked by a visitor. Looking out over a hillside where the flint and slate ledges cut up through the thin soil, this stranger had said:

"Doesn't look like much of a farming country around here. What do you raise?"

The farmer looked at him steadily. "Men," he said.

The Snows of Yesterycar

. . . AN EARLY summer visitor driving through a deep gorge, scarcely touched at any part of the day by sunshine, found a man busily shoveling snow which had evidently drifted deep across the road.

"You must have had lots of snow here last winter," he remarked as he drove by.

From *New England Joke Lore,* The Tonic of Yankee Humor, by Arthur G. Crandall, p. 18. Copyright, 1922, by F. A. Davis Company. Philadelphia.

"Oh! no," was the reply, "this is winter before last's snow."

God and the New Hampshire Farmer

A FARMER was working his small rocky plot on a back road when a curate who was new to the district came along. He stopped to talk and in the course of the conversation remarked, "You and God certainly have done a nice piece of work here." "Yeah," the man answered, "you ought to have seen it when God had it all alone."

Rock Farm

[A] MAINE farmer . . . was asked by a summer visitor how there happened to be so many rocks on his farm. "Glacier brought 'em," he said. What was he going to do about it? the summer visitor asked. "Wait for another glacier to take 'em away again," he said.

Building Wall

ONE OF our [Maine] country men was building a stone wall, as everybody did when I was a boy. This particular wall was four feet wide and three feet high. A neighbor came by and asked the old farmer why he was building such an odd-shaped wall—wider than it was high. Without looking up from his work, the farmer said, "So if it ever blows over it'll be higher than it was before."

Answering One Question by Asking Another

A WAGER was laid on the Yankee peculiarity of answering one question by

From "Lancaster," by Ola G. Veazie. Manuscripts of the Federal Writers' Project of the Works Progress Administration for the State of New Hampshire.

From "Maine," by Arthur Bartlett, *Holiday,* Vol. II (August, 1947), No. 8, p. 87, Copyright, 1947, by The Curtis Publishing Company. Philadelphia.

From *Rufus Jones' Selected Stories of Native Maine Humor,* edited by Nixon Orwin Rush, pp. 13–14. Copyright, 1945, by Clark University Library. Worcester, Massachusetts. 1946.

From *The American Joe Miller:* A Collection of Yankee Wit and Humour, Compiled by Robert Kempt, p. 32. Entered at Stationer's Hall. London: Adams and Francis. 1865.
This trait . . . is, I take it, a relic of the inquisitorial character of the old colonial days, when every stranger was expected to give an account of himself, or be set down as a suspicious character.—Samuel Adams Drake, *The Pine-Tree Coast* (Boston, 1891), p. 73.

asking another. To decide the bet a Down-Easter was interrogated. "I want you," said the better, "to give me a straightforward answer to a plain question." "I kin du it, mister," said the Yankee. "Then why is it New Englanders always answer a question by asking one in return?" *"Du they?"* was Jonathan's reply.

The Man from Monkton

To THOSE of rural districts who seldom travel far from the home fireside, there are suggestions of possible interest and entertainment in conversing with strange frequenters of the highway. This was especially true of earlier days when, because of frugal habits and rather unsatisfactory public roads, unfamiliar faces in the highways were few indeed.

It is not surprising therefore that when a real old gentleman who had served his community and even his state acceptably in his more active days, observed an absolute stranger walking rapidly up the road, he should have meandered out to the front gate for a little closer inspection.

The traveler was evidently in haste, but was brought up to a short turn with an interrogation from the old gentleman that it would have been very impolite to have ignored. Then followed a conversation which is yet occasionally referred to after more than half a century.

"You seem to be in a hurry today."

"Yes, I am."

"Where did you come from?"

"I came from Monkton."

"When did you leave there?"

"Day before yesterday."

"Where did you stay last night?"

"I stayed in Goshen."

"Where are you going today?"

"I am going to Jericho."

"What are you going to Jericho for?"

"I am going to school."

"A man as old as you going to school! What are you going to school for?"

"I am going to school to see if I can't learn how to mind my own business."

Taunton's Seasons

THE plenty in season, the scarcity when the run of fish was gone, has passed into the myths of a town of the Old Colony. A traveler in the frozen winter, meeting an emaciated villager, asks the name of the place; a weak voice drawls out, "Taunton, Good Lord!" Returning in the genial spring, the sun shining, the streams unlocked, the herring in full run, he meets the same person, now erect, plump, and audacious. To the same question the renovated citizen answers, "Taunton!! and be d——d to you!"

Jim Eldredge's Old Mill

A DISCRIMINATING lady from Baltimore, with an indulgent eye for Dutch effects, sallied forth one May morning to buy an old windmill. She was the first to conceive the idea that such an interesting annex to her cottage would make unique quarters for her guests. As old windmills, however, are not to be acquired off-hand at any chain store, the pursuit led her many a mile from one end of the Cape to the other. Success came in the end. She chanced upon a fine old specimen in Falmouth, had it transported tenderly to Chatham, and then carried through her attractive plan to its least detail, which was roses rambling over the arms of the mill. Imagine her surprise when shortly afterwards a veteran character of the neighborhood strolled around, and exclaimed, "Well, well, I'm glad to see Jim Eldredge's old mill back in Chatham. You know, a man from Falmouth came here fifteen or twenty years ago and took it away. Sort of wanted to decorate his grounds."

Characters

DOWN ON THE Cape . . . there used to be a stage line from the railway station in a town to a beach resort a few miles distant. On one occasion the driver of this stage had as a passenger a young fellow who was returning to the city after a two-weeks' stay at the resort.

"Uncle," said this young chap, "I'll say this for you. You certainly have some queer characters here on Cape Cod."

The driver nodded, "Um-hm," he agreed gravely. "This is the season for 'em; they come on about every train now."

From *Cape Cod Ahoy!*, A Travel Book for the Summer Visitor, by Arthur Wilson Tarbell, p. 103. Copyright, 1932, by Arthur Wilson Tarbell. Boston: A. T. Ramsay & Company.

From *Cape Cod Yesterdays*, by Joseph C. Lincoln, p. 259. Copyright, 1935, by Joseph C. Lincoln and Harold Brett. Boston: Little, Brown and Company.

Migratory Birds

ONE OF THE neighbors in East Alstead was ill and his doctor was there taking care of him. And one of the summer neighbors came in to visit and to sympathize with the family in their alarm over the illness of this man. Presently the doctor left and this neighbor asked if they had called in any consulting doctor. And the family said no, they hadn't. If some consulting doctor were needed, they felt sure their family doctor would know it and suggest it and so they hadn't suggested anything.

"Well," said the summer neighbor, "if I felt the doctor wasn't doing everything *possible* I should *cast him aside* and get another."

And she fluttered around a bit about it and left. Then the mother of the family leaned back in her chair and said: "The summer people come and flutter around a while and then they go away." She was comparing the summer people to the birds that migrate: they come in the spring, flutter around a while and then they go away, leaving the country to the year-round people.

Exhuming the Remains

AN INCIDENT told in many Vermont communities for two generations and always as a local occurrence has to do with the transfer of an ancient cemetery to a new location. All consents had been obtained except in the case of a comparatively recent grave. The occupant had been buried only seventy years and had two elderly grandnephews still living. One of them refused consent for a long time, but finally gave in, though he would have nothing whatever to do with the business of transfer. After it was over the two old brothers were sitting on the front porch and the following dialogue ensued:

"Did they?"
"Yep."
"Were you thar?"
"Yep."
"How was the box?"
"Purty nigh gone."
"Coffin?"
"Sorta moldy."
"D'ja look in?"
"Yep."
"How was Uncle John?"
"Kinda poorly."

As told by Edith Newlin Chase, Alstead, New Hampshire, February 12, 1964. Recorded by B. A. Botkin.

Bringing in the Log

SAM SLICK tells the following story:—

Squire Peleg Sandford and all his family were all of them the most awful passionate folks that ever lived, when they chose; and then they could keep in their temper, and be as cool as cucumbers. One night old Peleg, as he was called, told his son Gucom, a boy of fourteen years old, to go and bring in a back-log for the fire. Back-log, you know, Squire, in a wood-fire, is always the biggest stick that one can find or carry. It takes a stout junk of a boy to lift one.

Well, as soon as Gucom goes to fetch the log, the old squire drags forward the coals, and fixes the fire so as to leave a bed for it, and stands by, ready to fit it in its place. Presently in comes Gucom with a little cut-stick, no bigger than his leg, and throws it on. Uncle Peleg got so mad, he never said a word, but just seized his riding-whip, and gave him an awful whippin'. He tanned his hide properly for him, you may depend.

"Now," says he, "go, sir, and bring in a proper back-log."

Gucom was clear grit as well as the old man, for he was a chip of the old block, and no mistake; so out he goes without so much as sayin' a word, but instead of goin' to the wood-pile, he walks off altogether, and stayed away eight years, till he was one-and-twenty and his own master.—Well, as soon as he was a man grown, and lawfully on his own hook, he took it in his head one day he'd go home and see his father and mother agin, and show them that he was alive and kicking; for they didn't know whether he was dead or not, never havin' heard of or from him one blessed word all that time. When he arrived at the old house, daylight was down, and the lights lit, and as he passed the keepin' room winder, he looked in, and there was the old Squire sittin' in the chair he was eight years afore, when he ordered in the back-log, and gave him such an unmerciful whippin'. So what does Gucom do but stop at the wood-pile, and pick up a most hugaceous log, (for he had grow'd to be a whappin' big fellow then,) and openin' the door, marches in and lays it down upon the hearth, and then lookin' up, says he—

"Father, I've brought you in the back-log."

Uncle Peleg was struck up all of a heap; he couldn't believe his own eyes, that the six-footer was the boy he had cowhided, and he couldn't believe his own ears when he heard him call him father; a man from the grave wouldn't have surprised him more; he was quite onfakalized and bedumbed for a minute. But he came to right off, and iced down to a freezin' point in no time.

"What did you say?" said he.

"That I have brought you in the back-log, sir, you sent me out for."

From *Comic Metamorphoses*, Being a Perfect Encyclopedia of Fun and Humor ... , by Dr. W. Valentine, pp. 176–177. Entered according to an Act of Congress, in the year 1855, by Garrett & Company, in the Clerk's Office of the District Court for the Southern District of New York. New York: Dick and Fitzgerald.

"Well then, you've been an amazin' long time a fetchin' it," said he, "that's all I can say. Draw the coals forward, put it on, and then go to bed."

SALT WATER YANKEES

Ma'am Hackett's Garden

FISHING on the Banks is largely carried on by fast-sailing well-equipped schooners. They carry fresh vegetables, frozen meats, and canned goods to eat, and the crew has the best of fare. It requires three or four months to lay in a cargo of cod. The decision as to just where a schooner shall fish depends a great deal on the depth of the water and the character of the bottom. By constant sounding with the lead line an expert captain gets to know the realm beneath the waters very thoroughly. The lead has a hollow at its lower extremity in which a little grease is inserted, so that a sample of the sea bottom may be secured. The story is told of a certain old Nantucket skipper who could invariably tell just where his vessel was by examining the soil his lead brought up. In order to perplex him his crew once put some garden loam from the home island in the cup of the lead, made a pretence of sounding, and then asked the skipper to name the position of the schooner. The old fisherman tasted the dirt on the lead— his favorite method of determining its individuality—and suddenly exclaimed, "Nantucket's sunk, and here we are right over Ma'am Hackett's garden!"

Following the Wrong Gulls

"IT's shutting in thick over the whole of the bay," Cap'n Eldad told the lad at the wheel, who was a green hand and off-Cape at that. "Better let her go for home." And he started down the companionway.

"But what course shall I steer?" the youth called after him; for "home" was in Truro, and the vessel was in the middle of Cape Cod Bay.

"Follow the gulls," replied Cap'n Eldad. "They'll take you straight into Pamet Harbor."

The skipper turned in. He awoke six hours later—long beyond any

From *New England, A Human Interest Geographical Reader,* by Clifton Johnson, pp. 84–86. Copyright, 1917, by The Macmillan Company. New York and London

From *Cape Cod Pilot,* by Jeremiah Digges, with Editorial and Research Assistance of the Members of the Federal Writers' Project, p. 206. American Guide Series, Federal Writers' Project, Works Progress Administration for the State of Massachusetts. Copyright, 1937, by Poor Richard Associates. Provincetown and New York: Modern Pilgrim Press and the Viking Press.

reasonable running time—came on deck, and found the vessel off the Back Shore of the Cape. What in 'tarnity's name, he wanted to know, was his helmsman trying to do—go a furrin viage?

"I've been following the gulls, like you told me," the lad replied.

"Why, you fog-brained farmer! You've been following Chatham gulls, not Truro gulls!"

The Captain's Hat

THEIR knowledge of the weather comes of lifelong study. There is the story, for instance, of old Cap'n Phineas Eldridge, retired skipper who took to growing turnips on a farm in Eastham, but who had grown weatherwise through many years in command of a coasting schooner. One evening the Cap'n was late for supper, and his wife, glancing out the window, saw a light flitting about the turnip field. Then the Cap'n dashed in, spun the telephone crank and shouted, "Give me Chatham, quick! Hello, Chatham? I want Sam Paine, the postmaster. Hey, Sam! My hat's just blowed off and got clear of me, but she's scudding due south in this breeze, and allowing for the reef in the brim, I calculate she'll just about make it to your place in fourteen minutes more. Mail her back to me, will you, Sam?"

The hat, of course, fetched up on the specified doorstep in Chatham, in exactly fourteen minutes after the Cap'n hung up the receiver, and was sent back to him next morning by parcel post.

How Long from Port?

A SIX months' North Atlantic voyage, officially called a " 'tween seasons" voyage, unofficially called a "plum-pudding voyage," was much scorned by the sturdy old-timers of New Bedford. Such a voyage was generally carried on by Provincetown brigs and schooners. One old New Bedford skipper, who had been coerced against his inclination to make such a voyage, was busily engaged casting off from the wharf when his agent approached and whispered in his ear, "Captain Jones, you've forgotten to kiss your wife good-bye!" Without shifting his gaze from aloft, the captain demanded— "What's ailin' her? I'm only going to be gone six months."

There have been many yarns told illustrative of the extreme length and precarious nature of a whaleman's voyages. One captain reported upon his return from a four years' fruitless search that he hadn't a single barrel of oil or a single pound of bone aboard, but he'd "had a damn fine sail!" A

Ibid., pp. 10–11.

From *The Yankee Whaler*, by Clifford W. Ashley, p. 103. Copyright, 1926 and 1938, by Clifford W. Ashley. Boston: Houghton Mifflin Company.

California clipper is said to have once hailed a whaler in the neighborhood of the Horn and to have asked, "How long from port?" One of a row of ragged and long-bearded men, who were lined up at the rail, answered, "We don't remember, but we were young men when we started!"

Counting the Children

WHEN the vessels left, the wives assembled on the wharves to say good-by, and it was a convention that everyone keep a stiff upper lip.

"We Provincetown women," one banker's wife told me, "would watch an off-Cape bride sharp to see she didn't show a tear. That's no way to see a man off when he's going to be away for months maybe."

"How many children have you, Captain Davis?" I asked an old-timer.

"Wife," he said, "how many times have I been bankin' since we was married?"

Whalers' Bastards

THERE were transgressions. There were occasional sons and daughters born to couples while the husband had been at sea for a couple of years. One such occasion was the cause of a visit to the mother by a committee of neighbors from the village church.

"Mrs. Jones." began the elder solemnly, "there is something that ought to be explained. You have just given birth to a son, and yet your husband has been at sea for the past two years and over. Have you anything to say in explanation?"

"Why, yes," replied the mother, with evident sincerity. "John has written to me several times since he has been away."

Captain Peleg's Letter

"Now then, Arathusy," Captain Peleg told his wife, "it's twenty minutes to sailing-hour. Better start your crying and get it over with, so's I won't

From *Time and the Town, A Provincetown Chronicle*, by Mary Heaton Vorse, p. 114. Copyright, 1942, by Mary Heaton Vorse. New York: The Dial Press.

From *Tales and Trails of Martha's Vineyard*, by Joseph C. Allen, p. 66. Copyright, 1938, by Joseph C. Allen. Boston: Little, Brown and Company.

From *Cape Cod Pilot*, by Jeremiah Digges, with Editorial and Research Assistance of the Members of the Federal Writers' Project, p. 65. American Guide Series, Federal Writers' Project, Works Progress Administration for the State of Massachusetts. Copyright, 1937, by Poor Richard Associates. Provincetown and New York: Modern Pilgrim Press and the Viking Press.

be holding up the vessel."

As he pursed his lips and began tidying up his ditty-box, an obedient sob escaped his wife.

"Oh, Peleg, 'twouldn't be so hard, if you'd only write me a letter while you're away on these etarnal long v'yages! Promise me, Peleg, you'll write this time—just one letter!"

The Captain groaned and promised. And eighteen months later, Arathusy, all a-tremble, tore open an envelope and read:

> *Hong Kong, China,*
> *May 21, 1854.*

Dear Arathusy:
> *I am here and you are there.*
> *P. Hawes.*

Captain Eleazer's *Bulldog*

THERE is no question but that these men loved a good ship, a fast ship. Among the thousand Cape Cod yarns that are variations on this theme is the one about Captain Eleazer, skipper of one of the trimmest schooners in the "Injies trade." His vessel, the *Bulldog*, was "built to split a drop of water into a half moon while she heeled," and he had let the town know he was proud of her. He married a girl name Abigail Bangs, and townsfolk began asking him if he planned to change the name of the vessel to the *Abigail S* as a token of affection for his bride. His reply was, "No, I don't see fitten for to change the vessel's name. But if Abigail keeps on steady being a good girl like she is, I've been thinking I might have her rechristened Bulldog."

The Captain's Prescription

MANY old-time ships carried in the medicine chest what was called the "symptom book," in which were detailed such symptoms as were likely to develop in certain diseases. The diagnosis being thus disclosed, instructions were given to administer such and such a dose of remedy number so

---

Ibid., p. 69.

From *The Nantucket Scrap Basket*, Being a Collection of Characteristic Stories and Sayings of the People of the Town and Island of Nantucket, Massachusetts. Compiled, Edited and Arranged by William F. Macy and Roland B. Hussey and Published for the Benefit of "The Sons and Daughters of Nantucket," pp. 13–14. Copyright, 1916, by William F. Macy and Roland B. Hussey. Nantucket: The Inquirer and Mirror Press. 1916.

and so from the medicine chest. One day a sick sailor having developed the symptoms calling for number eleven, the captain found to his dismay that the bottle supposed to contain that number was empty. However, not to be stumped by a little thing like that, he administered equal parts of number six and number five to the amount of the dose directed for number eleven. The story has it that the man was pretty sick for a time, but that he finally pulled through, though whether owing to a strong constitution or to the captain's ingenuity, deponent sayeth not.

Thar She Blows!

WE WAS cruising down the Mozambique Channel under reefed tops'ls and the wind blowin' more'n half a gale, two years outer New Bedford an' no ile. An' the masthead lookout shouts, "Thar she blows!"

An' I goes aft.

"Cap'n Simmons," sez I (his being the same name as mine, but no kith or kin, thank God!) "the man at the masthead sez, 'Thar she blows!' Shall I lower?"

"Mr. Simmons," sez the cap'n, "it's blowin' a little too peart an' I don't see fittin' fer to lower."

An' I goes forrard.

An' the man at the masthead sings out, "Thar she blows an' breaches!"

An' I goes aft.

"Cap'n Simmons," sez I, "the lookout at the masthead sez, 'Thar she blows an' breaches!' Shall I lower?"

"Mr. Simmons," sez the cap'n, "it's blowin' too peart an' I don't see fittin' fer to lower."

An' I goes forrard.

An' the lookout at the masthead sings out, "Thar she blows an' breaches, an' sparm at that!"

An' I goes aft.

"Cap'n Simmons," sez I, "the lookout sez, 'Thar she blows an' breaches, an' sparm at that!' Shall I lower?"

"Mr. Simmons," sez he, "it's blowin' too peart an' I don't see fittin' fer to lower, but if so be you sees fittin' fer to lower, Mr. Simmons, why lower, an' be good an' God damned to ye."

An' I lowers an' goes on the whale, an' when I comes within seventy-five foot of her I sez, "Put me jest three seas nearer, fer I'm hell with the long harpoon." An' I darted the iron an' it tuk.

When I comes alongside the ship, Cap'n Simmons stands in the gangway. "Mr. Simmons," sez he, "you are the finest mate that ever sailed in

From *History of New Bedford*, by Zephaniah Pease. Cited in *Sea Language Comes Ashore*, by Joanna Carver Colcord, p. 190. Copyright, 1945, by Cornell Maritime Press. New York.

this ship. Below in the locker on the port side there's rum and seegars at your sarvice."

"Cap'n Simmons," sez I, "I don't want your rum, no more your seegars. All I want of you, Cap'n Simmons, is plain seevility, an' that of the commonest, God damndest kind."

An' I goes forrard.

The Stammering Sailor

A stuttering foremast hand, seeing a shipmate fall overboard, rushed aft to tell the captain, but so terrified and excited was he that he could only mouth helplessly, "B-b-b-b—!" "Sing it, man," roared the captain, "sing it!" Whereupon the sailor (for 'tis well known that stutterers can always sing) chanted:

> "Overboard goes Barnabas—
> Half a mile astarn of us."

The Seagoing Coffin

IT WAS characteristic of Cotton Mather and his followers that they enjoyed the contemplation of death; their descendants have not changed the subject matter, but they have a lighter touch. As proof of this, Joe Lincoln once told me of his effort to find the source of a story that is told in nearly every town on the Cape. In each place the oldest inhabitants can tell you the exact spot where the incident occurred, and the names of the *dramatis personae*.

Aunt Emma, it seems, was near her end, and the only maker of caskets in the vicinity was Cap'n Zeke, the boat builder. He had promised to have a coffin ready, but each time the family inquired he had done nothing about it. Finally they went to him with anxious insistence, for Aunt Emma was fading fast.

"I'm mighty sorry," said Cap'n Zeke; "fact is I've been so busy with this thu'ty-footer I just couldn't put my mind to anythin' else. But I'll have her for ye day-after-t'morrer mornin'.'"

Cap'n Zeke was as good as his word. The coffin got to the house as he

From *The Nantucket Scrap Basket,* Being a Collection of Characteristic Stories and Sayings of the People of the Town and Island of Nantucket, Massachusetts. Compiled, Edited and Arranged by William F. Macy and Roland B. Hussey and Published for the Benefit of "The Sons and Daughters of Nantucket," p. 15. Copyright, 1916, by William F. Macy and Roland B. Hussey. Nantucket: The Inquirer and Mirror Press. 1916.

From *As Much As I Dare,* A Personal Recollection, by Burges Johnson, p. 31. Copyright, 1944, by Ives Washburn, Inc. New York.

had promised and just in time. But he had been a little bit absent-minded and had put a centerboard in it.

This same story is ancient folklore along the Maine coast, but down there they tell you that the Cap'n added a rudder.

She Sleeps Six

. . . CAPE fishermen, you are to know, rate the size of their boats not by their length but by the number of men they can sleep. "She sleeps four" or "she sleeps five" is the way they phrase it. One day a certain distant rich man died who had loved this land, and his last request was to be buried in a mausoleum at a Cape cemetery by the sea. Not long afterwards an old fishing skipper, looking into it one morning through the finely grilled doors, was accosted by a passerby with the remark:

"That's a grand tomb, Cap'n Jim."

"Yes, sir, this is a mighty good 'un," was the captain's reply, "she's here for keeps, and she sleeps six."

Cap'n Tibbett and the Body

ALONG the Maine coast—I have been told several places where it occurred —two farmers were gathering kelp along the beach for fertilizer, when they came upon a corpse. Neither recognized it, but one said he thought it might be old Cap'n Tibbett who lived alone in a cabin down on the point. They thought they had better go out to the cabin and see, before reporting their discovery.

They reached the cabin, knocked on the door and old Cap'n Tibbett opened it.

"Well," said one of them, "we're mighty relieved. We found a body down in the kelp and thought it might be you."

"H'm," said Cap'n Tibbett, rolling his quid. "Found a body, did you? Was it wearing a pea-jacket?"

"Yep, had on a pea-jacket!"

"Corduroy pants?"

"Yep."

"Boots?"

"Yep."

From *Cape Cod Ahoy!*, A Travel Book for the Summer Visitor, by Arthur Wilson Tarbell, p. 102. Copyright, 1932, by Arthur Wilson Tarbell. Boston: A. T. Ramsay & Company.

From *As Much As I Dare*, A Personal Recollection, by Burges Johnson, pp. 32–33. Copyright, 1944, by Ives Washburn, Inc. New York.

"Was they knee-boots or these here thigh-boots?"
"They was knee-boots."
"Well, then—'twan't me."

A Wreck's a Wreck

. . . Old Chrissy was an old rascal of a woman that was the head of a gang of [Block Island] wreckers. They lured ships in with false lights, and they killed the sailors and passengers, so there wouldn't be any tales told. Old Chrissy took charge of the killing. She had a big club and she'd hist her skirt and wade out in the surf and clout the people on the head as they swam in or floated in. She called a wreck a wrack, the way the Block Islanders do. That's the way she pronounced it. One night, she and her gang lured a ship up on the reef, and the sailors were floating in, and old Chrissy was out there clouting them on their heads. One poor fellow floated up, and it was one of old Chrissy's sons, who'd left the island and gone to the mainland to be a sailor. He looked up at old Chrissy and said, "Hello, Ma." Old Chrissy didn't hesitate. She gave him a clout on the head with her club. "A son's a son," she said, "but a wrack's a wrack."

A Long Wreck Hook for the Preacher

. . . I heard a Block Island [1] the other day. Johnny Bindloss told it. Johnny had it years ago from his grandfather, old man William Park Bindloss. He was a stone mason who specialized in lighthouses. He built South East Light on Block Island, and he lived over there a year or two and got acquainted. In those days, according to the general talk, the islanders got the better part of their bread and butter salvaging off wrecks. There'd be wrecks on the reefs all during the winter, coasting vessels mostly, and the stuff in them would wash up on the beach. The islanders would stand on the beach all day and all night, hooking for the stuff with poles that had bent nails on the ends of them. They were called wreck hooks. Everybody would line up down there and hook—little children, great-grandmothers, *every*body that could walk. The competition got so thick that they all agreed on a standard-length hook. Everybody had to use the same length. Around that time, a preacher from the mainland came over and settled on the island to preach the word of God and make a

---

As told by Charlie Brayman. From "Dragger Captain," by Joseph Mitchell in *The New Yorker*, Vol. XXII (January 11, 1947), No. 48, p. 42. Copyright, 1947, by The F-R. Publishing Corporation. New York.

As told by Ellery Franklin Thompson. From "Dragger Captain," by Joseph Mitchell in *The New Yorker*, Vol. XXII (January 11, 1947), No. 48, pp. 41–42. Copyright, 1947, by The F-R. Publishing Corporation. New York.
[1] They also collect Block Island stories, or Block Islands.—J: M.

living for himself. The islanders listened to him, but they didn't offer to pay him anything. Along about February, he got real lean and raggedy. He was nothing but skin and bones. The islanders didn't want him to starve to death over there. For one thing, they'd have to bury him. So they held a meeting and argued the matter back and forth. One man made a motion they should take up a collection for the preacher, but this man had a reputation for being simple and his motion was so idiotic they didn't even discuss it. Some wanted each family to give the preacher a peck of potatoes or a turnip or two, and some were for giving him a fish whenever there was a good big catch. They couldn't agree. They argued until late that night. Finally, they decided they'd let him have a wreck hook an inch and a half longer than all the rest. If he couldn't get a living with that, he could starve to death.

Anecdote Characteristic of Sailors

SOON after the last war [of 1812], one of our frigates, bound into Boston, anchored for a few days off Salem. The inhabitants of the town, having ascertained that the ship would remain over Sunday, sent an invitation to the officers and crew to attend service on shore. They accepted it; and on Sunday morning, about meeting time, arrived at the wharf in gallant trim; the officers in the usual naval uniform, and the sailors in that of theirs. From the wharf, where they were met by the authorities of the church, they marched to the meeting house, the sailors under the command of the boatswain. On reaching the house, the officers were conducted to seats on the lower floor; but the sailors, choosing, as they expressed it, "to sit aloft," were shown into the gallery, where, after going through various evolutions, by order of the boatswain, for purpose as he said of making "handsome stowage," they were finally all comfortably seated. The services commenced and were continued without interruption until the minister had got pretty well advanced in his sermon. He had chosen a text adapted to the occasion, and being very anxious for the spiritual welfare of these sons of the ocean, was uncommonly warm and eloquent in his discourse. The sailors, not used to preaching, began to grow uneasy, and the boatswain in particular; but no great insubordination had as yet shown itself. The minister, observing the commotion in the gallery, and thinking it to be the genuine signs of conviction, now directed his sermon more particularly to this portion of his "sea-faring brethren," and that they might the better understand his meaning, he framed his language in similes and figures adapted to their comprehension. He compared a sinner in this life, without religion, to a ship of war in a violent gale, without sufficient strength to enable her to ride it out—the first was as surely on his course to hell as the ship was to be wrecked. He then proceeded to describe a ship in this condition—her rigging broken—her sails lost, or torn in pieces by the furious wind—her groaning masts expected every moment to go by the board—her rudder unshipped, and the unmanageable vessel drifting at the mercy of the winds and waves. "What appalling cry is that which now rises on the blast, benumbing all as with the fear of death? Hark! 'We're lost—the ship is running on a lee shore, and in a few minutes' "—"Avast, there," cried the boatswain, who, throughout the description, had been up and down in his seat at least a dozen times, thinking all the while it was the ship that was going to hell, and being so much carried away by the excitement of the moment, that fancying himself on shipboard, he blew his whistle with tremendous energy, and cried out in a stentorian voice, "Tumble up, tumble up, my lads, and furl every d——d rag, loose the foretopmost-staysail, double reef the mizzen-topsail, jump into the chains, one of you, with the lead—cheerily, men, cheerily, *and we'll weather hell in spite of damnation!*" [1]

. . . I like better this story of the stout old fisherman who in church so unexpectedly answered his pastor's thrilling exhortation, "Supposing, my brethren, that any of you should be overtaken in the bay by a northeast storm, your hearts trembling with fear, and nothing but death before, whither would your thoughts turn? what would you do?"—with the instant inspiration of common-sense, "I'd hoist the foresail and scud away for Squam!" [2]

YANKEE PREACHERS

Fisherman's Reward

To ILLUSTRATE and Demonstrate the Providence of God our Saviour over the Business of the Fisherman, I will Entertain you with Two short Modern Histories. . . . When our Mr. Brock lived on the Isles of Shoals, he brought the Fishermen into an Agreement that besides the Lord's Day

---

[1] From *The Old American Comic Almanac,* with Whims, Scraps and Oddities from the Land of Johnny Bull, Brother Jonathan and Mons. Nontongpaw, New Series, Whole Number IX, Number I, p. 33. Entered, according to an Act of Congress in the year 1838, by Samuel N. Dickinson, in the Clerk's Office of the District Court of Massachusetts. Boston. 1839.

[2] From *Among the Isles of Shoals,* by Celia Thaxter, p. 45. Entered according to Act of Congress, in the year 1873, by James R. Osgood & Co., in the Office of the Librarian of Congress, at Washington. Boston.

From *The Fisherman's Calling,* A Brief Essay to Serve the Great Interests of Religion among Our Fishermen, by Cotton Mather, pp. 22–24. Boston: T. Green. 1712.

they would Spend one Day every Month together in the Worship of the Glorious Lord. A certain day which by their Agreement belonged unto the Exercises of Religion being arrived, they came to Mr. Brock, and asked him, that they might put by their Meeting and go a Fishing, because they had Lost many Days by the Foulness of the Weather. He, seeing that without and against his consent they resolved upon doing what they asked of him, replied, "If you will go away I say unto you, 'Catch Fish if you can!' But as for you that will tarry, and Worship our Lord Jesus Christ this day, I will pray unto Him for you that you may afterwards take Fish till you are weary." Thirty Men went away from the Meeting and Five tarried. The Thirty that went away from the Meeting with all their Craft could Catch but four Fishes. The Five which tarried went forth afterwards and *they* took *five Hundred*. The Fishermen were after this Readier to hearken unto the Voice of their Teacher.

Prayer for Rain

ONE summer, in the early years of the town [of Goshen], there was a worse drouth than any other in the memory of the oldest inhabitant. The grass fields became brown and crisp, the brooks dried, and the highways sent up clouds of dust with every scurry of wind. Several farmers consulted and decided to ask their pastor to pray in the pulpit for more favorable weather conditions.

The following Sunday, as the old pastor was reading notices handed in on slips of paper, he came to the request that a special prayer be made for rain. After glancing at it, he looked through a window at the cloudless, unrelenting blue sky, and observed the direction of a light wind that was blowing. Then he said to his congregation: "I have been asked to pray for rain and will make the prayer if you wish; but I do not think it will do much good as long as the wind remains in the northwest." [1]

Of the local clerics the best-remembered was Aaron Kinne, a preacher of the old type, who lived in Egremont in 1803 and for twenty years sermonized in the various towns of southern Berkshire. During a severe drought a special meeting was called that all members of the church might pray for rain. The crops were drying up and the meadows looked as if they had been scorched by fire. Mr. Kinne was asked to lead the meeting, and when the congregation had gathered, he called loud and long upon the Almighty to send rain to the Berkshires, especially to Egremont and the adjoining town of Alford. Then, closing his prayer, he paused and added

[1] From *Historic Hampshire in the Connecticut Valley*, Happenings in a Charming Old New England County from the Time of the Dinosaur Down to About 1900, by Clifton Johnson, pp. 298–299. Copyright, 1932, by The Northampton Historical Society. Springfield, Massachusetts: Milton Bradley Company.

as an afterthought, "But after all our petitions, O God, we would not presume to dictate, but we would advise." [2]

In the long ago, there lived an old man who believed, firmly, in the efficacy of prayer and during a season of pronounced drought, at the weekly meetin', rose to pray and said, "Oh Lord, we need rain bad, send us rain. We don't want a rippin', rarin', tearin' rain that'll harrer up the face of Natur, but a drizzlin', drozzlin', sozzlin' rain, one that'll last all night and putty much all day, Oh Lord." [3]

. . . It is narrated of him that on one of these occasions, there had been for a long time no rain, and the earth was dry and parched. "Master John" [Ballantine] prayed earnestly for the dews upon the mown grass, and showers that water the earth; and after several weekly petitions, his prayers were answered. The windows of heaven were opened, and down came the torrents, that made up the Jefferson flood. The river rose to an unprecedented height. The meadows were overflowed, and still the waters increased so as really to alarm the people. Sunday came, and with it, "Master John," in the sacred desk, indicating by his manner that something was to be done, and that quickly. He modestly referred to the earnest petitions he had offered up for the "cisterns of the sky," and the discharge of their contents upon "the thirsty ridges of the field," and how abundantly that petition had been answered; and in view of the fact, that apparently a deluge was impending, he broke out into the following eloquent supplication: "Lord, Lord, stay thy hand! O, stay thy hand! Enough! enough! art thou a going to drown us out?" * It is said that the rain ceased, the water subsided, and the woodchucks, and other dwellers in the holes of the earth, who had been drowned out, as "Master John"

---

[2] From *The Berkshire Hills*, Compiled and Written by Members of the Federal Writers' Project of the Works Progress Administration for Massachusetts, p. 179. Copyright, 1939, by The Berkshire Hills Conference, Inc. New York: Duell, Sloan and Pearce.

[3] By Carrie Ordway. From *More New Hampshire Folk Tales*, collected by Mrs. Moody P. Gore and Mrs. Guy E. Speare, p. 238. Copyright, 1936, by Mrs. Guy E. Speare. Plymouth, New Hampshire: Compiled and published by Mrs. Guy E. Speare.

Confer the anecdote of the Scotch minister cited from Dean Ramsay's *Reminiscences of Scottish Life and Character* in *Old New England Traits*, by George Lunt (1873, p. 126): "At one time when the crops were much laid by continuous rains, and wind was earnestly desired in order to restore them to a condition fit for the sickle,—'A minister,' he says, 'in his Sabbath services expressed their wants in prayer, as follows: "O Lord, we pray thee to send us wind, no a rantin' tantin', tearin' wind, but a noohin' (noughin'?), soughin', winnin' wind." '"

feared the people would have been, returned to their burrows, or dug new holes above high water mark. . . .[4]

. . . The Van Dyke yarn most often heard is of a spring when his drive was hung up by low water. With a crew of over two hundred idle, their French-Canadian boss came and asked him:

"Well, Mister Van Dyke, maybe you t'ink pretty good plan I go ask Padre say mass for some rain, so river he rise and we go along."

"Here's ten dollars," said Van Dyke, "and tell that priest to pray like hell!"

That was Friday night. The priest said mass and next day it rained. All over the week end the rain poured down and from upriver came such an angry flood that the huge long logs were carried by thousands up creeks and out onto meadows, to bring Van Dyke only damage suits in place of a whole year's profit in logs. In a frenzy he called in his river boss and gave him a hundred-dollar bill.

"Now tell that Goddamned son of a bitch to shut off the water up there!" he roared.[5]

Prayer for Wind

IN THE early part of his ministry particularly, it was the custom of the fishermen to make two trips during the season to the Banks. So that during the summer months, some of the vessels were going and coming at the same time. If the wind was west, it would be fair only for those going down to the Banks; and if east, only fair for those coming home, and dead ahead for the return fleet. Mr. Damon understood this, and his benevolent heart shaped his prayers to the contingency by introducing the following passage:

"We pray, O Lord, that thou wilt watch over our mariners that go down to do business upon the mighty deep, keep them in the hollow of thy hand; and we pray thee, that thou wilt send a side-wind so that their vessels may pass and repass."

---

[4] From *The Westfield Jubilee:* A Report of the Celebration at Westfield, Mass., on the Two Hundredth Anniversary of the Incorporation of the Town, October 6, 1869, with the Historical Address of the Hon. William G. Bates, and other Speeches and Poems of the Occasion, with an Appendix, Containing Historical Documents of Local Interest, p. 178. Westfield, Massachusetts: Clark & Story, Publishers. 1870.

[*] "Lord, Lord, stay thy hand! Oh, stay thy hand! Enough! Enough! Art thou goin' to drown us out like woodchucks?"—Merle Dixon Graves, *Bubblin's an' B'ilin's at the Center* (Rutland, 1934), p. 15.

[5] From *The Great White Hills of New Hampshire,* by Ernest Poole, pp. 35–36. Copyright, 1946, by Ernest Poole. Garden City, New York: Doubleday & Company, Inc.

From *Truro—Cape Cod, or Land Marks and Sea Marks,* by Shebnah Rich, p. 292. Second Edition, Revised and Corrected. Copyright, 1883, by D. Lothrop and Company. Boston. 1884.

"Schooner Ashore!"

[IN 1876 it was still a misdemeanor in Massachusetts to perform any labor on Sunday, except work of necessity or charity, including the preservation of property which might be lost by delay.]

. . . A [Cape Cod] clergyman was once holding forth to his congregation on Sunday morning—on the vanity of human riches, perhaps—when a man rushed in with the alarm, "Skewner ashore!" The audience arose *en masse,* and made a stampede for the doors, but were arrested by the voice of their shepherd, who exclaimed in stentorian tones, "Brethren, before you leave, I've one last word to give ye," at the same time descending the pulpit stairs and walking deliberately down the aisle, "and that is," continued he, as he joined the crowd at the door, "let's all start fair!" and off he went like arrow from bow, and was the first man on the scene of "accessible value." . . .

Minister and Fish[1]

BLUEFISH are more abundant during some years than during others. They dislike cool water; but whenever the temperature of the sea ranges from sixty to seventy-five degrees, the bay is likely to be full of them. Their coming and going have been mysterious. From the year 1659 to the year 1763, they were recorded as plentiful about Nantucket and the south shore of Barnstable County during the summers; but in the year 1764 they disappeared suddenly, and it is stated that they were not seen again in northern waters, except in small schools, until the year 1810; when and thereafter they returned in large numbers annually to Buzzard's Bay. There is a tradition that during their absence their return was annually expected and watched for all along the shore. At last a large school came into the bay on a Sunday morning in June, and the lads who discovered them hurried to the meeting-house to proclaim the glad tidings. The doors were wide open, the preacher was expounding, when a shrill cry rang in: "Bluefish in the bay!" In a twinkling the meeting-house was emptied, and every boat belonging to the village was soon spreading its sails for the open water. This action was not without precedent. I have read in the annals of Truro, on Cape Cod, that in February, 1755, the people were assembled in their meeting-house for the ordination of the town's minister; when, on account of certain news received at the door, it was "Voted that as many of the inhabitants are called away from the meeting by news of a whale in the bay, this meeting be adjourned." They wanted a whale before

From *Humorous Phases of the Law,* by Irving Browne, pp. 19, 22–23. Copyright, 1876, by Irving Browne. San Francisco: Summer Whitney & Company.

[1] From *The Old Colony Town and Other Sketches,* by William Root Bliss, pp. 61–62. Copyright, 1893, by William Root Bliss. Boston and New York: Houghton, Mifflin and Company.

they wanted a preacher. There are many people who have the same want now.

"[The blackfish are] something like small whales," the fisherman responded, "and I've seen 'em that'd weigh a ton. They're no good to eat, but we cut off the fat and boil it in great big kittles by the shore for the oil. We used to get 'em every year, but now only once in a long time. The biggest capture we ever made numbered fourteen hundred and five. They go just like a flock of sheep, and all you have to do is to get behind 'em with your boats and drive 'em up on shore and lance 'em. When it was known that this school of blackfish was in the bay every boat in town went out to drive 'em. The minister was there with the rest of us, and he give a little girl a Bible afterward for tellin' him about the blackfish in time so he could go. We all hollered and pounded the sides of the boats and made as much noise as we could. Everybody but the minister was swearing and ripping out the toughest words they knew. You'd thought they'd been ashamed to use such language before him, but he was so excited he didn't notice it. Besides, he was making such a racket himself that he had no chance to hear the rest. Well, he had a good strong voice and was a great hollerer anyway. He was shouting: 'Praise the Lord! *Bless* the Lord for so great a gift to this little place.'

"In two hours the fish was all run up on the shore and killed, and when the time come to divide profits there was fifty dollars for every man who had a hand in the job, and that was most all the men in town." [2]

The World, the Flesh, and the Devil

A CERTAIN minister, who had some unpleasantness with the church, took as his text, "The world, the flesh, and the devil," and said, "I shall touch lightly upon the world, hasten to the flesh, and pass on to the devil, when I will give it to you hot as you can sup it."

A Timely Text

A "good sermonizer" was the Reverend Timothy Alden, of Old Yarmouth, with a nice eye for timeliness in the choice of his texts. For fifty

[2] From *Highways and Byways of New England,* Including the States of Massachusetts, New Hampshire, Rhode Island, Connecticut, Vermont and Maine, Written and Illustrated by Clifton Johnson, pp. 195–196. Copyright, 1915, by The Macmillan Company. New York and London. 1916.

From *Truro—Cape Cod, or Land Marks and Sea Marks,* by Shebnah Rich, p. 314. Second Edition, Revised and Corrected. Copyright, 1883, by D. Lothrop and Company. Boston. 1884.

From *Cape Cod Pilot,* by Jeremiah Digges, with Editorial and Research Assistance of the Members of the Federal Writers' Project, p. 66. American Guide Series, Federal Writers' Project, Works Progress Administration for the State of Massachusetts. Copyright, 1937, by Poor Richard Associates. Provincetown and New York: Modern Pilgrim Press and the Viking Press.

years his little flock had faithfully supplied firewood for the parsonage, in
accordance with his salary agreement, and for fifty years the Reverend
Alden sermonized in return, ever finding the word of God that best befitted
the occasion. But one cold winter in the 1790's, the day set for delivery
of his firewood passed, and it appeared that this little item had been let to
lapse. The following Sabbath, the pastor announced his text from
Proverbs XXVI, 20:

"Where no wood is, there the fire goeth out."

The Rev. Mr. Bulkley's Advice

THE following humorous story, in which Mr. Bulkley the first minister in
this town was concerned, is from an ancient publication.

"The Rev. Mr. Bulkley of Colchester, Conn., was famous in his day
as a casuist and sage counsellor. A church in his neighborhood had fallen
into unhappy divisions and contentions, which they were unable to adjust
among themselves. They deputed one of their number to the venerable
Bulkley, for his services; with a request that he would send it to them in
writing. The matters were taken into serious consideration, and the advice,
with much deliberation, committed to writing. It so happened, that Mr.
Bulkley had a farm in an extreme part of the town, upon which he entrusted
a tenant; in superscribing the two letters, the one for the church was
directed to the tenant, and the one for the tenant to the church. The
church was convened to hear the advice which was to settle all their dis-
putes. The moderator read as follows: *You will see to the repair of the
fences, that they be built high and strong, and you will take special care
of the old black bull.* This mystical advice puzzled the church at first,
but an interpreter among the more discerning ones was soon found, who
said, Brethren, this is the very advice we most need; the directions to
repair the fences is to admonish us to take good heed in the admission and
government of our members: we must guard the church by our master's
laws, and keep out strange cattle from the fold. And we must in a particular
manner set a watchful guard over the *Devil,* the old black bull, who has
done so much hurt of late. All perceived the wisdom and fitness of Mr.
Bulkley's advice, and resolved to be governed by it. The consequence was,
all the animosities subsided and harmony was restored to the long afflicted
church. What the subject of the letter sent to the tenant was, and what
good effect it had upon him, the story does not tell."

From *Connecticut Historical Collections,* Containing a General Collection of Interesting Facts, Traditions, Biographical Sketches, Anecdotes, &c., Relating to the History and Antiquities of Every Town in Connecticut, with Geographical Descriptions,
by John Warner Barber, p. 308. Entered according to the Act of Congress, in the
year 1836, by John W. Barber and A. Willard, in the Clerk's Office of the District
Court of Connecticut. New Haven and Hartford.

Johnny-Cake under the Stove

LIKE all Berkshire towns, Washington has a story or two worth telling. One concerns the Reverend Braman Ayers, possibly the last of the old-time "A-h-men!" Methodist ministers who preached here, a man who mixed wit and ingenuity with religion to the disparagement of neither. One fine spring day he paid a visit to his brother's home. Driving past, he sniffed the smell of his sister-in-law's tasty johnny-cake, and quite designedly he reined his horse into his brother's yard at high noon. Invited to eat dinner with the family, the minister seated himself at the table, apparently oblivious of the dismay on his sister-in-law's face.

"Johnny-cake indeed!" she probably muttered to herself as she deftly slid the cake out of the oven. "If Brother Ayers eats one piece, he'll eat two; and if he eats two, he'll certainly eat three; and if he eats three—"

Silently imploring the Lord to remember her virtues and be as lenient as possible with her transgression, she shoved the fragrant yellow cake out of sight. In its place, wheat bread was set in prominence on the red table-cloth, while the parson's hostess reminded him, in somewhat of a hurry, "Brother, it's time to say grace."

"Oh Lord," began the Reverend, sniffing for direction, "bless this food prepared for our use, and bless the johnny-cake"—sniffing triumphantly—*"under the stove!* A-h-men!"

The Dominie and the Horse

THE longest pastorate in the church was that of Charles Gleason, the second pastor, who was ordained October, 1744 and died May, 1790. The next pastorate in point of years was the fourth, Abiel Williams, reaching from 1799 to 1831. The people of the town called him "Priest Williams" and a more genial, kindly pastor never rejoiced the hearts of his parishioners. He was past master in his knowledge of cattle, horses and land. There is a story, probably apocryphal, that one Sabbath when a farmer drove up with a fine horse, the good old dominie laid his hand upon the horse's side and said, "If it was not Sunday, how much would you take for that horse?"

From *The Berkshire Hills*, Compiled and Written by Members of the Federal Writers' Project of the Works Progress Administration for Massachusetts, pp. 224–225. Copyright, 1939, by The Berkshire Hills Conference, Inc. New York: Duell, Sloan and Pearce.

From *Black Tavern Tales, Stories of Old New England*, by Charles L. Goodell, p. 36. Copyright, 1932, by Charles L. Goodell. Brooklyn: Willis McDonald & Co.

YANKEES AND INDIANS

Wickhegan

[*Wickhegan* is] an Indian word meaning in general an official document, more particularly the written permission granted by a chief to hunt on his tribe's territory; also a fine or the price of a permit. The story is that an Old Town Indian got drunk and was arrested and brought before the municipal court in Bangor. The judge fined him ten dollars but remitted the fine on condition that he would not get drunk again. The Indian began to fumble in his pocket and produce money. The judge started to explain that he need not pay now. But the Indian answered, "No judge, I pay *wickhegan*. I might die and go to Happy Hunting Ground and the Great Spirit would ask me if I owed anybody. Then I would remember my fine and would have to hunt all over hell, judge, to find you."

When the Powder Grows

A WHITE trader sold a quantity of powder to an Indian, and imposed upon him by making him believe it was a grain which grew like wheat, by sowing it upon the ground. He was greatly elated by the prospect, not only of raising his own powder, but of being able to supply others, and thereby becoming immensely rich. Having prepared his ground with great care, he sowed his powder with the utmost exactness in the spring. Month after month passed away, but his powder did not even sprout, and winter came before he was satisfied that he had been deceived. He said nothing; but some time after, when the trader had forgotten the trick, the same Indian succeeded in getting credit of him to a large amount. The time set for payment having expired, he sought out the Indian at his residence, and demanded payment for his goods. The Indian heard his demand with great complaisance; then looking him shrewdly in the eye, said, *"Me pay you when my powder grow."* This was enough. The guilty white man quickly retraced his steps.

Head Work

As Gov. JOSEPH DUDLEY, of Massachusetts, observed an able-bodied In-

From "A Word-List from Aroostook," by J. W. Carr and G. D. Chase, in *Dialect Notes*, Vol. III (Part V, 1909), p. 418. Publication of the American Dialect Society. New Haven, Connecticut.

From *The Early History of New England*, Illustrated by Numerous Interesting Incidents, by Rev. Henry White, p. 238. Entered according to an Act of Congress, in the year 1841, by Rev. Henry White, in the Clerk's Office of the District Court of New Hampshire. Boston: Sanborn, Carter, Bazin & Co. [n. d.]

Ibid., pp. 236–237.

dian, half naked, come and look on, as a pastime, to see his men work, he asked him why he did not work, *and get some clothes to cover himself.* The Indian answered by asking him why *he* did not work. The governor, pointing with his finger to his head, said, *"I work head work,* and so have no need to work with my hands as you should." The governor told him he wanted a calf killed, and that if he would go and do it, he would give him a shilling. He accepted the offer, and went immediately and killed the calf, and then went sauntering about as before. The governor, on observing what he had done, asked him why he did not dress the calf before he left it. The Indian answered, *"No, no, Coponoh,* (governor,) that was not in the bargain. I was to have a shilling for killing him. Am he no dead, Coponoh?" The governor, seeing himself outwitted, told him to dress it and he would give him another shilling.

This Indian having several times outwitted the governor, he, falling in with him some time after, asked him by what means he had cheated and deceived him so many times. He answered, pointing with his finger to his head, *"Head work, Coponoh, head work!"*

A New Way to Make People Happy

MR. WINSLOW, returning from Connecticut to Plymouth, left his bark at Narragansett, and intending to return home by land, took the opportunity to make a visit to Massasoit, who, with his accustomed kindness, offered to conduct him home. But before they set out, Massasoit secretly despatched one of his men to Plymouth with a message, signifying that Mr. Winslow was dead, carefully directing his courier to tell the place where he was killed, and the time of the fatal catastrophe. The surprise and joy produced by Mr. Winslow's return must have satisfied even Massasoit's ardent affection, when the next day he brought him home to his weeping family. When asked why he had sent this account, both false and distressing, he answered that it was their manner to do so, to heighten the pleasure of meeting after an absence.

Indian Justice

[IN 1720] Jacob [Spalding] one day purchased of an Indian a deer skin,

From *The Early History of New England,* Illustrated by Numerous Interesting Incidents, by Rev. Henry White, pp. 225–226. Entered according to an Act of Congress, in the year 1841, by Rev. Henry White, in the Clerk's Office of the District Court of New Hampshire. Boston: Sanborn, Carter, Bazin & Co. [n. d.]

From *Connecticut Historical Collections,* Containing a General Collection of Interesting Facts, Traditions, Biographical Sketches, Anecdotes, &c., Relating to the History and Antiquities of Every Town in Connecticut, with Geographical Descriptions, by John Warner Barber, p. 427. Entered according to the Act of Congress, in the year 1836, by John W. Barber and A. Willard, in the Clerk's Office, of the District Court of Connecticut. New Haven and Hartford.

for which he paid him a *tenor bill*. The latter, somewhat intoxicated, forgot soon after that he had received it, and asked for the money a second
time. Jacob of course paid no attention to such an unwarrantable demand,
and the Indian went away muttering revenge. The next day while shingling
a barn, Jacob saw him returning with two companions. He leaped from the
roof, met them, and was again asked to pay the price of the deer skin.
He refused to comply, till one of the company, who appeared to be the
Sachem of his tribe, said he had come to see "fair play," and avowed it to
be honorable for two Indians to contend with one white man. Jacob therefore imagined he would have a rather difficult task to accomplish, but
plucking up courage, he exerted himself to the utmost, and on the very
first encounter, *laid them both* upon the ground and gave them a "sound
drubbing." The other who was looking on, was not at all disposed to
assist his brethren, and gave them no other encouragement than, "Poor
dogs, poor dogs; me hope he kill you both!!" However, Jacob, after
"pounding them" a short time, suffered them to escape. But the next day
he saw them coming again, and the individual who imagined himself his
creditor, bearing a rifle which he was in the act of loading. But in thrusting
his hand into his pocket to find the ball, he drew out the identical *bill* which
he had received two days before! Conscience-struck, he said to Jacob, who
was coming to meet him, "Me believe now, Jacob, you paid me de tenor
bill." After this confession, Jacob addressed the person who had come to
see "fair play." "You," said he, "that have come to see fair play, what do
you advise us to do with him?" "Tie him to de tree and whip him," was
the reply, which was done accordingly. And here a circumstance occurred
which shows to what extent the Indians carried their principle of honor.
The individual in question, after this humiliating treatment, became so
dejected that he fled from his tribe and was never heard of afterwards.

The Englishman with Two Heads

ABOUT the 15*th* of *August*, Captain *Mosely* with sixty Men, met with a
company, judged about three hundred *Indians*, in a plain place where few
Trees were, and on both sides preparations were making for a Battle; all
being ready on both sides to fight, Captain *Moseley* plucked off his Peri-
wig, and put it into his Breeches, because it should not hinder him in fighting. As soon as the *Indians* saw that, they fell a Howling and Yelling most
hideously, and said, *Umh, umh, me no stawmerre fight Engis mon, Engis
mon get two hed, Engis mon got two hed; if me cut off un hed, he got noder,
a put on beder as dis;* with such like words in broken *English*, and away
they all fled and could not be overtaken, nor seen any more afterwards.

From *The Present State of New-England* . . . faithfully composed by a Merchant
of Boston, and communicated to his Friend in London (London, 1675), p. 12. In
The Old Farmer and His Almanack, by George Lyman Kittredge, p. 354. Copyright,
1904, by Horace E. Ware. Boston: William Ware and Company.

Justice Waban

THE following is handed down as a true copy of a warrant issued by an Indian magistrate.—"You, you big constable, quick you catchum Jeremiah Offscow, strong you holdum, safe you bringum afore me.

"Thomas Waban, Justice peace."

When Waban became superannuated, a younger magistrate was appointed to succeed him. Cherishing that respect for age and long experience, for which the Indians are remarkable, the new officer waited on the old one for advice. Having stated a variety of cases and received satisfactory answers, he at length proposed the following:—"when Indians get drunk and quarrel and fight and act like Divvil, what you do dan?"—"Hah! tie um all up, and whip um plaintiff, whip um fendant and whip um witness."

YANKEE HUSBANDS AND WIVES

Abraham Underhill's Wife

. . . ABRAHAM UNDERHILL . . . owned a tavern here in the early days. It seems he was a rare old tippler but he had a smart and thrifty wife. She was also deeply pious. She bore her lot uncomplainingly despite Abraham's jovial ways. One time, after she had risen in the middle of the night to set out a hot meal for him and some of his cronies, who had returned to the tavern none too sober, a friend condoled with her. "Oh, well," said Mrs. Underhill, "all of Abraham's enjoyment will have to be in this world, and I mean to see that he gets as much as possible."

The Reformed Wife

THE following pleasant and unusual circumstance is said to have taken

From *History of the Town of Natick, Mass.*, from the Days of the Apostolic Eliot, MDCL, to the Present Time, MDCCCXXX, by William Biglow, p. 85. Boston: Published by Marsh, Capen, & Lyon. 1830.

For a discussion of Waban and this anecdote and its variants, see George Lyman Kittredge, *The Old Farmer and His Almanack* (Boston, 1904), pp. 333–350.

As told by Zephine Humphrey. From *This Is Vermont*, by Walter and Margaret Hard, p. 79. Copyright, 1936, by Walter Hard and Margaret Hard. Brattleboro, Vermont: Stephen Daye Press.

From *Connecticut Historical Collections*, Containing a General Collection of Interesting Facts, Traditions, Biographical Sketches, Anecdotes, &c. Relating to the History and Antiquities of Every Town in Connecticut, with Geographical Descriptions, by John Warner Barber, p. 116. Entered according to the Act of Congress, in the year 1836, by John W. Barber and A. Willard, in the Clerk's Office, of the District Court of Connecticut. New Haven and Hartford.

place in Newington many years since. Mr. A—— of this place, who was a very religious and conscientious man, married for a wife, one of the most ill natured and troublesome women which could be found in the vicinity. This occasioned universal surprise wherever he was known, and one of his neighbors ventured to ask him the reasons which governed his choice. Mr. A—— replied, that having had but little or no trouble in the world, he was fearful of becoming too much attached to things of time and sense. And he thought by experiencing some afflictions, he should become more weaned from the world, and that he married such a woman as he thought would accomplish the object. The best part of the story is, that the wife hearing of the reasons why he married her, was much offended, and *out of revenge*, became one of the most pleasant and dutiful wives in the town, declaring that she was not going to be made a *pack horse*, to carry her husband to heaven.

The Will of the Lord

AMONG the Morse stories is that a certain deacon Morse, having lost his first wife some time previous, rode early one morning to the chosen one's door and without dismounting knocked, and inquired of the father for his daughter Betsey who hurried to the door. The Deacon without even saying good morning cried: "Betsey, it has been revealed to me that you are to become my wife."—"The will of the Lord be done!" exclaimed the maiden with corresponding taste and congeniality of feeling, anticipating her reward in the richest husband in New London Co. The marriage was a happy one and the brevity of the above courtship saved time to serve their generation.[1]

The Lees owned all the land along Bride Brook as far as the eye could see, but there was an ancient dispute as to whether the territory came under the authority of Lyme or New London. Finally it was decided to settle the matter by the time-honored method of trial by combat. Lyme's gladiators won. Their chief, one Reynold Marvin, claimed young Betty Lee's hand as a reward. The maiden was standing, like Rebecca, at the well when the swain made known his desires in most unorthodox fashion. "The Lord," began the pious suitor," has commanded me to marry

---

[1] From Historical Reminiscences of the Early Times in Marlboro, Massachusetts, and Prominent Events from 1860 to 1910, Including Brief Allusions to Many Individuals and an Account of the Celebration of the Two Hundred and Fiftieth Anniversary of the Incorporation of the Town, by Ella A. Bigelow, pp. 210–211. Copyright, 1910, City of Marlborough. Marlborough, Massachusetts: Times Publishing Company.

you." Betty dropped her eyes. It has been said she also dropped a plate she was wiping; and said, demurely:
"Then the Lord's will be done!"[2]

Thomas Hatch's Courtship

A PLEASANT story is told respecting his courtship. It is said that he was son of a farmer and served his father before learning the trade of a tailor. His wife was also a farmer's daughter, and in time of harvest assisted him in the fields, and was very expert in the use of the sickle. Two young men asked her hand in marriage and it was agreed that the one who should reap the larger piece in a given time should win the prize. The land was marked off and an equal proportion assigned to Miss Grace. She was the best reaper, and having decided that she would marry Thomas Hatch, she slyly cut over on the part set off to him, and in consequence Thomas came out ahead, claimed and received her hand in marriage.

Pulling the Rope

AT AN unknown time previous to 1762 Samuel and his brother Elisha appeared in Canaan. In 1770 Samuel built a house on the Blackberry River near the modern Samuel Forbes Bridge on the Lower Road to East Canaan. At an unknown time, possibly before he built his house, he became smitten of Lucy, daughter of Amos Peirce, a young lady who is said to have been his equal in physiognomy, physique and strength of will. On one point they seem to have agreed from the start, the desirability of getting married. Since Papa Peirce held a different view, an elopement was arranged, and the two coy titans rode off on the same unhappy horse into New York State where they were duly hitched. On returning to the homestead, Samuel pitched a rope over his new barn. "Now, my sweet," said he, "do you draw down on your end and I will draw on mine, and whichever draws the other over the roof is to rule this roost." They both pulled with no effect. "Now, my sweet," proposed Samuel, "do you come around on this side, and let us draw together." The sweet Lucy complied, and together they pulled the rope over the barn. "Let that be the way this house will be run," quoth Samuel.[1]

---

[2] From *Connecticut Trilogy*, by Marguerite Allis, with Drawings by the Author, p. 142. Copyright, 1934, by Marguerite Allis. New York: G. P. Putnam's Sons.

From *Genealogical Notes of Barnstable Families*, Being a Reprint of the Amos Otis Papers, Originally Published in The Barnstable Patriot, revised by C. F. Swift, Largely from Notes Made by the Author, Vol. I, p. 462. Entered according to Act of Congress, in the year 1885, by F. B. Goss, in the Office of the Librarian of Congress, at Washington. Barnstable, Mass.: F. B. & F. P. Goss, Publishers and Printers. 1888.

[1] From *The Housatonic, Puritan River*, by Chard Powers Smith, p. 258. Copyright, 1946, by Chard Powers Smith. New York and Toronto: Rinehart & Company, Incorporated.

Weddings were the grand exhibitions of fashion and occasions for the display of rank; to have a great wedding was to win a name in society. A story is told of one George Babcock, who was as shrewd as he was eccentric. Wishing to enforce the idea of family concord among the people, he at a certain time threw a rope over his house, and stationing his wife on the side opposite to himself, called to her, "Pull, Betty, pull!" Both pulled, but nothing was gained. He then asked Betty to join him at his end of the rope, remarking, "See now, my dear, how easily two can accomplish, when united, what is impossible to them when divided." The story has been a legacy of good to the town.[2]

Don't Hit That Post Again

ON THE western slope of Monument Mountain once stood the Pelton Farm, whose stone gatepost led to a tragi-comic episode. The wife and mother of the family occupying the house had died; as the funeral cortege was leaving the yard, the conveyance carrying the body hit the post. The force of the collision was so great that the corpse was thrown to the ground and the shock revived the woman, who not only showed signs of life but lived five years before she again passed away. Once more the funeral party started on its way, but this time when the hearse approached the post, the husband suddenly stopped the procession and solemnly warned the driver, "Be careful now, don't hit that post again!"

Breaking the Pitcher

THE following story seems to be told in about every town in the North Country and always about some rather vain and pompous gentleman. The man goes down cellar for a pitcher of cider and somehow stumbles. His wife hears him and calls down, "Did you break the pitcher?" This so angers

[2] From *Westerly (Rhode Island) and Its Witnesses,* For Two Hundred and Fifty Years, 1626–1876, Including Charlestown, Hopkinton, and Richmond, Until Their Separate Organization, with the Principal Points of Their Subsequent History, by Frederic Denison, A.M., pp. 142–143. Entered according to Act of Congress, in the year 1878, by Frederic Denison, in the Office of the Librarian of Congress, at Washington, D. C. Providence: Published by J. A. & R. A. Reid.

From *The Berkshire Hills,* Compiled and Written by Members of the Federal Writers' Project of the Works Progress Administration for Massachusetts, p. 162. Copyright, 1939, by The Berkshire Hills Conference, Inc. New York: Duell, Sloan and Pearce.

For mutations of this jest, see W. Carew Hazlitt, *Studies in Jocular Literature* (London, 1890), pp. 120–121. Mrs. Clifton Johnson (in a letter) relates the same story of Molly Webster, the Hadley witch.

From "Lancaster," by Ola G. Veazie. Manuscripts of the Federal Writers' Project of the Works Progress Administration for the State of New Hampshire.

the man, for he thinks that the good wife should ask him if he hurt himself, that he calls back, "No, by thunder, but I will," at which he hurls the precious pitcher at the cellar wall.

Rat or Mouse

. . . DER was hol' man an' hol' hwomans in Canada gat maree togedder w'en dey was hol' an' in t'ree day dey was set heat dinny, an' leetly maouse run on de haouse, an' hol' hwomans say, "See dat maouse." Hol' mans say, "It was rats," an' hol' hwomans say, "No, it was maouse." "Ah tol' you it was rats," he 'll said. "Maouse," she 'll said, an' dey holler "Rat," "Maouse," an' get so mad he 'll go 'way an' stay t'ree year. Den he 'll come back, an' she 'll was veree glad fer see it. "It was too bad you 'll go 'way so, jes' for leetly maouse." "Ant Ah 'll tol' you it was rats?" he 'll holler, and he 'll go, an' never come some more. . . .

The Old Couple and the Bear

. . . I'VE hearn tell o' tew ol' critters 'at got sot aidgeways an' come aout better 'n you tell on. They'd lived together thirty year, but bimeby they fell aout an' they'd mump raound all day 'thaout speakin', an' when it come night they'd turn the' backs tow-ards one other an' snore, an' purtend tu be asleep, each one wishin' 't t' other 'd speak, but nary one would n't fust. An' so it run on till one night in the fall o' the year they heered a turrible rumpus 'mongst the sheep in the yard, an' he ups an' dresses him an' goes aout. Arter quite a spell, an' he did n't come back, she slips on her gaownd an' shoes an' aout she goes tu see what's the matter ailded him, an' lo an' behol', he was clinched in with an almighty gret bear, the bear a-chawin' at him an' him a-huggin' as hard as the bear tu keep him f'm gittin' his hind claws intu his in'ards, which is onpleasant, as I know. "Go it, ol' man, go it, bear," says she, "it's the fust fight ever I see 'at I did n't keer which licked."

She stood lookin' on a leetle spell, with her fists on her hips, till she see the ol' man was a-gittin' tuckered, an' the bear a-hevin' the best on 't, an' then she up with a sled stake an' gin the bear a wollop on the head 't knocked him stiffer 'n a last, and then they hed a huggin' match over the carkis of the bear, an' lived tu gether as folks ortu, tu the eend of the' days.

From *Danvis Folks*, by Rowland E. Robinson, pp. 297–298. Copyright, 1894, by Rowland E. Robinson. Boston and New York: Houghton Mifflin Company.

Ibid., pp. 298–299.

Yankee Diligence

To WASTE either time or money was to a Yankee the breaking of the Ten Commandments. When a good old deacon had passed away, his relict, waiting in the darkened room for the funeral to begin, whispered to her daughter, "Hand me my knitting. I might knit a few bouts while the folks are gathering."

The Parsimonious Widower

IN VERMONT there is a story told me by old citizens in different communities, and in each place it is passed along as local history.

Henry Pease had been a widower for going on a year, and had tried to do for himself, but without much success. He was a parsimonious old fellow, or as the neighbors phrased it, "jest a mite near," and he would not afford hired help. So finally he began calling on the Widow Perkins, reputed to be an excellent cook. But the widow was cagey; she would not commit herself in any way until she had seen Henry's home. Properly chaperoned, she visited it and was quite outspoken about the untidiness and lack of repair, and especially the state of the old-fashioned oven which needed a new soapstone lining. When things were fixed up, she said, she'd like to see it again.

Henry busied himself about cleaning and simple repairs, but he could not bring himself to buy a new lining for the oven. Then he thought of the fine headstone on his late consort's grave, so he went up to the cemetery one night and carried away the slate stone. It split and sawed up nicely and the oven was as good as new.

When the widow came again she was greatly pleased by the look of everything, especially the oven, and agreed to bake a batch of biscuit in it and stay to lunch. Everything went smoothly for Henry until the slab of hot biscuit came to the table. On the bottom of the slab in reversed but sharply defined capitals the assembled company read: "Sacred to the memory of my beloved wife Mathilda."

From *Black Tavern Tales, Stories of Old New England,* by Charles L. Goodell, p. 138. Copyright, 1932, by Charles L. Goodell. Brooklyn: Willis McDonald & Co.

From *As Much As I Dare,* A Personal Recollection, by Burges Johnson, pp. 31–32. Copyright, 1944, by Ives Washburn, Inc. New York.

THE CLEVER AND THE FOOLISH

The Secret of True Economy

Two men met on the street one day, and in the course of conversation the one said to the other: "How do you manage to feed your large family with your small income?" "Well," he responded, "I'll tell you. I find out what they don't like and give 'em plenty of it."

Poor Butter

I REMEMBER once a man came in and asked, "Have you any poor butter?" I looked him straight in the eye, and he stared back. I said, with extreme truthfulness, "Yes, sir, I have." He said he'd take a pound, and I wrapped up some butter that almost threw me while I was tying the string. The next night the man came in again, and casually stated, "I'll take two more pounds of that butter."

While I held it down and reached for the wrapping paper I said, "I wish you'd tell me why you want this—I've been ripped up the back plenty of times for selling stuff like this."

He told me the secret. "My wife has two big booby boys by her first husband, and they're visiting us. They'll put a quarter of a pound of butter on a biscuit and swallow it, but by God this butter makes 'em stand back."

Selling the Dog

BENJAMIN GORHAM, son of Benjamin, (called Young Fiddler) resided in

From *The Nantucket Scrap Basket*, Being a Collection of Characteristic Stories and Sayings of the People of the Town and Island of Nantucket, Massachusetts, Revised, Expanded, and Rearranged by William F. Macy, p. 91. Copyright, 1916, by William F. Macy and Roland B. Hussey; 1930, by William F. Macy. Boston and New York: Houghton Mifflin Company.

From *Yankee Storekeeper*, by R. E. Gould, p. 74. Copyright, 1946, by Curtis Publishing Co. and R. E. Gould. New York and London: Whittlesey House, McGraw-Hill Book Company, Inc.

From *Genealogical Notes of Barnstable Families*, Being a Reprint of the Amos Otis Papers, Originally Published in The Barnstable Patriot, revised by C. F. Swift, Largely from Notes Made by the Author, Vol. I, p. 441. Entered according to Act of Congress, in the year 1885, by F. B. Goss, in the Office of the Librarian of Congress, at Washington. Barnstable, Mass.: F. B. & F. P. Goss, Publishers and Printers. 1888.

the house that formerly stood where Capt. John T. Hall's now stands. He had not the business capacity of his brothers; but was a man of wit and a boon companion. The following story is told of him, and illustrates his general character: When a boy he had a dog that was very troublesome, and annoyed his mother very much. One day he went home and with a serious air said, "Mother, I have sold my dog." "I am very glad, Benjamin, she was so troublesome—how much did you get for her?" "$500." "Did you, Benjamin!" "Yes, mother, I did, most certainly." "What did you get your pay in, Benjamin?" "Aye, that's it,—in bitch pups, at $50 apiece." This story is the origin of the common saying, applied to a man who makes a bad barter trade: "He got his pay in bitch pups."

Misfits

It's turrible resky a-gittin' one thing 'at 's a leetle cuter 'n the rest o' yer belongin's. . . . Oncet I got me a new awl 'at put me clean aout 'n consait o' my ol' kit, an' cost me more 'n a month's airnin's a-buyin' new tools 'at I didn't need, an' some on 'em jest useless consarns.

I've knowed a feller tu git a patch sot on a boot 'at looked so much better 'n the rest on 't 'at he hed tu git a new pair an' then a suit o' clo's tu match, an' then his womern must up an' hev a new caliker gaownd. But the beatinest was Ros'l Drake's door, a bran new front door 'at he bid off tu Amos Wilkinses vandue. Do' know haow Amos come tu hev it, but he hed it, an' Ros'l he bid it off, an' took it hum an' sot it in the barn, and at fust his womern sputtered 'baout his buyin' of it, an' they hed a notion o' puttin' on 't in the place o' their ol' front door, but it wouldn't fit, an' they cal'lated ef it did it 'ould make the hul haouse look humblier 'n ever. But it would n't du to waste that aire door, 'at was paneled an' hed a big brass knocker, an' so what d' they du finally but turn tu an' build them a new haouse tu fit that aire door, which the ol' one was plenty good 'nough.

Wal . . . they hed tu mortgage the' place, an' finally lost it, ol' haouse, new haouse, front door an' all, an' went off over intu Adam's Gore tu live in a lawg haouse, an' glad 'nough tu git sech shelter.

Getting More for His Money

. . . [A] MAN . . . complained because a Boston dentist charged him $5.00 for pulling his tooth.

From *Danvis Folks,* by Rowland E. Robinson, pp. 254–255. Copyright, 1894, by Rowland E. Robinson. Boston and New York: Houghton Mifflin Company.

From *The Story of a Father and Son* or "Unscrewing the Inscrutable," Third Edition, p. 51. Cambridge, Massachusetts: Elliott Addressing Machine Company.

He complained that the Boston dentist had pulled his tooth in about one second, and he thought $5.00 was an overcharge because a few years before a New Hampshire dentist had dragged him all over his office for about ten minutes to pull one tooth and had only charged him $7.50.

He said the New Hampshire dentist had given him a lot more for his money.

Recognizing the Broom

ONE of Poland's queer characters was Hanson Orr, the hired man of some of Mrs. Keen's people. He had a number of quips that he got off occasionally, such as, when trying to establish what day it was: "Is it Thursday or Friday or some day next week?"

On most occasions he was somewhat dull. Once some visitors took a picture of him as he was sweeping in the barn doorway, unknown to him. They showed him the picture and asked him if he recognized the man. Hanson studied it; no, he didn't know as he did.

"Why, it's you, Hanson!" the jokers cried.

Hanson looked disgruntled, and said: "Thought that broom looked familiar."

The Double Hitch

[A] PARSON at Ashfield, Massachusetts . . . mounted his horse one afternoon to make parish calls. He was, of course, offered a glass of toddy at each house he visited, and by the time he came to make his last call was unmistakably feeling the effects of the drinks he had taken. But he dismounted at the last house, drew the bridle rein over his horse's head, and threw it over the hitching post. While he was inside making his call, during which he had another drink, his horse got loose, but was promptly caught by a neighbor who secured the animal to the post again by passing the rein through the augur hole near the top and then looping it over the post. When the minister finished his call and came out to go home he had difficulty unhitching his horse. Finally, after he had delayed some time, members of the family who had been watching came to his assistance. Glassy-eyed but dignified, the D.D. explained the situation.

"Friends," he said, "since I have been in your house one of the most remarkable miracles ever known has occurred, for my horse has in some manner crawled through the hole in this post, and I cannot persuade him to return."

By Elsie Keen, Poland, Maine. Manuscripts of the Federal Writers' Project of the Works Progress Administration for the State of Maine.

From *Yankee Folk*, by Edwin Valentine Mitchell, pp. 104–105. Copyright, 1948, by Edwin Valentine Mitchell. New York: The Vanguard Press, Inc.

Spelling His Name

. . . OCTAVE [Nadeau] told us about his cousin's argument at the Post Office the day before. This cousin had but lately arrived from some back-woods hamlet in Quebec, and was expecting a letter from his wife. Said Octave:

"My cousin hask de Postmaster, 'You got a letter for me?' ' What's your name?' Postmaster say. My cousin say, 'My name Joe.' 'What's your last name?' the Postmaster hask him. 'Joe Vouvoulonceau,' my cousin tell him. 'How you spell dat?' Postmaster say. Joe gittin' madder all de time. 'Can't *you* spell heem needer?' Postmaster shake hees head. Joe say, 'Mon Dieu! You better sell dat post*hoffice* and buy school-*house!*' "

The Thief's Defense

I THINK it was Jonathan N. Hazard who missed his axe, and on meeting black Jim Tefft (a noted thief, whom he suspected), asked him when he was going to bring back the axe he stole from him. Jim seemed horrified at the charge and defended himself stoutly. Jonathan expressed surprise at Jim's alleged innocence, and remarked that he could not think of any one else who would steal it! But Jim got in the last word when he rejoined. "Mr. Hazard, you may depend upon it, there is a great deal stole around here on my credit!" . . .

Not Bright

A FARM-HAND who had not been considered very bright was accidentally killed, and his family took the matter to court to try to get some damages from his employer. During the questioning in court, the judge asked the employer if the laborer was foolish. The employer replied, "No." When asked if he was bright, he replied, "No." The judge asked him to explain, and he said: "Wal, Judge, I ain't bright and you ain't bright, but if any one called us foolish we'd be madder'n hell."

From *Maine Stories*, by John William Stolle, aided and abetted by M. S. (Boob) Snowman, p. 25. Copyright, 1953, by John William Stolle. Bangor, Maine: H. P. Snowman, printer.

From *The Jonny-Cake Papers of "Shepherd Tom,"* Together with Reminiscences of Narragansett Schools of Former Days, by Thomas Robinson Hazard, with a Bio-graphical Sketch and Notes by Rowland Gibson Hazard, p. 333. Copyright, 1915, by Rowland G. Hazard. Boston: Printed for the Subscribers.

From "Littleton," by Ola G. Veazie. Manuscripts of the Federal Writers' Project of the Works Progress Administration for the State of New Hampshire.

An Honest Man

SOME time ago there lived in Stonington a farmer with political aspirations. The reputation he acquired in the course of satisfying his ambitions was not altogether savory. One day a colleague of his met an old farmer who came from the politician's district and asked: "What do you think of the man out your way?"

The old gentleman stroked his beard and looked wise, but said nothing.

"Would you call him an honest man, or a liar?" persisted the colleague.

After more stroking of the beard the old man replied slowly, "We-ell, I wouldn't go so fur as to call.him a liar—but I heered tell by them as knows him that when he wants his pigs to come for their feed, he has to git somebody else to call 'em."

Uncle Jed

"UNCLE JED," said Ezra one day, "ben't you gittin' a leetle hard of hearin'?"

"Yes," said Uncle Jed, "I'm afraid I'm gittin' a mite deef."

Whereupon Ezra made Uncle Jed go down to Boston to see an ear doctor.

Uncle Jed came back. And Ezra asked what happened. "Well," said Uncle Jed, "that doctor asked me if I had been drinkin' any. And I said, 'Yes, I been drinkin' a mite.'

"And then the doctor said, 'Well, Jed, I might just as well tell you now that if you don't want to lose your hearin', you've got to give up drinkin'.'

"Well," said Uncle Jed, "I though it over; and then I said, 'Doc, I like what I've been drinkin' so much better than what I've been a-hearin' [lately] that I reckon I'll jest keep on gittin' deef!' "

A Shovel for "Uncle Ed"

"UNCLE ED" IS on relief, employed on the Middlebury highways. He is complaining to the foreman, "It ain't fair, an' you know it. I want a shovel."

Manuscripts of the Federal Writers' Project of the Works Progress Administration for the State of Connecticut.

From *The Public Papers and Addresses of Franklin D. Roosevelt,* edited by Samuel Rosenman, The 1940 Volume, p. 34. Copyright, 1941, by Franklin Delano Roosevelt. New York: The Macmillan Company.

From "Some Characteristics of Northern Vermont Wit," by Robert Davis, *Proceedings of the Vermont Historical Society,* New Series, Vol. V (December, 1937), No. 4, p. 321. Copyright, 1937, by the Vermont Historical Society. Montpelier, Vermont.

"Never you mind, Uncle Ed, about a shovel; you're on the payroll all right; you'll get your pay."

"Yes, I will mind, too. It's my rights to have a shovel, and I mean to have a shovel ef I have to write t' Congress about it. Kin I have a shovel or can't I?"

"Now, Uncle Ed, go easy. You're goin' t' get y'r money all right, don't you worry."

"It ain't fair. I want a shovel. Ev'ybody but me's got sunthin' t' lean on."

The Laziest Man in Vermont

LAZY? Yes, Nathan is it, one hundred and thirty-three per cent. When he was young his pa got him a job working to New York. He worked with the cleaners in them sky scrapings. Yes, he was one of the brass polishers. No, he didn't wipe none. He was the one what walked ahead and went "Huh-Huh" on the doorknobs.

When me and him got married he used to snore pretty vocal. I got used to it and couldn't sleep without it. But his snoring died out on him. It was then he hired the hired man to snore for him.

His prize? Yes, the committee come up from the Center to give him the ten dollars for being the laziest man north of the Massachusetts line. Nathan was in the orchard when they come, watching nature.

"Boys," Nathan said, "are y' bent on givin' this t' me? Y're makin me a lotta trouble. How be it, ef y're set on it, d' y' mind rollin' me over an' puttin' it in my backside pocket?"

The sheriff's funeral? Yes, that was a grand sight. Nathan was real interested. He was restin' in the Cape Cod hammick when it passed our gate. I come out and told him who all was in the carriages and autamobiles, his kinfolk and his nephews and nieces wavin' to him.

Nathan was kinda peeved.

"Just my luck," he said. "T' be facin' th' other way."

Wife Sitter

. . . BENNY CLEVELAND, whose house still stands in Eagle Lane, . . . was a jack-of-all-trades, and specialized in doing odd jobs for women whose

---

Ibid., pp. 330–331.

From *Of Whales and Women,* One Man's View of Nantucket History, by Frank B. Gilbreth, Jr., p. 188. Copyright, 1956, by Frank B. Gilbreth, Jr. New York: Thomas Y. Crowell Company.

husbands were away at sea. He was a rather vague citizen, and so innocent and harmless that no scandal could ever attach itself to him. As a result, when women were ill or expecting babies, and their husbands were away, they sometimes hired Benny to sleep in their houses.

Looking for more business along this line, Benny ran a newspaper advertisement which has become something of a classic:

"Women slept with, twenty-five cents a night," said the ad. "Nervous women, fifteen cents extra."

Two Round Trips

. . . [An] old Nantucketer . . . married an off-islander—a woman from Maine. The woman died and the widower presented himself at the ticket window, and asked for two round-trip tickets to Bangor.

The ticket agent said, "But you don't want two round-trips, Obed. You want one round-trip and one one-way"—because a dead person can travel on a passenger ticket, and ride in the baggage car, instead of the coach.

But the old man said No—he wanted two round-trips.

The ticket agent tried to explain, but the widower interrupted. He knew what he was doing, he said. He wanted a round-trip for himself and another for his wife, because she was coming back with him in a few days. And then *he* explained.

If he had the funeral in Nantucket, all her off-island folks would come, he said, and he'd have them on his hands for the summer. So he was going to take her to Maine and let them look at her. And then he would bring her back and bury her. And they would have no excuse for a visit.

Sylvester and John

. . . Sylvester had a younger brother named John, between whom and himself a coolness had existed for many years, so intense that they never spoke to each other. Old Jimmy Helme, who delighted in making peace among his neighbors, had often sought to reconcile the brothers, but without effect. One day as Jimmy was standing at the Four Corners with Sylvester, he saw John coming along on the other side. "Now," said

From *An Island Patchwork*, by Eleanor Early, p. 31. Copyright, 1941, by Eleanor Early. Boston and New York: Houghton Mifflin Company.

From *The Jonny-Cake Papers of "Shepherd Tom,"* Together With Reminiscences of Narragansett Schools of Former Days, by Thomas Robinson Hazard, with a Biographical Sketch and Notes by Rowland Gibson Hazard, pp. 165–166. Copyright, 1915, by Rowland G. Hazard. Boston: Printed for the Subscribers.

Jimmy, "do speak to John, and I know he will speak to you." "I would do so, Mr. Helme, to oblige you," said Sylvester, "but I know he won't speak to me!" "Well, now," rejoined Jimmy, "do just try and see." So when John got opposite to where they stood, Sylvester halloaed across the street, "John!" John stopped, and Sylvester continued, "When are you going to bring home that iron bar you stole from me, you thief?" Without saying a word John passed on. "There, Mr. Helme," said Sylvester, "I told you it would be no use!"

When on his death-bed, Sylvester relented and sent for his brother John. When John came to his bed-side, Sylvester told him he would like to make up with him before he died, to which John readily assented, whereupon they shook hands and exchanged many friendly greetings. The interview lasted for an hour or more, when John shook his brother's hand, bidding him an affectionate good-bye. Just as John was closing the door behind him, Sylvester called him back and said, "Now, John, we are good friends, ain't we, just as if nothing had ever happened?" "Yes, brother Sylvester," replied John, "that is just as I feel." "Just so," said Sylvester, "but remember, John, this is only in case I don't get well again. If I do, why then we are to be just as we were before." "Yes, brother Sylvester," said John, "that is just as I understand it, and should have said so before, only I didn't think there was any chance of your ever leaving your bed again alive." . . .

How the Old Lady Beat John

ONE stormy winter night, after midnight, I was sitting here reading, the rest of the family having gone to sleep long before, when old Dr. Strong thundered at the door-knocker, and made noise enough to wake the Seven Sleepers. It is a way he has, and neither my wife nor the girls, who were roused out of slumber, nor I myself, had any question who was at the door. I let him in myself, and a tempest of wind and snow with him. The blast that drove him into my arms also put out the hall lights, whirled into the library, and flared the reading-lamp so that it broke the chimney and blazed up to a colored tissue-paper affair which Susie had put over the shade, set it on fire, and for a moment threatened a general conflagration of papers and books on the table.

"Shut the door yourself!" I shouted, and rushed in here to put out the fire. That done, I went back and found the old doctor out of breath, in

From *Among the Northern Hills,* by W. C. Prime, pp. 124–127. Copyright, 1895, by Harper & Brothers. New York.

Of the many . . . stories that lawyers tell, I think the one that takes the prize is the yarn about an old widow in a little town not far from our home . . . such is the power that hatred can bring to some of these people in the hills.—Ernest Poole, *The Great White Hills* (Garden City, 1946), pp. 230–231.

the dark, trying to shut the door against the wind. It took the strength of both of us to do it. Then I told him to find his way to the library, for he knew it, and I went off in search of another lamp.

When I came back he was just recovering his wind, and, after a gasp or two, told me his errand. "Old Mrs. Norton is dying. She can't live till morning. She's alive now only on stimulants. She wants to make a will, and I have come for you."

"A nice night," I said, "for a two-mile drive, to make a will for a woman who hasn't a cent in the world to leave. Why didn't you tell her so, and have done with it."

"Now look here," said the doctor, "this is a case of an old woman and old neighbor and friend, and she wants you to do something for her, and you'll do it, if it's only to comfort her last hours. Get your things and come with me. We shall not find her alive if you don't hurry, and you'll be sorry if that happens."

The upshot of it was that I went. We had a fearful drive out to the farm-house on the flat, which you are asking about. Mrs. Norton was the widow of John Norton, who had died forty odd years before this. John Norton when he married her was a widower with one son—John. He was a man of considerable property, and when he died left a widow, that son John by his first wife, and two sons by his second wife. The elder son, John, had never been on very warm terms with his step-mother, and for some years had had no intercourse with the family.

I found the old lady lying in the big room, on a great bedstead on one side of the room, opposite to the broad chimney, in which was a roaring fire, the only light in the room. After the doctor had spoken to her and administered something—a stimulant, I suppose—he came over to me and said in a whisper: "Hurry up; she's very weak."

I had brought paper and pen and ink with me. I found a stand and a candle, placed them at the head of the bed, and, after saying a few words to her, told her I was ready to prepare the will, if she would now go on and tell me what she wanted to do. I wrote the introductory phrase rapidly, and, leaning over towards her, said: "Now go on, Mrs. Norton." Her voice was quite faint, and she seemed to speak with an effort. She said: "First of all I want to give the farm to my sons Harry and James; just put that down." "But," said I, "you can't do that, Mrs. Norton; the farm isn't yours to give away."

"The farm isn't mine?" she said, in a voice decidedly stronger than before.

"No; the farm isn't yours. You have only a life interest in it."

"This farm, that I've run for goin' on forty-three year next spring, isn't mine to do what I please with it! Why not, Judge? I'd like to know what you mean!"

"Why, Mr. Norton, your husband, gave you a life estate in all his property, and on your death the farm goes to his son John, and your children get the village houses. I have explained that to you very often before."

"And when I die John Norton is to have this house and farm, whether I will or no?"

"Just so. It will be his."

"Then I ain't going to die!" said the old woman, in a clear and decidedly ringing and healthy voice. And, so saying, she threw her feet over the front of the bed, sat up, gathered a blanket and coverlet about her, straightened up her gaunt form, walked across the room, and sat down in a great chair before the fire.

The doctor and I came home. That was fifteen years ago. The old lady's alive to-day. And she accomplished her intent. She beat John, after all. He died four years ago, in Boston, and I don't know what will he left. But whoever comes into the farmhouse when she goes out, it will not be John. And since John's death the farm has been better kept, and everything about it is in vastly better condition for strangers than it would have been for John.

A Careless Cuss

JOB NICKERSON was called upon by his neighbor, Caleb Tilton. (The call was made in the very early morning, not that it matters.)

Said Caleb, "Job, your son Nathan has been calling pretty regularly on my daughter Debbie. He's done her wrong, and if something isn't done mighty sudden there's going to be a bastard in my family!"

"By Godfrey!" ejaculated Job. "Nathan is the most careless cuss that ever drew the breath of life! Just this morning he busted a hoe-handle for me!"

Salmon or Cod?

ONE DAY . . . Smith caught a fine salmon, which he took into his house and showed to his wife, saying, "What shall we do with this salmon?" Said his wife, "You're going down to —— tomorrow, aren't you? "Yes," said Smith. "Take it and on your way stop at Parson Jones's and make him a present of it." He said he would. His wife packed it in a cloth and sewed it up very neatly, and the next morning he put it in the box of his vehicle and started off. He stopped to dine at a tavern on the way, and told the landlord what he was going to do with it. The landlord went out

From *Tales and Trails of Martha's Vineyard,* by Joseph C. Allen, pp. 92–93. Copyright, 1938, by Joseph C. Allen. Boston: Little, Brown and Company.

From *Half a Century with Judges and Lawyers,* by Joseph A. Willard, pp. 302–303. Copyright, 1895, by Joseph A. Willard. Boston and New York: Houghton Mifflin Company.

and got the salmon, brought it into the house, took it out of the cloth, put in a lot of dried codfish, hay, and stone, sewed up the cloth neatly, and put it back into the vehicle. Smith went on, stopped at Parson Jones's, and told him that he and his wife thought that they would make him a present of a salmon. He took out the bundle, left it there, and then went on to the next town. After having transacted his business, he started for home the next morning, stopping at the parson's on the way to inquire how they liked the salmon. They began laughing, and when he asked what they were laughing about they told him that he didn't bring any salmon, and showed him what he had brought. He was somewhat amazed, but thought that they had better sew up the material he had brought and he would take it back. So it was sewed up, and he put it in his box. Again he stopped at the same tavern to dine, and when he saw the landlord he told him what had happened. The landlord went out, got the bundle, took out the stuff, replaced the salmon, and sewed up the bundle. Then Mr. Smith went home, and after having unharnessed his horse he went into the house and sat down. His wife said: "Why, Smith, you seem to be in a quandary; what's the matter?" He said: "I thought I carried a good salmon down to Parson Jones, but it turned out to be nothing but a lot of dried salt fish, hay, and stones." "Pooh!" said his wife; "didn't I sew him up and don't I know? Where is it?" "In the box in the vehicle in the barn." "Get it, and bring it here," said his wife. He brought it in, opened it, and there was the salmon. "Ah," said Smith, shaking his fist at the salmon, "you're dashed good salmon on the Kennebec, but down on the Penobscot you're nothing but a cod."

Eggs Is Eggs

ONE day a man brought in a dozen of extra large eggs and so tried to get a fancy price for them. The storekeeper refused, saying "Eggs is eggs." The next week he brought in a dozen bantam eggs, and when the store-keeper started to object, quietly remarked, "Eggs is eggs."

Answering the Reproof

THE minister was reproving a neighbor for his profanity. In an apologetic way the man said: "Mr. Clark, you pray and I swear and we don't either of us mean anything by it."

From "Littleton," by Ola G. Veazie. Manuscripts of the Federal Writers' Project of the Works Progress Administration for the State of New Hampshire.

By Augustus K. Small, Portland, Maine. Manuscripts of the Federal Writers' Project of the Works Progress Administration for the State of Maine.

Painting the Meeting-House

IN ONE of the towns of New England, since the commencement of the reform in temperance, at a meeting held for the transaction of business, a proposition was introduced and carried for painting the meeting-house. Of course it was necessary to decide what color it should be painted. One gentleman proposed white; another, green; another, yellow; another, red; and reasons were offered for each. At last says one: "Mr. Moderator, I move that it be painted *rum* color, and I will give a reason. There is Captain ——, who sits near you, has had his *face* painted *rum* color these fifteen years; and it grows *brighter and brighter every year*."

The Order of Their Going

A YANKEE pedlar with his cart, overtaking another of his class on the road, was thus addressed: "Hallo, what do you carry?" "Drugs and medicines," was the reply. "Good," returned the other, "you may go ahead; I carry grave-stones."

Whittling without a Purpose

A YOUNG Yankee had formed an attachment for the daughter of a rich old farmer, and after agreeing with the "bonnie lassie" went to the old farmer to ask his consent; and during the ceremony, which was an awkward one with Jonathan, he whittled away at a stick. The old man watched the movements of the knife, at the same time continuing to talk on the prospects of his future son-in-law, as he supposed, until the stick was dwindled down to naught. He then spoke as follows:—"You have fine property, you have steady habits; good enough looking; but you can't have my daughter. Had you made something, no matter what, of the stick you whittled away, you could have had her; as it is you cannot. Your property will go as the stick did, little by little, until all is gone, and your family reduced to want. I have read your character; you have my answer."

From *The Christian Almanac, for New-England,* for the Year of Our Lord and Saviour, Jesus Christ, 1831, Vol. II, No. 3, p. 24. Boston: Published by Lincoln & Edmands, for the American Tract Society.

From *The American Joe Miller:* A Collection of Yankee Wit and Humour, Compiled by Robert Kempt, p. 175. Entered at Stationer's Hall. London: Adams and Francis. 1865.

Ibid., pp. 18–19.

A Couple of Reasons Too Many

... (A) MAPLE-SUGAR man in Vermont ... was sued for returning a borrowed sap-kettle in a damaged condition, and pleaded in defence— first, that the kettle was sound when he returned it; secondly, that it was cracked when he borrowed it; and thirdly, that he never had the sap-kettle. ...

The Ungallant Suitor

A CONNECTICUT Jonathan, in taking a walk with his *dearest*, came to a toll bridge, when he, as honestly as he was wont to be, said, after paying his toll (which was one cent), "Come, Suke, you must pay your own toll, for just as like 's not I shan't have you after all."

The Captain's Pudding

THE following story is told of a Yankee captain and his mate:—Whenever there was a plum-pudding made, by the captain's orders, all the plums were put into one end of it, and that end placed next to the captain, who, after helping himself, passed it to the mate, who never found any plums in his part of it. After this game had been played for some time, the mate prevailed on the steward to place the end which had no plums in it next to the captain. The captain no sooner perceived that the pudding had the wrong end turned towards him, than picking up the dish, and turning it round, as if to examine the china, he said: "This dish cost me two shillings in Liverpool"; and put it down, as if without design, with the plum end next to himself. "Is it possible?" said the mate, taking up the dish. "I shouldn't suppose it was worth more than a shilling." And, as if in perfect innocence, he put down the dish with the plums next to himself. The captain looked at the mate; the mate looked at the captain. The captain laughed; the mate laughed. "I tell you what, young one," said the captain, "you've found me out, so we will just cut the pudding lengthwise this time, and have the plums fairly distributed hereafter."

Ibid., p. 3

From *The National Comic Almanac for the Year 1836*, Calculated for Each State in the Union, With Humorous Stories and Anecdotes, [n.p.]. Entered according to Act of Congress, in the year 1835, in the Clerk's Office of the District Court of Massachusetts. Published by the President of the American Eating Club.

From *The American Joe Miller:* A Collection of Yankee Wit and Humour, Compiled by Robert Kempt, p. 123. Entered at Stationer's Hall. London: Adams and Francis. 1865.

Diploma Digging

ONE of the old herb doctors who flourished years ago in Maine would never admit his lack of any remedy. An acquaintance once said to him: "See here, doc, have you any diploma?"

"Wal, no, I ain't got none on hand, but I'm going to dig some just as soon as the ground thaws out in the spring."

Damaging the Engine

A MAN was sitting on the track of the New London road, when the train came along and pitched him head over heels into the bushes. The train stopped and backed to pick up the body, when the man coolly informed the conductor, as he brushed the dirt from his coat sleeves, that if he "had damaged the engine any he was ready to settle for it," and walked off home.

He Might as Well Have Et

A CLERGYMAN was having dinner with a parishioner preceding an afternoon service. He ate very sparingly, explaining that it was not well to eat too hearty a meal before preaching.

The housewife was unable to attend the service, so when her husband returned she inquired, "And how was he?"

"Oh, well," he replied, wearily, "he might as well have et."

Quite a Storm

ON A summer afternoon the Sewing Circle met at the home of Mrs. Bennett. A thunderstorm of terrific violence broke during the session and the terrified ladies cowered together. "Old Man" Bennett, who was noted for

From *The (Old) Farmer's Almanack,* Calculated on a New and Improved Plan for the Year of Our Lord 1927, No. 135, by Robert B. Thomas, p. 44. Copyright, 1926, by The Old Farmer's Almanac, Incorporated. Boston, Massachusetts.

From *The American Joe Miller:* A Collection of Yankee Wit and Humour, Compiled by Robert Kempt, p. 128. Entered at Stationer's Hall. London: Adams and Francis. 1865.

From *The (Old) Farmer's Almanack,* Calculated on a New and Improved Plan for the Year of Our Lord 1927, No. 135, by Robert B. Thomas, p. 43. Copyright, 1926, by The Old Farmer's Almanac, Incorporated. Boston, Massachusetts.

Manuscripts of the Federal Writers' Project of the Works Progress Administration for the State of Connecticut.

his fearlessness, undertook to calm them. With a great show of bravery he strode to the front door, flung it open and shook his fist at the sky shouting, "Durn ye! If ye're so danged powerful, come on and strike that ole hornbeam tree!" As if in answer to his challenge, there was a vivid flash accompanied by a deafening crack, and the tough wood of the hornbeam was split asunder. "Old Man" Bennett returned to the Circle and sat down meekly. "Waal," he said, " 'tis quite a storm, ain't it?"

Saving a Fuss

IT IS told that the night [Uncle "Liphey" Paddock] died, he roused and inquired of the "watcher" [term used for night nurse in those days] what the hour was. It was then near midnight. He asked what time the tide changed, and was told. "Well," he said, "you go out and get the 'board' [there was always a board kept in certain households for "laying out" bodies] and bring it here, for I'll die about the time the tide turns, and I don't want you people running around all excited after a board, and ev'rybody hollerin', 'Is Liphey Paddock dead? Has Liphey Paddock died?' You jest git the board, now, and we'll save lots of that fussin'."

Timothy Crumb's Courtship

TIM had hired by the month to Squire Champlin, who lived on a farm a little north-west of where the Kingston depot is now situated. Tim had taken a shine to Sal, and after three or four sittings up with her, had engaged to wait on her to meeting the next Sunday. So Tim got up early in the morning, and after getting through his chores and breakfast, he thought before dressing up to wait on Sal, he would go to the river and wash off. Accordingly he went down and undressed, hanging his red shirt, which was a little sweaty, in a swamp blueberry bush to dry while he was in the water. It so happened that Deacon Brown's old bull Wrinkle was lying on a little knoll near by, unnoticed by Tim. The sight of Tim's red shirt was not at all pleasing to old Wrinkle, who now got up and began to paw the ground and bellow. This did not, however, move Tim, as he had heard Wrinkle

From *The Nantucket Scrap Basket*, Being a Collection of Characteristic Stories and Sayings of the People of the Town and Island of Nantucket, Massachusetts, Compiled, Edited and Arranged by William F. Macy and Roland B. Hussey, and published for the benefit of "The Sons and Daughters of Nantucket," p. 95. Copyright, 1916, by William F. Macy and Roland B. Hussey. Nantucket: The Inquirer and Mirror Press.

From *The Jonny-Cake Papers of "Shepherd Tom,"* Together with Reminiscences of Narragansett Schools of Former Days, by Thomas Robinson Hazard, with a Biographical Sketch and Notes by Rowland Gibson Hazard, pp. 119–122. Copyright, 1915, by Rowland G. Hazard. Boston: Printed for the Subscribers.

making pretenses of the kind several times before. Bime'by, however, old Wrinkle made for the red shirt, and before Tim could interfere, the enraged beast tossed it in the air and then stamped it into the ground, and when Tim started to the rescue of his under garment, the old sarpent, not apparently recognizing him with his clothes off, gave chase to the naked biped, following Tim on the run, bellowing and shaking his horns as he went, right into the river. Things began to look rather squally, and just as the old varmint seemed getting ready to make a dive with both horns set for action, Tim seized the branches of a swamp white oak that hung over the water, and swung himself on a big limb out of reach of old Wrinkle, who now placed himself just beneath where Tim sat, roaring at the top of his voice and making sundry other threatening demonstrations. Tim, however, felt safe where he was, so far as Wrinkle was concerned, although he had some misgivings whether or not Sal Brown might not, in consequence of his enforced neglect to keep his engagement, permit that other fellow, Jim Arlington, who, too, was after her, to wait on her to hear Elder Northup preach. All at once, Tim heard a buzzing over his head, and looking up saw, to his horror, not more than two yards above his head, a hornets' nest, nigh upon as big as a bushel basket, covered all over with the worst kind of black hornets, who, he could readily see, were getting ready to attack him. Tim took in the situation at once, and saw plainly that there was but one chance for him, desperate as it was. So seizing, with both hands, the limb on which he sat, he lowered himself quickly down a-straddle of old Wrinkle's neck, seizing a horn in each hand at the same moment, the better to enable him to retain his uneasy position. Just as he lighted on the neck of old Wrinkle, about two quarts of hornets dropped on Tim's bare neck and shoulders, about half a pint of which slopped over and fell straight into old Wrinkle's left ear. This did not help matters at all, but made the bull madder than ever, who now started off on the run for the deacon's house, plunging and roaring as he went. Sally Brown had dressed herself to go to meeting, and was waiting in the great-room for Tim, when hearing old Wrinkle making such a catouse, she stepped to the front door to see what was the matter. Just as Sally with her arms akimbo had placed herself in the open door-way, Wrinkle and Tim reached a high chestnut rail fence that was within about two rods of where she stood. Sal recognized Wrinkle at first sight, but was somewhat doubtful of the identity of Tim, as she exclaimed: "For the Lord's sake, is that you, Tim, or the dev—" She meant to say devil, and would have done so had she been allowed time, but before Sal got the last syllable out, old Wrinkle made a desperate dive through the fence, making kindling splinters of the big chestnut rails, and ejecting Tim with such velocity from his neck and horns, that, after making three complete somersaults in the heavens, the nether parts of his body struck Sally Brown about midships, a big toe just grazing each side of her diaphragm as they passed, more like a forked thunder-bolt or streak of lightning, than anything with human legs, and knocked her clean through the kitchen door, where she fell flat with her face towards the ceiling. As for Tim, he gathered himself up without saying a word, and rushed out of the back door into the big swamp near by, and pursuing a circuitous route in the bushes, recovered his red shirt and other clothes, and then made a bee-line west. A week afterwards, Jim Knowles, who had been out West to reconnoitre, reported that on his return from the Genesee country, in crossing the Connecticut river below Hartford, he passed Tim paddling a white pine log with a piece of bark, in an opposite direction, which was the last ever heard of Timothy Crumb in Narragansett.

III. STOUT FELLOWS AND HARD LIARS

The humor of hyperbole, as well as that of ironical understatement, is quite in accordance with the New England character.
—GEORGE LYMAN KITTREDGE

In 1661 a man in Eastham was fined one pound for lying about a whale. This is supposed to be the original "Fish Story."
—SHEBNAH RICH

. . . there's a putty consid'able sight o' things in this world that's true; and then ag'in there's a sight o' things that ain't true. Now, my old gran'ther used to say, "Boys," says he, "if ye want to lead a pleasant and prosperous life, ye must contrive allers to keep jest the happy medium between truth and falsehood." Now, that are's my doctrine.
—SAM LAWSON, in *Oldtown Fireside Stories,*
by Harriet Beecher Stowe

1. "OVERPLUS OF EXPRESSION"

A LTHOUGH the Yankee is distinguished from his tall-talking Southern and Western compatriots by his "reluctant" eloquence, the others have no monopoly on either hyperbole or humorous exaggeration. Like most American folk metaphor, Yankee sayings have that "overplus of expression" which for James Russell Lowell constituted the tendency of humor as over against the "logical precision" of wit.[1] Following this distinction, it might be said that, far from being incompatible with the understatement of Yankee wit, humorous exaggeration flourishes among Yankee story-tellers no less than in more exuberant regions.

---

[1] Introduction to "The Biglow Papers: Second Series," in *The Poetical Works of James Russell Lowell* (Boston, 1885), p. 225.

Yankee hyperbole takes the form not only of folk metaphor ("Cold as the north side of a Jenooary gravestone by starlight"[1]) but also of the intensifying extravagances of the jest books and almanacs:

> There is a man living down East whose *feet* are so *large* that he pulls his *pantaloons* over his *head*.
> There is a fellow down East so powerful in the arms that he is employed to *squeeze tar out of pine trees*.
> There is a man in Vermont so tall that whenever it rains, he gets his hat wet a quarter of an hour before the rain reaches any one else.[2]

This sort of "tall talk" is so much in the spirit of the tall tale that the latter may be described as an expanded hyperbole, built up into a tale by the use of circumstantial narrative calculated to make it plausible.[3]

Because of the prevalence of the "broad grin" in both our folk speech and story-telling, humorous exaggeration has been singled out (especially by British critics) as the distinguishing trait of American humor, correlated with American geography.

> In considering the nature of American humor, it is obvious that broad exaggeration is its great characteristic. It is essentially *outré*. No people seek to raise the laugh by such extravagant means as the Yankees [*i.e.*, Americans]. Their ordinary speech is hyperbole, or tall talk. They never go out shooting unless with the long bow. . . . The humor of a people always reflects the character of that people, and character, as we all know, is influenced in no small measure by country and climate. Our American brethren are born, or as they themselves say "raised," in a country whose physical features have been planned on a scale far surpassing in magnitude— not unfrequently in beauty also—those of every other country in the world. . . . Into this Brobdingnag of our cousins Munchausen emigrated early, and the genius of the celebrated German Baron still continues to control its people.[4]

And for the reason, perhaps, that the West eclipses the East in the magnitude of its natural features, as well as of its boasting and boosting, it has been said that "It is no use for an Eastern man to try to tell a big story when there is a Western man about."[5]

---

[1] *Ibid.*, p. 224.

[2] *Turner's Comic Almanack,* for 1838, 1840, and 1843, respectively. See also "The Yankee Joe Miller" above.

[3] Since this was written, there has come to hand C. Grant Loomis's collection of "Jonathanisms: American Epigrammatic Hyperbole," in *Western Folklore,* Vol. VI, (July, 1947), No. 3. pp. 211–227. Dr. Loomis, an indefatigable collector of tall tales from printed sources, here attempts to establish the use of the word "Jonathanism" (originally a Yankeeism or Americanism) to mean an "American epigrammatic hyperbole" and adds: "A Jonathanism is an integral element of tall-tale lore and is, perhaps, the initiating force behind the longer, exaggerated anecdote."

[4] Robert Kempt, *The American Joe Miller* (London, 1865), pp. vi–vii.

[5] "A Western Man Takes the Lead Again as Usual," *Phinney's Calendar, or Western Almanac* . . . 1880, (n. p.).

2. "I Came to New England Seeking Wonders"

Besides humorous exaggeration, the tall tale involves artful mendacity. Because the dèceived and deceiving imagination finds a fertile soil and a congenial atmosphere in a new country, especially as seen by the traveler, the "earliest remains (of the American tall tale) are embedded in a matrix of travelers' tales."[1] "I came to New England seeking wonders"[2] is the burden of most colonists and colonial travelers. Compounded of "folklore, mendacity, and humor," with varying degrees of accuracy of observation and falseness of hypotheses and varying proportions of misinformation and fantasy, travelers' tales share with tall tales the desire to improve on actual happenings.

> The perpetrators of such oral fictions were not mere liars. They were artists in ascertaining the limits of their victim's capacity for being deceived. If these limits could not be found, so much the better.[3]

Similarly keyed to the love of marvels and a belief in the impossible are the early histories of New England. The very titles of such books—Edward Johnson's *The Wonder-Working Providence of Sion's Saviour in New England* (1654), John Josselyn's *New England Rarities Discovered* (1672), Increase Mather's *Remarkable Providences Illustrative of the Earlier Days of American Colonisation* (1684)—show a readiness to confuse science with superstition and faith with credulousness, if not, as in Samuel Peters' *General History of Connecticut* (1790), history with fiction. With grim piety and unconscious humor, these historians relate true-tall tales of hardships, plagues, storms, disasters, witchcraft, and other "singular occurrences" and "memorable accidents" as well as freaks of nature.[4]

In the same category of true-tall tales are the accounts of early settlers' experiences on the New England border, amidst the terrors of the wilderness and wild animals—bears, wolves, wild-cats, panthers. When John Strong thrust his hand into the mouth of a bear in whose embrace he was locked and held on to its tongue until he freed himself by a supreme effort, he was in the miraculous tradition of Munchausen and Davy Crockett. Such marvels are heightened by the early settlers' superstitious beliefs in the anthropomorphic intelligence or benevolence of the bear.

3. Local Pride and Prejudice

If Yankees have made any distinctive contributions to American tall tales, these are in the field of hunting and fishing. According to one old

---

[1] James R. Masterson, "Travelers' Tales of Colonial Natural History," I, *Journal of American Folklore*, Vol. 59 (January–March, 1946), No. 231, p. 51.

[2] *The Journal of William Jefferay, Gentleman* . . . A Diary That Might Have Been, edited by John Osborne Austin (Providence, 1899), p. 18.

[3] Masterson, *op. cit.*, II, *Journal of American Folklore*, Vol. 59 (April–June, 1946), No. 232, p. 187.

[4] See Part Two below.

Maine guide, "The only difference between a hunter and a fisherman is that the fisherman expects to be branded a liar and therefore exercises some control over his imagination."[1] When hunting became a sport, hunters' brags were told for their own sake, as part of the sociability of the campfire; and stories of fearsome critters grew up as tales to prank tenderfeet. The sea, with its whales, cod, sea serpents, fogs, and storms, and the rivers, with their remarkable runs of fish or schools of fish frozen in the ice, rival the woods as a source of New England lying tales.

The New England country also has its strong men and giants, who perform seemingly impossible feats of lifting, toting, throwing, walking, etc.,[2] and its prodigious eaters and drinkers. Tough yarns of rich land, poor land, and hard land (symbolized by New England's stony fields and stone walls); of freaks of climate and weather; and of the folk etymology of place names match those of other regions.

Other tall tales originate in satirical hoaxes and libels, provoked by factional and regional rivalry and quarrels. In this category are the whopping brags and feuding taunts of local patriots, as in *The Jonny-Cake Papers of "Shepherd Tom" Hazard* (1880). Thus New Englanders use artful exaggeration to strengthen pride or prejudice, faith or skepticism.

When Thoreau asked a minister from Truro what the fishermen did in the winter, the other replied: "Nothing, but go a-visiting, sit about, and tell stories, though they worked hard in the summer, and it is not a long vacation they get." And wherever Yankees seek a vacation from toil, and visit and sit about, as in the country store, the "master hand at telling stories" is likely to be the one who can tell the biggest lies.

B. A. B.

MONSTROSITIES OF MIRTH

Hard Lying

THERE lives in New Hampshire a man called Joe, a fellow noted for the tough lies he can tell. A correspondent informs us that Joe called in at Holton's lately, and found him almost choked with smoke, when he suggested, "You don't know as much about managing smoky chimneys as I do, squire, or you'd cure 'em." "Ah! said Holton, with interest, "did you ever see a smoky chimney cured?" "Seen it?" said old Joe, "I think I have. I

---

[1] Raymond R. Camp, "The Hunter Bags a Tale," *The New York Times Magazine*, December 15, 1946, p. 54.

[2] For examples see Richard M. Dorson, *Jonathan Draws the Long Bow* (Cambridge, 1946), pp. 121 ff.

From *The American Joe Miller:* A Collection of Yankee Wit and Humour, Compiled by Robert Kempt, pp. 4–5. Entered at Stationer's Hall. London: Adams and Francis. 1865.

had the worst one in Seaboard county once, and I cured it a little too much." "How was that?" asked Holton. "Why, you see," said Joe, "I built a little house out yonder, at Wolf Hollow, ten or twelve years ago. Jim Bush, the fellow that built the chimneys, kept blind drunk three-quarters of the time, and crazy drunk the other. I told him I thought he'd have something wrong; but he stuck to it and finished the house. Well, we moved in, and built a fire the next morning to boil the tea-kettle. All the smoke came through the room and went out of the windows; not a bit went up the flues. We tried it for two or three days, and it got worse and worse. By and by it came on to rain, and the rain began to come down the chimney. It put the fire out in a minute, and directly it came down by the pailful. We had to get the baby off the floor as soon as we could, or it would have been drowned. In fifteen minutes the water stood knee deep on the floor. I pretty soon saw what was the matter. The drunken cuss had put the chimney wrong end up, and it drawed downwards. It gathered all the rain within a hundred yards, and poured it down by bucketfuls." "Well, that was unfortunate," remarked Holton, "but what in the world did you do with the house? Surely you never cured that chimney?" "Didn't I, though?" answered old Joe; "yes, I did." "How?" asked Holton. "Turned it the other end up," said the incorrigible, "and then you ought to have seen it draw. That was the way I cured it too much." "Drew too much?" asked Holton. "Well, squire, you may judge for yourself," said old Joe. "Pretty soon after we got the chimney down the other end up, I missed one of the chairs out of the room, and directly I see'd another of 'em shooting towards the fireplace. Next the table went, and I see the back log going up. Then I grabbed the old woman under one arm and the baby under t'other and started; but just as I got to the door I see'd the cat going across the floor backwards, holding on with her claws to the carpet, yelling awfully. It wasn't no use. I just see her going over the top of the chimney, and that was the last of her." "Well, what did you do then?" asked Holton; "of course you could not live in such a house?" "Couldn't I, though?" said Joe; "but I did; I put a poultice on the jamb of the fireplace, and that drawed t'other way, so we had no more trouble." This is what we call hard lying.

The Man Who Bottled Up the Thunder

ONE evening in Mr. Smiley's baker shop the topic of thunder showers came up. A man asked Mr. Smiley to tell about the big thunder shower which he experienced last summer. Mr. Smiley's story is as follows:

"Last summer I was helping my father to get in the hay before the storm. We were almost through when it began to rain and thunder. Suddenly a

By Fred Smith, Fayette, Maine. Manuscripts of the Federal Writers' Project of the Works Progress Administration for the State of Maine.

big round ball of fire fell from the sky bouncing along the ground and went right plump into a wood-chuck hole. Looking around, I saw a large flat stone which I picked up and placed over the wood-chuck hole to keep the ball of fire from coming out, then thought no more about it. The other day I was up in the same field when I remembered about last summer, and sure enough there was the same rock still over the wood-chuck hole. Walking over to the rock, I removed it, when suddenly two tremendous crashes of thunder came out of the hole. I had bottled the thunder last summer and just released it the other day."

He is still referred to as "Mr. Smiley, the man who bottled up the thunder."

The Man That Cut Bread So Fast with the Shoe-Knife

. . . WAL the' was a shoemaker 't lived in Connecticut, an' my father knowed him, 'at hed a knife julluk this . . . the cutest thing t' cut bread with't ever was, but he wouldn't let nob'dy but his own self use it, so they use ter send fer him to all gret duins t' cut the' bread fer 'em. Wal, arter he'd ben a-cuttin' raoun' fer three, fo' year, they sent fer him one July to go t' Colonel Leavenworth's gret shearin'. He kep' a thousan' sheep, an' hed twenty shearers, an' made a big splonto, "wine in quart mugs an' straw-b'ries rolled in cream," he use ter brag about, but they wan't on'y pint mugs 'n not filled very often at that, an' the wine was cider, an' the' wan't more 'n tew strawb'ries apiece, 'n' they was dried apples. Wal, the shoemaker come with his knife keener 'n ever, an' the han's an' comp'ny hed all got washed up for dinner with the' clean clo's on, an' stood raound watchin' on him cut the bread, ker slice, ker slice, faster 'n a gal could pick up the slices, off 'm a loaf 't he hel' agin his breast. He done it so neat 't they cheered him, which he got kinder 'xcited, an' tried t' cut faster 'n ever, an' the next lick he gin the loaf he cut hisself clean in tew, an' the man 'at stood behind him clean in tew, an' badly waounded the next one. They sot tew an' stuck 'em together so 't they lived, but it spilte the shoemaker's bread-cuttin' business, an' he hed to go back to shoemakin' an' starvin', julluk me.

From *Uncle Lisha's Shop*, Life in a Corner of Yankeeland, by Rowland E. Robinson, p. 32. Copyright, 1910, by Forest and Stream Publishing Co. New York. 1902.

Nantucket "Sleigh Ride"

A HARPOONED whale will usually "sound" at once, often going down very deep and remaining under for the better part of an hour. On rising to the surface, he will often "run," that is, swim away at high speed, dragging the boat after him by the whale line. From time immemorial this method of marine travel has been known as a "Nantucket sleigh ride" and a very exciting trip it can be.

One old whaleman given to "drawing the long bow" once entertained an interested group of summer folks with a story the truth of which we do not vouch for, but we give it for what it is worth: "We was fast to an old bull whale, an' the minute he broke water he started off to looard lickety-split. Sufferin' cats! How that whale did travel! We fleeted aft's fur's we could git, but even then the water poured over the gunnel for'ard and kep' us all bailing's hard's we could to keep her afloat. All of a sudden I happened to look aft, an' there was an empty whale boat follerin' in our wake astarn. For a minute or so she follered us close; then we gained on her an' gradually she fell off an' swung round into the troth o' the sea. The next wave struck her, an' smash! she went, all to smithereens, an' that was the last we seen of her."

"But what was it? Where'd the other boat come from?"

"Wal, believe it or not! 'twas a mystery to *us* till we got aboard ship and h'isted our boat up on the davits. Then we see her plankin' was as clean as the day she come out o' the shop. You see that thar whale went so fast he pulled our boat clean out o' the paint, an' what we seen was jest that shell o' paint follerin' after us!"

STRONG MEN

John Strong and the Bear

ONE fall the bears were making destructive work in his cornfield; he found

From *The Nantucket Scrap Basket,* Being a Collection of Characteristic Stories and Sayings of the People of the Town and Island of Nantucket, Massachusetts, Second Edition, Revised, Expanded and Rearranged by William F. Macy, pp. 28–29. Copyright, 1916, by William F. Macy and Roland B. Hussey. Copyright, 1930, by William F. Macy. Boston and New York: Houghton Mifflin Company. 1930.

From "Addison," by Hon. John Strong, in *The Vermont Historical Gazetteer: A Magazine, Embracing a History of Each Town, Civil, Ecclesiastical, Biographical and Military,* edited by Abby Maria Hemenway, in Three Volumes, Vol. I, p. 8. Entered according to Act of Congress, in the year 1859, by Abby Maria Hemenway, in the Clerk's Office of the District Court of the District of Vermont. Burlington, Vermont: Published by Miss A. M. Hemenway. 1867.

where they came in, and placed his trap in their road. The second morning he found his trap gone, and plenty of signs that a large bear had taken it; he got two of his neighbors, Kellogg and Pangborn, to go with him. They had two guns and an axe, and three dogs. After following the track for some two miles, they heard the dogs, and as they came up they found the bear with her back against a large stub, cuffing the dogs whenever they came within reach. The trap was on one of her hind legs. Kellogg proposed to shoot the bear, but Strong said he could kill her with his axe as well as to waste a charge of ammunition, which was scarce and difficult to get. So taking the axe, and remembering his encounter on the lake, he turned the bit of the axe, intending to split her head open. He approached cautiously, and when near enough, gave the blow with tremendous force, but the bear, with all the skill of a practised boxer, caught the axe as it was descending; with one of her paws knocking it out of his hand, at the same time catching him with the other, she drew him up for the death-hug; as she did so, endeavoring to grab his throat in her mouth. One moment more, and he would have been a mangled corpse. The first effort, he avoided by bending his head close upon his breast; the second, by running his left hand into her open mouth and down her throat, until he could hook the ends of his fingers into the roots of her tongue. This hold he kept until the end, although every time the bear closed her mouth his thumb was crushed and ground between her grinders, her mouth being so narrow that it was impossible to put it out of the way. He now called on Kellogg for God's sake to shoot the bear, but this he dared not do, for fear of shooting Strong; for as soon as he got the bear by the tongue, she endeavored to get rid of him by plunging and rolling about, so that one moment the bear was on top, and the next Strong. In these struggles they came where the axe had been thrown at first. This Strong seized with his right hand, and striking the bear in the small of the back, severed it at a blow. This so paralyzed her that she loosened her hug, and he snatched his hand from her mouth, and cleared himself of her reach. The men then dispatched her with their guns. His mutilated thumb he carried, as a memento of the fight, to his dying day.

Stout Jeffrey

LESS than two miles to the south-easterly from this bridge stands the

From *Recollections of Olden Times:* Rowland Robinson of Narragansett and His Unfortunate Daughter, with Genealogies of the Robinson and Hazard Families of Rhode Island, by Thomas R. Hazard, "Shepherd Tom," in His Eighty-First and Eighty-Second Years; Also Genealogical Sketch of the Hazards of the Middle States, by Willis P. Hazard, of Westchester, Pa., pp. 70–71. Entered according to Act of Congress, in the year 1879, by John P. Sanborn, in the Office of the Librarian of Congress, at Washington, D. C. Newport, Rhode Island.

Governor George Brown house, which was occupied by Geoffrey Hazard, called "Stout Jeffrey," who if the half that is told be true, must have approached nearer in physical strength to the fabled Hercules than almost any other man known in modern times. I have heard old people say that Stout Jeffrey was remarkably broad across the shoulders, and so thick through the chest that when he stood with his face fronting you his head looked as if it were set unnaturally far back on his shoulders, and that when his back was towards you, it looked as though he stooped, his head seeming to project so far in the contrary direction.

Most marvelous stories used to be told and vouched for within my memory of the feats of strength performed by Stout Jeffrey, and also those of a sister who married a Wilcox. There may now be seen on the lawn in front of Rowland Hazard's house at Peacedale, in Narragansett, a blue stone [1] weighing by the scales sixteen hundred and twenty pounds, that Mr. Hazard had drawn with oxen some years ago from Stout Jeffrey's homestead in Boston Neck, with which the following tradition is associated. Several negroes were engaged in laying a wall on the premises, when Stout Jeffrey, chancing to observe a large stone lying near by that they had neglected to build into the wall, asked why they had left it out. "Cos, massa, it be too heavy," was the reply. Thereupon Stout Jeffrey stooped down and taking the stone partly on his knees, carried it some twenty feet from the wall and dropping it on the ground said, "Let *that stone* lie there until a man is found strong enough to put it back again."

It was said that Stout Jeffrey and his sister would alternately lift in playful sport a full barrel of cider—thirty-one gallons—by the chimes and holding it up drink at its bung—a thing hard to believe in these degenerate days.

Jonas Lord

THERE was a man by the name of Jonas Lord, who was born in 1820 and died in 1900. He was a massive man, well over six feet tall, and very strong. He was so strong and powerful that he would never wind his own watch; some one else would always do it for him. His fingers were thick and without much feeling and he was apt to wind the stem right off.

---

[1] A bronze tablet set into the surface of the stone bears this legend:

> Stout Jeffrey Hazard lifted this Stone,
> In pounds just sixteen twenty one,
> In South Kingstown he lived and died,
> God save us all from sinful Pride.
> —R. G. H., *ibid.*, p. 397.

By L. Crosberry, S. Wells, W. Richards, W. Morrill, and Mrs. J. Hart, Wayne, Maine. Manuscripts of the Federal Writers' Project of the Works Progress Administration for the State of Maine.

In the machine shop where Jonas Lord worked it was necessary every week for each man to bring his anvil weighing 400 pounds to the blacksmith shop to be refinished. This generally required two men and the use of a wheelbarrow, but to Jonas Lord it was a simple matter. He just placed the anvil under his arm as if it were a newspaper and walked over to the blacksmith shop, had it refinished, and returned with it. One day the men in the shop waylaid him when he had the anvil under his arm and talked to him for a half an hour. Jonas Lord stood there all that time without as much as shifting the position of the anvil.

One day in the tool shop a large die used for stamping out scythes by means of a trip hammer had to be removed. This die weighed 600 pounds and generally required several men to move it. When it was time for the die to be moved, all the men seemed to have disappeared except Jonas. He shouted for them and, receiving no answer, he moved the die by himself, carrying it about one hundred feet to the machine shop.

Shortly after Jonas Lord came to work at this machine shop and was learning the trade, there were many practical jokes played on him, until finally he informed all the men that the next man that tried to plague him would receive as good as he gave. That very afternoon the boss walked into the shop and told young Lord to clean up the mess around the boiler. As a rule in those days the ashes and clinkers were removed and placed in a big iron vat to cool off and then removed. This work was not young Lord's work, so he wasn't over-anxious to do it. The boss realized this and sarcastically said, "Come on, why don't you pick up the vat and the ashes and lug them out? You're big enough." With that young Lord got mad and picked up the vat with one arm and the boss with the other and went outside and dumped the ashes out first and then dropped the boss on top of the ashes.

The proprietor of the hardware store in Wayne was endeavoring to sell a mowing machine to a customer, who refused to buy unless the machine was demonstrated. Just at this moment Jonas Lord came into the store, and the proprietor asked Jonas to take the man out and demonstrate the machine. Jonas stepped between the two shafts of the machine and told the customer to get on. Picking up the shafts as if he were a horse, he started across the nearby field. Realizing that the man hadn't put the machine in gear, Jonas turned around and said, "What the heck is the matter with you? Put the machine in gear." He towed the machine down the field and back again with little effort. Needless to say, the machine was sold.

Jigger Johnson, River Boss

THERE were river bosses who claimed to know every rock, eddy and white-

From *The Great White Hills of New Hampshire,* by Ernest Poole, pp. 55–57. Copyright, 1946, by Ernest Poole. Garden City, New York: Doubleday & Company, Inc.

water stretch in our mountain rivers and creeks. Jim Smart knew the Androscoggin as a man knows a cantankerous wife, and on that same river Dan Bossy was called the "cattiest" man who ever drove logs. But for toughness, Jigger Johnson held first place. From Maine at the age of twelve he had come into the woods and had worked and fought his way by twenty up to a job as woods and river boss. He often drove crews to open revolt but, though only five feet six, he would face the rebels with peavy or ax and threaten to kill any man who failed to get right back on the job. Stories are still told of his battles. When stripped, his whole body showed the scars left by scores of calked boots; but men left his head alone, for his bite was swift and his teeth were strong. He is said to have bitten off a man's ear and spit it out when the fight was done. When once with his crew he went into Berlin and got thoroughly soused, some of his men laid for him on the dark road back to camp and "calked" him well and, with both his arms and legs broken, left him for dead. But Jigger managed to wriggle and roll to a neighboring pigsty, rolled into manure to keep warm and so slept off his drunk, was found by a forest ranger and taken to a hospital, whence a month later he emerged limping a bit but still going strong. And when one of the lads who had "calked" him met him on the street that night, the logger left Berlin on the run, for he thought he had seen Jigger's ghost!

Famed for his use of the Bible, he called one logger "dirtier than the combined britches of Mathew, Mark, Luke and John"; and [said] of another, that in Berlin with the gals he could "beat old King Solomon hisself"! In barrooms men all stopped to listen in admiration while Jigger swore; and when he bellowed logger ballads, they said it rocked the floor. Joe Dodge, who is himself some epicure in profanity, declares that never has he heard anything equal to Jigger's line. Dodge knew him well in his old age; for when Jigger quit as camp boss about twenty years ago, he took a job in the Forest Service and built part of a Carter Dome trail.

"I used to see him there," said Dodge. "He would work all summer, save four hundred bucks and then go on one hell of a bender. Now and then we used to harbor him here in Pinkham Notch Camp on his jubilees, and while he was working on the trail we often took him up cigars. Then he got a fire-lookout job on Chocorua and later on Carter Dome; and there he served well through dangerous times when the woods were dry; but in wet spells, with nothing to do, he drank himself into d.t.'s on a home brew that he called Eagle Sweat. When for that the Service fired him, down near Chocorua he trapped for years, and in wildcats he could lick his weight. He loved to take a cat alive. Trapping one fall, he found the carcass of a deer with throat and shoulder torn by a cat. Figuring that the killer would be back to feed at dusk, Jigger climbed into a hemlock close by. Dark came and then *two* cats appeared. Jigger quietly hitched himself out on a limb; and when both were well into the guts of the deer, he jumped and crashed down on the pair. The battle took him quite some time but at the end he had a cat tucked clawing and spitting under each arm. Four miles he hiked to his cabin below and, whenever a cat got restless, Jigger would bang him on the head. At home he threw one in the wood box and nailed down the lid; the other he tied with telephone wire to his bedpost and then went to sleep. He kicked the cat each time she yowled, so by morning she was dead; but the other one he shipped in a crate to Portland, to a sporting-goods firm that wanted a live cat in their window.

"He got four or five cats each fall. Catching one on the side of Madison, he hog-tied her and brought her to a Forest Service guard station near here. By that time old Jigger was all clawed up, so he threw the cat into the dynamite room and went to Gorham on a drunk. At the station the guard and his wife spent a bad night. She was soon to have a baby and it got on her nerves to hear the big cat screeching and clawing around in that room filled with dynamite and percussion caps. They flagged cars on the road till one kind soul went to Gorham and brought Jigger back. Drunker than a billy goat, he walked right in and grabbed the cat, who had scattered percussion caps over the floor!"

But in the fall of 1935, having caught and killed a six-foot lynx, he brought it to town for the bounty and spent the money on a drunk, and then, on the way back to his traps, crashed his flivver into a telegraph pole. So Jigger lived and so he died.[1]

Old Sam Hewes, River Man

Lines written some time ago to commemorate the personality and exploits of the doughty Samuel Hewes, whose grave may be seen today beside his wife's in the cemetery at South Fairlee, Vermont:

> When I was a little feller, the funniest man that I ever saw
> Was Old Sam Hewes.
> He hadn't any palate, and he talked with a hee and a haw,
> Did Old Sam Hewes.
> He'd been a hard old ticket, is what the people said,
> Had Old Sam Hewes.
> He'd broad and brawny shoulders and a great big bushy head,
> Had Old Sam Hewes.
> He was the biggest and the stoutest of any man in town,
> Was Old Sam Hewes.
> At fighting and at wrestling he could put the strongest down,
> Could Old Sam Hewes.
> Across the lake at Plattsburg he had fought the British there,
> Had Old Sam Hewes.

---

[1] Cf. "Saga of the Jigger [Jones]" in Stewart H. Holbrook's *Holy Old Mackinaw* (New York, 1938), pp. 1–13.

From Fairlee, Vermont. Manuscripts of the Federal Writers' Project of the Works Progress Administration for the State of Vermont.

He was wounded by a bullet but he didn't seem to care,
>> Did Old Sam Hewes.
Our men they were retreating, and they called on him to follow,
>> To Old Sam Hewes.
The British tried to take him but he beat them out all hollow,
>> Did Old Sam Hewes.
Two red coats with their bayonets came to him on the run,
>> At Old Sam Hewes.
But he knocked aside those bayonets and he hit them with his gun,
>> Did Old Sam Hewes.
And then he reached and grabbed them, one under each arm,
>> Did Old Sam Hewes.
And he brought them into camp without suffering further harm,
>> Did Old Sam Hewes.
He'd taken for his wife a grim old Indian squaw,
>> Had Old Sam Hewes.
She hadn't any beauty that any ever saw,
>> But Old Sam Hewes.
They were happy and contented as any man and wife,
>> She and Old Sam Hewes.
And he cherished her and loved her until the end of life,
>> Did Old Sam Hewes.
I saw their graves to-day where they're sleeping side by side,
The brawny and mighty Samuel and his dusky Indian bride.
>> God rest them,
>> Her and Old Sam Hewes.

REMARKABLE HUNTING AND SHOOTING

Jonathan's Hunting Excursion

"DID you ever hear of the scrape that I and uncle Zekiel had duckin' on 't on the Connecticut?" asked Jonathan Timbertoes, while amusing his old Dutch hostess, who had agreed to entertain him under the roof of her log cottage, for and in consideration of a bran new tin milk-pan. "No, I never did; do tell it," said Aunt Pumkins. "Well—you must know that I and uncle Zeke took it into our heads on Saturday's afternoon to go a gunning after ducks, in father's skiff; so in we got and sculled down the river; a proper sight of ducks flew backwards and forwards I tell ye—and by'm-by a few on 'em lit down by the mash, and went to feeding. I catched up my powder-horn to prime, and it slipped right out of my hand and sunk to the bottom of the river. The water was amazingly clear, and I could see it on the bottom. Now I couldn't swim a jot, so sez I to uncle Zeke, you're a

From *The Farmer's Almanack*, Calculated on a New and Improved Plan, for the Year of Our Lord 1836, by Robert B. Thomas. Entered according to Act of Congress, in the year 1835, by Carter, Hendee and Co., in the Clerk's Office of the District Court of Massachusetts. Boston.

pretty clever fellow, just let me take your powder-horn to prime. And don't you think, the stingy critter wouldn't. Well, says I, you're a pretty good diver, 'un if you'll dive and get it, I'll give you primin. I thought he'd leave his powder-horn; but he didn't, but stuck it in his pocket, and down he went—and there he staid"—here the old lady opened her eyes with wonder and surprise, and a pause of some minutes ensued, when Jonathan added,—"I looked down, and what do you think the critter was doin?" "Lord!" exclaimed the old lady, "I'm sure I don't know." "There he was," said our hero, "setting right on the bottom of the river, pouring the powder out of my horn into hizen."

Slow Powder

THIS IS about muzzle-loading guns and powder. That's what suggested this story. My father recalled that Tilly Davis who lived in Langdon was reputed to be the quickest man in New Hampshire. He planted some corn one year—I know just where it was—and the chipmunks bothered it. He went down to Tim Tufts' store in Alstead to get some powder. He never liked Tufts and he told this story himself. He smoked a pipe and on the way it blew into the powder. He jumped out of the wagon, put the keg beside the road, took a saw and sawed it in two, and saved half the powder.

When he got home he loaded his gun and went out to shoot those chipmunks. There they were, lined up on the wall, and he shot and shot, but he couldn't see that he was getting any of them. He went to see what the trouble was, and when he got there he could hear the shot coming along— Old Tufts' powder was that slow.

Captain Paddock's Whale Iron

ONE of the most singular incidents in connection with the exploits of Nantucket's whalemen and whaleships was that of Peter Paddock. Captain Paddock struck a whale in the Pacific ocean and "lost his iron," the whale escaping. Thirteen years later, while on another voyage in the Pacific, he struck a whale and when it was being cut up, the iron which he lost so many years previous was found imbedded in the flesh. It bore his own initials "P. P.," and was easily identified as the lost iron. That Captain Paddock should strike the same whale after a lapse of thirteen years

As told by Elsie Goodenow, South Acworth, New Hampshire, February 12, 1964. Recorded by B. A. Botkin.

From *The Nantucket Scrap Basket,* Being a Collection of Characteristic Stories and Sayings of the People of the Town and Island of Nantucket, Massachusetts, Second Edition, Revised, Expanded and Rearranged by William F. Macy, pp. 29–30. Copyright, 1916, by William F. Macy and Roland B. Hussey. Copyright, 1930, by William F. Macy. Boston and New York: Houghton Mifflin Company. 1930.

and thus recover his iron himself was considered most remarkable by the Nantucket whalemen.

Sharp Shooting

October 1st. It's common for the Soldiers to fire at a target fix'd in the stream at the bottom of the *common.* A countryman stood by a few days ago, and laugh'd very heartily at a whole regiment's firing, and not one being able to hit it. The officer observ'd him, and ask'd why he laugh'd? Perhaps you'll be affronted if I tell you, reply'd the countryman. No, he would not, he said. *Why then,* says he, I laugh to see how awkward they fire. *Why,* I'll be bound I hit it ten times running. Ah! will you, reply'd the officer; come try: Soldiers, go and bring five of the best guns, and load 'em for this honest man. Why, you need not bring so many: let me have any one that comes to hand, reply'd the other, but I chuse to load *myself.* He accordingly loaded, and ask'd the officer where he should fire? He reply'd, to the right—when he pull'd tricker, and drove the ball as near the right as possible. The officer was amaz'd—and said he could not do it again, as that was only by chance. He loaded again. Where shall I fire? *To the left*—when he perform'd as well as before. Come! once more, says the officer.—He prepar'd the third time.—Where shall I fire *naow?*—*In the Center.*—He took aim, and the ball went as exact in the middle as possible. The officers as well as soldiers *star'd,* and tho't the Devil was in the man. *Why,* says the countryman, I'll tell you *naow.* I have got a *boy* at home that will toss up an apple and shoot out all the seeds as it's coming down.

A Gone Coon

IN THE Western States, where the raccoon is plentiful, they use the abbreviation *'coon* when speaking of people. When at New York, I went into a hairdresser's shop to have my hair cut; there were two young men from the west—one under the barber's hands, the other standing by him.

From *Letters of John Andrews, Esq., of Boston, 1772–1776,* Compiled and Edited from the Original Mss., with an Introduction, by Winthrop Sargent, Reprinted from the Proceedings of the Massachusetts Historical Society, pp. 58–59. Cambridge: Press of John Wilson and Sons. 1866.

From *A Diary in America,* with Remarks on Its Institutions, by Capt. [Frederick] Marryat, C. B., Vol. II, pp. 37–38. Entered according to the Act of Congress, in the year 1838, by F. Marryat, in the Clerk's Office of the District Court for the Eastern District of Pennsylvania. Philadelphia: Carey & Hart. 1839.

"I say," said the one who was having his hair cut, "I hear Captain M—— is in this country."

"Yes," replied the other, "so they say; I should like to see the *'coon*."

"I'm a *gone 'coon*" implies "I am distressed—*or* rüined—*or* lost." I once asked the origin of this expression, and was very gravely told as follows:—

There is a Captain Martin Scott in the United States army who is a remarkable shot with a rifle. He was raised, I believe, in Vermont. His fame was so considerable through the State, that even the animals were aware of it. He went out one morning with his rifle, and spying a raccoon upon the upper branches of a high tree, brought his gun up to his shoulder; when the raccoon, perceiving it, raised his paw up for a parley. "I beg your pardon, mister," said the raccoon, very politely; "but may I ask you if your name is *Scott?*"—"Yes," replied the captain.—"*Martin* Scott?" continued the raccoon.—"Yes," replied the captain.—"*Captain* Martin Scott?" still continued the animal.—"Yes," replied the captain, "Captain Martin Scott."—"Oh! then," says the animal, "I may just as well come down, for I'm a *gone 'coon*."

The Double-Barreled Shotgun

RIGHT down to this day I can't hardly think about gramp without remembering his account of the muzzle-loading, double-barreled shotgun he had when he was a young man. He said he figured on going hunting, so he put in two charges of powder. When he come to look for his shot, he found he'd used it all up, and he didn't want to take the trouble of getting out his bronze bullet mold and casting more. He scratched around in the shop and happened on a box of tacks. He shook some of the tacks into one barrel, but tacks was kind of scarce, too, and he didn't want to use them all. He saw an old broken jackknife lying around, and he just dropped that down the other barrel.

Then he took a turn around the woods, but he didn't see nothing. He walked right around the north pasture and up through the woodlot, and nary a sign of game. Finally he got disgusted and started home through the sugar bush.

And then right next to the sugarhouse, a rabbit set up on its hind legs and looked at him. He got ready to shoot, and just as the rabbit dropped down, he fired. He fired the barrel with the knife in it first. The knife was so heavy that it went low and split the rabbit's skin right down the middle. The skin flapped open and flew up just as he fired the other barrel, with

From "Grandpa Was Quite a Fellow," by Walter Needham, as recorded by Barrows Mussey, in *The Saturday Evening Post*, Vol. 219 (November 9, 1946), No. 19, p. 13. Copyright, 1946, by The Curtis Publishing Company. Springfield, Ohio.

the tacks. Those tacks spread the hide neat and tight on the back wall of the sugarhouse. . . .

Old Town Tall Tales

THE CAT WITH THE WOODEN LEG

THERE was a trapper used to live out back here in the woods, and every winter he set a lot of traps. He had a tiger cat that used to follow him around and that cat got to be such a good hunter that he was able to get all his food out in the woods. The trapper didn't have to feed him at all, in fact the cat got so that it wouldn't eat anything unless it killed it himself. One day the cat was out huntin' all alone and he got one of his front paws caught in a trap. When the trapper found him the paw was half chewed off and he got the cat out of the trap and took it home. That paw was so bad that the man had to cut it off. It healed all right, but the cat kept gettin' thinner because it couldn't enjoy the food the trapper gave it. By and by the man said, "I'll have to do something or I'll lose that cat sure," so he got a little piece of cedar and whittled out a wooden leg for the cat and he tacked some leather on the little piece of wood to make a socket to fit on the stump of the cat's leg. He made leather straps to go around the cat's body to hold the leg in place. Well, when the cat first got that wooden leg on it used to shake its paw tryin' to get the thing off, but by and by it got used to it and the cat got so it could prance around in great style. As soon as it got so it could run real well it started goin' out into the woods again to look for game. The trapper knew the cat was gettin' it, too, because it started to fatten up. That fellow got kind of interested so one day he followed the cat out to see how it managed with that wooden leg, and he saw the cat creep up on something and grab it with one paw and hit it over the head with that wooden leg.

BRINGING IN THE BEAR

There was another about a fellow that invited a couple of friends of his from New York to come up and learn something about bear huntin'. The three of them got out in the woods and this fellow told his friends that he'd go ahead and do a little scoutin'. By and by they saw their guide comin' tearin' through the woods with a bear after him. "Get out of the way, boys," the fellow hollered. "I'm takin' this one back to the camp alive."

As told by Mike Pelletier, Old Town, Maine. Manuscripts of the Federal Writers' Project of the Works Progress Administration for the State of Maine.

Tagging a Deer

There was a fourteen-year-old boy shot a deer over here in Milford a few years ago. Now this story is really true: I know myself, it's a fact. This boy's father taught him to always tag a deer he shot so that no one else could claim it. Well, when the boy shot this deer he slipped his tag on to the deer's horns, but when he was turned the other way for a minute the deer jumped up and made off. Sometimes, you know, when a deer is hit it'll drop, but it's apt to get up and run away if it's able to. That deer got out of sight before the boy got over his surprise, but the boy started to follow along the tracks in the hope of catchin' up. By and by he heard a shot ahead and when he got up there he found two men skinnin' his deer.

He told the men that the deer belonged to him, and to prove it he showed them the tag on the deer's horns. One of the men looked at the tag and says, "All right, boy, the deer is yours. Anybody that can tag a deer that was goin' as fast as that one was when we saw it certainly deserves the animal."

Tying a Knot in a Panther's Tail

. . . WE WAS go huntin' for deer. Ah guess so, an' da was leetly mite snow on de graoun'. Wal seh, we'll see it track, we ant know what he was be, an' we'll folla dat, oh, long, long tam. Bamby he'll go in hole in rock, leetly laidge, you know, 'baout tree, fo', prob'ly seex tam big dis shantee was. Wal, seh, boy, Ah'll left it ma brudder-law for watch dat holes, an' Ah'll go 'raoun' back side laidge see all what Ah'll see. Ah'll look veree caffly, an' what you tink Ah'll fin' it? Leetly crack in rock 'baout so wide ma tree finger of it, an' dat panter hees tail steek off of it 'baout so long ma arm, prob'ly, where he'll push hind fust in dat holes. An' he'll weegly hees tail so (waving his forefinger slowly). Wal, Ah'll tink for spell what Ah do. Den Ah'll go cut off strong steek so big half ma wris' and two foots long. Den Ah'll tek hol' dat tails an' tied knot in him, veree caffly, den Ah'll run steek t'rough an' pull knot hard! Oh, bah gosh! you'll oughty hear dat panters yaller an' holla! Wus as fo' honded tousan' cat! Yes, seh! Oh, he'll hugly, Ah tol' you! but he can' help it, he can' gat it loose 'less he pull up hees tails off. Wal, seh, Ah'll lafft at it, Ah can' help it, mos' Ah'll split off ma side. Den Ah'll go 'raoun' ma brudder-law, an' he'll be scare mos' dead, an' goin' runned way. Ah'll tol' heem, Ah goin' in dat holes shoot dat panters. "Oh, gosh!" he'll ax me, "he tore you dead more as forty piece!" Ah'll say, "Ah so good man Ah'll don't 'fraid me." Den Ah'll crawl

From *Sam Lovel's Camps*, Uncle Lisha's Friends under Bark and Canvas, A Sequel to Uncle Lisha's Shop, by Rowland E. Robinson, pp. 65–66. Copyright, 1889, by Forest and Stream Publishing Co. New York. 1899.

in dat holes an' Ah'll shoot it, boom! raght 'tween hees head! An' bamby pooty soon he ant yaller some more, be all still as mices. Den Ah'll come off de holes an' Ah'll tol' ma brudder-law he'll crawl in an' pull off dat panters. He'll pooty 'fraid for go, but bamby he go. He touch hol' of it, he can' pull it cause hees tail tie, but he ant know. "Bah gosh!" he say, "dat panters more heavy as two ton! Ah can' pull it!" Den Ah'll go 'raoun' an' taked off dat steek, an' holla "pull!" an' ma brudder-law pull more harder he can—boom! he go tumbly on hees back, dat panters on top of it! Oh! 'f he ant scare, ma brudder-law. Yas seh! Wal, seh, boy . . . 'f you ant mek b'lieve dat stories you go Canada 'long to me Ah show you de steek. Ma brudder-law he'll saved it. Ah ant never tol' you stories so true lak dat, seh!

Duck Hunting Yarn

HAD pretty good hunting along about this time last year. 'Twas up at Cold Pond, over Tioga way. Folks sure knew what they was talking about when they named that place, Cold Pond, sure gets cold there, early too. It must have been about the first of November as I remember. That morning I had found a thin crust of ice on the watering trough in my barnyard when I led Dol out to drink.

Well, it was getting along towards nightfall, and I had been all over that god-forsaken section, clean from the Banty Place I had walked, across the swamp lands, and swinging across the side of Ragged Mountain. I was heading back to where I had started from, coming back by way of the old road that leads past this here Cold Pond. I figgered it would be shorter, and the sun was going down behind Forbes.

Hadn't shot a thing all day except a couple of "hogs"—figgered that their noses would pay for a couple boxes of shot. Well, as I was going to say, I was passing along the edge of the pond, sort of in the alders and brush when I heard a commotion. Hadn't been paying much attention to what was going on around me, was just moseying along towards home. I looked out onto the water and there was a whole flock of ducks; big fat ones, must have been nigh two hundred of them, maybe more. It was getting dusky, and they had settled for the night. 'Twas mighty cold up thereabouts, too.

I histed up my gun and took a pot shot, right into the middle of them. They looked fat and good, and I just didn't want to go home with nothing to show for my trouble. There was an awful quacking and squalling among them birds, but not a one flew off—I couldn't rightly figure out why they didn't get out of there quicker than scat.

By Harry E. Flanders. Manuscripts of the Federal Writers' Project of the Works Progress Administration for the State of New Hampshire.

Well, sir, to make a long story short I found that them there birds had been frozen into the ice that had formed over the northern part of the pond where they had lit. There warn't no ice near the edge of shore, but right over the deepest part, where it is so deep that no man has ever been able to plumb the bottom, the ice had formed several inches thick. I figger they must have been there since the night before, but of course, maybe the ice may have formed that night since the sun left Cold Pond. Mighty chilly place up there you know.

I climbed into a boat that some fishermen had left on the shore and rowed out to that ice patch. I kinda wanted to see if I had shot any of them ducks, and if I hadn't gotten any, why, I could walk around on the ice, wring a few necks, and cut my legal limit of birds out of the ice. But I didn't figure on how scared them ducks would be when I walked into the middle of them.

They put up the gol-durndest hullaballoo you ever heard and started to flap their wings real excited like. I was about in the middle of the ice cake then and the whole kit and kaboodle of them was a flapping and a quacking —they made quite a wind with their threshing around like that.

I was some surprised, now let me tell you, when that cake of ice began to lift out of the water. There were so many ducks frozen into the ice that when they got to flapping their wings, all together, they lifted the ice plumb off the pond, and the next thing I knew there I was, in the middle of a bunch of ducks, sailing over the trees. Right over Ragged Mountain and Kearsarge we went, them gol-durned birds flapping their wings to beat sixty.

Scairt? Hell no! I always had wanted to fly around up in the air and see what it was going to feel like to go to heaven, but just never had gotten around to it, and here was my chance to see what things looked like from up in the air.

Course I could have wrung their necks, one by one, and let myself down to earth again, easy like, but I was beginning to enjoy myself now. Course the ice was kind of cold, but I ain't one to ask for everything. They headed south, and we just kept on flying until the ice melted from the heat of the sun.

The Green Duck Hunter and the Live Decoy

IF ONE can get the market gunner of yesterday talking, he will tell you many stories of the city greenhorn and his performances alongshore or on the marshes. He will enjoy telling them, too, and his sulphurous comments are as interesting as the yarns themselves. Here is one.

The hero was a young fellow who came to the village in the duck season. He was not equipped for the sport, but he overcame that obstacle by borrowing a gunning float, a gun and one live decoy duck. They told him where, at the marshy edge of one of the inlets, he might find game. He rowed to that spot, put on his lone decoy, anchored his float and prepared for slaughter. The decoy was what the townsman who had lent it to him called a "first-class quacker." The decoy quacked and swam about and the gunner crouched and shivered and waited.

His wait was not a long one. In from the sea and down toward him swooped a tremendous flock of wild fowl. It was such a huge flock that, in his frenzy of excitement, he forgot to take aim, but blazed away in the direction of everything in general. The wild fowl clamorously soared to safety, but the gunner, peeping out over the edge of his float, was thrilled by the sight of a dead duck. He had actually killed something with his very first shot. He had, but it was the decoy he had borrowed. The "first class quacker" was noisy no longer, but its owner was talkative later on.

Jotham Stories

"MY GRANDFATHER," says Jotham, "was a great hunter. On stormy days like this he would take down his old long, single-barrelled gun and go out and bring home all kinds of game, mostly ducks and geese. In his day the ducks and geese bred around here and you could get 'em any time, but the best shooting was in the early fall on a northeaster. The heavy waves down on the coast drive the birds out of their feeding grounds and they come up to the fresh-water ponds inland to drink and get a change of feed. It is the same way with the shore birds, yellow-legs and plover and the like, though in my grandfather's day they didn't care much about such small game. Bigger birds were plenty enough. Grandfather used to hate yellow-legs, though, for they are telltales.

"Once he went over to Muddy Pond loaded for duck. It is a great place for ducks. In those days they used to come in there and sometimes pack it solid full. You could hardly see the pond for the ducks in it. Grandfather always knew just the right day to go, and this time when he looked down on the pond from the hill he saw hardly any water at all, nothing much but ducks. It was the chance of his life. He slipped down the hill among the scrubs to the cedars and then began to creep carefully up. You know what the pond is like, perfectly round and only a couple of acres or so, with a rim of marsh and then another big rim of swamp cedars, then the hills all about, neither inlet nor outlet; a queer pond anyway, and queer things happen on it, same as they did that day. Grandfather had got half way through the swamp cedars when he came to a little opening which he

From *Old Plymouth Trails,* by Winthrop Packard, pp. 204–213. Copyright, 1920, by Winthrop Packard. Boston: Small, Maynard & Company, Publishers.

had to cross. Just then there came up on the east wind a big flock of telltales, 762 of them, whirling over the hills without a sound till they saw him.
Then they began to yelp."

"Look here, Jotham," I am always careful to say at this point, "how
could he tell that there were just 762 of them? He couldn't count so many
as they flew."

"Didn't have to count 'em as they flew," answers Jotham. "He counted
'em after he had shot 'em.

"Well, they began to yelp 'Look out for him! Look out for him!' and the
ducks knew what that meant. All that great blanket of ducks uncovered
the pond with one motion. Grandfather said it was just like a curtain rising
straight up, for they were all black ducks. There is no other duck can go
straight up in the air. Other ducks slide off on a slant against the wind."

How Jotham manages to put the lonely quaver of the yellow-leg's call
into that phrase "Look out for him! Look out for him!" with its four-note
repetition is more than I know, but he always does, and you can see the big
flock swing through the mist as he says it.

"Grandfather was pretty mad to lose that chance at good game and he
made up his mind that he'd take it out of the telltales, so he began to
whistle 'em back. He was a master hand at any wild call and pretty soon
he lit the flock. There they were, a rim of yellow-legs all around the pond,
a perfect circle except in one place, where some dogwood bushes made down
to the water's edge. Then granddad had a great idea. He saw his chance to
kill every one of those infernal telltales where they sat. He studied on the
size of that circle for a minute. Then he put the long barrel of that old
gun between two swamp cedar stumps and bent on it carefully. He kept
doing this, looking at the circle, then bending the gun barrel till he had the
gun bent just on the curve of the circle of yellow-legs sitting round the
pond. Then he smiled for he knew he had 'em. He crept carefully into the
dogwood bushes till he was in just the right place, took a good aim round
that circle, and then he onlatched on 'em.

"Well, he'd figured that circle just right. The shot swung round it and
killed every one of them seven hundred and sixty-two yellow-legs right
where they stood. But tarnation; he'd forgotten all about himself, he was
so interested in the science of it. The back of his neck was right in that
circle and the shot came round true as could be and hit him right there.
The force of it was pretty well spent going so far and killing so many
yellow-legs, but it dented some bits of dogwood leaves right into his system
and he had dogwood poisoning pretty bad. He used to have it every year
after that, about the time the first northeaster set in."

Anybody who knows Muddy Pond will know that Jotham's story ought
to be true, for the pond is there to prove it, just as he describes it.

"Of course," says Jotham at this point, "that was skill. Not one hunter
in a hundred would have thought to bend his gun so as to throw the shot in
a circle or would have been able to estimate the amount of the curve so
exactly right. Another thing happened to my grandfather over at that pond
that was part skill and part luck. He was on his way home from partridge

shooting one day just before Thanksgiving. He found he was out of shot just before he got to the pond. His flask had leaked and let every bit of the shot out, and when he came to load up after shooting his last partridge he stopped with the powder, for there was no shot to put in. Just then he came in sight of the pond and there were seven geese swimming round in it; and that the day before Thanksgiving!

"It was a tough time to be without any shot, but grandfather was equal to the emergency. He simply left his ramrod right in the gun, put on a cap, and began to worm his way through the cedars to the shore, where he could get a good, close shot at the geese. Just as he did this another hunter who was no kind of a shot, came to the other side of the pond and saw the birds. He was one of the kind that have the buck fever at the sight of game, and he put up his gun and shot slam at the flock, too far away to do any execution, then he let out a yell and began to run down to the shore as fast as he could go.

"Of course he scared the geese and they lit out, swinging right by grandfather. Grandfather was a nervy hunter. He held his fire till he got the heads of those seven geese right in line, and then he shot and strung 'em all right through the eyes with the ramrod. Granddad couldn't quite see where he had hit 'em, but when the smoke cleared away he saw the seven geese still flying and his ramrod going off with 'em, and he was some considerable astonished and a good deal put about at losing his ramrod.

"Now here's the queer part of it: Those seven geese were blinded, of course, with a ramrod strung right through their eyes, but the life in a wild goose is powerful strong and they kept on flying just the same, until they went out of sight, right in the direction of granddad's home. But he got home and had hung up his gun without seeing anything more of them and he thought his ramrod was sure gone for good. Then grandmother came to him, kind of scared, saying she heard spirit rappings on the pantry wall. Granddad heard the noise, a sort of tapping, but he couldn't see anything until he looked out the pantry window.

"Yes, there they were seven of 'em, hung on the ramrod and the ramrod hung on a blind-hook, just outside granddad's pantry window, their wings still flapping a little and making that rapping sound, just as if they were knocking to be let in at the pantry of the man that had shot 'em. All the relations used to come to grandfather's for Thanksgiving, and thirty-five of 'em sat down to dinner that year and every one of 'em had all the roast goose they could eat."

Frightened or injured game birds do perform strange feats as many an honest huntsman will tell you. I myself have a neighbor, no relative of Jotham's who shot at a partridge in the woods a quarter of a mile from his house and saw the bird fly away. When he got home a half-hour later he found his pantry window broken and a partridge lying dead on the pantry floor, either the one he had shot at or another just as good—and as the proverb has it, one story is good until another one is told. Jotham usually caps his list with the following:

"I guess the greatest wild goose hunting grandfather ever did was the time the big flock got caught in the ice storm. It came in November, a foot of soft snow and then one of those rainstorms that freeze as soon as the rain touches anything. Every twig on the trees that storm was as big as your wrist with ice and there was an inch or two of clear ice on everything and more coming all the time, when grandfather heard a big flock of wild geese honking. They didn't seem to be going over, but their voices hung in the air right over the big steep hill from the barn up into the back pasture. After they'd been honking up there for some time grandfather went up to see what it was all about, but he didn't take his gun. As he climbed the hill through the wet snow he heard 'em plainer and plainer, and when he got to the top he saw a most 'strodinary sight. There was a good-sized flock, ninety-seven geese, to be exact, that had got so iced up that they had to settle on the top of the hill.

"The ice had formed on their feathers as they flew and they were so weighted down they couldn't fly and they were getting more and more iced up every minute. Granddad didn't care to go back for his gun for fear some of the other nimrods in the neighborhood would come on the scene and bag the game first, but there wasn't any need of a gun. All he had to do was to drive 'em home. They were terribly iced up, but their legs were still free and he chased 'em about for some time before he got 'em started down hill. But once over the edge of the hill the weight of the ice on 'em turned 'em right over and over, and so they rolled on down. It was a wet snow and as they rolled they took up more and more of it till by the time they came slap up against the side of the barn every single goose was sealed up in the middle of a hard, round snowball. They all stopped there and all that grandfather had to do was to pile them up, and there they were, in cold storage for the winter. Every time the family wanted roast goose they went out and split open a snowball. The folks in granddad's time used often to freeze their fresh meat and keep it out in the snow all winter, but he was the only one that I ever heard of that stored wild geese in that way."

FISHERMAN'S LUCK

Grant's Tame Trout

THE sage of Beaver Camp sat sunning himself on the bench beside the cook camp, the bench so widely known as the scene of countless weary hours

From "The Tame Trout," by Samuel T. Farquhar, *California Folklore Quarterly*, Vol. III (July, 1944), No. 3, pp. 177–178. Copyright, 1944, by the California Folklore Society. Berkeley and Los Angeles: Published for the California Folklore Society by the University of California Press. Reprinted from *The Tame Trout and Other Fairy Tales*, narrated by Ed Grant of Beaver Pond, Maine, chronicled by Francis I. Maule of Philadelphia. Phillips: Maine Woods and Woodsman Print. 1904.

of that perpetual toiler. He seemed to be smoking an old black pipe, whereas he was only dropping matches into its empty bowl at intervals of three minutes, agreeable to the terms of his contract with the American Match trust.

As he so sat and pondered, the writer, at the time a recent arrival, approached and said: "Mr. Grant, I wish you would give me the true history of your wonderful success in taming a trout. I have heard of it in all parts of the world but I have always longed to hear the story direct from headquarters."

"Well, it really ain't so much of a story," replied the famous chronicler. "It was this way. Nine year ago the eleventh day of last June, I was fishin' out there in the pads, and right under that third yaller leaf to the right of the channel—yes, that one with the rip in it—I ketched a trout 'bout six inches long. I never see a more intelligent lookin' little feller— high forehead, smooth face, round, dimpled chin, and a most uncommon bright, sparkling, knowin' eye.

"I always allowed that with patience and cunning a real young trout (when they gets to a heft of 10 or 15 pounds there ain't no teachin' them nothin') could be tamed jest like a dog or cat.

"There was a little water in the boat and he swims around in it all right till I goes ashore and then I gets a tub we had, made of the half of a pork barrel, fills it with water and bores a little small hole through the side close down to the bottom and stops the hole with a peg.

"I sets this tub away back in a dark corner of the camp and every night after the little fellow gets asleep I slip in, in my stockin' feet, and pulls out the peg softly and lets out jest a little mite of the water. I does this night after night so mighty sly that the little chap never suspected nothin' and he was a-livin' hale and hearty for three weeks on the bottom of that tub as dry as a cook stove, and then I knowed he was fit for trainin'.

"So I took him out o' doors and let him wiggle awhile on the path and soon got to feedin' him out of my hand. Pretty soon after that when I walked somewhat slow (I'm naturally quite a slow walker some folks think) he could follow me right good all round the clearin', but sometimes his fins did get ketched up in the brush jest a mite and I had to go back and swamp out a little trail for him; bein' a trout, of course he could easy follow a spotted line.

"Well, as time went on, he got to follerin' me most everywhere and hardly ever lost sight of me, and me and him was great friends, sure enough.

"Near about sundown one evening, I went out to the spring back of the camp, same one as you cross goin' to Little Island, to get some butter out of a pail, and, of course, he comes trottin' along behind. There was no wind that night, I remember, and I could hear his poor little fins a-raspin' on the chips where we'd been gettin' out splits in the cedar swamp. Well, sir, he follered me close up and came out onto the logs across the brook and jest as I was a-stoopin' down over the pail I heard a kee-plunk! behind me and Gorry! if he hadn't slipped through a chink between them logs

and was drowned before my very eyes before I could reach him, so he was."
Here a tear started from the good old man's eye on a very dusty trip down
his time-stained cheek.

"Of course I was terrible cut up at first—I couldn't do a stroke of work
for three weeks—but I got to thinkin' that as it was comin' on cold (it was in
late November then) and snow would soon be here and he, poor little cuss,
wasn't rugged enough for snow-shoein' and he couldn't foller me afoot all
winter no how, and as he couldn't live without me, mebby it was jest as well
after all he was took off that way. Do you know, Mister, some folks around
here don't believe a word of this, but if you'll come down to the spring with
me, right now, I'll show you the very identical chink he dropped through
that night, so I will. I've never allowed anyone to move it. No, sir! nor
I never will."

Here the old man dropped match number thirty-seven [1] into his pipe
and sucked at it hard in silence, while I crept softly away on tiptoes. I
never could bring myself to speak of it again, after seeing him so deeply
moved—I never could.

Catching Trout by Tickling

THE biggest trout I ever caught was in the month of March, many years
ago, just after the old Peace Dale milldam was carried away in a freshet.
As I was sauntering along the bank of the Saucatucket river, some ten or
fifteen rods below the dam, I saw a big speckled trout side of a rock, and
I just thought I would try the English method of catching trout where the
water is cold, by tickling! So I just put my hand down slily behind the
tail of the fish, and making a sort of half-moon or rather crescent with my
fingers and palm, I carried my hand beneath him and manipulated him
gently with the tips of my fingers. Whether it was the warmth of my
fingers, or what, I don't know, but the trout did not move otherwise than to
rise gradually to the surface of the water, my hand following him all the
while, with the ends of my fingers occasionally gently tickling him, until he
got his back almost out of water, when with a sudden jerk I landed him on
the bank. I took him home and found he just turned the steelyards at three
pounds and one-half.

---

[1] Ed Grant's regular allowance is one pound of tobacco to each gross of matches
used.—S. T. F.

From *The Jonny-Cake Papers of "Shepherd Tom,"* Together With Reminiscences of
Narragansett Schools of Former Days, by Thomas Robinson Hazard, With a Biographical Sketch and Notes by Rowland Gibson Hazard, pp. 356–357. Copyright,
1915, by Rowland G. Hazard. Boston: Printed for the Subscribers.

A Creel of Big Ones

As A TELLER of tall tales, the American fresh-water fisherman is perhaps in a class by himself. He is forever concocting them and forever telling them. Around a campfire up in our New England corner [Northfield, Vermont] where freely wagging tongues are gay, such yarns will acquire impressive dimensions. Here are some samples:

EASY FISHING

"How did I get that big salmon in that basket? I got him easy, believe it or not, brother. I been still-fishin' off these rocks all morning, not gettin' a thing, till that durned fish-hawk—he's got a nest up there on Pisgah—came flyin' round an' divin' for fish. I saw him dive and come up with that salmon. Then he started to fly plumb over me. I just clapped my hands, an' the noise startled him so—yes sir!—he dropped that fish, an' it lit bang in the basket. Easiest fishin' I ever done. Yes—sir!"

THE HOOPAJUBA

"Hoopajubas? Oh, they live like the golden trout in the deepest and coldest part of a lake. How to catch them? Well, you get hold of a water-augur. You row out to the deepest springhole and bore a hole in the water with it. Then you row ashore, hide in the bushes and make a noise like a mudworm. The hoopajuba comes out of the hole, grabs his tail in his mouth, and starts rolling toward you like a hoop. You stick out an arm, run it through his hoop, and you have him! That's the way to catch a hoopajuba."

TRUTHFUL JAKE

"Old Jake Ackley, fishin' for bass on Scrabble Pond, back in prohibition days, allus had a pint of moonshine under the seat of his boat—figgered if he drunk enough of it, the skeeters would get drunk an' leave him alone. Every time Jake tossed a hook over, a big bass would twitch the worm off, an' Jake got good an' sore; so he swashed a big worm around in his moonshine, hooked him on, an 'slung him overboard. There was an awful fuss in the water, an' Jake hauled up the bass with that big worm wound around its neck strangling it to death, an' Jake says that worm was a-sayin', 'You bit me once, dog-gone you, now you try it again!' Powerful stuff they made in them days, up Scrabble way."

By Arthur Wallace Peach. *The New York Times Magazine,* April 11, 1948, p. 18.

Simple Explanation

The rainbow trout weighed four pounds but its color was unusually clear, light silver. The fisherman who caught him said: "I was fishing the Battenkill, crossed a fairly deep hole, and stumbled over a keg. I heard a noise in it, so rolled it ashore, and still something kept making a noise inside. I broke the keg open, and, gentlemen, that big rainbow was in there! Explain it? Easy. I figure that when he was a little chap he slipped in through the bunghole, and, finding plenty of insects, just stayed inside, fed on the bugs, and kept growing. Then I came along, opened the keg, and by gosh, there he was!"

Saturation Point

"Man, I sure got these bass a funny way. I like to fish early; so I went down to Number Ten pond 'fore dawn. Fog so thick I couldn't see nothin', but I cast out an' I got these six bass, one after tuther. Then it cleared, and I saw I hadn't been fishin' in the pond at all but in the fog! Those durned bass had come out of the lake and the fog was so thick they was swimmin' around in it grabbin' mosquitos. I 'low you don't see fog that thick often!"

Expert Advice

He was a greenhorn, so the yarn goes, and one of the older guides was assigned to him on the theory that the placid veteran would not be offended at the amateur's annoying mannerisms. Patiently, the veteran coached the amateur, who finally managed to hook a trout. It was a small one, and he reeled it speedily up to the tip of his rod, where it hung, flapping and flopping. Then he turned to the guide and asked, "Now, what'll I do?" It was too much. The old guide stared at him a moment, and then said gently: "I'll tell you what—climb up the pole and stab it to death."

The Law

"He come up to my house back on Bull Run Road, all dolled up to go fishin'. Chap I never see before. Think he was stayin' down at the inn. An' he was worried 'cause he had jest heard that in Vermont the limit is six inches fer a trout. Since he had nothin' to measure with, I cut a stick, just six inches, an' off he went. He come to the house about three hours later— an' he didn't have nary a trout. Surprised me—'cause the fishin' in the Run is mighty good. So I sez, sez I, 'Funny you didn't get no fish, friend.' An' he sez, kinda sad: 'I caught plenty, but they was either under six inches or over; so I tossed 'em back.'"

OUTBOARD MOTOR

The twenty-pound lake trout hung majestically outside the fishing camp, and beside it were two smaller ones. "How'd we catch 'em? Funny thing, the way it happened—mighty funny. I and my old fishin' pal, Jim, were trollin' down in the North Cove, usin' a light canoe, and I hooked into that big fellow. I had quite a wrastle with him, an' since I was usin' a heavy rig, I didn't want to horse him too much; an' then the canoe began to move along slow. So I said to Jim, 'Guess I'll let him tire himself out—jest hang on an' let him go. You might as well bait up and fish too.' So Jim put out his rig, an' that husky towed us clean across the Cove an' Jim picked up those two smaller fellers on the way."

The Man That Liked to Fish

. . . GREAT many while 'go, w'en de tam was hol', dar was one man Canada was lak for feesh so much he ant do mos' not'ing but dat. W'en his corn ought for be plant his waf was plant it, if he gat plant 't all, an' he go feeshin'. W'en his corn was ought for be hoe, he go feeshin'. W'en it was tam for cut off, his waf cut it off, an' de mans go feeshin' an' de sem for husk it, an' jes' de sem for rip his wheat, an' t'rash it, his waf he do it, all of it. An' w'en his hwood was ought for be cut he go feeshin' in de ice. An' w'en de Govny want it for go faght de Hinjin an' de Angleesh, he 'll run 'way an' go feeshin', so bamby de pries' he 'll gat mad at it an' he tol' it 'f he ant 'have hese'f for be so shiflin', he goin' turn it into kingfishin' an' den see 'f he 'll gat 'nough feeshin'.

De mans he some scare an' promise for be better, 'fore soon he fregit an' go feeshin' all de tam jes' de sem. Den de pries', Oh, haow he 'll was mad an' turn dat man into kingfishin' raght off. De man he was surprise prob'bly, for feel hese'f such leetly feller all cover wid fedder, but pooty soon he feel glad for t'ink he 'll ant gat for wear clo's dat was trouble for git, an' can go feeshin' all de tam.

He go up de river, "K-r-r-r-r," an' he go daown de river, "K-r-r-r-r," an' wen he see leetly feesh, 'baout so big he can swaller, "splosh," he jomp on it an' flew on a tree for heat it an' say, "T'ank you, Père Jerome, it was funs for be kingfishin'." When he was flew pas' hees hown haouse on de river an' see hees waf homp hees back hoein' an' rippin' in de sun an' hees chillren cry for hongry he 'll holler "K-r-r-r-r," jes' lak he was laught at it, he such gre't wicked.

Wal, seh, he 'll had good tam all summer an' long in de fall 'fore it come col'. Den he ant hear de sing bird yaller any more 'cause dey all gone

From *Uncle Lisha's Outing*, by Rowland E. Robinson, pp. 217–218. Copyright, 1897, by Rowland E. Robinson. Boston and New York: Houghton Mifflin and Company.

'cep' de jay an' de hwoodpeckit; den de river froze on top, but he 'll ant know 'nough for go to de warm wedder. He guess he was be hable for stay jes' long anybody. One morny de river was be froze on top, but he 'll ant know when he go for his breakfis' an' he go "K-r-r-r-r," lookin' for see some feesh, an' bamby he 'll see leetly feesh swim under de ice an' he holler "K-r-r-r-r" an' go firs' head raght on top of it, "Floop," an' bus' his head on de ice an' broke his brain all off an' dat was de en' of it.

REMARKABLE ANIMAL BEHAVIOR

A Gone Fish

Tom Rodman's grog was held to be the best in the County. Squire Hooper and his old crony, Gran'ther Holland, differed on this point alone, for Gran'ther Holland always upheld the peculiar merit of Elisha Watson's drink. These two rumsellers were keen rivals in the groggery business, both managing to keep their customers in debt, and in the end taking even their farms at forced sale. In short, they were a precious pair. The story runs that one foggy summer morning, Gran'ther Holland sent word to Squire Hooper that it was a likely day to go tautogin' on Peaked Rock. They often fished together, and were the best of friends, quarreling only on the point of drink. So, taking their heavy chestnut saplin peeled poles, they went down to the Peaked Rock, then still standing upright on the ledge where Whimsy Cot, now the property of Mrs. Irving Fisher, of New Haven, stands overlooking the rock. The day turned out badly—hot and hotter till the sun burned off the fog, so the tautog got shy and lay swinging in the tide waiting for the twilight; the anglers lost their bait, and their tempers also; now and then by chance they "stole" a chogset, pest of the tautog fisherman. Most of these wily thieves dropped back, and of course told their friends below, *who* was after them. A few were saved for the frying-pan. No fish has a finer flavor, when properly fried. Along about noon Gran'ther Holland growled out, "Le's give up, and go on home, no use brilin' here any longer." "All right," says Squire Hooper, "I'll jest fish up my last crab." So he tied her on good and solid, and hadn't more 'n got his line down when he felt a big one take holt, and bore down hard on his big pole, to hist him out. The big tautog, soon's he felt the pull, sung out with fright, "Chogsetties, who in hell has got hold of that thar dam pole?" "Squire Hooper! ole boy, Squire Hooper!" Hearing this, the big fish groaned out, "Good-bye, boys, I guess I'm a goner. *I'll be to Tom Rodman's afore sunset.*"

By Rowland Gibson Hazard in *The Jonny-Cake Papers of "Shepherd Tom,"* Together with Reminiscences of Narragansett Schools of Former Days, by Thomas Robinson Hazard, With a Biographical Sketch and Notes by Rowland Gibson Hazard, pp. 399–400. Copyright, 1915, by Rowland G. Hazard. Boston: Printed for the Subscribers.

The Mink Story

ON A Maine Lake famous for its sporty landlocked salmon, I often listened with my son to the yarns of our guide. Charlie, sparsely built man, past middle age, a great tobacco-chewer and a first-class guide, was a good companion. Perhaps for the boy's edification he told this story.

One day, something that was said about animal life in the vicinity of Grand Lake Stream gave Charlie a lead which he promptly followed.

"Did I ever tell you," he said, a far-away look in his eyes indicating that his powers of imagination were at work—"did I ever tell you the funny thing that happened to me last summer?

"Along the middle uv May," he began, "I'd been up the lake to see if there wuz any loose logs floatin' round in Sobsen's Bay. About the middle uv the afternoon it begun to rain real hard so I paddled ashore, got under a spruce near the head uv a cove nigh where a little brook come into the lake, an' set down an' filled my pipe fur a smoke. By'n' by, seein' trout wuz risin' towards the mouth uv the brook, I set up my rod an' put on a couple uv flies—a Silver Doctor and for the dropper a new one that I tied myself. The fish warn't much for size—most half-pounders—a few wuz bigger.

"They come along pretty good and when I took one off the hook I'd throw him back into the stern. As I stood up an' started to shove off when it stopped rainin', I looked round but there warn't a single fish in the canoe! Not ˉone!

"I wuz stumped for sure," Charlie said, ejecting a quid into the water and taking out his knife to cut off a fresh chew. "Where in tophet hed them trout gone? It bothered me, for they warn't big enough to flop overboard themselves, and anyway I would hev heered 'em. I looked 'round but couldn't see nothin', so I set down and lighted my pipe ag'in, to think it over. Arter a while I begun to fish some more. The fust trout I lost. The next one wuz a little feller that I hedn't orter've kept but I wanted to see what in heck wuz up so I throwed him behind me in the canoe jest the way I had been 'doin' before. I kep' kinder quiet, didn't look back, but kep' on fishin' till I got a couple more. When I'd throwed the last one up along with the others I turned round a little so I could see what wuz goin' on, but keepin' quiet and not makin' no noise. What do you s'pose I saw? A brown head with little shiny eyes and bristlin' whiskers come up over the side uv the canoe! It wuz a mink! When he saw me he dodged back quick. I kep' still, didn't move none, and in less'n a minute Mister Mink's head popped up ag'in. Then all to onct his neck and shoulders come over th' edge an' before you could say 'scat' he picked up one uv them trout in his mouth an' wuz off like a flash. I waited and it warn't long before he

By Charles E. Goodspeed. From *A Treasury of Fishing Stories*, compiled by Charles E. Goodspeed, pp. 391–393. Copyright, 1946, by A. S. Barnes and Company, Inc. New York. Originally printed, in a slightly different version, in *Angling in America*, Its Early History and Literature, by Charles Eliot Goodspeed, pp. 321–322. Copyright, 1939, by Charles E. Goodspeed. Boston: Houghton Mifflin Company.

come back for the other fish. This time I turned way round an' watched him, but he didn't go fur. There wuz a rotten birch stump under the trees 'bout ten foot off, an' the mink hed dug out a hole under it. When I looked in it, thar wuz eight nice trout lyin' side by side, the big ones underneath, jest as neat as my old woman'd lay 'em on a dish.

"Now," said Charlie, "here's what happened. Fust I counted them trout to see if they wuz all there. One wuz missin', so I looked round, but not seein' him nowheres, I picked the rest up out uv the hole where they wuz and went back to the canoe. Jest as I wuz goin' to step in I happened to look down, and that missin' trout wuz lyin' right on the ground. I a'most stepped on it. He wuz jest where the mink dropped him when he saw how small he wuz."

Charlie paused for a reminiscent chuckle.

"A mighty cute one that mink wuz. The little trout warn't more'n seven inches an' the mink had tried to cover him up with leaves."

Again Charlie stopped, this time to avoid what promised to be a lame conclusion of his story. "An' mebbe," he meditatively said, "mebbe that mink thought I wuz a game-ward'n!"

Why I Never Shoot Bears

FRED JENNES, veteran woods guide of Greenville, Maine, tells this tall tale and swears by all the Bibles in Piscataquis county that it is gospel truth:

"Do you know why I don't kill bears?" he asked. "No! Well, it's this way. Three years ago this June I was on a fishing trip up to Grand Lake. I had been out on the water pretty nearly all of one day and, getting tired, paddled back to camp. I hauled the canoe up on the sandy beach and started for the shack.

"When I got within about 100 feet of the place I saw the front door was open. I peeked in. There stood a big black bear just pulling the cork out of my molasses jug with his teeth. Out came the sticky syrup all over the floor. Bruin lapped up some of it and then rubbed his right paw into the rest—smeared it all over.

"So I crept around behind the camp, stuck my head in the window and yelled. He shot through the door like a bullet and headed for the lake. I never saw such an odd gait on a bear before—sort of mixture of running and galloping. And all on three legs. He was holding up the paw daubed with molasses.

"From where I stood it looked as if the critter had sat down on the shore and was holding his sweetened paw up to the air. It was June and the air was full of flies, mosquitoes and black midges. I could see that they were

From the *Boston Traveler*, June 1, 1938. Reprinted in *Angling in America*, Its Early History and Literature, by Charles Eliot Goodspeed, pp. 323–324. Copyright, 1939, by Charles E. Goodspeed. Boston: Houghton Mifflin Company.

swarming around that molasses foot. Soon it was covered with flies feasting on that stuff.

"Suddenly he waded out in the water and stood up. He was in to his shoulders. He placed the sweetened paw down close to the surface and the next thing I saw a fine trout jump clear of the water at those flies.

"Every time a fish leaped clear of the water, Bruin would give it a cuff that sent it ashore and far up the beach.

"Finally as he saw the pile of trout on the sand he seemed to think he had enough. He waded ashore lapping off the insects and I expected he would sit down and gobble every fish. I recalled that all I had caught that day was two small fish.

"Well, sir, he had a fine feed, and when he had eaten half a dozen fine big trout, he paused, looked over at the bushes where I was and actually laid the remaining fish in a row. Then he ambled off up the shore and oddly enough kept looking back over his shoulder.

"I walked down to the beach and true enough there were half a dozen wonderful trout. At the edge of the woods the bear stopped and was standing up. As loud as I could, I yelled, 'Thanks old man!' Do you know he actually waved a paw at me and dove into the thicket. I honestly think he left me those fish to pay for my spilled molasses. No, *sir,* I never shoot bears."

The Hawk Feather That Ate the Chicken Feathers

. . . One tam Ah'll was leetly boy an' leeve in Canada, mah mudder was mek it some bed fedder of geese's fedder an' she was gat it mos' all stuff up but leetly maght he ant gat nough fedder. Den mah fader was keel two hawk was come raoun' for ketch de chicklin, an' mah mudder was pull de fedder for feenish his bed of it. It was very nice plump beds, an' dey keep it for de bes' one for w'en company come see it, an' nex' year mah gran'pere an' gran'mere come for visit all naght, an', seh, gran'mere was gre't big hol' hwomans, an' w'en he come on de room in de morñy he was r-r-r-rubby, r-r-r-rubby heself an' grunt very hard, an' w'en mah mudder ax it what de matter, she say de bed rope cut him all in chonk, 'cause de bed fedder was so t'in, an' mah mudder was supprise mos' for be mad for have it say so 'baout hees bes' bed, but w'en he ex-amine he fin' honly de hawk fedder, de res' it was all heat up. . . .

Tall Tales from the Maine Woods

THE THREE BEARS

"FELLER NAME of Avon Stevens watched camp fer a loggin' company one summer way back on Chamberlin Lake. Avon was awful techy about bears breakin' into the camp while he was asleep, so he build his bunk on a platform seven feet above the floor. One afternoon he was layin' there in his crow's nest, jest dozin' off, when in walked three bears—an old he-one, a she-one, and their cub. Avon was scared plumb speechless, and hild his breath. The old she-bear, she snooped around and looked over Avon's curtains, shelf trimmin's and cookin' utensils, while the cub sot down on a bench and went to pawrin' over the pages of a Sears, Roebuck catalog. The old he-bear, he took to rummagin' around the spice cabinet, pawrin' over packages of pepper, mustard, cinnamon and so forth. Avon says it was so quiet it was painful; when all of a sudden the old he-bear blurted out, in a deep bass tone o' voice, 'I wonder where he keeps his cream o' tartar?' "

THE STOVE PIPE

"Sherm Ludlow, one of the best beaver poachers in the State [of Maine], says he built a trappin' cabin one fall up Mooseleak way, luggin' in the window sash, tar paper, beddin', stove-pipe and so forth, a pack load at a time. It so happened that he'd lugged in the stove-pipe before the cabin was finished. On his last trip he brought in a sheet iron stove, but when he went to set it up the joint of stove-pipe with the damper into it was missin'. Sherm hunted fer it high and low, and finally give it up. About the time he'd begun buildin' his camp, a family of beaver hed started buildin' a dam across the brook a few rods from the camp site. When Sherm went down to the brook fer a pail of water that evenin', he took a look at the dam to see how the beaver was gettin' along with their work. 'I hope t' hev my tobaccer taken away from me, and be sentenced t' live three months in de Province,' Sherm says, 'ef dem sinful beaver hedn't stole my joint of stove-pipe with the damper into it, and built it into the dam, t' regulate the flow of water.' "

From *Maine Stories,* by John William Stolle, aided and abetted by M. S. (Boob) Snowman, pp. 16, 21–22, 24, 55, 70. Copyright, 1953, by John William Stolle. Bangor, Maine: H. P. Snowman, printer.

I have tried to record the actual language of interesting old timers I have met [while I farmed, logged, and worked as a guide and Forest Service lookout in Aristook County from 1905 to 1945], most of whom have beaten me to the Happy Hunting Ground. The names of most of the places mentioned in the narrative as well as the names of people (with the exception of Elmer Dearborn and Lewis Brown) are fictitious.—Foreword, J. W. S.

BIG EATING

"This Parmer," Sam said, "could stow away more vittles than three husky men. Went to a big reunion one time and it seems his train back home left before the big barbecue feast was due to start, so the committee on refreshments rigged him a special feed, consistin' of a roast sucklin' pig, with potatoes, turnips, and all the usual trimmin's. After he'd been gorgin' himself fer about an hour one of the committee looked into the big dinin' room and ast him if there was anything more he would like. 'Why, yes,' Parmer says, 'if you've got any more o' them small hogs, fetch me in another one.'"

THE LOST SHOAT

. . . Billy Carter led off with a tale about a shoat he had lost several years ago.

"This shoat," Billy went on, as he puffed away on his corn cob pipe, "disappeared from his pen one night right after hayin'. Wa'n't no sign o' where he'd climb out er broke out, so I cal'lated some thievin' neighbor o' mine had made off with him. I didn't say nothin' to nobody about it, on the theery that sooner er later I'd hear a rumor and find out who done it. After the pig hed bein missin' about three weeks, I went out one Sunday afternoon to look at a back field I hed sowed to buckwheat, t' see if 'twa'n't 'bout ready t' cut. In a back corner o' the field I seen somebuddy pullin' up an armful o' buckwheat, and luggin' it inta the woods. 'Twas quite a ways off, and I couldn't make out who in Tophet it was, so I snuk along jest inside the aidge o' the woods so's t' git up closer and find out who 'twas. Ever' now and agin, whoever 'twas, would go git another armful o' buckwheat and lug it inta the woods. Bye and bye I got up t' where I could see a square pen, logged up about four logs high. I looked inta the pen and there was my *shoat*! And here come a bear, with another armful o' buckwheat! That son-of-a —— was fattenin' up that hog to butcher that fall 'fore he hibernated."

LEGAL TENDER

"Every time I look at a hammer handle [Ben Nesbit said,] I think of the yarn my father used to tell about a hired man he once had, back in the good old pod auger days, when money wuz scurce, and they wuz a good deal of barterin' done. In them times farmers used to make axe handles, when the weather wuz too bad to work outdoors. When they got a good supply made ahead, they'd take them down to the Village and trade 'em in fer groceries.

"This hired man Father used to tell about came from the Province. He wuz one o' these here drifters—here today, and gone tomorrow; and he'd never worked in the State o' Maine before. After he'd worked fer Father a week, the itch got into his feet, and he allowed he'd draw his pay, and move on. So Father figgered up how much wuz due him, and give him an armful of axe-handles.

" 'What's this fer?' the feller wanted to know.

" 'That's yer wages,' Father told him.

" 'Wages, hell!' the feller sez, 'I want my money!'

" 'That's all the money ye'll *git*,' Father sez. 'Take them handles to the Village and swap 'em fer anything ye want—clothes, terbaccer, rum, er anythin' in the store!'

"The feller see 'twa'n't no use to argue, so he took up his bundle and struck fer the Village, where he hunted up a speakeasy fust thing to squench his week-old thirst. He still hed a little money left from another job he'd worked at, so he ordered a slub o' rum, and partly out of deviltry, and partly to test Father's claim that axe-handles wuz legal tender, he laid one of his axe-handles down on the bar. He shore wuz surprised when the bartender took the handle, put it under the bar, and came up with a hammer handle and two hatchet handles in change!"

LOCAL WONDERS

The Mosquitoes with the Canvas Britches

CAPT. JONES, of Stonington, is responsible for the following: On his passage from New York a few years ago he observed, one summer afternoon, a heavy cloud arise from the land, and, to his great surprise, approach the vessel. Suddenly it broke near him and covered the deck with millions of musquitoes, while part of the flock went through the mainsail, leaving nothing but bolt ropes hanging idly to the spars. Corroborative evidence to this astonishing tale was found in the person of a "down-east skipper," who heard the story, and who, on comparing dates with the narrator, declared that two days afterwards he was boarded by the same flock of musquitoes, and they all wore canvas breeches.

Frozen Death

THE events described herewith took place within 20 miles of Montpelier,

From *Phinney's Calendar, or Western Almanac, for the Year of Our Lord 1873,* by George R. Perkins. Buffalo, New York: Published by James M. Lent.

By Robert Wilson, in *The (Old) Farmer's Almanack,* Calculated on a New and Improved Plan for the Year of Our Lord 1943, by Robert B. Thomas, pp. 50, 83. Copyright, 1942, by Mabel M. Swan. Dublin, New Hampshire: Yankee, Inc.

Cf. Charles Edward Crane, *Winter in Vermont* (New York, 1941), p. 85, who cites this story (under the title, "Human Hibernation") from an old clipping in a scrapbook belonging to Elbert S. Stevens, of Bridgewater Corners. The clipping, of unknown source, date, and authorship, was reprinted in the *Rutland Herald,* May 24, 1939.

Vermont. They were first found recorded in a local diary which the author verified with an old man who vouched for their truth—and said his father was among those operated on. The practise is not commonly carried on today.

"*January 7*—I went on the mountain today and witnessed what to me was a horrible sight. It seems that the dwellers there who are unable either from age or other reasons to contribute to the support of their families are disposed of in the winter months.

"I will describe what I saw. Six persons, four men and two women, one man a cripple about thirty years old, the other five past the age of usefulness, lay on the earthy floor of the cabin drugged into insensibility, while members of the families were gathered about them in apparent indifference. In a short time the unconscious bodies were inspected by one man who said: 'They are ready.' They were then stripped of all their clothing except a single garment. The bodies were carried outside and laid on logs exposed to the bitter cold mountain air, the operation having been delayed several days for suitable weather.

"Soon the noses, ears, and fingers began to turn white, then the limbs and faces assumed a tallowy look. I could stand the cold no longer and went inside, where I found the friends in cheerful conversation. In about an hour I went out and looked at the bodies. They were fast freezing.

"Again I went inside where the men were smoking their clay pipes but silence had fallen on them. Perhaps they were thinking that the time would come when they would be carried out in the same way. I could not shut out the sight of the freezing bodies outside, neither could I bear to be in darkness, but I piled on the wood in the cavernous fireplace and, seated on a single block, passed the dreary night, terror-stricken by the horrible sights I had witnessed.

"*January 8*—Day came at length but did not dissipate the terror that filled me. The frozen bodies became visibly white on the snow that lay in huge drifts about them. The women gathered about the fire and soon began to prepare breakfast. The men awoke and affairs assumed a more cheerful aspect.

"After breakfast the men lighted their pipes and some of them took a yoke of oxen and went off into the forest, while others proceeded to nail together boards making a box about ten feet long and half as high and wide. When this was completed they placed about two feet of straw in the bottom. Then they laid three frozen bodies in the straw. Then the faces and upper part of the bodies were covered with a cloth; more straw was put in the box and the other three bodies placed on top, and covered the same as the first ones, with cloth and straw.

"Boards were then firmly nailed on top to protect the bodies from being injured by carnivorous animals that made their home on these mountains. By this time the men who had gone off with the ox team returned with a huge load of spruce and hemlock boughs which they unloaded at the foot of a steep ledge, came to the house and loaded the box containing the bodies on the sled, and drew it near the load of boughs.

"These were soon piled on and around the box and it was left to be covered with snow, which I was told would lie in drifts twenty feet deep over this rude tomb. 'We shall want our men to plant our corn next spring,' said the wife of one of the frozen men, 'and if you want to see them resuscitated, you come here about the tenth of next May.'

"With this agreement I left the mountaineers, living and frozen, to their fate and returned to my home in Boston, where it was weeks before I was fairly myself."

Turning the leaves of the diary, I came to the following entry:

"*May 10*—I arrived here at ten a.m. after riding about four hours over muddy, unsettled roads. The weather here is warm and pleasant, most of the snow is gone except where there are drifts in the fence corners and hollows. But nature is not yet dressed in green.

"I found the same parties here I left last January. They were ready to disinter the bodies, but I had no expectations of finding life there. A feeling that I could not resist, however, impelled me to come and see.

"We repaired at once to the well-remembered spot at the ledge. The snow had melted from the top of the brush, but still lay deep around the bottom of the pile. The men commenced work at once, some shoveling, and others tearing away the brush. Soon the box was visible. The cover was taken off, the layers of straw removed, and the bodies, frozen and apparently lifeless, lifted out and laid on the snow.

"Large troughs made out of hemlock logs were placed nearby filled with tepid water, into which the bodies were placed separately with the head slightly raised. Boiling water was then poured into the trough from kettles hung on poles nearby until the water was as hot as I could hold my hand in. Hemlock boughs had been put in the boiling water in such quantities that they had given the water the color of wine.

"After lying in the bath about an hour, color began to return to the bodies, when all hands began rubbing and chafing them. This continued about an hour when a slight twitching of the muscles followed by audible gasps, showed that vitality was returning.

"Spirits were then given in small quantities and allowed to trickle down their throats. Soon they could swallow and more was given them when their eyes opened and they began to talk, and finally sat up in their bath-tubs.

"They were taken out and assisted to the house where after a hearty meal they seemed as well as ever and in no wise injured, but rather, refreshed by their long sleep of four months."

Human Hibernation: The Mystery Solved

AMONG THE many with whom I discussed this mystery [of "frozen sleep"

From *Yankee Yarns*, by Alton H. Blackington, pp. 144, 146–149. Copyright, 1954, by Alton H. Blackington. New York: Reprinted by permission of Dodd, Mead & Company.

treatment] was Roland Wells Robbins, a local archeologist with a penchant for digging up facts. . . .

* * * * *

Mr. Robbins toured the towns within a twenty-five miles radius of Mont-pelier, where the freezings were said to have taken place. Almost everyone knew the story, but no one could add anything new.

Hoping someone would yet come forward with the information he wanted, Robbins prepared a lengthy article which was published in the 1949 winter edition of *Vermont Life,* the official publication of the State of Vermont. The following (spring 1950) issue said editorially, "The article on 'Human Hibernation' evoked an avalanche of letters, phone calls and newspaper comment. One columnist suggests that [the mysterious author who signed himself] 'A.M.' might have been some member of the Atkins family, who owned and published the *Argus & Patriot* in 1887. Several members of that family have initials 'M.A.' which might simply be reversed."

But Robbins had already interviewed Miss Elaine Atkins, editor and publisher of the Montpelier *Argus* (now a daily) and reached another dead end. Old office records had been destroyed by flood or by fire; there was nothing left to identify old-time contributors.

Among the letters which Robbins received, one from Florida seemed promising. Mrs. Mabel E. Hynes wrote, "The A.M. you are looking for was my grandfather, Allen Morse." Robbins would have liked to have jumped a plane that very day, but his [archeological] duties at the [site of the First] Iron Works kept him in Saugus, and impatiently he sweated it out until Mrs. Hynes returned to her home in Massachusetts where he could talk to her.

This is what he learned: Allen Morse was born in Woodbury, Vermont, on December 21, 1835. The family moved to Calais, Vermont, in 1840, and there he lived most of his life. He had four children, three girls and one boy. The eldest girl, Alice May Morse (Mrs. Hynes' mother), secured her first employment in the *Argus & Patriot* office in Montpelier and "took board and room" with the publisher, Hiram Atkins.

Like most Vermonters, Allen Morse devoted much of his time to farming, but he was also of a literary bent and frequently wrote pieces for the *New England Homestead* and for *Farm & Fireside.* That he was progressive and thrifty is shown by his purchasing the first parlor organ and the first sewing machine in that section of Vermont. The organ was used freely for Sunday night gatherings, but neighbors were charged by the yard when they borrowed the sewing machine.

Allen Morse was noted as story teller, and no family reunion or Christmas party went by that he wasn't called upon to spin a few yarns. Benjamin Morse, his cousin, was runner-up, and considerable rivalry existed between A.M. and B.M. to see who could tell the tallest tale.

Benjamin's favorite spell-binder concerned a grave which burst into flame, and not to be outdone, Allen Morse concocted his freezing story, using familiar local spots to make it sound real. The cabin where the bodies were prepared was an old deserted log house near the Morse farm, and the ledge where they lay under the snow was Eagle Ledge, on the road between Calais and East Elmore. And incidentally, the snow has been known to drift to a depth of twenty feet and more at that particular place.

The "Uncle William" mentioned was a brother-in-law, William Noyes.

Mrs. Hynes explained, "My mother left the *Argus & Patriot* after she married and moved to Connecticut, but she frequently came back to Vermont for short visits. Around the middle of December, 1887, she called on her former employer, Hiram Atkins, and suggested he print her father's favorite story on his birthday."

Editor Atkins read over the handwritten pages about the alleged freezings and smiled. "I'll print it if you'll set it." So, borrowing an apron and a composing stick, Allen Morse's daughter set the type from which "A Strange Tale, by A.M." was printed on her father's fifty-second birthday, December 21, 1887.

Over in Bridgewater, Mrs. Hannah Stevens, interested by the story, cut it out and pasted it into her scrapbook, never dreaming that half a century later, authors, editors, newspaper reporters and photographers would be pestering her son Elbert for just a peek at the old clipping. And how surprised "A.M." would have been to read in all the books and papers and magazines this tall tale he had invented in his effort to tell a bigger lie than his cousin!

In spite of the fact that this famous Vermont legend has been debunked, it will still be told when Yankee families gather round their firesides on future winter nights. Fiction though it was, it caught the public's interest, and fooled not a few. And, considering what has been accomplished since that time with low-temperature treatments in medical research, who can say that it was not prophetic?

Fog Yarn

THE fogs that sometimes envelop Nantucket gave rise to a pleasant fiction, which smacks of the salt. A whaling ship, outward-bound, having been caught in one of unusual density in leaving the port, the captain made a peculiar mark in it [the fog] with a harpoon, and on his return, after a three years' cruise, fell in with the harbor at the very same spot.

From *Nooks and Corners of the New England Coast,* by Samuel Adams Drake, p. 349. Entered according to Act of Congress, in the year 1875, by Harper & Brothers, in the Office of the Librarian of Congress, at Washington. New York.

Shingling Out onto the Fog

A RATHER loquacious individual was endeavoring to draw an old man into conversation, but hitherto without much success, the old fellow having sufficient discernment to see that his object was to make a little sport for the passengers at his expense. At length says loquacious individual: "I suppose you consider Down East a right smart place; but I guess it would puzzle them to get up quite so thick a fog as we are having here this morning, wouldn't it?" "Well," said the old man, "I don't know about that. I hired one of your Massachusetts chaps to work for me last summer, and one rather foggy mornin' I sent him down to the meadow to lay a few courses of shingle on a new barn I was finishin' off. At dinner-time the fellow came up, and, sez he, 'That's an almighty long barn of yourn.' Sez I, 'Not very long.' 'Well,' sez he, 'I've been to work all this forenoon, and haven't got one course laid yet.' 'Well,' sez I, 'you're a lazy fellow, that's all I've got to say.' And so after dinner I went down to see what he'd been about, and I'll be thundered ef he hadn't shingled more than a hundred foot *right out on to the fog*."

Maine's Woodland Terrors

IT IS feared that some of the creatures which infest the woods of Aroostook, Piscataquis, and Penobscot counties, especially in the lumbering season, have had their mischievous qualities magnified in local myths for the silencing of fretful children and the stimulation of generosity on the part of green choppers. It is the newcomer in a lumber-camp who is expected to supply the occasional quart of whiskey that shall pacify Razor-shins, and to do a little more than his share of the breakfast-getting, errand-running, and so on, in order to quiet the hostility of the will-am-alones. Like the duppies and rolling calves of the West Indies, these creatures are not seen as often as they were, for they have a fixed hostility to schools, never venturing within ten miles of one.

The will-am-alone is a quick little animal, like a squirrel, that rolls in its fingers poison-lichens into balls and drops them into the ears and on the eyelids of sleeping men in camp, causing them to have strange dreams and headaches and to see unusual objects in the snow. It is the hardest drinkers in the camp who are said to be most easily and most often affected by the poison. The liquor in prohibition States is always plentiful and bad,

From *The American Joe Miller:* A Collection of Yankee Wit and Humour, Compiled by Robert Kempt, pp. 57–58. Entered at Stationer's Hall. London. Adams and Francis. 1865.

From *American Myths and Legends*, by Charles M. Skinner, Vol. I, pp. 34–38. Copyright, 1903, by J. B. Lippincott. Philadelphia and London.

and in combination with the pellets of the will-am-alones is nearly fatal.

More odd than this animal is the side-hill winder, a rabbit-like creature so called because he winds about steep hills in only one direction; and in order that his back may be kept level, the down-hill legs are longer than the up-hill pair. He is seldom caught; but the way to kill him is to head him off with dogs when he is corkscrewing up a mountain. As the winder turns, his long legs come on the up-hill side and tip him over, an easy prey. His fat is a cure for diseases caused by the will-am-alone, but to eat his flesh is to die a hard and sudden death.

Much to be dreaded is the ding-ball, a panther whose last tail-joint is ball shaped and bare of flesh. With this weapon it cracks its victim's skull. There is no record of a survival from the blow of a ding-ball. In older traditions it sang with a human voice, thus luring the incautious from their cabins to have their sconces broken in the dark. It is fond of human flesh, and will sing all night for a meal of Indians.

An unpleasant person is Razor-shins, a deathless red man who works for such as are kind to him, but mutilates that larger number of the ignorant who neglect to pay tribute. Keep Razor-shins supplied with fire-water,— a jug at every full moon,—and he will now and then fell a tree for you with his sharp shin-bones, if nobody is around, or will clear up a bit of road. But fail in this, and you must be prepared to give up your scalp, which he can slice from your head with a single kick, or he will clip off your ears and leave cuts on you that will look like sabre-strokes. When a green hand arrives in a lumber-camp it is his duty to slake the thirst of Razor-shins. He puts a jug of virulent Bangor whiskey at the door. The best proof that the Indian gets it is shown in the odor of breathed alcohol that pervades the premises all night and the emptiness of the jug in the morning.

Where French Canucks are employed at chopping, you must look to see them all quit work if a white owl flies from any tree they are felling; and they must not look back nor speak to it, for it is a ghost and will trouble them unless they leave that part of the wood for fully thirty days.

But worst of all is the windigo, that ranges from Labrador to Moosehead Lake, preferring the least populous and thickest wooded districts. A Canadian Indian known as Sole-o'-your-foot is the only man who ever saw one and lived—for merely to look upon the windigo is doom, and to cross his track is deadly peril. There is no need to cross the track, for it is plain enough. His footprints are twenty-four inches long, and in the middle of each impress is a red spot, showing where his blood has oozed through a hole in his mocassin; for the windigo, dark and huge and shadowy as he seems, has yet a human shape and many human attributes. The belief in this monster is so genuine that lumbermen have secured a monopoly of certain jobs by scaring competitors out of the neighborhood through the simple device of tramping past their camp in furcovered snow-shoes and squeezing a drop of beef blood or paint into each footprint. There was at one time a general flight of Indian choppers from a lumber district in Canada, and nothing could persuade them to return to work; for the track of the windigo had been seen. It was found that this particular windigo was an Irishman who wanted that territory for himself and his friends; but the Indians would not be convinced. They kept away for the rest of the season. The stealthy stride of the monster makes every lumberman's blood run as cold as the Androscoggin under its ice roof, and its voice is like the moaning of the pines.

The Tote-Road Shagamaw

FROM the Rangeley Lakes to the Allegash and across in New Brunswick loggers tell of an animal which has puzzled many a man, even those who were not strangers in the woods. Frequently the report is circulated that the tracks of a bear have been seen near camp, but a little later this is denied and moose tracks are reported instead. Heated arguments among the men, sometimes resulting in fist fights, are likely to follow. It is rightly considered an insult to a woodsman to accuse him of not being able to distinguish the track of either of these animals. To only a few of the old timber cruisers and rivermen is the explanation of these changing tracks known. Gus Demo, of Oldtown, Maine, who has hunted and trapped and logged in the Maine woods for 40 years, once came upon what he recognized as the tracks of a moose. After following it for about 80 rods it changed abruptly into unmistakable bear tracks; another 80 rods and it changed to moose tracks again. It was soon observed by Mr. Demo that these changes took place precisely every quarter of a mile, and, furthermore, that whatever was making the tracks always followed a tote road or a blazed line through the woods. Coming up within sight of the animal, Gus saw that it had front feet like a bear's and hind feet like those of a moose, and that it was pacing carefully, taking exactly a yard at a step. Suddenly it stopped, looked all about, and swung as on a pivot, then inverting itself and walking on its front feet only, it resumed its pacing. Mr. Demo was only an instant in recognizing by the witness trees that the place where the animal changed was a section corner. From this fact he reasoned that the shagamaw must have been originally a very imitative animal, which, from watching surveyors, timber cruisers, and trappers patiently following lines through the woods, contracted the habit itself. He figures that the shagamaw can count only as high as 440; therefore it must invert itself every quarter of a mile.

From *Fearsome Creatures of the Lumberwoods, With a Few Desert and Mountain Beasts,* by William T. Cox, p. 23. Copyright, 1911, by William T. Cox. Washington, D. C.: Press of Judd & Detweiler, Inc.

Gazerium and Snydae

FROM Maine comes news of two extinct creatures, the *gazerium* and the *snydae*. Both, according to Richard G. Kendall, a specialist in unearthly zoölogy highly esteemed in that great State, were found only along the Kennebec river, and were favorite delicacies of the Kennebec Indians and the early white settlers. Kendall says that the *gazerium* resembled a shrimp, but had two legs forward and only one aft, and that it fed chiefly upon the *snydae,* which were minute forms of marine life. The *snydae,* in turn, fed upon the eggs of the *gazerium,* so the two species gradually exterminated each other. He adds:

The Kennebecs usually cooked the *gazerium* in deep fat. It tasted something like a French fried potato, with just a hint of the flavor of cocktail sauce imparted to it by its diet of *snydae.*[1]

Gyascutus

DURING my boyhood on a Vermont farm the *gyascutus* or cute cuss, was not a rare barnyard animal. He or the female of the species, *gyascuta,* which we affectionately called the *cuter cuss,* were as necessary as the cow to most Vermont farmers. Indeed, without the *gyascutus,* dairy farming in Vermont would have been restricted to the narrow lowlands, the riverside meadows that probably do not account for more than one-tenth of one per cent. of Vermont's acreage. . . .

Obviously, the ordinary cow cannot clamber over Vermont pastures. The early settlers, bringing cows from other States, quickly learned this, and for several years a problem worse than the Indians . . . was that of getting cows to and from pasture. It took two men for each cow and the task was comparable to teaching her to go up and down a ladder.

But the *gyascutus* had legs shorter on one side than on the other, so it could circumambulate the Vermont hills with the greatest ease. The Vermonters immediately understood they must have cows with the *gyascutus's* running gear, so they domesticated the creature and by interbreeding developed a new breed of cattle. Today, as all Americans should know, all Vermont calves are born with legs shorter on one side than the other. . . .

From *Supplement I: The American Language,* An Inquiry into the Development of English in the United States, by H. L. Mencken, p. 251. Copyright, 1945, by Alfred A. Knopf, Inc. New York.

[1] "Journal of a Journeyman," Portland *Press Herald,* March 20, 1944.—H. L. M.

From "A Cuter Cuss for a Pet," by William H. Heath, in the Haverhill (Mass.) *Gazette,* March 18, 1944, p. 4. Cited in *Supplement I: The American Language,* An Inquiry into the Development of English in the United States, by H. L. Mencken, pp. 247–248. Copyright, 1945, by Alfred A. Knopf, Inc. New York.

[1] Mr. Heath, in March, 1944, asked his father in Vermont to search the attic of the family homestead "for an old snapshot of the female of the species that was a pet of my boyhood." Unfortunately, it could not be found.—H. L. M.

Some *gyascutuses,* or *gyuscuti,* survived in an unadulterated state even as recently as the period of my boyhood. They were cherished by the farmers as evidence of Providence's concern for their welfare. We recall one especially affectionate *gyascuta* that was strongly attached to us in our early youth. How many times we have trudged to school in tears at the sight of the *cuter cuss's* attempts to follow us on a road made for legs of equal length.[1]

The Come-at-a-Body

REPORTED by Mr. B. B. Bickford of Gorham, N. H. Not found outside the White Mountains. A short, stubby, rather small animal, resembling a woodchuck but having very soft, velvety, kitten-like fur. Harmless, but surprising. Has the terrifying habit of suddenly rushing directly at you from the brush, then stopping only a few inches away and spitting like a cat. A strong mink-like scent is thrown, and the Come-at-a-Body rushes away.

From *Fearsome Critters,* by Henry H. Tryon, p. 13. Copyright, 1939, by Idlewild Press. Cornwall, New York.

PART TWO

MYTHS, LEGENDS, AND TRADITIONS

*Jonathan is conscious still that he lives in the world
of the Unseen as well as of the Seen.*
—JAMES RUSSELL LOWELL

*. . . fabulous rumors naturally grow out of the
very body of all surprising terrible events—as the
smitten tree gives birth to its fungi.*
—HERMAN MELVILLE

*Tradition . . . sometimes brings down truth that
history has let slip, but is oftener the wild babble
of the time, such as was formerly spoken at the fireside and now congeals in newspapers.*
—NATHANIEL HAWTHORNE

*It may be said, then, that while History has its
truth, the Legend has its own; both taking for their
end the portrayal of Man as he has existed in every
age,—a creature in whom the imagination is supreme, and who performs deeds terrible or heroic
according as it may be aroused into action.*
—SAMUEL ADAMS DRAKE

I. WONDERS OF THE INVISIBLE WORLD

Such Divine Judgements, Tempests, Floods, Earth-quakes, Thunders as are unusual, strange Apparitions, or what ever else shall happen that is Prodigious, Witchcrafts, Diabolical Possessions, Remarkable Judgements upon noted Sinners, eminent Deliverances, and Answers of Prayer, are to be reckoned among Illustrious Providences.—INCREASE MATHER

. . . these with many other stories they told me, the credit whereof I will neither impeach nor inforce, but shall satisfie my self, and I hope the Reader hereof, with the saying of a wise, learned and honourable knight, that there are many stranger things in the world, than are to be seen between *London and Stanes.*
—JOHN JOSSELYN

1. PROVIDENCES AND PRODIGIES

THE early history of New England is filled with accounts of "surprising terrible events" and "fabulous rumors" no less marvelous than the local wonders of travelers' and tall tales and similarly arising out of a pious or playful belief in the impossible. For before the New Englander became a Yankee, he was a Puritan; and the superstitious seventeenth century gave credence and currency to remarkable providences and memorable accidents such as were recorded by the Mathers for the improvement of religion and by historians like Edward Johnson intent on showing the "wonder-working providence of Sion's Saviour in New England."

In their desire to found a great church and a great state in Massachusetts the Puritans were convinced that God showed a providential regard for his children by delivering them from the perils of the sea and the wilderness, protecting them from the Indians, and otherwise providing for their needs. At the same time, "*these* too were tryed with very humbling circumstances," and in answer to "fervent prayers" God often "condescended" an "extraordinary account" for the "quieting of their afflicted spirits." Such was the vision of the New Haven Specter Ship which appeared in the sky over New Haven harbor in June, 1647, and revealed to the "admiring spectators" the "tragick end" of the ship of which they had had no news for six months.

These prodigies differed from the omens of the ancients in that they were providential rather than accidental, but they invoked the same awe and dread of the shadows that coming events cast before them. Thus, in his history of King Philip's war, Increase Mather declared that "It is a common observation, verified by the experience of many ages, that great and publick calamityes seldome come upon any place without prodigious warnings to forerun and signify what is to be expected."

Two notable accounts have come down to us of public calamities that failed to materialize, with heroi-comic rather than tragic effects and implications. In April, 1775, a baseless rumor of impending British invasion swept the town of Ipswich and threw the populace into a ridiculous frenzy of terror and flight, which Whittier rationalizes as "a prudent and wholesome regard to their own comfort and safety" and the safety of their "hard-gained property." Earlier, on a July night in 1758, the alarmed residents of Windham were routed from their beds by the fiendish outcries of what they took to be attacking Indians but what proved to be bull frogs fighting for water in a nearly dried-up pond.

2. History *versus* Myth

Erroneous perception such as underlay the Ipswich and Windham frights also gave rise to legends like the *Palatine* Light. Tradition says that in the first half of the eighteenth century (1752, according to one source), the ship *Palatine* "sailed from some German port, laden with well-to-do emigrants, bound to Philadelphia; that the captain died or was killed on the passage; that the officers and crew starved and plundered the helpless emigrants, and finally, in their boats, abandoned the vessel, which drifted ashore. . . . The ship was undoubtedly burned." [1]

So much for "history." Now for myth.

A part of her legend is that she was somehow changed into a ship of fire, rising up from the waters of Block Island Sound, which separates the Island from the main land, and gracefully sailing on this tack or that, mysteriously manned by an invisible captain and crew, until hull, spars, ropes, and sails all slowly vanished in the air or settled down into the deep. Nor was all of this a myth, or an *ignis fatuus*. For there is ample evidence that a very strange light once performed very strange freaks over those waters. . . .

Upon analyzing the legend and attempting to find a satisfactory explanation, Reverend S. T. Livermore arrived at the conclusion that there was no connection between the burning of the *Palatine* [2] (by pillaging Block Islanders, according to a tradition which Reverend Livermore stoutly denies) and the *Palatine* Light, and that possibly the latter "was fed by gas rising through the water." At the same time he admits: "Of this phenomenon no satisfactory explanation has ever been given, while much talent has been employed in making it instrumental in gratifying the taste for the marvelous."

3. Nature Myths

In 1817 a similar zeal for the truth led the Linnean Society of Boston to undertake an investigation of the Gloucester sea-serpent, taking the sworn

---

[1] For this and subsequent passages regarding the *Palatine* Light, see Rev. S. T. Livermore, *Block Island* (Hartford, 1882), pp. 92–105.

[2] The records show that the ship was wrecked in the Bay of Bengal in 1784.

depositions of twelve witnesses. Yet, for all its scientific effort in collecting testimony, the Committee fell into the vulgar and absurd error of a false hypothesis, declaring that a common land-snake, found on shore shortly after the appearance of the serpent, was "of the same species."

The history of the sea-serpent proves that, far from being killed by the historical and scientific impulse, the myth-making imagination may exist alongside of it and that in building up elaborate hypotheses based on hearsay or misinformation, myth often resembles tall tale as a form of hoaxing and practical joking. This is especially true in the realm of natural history, where attempts to establish corroborative evidence recall Defoe's method, as in "The Strange Apparition of Mrs. Veal," of employing "ingenious confirmation" to divert attention from the basis in "anonymous evidence."

Far from being limited to the common people, myth, like superstition, is also found among the learned men of early New England, often in the same breath with a scientific statement. Thus, in addition to his snake stories, Cotton Mather, in 1717, sent the Royal Society a miraculous cure for snakebite—*Ophiophuga, Cottonis Mather.*

> A *Poultiss* of this bruised and laid to the Part Bitten by the *Rattle-Snake,* it immediately fetches out the *Deadly Poyson:* it's also remarkable, that if put into the *Shoes,* no *Serpent* will dare to come near them. A *Tea* of it is a good *Ophthalmiack.*[1]

4. GHOST-RIDDEN AND DEVIL-DOOMED

As a corollary to the belief in providence or divine intervention (supernatural phenomena), the seventeenth century believed in "diabolical operations" (preternatural phenomena). As Melville says, "in maritime life, far more than in that of terra firma, wild rumors abound, wherever there is any adequate reality for them to cling to." Perhaps the noblest and terriblest embodiment of the maleficent forces of the universe is Moby-Dick, the white whale, the "rumors and portents" of whose savagery, ubiquitousness, immortality, and whiteness fired the apocalyptic imagination of Melville.

With the accusing ghost who returns to avenge a wrong or the devil-doomed spirit condemned to the endless repetition of a Sisyphean task, as with the doom that follows a prophetic curse, and like occult tales, we are once more in the kingdom of morality, where the sense of a divine order, as well as the taste for the marvelous, is satisfied by retributive or poetic justice.

B. A. B.

---

[1] George Lyman Kittredge, *Letters of Samuel Lee and Samuel Sewall Relating to New England and the Indians, The Publications of the Colonial Society of Massachusetts* (Cambridge, 1912), p. 184.

SINGULAR OCCURRENCES

The New Haven Specter Ship

BEHOLD, a fourth colony of New-English Christians, in a manner *stolen* into the world, and a colony, indeed, *constellated* with many stars of the first magnitude. The colony was under the conduct of as holy, and as prudent, and as genteel persons as most that ever visited these nooks of America; and yet *these* too were tryed with very humbling circumstances.

Being Londoners, or merchants and men of traffick and business, their design was in a manner wholly to apply themselves unto *trade;* but the design failing, they found their great estates sink so fast, that they must quickly *do something.* Whereupon in the year 1646, gathering together almost all the strength which was left them, they built one ship more, which they fraighted for England with the best part of their tradable estates; and sundry of their eminent persons embarked themselves in her for the voyage. But, alas! the ship was never after heard of: she foundred in the sea; and in her were lost, not only the *hopes* of their future trade, but also the *lives* of several excellent persons, as well as divers *manuscripts* of some great men in the country, sent over for the service of the church, which were now buried in the ocean. The fuller story of that grievous matter, let the reader with a just astonishment accept from the pen of the reverend person who is now the pastor of New-Haven. I wrote unto him for it, and was thus answered:

"REVEREND AND DEAR SIR—

"In compliance with your desires, I now give you the relation of that APPARITION of a SHIP IN THE AIR, which I have received from the most credible, judicious and curious surviving observers of it.

"In the year 1647, besides much other lading, a far more rich treasure of passengers, (five or six of which were persons of chief note and worth in New Haven) put themselves on board a new ship, built at Rhode Island, of about 150 tuns; but so walty, that the master (Lamberton) often said she would prove their grave. In the month of January, cutting their way through much ice, on which they were accompanied with the Reverend Mr. Davenport, besides many other friends, with many fears, as well as prayers and tears, they set sail. Mr. Davenport, in prayer, with an observable emphasis, used these words: 'Lord, if it be thy pleasure to bury these

From *Magnalia Christi Americana;* or, The Ecclesiastical History of New England, from Its First Planting, in the year 1620, unto the Year of Our Lord 1698, in Seven Books, by Cotton Mather, Volume I, pp. 83–84. Entered, according to Act of Congress, in the year 1852, by Silas Andrus & Son, in the Clerk's Office of the District Court of Connecticut. Hartford. 1853.

our friends in the bottom of the sea, they are thine; save them!' The spring following, no tidings of these friends arrived with the ships from England: New Haven's heart began to fail her: this put the godly people on much prayer, both publick and private, 'that the Lord would (if it was his pleasure) let them hear what he had done with their dear friends, and prepare them with a suitable submission to his Holy Will.' In June next ensuing, a great thunder storm arose out of the north-west; after which (the hemisphere being serene) about an hour before sun-set, a ship of like dimensions with the aforesaid, with her canvas and colours abroad (though the wind northernly) appeared in the air coming up from our harbour's mouth, which lyes southward from the town, seemingly with her sails filled under a fresh gale, holding her course north, and continuing under observation, sailing against the wind for the space of half an hour.

"Many were drawn to behold this great work of God; yea, the very children cryed out, 'There's a brave ship!' At length, crowding up as far as there is usually water sufficient for such a vessel, and so near some of the spectators, as that they imagined a man might hurl a stone on board her, her *main-top* seemed to be blown off, but left hanging in the shrouds; then her *mizzen-top;* then all her *masting* seemed blown away by the board: quickly after the *hulk* brought unto a careen, she overset, and so vanished into a smoaky cloud, which in some time dissipated, leaving, as everywhere else, a clear air. The admiring spectators could distinguish the several colours of each part, the principal rigging, and such proportions, as caused not only the generality of persons to say, 'This was the mould of their ship, and this was her tragick end,' but Mr. Davenport also in publick declared to this effect, 'That God had condescended, for the quieting of their afflicted spirits, this extraordinary account of his sovereign disposal of those for whom so many fervent prayers were made continually.' Thus I am Sir,   "Your humble servant,

                                                  "JAMES PIERPONT"

Reader, there being yet living so many credible gentlemen, that were eyewitness of this *wonderful* thing, I venture to publish it for a thing as *undoubted* as 'tis wonderful.

The Moodus Noises

CONTEMPORARY ACCOUNTS [1]

FROM time immemorial, East Haddam has been the seat of uncommon subterranean noises, called Moodus noises. The Indian name of the town

---

[1] From *Connecticut Historical Collections*, Containing A General Collection of Interesting Facts, Traditions, Biographical Sketches, Anecdotes, &c., Relating to the History and Antiquities of Every Town in Connecticut, with Geographical Descriptions, by John Warner Barber, pp. 525–528. Entered according to the Act of Congress, in the year 1836, by John W. Barber and A. Willard, in the Clerk's Office, of the District Court of Connecticut. New Haven and Hartford.

was *Mackimoodus,* which in English is the *place of noises;* a name given with the utmost propriety to the place. The accounts given of the noises and quakings there are very remarkable. Were it not that the people are accustomed to them,- they would occasion great alarm. The Rev. Mr. Hosmer, in a letter to Mr. Prince, of Boston, written August 13th, 1729, gives this account of them:—"As to the earthquakes, I have something considerable and awful to tell you. Earthquakes have been here, (and no where but in this precinct, as can be discerned; that is, they seem to have their centre, rise and origin among us,) as has been observed for more than thirty years. I have been informed, that in this place, before the English settlements, there were great numbers of Indian inhabitants, and that it was a place of extraordinary *Indian Pawaws,* or in short, that it was a place where the Indians drove a prodigious trade at worshipping the devil. Also I was informed, that, many years past, an old Indian was asked, What was the reason of the noises in this place? To which he replied, that the Indian's God was very angry because Englishman's God was come here.

"Now whether there be any thing diabolical in these things, I know not; but this I know, that God Almighty is to be seen and trembled at, in what has been often heard among us. Whether it be fire or air distressed in the subterraneous caverns of the earth, cannot be known; for there is no eruption, no explosion perceptible, but by sounds and tremors, which sometimes are very fearful and dreadful. I have myself heard eight or ten sounds successively, and imitating small arms, in the space of five minutes. I have, I suppose, heard several hundreds of them within twenty years; some more, some less terrible. Sometimes we have heard them almost every day, and great numbers of them in the space of a year. Often times I have observed them to be coming down from the north, imitating slow thunder, until the sound came near or right under, and then there seemed to be a breaking like the noise of a cannon shot, or severe thunder, which shakes the houses, and all that is in them. They have in a manner ceased; since the great earthquake. As I remember, there have been but two heard since that time, and those but moderate."

A worthy gentleman, about six years since, gave the following account of them. "The awful noises, of which Mr. Hosmer gave an account, in his historical minutes, and concerning which you desire further information, continue to the present time. The effects they produce, are various as the intermediate degrees between the roar of a cannon and the noise of a pistol. The concussions of the earth, made at the same time, are as much diversified as the sounds in the air. The shock they give to a dwelling house, is the same as the falling of logs on the floor. The smaller shocks produced no emotions of terror or fear in the minds of the inhabitants. They are spoken of as usual occurrences, and are called Moodus noises. But when they are so violent as to be felt in the adjacent towns, they are called earthquakes. During my residence here, which has been almost thirty-six years, I have invariably observed, after some of the most violent of these shocks, that an account has been published in the newspapers, of a small shock of an earthquake, at New London and Hartford. Nor do I believe, in all that period, there has been any account published of an earthquake in Connecticut, which was not far more violent here than in any other place. By recurring to the newspapers, you will find, that an earthquake was noticed on the 18th May, 1791, about 10 o'clock, P.M. It was perceived as far distant as Boston and New York. A few minutes after there was another shock, which was perceptible at the distance of seventy miles. Here, at that time, the concussion of the earth, and the roaring of the atmosphere, were most tremendous. Consternation and dread filled every house. Many chimnies[*sic*] were untopped and walls thrown down. It was a night much to be remembered; for besides the two shocks which were noticed at a distance during the night there was here a succession of shocks, to the number of twenty, perhaps thirty; the effects of which, like all others, decreased in every direction, in proportion to the distances. The next day, stones of several tons weight, were found removed from their places; and apertures in the earth, and fissures in immovable rocks, ascertained the places where the explosions were made. Since that time, the noises and shocks have been less frequent than before; though not a year passeth over us, but some of them are perceptible." *

Mount Tom is situated at the junction of Moodus with Salmon river. . . . This mountain seems to be situated about the centre from which the Moodus noises proceed. The severest shocks are felt as far N. Easterly as Boston, and as far S. West as New York, and there noticed as earthquakes. In 1816 and 1817, in the night, these noises were more than usually violent. A person was on Mount Tom about 15 years since, at the time these noises were heard. It appeared to this person as though a stone or large body fell underneath the ground directly under his feet, and grated down to a considerable distance in the depths below. The cause of these noises is explained by some to be mineral or chemical combinations, exploding at a depth of many thousand feet beneath the surface of the earth. The jar is similar to that of exploded gun powder.

*   *   *   *   *

. . . "Various have been the conjectures concerning the cause of these earthquakes or Moodus noises, as they are called. The following account has gained credit with many persons.—It is reported that, between 20 and 30 years ago, a transient person came to this town, who called himself Doctor Steel, from Great Britain, who having had information respecting those noises, made critical observation at different times and in different places, till at length he dug up two pearls of great value, which he called Carbuncles, near Salmon river;—and that he told people the noises would be discontinued for many years, as he had taken away their cause; but as he had discovered others in miniature, they would be again heard in process of time. The best evidence of the authenticity of this story is, that

---

* The foregoing account is from Trumbull's *History of Connecticut.*

it has happened agreeably to his prophecy. The noises did cease for many years, and have again been heard for two or three years past, and they increase—three shocks have been felt in a short space, one of which acording to a late paper was felt at New London, though it was by the account much more considerable in this and the adjacent towns." *

AN INTERVIEW [2]

I inquired particularly about these noises of two men who were sitting on the post office piazza. "We still have one once in a while," the older man said. "The ground shakes and there's a noise like a cannon going off or a rumblin' like thunder. It woke me up once in the night and the dishes were rattling on the buttery shelves. You remember old Hardy, don't you, Fred?"

"Yes," the younger man replied, "he gave me a horse-whipping one time when I was a boy."

"Well," the older man resumed, "he tells of being at work on the medder one day when the ground shook so strong that it brought the cattle down on their knees. The noises are made by gas and dead air exploding underground. They start a mile and a half from here on Cave Hill. Right in the side of that high hill there's a cave you can walk into for about forty rods. You can keep going until the air gets so stagnant that your light goes out. Then it's time for you to start back."

"We use to have quite a famous drum corps here," Fred remarked, "and some one made up a piece of poetry about that and the Moodus earthquake. The words were:

> "A man from Texas tall and stout
> Stuck up his nose and hollered out,
> 'Oh, what is that infernal noise?'
> 'Twas nothing but the Drum Corps boys."

The Windham Frogs

MUCH pleasantry has been indulged at the expense of the inhabitants of Windham, on account of a singular occurrence which happened in the year

---

* From the *Connecticut Gazette* (New London), August 20, 1790, No. 1397, dated "East Haddam, August 5, 1790."

[2] From *Highways and Byways of New England,* Including the States of Massachusetts, New Hampshire, Rhode Island, Connecticut, Vermont and Maine, Written and Illustrated by Clifton Johnson, pp. 278–279. Copyright, 1915, by The Macmillan Company. New York and London. 1916.

From *Connecticut Historical Collections,* Containing a General Collection of Interesting Facts, Traditions, Biographical Sketches, Anecdotes, &c., Relating to the History and Antiquities of Every Town in Connecticut, with Geographical Descriptions, by John Warner Barber, pp. 446–447. Entered according to the Act of Congress, in the year 1836, by John W. Barber and A. Willard, in the Clerk's Office, of the District Court of Connecticut. New Haven and Hartford.

1758, by which the inhabitants were very much frightened. The following is from a sheet recently printed in the county, entitled "Lawyers and Bullfrogs," and will show the cause of the fright. . . .

"On a dark cloudy dismal night in the month of July, A.D. 1758, the inhabitants of Windham, a small town in the Eastern part of Connecticut, had retired to rest, and for several hours, all were wrapped in profound repose—when suddenly, soon after midnight, the slumbers of the peaceful inhabitants were disturbed by a most terrific noise in the sky right over their heads, which to many, seemed the yells and screeches of infuriated Indians, and others had no other way of accounting for the awful sounds which still kept increasing, but by supposing the day of judgment had certainly come, and to their terrified imaginations, the awful uproar in the air, seemed the immediate precursor of the clangor of the last trumpet.—At intervals, many supposed they could distinguish the calling out of the particular names, as of Cols. DYER and ELDERKIN, two eminent lawyers, and this increased the general terror. . . . But soon there was a rush from every house, the tumult in the air still increasing—old and young, male and female, poured forth into the streets, *'in puris naturalibus,'* entirely forgetful, in their hurry and consternation, of their nether habiliments, and with eyes upturned tried to pierce the almost palpable darkness.—My venerable informant, who well recollects the event, says that some daring 'spirits' concluding there was nothing supernatural in the hubbub and uproar over head, but rather, that they heard the yells of Indians commencing a midnight attack, loaded their guns and sallied forth to meet the invading foes. These valiant heroes on ascending the hill that bounds the village on the East, perceived that the sounds came from that quarter, and not from the skies, as first believed, but their courage would not permit them to proceed to the daring extremity of advancing Eastward, until they had discovered the real cause of alarm and distress, which pervaded the whole village.—Towards morning the sounds in the air seemed to die away. . . . In the morning, the whole cause of alarm, which produced such distressing apprehensions among the good people of the town, was apparent to all who took the trouble to go to a certain mill pond situated about three fourths of a mile Eastward of the village.—This pond, hereafter, in the *annals of Fame,* forever to be called the FROG POND, in consequence of a severe drought, which had prevailed many weeks had become nearly dry, and the Bull Frogs, (with which it was densely *populated,*) at the mill fought a pitched battle on the sides of the ditch which ran through it, for the possession and enjoyment of the fluid which remained.—Long and obstinately was the contest maintained; and many thousands of the combatants were found defunct, on both sides of the ditch, the next morning.—It had been uncommonly still, for several hours before the battle commenced, but suddenly, as if by a preconcerted agreement, every frog on one side of the ditch, raised the war cry, Col. Dyer, Col. Dyer, and at the same instant, from the opposite side, resounded the adverse shout of Elderkin too, Elderkin too.—Owing to some peculiar state of the atmosphere, the awful noises and cries appeared, to the distressed Windhamites, to be directly over their heads. . . ."

The Great Ipswich Fright

THE 21st of April, 1775, witnessed an awful commotion in the little village of Ipswich. Old men, and boys, (the middle aged had marched to Lexington some days before,) and all the women in the place who were not bedridden or sick, came rushing as with one accord to the green in front of the meeting-house. A rumor, which no one attempted to trace or authenticate, spread from lip to lip that the British regulars had landed on the coast and were marching upon the town. A scene of indescribable terror and confusion followed. Defence was out of the question, as the young and able-bodied men of the entire region round about had marched to Cambridge and Lexington. The news of the battle at the latter place, exaggerated in all its details, had been just received; terrible stories of the atrocities committed by the dreaded "regulars" had been related; and it was believed that nothing short of a general extermination of the patriots,—men, women, and children,—was contemplated by the British commander. Almost simultaneously the people of Beverly, a village a few miles distant, were smitten with the same terror. How the rumor was communicated no one could tell. It was there believed that the enemy had fallen upon Ipswich, and massacred the inhabitants without regard to age or sex.

It was about the middle of the afternoon of this day that the people of Newbury, ten miles farther north, assembled in an informal meeting at the town-house to hear accounts from the Lexington fight and to consider what action was necessary in consequence of that event. Parson Carey was about opening the meeting with prayer when hurried hoof-beats sounded up the street, and a messenger, loose-haired and panting for breath, rushed up the staircase. "Turn out, turn out, for God's sake," he cried, "or you will be all killed! The regulars are marching on us; they are at Ipswich now, cutting and slashing all before them!" Universal consternation was the immediate result of this fearful announcement; Parson Carey's prayer died on his lips; the congregation dispersed over the town, carrying to every house the tidings that the regulars had come. Men on horseback went galloping up and down the streets shouting the alarm. Women and children echoed it from every corner. The panic became irresistible, uncontrollable. Cries were heard that the dreaded invaders had reached Oldtown Bridge, a little distance from the village, and that they were killing all

From *Prose Works of John Greenleaf Whittier,* Vol. II, pp. 115–121. Entered according to Act of Congress, in the year 1866, by John Greenleaf Whittier, in the Clerk's Office of the District Court of the District of Massachusetts. Boston: Ticknor and Fields.

For an earlier account, see Joshua Coffin, *A Sketch of the History of Newbury, Newburyport, and West Newbury, from 1635 to 1845* (Boston, 1845), pp. 245–247.

whom they encountered. Flight was resolved upon. All the horses and vehicles in the town were put in requisition; men, women, and children hurried as for life towards the north. Some threw their silver and pewter ware and other valuables-into wells. Large numbers crossed the Merrimac, and spent the night in the deserted houses of Salisbury, whose inhabitants, stricken by the strange terror, had fled into New Hampshire to take up their lodgings in dwellings also abandoned by their owners.

A few individuals refused to fly with the multitude; some, unable to move by reason of sickness, were left behind by their relatives. One old gentleman, whose excessive corpulence rendered retreat on his part impossible, made a virtue of necessity; and, seating himself in his door-way with his loaded king's arm, upbraided his more nimble neighbors, advising them to do as he did, and "stop and shoot the devils." Many ludicrous instances of the intensity of the terror might be related. One man got his family into a boat to go to Ram Island for safety. He imagined he was pursued by the enemy through the dusk of the evening, and was annoyed by the crying of an infant in the after part of the boat. "Do throw that squalling brat overboard," he called to his wife, "or we shall be all discovered and killed." A poor woman ran four or five miles up the river and stopped to take breath and nurse her child, when she found to her great horror that she had brought off the cat instead of the baby!

All through that memorable night the terror swept onward towards the north with a speed which seems almost miraculous, producing everywhere the same results. At midnight a horseman, clad only in shirt and breeches, dashed by our grandfather's door, in Haverhill, twenty miles up the river. "Turn out! Get a musket! Turn out!" he shouted; "the regulars are landing on Plum Island!"—"I'm glad of it," responded the old gentleman from his chamber-window; "I wish they were all there, and obliged to stay there." When it is understood that Plum Island is little more than a naked sand-ridge, the benevolence of this wish can be readily appreciated.

All the boats on the river were constantly employed for several hours in conveying across the terrified fugitives. Through "the dead waste and middle of the night" they fled over the border into New Hampshire. Some feared to take the frequented roads, and wandered over wooded hills and through swamps where the snows of the late winter had scarcely melted. They heard the tramp and outcry of those behind them, and fancied that the sounds were made by pursuing enemies. Fast as they fled, the terror, by some unaccountable means, outstripped them. They found houses deserted and streets strewn with household-stuffs abandoned in the hurry of escape. Towards morning, however, the tide partially turned. Grown men began to feel ashamed of their fears. The old Anglo-Saxon hardihood paused and looked the terror in its face. Single or in small parties, armed with such weapons as they found at hand,—among which long poles, sharpened and charred at the end, were conspicuous,—they began to retrace their steps. In the mean time such of the good people of Ipswich as were unable or unwilling to leave their homes became convinced that the terrible rumor which had nearly depopulated their settlement was unfounded.

Among those who had there awaited the onslaught of the regulars was a young man from Exeter, New Hampshire. Becoming satisfied that the whole matter was a delusion, he mounted his horse and followed after the retreating multitude, undeceiving all whom he overtook. Late at night he reached Newburyport, greatly to the relief of its sleepless inhabitants and hurried across the river, proclaiming as he rode the welcome tidings. The sun rose upon haggard and jaded fugitives, worn with excitement and fatigue, slowly returning homeward, their satisfaction at the absence of danger somewhat moderated by an unpleasant consciousness of the ludicrous scenes of their premature night flitting.

Any inference which might be drawn from the foregoing narrative derogatory to the character of the people of New England at that day, on the score of courage, would be essentially erroneous. It is true, they were not the men to court danger or rashly throw away their lives for the mere glory of the sacrifice. They had always a prudent and wholesome regard to their own comfort and safety; they justly looked upon sound heads and limbs as better than broken ones; life was to them too serious and important, and their hard-gained property too valuable, to be lightly hazarded. They never attempted to cheat themselves by under-estimating the difficulty to be encountered or shutting their eyes to its probable consequences. Cautious, wary, schooled in the subtle strategy of Indian warfare, where self-preservation is by no means a secondary object, they had little in common with the reckless enthusiasm of their French allies or the stolid indifference of the fighting machines of the British regular army. When danger could no longer be avoided, they met it with firmness and iron endurance, but with a very vivid appreciation of its magnitude. Indeed, it must be admitted by all who are familiar with the history of our fathers, that the element of fear held an important place among their characteristics. It exaggerated all the dangers of their earthly pilgrimage, and peopled the future with shapes of evil. Their fear of Satan invested him with some of the attributes of Omnipotence, and almost reached the point of reverence. The slightest shock of an earthquake filled all hearts with terror. Stout men trembled by their hearths with dread of some paralytic old woman supposed to be a witch. And when they believed themselves called upon to grapple with these terrors, and endure the afflictions of their allotment, they brought to the trial a capability of suffering undiminished by the chloroform of modern philosophy. They were heroic in endurance. Panics like the one we have described might bow and sway them like reeds in the wind; but they stood up like the oaks of their own forests beneath the thunder and the hail of actual calamity.

It was certainly lucky for the good people of Essex County that no wicked wag of a Tory undertook to immortalize in rhyme their ridiculous hegira, as Judge Hopkinson did the famous Battle of the Kegs in Philadelphia. Like the more recent Madawaska war in Maine, the great

Chepatchet demonstration in Rhode Island, and the "Sauk fuss" of Wisconsin, it remains to this day "unsyllabled, unsung"; and the fast-fading memory of age alone preserves the unwritten history of the great Ipswich fright.

The Palatine Light

. . . LOOKING from McSparran Hill, Block Island is plainly to be seen in all its breadth, some twenty miles to the south, with Montauk Point, the eastern extremity of Long Island, lying some few leagues to the westward of it. From this point, too, if unbroken tradition can be relied upon, there was formerly seen occasionally at night the "Palatine ship" all in flames, hovering about the island, where the legend asserts a ship freighted with emigrants and their effects from Germany in the first half of the eighteenth century was purposely—as some said—run on shore by her captain and crew, for the sake of plunder, whilst others said that the vessel was decoyed one dark stormy night by means of false lights arranged by the islanders with like intent. I remember hearing, when quite young, of an islander by the name of ——, who was generally well and in his right mind except at the season of the year when the Palatine ship was wrecked, and after being stripped of everything of value was set on fire by the land pirates and burned with all the crew and passengers on board. At this particular season this old man, it was said, always became madly insane, and would rave about seeing a ship all ablaze, with men falling from her burning rigging and shrouds, and ever and anon shrink in horror from the spectres of two women, whose hands he cut off or disabled by blows from a cutlass, as they sought to cling to the gunwale of the last boat that left the burning ship and all on board to their fate that not one might remain alive to bear witness of the terrible catastrophe and crime. Whether the legend is true or false I know not, though I do know that many Block Islanders, in my early days, firmly believed that the burning Palatine ship was often seen near the island.

My father became possessed, by will of his uncle, Rowland Robinson, of two or more farms on Block Island, which he leased for some years, and finally sold to several different purchasers. This gave occasion for some of the leading and most intelligent men, as well as others from Block Island, to visit our house in Narragansett, and sometimes pass the night. Of course I was always curious to hear about the old Palatine ship, and I

From *Recollections of Olden Times:* Rowland Robinson of Narragansett and His Unfortunate Daughter, With Genealogies of the Robinson and Hazard Families of Rhode Island, by Thomas R. Hazard, "Shepherd Tom," in His Eighty-First and Eighty-Second Years, Also Genealogical Sketch of the Hazards of the Middle States, by Willis P. Hazard, of Westchester, Pa., pp. 127–129. Entered according to Act of Congress, in the year 1879, by John P. Sanborn, in the Office of the Librarian of Congress, at Washington, D. C. Newport, Rhode Island.

do not remember an instance wherein these several visitors did not bear testimony to the verity of the phenomenon. On one occasion I remember asking the late George Sheffield, who had just arrived at our house from Block Island, what he thought the weather would be, to which he replied that it would continue fair, but directly hesitated, and said to Shedrick Card—a venerable old patriarch, who happened to accompany him—, "Mr. Card, the old Palatine loomed up high last night, didn't she?" Mr. Card answered in the affirmative, when the other rejoined, addressing his words to me, "I was mistaken; it will be stormy soon." It was evident that neither of these men, both of whom were very intelligent, had the least doubt of their having seen the ship all in flames the night before, and that her *bona fide* appearance was no more than an ordinary occurrence.

Since the conclusion of these papers in printed form, I have received a very interesting letter from Mr. Benjamin Congdon, who, I remember, lived many years ago in a house that stood north of the Walcott farm and west of the road in Point Judith. Mr. Congdon is now in his ninetieth year and was considered by all who knew him in Rhode Island to be a man of unusual intelligence and probity. I make the following extracts from his letter which is dated "Napoli, Cattaraugus Co., New York, March 4, 1878."

"In 1800, my elder brother attended Robert Rogers' Academy in Newport. I was then twelve years old. My father had a school kept in a small house, on our farm, for a number of years, by the late Thomas Perry, who kept the best school I was ever in. Mr. Perry afterwards moved to Westerly, and was chosen cashier of the Washington Bank, which position he retained until his death, when his son Charles succeeded him, who, I think, remains cashier of the same bank still, now seventy years since his father first assumed the same position. I can recollect well when Washington's second term expired, in 1797; when John Adams became President, followed by Jefferson, and then Madison, who was President during the War of 1812. About the burning Palatine ship you speak of in your interesting papers, I may say that I have seen her eight or ten times or more. In those early days nobody doubted her being sent by an Almighty Power to punish those wicked men who murdered her passengers and crew. After the last of these were dead she was never more seen. We lived when I was young, in Charlestown, directly opposite Block Island, where we used to have a plain view of the burning ship."

MYSTERIOUS CREATURES

The Reverend Samuel Peters' Contributions to the Natural History of Connecticut

CATERPILLARS AND WILD PIGEONS [1]

IN 1768 the inhabitants of Connecticut River were as much alarmed by an army of caterpillars as those of Windham were at the frogs; and no one found reason to jest at their fears. These worms came in one night and covered the earth, on both sides of the river, to an extent of three miles in front and two in depth. They marched with great speed, and eat up everything green for the space of one hundred miles, in spite of rivers, ditches, fires, and the united efforts of 1,000 men. They were, in general, two inches long, had white bodies covered with thorns, and red throats. When they had finished their work they went down to the river Connecticut, where they died, poisoning the waters, until they were washed into the sea. This calamity was imputed by some to the vast number of logs and trees lying in the creeks, and to cinders, smoke, and fires, made to consume the waste wood for three or four hundred miles up the Connecticut River; while others thought it augurated future evils, similar to those of Egypt. The inhabitants of the Verdmonts [Vermont] would unavoidably have perished with famine, in consequence of the devastation of these worms, had not a remarkable Providence filled the wilderness with wild pigeons, which were killed by sticks as they sat upon the branches of the trees, in such multitudes that 30,000 people lived on them for three weeks. If a natural cause may be assigned for the coming of the frogs and caterpillars, yet the visit of the pigeons to the wilderness in August has been necessarily ascribed to the interposition of infinite Power and Goodness. Happy will it be for America, if the smiling providence of Heaven produces gratitude, repentance, and obedience amongst her children!

THE WHAPPERKNOCKER [2]

The whapperknocker is somewhat larger than a weasel, and of a beautiful brown colour. He lives in the woods on worms and birds; is so wild

---

[1] From *The Rev. Samuel Peters' LL.D. General History of Connecticut* . . . to Which Are Added Additions to Appendix, Notes, and Extracts from Letters, Verifying Many Important Statements, by Samuel Jarvis McCormick, pp. 131–132. Copyright, 1877, by D. Appleton and Company. New York.

A good deal of the natural lore, as well as the professed history, of the *General History of Connecticut*, by Samuel Peters, seems to be the product of the myth-making imagination. This history was first published in London in 1781, and an American edition . . . was published in New Haven in 1829. Apparently Peters was determined to be interesting, even to the extent of cracking credibility.—George Philip Krapp, *The English Language in America* (New York, 1925), I: 109.

[2] *Ibid.*, pp. 182–183.

that no one can tame him, and, as he never quits his harbour in the day-time, is only to be taken by traps in the night. Of the skins of these animals —which are covered with an exceedingly fine fur—are made muffs, at the price of thirty or forty guineas apiece; so that it is not without reason the ladies pride themselves on the possession of this small appurtenance of female habiliment.

THE CUBA [3]

The cuba I suppose to be peculiar to New England. The male is of the size of a large cat; has four long tushes sharp as a razor; he is very active in defending himself, and, if he has the first blow, will spoil a dog before he yields. His lady is peaceable and harmless, and depends for protection on her spouse, and, as he has more courage than prudence, always attends him to moderate his temper. She sees danger, and he fears it not. She chatters at him while he is busy preparing for battle, and, if she thinks the danger is too great, she runs to him and clings about his neck, screaming her extreme distress; his wrath abates; and by her advice, they fly to their caves. In like manner, when he is chained, and irritated into the greatest rage by an impertinent dog, his lady, who is never chained, will fly about his neck and kiss him, and in half a minute restore him to calmness. He is very tender of his family, and never forsakes them till death dissolves their union. What further shows the magnanimity of this little animal, he never manifests the least anger toward his lady, though I have often seen her extremely loquacious, and, as I guessed, impertinent to him. How happy would the rational part of creation become if they would follow the example of these irrational beasts! I the more readily suppose the cuba to be peculiar to New England, not only from my never having yet seen the creature described, but also on account of its perverse observance of carnival and neglect of *carême*.

THE DEW-MINK [4]

. . . The dew-mink, so named for its articulating those syllables, is black and white, and the size of an English robin. Its flesh is delicious. . . .

THE HUMILITY [5]

. . . The humility is so called because it speaks the word humility, and seldom mounts high in the air. Its legs are long enough to enable it to outrun a dog for a little way; its wings long and narrow; body maigre and of the size of a blackbird's; plumage variegated with white, black, blue,

---

[3] *Ibid.*, pp. 183–184.
[4] *Ibid.*, p. 186.
[5] *Ibid.*, p. 186.

and red. It lives on tadpoles, spawn, and worms; has an eye more piercing than the falcon, and the swiftness of an eagle; hence it can never be shot, for it sees the sparks of fire even before it enkindles the powder, and by the extreme rapidity of its flight gets out of reach in an instant. It is never known to light upon a tree, but is always seen upon the ground or wing. These birds appear in New England in summer only; what becomes of them afterwards is not discovered. They are caught in snares, but can never be tamed.

THE WHIPPOORWILL [6]

The whippoorwill has so named itself by its nocturnal songs. It is also called the Pope, by reason of its darting with great swiftness from the clouds to the ground and bawling out Pope, which alarms young people and the fanatics very much, especially as they know it to be an ominous bird. However, it has hitherto proved friendly, always giving travellers and others notice of an approaching storm by saluting them every minute by Pope! pope! It flies only a little before sunset, unless for this purpose of giving notice of a storm. It never deceives the people with false news. If the tempest is to continue long, the augurs appear in flocks, and nothing can be heard but Pope! pope! The whippoorwill is about the size of a cuckoo, has a short beak, long and narrow wings, a large head, and mouth enormous, yet is not a bird of prey. Under its throat is a pocket, which it fills with air at pleasure, whereby it sounds forth the fatal word Pope in the day, and Whip-her-I-will in the night. The superstitious inhabitants would have exorcised this harmless bird long ago, as an emissary from Rome and an enemy to the American Vine, had they not found out that it frequents New England only in the summer, and prefers the wilderness to a palace. Nevertheless, many cannot but believe it a spy from some foreign court, an agent of antichrist, a lover of persecution, and an enemy of Protestants, because it sings of whipping and of the Pope, which they think portends misery and a change of religion.

BELLED SNAKES [7]

. . . The belled or rattle-snakes are large, and will gorge a common cat. They are seldom seen from their rocky dens. Their bite is mortal if not speedily cured; yet they are generous, and without guile; before they bite they rattle their bell three or four times, but after that their motion is swift and stroke sure. The Indians discovered and informed the English of a weed, common in the country, which, mixed with spittle, will extract the poison.

---

[6] *Ibid.*, pp. 186–187.
[7] *Ibid.*, pp. 188–189.

TREE-FROGS [8]

The toads and frogs are plenty in the spring of the year. The tree-frogs, whippoorwills, and whooping owls serenade the inhabitants every night with music far excelling the harmony of the trumpet, drum, and jews-harp.

The tree-frog cannot be called an insect, a reptile, or one of the winged host; he has four legs, the two foremost short, with claws as sharp as those of a squirrel; the hind-legs five inches long, and folding by three joints. His body is about as big as the first joint of a man's thumb. Under his throat is a wind-bag, which assists him in singing the word I-sa-ac all the night. When it rains, and is very dark, he sings the loudest. His voice is not so pleasing as that of the nightingale; but this would be a venial imperfection, if he would but keep silence on Saturday nights, and not forever prefer I-sa-ac to Abraham and Jacob. He has more elasticity in his long legs than any other creature yet known. By this means he will leap five yards up a tree, fastening himself to it by his fore-legs, and in a moment will hop or spring as far from one tree to another. It is from the singing of this tree-frog that the Americans have acquired the name of Little Isaac. Indeed, like a certain part of them, the creature appears very devout, noisy, arbitrary, and phlegmatic, and associates with none but what agree with him in his ways.

Cotton Mather's Snake Stories

COTTON MATHER sent the Royal Society two good snake stories in 1712. They are reported, with some changes in form, in the Philosophical Transactions [No. 339 (for April–June, 1714), xxix, 68]. I give them from a copy of the original letter.

A Traveller in this Countrey mett and killed a *Rattlesnake;* but suffered the Angry *Snake* to give a Bite before he died unto ye lower end of the Switch, with ye lashes of which he had first spoiled his leaping. He rode on, & a fly disturbing him on one of his Temples, he rubb'd ye place, wth ye upper end of the Switch in his hand, unto which ye poison below had so permeated, that ye Head of ye poor Man Swell'd immediately, and (as I remember) he died upon it. . . . At Cape *Fear,* one of or people Sporting with a *Rattlesnake,* provoked him, & suffered him to

---

[8] *Ibid.*, p. 189.

From *Letters of Samuel Lee and Samuel Sewall Relating to New England and the Indians*, edited by George Lyman Kittredge, p. 174. Reprinted from *The Publications of the Colonial Society of Massachusetts*, Vol. XIV. Cambridge: John Wilson and Son, University Press. 1912.

bite ye edge of a Good Broad Ax; whereupon, immediately ye Colour of the Steeled Iron changed, & at the first blow he gave, when he went after this to use his Axe, ye discoloured part of ye Bitten Iron, broke off without any more ado. I know not whether I have now Sprung a New Game, for the Gentlemen, that are hunting after ye Liquor *Alkahest*.[1]

The New England Sea-Serpent

ON AUGUST 18th, 1817, the Linnean Society of Boston formed a committee [2] "for the purpose of collecting any evidence which may exist respecting a remarkable animal, denominated a *Sea Serpent*, reported to have been seen in and near the Harbour of Gloucester."

* * * * *

The Committee's report was published as a small pamphlet [3] (now very scarce) in December, 1817. It contained, *inter alia*, the sworn depositions of twelve witnesses.[4] Before giving extracts from these, it seems worth while to reproduce the very excellent rules which the Committee laid down to govern its investigations.

"*Boston, Aug.* 19, 1817.

"The Committee appointed by the Linnean Society . . . have concluded on the following method of proceeding in the execution of their commission.

I. The examination to be confined to persons professing actually to have seen the animal in question.

II. Such persons to be examined as may be met with by either of the Committee, or by Hon. Lonson Nash of Gloucester, who is to be requested by a letter addressed to him from the Committee to undertake this service.

III. All testimony on the subject to be taken in writing, and after being deliberately read to the person testifying, to be signed by him, and sworn to before a magistrate. The examinations to be separate, and

---

[1] Letter of Nov. 27, 1712 (addressed to Richard Waller, the Secretary of the Royal Society). In the archives of the Society. From a copy kindly lent me by our associate Mr. Frederick Lewis Gay. The alkahest, or universal solvent, was passionately sought after in the seventeenth and eighteenth centuries.—G. L. K.

From *The Case for the Sea-Serpent*, by Lieut.-Commander R. T. Gould, pp. 29–32, 53–60. New York: G. P. Putnam's Sons. 1934.

[2] John Davis, Jacob Bigelow, and Francis C Gray.—R. T. G.

[3] REPORT/of a/COMMITTEE/of the/LINNEAN SOCIETY OF NEW ENG-LAND/relative/to a large marine animal/supposed to be/A SERPENT,/seen near Cape Ann, Massachusetts,/in/August 1817.//BOSTON:/published by Cummings and Hilliard,/No. 1, Cornhill.//Univ. Press . . . Hillard and Metcalf./1817.

Small 8vo., gray paper cover. 10½″ x 6½″. 52 pp., 2 plates.—R. T. G.

[4] Their names, reminiscent of Widecombe Fair, were: Amos Story, Solomon Allen, Eppes Ellery, Wm. H. Foster, Matthew Gaffney, James Mansfield, John Johnston, Wm. B. Pearson, Sewall Toppan, Robert Bragg, Wm. Somerby, and Elkanah Finney. —R. T. G.

the matter testified by any witness not to be communicated until the whole evidence be taken.

IV. The persons testifying to be requested first to relate their recollections on the subject, which being taken down, the following questions to be proposed, if not rendered unnecessary by the statement given:

QUESTIONS

1. When did you first see this animal?
2. How often and how long at a time?
3. At what times of the day?
4. At what distance?
5. How near the shore?
6. What was its general appearance?
7. Was it in motion or at rest?
8. How fast did it move, and in what direction?
9. What parts of it were above the water and how high?
10. Did it appear jointed or only serpentine?
11. If serpentine, were its sinuosities vertical or horizontal?
12. How many distinct portions were out of water at one time?
13. What were its colour, length, and thickness?
14. Did it appear smooth or rough?
15. What were the size and shape of its head, and had the head ears, horns, or other appendages?
16. Describe its eyes and mouth.
17. Had it gills or breathing holes, and where?
18. Had it fins or legs, and where?
19. Had it a mane or hairs, and where?
20. How did its tail terminate?
21. Did it utter any sound?
22. Did it appear to pursue, avoid, or notice any thing?
23. Did you see more than one?
24. How many persons saw it?
25. State any other remarkable fact."

* * * * *

One creature only was seen. It frequented Gloucester harbour from August 10th (or, possibly, a few days earlier) to August 23rd, after which it proceeded northward, being seen *en route* on August 28th, and in Long Island Sound on October 3rd and 5th. It was observed by many persons simultaneously, for periods ranging from a few minutes to two hours and upwards, and at distances varying from a few feet to a mile.

It was seen at all times of the day, sometimes in rapid motion, sometimes at rest. When moving, it appeared to curve its back in vertical undulations; when at rest, its back seemed, at times, to be undulating, and at others smooth. It presented the appearance of an enormous serpent, of a black or dark-brown colour, its body (so far as this could be seen) having a diameter of something under three feet, tapering slightly towards the extremities. Its length was variously assessed at from seventy to one hundred and twenty feet. Its skin appeared smooth to most of the witnesses, but rough to two.

The head was generally described as like a serpent's. Three witnesses deposed to seeing a long tongue projected almost vertically from the mouth. One witness only spoke of seeing the eye, bright and resembling that of an ox. No legs, fins, gills or mane were observed. There was great unanimity of opinion as to the monster's extreme lateral flexibility.

It appeared to take little notice of surrounding objects, human beings, and even gunshots. It was not heard to utter any sounds. On two occasions it was seen, or believed to be seen, lying partly on the shore and partly in the water.

It is, I think, difficult for any person of unbiased mind to read through the depositions without being struck by their weight and general agreement. Something of the latter, no doubt, must be regarded as artificial. Had the witnesses made entirely independent statements, one would not expect to find them all deposing, with only the slightest of verbal changes, that they had seen "a strange marine animal," which they "believed to be a serpent." One imagines that this formula was submitted to them—in substitution, possibly, for some much more terse and vigorous description—by Mr. Lonson Nash; and that they accepted it as sufficiently conveying their meaning. Broadly speaking, one imagines that while Nash probably acted up to the spirit of his instructions, directing "the examinations to be separate, and the matter testified by any witness not to be communicated until the whole evidence be taken," he performed (perhaps unconsciously) the functions of a compiler and editor, bringing the various accounts into a slightly misleading state of general uniformity—uniformity of language, be it noted, not of fact. I do not suggest that he took any liberties with the reported facts—his comments on Allen's evidence are sufficient proof that he did not.

The evidence afforded by the depositions is, as already remarked, entitled to very serious consideration. Unfortunately, the Committee went out of their way to stultify the valuable work which they had performed. Not content with merely collecting testimony—a task which they had accomplished most admirably- -they cast about for a hypothesis which should explain this, and be incorporated in their report. Such an hypothesis, accordingly, will be found appended to the depositions; and a very singular one it is.

About a month after the "strange marine animal" had quitted Gloucester harbour, a small black snake of somewhat curious appearance was found by two boys on the beach at Loblolly Cove.[1] Alarmed, they summoned their father. This brave fellow attacked the savage reptile—which

---

[1] On the east side of Cape Ann peninsula.—R. T. G.

was fully three feet long—with a pitchfork, and ultimately slew it. It was bought by a resident named Beach, who presented it to the Committee; apparently on the slender chance that its appearance might in some way be connected with the monster recently seen in the harbour. It appears that the local pothouse-pundits were firmly of opinion that the latter had visited Gloucester's shores to deposit its eggs thereon.

The Committee received the snake, and the suggestion, with great gravity. They examined and dissected the carcase, and were delighted to find that its back exhibited a series of small humps, or bunches. Nothing further, surely, was necessary. Devoting some four pages of their report to a minute comparison of the snake's anatomy with the reported characteristics of the "strange marine animal," they concluded as follows:

"On the whole, as these two animals agree in so many conspicuous, important and peculiar characters, and as no material difference between them has yet been clearly pointed out, excepting that of size, the Society will probably feel justified in considering them individuals of the same species, and entitled to the same name, until a more close examination of the great Serpent shall have disclosed some difference of structure, important enough to constitute a specific distinction."

Holding this remarkable opinion, they christened their newly-acquired specimen *Scioliophis Atlanticus*, and appended to their report an anatomical description of it, illustrated by two plates. By so doing, they made a rod for their own backs; since European naturalists, headed by H. M. D. de Blainville,[1] immediately pointed out to them that their juvenile sea-serpent was nothing more than a common black snake (*Coluber constrictor*) in a diseased condition. Moreover, since the Committee had gone out of their way to assert a close connection between their small, common land-snake and the huge sea-creature seen off Gloucester, it is scarcely surprising that those competent to form an opinion should have concluded that persons capable of so egregious a blunder in a simple point of identification were not the safest guides to accurate information regarding a strange and huge creature of unknown species which they had not personally examined.

For good reason, therefore, scientific men in general received the Committee's report with a "calmness bordering on indifference." The vulgar, on the other hand, were at no loss to suggest, in pretty plain language, that the Gloucester monster was a myth, and that those who professed to have seen it were drawing the long bow. This, of course, was almost inevitable. The story was strange and improbable; it rested on the assertions of a comparatively small number of persons living in the same town; and it provided their less-favoured neighbours with a most excellent means of poking fun at Gloucester credulity and vaunting their own superior perspicacity and common sense. In consequence, the sober tales of the Gloucester witnesses were, in no long time, distorted, parodied and (to a great

---

[1] *Journal de Physique* . . . , Vol. LXXXVI (Paris, 1818).—R. T. G.

extent) laughed out of court. Practical jokers sent in marvellous reports of apocryphal "sea-serpents"; not supporting—or, indeed, designed to support—the slightest examination. The Press, with one or two honourable exceptions, followed on the same side—after its fashion. And about a year after the "sea-serpent's" last appearance off Gloucester an event occurred which, designedly or not, helped materially to throw ridicule on the whole matter.

I am uncertain whether it should be regarded as a malicious hoax, a misfired practical joke, or an honest blunder. Personally, I incline to the second hypothesis. Here are the facts, as related by Colonel Perkins many years afterwards: [1]

". . . As it happened, a circumstance took place which did not do much credit to the actors in it, but which served to fortify the unbelief of our southern brethren. Believing that the possession of the sea-serpent would be a fortune to those who should have him in their power, many boats were fitted out from Cape Ann and other places in the neighbourhood of his haunts, armed with harpoons and other implements, and manned with persons used to the whale fishery, in hopes of getting near enough to him to fasten their harpoons in his side.

"Among others a Captain Rich . . . of Boston, took command of a party, which was fitted out at some expense, and went into the bay,[2] where they cruised along shore two or three days without seeing the serpent. With a view, however, to keeping the joke for themselves, they . . . spread a report that they had caught the serpent, or what had been taken for one, and that he was to be seen at a place [3] mentioned in the advertisement.[4]

"Thousands were flocking to see this wonder, when it was found to be no other than a large horse macquerel,[5] which (though a great natural curiosity, weighing sometimes 600 or 700 pounds) very much disappointed those, who had been induced to visit it. Those who had declared their disbelief of the existence of the Sea-serpent amongst themselves were delighted to find their opinions were confirmed, and gave themselves great credit for their judgment and discrimination. The report spread from Boston to New Orleans, that what had been thought by some persons to be a sea-serpent had proved to be a horse macquerel, and even those who had been believers now supposed that those who had reported that they had seen the serpent had either misrepresented or had been themselves deceived. As no report of the snake having been seen after the capture of the macquerel was made, during that year, Captain Rich had the laugh with him, until circumstances, which have transpired since, have borne rather against him."

---

[1] *Boston Daily Advertiser*, 25, xi. 1848.—R. T. G.
[2] Massachusetts Bay.—R. T. G.
[3] At Boston.—R. T. G.
[4] In the *Boston Daily Advertiser*, and other local papers, 3, ix. 1819.—R. T. G.
[5] Or tunny [tuna].—R. T. G.

It is fair to add, though, that Captain Richard Rich protested in print, and immediately, against the general impression that he had tried to perpetrate a silly hoax. Writing in the *Boston Weekly Messenger* of September 17th, 1818, he contended that he had repeatedly observed, in the course of his cruise in Massachusetts Bay, the appearance of a creature similar to that seen off Gloucester the year before—that he had finally captured it—and that it had proved to be a tunny. He continues:

". . . If I am asked—how is it possible for a Fish like this to produce such a wonderful appearance, I can only answer: 'His peculiar movement and his velocity produced a greater deception than I ever saw before, and the describing his body as being like kegs fastened together, struck me so forcibly, that had I not followed it up and discovered the deception, I should have given my testimony to the long list already given, of the existence of a Sea Serpent on our coast.'

"I now take my leave of the public, hoping they will do me the justice to say that I used no deception.

"RICHARD RICH."

I have a strong impression that the public took no such action. The discrepancies between Rich's assertions—and his tunny—and the Gloucester depositions are more than Appella himself could stomach.

As Perkins notes, the dime-show staged by Rich put an end, for a time, to the reports of sea-serpents off the New England coast. Rich's joke, if it were a joke, had obviously fallen exceedingly flat; the public was no longer amused by hoaxes, and these in their turn had effectually discredited, in advance, any further similar reports. **. . .**

Caldera Dick

CALDERA DICK WAS a monstrous old bull sperm whale. There were others big and tough and mean, but Caldera Dick was bigger, tougher, meaner—and smarter—than any other whale that ever lived. The ocean for a circuit of several hundred miles about Caldera was his dooryard, though he didn't always stay at home. (Caldera is a little seaport on the coast of Chile.) At times he'd get around Cape Horn into the Atlantic, or he'd turn up in the Japan Sea, or you might hear of ships running afoul of him almost any-

As told by Captain Benjamin Doane to Benjamin D. Doane. From *The Rainbow Book of American Folk Tales and Legends,* by Maria Leach, pp. 262–266. Copyright, 1958, by Maria Leach. Cleveland and New York: The World Publishing Company.

On the sixth day of May (1846), we again made the coast of Chile, about Caldera, the mention of which, to old whalemen, would suggest the story of Caldera Dick. It was long before my time that he flourished and fell. His career covered the whole history of the whale fisheries in the South Seas from early Colonial times, and succeeding generations of whalers tried in vain to capture him.—Captain Benjamin Doane, p. 262.

where that boats were lowered for whales. But mostly he ranged off Caldera.

The difficulty was not in striking him and getting fast. He seemed to invite that. He'd lie still and calm as you please while a boat was put on to him, but once the dart was made and the harpoon fairly settled in his tough old hide, there was the devil to pay and no pitch hot. He seemed to have a fancy for collecting harpoons. Leastwise, he took all that came his way and never gave any back, until last of all, when he was finally bested, he was so studded with iron, it was a wonder he could float. And nobody ever thrust a lance into him, either, but the one that finished him. He was too smart for that.

---

* * * * *

This is the story of Caldera Dick as told to me when I was a small boy by my grandfather, Captain Benjamin Doane, who in the years 1845-6-7, a young man in his early twenties, was boatsteerer (harpooner) in the whaleship *Athol,* Captain James D. Coffin, out of Saint John, New Brunswick. The [preceding note] is from his unpublished memoirs.

It was my grandfather's later belief that the stories of Caldera Dick, as told in the forecastles of whaling ships, were the basis of Herman Melville's great novel, *Moby Dick,* published in 1851.—Benjamin D. Doane, p. 266.

* * * * *

There were other notoriously great and savage whales, whose reputations were enlarged wherever whalemen got together for a gam: Mocha Dick and Galera Dick, whose names were derived from the regions in which they were usually encountered—the seas around the island of Mocha, off the southern coast of Chile, and the seas off Galera, a little cape on the coast of Peru. It seems likely that Melville heard the stories about all three Dicks, for he was whaling in those parts in the year 1841. And I suspect that he turned them all to whatever purpose suited his imaginative mind. The probable inspiration for *Moby Dick,* however, was the sinking of the whaleship *Essex,* rammed and sunk by a sperm whale in mid-Pacific in the year 1820.

Of the three Dicks, Mocha Dick, at least, was often described as white, or as having a great white scar. Since Melville made his Moby Dick a white whale, perhaps the island of Mocha may rise and take a bow in claim of literary honors. I do not remember my grandfather describing Caldera Dick as white, and the references available to me about Galera Dick are vague in detail, describing him only as a great legendary rogue whale. But whether the Dick was white or black, his legend persisted through the life of the sperm-whale fishery. The name was always Dick, however, whether Mocha, Galera, or Caldera claimed him. And if Caldera Dick was taken, as my grandfather says, "long before my time," he was supplanted by Mocha Dick or by Galera Dick, for whalemen kept the story alive and current.

Perhaps there were three whales. Perhaps the three were one, with three names. Perhaps they were *all* whales—all whales, that is, with the gumption, courage, and honor to fight for their lives and turn upon their hunters. The prowess laid to these legendary whales was often encountered in whales to which no legend was attached. Countless whales smashed the boats of their pursuers, thrashed madly in the wreckage, and escaped, leaving death and destruction behind them. At the time, the crew would probably consider the matter all in the day's work, thanking God that such work did not occur every day. But, next voyage, in a new ship, with green hands to impress—well, what old whaleman would admit to defeat by any run-of-the-mill whale? Only the whale of whales, Caldera Dick, or Galera Dick, or a white whale named Mocha Dick, beyond taking by mortal man, could get the best of *them.*— Benjamin D. Doane, pp. 309–310.

His favorite game was to wait until the boat was fast, then try to get her with a flip of his flukes. Often as not, that was all there was to it: kindling wood and men flying through the air, to plop back into the sea, smashed and stunned, where old Dick could leisurely give his undivided attention to each bit of wreckage and to each desperately clinging or swimming whaleman that had survived the first blow. He'd come back among the wreckage and maneuver around through it, using his great flukes to toss any bit of it he could see or feel sky high again, as long as there was anything left that he could find.

Sometimes the boatheader would be skilful enough to sheer the boat off and escape that first thrust of the flukes. When that happened old Dick would sound, diving down into the depths, taking fathom after fathom of line after him, just as any ordinary whale might do. Then instead of coming to the surface, way off as far as the line was out, and running away, hell bent, with the boat towing after and the men hauling up to get close enough for the boatheader to use his lance and make the kill, Caldera Dick would come up right underneath the boat, so fast that the whole length of him would shoot out of water, and the boat, along with such of the men that hadn't made it over the side in time being chomped to death and matchwood in his jaws. Then he'd mill around through the wreckage, making little pieces out of big ones and dead men out of live ones until there was nothing left—and it was a lucky man who managed to swim fast and far enough to be out of the way, and perhaps get picked up later by the ship if it could find him.

Caldera Dick was resourceful, too. He would vary his tactics to meet the emergency, and if one method didn't work he'd try something else. He was a scourge and a terror, but he was also a terrific challenge. There were no craven hearts among the men who followed the sperm-whaling, and though boat after boat was smashed and many lives were lost in encounters with Caldera Dick, the boats never hung in the davits because of his presence but were lowered with all haste to take him on, and the men eager to have at him.

But Caldera Dick met his nemesis at last at the hands of an old Nantucket captain who devised a scheme that defied all whale philosophy. This old fellow had been bested by the great whale more than once, and it preyed upon his mind. He couldn't sleep at night, but lay in his bunk, brooding and figuring. One night a plan came to him and immediately he set to work to carry it out. The plan that came to mind was a method of taking whales that has been used by the Eskimos longer than anyone can remember, and a very simple plan it was.

First he got the cooper to make a cask—oval, instead of normal cask shape—strongly bound with iron hoops, and with the heads braced from the inside so it couldn't be stove in. The cask was then harnessed securely with ropes and a whale line made fast to it. Then the whole apparatus was stowed in the starboard boat, which was not to be lowered until they should fall in with Caldera Dick again—which happened off Caldera.

On that day the starboard boat lowered, and the captain himself took the steering oar. Caldera Dick lay quiet, as was his wont, while the boat was put on. The harpooner was told to stand up. He faced around toward the whale, readied his two harpoons, braced himself against the crotch of the boat, and as it fairly touched the whale, darted first one and then the other into him, sinking them both home. And in almost the same instant he heaved overboard the tub of line and the cask fastened to it. The men at the oars, the pick of the ship's crew, were meanwhile following the captain's orders without even so much as a turn of the head to see what was going on, and by great skill that deadly first thrust of the flukes was avoided.

Poor Caldera Dick. Following his usual routine, sounding and coming up from below, he found no boat there to grind in his jaws—only a cask floating lightly on the water. The boat was heading back for the ship as fast as ever stout oars with strong backs to bend them could take her. So Caldera Dick gave his attention to the cask. He took it in his jaws, but it squirted out; he knocked it galley-west with his flukes, but it plopped back into the sea, unharmed. Confounded and puzzled, after several tries, Caldera Dick did what he had never done before. He tried to escape. Away he went, with the line paid out behind him, and the cask smacking along into the waves at the end of it. Dick sounded, and the cask followed him down, a powerful drag upon him. He surfaced; he sounded; he ran straight away and in circles, but always the cask was there, dragging, dragging, wearing him down. And always the whaleship managed to keep him in sight, until, utterly exhausted and gallied, he lay still upon the surface. Then the starboard boat was lowered again, and Caldera Dick succumbed to the lance of his tormentor.

HAUNTS AND SPECTERS

Ocean-Born Mary

No STATE has more tales of witches and ghosts with which to while away the winter evenings than New Hampshire. And of all the tales of New Hampshire ghosts, I like best the story of Ocean-Born Mary. I like it so much that I made a visit to the haunted house in which folks say her ghost still walks, and I heard her story from the lips of eighty-year-old Mrs. Roy who lives there.

I arrived at the house, which is on the side of a steep mountain south of

From *The Hurricane's Children*, Tales from Your Neck o' the Woods, by Carl Carmer, pp. 29–37. Copyright, 1937, by Carl Carmer. New York and Toronto: Farrar & Rinehart, Inc.

the village of Henniker, just at twilight. Mrs. Roy was in the yard gathering herbs, but she kindly led me through the old green doorway built many years before the American Revolution. We sat in the front room, the eagle room, she calls it, because someone, possibly Ocean-Born Mary herself, painted above the fireplace long ago an American eagle with a band of sixteen stars above him. There she told me the story while the light left the New Hampshire hills and the room grew gray and dark and the white-spindled old stairway to the second story creaked mysteriously.

In the year 1720 Mrs. Roy said, a group of emigrants from Londonderry, Ireland, took ship for America, expecting to join relatives and friends living in Londonderry, New Hampshire. As they were nearing the Massachusetts coast a sinister-looking frigate flying no flag bore down upon their unarmed boat, fired a gun across her bows, forcing her to heave to. Then, while the crew stood helpless, white and silent, and the emigrants kneeled on the deck in prayer for deliverance, a boat put out from the stranger bearing sunburned men. They clambered aboard the emigrant ship, terrified the passengers and crew with their weapons, and bound them securely.

Their leader, whom they called Captain Pedro, was a tall dark man who said little. Though he looked Spanish he talked perfect English when he ordered his captives to prepare for immediate death. As he spoke, a faint cry came from below deck, and he suddenly wheeled about and hastened down the companionway. In a cabin below he came upon a mother and her newborn girl baby. He said to her: "Madam, if I may be allowed to name this little girl after my own mother, I will not harm this ship or its passengers." The mother gladly gave consent, and the pirate captain said: "Her name shall be Mary."

Then he went back on deck and ordered all the captives released and his own men into their boat. In a few moments he was on his way back to the frigate. Just as the emigrants were rejoicing over their good fortune, however, they were again panic-stricken by the captain's return. He carried with him a bolt of grayish green tapestry silk, exquisitely embroidered in a flower pattern. He strode down to the mother's cabin. "For your little daughter's wedding dress," he said, and returned to his boat.

The emigrants landed safely, but soon thereafter in Boston Ocean-Born Mary's father died. Then the mother took the little girl into New Hampshire hills. More than a score of years went by, and Ocean-Born Mary was a wife and herself the mother of four boys. She was six feet tall now, with red hair, very white skin, and green eyes. All over the state people talked of her beauty. And many grieved for her when she was left a widow with her four small sons to bring up.

But Captain Pedro had never forgotten the girl named for his mother. He was getting old now and longed for a more peaceful life—somewhere distant from the scenes of his criminal career. And so he came to Henniker to build a peaceful refuge from his own past and to be near his mother's namesake. He brought with him black slaves and his ship's carpenters and a few of his pirate crew. They chose a spot completely out of sight of any human dwelling and there they built a stately Colonial house with high handrailings on the stair like those on the bridge of the captain's ship and a sloping floor in the rear rooms like the slanting surface of a deck. Then he invited Ocean-Born Mary to come to live in the house, take care of him in his old age, and bring up her sons there. She accepted and became a fitting and beautiful mistress of the stately house. The captain presented her with a coach-and-four, and neighbors smiled to see her riding in it with her four tall sons. One day the captain returned from the seacoast with an enormous wooden chest. At midnight he and one of his pirate men staggered out of the high side door of the house carrying it on their shoulders, and Ocean-Born Mary heard the sound of shovels in the earth, then a low groan, and silence. The captain came back to the house alone and no one ever saw his pirate helper again.

It was over a year later that Ocean-Born Mary came home from a drive in her coach one late afternoon to find the house deserted. But in the orchard behind the house she found the body of the captain. He had been run through with a sailor's cutlass. She had her slaves bring the body into the house and there she supervised the captain's burial under the eight-by-three-foot stone slab in front of the big kitchen hearth—just as he had directed her to do in case of his death.

Ocean-Born Mary lived on in the old house. Her sons, grown to be men and all of them over six-foot-eight, left her to fight against the British king in the American Revolution. When they returned they took houses of their own. But Ocean-Born Mary lived on alone in the big house until 1814, when she died at the age of ninety-four.

The house was long unoccupied after that. Then people began to talk about the strange things that went on there. They still do. They say that strange lights appear in the windows at midnight. Some curious folks who went there at twilight claimed that they saw a very tall woman of great beauty walking down the high-railinged stair. Others say that on warm spring nights just after darkness has followed the twilight, a coach-and-four drives up to the old entrance and a tall woman steps out and hurries into the house. Immediately after that there come, from the old orchard back of the house, fearful groans as of a man in mortal pain.

Mediums and other people who claim supernatural power frequently visit Mrs. Roy in the old house. Some of them say that surely there is something of mysterious interest under the eight-by-three stone slab in the kitchen. I asked Mrs. Roy why she didn't have the slab lifted to see if the bones of the captain are there. She said that it would cost a hundred and fifty dollars and she thought that so much money as that would buy a lot of things more useful to her than a skeleton. One of the mediums not long ago said that she had summoned up the captain's spirit and talked to it. She said that she told the captain Mrs. Roy was a nice lady and that he ought to let her know somehow where his treasure is buried—but the captain just said: "I buried it. Let her *find* it."

When I heard all this for the first time I thought somebody had just made up a fancy story for me that had few words of truth in it. But now that I have seen a piece of Ocean-Born Mary's wedding gown—the gray-green silk embroidered in a flower pattern—and the strange eight-by-three hearthstone that looks like the top of a coffin with a hole drilled in the middle of it—and the house itself looking dark and haunted in the late twilight—and listened to Mrs. Roy—I'm not sure where truth ends and fancy begins. At any rate, many folks in New Hampshire love to tell this story on winter evenings before their birch-log fires, or on their porches on summer evenings when the stars are very bright above the mountaintops.

The Ghosts of Georges Bank

HER decks and spars aglitter in the moonlight, the new schooner *Charles Haskell* was like a queen enthroned as she sat chocked on the ways at Essex. At that time—December, 1869—Story's boatyard was already more than a hundred years old; and all the miracles which that institution could perform with white oak and tall spruce had been lavished on the new craft. Yes, like a queen she was, and the moon over the bay that night was giving her a train of pure gold—and none too good for her!

The boatyard was through with her now. Everything those magicians could do for her had been done. Rigging and a suit of sails, ground tackle and gear—give her these, with an able crew, and she was ready for sea. Give her as she deserved of these, and she would be the match of any sea she met, of any gale that blew. Yes, even of Georges Bank in the winter!

A worker walked through the deserted boatyard that night down to the ways, and climbed aboard the new schooner for one last look. He inspected the deck and then started down the forecastle companion. His foot slipped. Next morning, they found a man aboard the *Charles Haskell*, a man lying at the foot of the companion ladder—dead of a broken neck.

The skipper for whom the *Charles Haskell* was built refused her. She was perfect, he said. She was a beauty. She was everything they said she was. But no contract on earth could make him take her; because for his business, he said, she was now disqualified.

His business was winter-fishing on Georges Bank.

*   *   *   *   *

There have been in this fishery any number of forebodings, premonitions of tragedy, placed on record by virtue of their weird fulfillment. What part of such a "premonition" is really afterthought I do not know; nor do I care, for what interests me is not whether these things actually took

From *In Great Waters*, The Story of the Portuguese Fishermen, by Jeremiah Digges, pp. 104–105, 107–108, 109–110, 112–121. Copyright, 1941, by Josef Berger. New York: The Macmillan Company.

place as related, but the fact that they were *said* to have taken place.

One such instance was set down in the journal of Captain J. Wenzell of the Gloucester schooner *Sachem.* She had been fishing on Brown's Bank, but on September 7, 1871, ran up to cruise Georges. That night John Nelson, cook, went aft and begged the skipper to "get off Georges Bank." Making no bones about it, he explained that he had just waked from a dream. He had seen "women, dressed all in white, and standing in the rain." Twice before, cook said, he had had this same dream, and each time he had been shipwrecked. "For God's sake, skipper, get off Georges Bank!"

A little later it breezed up. At one-thirty A.M. the *Sachem* was hove to under close-reefed foresail. Then, from the forecastle, one of the men yelled that the vessel was filling. Captain Wenzell went below and found six inches of water. Pumps were manned, bucket bailing was got under way, and cook was ordered to provision a boat. Believing the leak was under the port bow, the captain wore around and hove to on the other tack, in the hope that this might bring the leak out of water.

But nothing was effective against cook's "women dressed all in white." With a strong breeze blowing, the *Sachem* signaled the Gloucester schooner *Pescador,* and shortly afterward, at great risk to both crews, the men were got off the leaking vessel.

At two o'clock the *Sachem* rolled on her side, settled by the bow, and went down.

* * * * *

Although tragedy on Georges Bank has been a continued story, even beyond the motorization of the fleet and into the present, with its wireless, Coast Guard cutters, planes, and other aids to mariners, the dread of a winter's gale on those grounds today is nothing like what it was in the days of sail. Then disaster lay in "going adrift"—parting the cable and running, wholly out of hand, to almost certain collision, and in that case, certain death.

The Georges fleet was a large one. Fishing ports from Cape Cod down to Newfoundland were represented among the craft there, and frequently from the rigging a man could count between two and three hundred sail. Where one vessel had good luck, others flocked to be "on the fish." And the result was that the fleet usually bunched itself over a few small spots on the bank.

In good weather this was well enough; but it multiplied the risks many times in a storm. For if the gale should overtake a schooner in those days, all her crew could do was to snug down, pay out a good string to the anchor, and hope for the best while they tried to ride it out. From then on, if anything less than the best happened, it happened first to that all-important part of their equipment, the ground tackle; the anchor would drag, or the cable part under the strain.

A single vessel, once set adrift in those crowded waters, was sure to spread destruction. If she struck another, both went down. But usually, before this happened, several vessels lying in her path had cut their own cables and gone adrift themselves, to get out of her way. Cutting cable was a last resort, but on each craft a man stood ready with the axe. And as each was forced to cut loose, by so much more were the others in the fleet endangered. Thus death went snowballing over Georges Bank on such a night.

*   *   *   *   *

Taking Georges Bank into account for what it was, and for what it meant to these men, it may be easier to understand the refusal of the skipper to accept that beautiful new schooner, the *Charles Haskell.* A man had died on board, while the craft was still on the ways. And that was an omen—a sure sign she was unfit for the Georges Bank winter fishery. But a year passed, and another Gloucester skipper did take her out. And now, let us go back to her story.

"Yes, sir, gentlemens," Joe Enos said in his remote, singsong manner while he tossed the lead out after the snoods, "we get a breeze o' wind tonight, yes, sir, gentlemens!"

Hand-lining for cod forty miles west of Georges North Shoal, the *Haskell's* crew were doing some fast fishing at the moment. But, busy as they were, a couple of the boys paused to glance at "the Portygee." Joe, the only Portuguese on board, didn't have a great deal to say, but already on this first trip of the new schooner he had proved himself an able fisherman; when he did talk the others listened, and when he took the trouble to mention "a breeze o' wind" the chances were that it was going to be no ordinary weather.

"What makes you think so, Portygee?" George Scott asked.

"You see the way the fish bite now?" Joe shook his head. "Fish don't take the hook like this—only when we got a breeze o' wind by 'm by. Yes, sir, gentlemens, a breeze o' wind!"

Faster and faster, the fat cod were being hauled aboard. Within five or six miles of one another, more than a hundred vessels could be seen from the deck of the *Charles Haskell,* and on each the scene was the same.

Around noon the wind hauled to east-northeast, and from then on rose steadily. At three o'clock Captain Clifford Curtis ordered the *Haskell's* crew to haul in their lines.

"All right, boys! Heave in strads and give her cable!"

The crew took off the "strads"—pieces of rope bound around the cable to prevent chafing in the hawsepipe—gave her eighty more fathoms of the string, and stradded her up again. Then they took in the foresail, putting a double reef in it before they furled it, so as to have it ready for hoisting in case they should go adrift. The fishing vessel of that day carried no triangular storm trysail, such as is used for steadying the modern power-driven vessel; instead, for the same purpose, three reefs were taken in the mainsail, a rig that was termed "balanced-reefed mainsail."

By nine o'clock that night, Joe Enos's "breeze o' wind" had become a full-fledged hurricane. On Georges Bank, at the time, were 290 vessels; and with the wind continuing from the east-northeast, the deadly North Shoal lay under the lee of the fleet.

On board the *Charles Haskell,* as on other vessels, all hands were called on deck. Captain Curtis stationed himself at the cable, axe in hand. From his post he could see the lights of one unlucky schooner after another, passing by like a ghastly parade through the sleet—vessels that had already broken adrift.

Within an hour, the *Haskell* herself was dragging anchor but before she had slipped far from her berth, the hook fouled something on the bottom and brought her up short. There she hung, giving and tautening by turns, when suddenly the men at the forward lookout yelled warning. Directly over the schooner's bowsprit, looking as if it were almost atop her, a light was riding.

Captain Curtis brought down his axe, the *Haskell* bounded off like a catapulted stick and silently the stranger swept by.

"Up with the foresail! You, Portygee, keep her due west!"

Joe Enos nodded understanding. It was the skipper's idea to get to the leeward of the fleet if he could, and at the same time work beyond the North Shoal; for between collision and running aground on that shoal, there was precious little to choose.

After half an hour of running, they raised another light, this time on the weather bow. Captain Curtis, thinking the vessel was riding at her anchor, called out:

"Hard up the helm!"

But the other fellow, coming bow-on, also had his wheel hove up hard. Too late the skipper discovered that he, too, was running adrift. There was no chance then to pay off; and from a wave-crest the *Haskell* crashed into the other craft, cutting her down just abaft the port rigging. The stranger was split nearly to the mainmast.

As the figures of passers-by on a dark street are caught by a flash of lightning and "stopped" for the instant, so the crew of the unknown vessel appeared to those aboard the *Haskell.* One or two could have jumped aboard from where they stood, but none moved. And in the next instant, vessel and crew had vanished.

The *Haskell's* main boom and main rigging on the starboard side had carried away in the crash. The bowsprit had broken off, but was still hanging there, thudding against the planking and threatening to bash in the bow. The men cut this stick free, and in order to keep the mast from starting, made a line fast to the jibstay, passed it through the hawsepipe, and then under the windlass.

When the wreck was cleared, Joe Enos went below. No one aboard the *Haskell* expected her to stay afloat. No vessel stayed afloat when this happened. But down in the forecastle, Joe found George Winters, pointing and laughing hysterically, and screaming, "She's dry! She's dry! I tell you, there ain't a drop in her!"

Joe wouldn't believe it. He took up the trap in the forecastle floor. There was no water underneath! Then he ran to tell the skipper. Captain Curtis had the men try the pump. Below deck, the *Charles Haskell* was dry as a bone!

"*Graças a Deos!*" said Joe Enos. Then he turned to the skipper. "Those poor fellers! I see the faces, captain—one, two mens. *Ai*, the faces!"

Captain Curtis nodded, and for a moment turned away and looked into the sleet. Then he asked Joe:

"Did you see what vessel she was?"

Joe didn't know. Neither did anyone else on board the *Charles Haskell.*

When they had returned to Gloucester, they learned that nine vessels had gone down on Georges that night. Wrecks of six had been witnessed by others standing by, or accounted for by the few survivors from among the crews. The craft which the *Charles Haskell* had rammed and sunk was one of the remaining three: schooners *A. E. Price* and *Martha Porter* of Gloucester, and the *Andrew Johnson* [1] of Salem. Captain Curtis knew the skippers of all three; but which it was that his own vessel had wrecked, he supposed he would never learn.

The *Charles Haskell* was run up on the flats near her owner's wharf, repaired, and refitted. While she was there, thousands came to look at her. Old fishermen could scarcely believe the story that she had survived a collision on Georges Bank; yet there she was, and what she did no other vessel had ever done in the history of Georges; nor would any be likely to do it again!

So said the old fellows; but they also shook their heads and told Captain Curtis that if 'twas them a-skipperin' her, they'd go find another berth. After what *she'd* done, they wouldn't want none of *her*, by God! Ten good men of Gloucester—or was it Salem—walking the water somewhere out there on Georges Bank!

Captain Curtis didn't laugh at the old men; on the contrary, he turned upon them, excited, angry.

"We ain't got no blood on our hands!" he said.

Nevertheless, Miles Joyce and James Allen wouldn't ship on her for another trip, and the skipper had to find men for their places. Joe Enos, Scotty, and the rest stuck by him.

They were glad they did; for on her next trip out, she ran straight down to Georges, sailing it like a queen, and for the next few days, did some beautiful fishing.

---

[1] Cf. W. H. Bishop, "Fish and Men in the Maine Islands," *Harper's New Monthly Magazine*, Vol. LXI (September, 1880), No. 364, pp. 506–507: "She [the *Haskell*] broke loose from her moorings in a gale on George's, and tore into and sank the *Andrew Johnson*, with all on board. For years after, the spectres of the drowned men were reputed to come aboard the *Haskell*[*sic*] at midnight and go through a dumbshow of fishing in regular form over the side, so that no crew could be got in Gloucester to sail her, and she would not have brought sixpence in the market."

There was nothing curious in the fact that all the men wanted the early watches. They always did that. And when it came to setting the watch, the skipper followed the custom of the time, calling the men around him to "thumb the hat." The crew stood in a circle, each man holding to the brim of the hat, thumb up. The skipper looked away, reached over, touched a thumb, and then counted ten from that one, going around the hat clockwise. The owner of the tenth thumb got first watch, and the business was repeated to determine who his watchmate should be, for the period from eight o'clock to ten. Then it was gone through again for the next two, and so on. There was nothing peculiar in the fact that Scotty and George Winters felt relieved when they were picked for first watch the night they arrived on Georges.

But the sixth day's work was over, fish stowed, crew long since asleep, when Harry Richardson and Joe Enos took their watch on deck. Shortly after twelve o'clock, while Joe was nodding over the wheelbox, he felt a frantic thumping at his side. He started, awoke, and faced his watchmate.

Shaking, unable at the moment to speak, young Harry Richardson pointed forward. Joe straightened up and stared over the wheel. In the starlit bow of the *Charles Haskell* he saw a little group of men.

"What's a matter them fellers?" Joe asked. "What's a matter they don't turn in?"

"Portygee," Harry Richardson softly croaked, "look at 'em again! Look at 'em! Them—*them ain't our boys!*"

Joe squinted, started forward, and after a couple of steps, stood still. The little knot of figures had grown! From somewhere, more had appeared! He could see that. And then he could see a man climb in over the rail, coming up from the starboard side. And another. Out of the waters of Georges Bank, men—figures, shadows in the shape of men—were boarding the schooner. Things of the imagination, yes; mere apparitions seen there in the starlight—but seen, Joe suddenly realized, not by one pair of eyes, but two!

Joe Enos stood still and watched. Then he turned to Harry.

"I go wake the skipper," he whispered.

As he turned, the younger man clutched at his arm. "No, you. don't! You don't leave this deck, Portygee! Not with me up here, you don't!"

It didn't matter to Joe *who* went for the skipper. Still staring at the bow, he was about to tell Harry to go when the men—the things up there in the bow—started to move.

"Look!" Joe said. "They come aft!"

Silently they were stationing themselves at the regular "berths" along the deck, baiting hooks, and heaving gossamer lines over the side. And as Joe watched, it became apparent that these beings, whatever they were, were paying no attention to himself and Harry Richardson. The waters from which they had arisen were calm tonight, peaceful, beneficent; in nothing was there harm.

"All right," Joe said at last to Harry Richardson. "We stay here. We don't say nothing, you and me. By 'm by, Scotty and O'Neill got the watch. We wait and see, no?"

And so the two men stayed at the wheelbox while fishermen fished for shadows, and out of the starshine, hauled up their subtile catch.

Three minutes after Joe Enos had called the new watch and settled himself in his bunk, there was a yell from the deck. He heard the thud of boots above him, pounding aft. Then all hands were called.

When Joe went up again, the crew of the *Charles Haskell* was gathered around the cabin companionway. The figures along the deck were still obviously tending their lines, still heaving over splashless leads and slatting airy shapes into the barrels.

"I see 'em!" Captain Curtis was saying to one of the men as Joe came near. "Ain't I got eyes? But I tell you, there's no blood on our hands!" Over and over he said it, and in his voice there was a strange mingling of anger and appeal.

"There's fair wind tonight for home, skipper," somebody said.

"Me, I ain't staying out here another night," another put in. "Not me— if I have to swim it back!"

Captain Curtis was for sticking it out, and in the argument voices rose —until one or another of the men glanced forward, and then all spoke in low tones again. For this there was no need. The *Charles Haskell's* extra hands turned now and then to one another, and smiled as their lips moved soundlessly; but for all else that went on aboard the vessel, they seemed to have deaf ears, sightless eyes.

The skipper, alone in his stand, gave in at last.

"All right, boys. Get in the anchor. We're going home."

Gingerly the men went about their work. It was slow. There was much hesitating, much backing away, for now the strangers were hauling in their lines, their work finished. But when they had gone through the motions of leaving everything shipshape, one by one they filed to the bow, stepped over the rail, and walked into the darkness of Georges Bank.

Twenty-four hours later, during the same watch, the *Charles Haskell* again was manned with the silent fishermen. But she was homeward bound now. She had passed the twin lights of Thacher's Island, and under a good breeze, was bowling past the welcome glimmer of sidelights carried on vessels from the home port.

In the small watches of the morning, she brought Eastern Point Light nearly abreast. Then the captain gave the order to bear about for Gloucester Harbor, and took the wheel himself.

At that moment, each of the strangers turned, looked aft at Captain Curtis, and then went to join his shipmates up in the bow. While the *Haskell's* men were trimming the sails, these others stood there, watching. Then from among them one stepped out, walked aft as far as the fore-rigging, and gazing intently at the helmsman, slowly shook his head. But the schooner was running fast for the mouth of Gloucester Harbor, and the skipper held her to her course. And so the lone figure mounted the rail, beckoned to his fellows, and was gone over the side. The others followed. And the last the *Haskell's* crew saw of them, they were slowly marching through the dawn—*towards Salem!*

We may think what we will of the things men say they've seen. We may explain these nightly visitors of the *Charles Haskell* into being, or we may explain them away. Whatever we care to make of them will be of no more substance than the ghost-fishes they themselves slatted into empty barrels.

But what men *do* because of the things they've "seen"—well, here is another matter. And the fact does remain that from the morning she arrived home from her second trip to Georges Bank, the schooner *Charles Haskell* was taboo in Gloucester. Captain Curtis could not find a crew for her. With good fishing in prospect, and not too many berths open for the men who gathered daily in Rogers Street, one might think that a dozen men could be found for the crew from among those hundreds who were looking for berths, crowd of motley temperament, men of many faiths and none.

Not a dozen, not five, not two, could be induced to ship on the *Charles Haskell*. But one—Joe Enos, the "Portygee"—did tell Captain Curtis he was willing to try it once more. And Joe was willing because, he said, now he understood. He knew what to do.

"Next time," Joe told the skipper, "we go to Georges, we fish, we set sail. But we don't take the vessel back to Gloucester, Cap'n! When we come back, we go to Salem. We take them fellers home first!"

But the captain, man of a colder, more practical race than Joe Enos's, did not understand; and for months the *Charles Haskell* lay idle at a Gloucester wharf. Finally, rather than keep her at a dead loss, her owners sold her off to a group in Digby, Nova Scotia.

Whether the wanderers of Georges Bank ever came on board the *Charles Haskell* again, I do not know. The next time I could find the schooner mentioned was in this little item in the ship-news column of the *Provincetown Beacon*, March 11, 1893:

On Thursday last, sch. *W. B. Keene*, was at Lewis Wharf, having on board a box belonging to a hand-horn of the type used by fishing vessels for giving fog warning. On the box, which had been newly split and but a few days in the water, was painted the name, "Charles Haskell." The *Keene* is fresh-haddocking this season on Georges Bank.

II. THE POWERS OF DARKNESS

Go tell Mankind, that there are Devils and Witches.—COTTON MATHER

. . . . If anything happened out of the common, the devil was in it. So say many to-day. . . . The persistent life of such local traditions as these [haunts of the Devil] fully attests to the belief of former generations of men in the active agency of the Evil One in human affairs.—SAMUEL ADAMS DRAKE

William Dean Howells used to come up here and he told me that, when things went wrong for months on end, old [New Hampshire] hill farmers used to say, "The Witch is in it." And by this they meant some dark heavy power of fate inexorably pressing down. —ERNEST POOLE

1. MONSTER OR GENTLEMAN?

THE coming of the Devil to New England might have been reckoned among remarkable providences inasmuch as it enabled the leaders of church and state to prove that God is greater than the Devil and that in exterminating the devilish sect of witches they (the leaders) were the chosen instruments of God. But in New England the Devil behaved much as he did everywhere else. He assumed divers animal shapes (according to his wont), from a blue boar (obviously copied from a tavern sign) to a skipping deer; he left giant footprints (rarely in the shape of a cloven foot) in numerous rocks; and he lent his name to rocks, caves, glens, and other natural objects, "whose singularity would seem to suggest more than mortal occupancy."

The Devil found himself at home in the New World. For one thing, he encountered there many devil-worshipers among the Indians, or at least many whites believing that Indians (like all pagans) were devil-worshipers.[1] As a matter of fact, the Indians "knew nothing, till the English told them, either of purgatory, or of the Devil," as Edward Augustus Kendall has said, in relating the "facetious tradition" of Purgatory, a chasm at Middletown, Rhode Island, where the Indian Devil is supposed to have killed a squaw and thrown her into Purgatory.[2] At the same time, it is true that the Indians had their trickster-heroes and mischief-makers, distinguished for their devilish craft and cunning, such as the Ojibwa Manobozho, whose exploits Longfellow, following Schoolcraft, attributed to the Iroquois Hiawatha, and the giant Maushope, commemorated in many Martha's Vineyard landmarks (the Devil's Den, the Devil's Bridge, the Devil's Head and Pillows) and in the Devil's Ash Heap, or Nantucket.

But whatever the place of the Devil in Indian religion and mythology, the Indian practice of magic, through powpows or wizards, had an important bearing on New England witchcraft in that it was a "constant reminder of the possibility of danger from witchcraft."[3]

---

[1] According to Trumbull, the Indians of New England "paid their principal homage to Hobbamocho. They imagined that he was an evil spirit, and did them mischief; and so, from fear, they worshiped him, to keep him in good humor."—Rev. Henry White, *The Early History of New England Illustrated by Numerous Interesting Incidents* (Boston, 9th ed., 1841), p. 312.

[2] See "Purgatory" below.

[3] George Lyman Kittredge, "Notes on Witchcraft," *American Antiquarian Society Proceedings,* N. S., Vol. XVIII (April, 1907), p. 196.

If the Devil often met his match in New England, that was because there were many Yankees like Jonathan Moulton, of whom it was said that "neither man nor devil could get the better of him in a trade." However, General Moulton, like Tom Walker (another avaricious Yankee who tried to cheat the Devil out of his due and failed),[1] was in this instance too smart for his own good. In "The Devil and Daniel Webster" Stephen Vincent Benét has told the story of one sharp Yankee who beat the Devil —a story without known traditional source, which may yet become folklore.

To Jabez Stone, in Benét's story, the devil appeared as a "soft-spoken dark-dressed stranger," wearing handsome black boots and a cane and driving a handsome buggy. This is in the older tradition of the devil as a gentleman, belying the many monstrous shapes that he assumes in New England witchcraft and sorcery. When the Devil came to make a contract with Jonathan Moulton, he was "dressed from top to toe in black velvet," and for Goody Hallett's benefit he was "dressed in fine French bombasset." Even when he exhibited himself to the bewitched Mercy Short in 1692,[2] "having the Figure of a Short and a Black Man . . . not taller than an ordinary Walking-Staff," with straight hair and a cloven foot, he wore a high-crowned hat as a concession to the gentlemanly tradition.

2. Dancing to the Devil's Fiddle

In his dealings with witches the Devil was his other monstrous self. Thus at the Devil's Hop Yard, at Chapman Falls, one mile outside of Millington, Connecticut, where "on stormy nights the old hags were wont to congregate . . . and cast spells and mumble incantations as they stirred their potions" in circular pot-holes in the rock, "His Satanic Majesty himself would sometimes attend these meetings, a lurid glow from his body lighting up the dismal scene. His customary seat was at the very edge of the precipice, where, with tail laid over his shoulder as a scepter, he would majestically direct the exercises." [3]

Such mumbo-jumbo was part of the folklore of witchcraft, which outlasted, as it antedated, the witchcraft delusion in New England. The history of the latter (probably the greatest single piece of work of the Devil in this region) differs from the witchcraft of folklore as mass-hallucination differs from sporadic beliefs. But the witchcraft cases also belong to folklore through their use of all the trappings and paraphernalia of black magic, possession, transformation, and divination. The "spectral evidence" which served to convict many an innocent victim was full of familiar witchcraft phenomena, based on erroneous perception, "expectant attention," and deliberate lies. Yet some of those accused of being witches

---

[1] See "The Devil and Tom Walker," *A Treasury of American Folklore* (New York, 1944), pp. 731–740.

[2] Cotton Mather, *A Brand Pluck'd Out of the Burning* (1693), reprinted in *Narratives of the Witchcraft Cases, 1648–1706*, edited by George Lincoln Burr (New York, 1914), p. 261.

[3] W. Harry Clemons, "The Legends of Machimoodus," in *The Connecticut Magazine*, Vol. VII (Series of 1902–1903), No. 5, p. 454.

must have believed themselves to be or had the reputation of being posses-
sors of extraordinary powers, such as the power to assume invisibility,
change shape, and afflict enemies with physical or mental illness, disease
or destruction of cattle or crops, storms, etc. Favorite types of New England witches are the storm-raising witch[1] and the witch-weaver.

In French-Canadian legends of the *loup-garou* witchcraft plays into the
hands of religion. Condemned for neglect of religious duties to "leave
their human form at stated intervals and do as the Devil directs them,"
the *loups-garous* can be restored to human form only by diawing blood
from them.

If the Devil was hard on New England, that was only to be expected,
since New England was hard on the Devil, employing every means, fair
or foul, at its disposal to fight and outwit him and his familiars.

B. A. B.

THE DEVIL IS IN IT

Old Trickey, the Devil-Doomed Sandman

TRICKEY was a fisherman, and as rough and unruly of disposition as the
wildest sea he ever rode out. He lived at the mouth of York River, but
just where, no one seems to know; but there were Trickeys in Kittery. He
was as prickly and irritable as the saltiest brine; and his ugliness and generally disreputable character for wickedness and malevolence were nowhere
to be questioned. All these made of him a privileged character, who, without let or hindrance, wrought in the devil's vineyard after his own inventions.

After he died it was said that on account of his misdeeds done in the
body, the devil condemned him to stay about the region of Bra'boat Harbor, and he was supposed to haunt the vicinity constantly. The curse was
upon him, and his doom was to bind and haul sand with a rope until the
devil was satisfied. Curse as he would, and fume and fret, it was useless
until his task was done. The devil had exacted so much sand, and so much
he would have, so old Trickey got at his work. When the storm began to
gather and the sand dunes inshore grew in size and number, when the brew
of the gale wet the nose of Cape Neddock, the wraith of old Trickey would
come shrieking along over the marshes and then he was at his Sisyphus-like

---

[1] A combination of the storm-breeder and the Flying Dutchman motifs is to be
seen in William Austin's legend of "Peter Rugg, the Missing Man." See *A Treasury
of American Folklore* (New York, 1944), pp. 742–750.

[2] From *Maine Pioneer Settlements: Old York*, by Herbert Milton Sylvester, pp.
311–313. Copyright, 1906, and 1909, by Herbert M. Sylvester. Boston: W. B. Clarke
Co. 1909.

labor, when the air was filled with his wailing cries, "More rope! More rope! More sand! More sand!" and there he wrought amid the rack of the storm. As the dusk deepened, the figure of old Trickey grew and grew, until racing inland with his load of sand he strode over the cabin roofs to disappear until the coming of the next gale. In the morning, the sands had shifted strangely, and as the sun shot its light across them, the village folk could not but observe the tremulousness of the atmosphere above them. It was old Trickey struggling with the devil over the scene of his labors of the night before, and after dark these sands were as much to be avoided as the graveyard a little way up the hill.

Nowadays, when the fogs roll in, and the sea and sky are one, and the winds begin to rise, and the growl of the surf on the harbor bar grows louder, the fisher folk say, "Old Trickey is binding and hauling sand to-night! God save the fishing-smacks from harm!"

The old jail at York is now used as a museum for such antiquities as the people there are able to keep from taking wings and flying away. Among the treasures there shown is the Bible once owned by Trickey, a cherished curiosity and an eerie thing, if what one may hear is to be taken without salt. It is said there is a spell upon it. It is ancient enough, and its joints are stiff and dry. As one opens it, the binding is somewhat reluctant in its yielding, and like many books made to-day it will not stay opened, but flies back with a vicious snap; and some say they cannot push its black covers apart; and so, it must be haunted, or "cursed." If old man Trickey had used it more frequently himself the old tome would have been more pliable, doubtless. However, it is an interesting relic, and as one fumbles at its discolored leaves, the story of its owner of long years ago smacks of reality, and out of the moaning of the sea and the wailing of the wind is readily conjured the tortured and maddened outcries of this devil-doomed sand-man.

Jonathan Moulton and the Devil

The legendary hero of Hampton is General Jonathan Moulton. He is no fictitious personage, but one of veritable flesh and blood, who, having acquired considerable celebrity in the old wars, lives on through the medium of a local legend.

The General, says the legend, encountered a far more notable adversary than Abenaki warriors or conjurers, among whom he had lived, and whom it was the passion of his life to exterminate.

In an evil hour his yearning to amass wealth suddenly led him to declare that he would sell his soul for the possession of unbounded riches. Think

From *A Book of New England Legends and Folk Lore,* in Prose and Poetry, by Samuel Adams Drake, New and Revised Edition, pp. 322–328. Copyright, 1883, 1901, by Samuel Adams Drake. Boston: Little, Brown, and Company. 1910.

of the Devil, and he is at your elbow. The fatal declaration was no sooner made—the General was sitting alone by his fireside—than a shower of sparks came down the chimney, out of which stepped a man dressed from top to toe in black velvet. The astonished Moulton noticed that the stranger's ruffles were not even smutted.

"Your servant, General!" quoth the stranger, suavely. "But let us make haste, if you please, for I am expected at the Governor's in a quarter of an hour," he added, picking up a live coal with his thumb and forefinger, and consulting his watch with it.

The General's wits began to desert him. Portsmouth was five leagues— long ones at that—from Hampton House, and his strange visitor talked, with the utmost unconcern, of getting there in fifteen minutes! His astonishment caused him to stammer out,—

"Then you must be the—"

"Tush! what signifies a name?" interrupted the stranger, with a deprecating wave of the hand. "Come, do we understand each other? Is it a bargain, or not?"

At the talismanic word "bargain" the General pricked up his ears. He had often been heard to say that neither man nor devil could get the better of him in a trade. He took out his jack-knife and began to whittle. The Devil took out his, and began to pare his nails.

"But what proof have I that you can perform what you promise?" demanded Moulton, pursing up his mouth and contracting his bushy eyebrows, like a man who is not to be taken in by mere appearances.

The fiend ran his fingers carelessly through his peruke, when a shower of golden guineas fell to the floor and rolled to the four corners of the room. The General quickly stooped to pick up one; but no sooner had his fingers closed upon it, than he dropped it with a yell. It was red-hot!

The Devil chuckled; "Try again," he said. But Moulton shook his head and retreated a step.

"Don't be afraid."

Moulton cautiously touched a coin; it was cool. He weighed it in his hand, and rung it on the table; it was full weight and true ring. Then he went down on his hands and knees, and began to gather up the guineas with feverish haste.

"Are you satisfied?" demanded Satan.

"Completely, your Majesty."

"Then to business. By the way, have you anything to drink in the house?"

"There is some Old Jamaica in the cupboard."

"Excellent! I am as thirsty as a Puritan on election-day," said the Devil, seating himself at the table, and negligently flinging his mantle back over his shoulder, so as to show the jewelled clasps of his doublet.

Moulton brought a decanter and a couple of glasses from the cupboard, filled one, and passed it to his infernal guest, who tasted it, and smacked his lips with the air of a connoisseur. Moulton watched every gesture.

"Does your Excellency not find it to your taste?" he ventured to ask; having the secret idea that he might get the Devil drunk, and so outwit him.

"H'm, I have drunk worse. But let me show you how to make a salamander," replied Satan, touching the lighted end of the taper to the liquor, which instantly burst into a spectral blue flame. The fiend then raised the tankard to the height of his eye, glanced approvingly at the blaze,—which to Moulton's disordered intellect resembled an adder's forked and agile tongue,—nodded, and said, patronizingly, "To our better acquaintance!" He then quaffed the contents at a single gulp.

Moulton shuddered; this was not the way he had been used to seeing healths drunk. He pretended, however, to drink, for fear of giving offence; but somehow the liquor choked him. The demon set down the tankard, and observed, in a matter-of-fact way that put his listener in a cold sweat: "Now that you are convinced I am able to make you the richest man in all the province, listen! Have I your ear? It is well! In consideration of your agreement, duly signed and sealed, to deliver your soul" —here he drew a parchment from his breast—"I engage, on my part, on the first day of every month, to fill your boots with golden elephants, like these before you. But mark me well," said Satan, holding up a forefinger glittering with diamonds, "if you try to play me any trick, you will repent it! I know you, Jonathan Moulton, and shall keep my eye upon you; so beware!"

Moulton flinched a little at this plain speech; but a thought seemed to strike him, and he brightened up. Satan opened the scroll, smoothed out the creases, dipped a pen in the inkhorn at his girdle, and pointing to a blank space, said, laconically, "Sign!"

Moulton hesitated.

"If you are afraid," sneered Satan, "why put me to all this trouble?" and he began to put the gold in his pocket.

His victim seized the pen; but his hand shook so that he could not write. He gulped down a mouthful of rum, stole a look at his infernal guest, who nodded his head by way of encouragement, and a second time approached his pen to the paper. The struggle was soon over. The unhappy Moulton wrote his name at the bottom of the fatal list, which he was astonished to see numbered some of the highest personages in the province. "I shall at least be in good company," he muttered.

"Good!" said Satan, rising and putting the scroll carefully away within his breast. "Rely on me, General, and be sure you keep faith. Remember!" So saying, the demon waved his hand, flung his mantle about him, and vanished up the chimney.

Satan performed his part of the contract to the letter. On the first day of every month the boots, which were hung on the crane in the fireplace the night before, were found in the morning stuffed full of guineas. It is true that Moulton had ransacked the village for the largest pair to be found, and had finally secured a brace of trooper's jack-boots, which came nearly up to the wearer's thigh; but the contract merely expressed boots, and the Devil does not stand upon trifles.

Moulton rolled in wealth; everything prospered. His neighbors regarded him first with envy, then with aversion, at last with fear. Not a few affirmed that he had entered into a league with the Evil One. Others shook their heads, saying, "What does it signify?—that man would outwit the Devil himself."

But one morning, when the fiend came as usual to fill the boots, what was his astonishment to find that he could not fill them. He poured in the guineas, but it was like pouring water into a rat-hole. The more he put in, the more the quantity seemed to diminish. In vain he persisted; the boots could not be filled.

The Devil scratched his ear. "I must look into this," he reflected. No sooner said, than he attempted to descend; but in doing so he found his progress suddenly stopped. A good reason. The chimney was choked up with guineas! Foaming with rage, the demon tore the boots from the crane. The crafty General had cut off the soles, leaving only the legs for the Devil to fill. The chamber was knee-deep with gold.

The Devil gave a horrible grin, and disappeared. The same night Hampton House was burned to the ground, the General only escaping in his shirt. He had been dreaming he was dead and in hell. His precious guineas were secreted in the wainscot, the ceiling, and other hiding-places known only to himself. He blasphemed, wept, and tore his hair. Suddenly he grew calm. After all, the loss was not irreparable, he reflected. Gold would melt, it is true; but he would find it all,—of course he would,—at day-break, run into a solid lump in the cellar,—every guinea. That is true of ordinary gold.

The General worked with the energy of despair, clearing away the rubbish. He refused all offers of assistance; he dared not accept them. But the gold had vanished. Whether it was really consumed, or had passed again into the massy entrails of the earth, will never be known. It is only certain that every vestige of it had disappeared.

When the General died and was buried, strange rumors began to circulate. To quiet them, the grave was opened; but when the lid was removed from the coffin, it was found to be empty.

Another legend runs to the effect that upon the death of his wife under —as evil report would have it—very suspicious circumstances, the General paid his court to a young woman who had been the companion of his deceased spouse. They were married. In the middle of the night the young bride awoke with a start. She felt an invisible hand trying to take off from her finger the wedding-ring that had once belonged to the dead and buried Mrs. Moulton. Shrieking with fright, she jumped out of bed, thus awaking her husband; who tried in vain to calm her fears. Candles were lighted and search made for the ring; but as it could never be found again, the ghostly visitor was supposed to have carried it away with her. This story is the same that is told by Whittier in the "New Wife and the Old."

The Devil and the Card-Players

IN A Connecticut village four men were visiting together one evening. At length one of them proposed that they should have a game of cards. They were aware of the wickedness of card-playing, and knew very well how scandalous the proposal was. Nevertheless, after a little argument, they agreed to play for a short time. On a stand in the corner of the kitchen was a candle whose flame had eaten nearly down to the socket. Said one of the men, "We'll just play till the candle burns out. There can't be much harm in that, I'm sure."

"Very good," said the others; "we'll stop when the candle burns out."

They played one game, two games, three games, and still the candle burned. The candle burned, and game followed game until morning came, and the first rays of daylight startled the four players.

Then they knew that Satan himself had been their companion through the night. Who but the Devil would have kept that candle burning for so many hours for such a purpose?

Cheating the Devil

A FARMER who had no money wanted a barn. Indeed, he wanted the barn very badly. The man had just a shed or two back of his little house, and it did not seem to him he could get along without a barn much longer possibly. Now, the Devil knew very well how the man was feeling; and one day he went to the man, and said he'd build him a barn. So they fixed up a bargain between them. For putting up the barn the Devil was to have the man's soul when he died; but the work must be done before the first rooster crew in the morning, or the bargain was off. All that night the man heard the Devil hammering and hammering away up the hill a little ways, where he was building the barn. A while before daylight the man got up, and went out the back door to where he had a slab shed he kept his hens in. He stopped before the door, and made an imitation of crowing, and the old rooster answered him. That knocked the bargain all to pieces, and the Devil got well cheated that time. The man got his barn free; but being of the Devil's building I don't suppose it was a very good one, or lasted very long.

From *What They Say in New England*, A Book of Signs, Sayings, and Superstitions, collected by Clifton Johnson, p. 237. Copyright, 1896, by Lee and Shepard. Boston.

Ibid., pp. 241–242.

The Loup-Garou

. . . Naow, wait till Ah'll goin' tol' you baout de loup garou. Ah dat was so bad ting, it mek me scare for tink of it ever sen Ah 'll leetly boy an' de hol' mans an' de hol' hwomans tol' of it. Den we 'll seet an' squeeze de fire, an' be scare fer look behin' of us, fer see de shadder creep, creep on de floor an' jomp on de wall, fer fred it be de loup garou.

*   *   *   *   *

. . . dey was dev' more as anyting. . . . Dev', dev'. Some tam dey was mans jes lak anybodee, and den dey was be wolfs, oh, more wusser as wolfs. Dey ketch dead mans in graveyards an' heat it, dey ketch live mans, an' heat it. Oh, dey was awfuls. Ah b'lieve dey ant gat some more in Canada, naow, but in de hol' tam dey had it. One tam, mah gran'-gran'mudder, he'll gat so hol' he'll mek off hees min's hee 'll die, an' mah gran'fader he 'll was go fer pries' in de naght, an' long, long way t'rough de hwood, an' he drivin' long on hees traine, can' hear no nowse 'cep' de snow scroonch, scroonch under de runner an' de hoss feet of it. Wal, seh, mah gran'pere was drovin' long, ant tink for much, 'cep' for hurry fas'. He 'll was goin' on smooze road t'rough de hwood wen hees hoss was beegin fer go slow an' he 'll can' mek it go fas', all he 'll wheep it. De hoss jes' pull hard lak he 'll draw more as two ton load an' sweat so he 'll smoke lak stimboat an' melt de snow on de road wid de drop of de sweat.

Bambye mah gran'pere look behin' of it, an', seh, he 'll see great beeg, beeg black dawg, mebby wolf, he do' know if it ant prob'ly, wid hees fore-foots off de graound an' can' pull back some more.

Mah gran'pere was mad, an' scare more as he 'll was mad, an' he stroke dat ting wid hees whip, an' dat ting jomp raght on de traine an' put hees before feet on mah gran'pere shoulder of it, so heavy, he mos' squeese him. Mah gran'pere feel of hees knife fer cut at it, cause ef you drew bleed of de loup garou he 'll turn mans raght off an' go away.

But he can' fin' hees knife, an' he 'll ant know what he 'll do. De hoss was scare an' run lak hol' hurricanes, 'cause de loup garou gat hees behin' foots off de graound an' can' pull back some more.

Mah gran'pere feel dat hell ting's hot bress froze hees neck, an' hees hairs bresh hees face lak needle, an' he 'll shut off hees heye, so he can' see dat awfuls yallar heye clost hees hown, an' he give up for tink he dead, jes' as de hoss run in de pries' gate, an' he holler an' de pries run aout an' say some word quick an' laoud an' de loup garou be mans raght off so quicker as you mek some wink an' run off in de hwood.

My gran'fader was so scare it was took more as mos half pant of de pries' whiskey-en-esprit to brought it to.

The Devil and the Loups-Garous

MANY years ago a man named Jean Dubroise lived in the village of St. Denis. He mocked the church and said that the Bon Dieu was non-existent. The crops grown upon his land were the finest in that part of Canada and in the winter his trap-line caught the largest number of animals with the finest fur. His house, barn, and fences were kept in repair and his neighbors could not account for this as he was never seen to do any work. It was told that from his house and farms strange wild noises issued and none of the villagers would set foot on his land at night. Even in the daytime, when a villager had to pass Jean Dubroise's house, he would cross himself and hurry away.

Alphonse Gaulin, returning home late one night from a dance where he had a few drinks of whisky, said, "What care I for the Devil? I go for a walk where I please and if the Devil come near me I give him a fine licking." So saying, Alphonse cut across Jean Dubroise's land as a short cut home. When he arrived near the house, he heard a horrible noise which came from the north and seemed to be something coming fast, like a rail-road train. This was queer, as there was no railroad anywhere near this farm. The nearer it came, the greater the noise. It came straight at Alphonse, who was now thoroughly frightened, and saying his act of con-trition he threw himself flat upon the ground, the while he promised the Bon Dieu that if he escaped alive he would always attend church and stop drinking and swearing. The noise had grown louder and at the height of about thirty feet over his head passed a great canoe. He could hear a snarling, a howling, a clanking of chains and evil noises of all kinds, like pieces of iron being shaken up in a kettle. The noise was so loud that his ears rang for ten minutes after the great canoe had passed.

The canoe came down to the ground near the door of Jean Dubroise's house, and Alphonse, from his hiding place, could see a huge man, who was sitting in the back of the canoe dressed in red from head to toe, swing a whip and lash the occupants of the canoe, the while shouting, "Come, get out of the canoe. There is much work to be done before morning." About twenty small elf-like creatures jumped out of the canoe and started plowing the land under the direction of the Devil and of Jean Dubroise, who had come out of the house. Now Alphonse knew the whole story. Jean Dubroise, who had mocked the priests and the church, had sold his soul to the Devil for burning and the Devil was paying him by working his farm every night with about twenty loups-garous. These were living men who, for not having attended to their religious duties, were compelled to leave their human form at stated intervals and do as the Devil directs them. They had to serve the Devil for various lengths of time. One who had not

By Edward Rousseau, Woonsocket, Rhode Island. Manuscripts of the Federal Writers' Project of the Works Progress Administration for the State of Rhode Island.

received communion for five years would have to serve the Devil for five years. Another who had not gone to confession for ten years would have to serve that length of time before he would be free of the Devil's spell.

Alphonse Gaulin was afraid to move and, lying on the ground, he watched the twenty loups-garous doing the farm work. They kept on working until just before dawn the Devil ordered them into the canoe and away the canoe dashed through the sky. Alphonse then rushed home and told his neighbors of what he had witnessed. While some of his neighbors thought that what he had seen was the Devil who came out of a whisky bottle, others believed and urged him to go to the curé and tell his story. He went to the parish house and told his story to the curé who promised to put an end to the Devil's coming to the village of St. Denis. The next day, while Jean Dubroise was away from his farm, the men of the parish, with the curé leading them, marched to the farm and upon arriving there the curé said Mass and then he sprinkled holy water all over the farm.

That night all the men of the parish and the curé hid themselves near the farmhouse of Jean Dubroise. Just before midnight they heard the Devil's canoe approaching. They were afraid, but knowing that the power of Bon Dieu was greater than that of the Devil, none moved from their hiding places. The canoe slid to earth and the Devil stepped out. When the foot of the Devil touched the earth he gave a great shout that shook the trees, for as every one knows the Devil is afraid of holy water. He shouted, raged, and tore up the ground. Thinking that Jean Dubroise had told the curé of his visits, he rushed to the house and, grabbing Jean, he hurried back to the canoe. Every time that the Devil's foot touched the ground terrifying groans of agony came from his lips. He threw Jean Dubroise into the canoe, jumped in himself, and then in a blast of flame that scorched the ground for many yards, the Devil, Jean Dubroise, and the canoe disappeared.

All this time the twenty loups-garous were wandering around with no one to direct them and as even a child knows, the only way to restore human form to these poor men is to draw blood from them. The men of the parish rushed upon the loups-garous and with knives cut them slightly so that the blood would flow. Almost immediately the loups-garous changed to human form and the men of St. Denis were astonished to find that they were friends who had been bewitched by the Devil. There was joy in St. Denis that day and a great feast was prepared. After eating, all of the people went to Mass and from that time on no man of St. Denis has mocked either the church or the curé nor has any one neglected his religious duties.

Why Purgatory Was Made

MANY years ago in the village of St. Ours lived a man by the name of Victor. Now Victor was a cunning good-for-nothing who wished to live without working and tried to cheat every one. All day long he would gamble with cards, even on Sunday. One day when his luck was bad, he lost all of his money.

That evening a stranger came to Victor's house and asked Victor to play cards with him. Victor explained to the stranger that he had lost all of his money playing cards and had nothing left to bet. The stranger replied, "If you will give your soul to me for burning, I'll give you this ring, and as long as you wear it, you will never lose when playing cards." Victor then knew that he was talking to the Devil but thought that this was a good bargain, as by winning at cards he would have plenty of money without working. So he agreed and the Devil said, "Here is the ring and when I need your soul I'll come and get you."

Victor put on the ring and went down to the Inn to play cards. For about three years Victor won every time that he played cards. He was very happy, as he had plenty of money. But one day the Devil suddenly appeared and said, "I have kept my promise. Now I want you to keep yours. On next Monday I will come for you, as I need your soul." Then the Devil disappeared, leaving Victor regretting that he had made such a bargain.

The next day Victor, trying to think of a way to cheat the Devil, was walking along the road when he met the Bon Dieu and St. Peter, who were traveling from village to village. St. Peter noticed the expression on Victor's face and said, "My son, what is the matter? Come, tell us. Maybe we can straighten things out for you." Victor told him of the trouble he was in and the Bon Dieu, who wanted to spite the Devil, said, "I will show you how you may cheat the Devil, but you must never gamble with other men, as you cannot lose, and that would be cheating." Victor promised that if he was delivered from the Devil's power, he would never play cards again and that he would go to work. So the Bon Dieu said, "Throw away the Devil's ring and when he comes for you play him a game of cards. You cannot lose, as I will put a charm upon you."

On Monday when the Devil came for him, Victor said, "Sit down and let us play a game of cards. If I lose, I'll go with you. If I win, I'll stay here." The Devil, seeing that Victor no longer wore the magic ring and believing that he himself would win, replied, "All right, if I don't beat you I'll go back to Hell alone." They played, but the Devil, unable to overcome the charm of the Bon Dieu, lost, and in a puff of smoke disappeared.

Now that Victor no longer feared the Devil, he soon forgot his promise

From "French-Canadian Folklore," Woonsocket, Rhode Island. Manuscripts of the Federal Writers' Project of the Works Progress Administration for the State of Rhode Island.

to the Bon Dieu, and instead of going to work he continued to gamble, and for many years Victor led an evil life. One day the Bon Dieu said to St. Peter, "Do you know that we have forgotten Victor and all this time he has been a gambler? He has broken his promise to me. You must go and get him." St. Peter said, "I am very busy now, so you had better send Death for him."

So Death was sent down to earth and he brought Victor to the gates of paradise. St. Peter would not let him in but told him to go and see his friend the Devil. Victor went to the Devil's abode far, far down below, but the Devil would not let him in, saying, "I won't have you here. You cheated me when you were on earth. Get out." Victor went back to the gates of paradise and said, "Now listen, great St. Peter, the Devil won't have me and I've got to sleep somewhere. Let me just hide behind the gates of paradise." St. Peter and the Bon Dieu discussed the matter and agreed to let Victor in if he promised never again to either gamble or to cheat any one. Victor promised and St. Peter let him in and told him to sit on a small white cloud behind the gates of paradise.

For a long time Victor remained quiet and had nothing to say. But this became wearisome, and at last Victor pulled out his cards and asked a neighbor, seated on a larger cloud above him, if he would like to play. "We will play for an exchange of places," said Victor, and he won the game. After he had moved to the second cloud, he said to his neighbor next above, "Would you like to play for each other's places?" Again Victor won, for the charm that the Bon Dieu had given him, long ago, was still powerful. This went on until Victor found himself seated beside the Great Throne. "Bon Dieu," said Victor, "will you play a little game with me for each other's place?" But the Bon Dieu said, "You are lucky to be here. Twice have you broken your promise to me and this time I'll put you where you will never again have any one to play cards with."

So the Bon Dieu made a place that was not as bad as Hell nor as good as Heaven and he called it Purgatory. It was a place of darkness and silence where a man's soul, by suffering, is purified from venial sins, and the man's soul is then admitted into Heaven. Victor was sent to Purgatory, where for many years he must suffer for the sins that he committed while on earth. Since that time every man who on earth is a gambler is sent to Purgatory when he dies so that he may suffer for his sins.

THE WITCH IS IN IT

How Old Betty Booker Rode Skipper Perkins Down to York

THESE two skippers, Mitchell and Perkins, were both Kittery salts, but of

From *Maine Pioneer Settlements: Old York*, by Herbert M. Sylvester, pp. 317–319. Copyright, 1906 and 1909, by Herbert M. Sylvester. Boston. W. B. Clarke Co. 1909.

the two Skipper Perkins was the worst curried. Old Betty Booker wanted some fish, and she suggested her need to the skipper, "Bring me a bit o' hal'but, skipper, when you git in ——."

"Show me your sixpence, ma'am," was the thrifty reply.

And with an ill-boding scowl, and a shake of—

"Her wicked head, with its wild gray hair,
And nose of a hawk, and eyes like a snake,"

she watched the skipper sail away. The sea beat him up and down. The gale tore his sails, and the fish sheered away from his trawls. His men got sick, and his schooner came home poorer than she went. Then it got bruited about that Betty Booker was making a witch-bridle for the skipper, and was going to ride him down to York some wild night, whereat, the skipper, when it came to his ears, got into a mortal terror. He was sure to be at home, always, before dusk; and his doors were barred double, and he quaked and shivered and shook until the sun came up. Finally Betty sent the skipper word that the first stormy night she would ride him to York.

Then he waited for the storm, and the storm came. The rain drove across Chauncey's Creek in blinding sheets; the winds wrenched and tore at the trees along shore, shaking the gables of the houses. Folk huddled about their slow fires with so much wet coming down the chimneys, and whispered awesomely that the witches were out.

Skipper Perkins not only barred his door double, but he piled all the movable furniture in his rooms against it, and then he waited for Betty Booker; nor was she long in coming. An unearthly wail came down the wind, and there was a scratching of a hundred witch-claws on his door, and above all sounded the cracked notes of Betty Booker's voice,—

"Bring me a bit o' hal'but, skipper!"

But the skipper piled the furniture higher against the door, and pushed against it with all his strength.

"Bring me a bit o' hal'but, skipper!"

With the cry of the hag, the gale rose higher, and with rougher buffetings it smote the old door that was built to look out on the sea; and then it began to open so the skipper felt a spatter of rain on his face. He heard the wild chatter of the witches, but he still held to his pushing, until he felt himself sliding along the rough floor. He made a leap for his bed, winding himself about in its coverings; the door flew open and in trooped the witches. They pounced upon the skipper, and stripped him to his skin; and while he cowered in his fear, old Betty bridled him and got upon his back, while the other witches climbed upon hers, and off they raced through the gale to York Harbor. When he lagged, they pricked him with their claws to make him go the faster; and so they rode him as long as they wished, to get him back to Kittery before cock-crow, more dead than alive.

"Don't say sixpence, skipper, to a poor old woman again," was Betty Booker's parting admonition, as she and her familiars vanished into the mists of the darkest part of the night.

After that the skipper took to his bed, where for three weeks he nursed his wounds and told his story to his neighbors.

In one of the old houses at Kittery, a part of which was being torn down not long ago, an old witch-bridle was found between the lathing and the outside boarding. It was made of the hair of the tail of a horse, strands of tow, and the inside bark of the yellow birch. A woman who happened to be present knew what it was, and seizing it with the tongs threw it into the fire. That there were such things seems to be well authenticated.

Old Deb and Other Old Colony Witches

"AFTER you pass Carver Green on the old road from the bay to Plymouth," said one of these women, "you will see a green hollow in a field. It is Witches' Hollow, and is green in winter and summer, and on moonlit nights witches have been seen dancing in it to the music of a fiddle played by an old black man. I never saw them, but I know people who saw witches dancing there. In a small house near the hollow, a little old woman lived who was a witch; she went by the name of Old Betty, and she danced on the green with the devil as a partner. There was an old man who lived in that neighborhood by himself; he was kind to Betty, giving her food and firewood. After a while he got tired of her and told her she must keep away. One day he caught her there and put her in a bag, and locked the bag in a closet, and put the key in his pocket, and went away to his work. While he was gone, she got out of the bag and unlocked the door. Then she got his pig, dog, cat, and rooster, put them into the bag, put the bag in the closet and hid herself. When the man came home the animals in the bag were making a dreadful noise. 'Ah, ha! Old Betty, there you are!' said the man. He took the bag and dashed it on his doorstone, and the old woman laughed and cried out, 'You hain't killed Old Betty yet!'"

Another story told by the old women was of two witches who lived in Plymouth woods, near the head of Buzzard's Bay, who never went out in the daytime; but in the evening twilight they walked out "casting spells." They cast a spell on a boy, compelling him to follow them home. Putting him to bed in a lower room, they went up a ladder into the loft. At midnight the boy saw them come down the ladder, go to the oven, and take out a quahog shell. Each witch rubbed it behind her ears and said "Whisk!" when each flew up the chimney. The boy got up and rubbed the shell behind his ears; immediately he went up the chimney and found himself standing outdoors beside the witches, who were sitting astride black horses in the yard. On seeing the boy one of them dismounted, went into the house and returned with a "witch bridle" and a bundle of straw. She flung the bridle over the straw, and out of it came a pony. The boy was put on the pony's back, and away the three cantered across a large meadow, until

From *The Old Colony Town and Other Sketches*, by William Root Bliss, pp. 104–112. Copyright, 1893, by William Root Bliss. Boston and New York: Houghton Mifflin Company.

they came to a brook. The witches cleared the brook at a leap; but the boy, when he cleared it, said to his pony, "A pretty good jump for a lousy calf!" Those words broke the spell; the pony vanished, the boy stood alone with the bridle and the straw. He now ran after the witches, and soon he came to an old deserted house in which he heard the sound of fiddles. He peeped in a window and saw a black man fiddling, and the two witches and other old women dancing around him. Frightened, he ran down the road until he came to a farmhouse. He knocked on the door, was admitted, and the next day the farmer carried him to his parents.

The old women who told the witch stories said that their grandmother had been personally acquainted with two witches, in the last century. One of these was named Deborah Borden, called at that day "Deb Burden," who was supposed to have caused a great deal of mischief in Wareham, Rochester, and Middleboro. It was thought to be necessary for farmers to keep in her good graces lest she should cause a murrain to come upon cattle, lest the rye refuse to head, and the corn to ear. She was a weaver of cloth and rag carpets. Woe to the unlucky housewife who worried Deb or hurried her at her looms! I will let one of the sisters relate her story of this sorceress. It is not probable that the relator had ever heard of Robert Burns' story of Tam O'Shanter and his gray mare Meg; but a running brook filled the same place in that story and in this:—

"Once my grandmother had a web of cloth in Deb's looms, so she sent my mother and a girl named Phebe after·it. The two girls were just as intimate as finger and thumb. They went to Deb's house and told her what my grandmother said, and it made her mad, 'cause she didn't like to be hurried. Near her back door was a tree full of red apples, and Phebe, said, 'Won't you please give me an apple?' and Deb said, 'Drat you! No, I won't!' My mother wasn't afraid, so she took an apple for Phebe and one for herself, and she said to Deb:—

" 'I ain't afraid of ye, ye old witch!'

" 'Ye ain't?' Deb screamed; 'then I'll make ye afraid afore ye git home!'

"They had a piece of woods to go through; in the middle of it there was a pair of bars, and on the other side of the bars there was a brook. Suddenly they heard a roaring and they saw a black bull coming. 'Oh!' said Phebe, 'Captain Besse's bull has got out and he will get us'; so they ran for the bars. They got through them and across the brook, when the bull leaped the bars and stopped on the edge of the brook and roared; then my mother knew it was old Deb Burden who was in the bull to frighten the girls, because the brook stopped the critter. Witches can't cross running water, you know.

"The girls reached home dreadfully frightened, and told what had happened. 'Never mind,' said my grandfather; 'I'll fix Debbie!' When she brought home the cloth, he came into the house and slipped behind her as she sat by the fire, and put a darning-needle through her dress and fastened her to the chair. Well, she sot; and every once in a while she said, 'I must go'; but she couldn't stir; she would be still for a while and then say, 'Why, I must go and tend my fire'; but she couldn't stir no more'n a milestone; and he kept her in the chair all day, and then he pulled out the needle and let her go. 'Scare my gal agin, ye old witch!' he said. You know witches can't do anything when steel is nigh, and that was the reason the darning-needle held her.

"Once Deb came to Thankful Haskell's in Rochester, and sot by the fire, and her daughter, fourteen year old, was sweeping the room, and she put the broom under Deb's chair. You can't insult a witch more than that, 'cause a broomstick is what they ride on when they go off on mischief. Deb was mad as a March hare, and she cussed the child. Next day the child was taken sick, and all the doctors gin her up, and they sent for old Dr. Bemis of Middleboro; he put on his spectacles and looked at her, and said he, 'This child is bewitched; go, somebody, and see what Deb is up to.' Mr. Haskell got on his horse and rode to Deb's house; there was nobody in but a big black cat; this was the devil, and witches always leave him to take care of the house when they go out. Mr. Haskell looked around for Deb, and he saw her down to the bottom of the garden by a pool of water, and she was making images out of clay and sticking in pins. As quick as he saw her he knew what ailed the child; so he laid his whip around her shoulders good, and said, 'Stop that, Deb, or you shall be burnt alive!' She whimpered, and the black cat came out and growled and spread his tail, but Mr. Haskell laid on the whip, and at last she screamed, 'Your young one shall git well!' and that child began to mend right off. The black cat disappeared all of a suddint and Mr. Haskell thought the earth opened and took him in."

"Moll Ellis was called the witch of Plymouth," said the other sister, taking up the story-telling. "She got a grudge agin Mr. Stevens, a man my grandfather worked for, and three years runnin' she cast a spell on the cattle and horses, and upsot his hay in a brook. My grandfather drove and Stevens was on the load, and when they came to the brook the oxen snorted, and the horses reared and sweat, and they all backed and the hay was upsot into the brook. One day Stevens said, 'I'll not stand this; I'll go and see what Moll Ellis is about.' So he went up to her house, and there she lay on her back a-chewin' and a-mutterin' dretful spell words, and as quick as Stevens saw her he knew what ailed his cattle; and he walked right up to the bed, and he told Moll, 'If you ever upset another load of hay I'll have you hung for a witch.' She was dretful scart, and promised she never would harm him again. When she was talking, a little black devil, that looked just like a bumblebee, flew into the window and popped down her throat; 't was the one she had sent out to scare the cattle and horses. When Moll died, they couldn't get the coffin out the door because it had a steel latch; they had to put it out the window."

The Man Who Could Send Rats

AFTER supper when my [New Hampshire] landlady had finished doing the dishes and had sat down to sew, we heard a rat in the walls. That reminded her of a chopper who several years ago came to the house to board a few days after he got through the winter in the woods, "and he say he can make the rats go just where he please—send them any place he want; and I say, 'You a nice man—doin' such things!'

"But he say, 'That's all right. It come very handy knowing to do that sometimes'; and I tell him I don't think much of man sending rats round. Well, he been long time in camp, and his clothes much dirty, and he want me to wash for him, and I say, 'No, you hire some other people what does washing here.' But he was a Frenchman and didn't want to spend noth-ings—these French, they come from Canada, you know, and they brings everything they will need and don't want to spen' one cent. They want to take they money all back to Canada. Then he ask will I let *him* do the wash, and so I did.

"When he ready to go home, an' we settle, he don't want pay fifty cent a day, and he say, 'You wouldn't charge so much to a poor workingman,' and I say, 'I would. You heat enough for two mans together, and I got have the price what I always have.' He want to pay twenty-five cents, but I won't take only my reg'lar price.

"So he went away, and that same day a lot of railway mens come, and the house was full up; and in the night we could not none of us sleep, the rats made so much noise. It was like any one move a trunk and throw a table on the floor—make jus' as much noise as that—and no one believe that was rats. The boarders, they want know the next morning if we hear that terrible noise—that scratch and bang—and they ask if we have ghosts. We never hear any rats before and we think that Frenchman, he go away mad and he mus' make the rats of all the peoples round here come down our place. We didn't have no cat. Every cat we use to have would get fits, and some day we find it turnin' round and grab on the wall and fall on the floor; and we think the cat might jump up on the cradle and scratch the baby, and we get frightened when the cat have fits, and we kill all the time. One of the boarder, he say he heard if you steal a cat, it keep well and never have that sickness same what all the before cats had. So I say, 'If you to steal a cat have a chance, I wish you to goodness would.'

"He kind of keep lookout for cats that day and he found one on the sidewalk 'bout two mile from here; and the boarders say we fed those other cats too much meat, so we didn't any more, and we had that cat eight or nine years and we got it yet. Soon as we got it that cat begun catch rats. It catch mos' as fifteen a day and it wouldn't never eat that rats once. It catch them all night and it not through catching the next morning, but it

From *New England and Its Neighbors*, written and illustrated by Clifton Johnson, pp. 30–32. Copyright, 1902, by The Macmillan Company. New York. 1912.

so tired then it would not kill, but bring them to the kitchen and leave them run round, and we have to take the broom. That make the boarders laugh.

"The next fall that Frenchman come again. It mos' night, and he go to the barn, but I know him as he pass the window. My husband he milking and he not in the dark remember the man. If he have he take a stick and break his neck. The man he ask if he can get board, and my husband he say, 'My wife manage all that.' So the man come and ask me. He have a bag on his back and it been rain hard and he all wet. He say he can't go any farther; and I say, '*You* the man what send the rats any place you want to. We got lots of rats that night you left. I guess you got you bag full of rats again. No, I not keep you.'

"He never sayed anythings, but jus' walk away down the road."

The Man Who Made Weather

ONE of these earlier local characters, whose story borders on the marvelous, was an old man, called "Uncle Kaler," who lived on Loudon Hill. Uncle Kaler had Finnish blood in his veins and was reputed to be a "wizard." By his magical art, Uncle Kaler could make amulets that would bring good luck to the sailor, love philters for despairing swains and forlorn damsels, and efficacious potions to cure the cattle that were bewitched. This weird enchanter could also make good weather or bad weather to order, although he sometimes overdid the matter, as the following tradition shows.

Uncle Kaler lived in an old house just below the millbrook, and the road from Cobbossee to the Hook ran close by his door. One warm misty evening in May, Uncle Kaler heard some horses speeding up the hill and stopping at his door. He opened it, and a man's voice came in from the darkness: "Is this Mr. Kaler?"

"It is, at your service."

"Well, my name is ——, and this lady with me is Miss —— of Pownalboro. We are on our way to Hallowell to be married. Her relatives don't like the match and are after us hot foot. Listen!"

Away down the river could be heard the long-drawn bay of hounds.

"You hear, old man! Now our horses are about used up, and if something isn't done they will overtake us; then there will be murder. You have the reputation of being a windjammer and wizard. Here are a hundred Spanish milled dollars for the worst weather you have got, and if it does the business, another hundred when I come back."

The old man made no reply, but went to a chest and taking out a small leather bag gave it to the stranger, saying, "Go back a little on the road,

From *Old Hallowell on the Kennebec*, by Emma Huntington Nason, pp. 290–292. Copyright, 1909, by Emma Huntington Nason. Augusta, Maine. 1909.
From "Van Ho," Loudon Hill.—E. H. N.

cut open the bag, squeeze out its contents, throw the bag away, then come back and resume your journey."

The man did as he was told, and returning in a short time said: "If you have played us false, something will happen to you."

"Rest easy," said Uncle Kaler. "Hark!" and away in the southwest was heard a low grumbling like distant thunder. It increased and deepened momentarily till it seemed as if a cyclone was tearing through the forest.

"What is it?" asked the stranger.

"A cloud-burst in the hills. It will be a sharp hound who follows your track in five minutes. Go in peace, and good luck go with you, from a man who can make good luck."

Away they dashed through the gathering storm and darkness, speeding to happiness, or the contrary, as the case may be with married people. Under the roaring thunder, and nearly deafened by the roar and crash of the raging torrent he had conjured, the old man went into the house saying to himself: "I am afraid I made that bagful too strong, but I don't know as I am sorry, for it would never do to have the young people caught."

The next morning the day broke clear and beautiful; but where, the day before, a peaceful little brook had flowed through a green pasture, and the little mill had clattered merrily grinding the few grists the neighbors brought, there was now a fearful gorge gullied down to the bedrock and choked up with uprooted trees and brush; the mill was gone and the big boulder that formed a part of its foundation had been swept away far out into the river, and now forms that impediment to navigation known as Mill Rock. If anyone will take notice at low tide they will see quite a large point stretching out into the river from the mouth of the brook; it is the debris of the cloudburst.

III. PLACE LORE

Local names . . . may always be regarded as records of the past, inviting and rewarding a careful historical interpretation.
—Isaac Taylor

. . . the anecdotes told to explain names are by their nature suspect; much like folk-etymologies, they are often ex post facto concoctions, attempts to rationalize the name.
—Frederic G. Cassidy

. . . the village street and the lonely farm and the hillside cabin became positively richer objects under the smutch of imputation; twitched with a grim effect the thinness of their mantle, shook out of its folds such crudity and levity as they might, and borrowed, for dignity, a shade of the darkness of Cenci-drama, of monstrous

legend, of old Greek tragedy, and thus helped themselves out for
the story-seeker more patient almost of anything than of flatness.
—HENRY JAMES

1. "A LOCAL HABITATION AND A NAME"

INTEREST in local names, as in local history generally, springs from local
pride and a desire to know one's past. And Yankees are endowed with
more than their share of both place-consciousness and curiosity. The
former is echoed in such fervid formulations as "I have never ceased to
feel my pulse quickened at the mention of the name of Westfield," [1] and
the latter in the rural New Englandism, "I want to know!" [2]

In their zeal for local history, Yankees have accumulated a vast amount
of local traditions, including place lore. As distinct from local legends
(such as the foregoing legends of haunts, specters, witches, and the Devil),
place lore proper is the lore of topographical features, landmarks, place-
names, settlement, environment, local objects and traits, local rivalries,
and everything else that comes under the head of *genius loci*. Much of
this lore is buried in the work of local historians, antiquarians, travel and
guidebook writers, local colorists, memoirists, and other chroniclers and
observers of the local scene. On the family bookshelf the town or county
history (generally sold by agents and by subscription) occupied a place
next to the Bible and the almanac; and in the continuity of oral tradition,
handed down from father to son, as well as in the living memory of old-
timers, local tradition was gospel, gossip, and guesswork.

Just as Yankees have insisted on their right to be "characters," especially "Yankee characters," so they have insisted on the right of every
locality to its characteristic traditions. And where recorded history has
failed to provide them, unwritten history or pseudo-history has been quick
to supply *ex post facto* accounts.

But even apocryphal explanations of history, including the history of
place-names, have indirect historical value, inasmuch as they "sometimes
furnish under the guise of fiction useful clues to the real facts" and (in
the case of place names), "whether fact or fiction, frequently shape and
control their forms and fortunes." [3] Outside of history, such explanations,
as Reverend Livermore said of the legend of the *Palatine* Light, afford
considerable gratification of the taste for the marvelous.

In the study of place-names Americans have the advantage of being
close to the beginnings and so to the documentary sources. Thus in the
accounts of early voyagers, as when Captain Gosnold tells us how he
named Cape Cod (which narrowly escaped being "Shoal Hope"), we see
geography as well as history in the making. In after-the-fact explanations

[1] *The Westfield Jubilee* (Westfield, 1870), p. 27.

[2] Samuel McChord Crothers, *The Gentle Reader* (Boston, 1903), p. 136.

[3] Robert L. Ramsay, Foreword to Frederic G. Cassidy's *The Place-Names of Dane
County, Wisconsin*, Publication of the American Dialect Society Number 7 (April,
1947), p. 5.

of place-names, a guess is occasionally right, but more often history is written or rewritten to suit the whims of romantic or facetious fancy.

At the root of many fanciful derivations is the need of making the unfamiliar familiar, according to the process of folk-etymology. This process results, on the one hand, in the garbling of Indian and foreign names into what sounds like the nearest English equivalent, and, on the other, in outlandish coinages or outrageous fabrications based on an assumed etymology. Other place-name stories originate in casual or accidental names, arising "either from an immediate circumstance attending the giving of the name, a happening, an object present, a natural feature of the landscape, or from memory association with other places or names." [1]

Among the more specious and spurious place-name stories Indian or pseudo-Indian fancies run a close second to the haunts of the Devil, in persistence and in mediocrity. For the folklorist they have the interest of migratory legends (*e.g.*, the Lovers' Leap and Pocahontas motifs)—a species of traveling local legend which always turns up like a bad penny. They also have the historical interest of period-pieces, since in both their style and their content, they reflect the taste of a past generation—a generation that apparently attempted to make amends for exterminating the Indian by romanticizing him, only to continue to kill him off by suicide, as if the only good Indian was an Indian who died for love. Indian legends also appealed to the taste for the exotic, seen, in another direction, in the naming of towns for places like Peru.

2. "MORE PATIENT ALMOST OF ANYTHING THAN OF FLATNESS"

Although place-names serve as a focus for all the "recorded incidents and the floating traditions" that hold local associations for Yankees, other place traditions occupy the borderland between history and folklore which is pseudo-history or pseudo-folklore. At various points these stories touch on the lore of local characters, tall tales, and customs. But their identification with a particular locale and the details of local color give them a special local flavor and a special appeal to local pride or prejudice.

Local bias creeps into origin legends like the Devil's Ash Heap, with their "deliberate slur born of malice"; into stories of neighborhood feuds, with their resultant splits and secessions; and into controversies over the relative merits of Narragansett and Boston brown bread and Massachusetts (or New England) and Rhode Island (or Manhattan) clam chowder.

Finally, since a good yarn knows no limitations of time or place, local rivalry reaches the point where several localities claim their version to be the original one.

B. A. B.

---

[1] George Philip Krapp, *The English Language in America* (New York, 1925), Vol. I, p. 188.

THE ART OF NAMING PLACES

There Are No Peruvians in Peru

. . . Not only has it pleased the good people of New England to decorate their towns with every name that is of note, in ancient or in modern, in profane or in sacred history, but they have often applied these names in immediate contempt of things; calling north, south; towns, shires; and hills, vales. A day's ride will carry a man from Middlesex to Jericho, and thence to Athens, Corinth, Hyde Park, Peru, Jamaica, Georgia, Bristol, China, Guildhall, *Vershire*, Scotland, Mount Tabor, Babylon, Bedlam, Padanaram and Cheapside. It is an even chance, but on reaching Mount Tabor, he finds a plain; and so of the other denominations; except, indeed, that he may be sure of wit and elegance in Athens, and splendid luxury in Corinth. He shall find Ash*ford* upon a hill; Dan*bury* and Marl*borough* where there is no *borough;* and Cumberland where the *Cymbri* was never heard of. Even names of original composition are equally destitute of meaning; there is no *borough* in New England, unless all its towns be boroughs, in fact though not in name; and yet we read of Dewey's*burgh* and Green's*borough.*

Hapless he, whose imagination is mocked with the name of his native village, far left under the canopy of other skies! When the sun rises, he sets forth, half promising himself to behold the dark and ivied battlements of its church, empurpled by the evening ray. Evening descends, and he is told that he has performed his journey; but, the church, the copse, the gardens and the cottages, where are they?

Nor is it enough that he reconciles himself to the new association, and learns that there may be a Delhi without palaces or pagodas, without baths or palm-trees, but with wide acres of stumps and trunks of trees, naked, gray and black; and here and there a hut of logs. This is not enough. The name returns upon him thrice in a day; he travels from Pekin in the morning, and he sleeps at Pekin at night. But the Pekin of the morning was a sea-port or a mountain; and the Pekin of the night is a cluster of saw-mills. Every state, and sometimes every county, recurs to the same names.

In the earlier periods of the colonies, the license was somewhat less extravagant; because, though names were arbitrarily borrowed and imposed, yet there was some motive, some sentiment, directing the choice; and names of places are rational, when they have reference to a historical fact, as much as when they are purely geographical. The name of a founder, or of the birth-place or residence of a founder, may be fairly given, upon principles of natural pride, or natural affection; and a kindred motive often

From *Travels through the Northern Parts of the United States, in the Year 1807 and 1808,* by Edward Augustus Kendall, Esq., Vol. I, pp. 117–121. New York: Printed and published by I. Rile 1809.

led the first colonists of New England to name their towns after the birth-places of former residences of their favorite clergy. But, now, little of this sort is regarded. There are no Peruvians in Peru, nor Chinese in China, nor aldermen nor giants in the glens and forests of Guildhall. It is matter of fact, that the choice is often made on no other principles than that a name sounds prettily on the ear. Persons, appointed on committees for naming towns, have told me, that their resource had been, to turn over a gazetteer, and cull from the alphabet a few well sounding names. The lists had been then submitted to the town-meeting, and the choice effected.

In a town in Maine, I was informed, that a different name from that which that town now bears, had been at first imposed by vote of the town-meeting; but, a principal inhabitant, who arrived a little too late, on promising his neighbors a cask of rum, procured the vote to be rescinded, and his own name to be received. Towns often change their names.

I heartily join in the regrets of those who wish that the Indian names of places had been more generally preserved; and this, not from any idle preference of a foreign language to my mother tongue, nor from any particular admiration of the sounds; but, from the agreement which those names possessed with the places they denoted. The savage has no temptation to that spirit of mean mimicry which so often disfigures lettered society; and he must call things by their right names, or it is in vain that he calls them by any. When he speaks of *the bend of river*, he means the bend of a river, and not a forest, a lake nor an island. It is the same when he speaks of an island, of a cataract, or of the basin at the cataract's foot. Such is the description of the Indian names that are still retained; and description, as being almost peculiar to these names, stamps them almost exclusively with the character of *classic*, in the whole nomenclature that embraces them. The rest exhibit a senseless heap; and if the reader turn with impatience from its barbarism, let him at least pity the pen that here commits it to paper!

Yankee Flavor

DURING the eighteenth century, by some alchemy, the Puritan was transmuted into the Yankee. Separated from the other colonies by the bottle-neck of the Dutch-speaking Hudson Valley, the New Englanders went their own ways. They still said *brook* and *notch*. The Maine people developed the use of *stream*. At first perhaps this denoted the water flowing from a certain pond or lake, so that Mopang Stream was said in distinction from Mopang Pond; it came, however, to mean any flowing water, between a brook and a river in size. The usage spread into northern New

From *Names on the Land*, A Historical Account of Place-Naming in the United States, by George R. Stewart, pp. 205–209. Copyright, 1945, by George R. Stewart. New York: Random House.

Hampshire and Vermont, and emigrants took it westward into the Adirondacks. *Intervale* was another northern word. Zadock Thompson, Vermont historian, explained it with rare exactitude:

> It may be derived from *inter*—within, and *vallis*—a vale, or valley; and in its specific signification, it denotes those alluvial flats, lying along the margins of streams, which have been, or occasionally are, overflowed.[1]

Another word arose from the frustrating process of attempting to lay out right-angled plots upon a spherical earth. The surveyors were sometimes left with a wedge-shaped piece of land lying between the boundaries of two towns and not included in either. Most of these were too small and badly shaped to be incorporated in their own right. Some were annexed to the adjoining towns, but others still remain as Coburn Gore, or Million Acre Gore, possessing individuality neither by the lay of the land nor by legislative act, but as mere left-overs.

New England was little affected by *-burgh* and *-ville*. As everywhere, the majority of the town-names were commonplace, but the legends and folk-tales attaching to a few of them do much to show the nature of the people. The accuracy of a tradition may always be questioned, but the very persistence of one shows the quality of the folk-mind and suggests that, even if merely invented for one town, it may well have functioned at the naming of another.

In 1781 the citizens of a small community in Maine petitioned for incorporation, and sent their minister, the Reverend Seth Noble, to Boston on this errand. As the clerk was filling out the papers, Mr. Noble stood by, in true Yankee fashion, quietly humming a tune to himself. When the clerk suddenly asked him, "What's the name?" he absent-mindedly thought of the tune, not the town, and replied "Bangor." The naming from a hymn-tune became a repeated folk-tale. Even one of the greatest of New Englanders gave it circulation: "named at a pinch from a psalm tune," as Mr. Emerson wrote, disparagingly.

Two years after Bangor, the town of Littleton in New Hampshire took its name. It continued the Connecticut tradition of the name manufactured from parts of others, here the two chief landowners, Moses Little and Tristram Dalton.

Illogically, as the religious fervor of the Puritans declined, Biblical names grew more numerous. Perhaps they began to seem less holy. Goshen and Canaan and Sharon might even be good for advertising, vaguely suggesting rich valleys flowing with milk and honey. Bozrah in Connecticut may also have brought to mind good pasturage from the mention of its sheep by the prophet Micah. On the other hand, its inhabitants braved the full-fledged threat of Jeremiah, 49, 13:

> I have sworn by myself, saith the Lord, that Bozrah shall become a desolation, a reproach, a waste, and a curse.

[1] For further discussion of the word, see "Interval(e)," below.

As the story runs, however, the name sprang from still another quotation. In 1786 the district applied for incorporation and asked to be called Bath. The rustic who presented this petition was dressed in some parti-colored homespun so strange as to cause someone to quote the query of Isaiah, 63, I:

> Who is this that cometh from Edom, with dyed garments from Bozrah?

And so the Assembly, in acknowledgment of an apt quotation, rejected Bath, and substituted Bozrah.

The re-naming of a certain town in Vermont shows that such affairs did not always pass without heat. It had been granted as Wildersburgh in 1780, but the name became unpopular. A town-meeting to replace it met in 1793. Various names were proposed, but the running was soon limited to two. Captain Joseph Thomson strenuously contended for Holden, in honor of the town in Massachusetts which had been his former home. Mr. Jonathan Sherman was equally vehement for Barre, because he had come from Barre, also in Massachusetts. The argument was so hot that some-one proposed a settlement by combat. The champions readily agreed.

The meeting then adjourned to a new barn-shed with a floor of rough hemlock planks. Space was cleared, and a pole was leveled waist-high. The combatants were to fight with their fists across this pole; but if one should knock the other down, he might follow up his advantage in any way he could.

Like two ancient warriors, they squared off—Thomson to lay on for Holden; Sherman, for Barre. Thomson was the more powerful; Sherman, the more lithe. After a little sparring, Thomson with a mighty blow knocked Sherman to the floor, and then leaping upon him began to pummel his head and face. But the supple Sherman squirmed so elusively that many of Thomson's blows merely barked his own knuckles on the hem-lock floor. And all the while Sherman was working his own fists adroitly from beneath. Suddenly Thomson groaned, and his blows grew weak. Sherman, throwing him off, sprang to his feet and claimed the victory by shouting in exultation, "There, the name is Barre, by God!"

This particular story was transmitted through the village doctor, an eye-witness. He may even be called a participant because, next day, he had to use his professional skill to extract from the victor's back and buttocks the hemlock splinters they had collected while he was writhing on the plank floor.

Less authenticated but even more illustrative of the folk-mind is the naming of Canton. Realists may point out that by 1798 the China trade had made Yankees familiar with the name of the most frequented far-eastern port, and also that *canton* was used in France and Switzerland to mean a district. According to the tale, however, Canton was named at the instance of a prominent citizen, who maintained that his Massachusetts town was antipodal to the Chinese city. Actually, such an opinion was startlingly wrong. No two places in the northern hemisphere could be antipodal. Even if Canton was thought to be the corresponding opposite spot in the northern hemisphere, the calculation was still 1,300 miles in error. The name, however, rapidly became popular.

Canton in Ohio was settled by New Englanders in 1805, and the name has spread to twenty-three states. Several of them tell the same story to explain their naming. The very perversity of the story is almost an argument for it. It seems just what a crotchety Yankee of 1798 would be likely to maintain. Moreover, the folk-mind is never scientifically exact. American children (and probably most American adults) still believe firmly that if they dug straight down through the earth, they would come out in China. Actually, they would emerge in the southern part of the Indian Ocean, west of Australia.

Names of the New England States

THE name of each of the six New England States originated as follows:

MASSACHUSETTS derived its name, as is supposed, from the blue appearance of its hills; the word in the Indian language, according to Roger Williams, signifying *Blue Hills*.[1]

CONNECTICUT derives its name from the river by which it is intersected, called by the natives Quonectacut. This word, according to some, signifies *the long river;* it has, however, been stated by others, that the meaning of the word is *River of Pines,* in allusion to the forests of pines that formerly stood on its banks.

As early as 1644, the Island of Rhode Island, on account of a fancied resemblance to the Isle of Rhodes, was called by that name, and by an easy declension it was afterwards called Rhode Island. This is supposed to be the origin of the name of the state of RHODE ISLAND.

NEW HAMPSHIRE derived its name from the county of Hampshire in England, the residence of Mason, to whom a patent embracing a considerable part of the state was given.

From *The Early History of New England,* Illustrated by Numerous Interesting Incidents, by Rev. Henry White, p. 303. Entered according to an Act of Congress, in the year 1841, by Rev. Henry White, in the Clerk's Office of the District Court of New Hampshire. Ninth edition. Boston: Sanborn, Carter, Bazin & Co.

[1] [Captain John] Smith wrote Massachuset as an Indian town. Though Smith may not have known it, the meaning is fairly clear, being the tribal name Mass-adchuseuck, "big-hill-people," which in English ears was blended with the name of the place, Mass-adchu-ut, "at-big-hills." Smith made of the Indian word an English plural to indicate the tribe, and so came Massachusetts.—George R. Stewart, *Names on the Land* (New York, 1945), pp. 37–38.

The provincial name of MAINE,[1] according to Williamson, was probably chosen in compliment to the queen of England, who had inherited a province of the same name in France.

VERMONT derived its name from the range of green mountains, which pass through it. *Verd* signifying green, and *mont*, mountain.

Nicknames of the New England States

Connecticut enjoys quite a number of sobriquets by which it is popularly known. Sometimes it is called the *Blue Law State* from the unenviable fame acquired by the first regulations of the government of New Haven Plantation, known as the Blue Laws. The valuable quarries of freestone, to which the State is largely indebted for its revenue, have procured for it the name of the *Freestone State,* while at other times it appears as the *Nutmeg State,* from the famous speculation in wooden spices, immortalized by Sam Slick, or, as a facetious native prefers to explain it, "because you will have to look for a grater!"

Maine obtains its name as the *Pine-Tree State* from the extensive pine-forests which cover its central and northern parts, while the occupation they afford to a large number of inhabitants, engaged in felling and rafting the trees, and in converting them into singles, boards, and the like, has made it also known as the *Lumber State.*

Massachusetts, known as the Colony of Massachusetts Bay before the formation of the present Union, still continues to be called the *Bay State.*

New Hampshire, originally so called by the early settlers, who wished to perpetuate the memory of the county from which many had emigrated, is now known as the *Granite State,* its mountains being largely composed of that material.

Rhode Island, the smallest State in the Union, is therefore affectionately called *Little Rhody.*

Vermont is generally, by simple translation of the original name given by the French settlers, called the *Green Mountain State,* the principal ridge of mountains within its boundaries being known by that name.

---

[1] In a New England charter of 1620 the lawyers wrote "the country of the Maine Land," words which suggest a general description rather than a name. Two years later, however, a charter was granted to two old sea-dogs of the Royal Navy, Sir Ferdinando Gorges and Captain John Mason, and in it the word had certainly ceased to be a description. Dated on August 10, 1622, the charter declared that "all that part of the mainland" the grantees "intend to name The Province of Maine." Some have thought that this name arose because of the greater number of islands off that northern coast, which made men have more reason to speak of "the main." Others have tried to connect it with the Province, or County, of Maine in France. But again, *main* as equaling *chief* or *important* would have been of good omen, if a little boastful. Moreover, about 1611 Captain Mason had served in the Orkneys, and must have known the name as used there.—*Ibid.,* pp. 41–42.

From *Americanisms; The English of the New World,* by M. Schele De Vere, pp. 658–662. Copyright, 1871, by Charles Scribner & Co. New York.

The Naming of Cape Cod

THE fifteenth day we had againe sight of the Land, which made ahead, being as wee thought an Iland, by reason of a large sound that appeared Westward betweene it and the Mayne, for comming to the West end thereof, we did perceive a large opening, we called it Shole-hope. Neere this Cape we came to Anchor in fifteene fadome, where wee tooke great store of Codfish, for which we altered the name, and called it Cape Cod. Here wee saw sculs of Herrings, Mackerels, and other small fish in great abundance. This is a low sandie shoare, but without danger, also wee came to Anchor again in sixteene fadome, faire by the Land in the latitude of 42 degrees. This Cape is well neere a mile broad, and lieth North-east by East. The Captaine went here ashoare and found the ground to be full of Pease, Strawberies, Hurtberies,[2] &c., as then unripe; the sand also by the shoare somewhat deepe, the firewood there by us taken in was of Cypresse, Birch, Wich-hazell and Beech. A young Indian came here to the captaine armed with his Bow and Arrows, and had certaine plates of Copper hanging at his Eares; hee shewed a willingnesse to help us in our occasions.

Why the White Mountains Are Called "White"

He [Darby Field],[1] however, found "store of Muscovy glass" and some crystals, which, supposing them to be diamonds, he carefully secured and brought away. These glittering masses, congealed, according to popular belief, like ice on the frozen regions of the [White] mountains, gave them the name of the Crystal Hills—a name the most poetic, the most suggestive, and the most fitting that has been applied to the highest summits since the day they were first discovered by Englishmen.

From "The Relation of Captaine Gosnol[d]'s Voyage to the North Part of Virginia, Begunne the Sixe-and-Twentieth of March, Anno 42 Elizabethae Reginae, 1602, and Delivered by Gabriel Archer, a Gentleman in the Said Voyage," in *Hakluytus Posthumus or Purchas His Pilgrimes* . . . (1625), IV, reprinted in *Forerunners and Competitors of the Pilgrims and Puritans,* edited for the New England Society of Brooklyn by Charles Herbert Levermore, Vol. I, pp. 45–46. Brooklyn, New York: Published for the Society. 1912.
1 Whortleberries.—C. H. L.

From *The Heart of the White Mountains, Their Legend and Scenery,* by Samuel Adams Drake, pp. 118, 119–121. Entered according to Act of Congress, in the year 1881, by Harper & Brothers, in the Office of the Librarian of Congress, at Washington. New York. 1882.
2 The first white man to ascend Mount Washington.—In . . . 1642 one Darby Field, an Irishman, with some others, traveled to an high mountain, called the White Hills, an hundred miles, or near upon, to the west of Saco. It is the highest hill in these parts of America. . . . There was a great expectation of some precious things to be found, either on the top or in the ascent, by the glistering of some white stones. Something was found like crystal, but nothing of value.—Rev. William Hubbard, *A General History of New England from the Discovery* to MDCLXXX (Boston, 1815, 1848), p. 381.

IT IS not precisely known when or how these granite peaks took the name of the White Mountains. We find them so designated in 1672 by Josselyn, who himself performed the feat of ascending the highest summit, of which a brief record is found in his "New England's Rarities." One cannot help saying of this book that either the author was a liar of the first magnitude, or else we have to regret the degeneracy of Nature, exhausted by her long travail; for this narrator gravely tells us of frogs which were as big as a child of a year old, and of poisonous serpents which the Indians caught with their bare hands, and ate alive with great gusto. These are rarities indeed.

The first mention I have met with of an Indian name for the White Mountains is in the narrative of John Gyles's captivity, printed in Boston in 1736, saying:

> These White Hills, at the head of Penobscot River, are by the Indians said to be much higher than those called Agiockochook, above Saco.

The similitude between the names White Mountains and Mont Blanc suggests the same idea, that color, rather than character, makes the first and strongest impression upon the beholder. Thus we have White Mountains and Green Mountains, Red Mountains and Black Mountains, the world over. The eye seizes a color before the mind fixes upon a distinctive feature, or the imagination a resemblance. It is stated, on the authority of Schoolcraft, that the Algonquins called these summits "White Rocks." Mariners, approaching from the open sea, descried what seemed a cloud-bank, rising from the landward horizon, when twenty leagues from the nearest coast, and before any other land was visible from the masthead. Thirty leagues distant in a direct line, in a clear midsummer day, the distant summits appeared of a pearly whiteness; observed again from a church steeple on the seacoast, with the sky partially overcast, they were whitish-gray, showing that the change from blue to white, or to cool tones approximating with white, is due to atmospheric conditions. The early writers succeed only imperfectly in accounting for this phenomenon, which for six months of the year at least has no connection whatever with the snows that cover the highest peaks only from the middle of October to the middle of April, a period during which few navigators of the sixteenth and seventeenth centuries visited our shores, or, indeed, ventured to put to sea at all.

Names in the White Mountains

WHAT a pity that the hills could not have kept the names which the Indian tribes gave to them! The names which the highest peaks of the great range bear were given to them in 1820, by a party from Lancaster. How absurd the order is! Beginning at "The Notch," and passing around

---

From *The White Hills; Their Legends, Landscape, and Poetry,* by Thomas Starr King, pp. 28–30. Entered according to Act of Congress, in the year 1859, by Crosby, Nichols and Company, in the Clerk's Office of the District Court of the District of Massachusetts. Boston: Crosby and Ainsworth. 1866.

to Gorham, these are the titles of the summits which are all seen from the village just spoken of: Webster, Clinton, Pleasant, Franklin, Monroe, Washington, Clay, Jefferson, Adams, Madison. What a wretched jumble! These are what we have taken in exchange for such Indian words as Agiochook, which is the baptismal title of Mount Washington, and for words like Ammonoosuc, Moosehillock, Contoocook, Pennacook, Pentucket. Think, too, of the absurd association of names which the three mountains that rise over the Franconia Notch are insulted with—Mount Lafayette, Mount Pleasant, and Mount Liberty! How much better to have given the highest peaks of both ranges the names of some great tribes or chiefs, such as Saugus, Passaconaway, Uncanoonuc, Wonnalancet, Weetamoo, Bomazeen, Winnepurkit, Kancamagus,—words that chime with Saco, and Merrimack, and Sebago, and Connecticut, and Ossipee, and Androscoggin.

Even the general name, "White Mountains," is usually inapplicable during the season in which visitors see them. All unwooded summits of tolerable eminence are white in the winter; and in the summer, the mountains of the Washington range, seen at a distance in the ordinary daylight, are pale, dim green. The first title, "Crystal Hills," which the white explorers gave them, it would have been better to have retained. But how much richer is the Indian name "Waumbek!" The full title they applied to them was Waumbek-Methna, which signifies, it is said, "Mountains with snowy foreheads." Yet not a public house in all the mountain region bears the name of Waumbek, which is so musical, and which might be so profitably exchanged for Alpine House, or Glen House, or Profile House, or Tip-Top House. We are surprised, indeed, that the appellation "Kan Ran Vugarty," signifying the continued likeness of a gull, which it is said one Indian tribe applied to the range, has not been adopted by some landlord as a title to a hotel, or in some village as the name of a river, on account of its barbarity.

Would this be worse than to give the name "Israel's River" to the charming stream, fed from the rills of Washington and Jefferson, which flows through the Jefferson meadows, and empties into the Connecticut? The Indian name was Singrawac. Yet no trace of this charming name is left in Jefferson or Lancaster. Think of putting "Mount Monroe," or "Mount Clay," or "Mount Franklin," or "Peabody River," or "Berlin Falls," or "Israel's River," into poetry. The White Mountains have lost the privilege of being enshrined in such sonorous rhythm and such melody as Longfellow has given to the Indian names in his lines. . . .

The Christening of Vermont

IT IS from the Green Mountains that the country has received the name

From *Travels through the Northern Parts of the United States, in the years 1807 and 1808,* by Edward Augustus Kendall, Esq., Vol. III, pp. 237-240. New York: Printed and published by I. Riley. 1809.

of *Vermont*. Of what is strangely called its baptism, as strange an account has been given, by the hand by which it was conferred. The narrative that I subjoin belongs to the history of Vermont, and is perhaps not uncharacteristic; and it is concluded with a criticism on a modern departure from what is represented to be the true orthography and pronunciation:

"VERD-MONT was a name given to the Green Mountain, in October, 1763, by the Rev. Dr. Peters, the first clergyman who paid a visit to the thirty thousand settlers in that country, in the presence of Colonel Taplin, Colonel Willes, Colonel Peters, Judge Peters and many others, who were proprietors of a large number of townships in that colony. The ceremony was performed on the top of a rock standing on a high mountain, then named Mount Pisgah, because it *provided* to the company, *a clear sight of Lake Champlain at the west, and of Connecticut River at the east;* and overlooked all the trees and hills in the vast wilderness at the north and south.

"The baptism was performed in the following manner and form, *viz:* Priest Peters stood on the pinnacle of the rock, when he received a bottle of *spirits* from Colonel Taplin; then, haranguing the company with a short history of the infant settlement, and the prospect of its becoming an impregnable barrier between the British colonies in the south, and late colonies of the French in the north, which might be returned in the next century to their late owners, for the sake of governing America by the different powers of Europe, he continued, 'We have here met on the rock Etam, standing on Mount Pisgah, which makes a part of *the everlasting hill,* the spine of Africa, Asia and America, holding together the terrestrial ball, and dividing the Atlantic from the Pacific Ocean, to dedicate and consecrate this extensive wilderness *to God manifested in human flesh,* and to give it a new name, worthy of the Athenians and ancient Spartans; which new name is *Verd-mont,* in token that her mountains and hills shall be ever green, and shall never die.'—And then poured the *spirits* around him, and cast the bottle on the rock Etam. The ceremony being over, the company descended Mount Pisgah, and took refreshment in a log-house, kept by Captain Otley, where they spent the night with great pleasure. After this, Priest Peters passed through most of the settlements, preaching and baptizing for the space of eight weeks; in which time he baptized nearly twelve hundred children and adults.

"Since Verdmont became a state, in union with the thirteen states of America, its general assembly have seen proper to change the spelling of *Verd*-mont, Green Mountain, to that of *Ver*-mont, Mountain of Maggots. Both words are French; and, if the former spelling is to give place to the latter, it will prove, that the state had rather be considered as a mountain of worms, than an ever-green mountain." [1]

After learning, from the inventor himself, that he formed the name

---

[1] *A History of the Rev. Hugh Peters, A.M. &c.* By the Rev. Samuel Peters, LL.D. New York. 1807.—E. A. K.

Vermont or *Verdmont* from the French language, we can pay no attention to the derivation of a topographer, who gives us a Latin etymology, *"Ver Mons,* Green Mountain"; [1] but, when we find a complaint instituted, of a departure from the original meaning of the word, such as involves a departure from its signification, we are naturally struck with the circumstance, that the word never was compounded and applied in any accurate form.

Green Mountain, in the singular, and not Green Mountains, was the name intended to be translated; and this is to be accounted for by the fact, that the mountains, of which only the southernmost part was known to the first settlers, were usually so spoken of—*the mountain.* But, for the name Green Mountain, *Ver Mons* is not Latin, and *Verd Mont* is not French.

The Naming of Auburn

BEFORE the post office was established, mail was brought from Worcester by a post rider who announced his arrival by the blast of a horn. From 1831 to 1840, stages from Worcester to Norwich stopped at the Tavern with the mail. At this time letters did not carry stamps; the amount charged was marked at the corner and collected by the postmaster on delivery. Thus mail was often held for weeks before being claimed. Almost as soon as the mail route was established, Ward began to experience difficulty in the delivery of mail. The similarity of the names of Ward and the more western town of Ware was so marked that the mail of the two towns was constantly getting mixed. A town meeting was held on November 14, 1836, to see what steps should be taken to insure more prompt delivery of business letters, to say nothing of personal mail and love letters.

Joseph Stone was elected chairman with Thomas Merriam, Alvah Drury, Israel Stone, Jr., and Hervey Bancroft. The committee reported at the adjourned meeting on November 28, 1836, and "recommended to the town (though not literally within the commission) to choose a Committee to prepare or cause to be prepared, a petition to the General Court, for the purpose aforesaid. . . .

The petition was granted and reads as follows:

Ch. 14
COMMONWEALTH OF MASSACHUSETTS
In the year One thousand eight hundred and thirty seven. An Act to change the name of the Town of Ward.

A *Historical Sketch of Auburn, Massachusetts,* From the Earliest Period to the Present Day, with Brief Accounts of Early Settlers and Prominent Citizens, Written and Compiled by the Federal Writers' Project of the Works Progress Administration for the State of Massachusetts, pp. 21, 22–23. Sponsored by the Auburn Centennial Committee. 1937.

Be it enacted by the Senate and House of Representatives in General Court assembled, and by the authority of the same, as follows: The name of the town of Ward in the County of Worcester is hereby changed to the name of Auburn, and said town shall henceforth be known and called by the said last mentioned name, anything in the Act whereby the said town was incorporated to the contrary notwithstanding.

House of Representatives February 15, 1837
Passed to be enacted
Julius Rockwell, Speaker
In Senate February 16, 1837
Passed to be enacted
Horace Mann, President

February 17th, 1837.
Approved,
Edward Everett.

There has been considerable speculation as to why the name of Auburn was selected. The most commonly accepted explanation is that the name was suggested by Oliver Goldsmith's poem, *The Deserted Village*. The poetic phrase, "Auburn, Sweet Village of the Plain" does not, however, describe Auburn, Massachusetts, with its rolling hills and valleys, and it seems safe to assume that the name was derived from another source. Joseph Stone, chairman of the naming committee, is said to have been the one to propose "Auburn." Stone was the great-great-grandson of Simon Stone, who, in 1636, settled on the banks of the Charles River in Watertown. The land remained in the Stone family until 1825, when a section of it, called Stone's Woods, was sold by David Stone and the heirs of C. Stone to George W. Brimmer, who was attracted by its natural beauty. The tract was a favorite spot of the Harvard College students, who called it "Sweet Auburn." Mr. Jacob Bigelow, secretary of the newly incorporated Horticultural Society of Boston, happened to visit the land with Mr. Brimmer, and proposed that the whole lot be purchased for a cemetery under the auspices of the Society. Accordingly, in 1831, the land was sold and Mount Auburn Cemetery established. A religious ceremony was held on Saturday, September 24, 1831, at which several members of the Stone family were present. Thus, it is probable that Auburn received its name from this lovely tract of land.

These Haddams

MARK TWAIN, in speaking of the way New Englanders mix up the names of their towns, tells the following:

"They tell a story of a stranger who was coming up the Connecticut river, and was trying his best to sleep; but every now and then the boat would stop and a man would thrust his head into the room. First he sang

From an old newspaper clipping scrapbook in the editor's possession.

out "Haddam!" and then "East Haddam!" and then "Haddam Neck!"
and then "North Haddam!" and then "Great Haddam!" "Little Had-
dam!" "Old Haddam!" "New Haddam!" "Old Haddam!" "Irish Had-
dam!" "Dutch Haddam!" "Haddam-Haddam!" and then the stranger
jumped out of bed, all excited, and says: "I'm a Methodist preacher, full
of grace, and forty years in service without guile! I'm a meek and lowly
Christian, but blast these Haddams. I wish the devil had 'em, I say!"

Which Dover?

REPETITION of place names, which is of frequent occurrence in New England, is sometimes confusing. Once in his youth my father and one of his
brothers became lost while driving home from a dance at Curtis's Grove
in Medfield, Massachusetts, to Framingham. Their horse did not know
the way any better than they did. After spending the dull watches of the
night wandering around back-country roads, they at length came to a
house. In answer to their summons, a man put his head out of an upper
window and asked what they wanted at such an hour.

"What town is this?" inquired my father.

"Dover," was the answer.

"Dover, Maine, or Dover, New Hampshire?" asked the brother.

"Dover, Massachusetts, you damn fool!" came the disgusted reply.

Lake Charcogg-Etc.-Maugg

. . . THE name came through many transmigrations. The first deed in
which the pond is named goes back to 1681—a deed giving to Governor
Winthrop the "land lying all along and from end to end upon the westerly
side of Chapnacongoe Pond toward Connecticut." Littlefield, the historian,
says Chapnacongoe Pond was intended for Chabanakongkomuin, now
known as Webster Lake. One must remember that in those early days
the Indians had no written language, so that the matter of spelling was
beyond their purview. Roger Williams' key to the Indian language and
the translation of the Bible by John Eliot was the first orderly arrangement of the Indian tongue. When I was a boy we called the name of the
lake "Junkermug." This you see is a phonetic spelling such as the Indians
themselves often used. When the name was reduced to print it took its

From *It's an Old New England Custom,* by Edwin Valentine Mitchell, p. 227. Copyright, 1946, by Edwin Valentine Mitchell. New York: The Vanguard Press, Inc.

From *Black Tavern Tales,* Stories of Old New England, by Charles L. Goodell, pp.
82–83. Copyright, 1932, by Charles L. Goodell. Brooklyn, New York: Willis Mc-
Donald & Co.

first expression in a form which has been maintained from that day to this, and which certainly has every claim to stand by itself unchanged. Keith's map which was in vogue in the early part of the last century had the name of the lake, Chaubunagungamaugg, so you will see that the abbreviation which took place on the last part of the name of the lake is without authority. That name eliminated "Chaubuna" without any reason whatever. In Kinnecut's *Indian Names of Worcester County*, we have Charchamonchogego and Charbunabungamaug. So you will see that if you wish to perpetuate the name which has back of it the full assent of the antiquarian and the students of the Indian tongue, the name must be written "Charcoggagoggmanchaugagoggchabunagungamaugg." . . .

The Origin of "Hoosic"—A Satire

ON THE borders of the stream now called by the name of Hoosick, as tradition saith, there formerly dwelt a good old lady, of rather a gossiping disposition, and who was possessed of an insatiable curiosity to learn, and an unconquerable desire to be the first to communicate, all the wonderful news in the vicinity. Among other things, she was prodigiously fond of hearing of all the lamentable cases of sickness far and near, and seemed to live on the pains and aches, the "gripes and grumbles" of her fellow creatures. With this fondness for the sad and horrible, she never failed to run out when the doctor was passing, and bawl out loud as she could— *"Doctor, who's sick?"* This she repeated so often, that at length the man of medicine grew tired of her importunities, and invented a hundred stories of improbable cases, with which he amused himself and ridiculed the old woman's love of the marvellous, but which she swallowed with the same avidity as she did her catechism.

At one time he told her he had been to see a patient who had the mortal borborigums, and that he had cured him completely by taking out his "insides" and washing them in soap suds and vinegar.

"Is it possible, doctor!" exclaimed the old woman. "Well, I hope the man will have a clean conscience after this."

At another time the doctor told her he had called to see a child that was born without any tongue.

"Oh me!" cried the old lady. "How will the poor thing ever talk!—is it a boy or a gal, doctor?"

"A girl," he replied.

"Ah, well," said she, "I ain't a bit afeared then but what it will talk well enough."

On a third occasion he told her he had been to visit a woman who was

From *Wehman's Idle Hours with the Humorists*, Brimful of Fun about Yankee Yarns, Western Sports, Boarding-House Hash, Rich College Scrapes, Wild Widows' Wit, and Tall Tales of Sailors and Marines, p. 27. New York: Published by Henry J. Wehman. [n. d.]

bitten by a rattlesnake. He said the patient was a great snuff taker, and as she was one day picking up blackberries, the snake, which was concealed among the briers, being highly enraged at the smell of the snuff, sprang from his lurking place and seized the woman by the end of the nose.

"Oh lord!" ejaculated the sympathizing listener, and giving her own nose a thorough wipe, "didn't it kill the woman?"

"No, by Jove," returned the doctor, "but it killed the snake."

But to return to the etymology. The doctor from being so often questioned by the old lady, "Who's sick?" at last began to call the neighborhood of her residence *Who's Sick;* and when asked by his own neighbors, "Which way are you riding to-day, doctor?" he would reply jocularly, "I'm going to *Who's sick*." This appellation was at first caught from the doctor and familiarly used by his neighbors, and afterwards by those more remote; and thus not only the neighborhood of the inquisitive old lady, but in process of time the whole stream and the valley on its borders, came by a slight alteration in its spelling, to be called by the name of *Hoosick*.

Point Judith

ABOUT two centuries ago a vessel was driving toward the coast in a gale, with rain and mist. The skipper's eyes were old and dim, so he got his daughter Judith to stand beside him at the helm, as he steered the vessel over the foaming surges. Presently she cried, "Land, father! I see land!" "Where away?" he asked. But he could not see what she described, and the roar of the wind drowned her voice, so he shouted, "Point, Judith! Point!" The girl pointed toward the quarter where she saw the breakers, and the old mariner changed his course and saved his ship from wreck. On reaching port he told the story of his daughter's readiness, and other captains, when they passed the cape in later days, gave to it the name of Point Judith.[1]

. . . I used to hear when a boy that "Point Judith point" was so called because it was first discovered by an old negro woman named Judith on board ship in a fog. The captain could not see the land with his spy-glass, and so he said to the old darky to point out the direction in which she saw it. Said he, "Point, Judy, point," and so when the captain saw it he put it down on his chart by that name, which has since been converted into "Point Judith," or "Pint Judy." Per contra, my brother Joseph tells me that Josiah Quincy, of Boston, during whose mayoralty the Cochituate water was introduced into the city and the great reservoir built near the capital, once told him that Point Judith was named after a relation of his,

[1] From *Myths & Legends of Our Own Land*, by Charles M. Skinner, Vol. II, p. 35. Copyright, 1896, by J. B. Lippincott Company. Philadelphia & London.

"Judith Quincy," who married a Mr. Hull and went at a very early date to live on Point Judith. . . .[2]

Lemon Fair River

THE [Lemon Fair] river's name is said to have grown out of an Indian massacre that occurred on the banks of the stream; the settlers referred to it as "the lamentable affair," and through constant usage this was shortened to Lemon Fair. A variant is the legend which traces the name to "leman fair," the old English phrase for "mistress fair." [1]

. . . Impossible stories are told to explain it, but it is still called Lemon Fair River, and the most likely explanation is that the strange name is only a Vermonter's attempt to render Les Monts Verts.[2]

Bride Brook

A STREAM which was the original west boundary of New London [Connecticut] was the scene of a very odd incident toward the end of winter in 1646. A young Saybrook couple wished to be married, and as the magistrate in their own place was away they sent word to Governor John Winthrop at New London that they would ride thither to have him perform the ceremony. He concluded to ride to meet them. Both he and the wedding party got as far as the boundary stream, and found it in flood and the ice broken up. They could not cross, but the marriage took place just the same. The governor on his side of the stream pronounced them man and wife, and they on the other side promised to love, honor, and obey. Since then the stream has been called "Bride Brook."

[2] From *Jonny-Cake Papers of "Shepherd Tom,"* Together with Reminiscences of Narragansett Schools of Former Days, by Thomas Robinson Hazard, With a Biographical Sketch and Notes by Rowland Gibson Hazard, pp. 306–307. Copyright, 1915, by Rowland G. Hazard. Boston: Printed for the Subscribers.

[1] From *Vermont:* A Guide to the Green Mountain State, written by Workers of the Federal Writers' Project of the Works Progress Administration for the State of Vermont, p. 317. American Guide Series. Copyright, 1937, by the Vermont State Planning Board. Boston: Houghton Mifflin Company.

[2] From *Names on the Land:* A Historical Account of Place-Naming in the United States, by George R. Stewart, p. 167. Copyright, 1945, by George R. Stewart. New York: Random House.

From *New England, A Human Interest Geographical Reader,* by Clifton Johnson, pp. 192–193. Copyright, 1917, by The Macmillan Company. New York and London.

Mingo Beach

As you go from Beverly to Manchester [, Massachusetts,] you will see the justly celebrated Mingo Beach about which there still echoes the tradition of Robin Mingo—a slave who had been promised his freedom on the day that the ebbing tide should leave a dry passage between Mingo's Beach and a rocky promontory called Becky's Ridge. He waited patiently for this great event, and then, one morning in 1773 when the receding tide did actually leave a dry passage, the kindly neighbors ran to tell him of the news. Awed and half terrified by the strange significance, they found the black man had indeed attained his freedom on that day, for he was lying dead—a smile upon his lips.

Sea-Gull Cliffs

FROM these creatures the locality has taken the name of Sea-Gull Cliffs.

It seems that these gulls were in danger of extermination until the people of the island awoke to the necessity of preserving them as one of its attractions. In the first place, some thoughtless person introduced foxes to the island. These animals soon drove the gulls to retreats inaccessible either to man or beast. Then came the caprice for wearing the snow-white breasts and wings on ladies' bonnets. This brought a swarm of eager hunters down upon the gulls, and soon drove them to make their rookeries still farther out, so that few remained in their old haunts. At this stage the law was invoked for their protection, much to the amusement of the lawmakers, be it said, who could not see why such a useless thing as a gull should be made to occupy their serious attention.

"I will tell you why, gentlemen," said the champion of the gulls of Grand Manan. "We islanders get our living by fishing. Now for one thing, the gulls show us where fish are schooling, for they fish as well as we; and so where we see gulls sailing about the water we steer our boats. We don't want them killed off, because, dumb creatures though they are, their instinct helps us to live."

By this time the provincial legislature had settled itself to listen.

"For another thing, gentlemen," the spokesman for the gulls went on, "our men are often caught out in the bay in a fog; and when that happens, the screams the gulls set up if a boat or a vessel comes near the cliffs— for you must know, gentlemen, that a gull can see enough farther than a man—often does us a good turn in a bad place, by letting us know where we are. We don't want the gulls destroyed, because they help to keep us from death by shipwreck. That's all I have to say."

The bill was passed without further speech-making.

The Devil's Ash Heap

WHILE MOSHOP was the first inhabitant of Martha's Vineyard of whom there is any authentic record, these same records concerning him plainly show that the land was well peopled in his time, as witness the following:—

Moshop was as kind hearted and wise as he was great and good, and to him all those in trouble came for counsel and advice. So it came to pass that a certain maiden whose poverty prevented her union with the youth of her choice came to the Great Chief. The fathers of the young people were petty chiefs and equal in rank, but the one was poor, the other rich, and the wealthy father would not permit his son to take a poor girl to wife.

The lovers, after talking the situation over, concluded that their only help lay in Moshop, and the girl, as the best pleader, was chosen to bear the petition. Then watching her opportunity when the chief, her father, had gone on a long hunt, the girl started on her journey to Aquinnah, and toiling up its steep slopes, for the heights in those days were 500 feet or more above the sea, she came into the presence. She was much frightened to see the great man loom so tall above her, but he spoke gently and she finally found courage to tell her story, receiving a prompt promise of aid.

It was appointed that the two lovers should meet the Giant on Sampson's Hill, Chappaquiddick, and there they came. While discussing the matter and canvassing every possible expedient, the elder took out his pipe and began to smoke. Now you must know that the pipe was in accord with the size of the man, and that it took many bales of tobacco to fill it, so that when he was through and proceeded to knock the ashes out into the sea there arose a tremendous hissing sound and great clouds of smoke and vapor which filled the whole region with a dense fog.

There was method in all this on the part of Moshop, but the lovers, who did not appreciate it, only thought he was a poky old giant and very slow to suggest a remedy for their very real woes. Imagine then their astonishment when, as the fog lifted, they beheld a beautiful island in the sea, gilded by the rising sun.

Thus was Nantucket born to meet the wants of a pair of Vineyard lovers. The marriage portion being now provided, the hard hearted parent relented and there was nothing to longer delay the ceremony which Moshop himself performed, and after celebrating the nuptials at his royal mansion in a fitting manner, he dismissed the pair to their new domain with his blessing.

From *The Story of Martha's Vineyard*, from the Lips of Its Inhabitants, Newspaper Files and Those Who Have Visited Its Shores, Including Stray Notes on Local History and Industries, Collected and Arranged by C. G. Hine, pp. 211–213. Entered, according to Act of Congress, in the year 1908, by C. G. Hine, in the office of the Librarian of Congress, Washington, D. C. New York: Hine Brothers.

So in Nantucket we have the authentic proof that the great Moshop once lived, and while it may gall our little neighbor to know that it was never intended in the original order of things and was merely created to fill a sudden emergency, it yet seems best to give the facts without bias.

Some there be who call Nantucket "The Devil's Ash Heap," but the reader can readily see that this is a deliberate slur born of malice and all manner of uncharitableness. The facts are as above stated.

LOCAL COLOR AND LOCAL RIVALRY

"Proper Bostonians"

THERE IS a story in Boston that in the palmy days of the twenties a Chicago banking house asked the Boston investment firm of Lee, Higginson & Co. for a letter of recommendation about a young Bostonian they were considering employing. Lee, Higginson could not say enough for the young man. His father, they wrote, was a Cabot, his mother a Lowell; farther back his background was a happy blend of Saltonstalls, Appletons, Peabodys, and others of Boston's First Families. The recommendation was given without hesitation.

Several days later came a curt acknowledgment from Chicago. Lee, Higginson was thanked for its trouble. Unfortunately, however, the material supplied on the young man was not exactly of the type the Chicago firm was seeking. "We were not," their letter declared, "contemplating using Mr. —— for breeding purposes."

[A] Boston woman . . . , reluctantly transplanted to another part of the country, returned to be asked how she liked being home again. Having been well taught in the Proper Boston school, she was taken aback. "Like it?" she said. "Why, I never thought of it that way. Liking Boston is like saluting the flag."

A visitor to Harvard sought to see the late Lawrence Lowell, then president of the university. Having been called to the nation's capital on a matter of business, Lowell could not be seen. The visitor was stopped by a secretary in the outer office. "The President is in Washington," she said, "seeing Mr. Taft."

At the age of eighty-eight "Aunt Sarah" [Palfrey] went to Europe all alone, shortly before World War I, for what she declared was her "last look around." She came back to this country to take up during her final illness the study of Hebrew. When a friend remonstrated with her for the effort this involved, she said that she had always intended to take up the language and had put it off far too long as it was. "I wish to be able," she said with some finality, "to greet my Creator in his native tongue."

Ex-Ambassador [Joseph P.] Kennedy has no illusions about being a Proper Bostonian. He would settle for the privilege of not being referred to in the Boston press as an Irishman. "I was born here," he says. "My children were born here. What the hell do I have to do to be an American?" [1]

* * * * *

In Boston . . . a small Hallowell boy . . . went to the Saltonstall house for his first overnight visit. That evening the Saltonstalls, fearing homesickness, left their young visitor's door open and were surprised to overhear him start his prayers: "Our Father who art in Heaven, Saltonstall be Thy name." Thinking the boy was upset, the Saltonstalls did nothing about it until the next morning. Then, apologetically, they admitted they had overheard his prayer and asked him if he always said it like that.

"Oh, no," he answered politely, "in our house we always say 'Hallowell by Thy name,' but in your house I thought I should say 'Saltonstall.' " [2]

* * * * *

A Boston woman was planning her first trip to the West. The travel agent asked, "How would you like to go? By Buffalo?" "Why, really," replied the lady, "I planned to go by train."

Two women from Boston were riding across the prairie and came upon a lone tombstone with the simple inscription: "John Jones—he came from Boston." They looked at it reverently, and finally one said, "How brief, but how sufficient."

Two Boston women went to the San Francisco Fair and ran into a hot spell. As they were stewing on Treasure Island, one said to the other, "My dear, I *never* expected to be so hot in San Francisco." "But, my dear," replied her companion, "you must remember that we are three thousand miles from the ocean."

A colleague from Leland Stanford insisted that once, when he was having tea in a Boston home, the lady of the house inquired, "How long did it

[1] From *The Proper Bostonians,* by Cleveland Amory, pp. 11, 25, 27, 140–141, 346. Copyright, 1947, by Cleveland Amory. New York: Reprinted by permission of E. P. Dutton & Company, Inc.

[2] From "High Society, U.S.A.," by Cleveland Amory, *Holiday,* Vol. 17 (March, 1955), No. 3, p. 48. Copyright, 1955, by The Curtis Publishing Company. Philadelphia, Pa. Reprinted by permission of Brandt & Brandt.

take you to come from Leland Stanford to Boston?" "About four days," replied my friend, "at least I was four nights on the train." "Why, really," said the hostess, "I never was on a train so long in my life. But then, of course, I'm here already." [3]

The Devil and the Wind in Boston

HIGH WINDS, especially on street corners, sometimes annoy [Boston] way-farers. According to an old legend, the Devil and a Gale of Wind were once strolling along Winter Street. When they reached Tremont Street corner the Devil said to his companion, "Wait here a minute; I've got to go in there," pointing to the Park Street Church. The Devil went in and never came out; but the Gale of Wind is still waiting for him at the corner, where at times he becomes quite obstreperous!

Damnation Alley

, . . OFF STATE STREET [Boston] we find Damnation Alley. As the story comes down to us, it seems that teamsters in the early days, meeting on this street and not being able to get by, said things to each other as they do today, for that matter, and this swearing gave the name to the street. The Town Fathers, we are told, got angry about it after a while and issued an order something like this: "Teamsters when they meet on these narrow streets must behave like good citizens, jump right down, and flip a coin to see who is to back out!"

The S.S. Pierce Pung

THE story is told—and how could it be anything but true—of a little Beacon Hill lass who had been permitted to take a wintry walk to the Charles River esplanade, but who had been told specifically not to hitch a ride, in the manner of the proletariat, on that sort of sleigh which in Yankee parlance is called a pung.

---

[3] From *Tales Out of School*, by George H. Chase, pp. 65–66. Copyright, 1947, by the President and Fellows of Harvard College. Cambridge, Mass.: Harvard University Press.

From *New England Colonial Life*, by Robert Means Lawrence, pp. 135–136. Copyright, 1927, by Robert Means Lawrence. Cambridge, Mass.: The Cosmos Press, Inc.

From *Hear Ye! Hear Ye! The New England Squeak and Other Stories*, Being the Strange Adventures of Heroic yet Primitive People, by James O. Fagan, pp. 24–25. Copyright, 1931, by James O. Fagan. Boston: Visitors Guide in the Old South Meeting House.

From *New England Comes Back*, by Lawrence Dame, with an Introduction by Stewart H. Holbrook, pp. 84–85. Copyright, 1940, by Random House, Inc. New York.

Back came the girl to her home. Her dress was wet and her stockings disheveled.

"Well, for Heaven's sake, what have you been doing?" asked Mama. The child hung her head. Then she sobbed out, "I hooked a ride."

"You naughty girl . . . ," began the fond parent.

"But, Mama, it was an S. S. Pierce pung!"

Why Boston Streets Are Crooked

THERE has been much speculation and a great deal of fun made in regard to the crooked and narrow streets of Boston, and they have been the subject of good-natured banter from wits of all ages, which we have borne with equanimity. There are even some to-day who in all seriousness will say, "My grandmother always said that Boston was laid out by the cows"; and the old conundrum that the streets of Boston were crooked because Boston was never dead enough to be laid out, is still with us.

Cape Cod Rivalries

ANOTHER pair of towns that do not always see eye to eye are Chatham and Harwich, as close together on the map as geography can get them, but miles apart in other respects. A Chatham man speaks of his Harwich neighbors as if they lived in trees and held on with their feet, while the Harwichean comes back at his detractor with tales like the following. A schooner, the Nancy M. Foster, of Digby, so he says, got aground on Shovelful Shoal, about twenty years ago. There was quite a sea running, enough to start her pounding badly, and since she was old, her seams opened up until she was half full. The crew didn't like the looks of things and went over the side, heading for the beach on planks and hatch covers and hen-coops—whatever they could find handy. One of them made pretty good weather of it, took the sea like a duck, and kept his plank headed bow on for the shore until he got close enough to see what was there. What he saw set him thinking: about a hundred hard-looking customers, waiting for him at the water's edge. An awful thought occurred to him.

"What town is this?" he hollered.

"Chatham," they yelled back.

"Good-bye," says he, and put his plank about and headed out to sea.

And so it goes: Provincetown has its fun with Truro; Truro's pride takes a fall before Orleans; and Harwich, perhaps in envy, tells stories

From *The Crooked & Narrow Streets of the Town of Boston, 1630–1822*, by Annie Haven Thwing, p. 7. Copyright, 1920, by Marshall Jones Company. Boston.

From *Mooncussers of Cape Cod*, by Henry C. Kittredge, pp. 17–18. Copyright, 1937, by Henry C. Kittredge. Boston and New York: Houghton Mifflin Company.

about Chatham. An old philosopher of Provincetown, who has watched three generations of Cape men, gives the conclusion of the whole matter when he says that he can tell as soon as he talks to a man what town he comes from: a Truroer, so he says, slouches along with a hangdog air, a regular countryman. Wellfleeters are blow-hards; they stick out their chests and talk big, when, come to find out, they haven't ten cents to their names. Easthamers are just the opposite; they walk around with a face a mile long and growl about hard times, when really they have long bank accounts; and you can tell a Barnstable man because he is always looking for a high time and will never refuse a drink.

How the Cranberry Came to Cape Cod

A SIGNIFICANT tale narrates how during an argument with the Rev. Richard Bourne the Indian pow-pow lost his temper and, chanting a bog-rhyme, mired Bourne's feet in quicksand. They then agreed to a contest of wits which lasted 15 days, during which Bourne was kept from thirst and starvation by a white dove which placed a succulent "cherry" in his mouth from time to time. Unable to cast a spell upon the dove, and exhausted from his own lack of food, the medicine-man finally fell to the ground and Bourne was free. In the meantime one "cherry" brought by the dove had fallen into the bog and had grown and multiplied. Thus the cranberry came to Cape Cod.

Provincetown and the Devil

PROVINCETOWN from its earliest days has been freer, richer in life than its neighbors. Back in 1727 Truro asked to be severed from Provincetown because of the goings-on there. Provincetown gloried in this separation and laughed to itself. Truro sitting discreetly in the folds of her moors looked down her nose at Provincetown and still does. The Cape early wrote, in legend, its opinion of the folk on Land's End.

Captain Jeremiah Snaggs lived up the Cape and he did not die in the odor of sanctity. The story is he tried to escape the devil by various devices. He dodged the devil in Barnstable, he eluded him in a hollow tree in Orleans, he escaped from him in Wellfleet by putting a jack-o-lantern

From *Massachusetts, A Guide to Its Places and People*, written and compiled by the Federal Writers' Project of the Works Progress Administration for the State of Massachusetts, p. 594. American Guide Series. Copyright, 1937, by George M. Nutting, Director of Publicity, Commonwealth of Massachusetts. Boston: Houghton Mifflin Company.

From *Time and the Town, A Provincetown Chronicle*, by Mary Heaton Vorse, p. 76. Copyright, 1942, by Mary Heaton Vorse. New York: The Dial Press.

Always the flight ends in Provincetown, and the conclusion is the same; but different Captains and different towns are used for the starting-point. Probably of late origin.—Elizabeth Reynard, *The Narrow Land* (Boston, 1934), p. 326.

which looked like him in a tree, but in Provincetown the devil caught up with him.

"Well," said Captain Jeremiah, "you caught me fair and squar'. Whar do we go from here?"

"Go?" said the devil. "Nowhar. Ain't we to Provincetown?"

Fishhouse Stories

IF YOU stopped inside the fishhouse you would hear stories of miraculous catches, of strange creatures seen—stories like that of Louis Tindrawers and his dory mate, Lopez, who were separated from their vessel by fog, and when the fog lifted the vessel was gone. They rowed for two days and two nights and finally came upon the back side, thinking themselves in hard luck, only to find they were the only ones left alive of their crew and that their vessel had been cut down by a steamer in the fog.

* * * * *

There is the story of the vessel that sounded her foghorn for twenty-four hours and heard no answering sound of conch. When the fog lifted not a dory was to be seen, yet these dories, attached to one another, triumphantly made Provincetown Harbor. They had been picked up by a Gloucester-man, put overboard at Race Point, and they rowed into harbor after having been given up for lost.

There is the tale of the young fisherman who was courting the same girl that his Old Man courted. He got the consent of the girl but the Old Man got the consent of her father. The lovers parted in tears. The girl did not dare go against her father's wishes. But the young suitor, overboard in a fog, made harbor first and when the vessel made port, after her trip, the Old Man weeping crocodile tears over the loss of his rival, the girl had vanished with the young suitor.

Some of the stories have a sourer ending, like that of the widow who had already spent the life-insurance money and was outraged at her husband's reappearance, going back to her folks to stay.

And the story of the man and his wife who got on none too well. They got on so badly indeed that each had consoled himself surreptitiously with another love. Finally the husband was lost at sea, the widow married again and put up a fine tablet, LOST AT SEA, in the cemetery. But there was quiet gossip that he had not been lost at all but had shared with her the life insurance and had settled down elsewhere and married his sweetheart, under another name, and that once a year he and his old wife met in Boston and went "on a time" to commemorate his death.

Fishermen's Races

THE stories of the fishermen's races in Gloucester are great stories of mag-

Ibid., pp. 165, 173–174.

Ibid., pp. 168–169.

nificent sailing; the race that brought the Lipton Cup to Provincetown is a great story. But the real stories and those that will never be recorded are those of the races to market.

The legend here in Provincetown is that the great highliners, like Captain Gaspy of the *Valerie* and Santos and Marion Perry and Joe King (Antoine Joaquin Sousa) of the *Jessie Costa* or Manuel Enos of the *Annie Perry,* never hove to in their race from the George's Banks. They left their fishing grounds with a "keep 'er full and drive 'er." Drive her they did. A coastwise steamer came to anchor in Provincetown Harbor reporting, "Had a fishing boat pass me sailing underwater."

They sailed their vessels with water swirling around the waist of the helmsman. They kept on canvas until the water came around the helmsman's neck. They tied their halyards aloft so they couldn't shorten sail. Fishermen claimed a good Provincetown boat sailed better when her cabin house was "most draggin'." They said that a vessel like the *Annie Perry* couldn't sail at all if her rail came up for air. There are stories of Gloucester boats winning races with "their sail just level with the water and their crew sitting on the keel."

A Town Divided

FOR many years [at Naples, Maine,] there has been strong political feeling between the Republican and Democratic parties. The feeling is not as intense as it once was, but nevertheless the antagonism is quite marked. Many years ago the feeling was so intense that there were two community flag poles, one for the Democrats and the other for the Republicans. A doctor was hired to administer to the needs of the people; and as he was an active worker in the Democratic party, the Republicans hired a practitioner of their views: hence two doctors. The churches were built with two front doors, and the Democrats sat on one side of the church and the Republicans sat on the other side. This feeling was even carried into education, and school houses were built with two front doors. The children of Republican parents entered one door and sat on that side of the room, the other side of the room being given over to the Democrats. To cap the climax, a superintendent of schools was hired who was a rabid Democrat. This did not suit the Republicans, and they hired a superintendent of their own political views. Each superintendent hired a teacher for each grade, and here arose a situation that became alarming. These grades had two teachers each, who taught in the same room the children of these political fanatics. The situation became so bad that the Maine legislature had to step in and settle the difficulty in 1904, and enact special legislation to govern the case. The strange feature of the whole thing is that the whole town took sides and the upheaval was not the work of any small group. While the natives grin sheepishly and tell about the affair, the listener can sense the tense feeling that still exists.

Naples, Maine. Manuscripts of the Federal Writers' Project of the Works Progress Administration for the State of Maine.

The Woman Who Sold Winds

THERE WAS a woman who lived in Taniscot, [Maine,] about the middle of the last century when it was a center of shipping and exported the oak and pine of its woods, the ice of its lakes, and the red brick made in the yards along its river banks to most of the world. She kept a sailors' boarding house, ostensibly, but she had a good trade on the side in selling winds.

Although one thinks of a witch, particularly a seaport witch, as a rather cosmopolitan person, this woman seems to have retained a good deal of local pride. So one evening when she heard two captains in her boarding house boasting of their respective vessels, which were waiting ready-laden for Boston, and of their general handiness and remarkable speed, she naturally took the side of the Taniscot captain—the other was an outsider from Bath maybe, or maybe Bangor. Anyway the woman made some excuse to call the Taniscot captain out of the room, where he sat arguing with the other man.

When she had him in the darkness of the hall, she whispered to him fiercely, "Bet him all you have, and I'll give and I'll give and I'll give you a wind, and you'll be in Boston by morning."

That sounded pretty impossible even to the Taniscot captain, but when a witch told you to do something in those days you did it, and asked no questions. So he went back and laid the bet with the other man and then roused up his crew and went down to his vessel and hauled up anchor in the dark—or what dark there was, for the moon was rising. There was a down-river wind rising too, of which there'd been no hint earlier in the evening, so they made good time with an outgoing tide. When they sailed into the ocean a strange thing happened: the following wind veered into the east— it was still a following wind. There was no tacking, no feeling about to keep the sheets filled, nothing at all for the captain and crew to do but set all sail and dance down the coast while the cook put the coffee to boil on the galley stove. Hour after hour went by, and the wind never faltered nor shifted again. Like a big broom sweeping a ball of paper before it, that breeze carried the Taniscot vessel straight to the entrance of Boston Harbor and then, with a sidewise flick, it tossed her in.

The moon was gone and the morning star was just beginning to pale and there was light on the eastern horizon when the ship came in to its usual berth at T Wharf after such a voyage as no Maine vessel ever has had before or since.

"Got in kind of early, didn't you, Captain?" asked the watchman, holding his lantern for the captain to step ashore.

The captain nodded.

"Had a fair wind," he said laconically.

From *Country Neighborhood,* by Elizabeth Coatsworth, pp. 61–62. Copyright, 1944, by Elizabeth Coatsworth Beston. New York: Reprinted by permission of The Macmillan Company.

Moving a Town down a Hill

NEWFANE, the shire town of Windham County, [Vermont,] is a real pretty village down in a valley off the West River. It has the county courthouse and the Grange and some other nice white clapboard buildings, and you'd think it had been there since the settlers took the land away from the Indians. It has, too— since just a few years before gramp was born. The place where Newfane is now used to be called Fayetteville; Newfane was right up on top of Newfane Hill. You'd probably call Newfane Hill a mountain; it's pretty steep, even for these parts. Newfane was built up there for protection from the Indians, and it would pretty near take a medium tank to attack the old site now.

Finally, in 1825, they decided the Indians wasn't going to bother them no more, and it really was a pretty smart climb up Newfane Hill, specially in mud time. So they took apart the courthouse and all the rest of the buildings, and drawed them down to Fayetteville by ox team, and set them up around the green like you see them now. Every so often, somebody tries to move the shire town from Newfane to Brattleboro, but I don't think they'll ever succeed. It used to be one of my neighbor John Gale's hobbies to stop them.

Ephraim Wright and the Underground Railroad

WE READ in history that Vermont was the first state in the Union to prohibit slavery. . . .

From the day when the name of the state was first adopted, no slave had been taken away from Vermont against his will. The fugitive who set foot upon her soil was safe, if not free.

Her north roads and her south roads were her underground railroads. There were Democrats who would send their teams to carry fugitives northward; while they themselves walked to a convention to shout for Douglas (the Democratic candidate for the presidency, in favor of slavery) and resolve that slavery must not be interfered with in states where it existed by law.

It is interesting to trace the underground railroad through this part of the state. Noah Safford, who lived near the foundry in a house that has been recently moved to Olive Street, [Springfield, Vermont] while spending winters in the south selling straw-cutters of his own manufacture, saw

From "Grandpa Was Quite a Fellow," by Walter Needham, as recorded by Barrows Mussey, *Saturday Evening Post,* Vol. 219 (Nov. 9, 1946), No. 19, p. 108. Copyright, 1946, by The Curtis Publishing Company. Philadelphia.

From *Folklore of Springfield,* by Mary Eva Baker, pp. 62–66. Copyright, 1922, by M. E. Baker. Springfield, Vermont: Publishers, The Altrurian Club of Springfield, Vt. 1922.

enough of slavery to make him vow eternal vengeance upon it. From that time his home was one of the most important stations where the fugitives were always safe—sometimes it might be weeks in the attic, again it might be only a few days in the barn.

His daughter, Mrs. Rebecca (Safford) Holmes, remembered when a little girl hearing teams drive up in the night and saw food carried to the barn in the morning; the following night she heard the sound of wheels again as fugitives were taken to the next station, which was usually Judge Pingree's office in Perkinsville. This office was a station where slaves were secreted, fed, and lodged, then sent to Col. Thomas Powers in Woodstock; from there to Deacon and Mrs. Morris' home in Strafford, which is just over the line in Orleans county. Judge Pingree had a very ingenious place for secreting these slaves. A movable panel by the fireplace gave entrance to a small closet, which was so arranged that none were ever discovered.

Ephraim Wright, a fugitive, remained with Mr. Safford for several years and was much afraid of being recaptured. One day he went to the store and came running back, asking to be hidden; for he saw, or thought he saw, what looked like his old master. It is said of him that he was as white as it is possible for a colored man to be.

This story is also told of him: From that time on he always walked with his head partially turned over his shoulder, that he might see anyone approaching from behind. One of the neighbors, meeting him one day, asked him what he should do if he saw his master coming. Ephraim replied, "I think I should fight."

He was a very large and powerful man, who had little fear from other men physically.

Ephraim Wright later married a fugitive girl who came here on the underground railway, escaping to Canada. The house, owned at the present time by Mrs. Will Nourse on South Street, was built for them. Ephraim and his wife became good citizens and, with their three children, united with the Congregational Church. He was the village barber for some time.

The Lost Child

WE HEARD the story about little Jacob Cady, who was lost [in 1770,] from Grandma Hodskins. The Cadys were the first settlers in East Alstead up on the hill where the Lawrences have their place now. One day Isaac Cady, the father, was out chopping wood and little three-year-old Jacob

As told by Mrs. Mary Burroughs, Alstead, New Hampshire, February 13, 1964. Recorded by B. A. Botkin.

For the original narrative see Seth S. Arnold, A. M. Pastor of the 1st Congregational Church, *Sermon Preached at Alstead,* on the First Sabbath in January, 1826, with Historical Sketches of the Town, Appendix, Embracing Historical Sketches of the Town of Alstead, pp. 22–24. Alstead, New Hampshire: Published by Newton and Tufts. 1826.

wanted to go see his father. So his mother let him go from the cabin. When the father came in, Jacob was not with him. They began to hunt and they began to call, but they couldn't find him anywhere. At last Isaac went off to the nearest neighbors some distance away. The neighbors joined in the search. Still they couldn't find him. At the end of three days they said there were four hundred men hunting for little Jacob Cady. A Colonel Bellows, for whom Bellows Falls was named, was one of the leaders of the search party.

They'd agreed that if they found him, in any condition, they would fire a musket once; if he was all right, they would fire twice. Night came on the third day, and still no sign of Jacob. Mrs. Cady and the neighboring women were gathered in the cabin. The poor mother was saying by this time that even to find him dead would be a comfort. Then she'd know he wasn't suffering from hunger or thirst or being hurt. Just then a shot rang out. It seemed an age before the second one was heard. Before too long back came the men with little Jacob. They had found him in a cave in the rocks on the other side of the pond some two miles or so away. Evidently when little Jacob heard the men going by all around him, calling, he thought they were Indians, and only crawled the deeper into his cave.

This story is told in the minister's sermon that gives us much of our early history. Grandma Hodskins added something else. They wondered that the little boy was in such good shape after three days with no food and no drink. But he said that there was a nice big black dog in that cave and he even sucked some milk from it.

IV. HISTORICAL TRADITIONS

Not everything orally transmitted is mere legend; there is traditional history as well as traditional folklore.—J. FRANK DOBIE

Some legends, unquestionably, are historically true, and many others are elaborations on historical fact. And a few no doubt are pure invention, concocted for sheer amusement or for some reason in the mind of the inventor.—STEWART H. HOLBROOK

To some extent, mythology is only the most ancient history and biography. So far from being false or fabulous in the common sense, it contains only enduring and essential truth, the I and you, the here and there, the now and then, being omitted. . . . We moderns, on the other hand, collect only the raw materials of biography and history, "memoirs to serve for a history," which itself is but materials to serve for a mythology. . . . Who knows what shape the fable of Columbus will at length assume, to be confounded with that of Jason and the expedition of the Argonauts. And Franklin,—there may be a line for him in the future classical dictionary, recording what that demigod did, and refer-

*ring him to some new genealogy. "Son of —— and ——. He
aided the Americans to gain their independence, instructed mankind in economy, and drew down lightning from the clouds."*
                                        ——HENRY D. THOREAU

1. TRADITION AND HISTORY

THE relation of tradition to history is not and probably never will be
clearly understood. Still more difficult to explain is the mixture of the
two in historical traditions. These include (1) legends of doubtful exploits
of historical personages and (2) traditions (of varying degrees of relia-
bility) of historical events which for one reason or another have become a
part of national tradition. The events related in historical traditions need
not have happened but they should be such as are believed to have happened.

The difference between historical traditions and local traditions (which
also involve history) is the difference between the "now and then" and
the "here and there." Both kinds of traditions may belong to a "family
of stories or beliefs." Just as migratory legends become attached to various
places, so they become attached to various persons, since a good yarn
knows no limitations of time, place, or character. The migratory type of
historical tradition is generally known as an historical legend, because, as
A. H. Krappe wisecracks, they are not historical at all. A case in point
is the stories of Lorenzo Dow. Historical traditions, proper, on the other
hand, are "isolated stories or beliefs," following John Fiske's distinction,
and conforming more or less to his definition of these as "untrustworthy
traditions of doubtful events." [1] Unlike unhistorical historical legends,
then, they may be semi-historical or pseudo-historical; and, as part of
national tradition, they may become an historical force.

At the same time historical traditions are no less credible than history
itself, which must necessarily contain a large amount of conjecture. Ordinarily, however, we expect the former to involve a greater proportion of
untruth because of the well-known unreliability of oral or popular tradition. But they are generally so convincing as to inspire the comment, "Well,
if it didn't happen that way, it *ought* to have happened." So no matter how
persistently and legitimately historians may pick holes in the story of Priscilla and John Alden, the popular imagination will stubbornly continue to
cherish it as one of its prized possessions, according to the following rea-
soning:

> Some of it is true, and I expect you to believe that part, but some of
> it is extremely untrue and I expect you to disbelieve that part. The
> trouble is that the true portion is harder to believe than the untrue por-
> tion; and, after all, the untrue portion may be true, because witnesses
> could only testify they'd never seen such things happen, and one's not
> having seen things happen doesn't keep them from happening. [2]

---

[1] *Myths and Myth-Makers* (Boston, 1898), p. 15.
[2] Frost Woodhull, "Folklore Shooting," *Southwestern Lore*, Publications of the
Texas Folklore Society Number IX (Austin and Dallas, 1931), p. 1.

2. THE BARDIC TRADITION

It is almost impossible to conceive of an historical character or event about which there has not grown up a body of legend or apocryphal anecdote. The natural affinity and attraction between history and legend points to a time before written history when the two were virtually indistinguishable. In this stage the bard, as singer or story-teller, is both historian and poet, "not always clearly differentiated from the medicine man and the soothsayer." [1] The special magic of the bard (like that of the good historian [2]) consists in giving us the sense of history (and literature) in the making. In the same way, tradition is both prophetic and creative.

Because of their prophetic and symbolic character, historical traditions—in songs and slogans as well as stories—are an integral part of a national tradition and of the heroes and other sacred symbols embodying it. That is because these traditions help, if not to interpret, to shape history, or, at least, "to remind us of the happenings that occasioned them." [3] Because these traditions also serve to illustrate traits of character and ideals, they easily pass into fable and illustrative anecdote. Not all anecdotes are folklore, but a good deal of folklore (as well as history) may be said to be in its anecdotage.

Likewise on account of their symbolic value, historical traditions are the materials of poetry. And working in this rich vein, in the fashion of the "national poet," [4] Longfellow and Whittier, particularly the former, have succeeded in stamping historical traditions indelibly upon the imagination of Americans, especially young Americans, and at the same time in stamping these traditions with the qualities of the American imagination. And this as much because as in spite of the liberties that a poet like Longfellow has taken with history [5] (as in "Paul Revere's Ride," "The Courtship of Miles Standish," and "Evangeline") and even mythology (as in "The Song of Hiawatha"). For, by poetic license, poetry and folklore have a way of fitting history to the requirements of the imagination, or poetic truth, tantamount to rewriting and perhaps distorting history but also (in rare prophetic moments) to *making* it.

3. THE YANKEE AS HERO: LEGEND AND MYTH

As hero or demigod, the Yankee does not stack up so well as, say, the Westerner. This may be due to the fact that in its insistence on the sacred right of the individual to be a character, New England may have bred

---

[1] Ludwig Lewisohn, *The Story of American Literature* (New York, 1939) p. xx.
[2] Cf. Samuel McChord Crothers: ". . . the great historian is one who has a certain prophetic gift. . . . He identifies himself so thoroughly with the age of which he writes that he always seems to be at the beginning of an era peering into the yet dim future."—"That History Should Be Readable," *The Gentle Reader* (Boston, 1903), p. 199.
[3] Henry F. Woods, *American Sayings* (New York, 1945), p. vii.
[4] Cf. "Longfellow Our National Poet," *Proceedings of the Massachusetts Historical Society,* February, 1907, pp. 564–582.
[5] *Ibid.*

eccentrics rather than heroes. Heroes have a way of transcending the merely personal, as well as the purely local, just as they have a way of transcending history, because their function is to embody certain ideal traits. And when we look at Yankee heroes, we are apt to be struck by the fact that so many of them are heroes in a state of arrested development, or· mere eccentrics.

As a "peculiar people," the Yankees are not heroic. For personal peculiarity or idiosyncrasy is the bane of the hero. Not every odd character, of course, can even boast of being a true eccentric (like Timothy Dexter), since the latter must be a person whose "oddities must be his chief claim to attention, and he must be known, more or less, throughout the nation." [1] The very greatness of his eccentricity, however, gives the Yankee eccentric a certain heroic stature.

Even when they rise above the limitations of mere eccentricity, Yankee heroes still tend to be local rather than national heroes. Thus Yankee leaders like John Adams and even Daniel Webster fail to attain the heroic stature of Washington and Lincoln, whereas Franklin and Paul Revere come nearer to appealing to the national (and popular) imagination. The fact is that the national hero, the culture-hero, requires a large proportion of myth as well as legend. Whereas legend simply explains or transforms history, myth explains or transforms nature and human nature. In his rôle of culture-bringer or culture-carrier, the hero appears as a demigod. And the only demigod among Yankees is the trickster-hero, the generic and ubiquitous Yankee peddler, trickster, and showman hero, from Sam Slick to P. T. Barnum, from Jack Downing to (even) Ethan Allen, whose tricks are tricks of the trade. As a "practical wag," Barnum, like Franklin, exemplifies and teaches the Yankee "art of getting on," and the more practical than heroic Yankee virtues of common sense, thrift, faculty, or "know-how," and handiness, as a means to security, self-respect, comfort, power, and prestige.

The Yankee peddler also possesses the heroic trait of restlessness. For the heroic spirit belongs to a "time of migrations," "a society cut loose from its roots." For the same reason the Yankee skipper and merchant-adventurer appeals to hero-worship.

But in spite of the mobility of the Yankee peddler and the Yankee skipper, a mobility which belongs to their time and which existed for the sake of moving and placing things rather than in movement for its own sake, and in spite of the readiness with which Yankees have left home to "New Englandize" the country, their genius is for staying put and digging in. To them even pioneering was a job rather than (as exploration was for the Connecticut Yankee John Ledyard) a gallant adventure.

For all these reasons, then, the Yankee mythus is plebeian and prosaic— workaday. It all boils down to the importance of work in the New England creed—an importance recognized by its place in the Puritan trinity of "Faith in God, faith in man, and faith in work." In commenting on the dry, unpoetic character of New England history as essentially a history ·of work, Lowell says: "So much downright work was perhaps never wrought

---

[1] Edmund Lester Pearson, *Books in Black or Red* (New York, 1923); p. 157.

on the earth's surface in the same space of time as during the first forty years after the settlement. But mere work is unpicturesque and void of sentiment."[1] And throughout New England history and folklore, we hear, not the horns of elfland faintly blowing, but the "noise of axe and hammer and saw, an apotheosis of dogged work, where, reversing the fairy-tale, nothing is left to luck, and, if there be any poetry, it is something that cannot be helped—the waste of the water over the dam."[2]

B. A. B.

FABLES AND SYMBOLS
Priscilla and John Alden

IN A very short time after the decease of Mrs. Standish [January 29th, 1621], the captain was led to think, that, if he could obtain Miss Priscilla Mullins, a daughter of Mr. William Mullins, the breach in his family would be happily repaired. He, therefore, according to the custom of those times, sent to ask Mr. Mullins' permission to visit his daughter. John Alden, the messenger, went and faithfully communicated the wishes of the captain. The old gentleman did not object, as he might have done, on account of the recency of Captain Standish's bereavement. He said it was perfectly agreeable to him, but the young lady must also be consulted. The damsel was then called into the room, and John Alden, who is said to have been a man of most excellent form with a fair and ruddy complexion, arose, and, in a very courteous and prepossessing manner, delivered his errand. Miss Mullins listened with respectful attention, and at last, after a considerable pause, fixing her eyes upon him, with an open and pleasant countenance, said, *Prithee, John, why do you not speak for yourself?* He blushed, and bowed, and took his leave, but with a look which indicated more than his diffidence would permit him otherwise to express. However, he soon renewed his visit, and it was not long before their nuptials were celebrated in ample form. From them are descended all of the name, Alden, in the United States. What report he made to his constituent, after the first interview, tradition does not unfold; but it is said, how true the writer knows not, that the captain never forgave him to the day of his death.

---

[1] *Among My Books*, (Everyman's Library), p. 181.
[2] *Ibid.*, p. 180.

From *Massachusetts Historical Collections*, Being a General Collection of Interesting Facts, Traditions, Biographical Sketches, Anecdotes, &c., Relating to the History and Antiquities of Every Town in Massachusetts, with Geographical Descriptions, by John Warner Barber, p. 500. Entered, according to Act of Congress, the year 1839, by Dorr, Howland & Co. In the Clerk's Office of the District Court of Massachusetts, Worcester.
Source: Alden's *A Collection of American Epitaphs* . . . , III.—J. W. B.

The Tinker and the Fencing-Master

. . . A TINKER with a cheese under his arm and a kettle of blacking in the hand, stopped at a tavern in a village in Massachusetts, where a French Fencing Master was teaching the art of fencing. He was challenging any one to try with him. Several did so and so expert was he, that he would soon disarm them. Presently the Tinker with his swab stick and his cheese under his arm took the floor and said he would try him. Although he disdained such a competitor as this tinker, yet to make sport for the company at the tinker's expense, he consented to try him. They went at it, but with all his skill he could not touch the tinker. Presently the tinker caught the fencing master's sword in his cheese and blacked one of his cheeks with the end of his swab stick, and the laugh turned on him instead of the tinker. He sweat and grew mad and exerted himself to the utmost to overcome the tinker. The next moment the tinker blacked the other cheek! The fencing master was now in a rage and threatened to kill him, but the tinker said coolly "don't you attempt that, for if you do, you are the dead man." The fencing master's sword dropped, and he said: "You are either Goffe, Whalley,[1] or the Devil, for there are no others in the world that can fence with me," and he was right, for it was one of these men, in the disguise of a tinker that stood before him.

The Angel of Hadley

DURING Philip's war, in 1676, Hadley was attacked on the morning of the

---

From "Further Reminiscences of the Valley of the Pawtuxet River and Its Branches," by Noah J. Arnold. in *The Narragansett Historical Register,* A Magazine Devoted to the Antiquities, Genealogy and Historical Matter Illustrating the History of the State of Rhode Island and Providence Planations, Vol. 7 (July 1889), No. 3, edited by James N. Arnold, p. 238. Copyright in the office of the Librarian of Congress at Washington, D. C. Providence, Rhode Island: The Narragansett Historical Publishing Company.

[1] They were two of Oliver Cromwell's ablest generals in the revolution in England, which dethroned and then beheaded Charles I, King of England. Their names were Goffe and Whalley, and [they] were reputed to be the best swordsmen in Europe. They were members of the Court that tried the king and voted the sentence of death upon him. After the restoration of Charles II, all those who were alive that were members of that Court had to flee from England to such places of refuge as they could find, or they would have been put to death. Goffe and Whalley came to this country, and kept secreted as well as they could.—N. J. A.

Cf. John Warner Barber, *Massachusetts Historical Collections* (Worcester 1839), p. 324, who places this episode, between the judge, disguised as a rustic, and a fencing-master, in Boston.

From *Massachusets Historical Collections,* Being a General Collection of Interesting Facts, Traditions, Biographical Sketches, Anecdotes, &c., Relating to the History and Antiquities of Every Town in Massachusetts, with Geographical Descriptions, by John Warner Barber, pp. 325–326. Entered, according to Act of Congress, in the year 1839, by Dorr, Howland & Co. in the Clerk's Office of the District Court of Massachusetts. Worcester.

Source: *Hoyt's Indian Wars,* p. 135.—J. W. B.

Cf. "The Gray Champion," by Nathaniel Hawthorne.

12th of June, by about seven hundred Indians. "In the preceding night, they approached the town, laid an ambuscade at the southern extremity, and advanced the main body towards the other, and at day-light the attack was commenced with great spirit; but the English, turning out, received them at the palisades. The Indians gained possession of a house at the north end of the street, and fired a barn, but were in a short time driven back with loss. The attack was renewed on other points, and the Indians, though warmly opposed, appeared determined on carrying the place; but a discharge of a piece of ordnance checked their fury and their ambuscade failing of their object, which was to attack the people who might be driven from the village, they drew off. Major Talcott, at Northampton, hearing the attack, hurried on, passed the river, and, joining the Hadley forces, precipitated the Indians into the woods. Only two or three men were lost by the English; the enemy's was not ascertained." "When the people were in great consternation, and rallying to oppose the Indians, a man of venerable aspect, differing from the inhabitants in his apparel, appeared, and, assuming command, arrayed them in the best manner for defence, evincing much knowledge of military tactics, and by his advice and example continued to animate the men throughout the attack. When the Indians drew off, the stranger disappeared, and nothing further was heard of him. Who the deliverer was, none could inform or conjecture, but by supposing, as was common at that day, that Hadley had been saved by its guardian angel. It will be recollected that at this time the two judges, Whalley and Goffe, were secreted in the village, at the house of the Rev. Mr. Russell. The supposed angel, then, was no other than Gen. Goffe, who, seeing the village in imminent danger, put all at risk, left his concealment, mixed with the inhabitants, and animated them to a vigorous defence. Whalley, being then superannuated, probably remained in his secluded chamber."

Lovel and the Indians

THERE is no doubt that farmer Lovel had read ancient history or he would not have been so ready in the emergency that befell him one time in the last century. He had settled among the New Hampshire hills near the site that is now occupied by the village of Washington and had a real good time there with bears and Indians. It was when he was splitting rails on Lovel Mountain—they named it for him afterward—that he found himself surrounded by six Indians, who told him that he was their prisoner. He agreed that they had the advantage over him and said that he would

From *Myths & Legends of Our Own Land*, by Charles M. Skinner, Vol. I, pp. 207–208. Copyright, 1896, by J. B. Lippincott Company. Philadelphia & London.

This ruse is attributed to many Indian-fighters, including Ford (Katharine M. Abbott, *Old Paths and Legends of New England*, New York, 1903, p. 413) and Weare (or Wyer) (Manuscripts of the Federal Writers' Project of the Works Progress Administration for the State of Maine).

go quietly along if they would allow him to finish the big chestnut log
that he was at work on. As he was a powerful fellow and was armed with
an axe worth any two of their tomahawks, and as he would be pretty sure
to have the life of at least one of them if they tried to drive him faster
than he wanted to go, they consented. He said that he would be ready all
the sooner if they would help him to pull the big log apart, and they agreed
to help him. Driving a wedge into the long split he asked them to take
hold, and when they had done this he knocked out the wedge with a single
blow and the twelve hands were caught tight in the closing wood. Struggle
as the savages might, they could not get free, and after calmly enjoying
the situation for a few minutes he walked slowly from one to the other
and split open the heads of all six. Then he went to work again splitting
up more chestnuts.

Captain Putnam and the British Major

IN THE TIME of the old French [and Indian] War much jealousy existed
between the British and provincial officers. A British major, deeming
himself insulted by General (then Captain) Putnam, sent him a challenge.
Putnam, instead of giving him a direct answer, requested the pleasure of
a personal interview with the major. He came to Putnam's tent, and found
him seated on a small keg, quietly smoking his pipe, and demanded what
communication, if any, Putnam had to make. "What you know," said
Putnam. "I'm but a poor miserable Yankee that never fired a pistol in
my life, and you must perceive that if we fight with pistols you have an
undue advantage of me. Here are two powder kegs. I have bored a hole,
and inserted a slow-match in each. If you will be so good as to seat yourself there, I will light the matches, and he who dares to sit the longest
without squirming shall be called the bravest fellow."

The tent was full of officers and men, who were heartily tickled with the
strange device of the "Old Wolf," and compelled the major by their
laughter and exhortation to squat. The signal was given, and the matches
lighted. Putnam continued smoking, quite indifferently, without watching
at all the progressive diminution of the matches—but the British officer,
though a brave fellow, could not help casting longing and lingering looks
downwards, and his terrors increased as the length of the match diminished.

The spectators withdrew, one by one, to get out of the expected explosion.
At length, the fire was within an inch of the keg. The major, unable to
endure longer, jumped up, and drawing out his match, cried out, "Putnam,
this is wilful murder; draw out your match; I yield." "My dear fellow,"
cried Putnam, "don't be in such a hurry. They're nothing but kegs of
onions!" The major was suddenly missing, having sneaked off.

From *The Rip-Rap Joker*, The Funniest and Spiciest Joker of the Times, p. 4. New
York: Benedict Publishing Company. [1860?]

Old Put's Wolf

IN THE year 1739, he [Gen. Putnam] removed from Salem to Pomfret, an inland fertile town in Connecticut, forty miles east of Hartford; having here purchased a considerable tract of land, he applied himself successfully to agriculture.

The first years on a new farm are not, however, exempt from disasters and disappointments, which can only be remedied by stubborn and patient industry. Our farmer, sufficiently occupied in building an house and barn, felling woods, making fences, sowing grain, planting orchards, and taking care of his stock, had to encounter, in turn, the calamities occasioned by a drought in summer, blast in harvest, loss of cattle in winter, and the desolation of his sheep-fold by wolves. In one night he had seventy fine sheep and goats killed, besides many lambs and kids wounded. This havoc was committed by a she wolf, which with her annual whelps, had for several years infested the vicinity. The young were commonly destroyed by the vigilance of the hunters, but the old one was too sagacious to come within reach of gunshot; upon being closely pursued she would generally fly to the western woods, and return the next winter with another litter of whelps.

This wolf at length became such an intolerable nuisance that Mr. Putnam entered into a combination with five of his neighbors to hunt alternately until they could destroy her. Two by rotation were to be constantly in pursuit. It was known that having lost the toes from one foot, by a steel trap, she made one track shorter than the other. By this vestige, the pursuers recognized in a light snow the route of this pernicious animal. Having followed her to Connecticut River and found she had turned back in a direct course towards Pomfret, they immediately returned, and by ten o'clock the next morning, the blood-hounds had driven her into a den, about three miles distant from the house of Mr. Putnam. The people soon collected with dogs, guns, straw, fire and sulphur to attack the common enemy. With this apparatus several unsuccessful efforts were made to force her from the den. The hounds came back badly wounded and refused to return. The smoke of blazing straw had no effect; nor did the fumes of burnt brimstone, with which the cavern was filled, compel her to quit the retirement.

Wearied with such fruitless attempts, which had brought the time to ten o'clock at night, Mr. Putnam tried once more to make his dog enter, but in vain; he proposed to his Negro man to go down into the cavern and shoot the wolf: the Negro declined the hazardous service. Then it was that the master, angry at the disappointment, and declaring that he was

From *The Life & Heroic Exploits of Israel Putnam, Major-General in the Revolutionary War*, by Colonel David Humphreys, pp. 8–12. Entered, according to the Act of Congress, in the year 1833, by Ezra Strong, in the Clerk's Office of the District Court of the Southern District of New York. New York. 1835.

ashamed to have a coward in his family, resolved himself to destroy the ferocious beast, lest she should escape through some unknown fissure of the rock. His neighbors strongly remonstrated against the perilous enterprise; but he, knowing that wild animals were intimidated by fire, and having provided several strips of birch-bark, the only combustible material which he could obtain, that would afford light in this deep and darksome cave, prepared for his descent. Having accordingly, divested himself of his coat and waistcoat, and having a long rope fastened round his legs, by which he might be pulled back, at a concerted signal, he entered head foremost with the blazing torch in his hand.

The aperture of the den, on the east side of a very high ledge of rocks, is about two feet square; from thence it descends obliquely fifteen feet, then running horizontally about ten more, it ascends gradually sixteen feet towards its termination. The sides of this subterraneous cavity are composed of smooth and solid rocks, which seem to have been divided from each other by some former earthquake. The top and bottom are also of stone, and the entrance in winter, being covered with ice, is exceedingly slippery. It is in no place high enough for a man to raise himself upright, nor in any part more than three feet in width.

Having groped his passage to the horizontal part of the den, the most terrifying darkness appeared in front of the dim circle of light afforded by his torch. It was silent as the house of death. None but monsters of the desert had ever before explored this solitary mansion of horror. Cautiously proceeding onward, he came to the ascent, which he slowly mounted on his hands and knees until he discovered the glaring eyeballs of the wolf, who was sitting at the extremity of the cavern. Started at the sight of fire, she gnashed her teeth, and gave a sullen growl. As soon as he had made the necessary discovery, he kicked the rope as a signal for pulling him out. The people at the mouth of the den who had listened with painful anxiety, hearing the growl of the wolf, and supposing their friend to be in the most imminent danger, drew him forth with such celerity that his shirt was stripped over his head and his skin severely lacerated. After he had adjusted his clothes, and loaded his gun with nine buck-shot, holding a torch in one hand and the musket in the other, he descended the second time. When he drew nearer than before, the wolf assuming a still more fierce and terrible appearance, howling, rolling her eyes, snapping her teeth, and dropping her head between her legs, was evidently in the attitude and on the point of springing at him. At this critical instant he levelled and fired at her head. Stunned by the shock, and suffocated with the smoke, he immediately found himself drawn out of the cave. But having refreshed himself, and permitted the smoke to dissipate, he went down the third time. Once more he came within sight of the wolf, who appearing very passive, he applied the torch to her nose, and perceiving her dead, he took hold of her ears, and then kicking the rope still tied round his legs, the people above with no small exultation dragged them both out together.

Yankee Doodle

. . . [IT WAS] Colonel Thomas Fitch, [of Norwalk, Connecticut,] whose shabbily dressed troops, which he led from here to the French and Indian War, inspired a British army surgeon, Dr. Shuckburgh, to write the derisive "Yankee Doodle." According to local tradition, Elizabeth Fitch, on leaving the house to bid good-bye to her brother, was dismayed by the ill-assorted costumes of the "cavalry." Exclaiming, "You must have uniforms of some kind," she ran into the chicken yard, and returning with a handful of feathers announced, "Soldiers should wear plumes," and directed each rider to put a feather in his cap. When Shuckburgh saw Fitch's men arriving at Fort Crailo, Rensselaer, New York, he is reputed to have exclaimed, "Now stab my vitals, they're macaronis!" sarcastically applying the slang of the day for fop, or dandy, and proceeded to write the song, which instantly caught popular fancy.

The Young Rebels

Sunday, January 29th (1775). . . . Shall close this by giving you a small anecdote, relating to some of our school lads—who as formerly in this season improv'd the Coast from Sherburn's hill down to School street. General Haldiman, improving the house that belongs to Old Cook, his servant took it upon him to cut up their coast and fling ashes upon it. The lads made a muster, and chose a committee to wait upon the General, who admitted them, and heard their complaint, which was couch'd in very genteel terms, complaining that their fathers before 'em had improv'd it as a coast for time immemorial, &ca. He order'd his servant to repair the damage, and acquainted the Governor with the affair, who observ'd that it was impossible to beat the notion of Liberty out of the people, as it was rooted in 'em *from their Childhood*.[1]

Near the centre of the [Boston] Common is a stone-rimmed body of water known as the Frog Pond. The old-time Boston boys used to slide down hill on to this pond, and they heaped up the snow to make a steeper descent. Just before the Revolution, the English soldiers who were camped on the Common destroyed the slides again and again while the boys were gone to school. The boys protested in vain to the soldiers, and then went to their general and complained. He asked who sent them.

"Nobody sent us, sir," one of them replied. "Your soldiers have spoiled our snow-slides and broken the ice where we skate. When we complained

From *Connecticut,* A Guide to Its Roads, Lore and People, written by Workers of the Federal Writers' Project of the Works Progress Administration for the State of Connecticut, p. 267. American Guide Series. Copyright, 1938, by Wilbur L. Cross. Boston: Houghton Mifflin Company.

From *Letters of John Andrews, Esq., of Boston, 1772-1776,* compiled and edited from the Original Mss., with an Introduction, by Winthrop Sargent, pp. 12-13. Reprinted from the Proceedings of the Massachusetts Historical Society. Cambridge: Press of John Wilson and Sons. 1866.

to them, they called us young rebels, and told us to help ourselves if we could. Now we will bear it no longer."

The general turned to an officer and exclaimed, "Good heavens! the very children draw in a love of liberty with the air they breathe."

Then he assured the boys that if any of the soldiers molested them again, they would be severely punished.[2]

The Original Brother Jonathan

WHEN General Washington, after being appointed Commander of the Army of Revolutionary War [June 15th, 1775,] came to Massachusetts to organize it, and make preparations for the defence of the country, he found a great want of ammunition and other means necessary to meet the powerful foe he had to contend with, and great difficulty to obtain them. If attacked in such condition, the cause at once might be hopeless. On one occasion, at that anxious period, a consultation of the officers and others was held, when it seemed no way could be devised to make such preparations as were necessary. His Excellency Jonathan Trumbull, the elder, was then Governor of the State of Connecticut, on whose judgment and aid the general placed the greatest reliance, and remarked: "We must consult 'Brother Jonathan' on the subject." The general did so, and the governor was successful in supplying many of the wants of the army. When difficulties arose, and the army was spread over the country, it became a by-word, "We must consult Brother Jonathan." The term Yankee is still applied to a portion, but "Brother Jonathan" has become a designation of the whole country, as John Bull is for England.

A Loyal Tory of Hancock

TRADITIONS and tales from the past are Hancock's chief contribution to the history of Berkshire. Her glory was at its peak during the years when the "Berkshire Boys" marched up the long valley to Bennington, and Tories received short shrift from the patriots.

A loyal Tory of Hancock, Richard Jackson, was accused of high treason against the Colonies when he was captured on his way to join the British near Bennington. Making no pretense of being other than a Royalist, ready

[2] From *New England, A Human Interest Geographical Reader,* by Clifton Johnson, pp. 66–67. Copyright, 1917, by The Macmillan Company. New York and London.

From *The American Joe Miller:* A Collection of Yankee Wit and Humour, Compiled by Robert Kempt, p. 116. Entered at Stationers' Hall. London: Adams and Francis. 1865.

From *The Berkshire Hills,* Compiled and Written by Members of the Federal Writers' Project of the Works Progress Administration for Massachusetts, pp. 51–52. Copyright, 1939, by The Berkshire Hills Conference, Inc. New York: Duell, Sloan and Pearce.

to fight for his king, he was taken to the jail at Great Barrington to await trial in Springfield. The jail was dilapidated and the guard lax, so that any prisoner could have escaped with ease. But Jackson's integrity was beyond question. Local tradition has it that he appealed to the sheriff.

"Let me go free that I may work and earn something."

"But—but—" stammered the sheriff, who respected Jackson, though he felt that this request was a little unorthodox.

"Have no fear, Sheriff, I shall come back at night," and he added grimly, "When it's time for me to be hanged, I'll be there."

Morning after morning Jackson was let out, did his day's work, and was safely locked up again at night. Finally in May it became the sheriff's duty to take him to Springfield. But seeing that his jailer was loath to leave his plowing and planting, Jackson suggested that he make the trip alone.

The sheriff, accustomed by this time to his prisoner's unusual requests, agreed, and his charge set off alone to trudge miles through the woods to his trial and execution, for there was no apparent hope of acquittal. In the woods of Tyringham he was overtaken by the Hon. Mr. Edwards, who was on his way to a meeting of the Executive Council in Boston.

"Whither are you bound?" asked Edwards. "To Springfield, sir, to be tried for my life," was the calm rejoinder.

Without disclosing his own identity, Edwards soon learned his companion's story. Pondering, he went on to Boston, while Jackson stopped in Springfield, was duly tried, and condemned to death. Meantime, the Executive Council, which at that time exercised power of release over those condemned to death, was listening to petitions for pardon. After all these had been read, Edwards asked the Council if a pardon was not to be granted to Mr. Jackson of Hancock. Earnestly addressing the assembly, Edwards told the story of Jackson's loyalty not only to his king, but to the laws and regulations of the Colony in so far as they implied no disloyalty to his English sovereign. The members of the Council hesitated, scarcely believing their ears, but when the story was proved true, they unanimously agreed that such a man as Jackson ought not to be sent to the gallows. An unconditional pardon was immediately made out and the loyal Tory returned to his family and farm in Hancock.

The early town records of Hancock lead one to wonder what kind of reception awaited Jackson after he cheated the noose. The town was militantly patriotic in Revolutionary times. Her sons served their country valiantly and as a rule Royalists received little tolerance from the Town Fathers. . . .

The Satisfied Redemptioner

BOTH before and after the Revolution, the poorer class of emigrants, in the lack of ready money, secured a passage to this country through shipping companies specially organized for that purpose, by signing a negotiable obligation for the amount of their passage ticket, whereby they were "bound to service for a term of years,"—more or less, according as the persons were single or had families. This class of persons was included in the famous rendition clause of the Constitution of the United States, Art. IV, Sect. 11, 3. They were familiarly known as "Redemptioners."

One of these was "held to service" by a planter in Westerly [, Rhode Island,] who had duly bought his paper. After serving very cheerfully and happily in his new relation for a season, he took occasion to express to his master or employer his entire satisfaction with his situation, and seriously averred that he wished his written obligation extended through his life. He was disquieted and depressed with the idea that he should finally, on the expiration of his service, be obliged to plan and toil for himself in a land of strangers. The farm to him was an Eden, and his employer was a father. He therefore proposed to have his obligation made perpetual in a new writing.

The appropriate paper for his life service, at his request, was duly prepared and presented for his signature. On taking the pen to sign the instrument, he hesitated, saying that he did not understand how the obligations of the old and new papers harmonized, as the time in the new in part overlapped the time in the old. Explanations were in vain. Finally the master proposed to destroy the old paper and thus clear the way. This was satisfactory. The old instrument was thrown under the forestick. The redemptioner again took his pen, but again hesitated. He seemed to be in a brown study. The employer inquired for the reason of his embarrassment. Was the paper satisfactory? Was it not just what he himself had proposed and dictated? It was allowed that the instrument was exactly what he had desired. "But," said the redemptioner, "I was thinking of some advice that my father once gave me. He gave me good counsel, and I only wish I had followed it more closely. He once said to me, 'My son, never sign your name to a paper of any kind.' As I have signed one paper, but have just got rid of it, I think I shall not sign another. So, sir, I kindly bid you a good-by." The redemptioner walked away a free man, and left the employer counting up his wits.

From *Westerly (Rhode Island) and Its Witnesses,* for Two Hundred and Fifty Years, 1626–1876, Including Charlestown, Hopkinton, and Richmond, Until Their Separate Organization, with the Principal Points of Their Subsequent History, by Rev. Frederic Denison, A.M., pp. 143–144. Entered according to Act of Congress, in the year 1878, by Frederic Denison, in the Office of the Librarian of Congress, at Washington, D. C. Providence: Published by J. A. & R. A. Reid.

The Yarn-Beam Cannon

HARD on the heels of the Revolution came Shays' Rebellion. The Berkshire farmers, oppressed by heavy taxes, hard times, and the almost worthless post-Revolutionary currency, understood better than the "city folks" in Boston the real purpose of Daniel Shays' uprising. Lee was in particularly hard straits. In the winter of 1787, a battle more comic than tragic took place between the Shaysites and the government troops under General Patterson, drawn up on a hill in East Lee. Uniformed troops these, with polished rifles and menacing cannon. Opposite, across Greenwater Brook, were lined up the ragged and hungry rebels. They had only a few old-fashioned muskets, little ammunition, and no cannon. But someone had an inspiration. "Bring out Mother Perry's yarn-beam," he cried; "we'll make it look like a cannon to scare the sheep across the way." Quickly the ponderous piece of weaving machinery, looking remarkably like a cannon, was mounted on a pair of ox-cart wheels. A ramrod and other military gadgets were flourished for the benefit of the enemy. Peter Wilcox roared the order, "Fire," and a blazing tarred rope was brandished like a fuse. Before the flames could damage Mother Perry's property, General Patterson's troops were in flight. In a twinkling, the hill they had occupied was bare.

Skipper Ireson's Ride

ON SUNDAY, the 30th of October [1808], the schooner Betty, commanded by Skipper Benjamin Ireson, arrived from the Grand Banks. Shortly after their arrival, the crew reported that at midnight on the previous Friday, when off Cape Cod lighthouse, they passed the schooner Active, of Portland, which was in a sinking condition; and that the skipper had refused to render any assistance to the unfortunate men on board the wreck. The excitement and indignation of the people upon the reception of this news can be better imagined than described. Two vessels, manned by willing volunteers, were immediately dispatched to the scene of the disaster, with the hope of their arrival in time to save the shipwrecked sailors. But their mission was a failure, and they returned with no tidings of the wreck. The resentment of the people was still further provoked when, on the following day, the sloop Swallow arrived, having on board

From *The Berkshire Hills*, Compiled and Written by Members of the Federal Writers' Project of the Works Progress Administration for Massachusetts, pp. 137–138. Copyright, 1939, by The Berkshire Hills Conference, Inc. New York: Duell, Sloan and Pearce.

From *The History and Traditions of Marblehead*, (Third Edition), by Samuel Roads, Jr., pp. 292–295. Copyright, 1880, by Samuel Roads, Jr. Marblehead: Press of N. Allen Lindsey & Co. 1897.

Captain Gibbons, the master of the ill-fated schooner. He corroborated the story told by the crew of the Betty, and stated that the Active sprang a leak at about eleven o'clock on Friday night. An hour later the Betty was spoken, "but contrary to the principles of humanity," she sailed away without giving any assistance. On Saturday, Captain Gibbons and three of the passengers were taken off the wreck by Mr. Hardy of Truro, in a whale boat. Four other persons were left on the wreck, but the storm increased so rapidly that it was found impossible to return to their rescue. Captain Gibbons was placed on board the revenue cutter Intent, and afterward went aboard the sloop Swallow, in which he came to Marblehead.[1]

This statement by one who had so narrowly escaped a watery grave made a deep impression upon the fishermen, and they determined to demonstrate their disapproval of Skipper Ireson's conduct by a signal act of vengeance. Accordingly on a bright moonlight night, the unfortunate skipper was suddenly seized by several powerful men and securely bound. He was then placed in a dory, and, besmeared from head to feet with tar and feathers, was dragged through the town, escorted by a multitude of men and boys. When opposite the locality now known as Workhouse Rocks, the bottom of the dory came out, and the prisoner finished the remainder of his ride to Salem in a cart. The authorities of that city forbade the entrance of the strange procession, and the crowd returned to Marblehead.

Throughout the entire proceeding, Mr. Ireson maintained a discreet silence, and when, on arriving at his own home, he was released from custody, his only remark was: "I thank you for my ride, gentlemen, but you will live to regret it."

His words were prophetic. When too late to make reparation for the wrong they had committed, the impulsive fishermen realized that they had perpetrated an act of the greatest injustice upon an innocent man.

At this late day, when for years his memory has been defamed throughout the land, and the fair name of the women of Marblehead has been sullied by the fictitious story of one of our best New England poets, it is but just that the true history of the affair should be written. Skipper Ireson was not more to blame than his crew and, it is believed, not at all. When the wreck was spoken and the cry of distress was heard, a terrific gale was blowing. There was a consultation on board the Betty as to the course to be pursued, and the crew decided not to endanger their own lives for the sake of saving others. Finding that they were resolute in their determination, Skipper Ireson proposed to lay by the wreck all night, or until the storm should abate, and then go to the rescue of the unfortunate men. To this they also demurred, and insisted upon proceeding on their homeward voyage without delay. On their arrival in Marblehead, fearing the just indignation of the people, they laid the entire blame upon the skipper. This version of the affair is generally accepted as true; and, for

---

[1] See *Boston Centinel*, *Essex Register*, and *Salem Gazette*, November, 1808.— S. R., Jr.

the credit of the town, be it said that it is one of the few incidents in its
entire history that its citizens have any reason to regret.[1]

Mrs. Bailey's Petticoat

THEY tell a story here [in Groton, Connecticut,] of the war of 1812 worth
relating: One day Commodore Hardy in the "Ramilies" and Sir Hugh

---

[1] Immediately upon the publication of the first edition of this book, Mr. Whittier
sent the author a letter in which he gracefully acknowledged himself mistaken as to
the facts in the case. He also gave directions that the letter should be published with
the poem in subsequent editions of his works. The letter, herewith printed, is published
with his permission.

OAK KNOLL, DANVERS, 5 mo, 18, 1880.

MY DEAR FRIEND: I heartily thank thee for a copy of thy *History of
Marblehead.* I have read it with great interest and think good use has
been made of the abundant material. No town in Essex County has a record
more honorable than Marblehead; no one has done more to develop the
industrial interests of our New England seaboard, and certainly none have
given such evidence of self-sacrificing patriotism. I am glad the story of it
has been at last told, and told so well. I have now no doubt that thy version
of Skipper Ireson's ride is the correct one. My verse was founded solely on a
fragment of rhyme which I heard from one of my early schoolmates, a native
of Marblehead.

I supposed the story to which it referred dated back at least a century. I
knew nothing of the participators, and the narrative of the ballad was pure
fancy. I am glad for the sake of truth and justice that the real facts are given
in thy book. I certainly would not knowingly do injustice to any one, dead
or living.

I am very truly thy friend,
JOHN G. WHITTIER.
—S. R., JR.

The "Chant of Flood Oirson," as it has been called, [the "fragment of rhyme"
referred to by Whittier] was current in the town years before Whittier wrote, and ran
in this wise:—

> Old Flood Oirson for his hord hort
> Was tor'd and further'd and coried in a cort,
> A becos he left five men on a wrack
> Was tor'd and further'd all over his back!

The true story was first published some twenty years ago by the late Rev. Charles
T. Brooks, minister and poet, in a newspaper, by way of introduction to his verses,
A Plea for Flood Ireson, written as an offset to Whittier's poem. . . .

Poor Ireson sailed another voyage as skipper, the following year, but never after.
Later in life he followed the dory-fishing in the bay, and used to peddle his catch in
a handcart through the streets. Although the best townspeople soon after the affair
became entirely satisfied that he had suffered unjustly, and treated him with respect, his
life was wrecked; and he drifted aimlessly till his death, only a year or two before
the appearance of Whittier's ballad. His name was Benjamin Ireson; "Flood," not
"Floyd," as Whittier gives it, being a nickname.—Edwin M. Bacon, *Historic Pilgrim-
ages in New England* (Boston, 1898), pp. 210–211, 212.

Pigott in the "Orpheus" hove in sight, and the people came to the conclusion that New London was to be attacked. Major Smith at once manned Fort Griswold with volunteers from the vicinity, while the women and children fled into the interior. At the last moment the Major found he had no wadding for his cannon, and sent out a squad in search of flannel for that purpose. Unfortunately all the houses and stores were closed, and they could secure none. Returning, they met on the street Mrs. Anna Bailey, who, on hearing their story, dropped her flannel petticoat, and told them to give it to the British at the cannon's mouth. The officers and garrison were greatly elated by the lady's spirit, and Hardy would no doubt have fared ill had he attacked. When the danger was over, Commodore Decatur gave a grand ball, at which Mrs. Bailey was the heroine of the occasion. Later her fame spread throughout the country, and she was visited by Lafayette, Monroe, Jackson, and other notables. "Mother Bailey" died in 1851 aged ninety-two years.

ROGUES, ECCENTRICS, AND HEROES

Captain Kidd Legends in New England

KIDD'S TOMB [1]

. . . [IN BOSTON] is King's Chapel, where the British officials and loyalist gentry worshipped in colonial days. Close to each of these buildings is an ancient cemetery with its lowly gray stones. Some say that in the King's Chapel churchyard the notorious pirate, Captain Kidd, lies buried. Before his reputation became as black as it did later, he was employed by the colonial governor of New England and certain others to go on a voyage to catch pirates. After a while rumors came that he had himself turned pirate. However, in a few years he appeared in Boston and delivered to the governor the treasure he had acquired in capturing various ships. This included 1111 ounces of gold, 2353 ounces of silver, 57 bags of sugar, and 41 bales of goods.

Orders came from England for his arrest, and he was locked up in Boston Jail. This was in 1699. The prison was a gloomy building with thick stone walls, ponderous oaken doors, and dark passages; and the keys that the jailer carried at his girdle weighed from one to three pounds each. Captain Kidd was later sent to London, where he was tried and hung. How his body happens to be in King's Chapel churchyard is not explained, but the statement is made that if a person will visit his tomb there at midnight, tap on it three times, and ask in a whisper, "Captain Kidd, for what were you hung?" the pirate will answer nothing.

---

[1] From *New Engalnd, A Human Interest Geographical Reader*, by Clifton Johnson, pp. 67–68. Copyright, 1917, by The Macmillan Company. New York and London.

KIDD'S GHOST [2]

A SHORT distance south of the town [of Northfield, Massachusetts] is Clark's Island, which has a curious legend of Captain Kidd. We are told that the pirate sailed up to this secluded spot, and he and his men brought on shore a heavy iron chest full of gold and jewelry and other precious loot. They dug a deep hole and lowered the chest into it. Then, in what was considered the proper old-fashioned pirate way, one of the crew was selected by lot, killed, and his body placed on top of the loose earth that had been thrown into the hole. His ghost was supposed to haunt the vicinity, and to forever guard the riches from audacious treasure-seekers.

From time to time, in the darkness of night when the gales howled, persons are said to have seen sailing up the stream a phantom ship, manned by a spectral crew, and commanded by a black-bearded ghost with the familiar features of Captain Kidd. Opposite the island the anchor was let go, and Kidd in a boat rowed by four sailors went ashore. After satisfying himself that the plunder was safe he returned to the ship and sailed down the river.

Some people doubt the whole story and ask how Captain Kidd ever navigated his ship up there past the rocky falls.

Tom Cook, the Leveler

IN THE year 1741 the little child of Cornelius Cook, the blacksmith of Westborough, Massachusetts, and of his wife Eunice, lay very close to death. As was the custom of the day, the good old parson, Dr. Parkman, and his deacons prayed earnestly over the boy, that the Lord's will be done; but his mother in her distress pleaded thus: "Only spare his life, and I care not what he becomes." Tom Cook recovered, and as years passed on it became evident by his mischievous and evil deeds that he had entered into a compact with the devil, perhaps by his mother's agonized words, perhaps by his own pledge. The last year of this compact was at an end, and the devil appeared to claim his own as Tom was dressing for another day's mischief. Tom had all his wits about him, for he lived upon them. "Wait, wait, can't you," he answered the imperative call of his visitor, "till I get my galluses on?" The devil acquiesced to this last request, when Tom promptly threw the suspenders in the fire, and therefore could never put them on nor be required to answer the devil's demands.

Tom Cook became well known throughout Massachusetts, and indeed throughout New England, as a most extraordinary thief. His name appears in the records of scores of New England towns; he was called "the honest thief"; and his own name for himself was "the leveller." He stole from

---

[2] *Ibid.*, p. 129.

From *Stage-Coach and Tavern Days,* by Alice Morse Earle, pp. 381–384. Copyright, 1900, by The Macmillan Company. New York and London.

the rich and well-to-do with the greatest boldness and dexterity, equalled by the kindness and delicacy of feeling shown in the bestowal of his booty upon the poor and needy. He stole the dinner from the wealthy farmer's kitchen and dropped it into the kettle or on the spit in a poor man's house. He stole meal and grain from passing wagons and gave it away before the drivers' eyes. A poor neighbor was ill, and her bed was poor. He went to a thrifty farm-house, selected the best feather bed in the house, tied it in a sheet, carried it downstairs and to the front door, and asked if he could leave his bundle there for a few days. The woman recognized him and forbade him to bring it within doors, and he went off with an easy conscience.

*   *   *   *   *

Tom Cook was most attractive in personal appearance; agile, well formed, well featured, with eyes of deepest blue, most piercing yet most kindly in expression. He was adored by children, and his pockets were ever filled with toys which he had stolen for their amusement. By older persons he was feared and disliked. He extorted from many wealthy farmers an annual toll, which exempted them from his depredations. One day a fire was seen rising from the chimney of a disused schoolhouse in Brookline, and Tom was caught within roasting a stolen goose, which he had taken from the wagon of a farmer on his way to market. The squire took him to the tavern, which was filled with farmers and carters, many of whom had been his victims. He was given his choice of trial and jail, or to run a gantlet of the men assembled. He chose the latter, and the long whips of the teamsters paid out many an old score of years' standing.

George White, Horse Thief

IN THE early years of this century there existed in eastern Massachusetts an organized band of thieves. It is said they were but one link in a chain of evil night-workers which, with a home or shelter in every community, reached from Cape Hatteras to Canada. This band was well organized, well trained, and well housed; it had skilful means of concealing stolen goods in innocent-faced cottages, in barns of honest thrift, and in wells and haystacks in simple dooryards. One mild-mannered and humble house had a deep cellar which could be entered by an ingeniously hidden broadside door in a woodshed; into this cave a stolen horse and wagon or a pursued load of cribbed goods might be driven, be shut in, and leave no outward sign. Other houses had secret cellars, a deep and wide one beneath a shallow, innocuous storage place for domestic potato and apple bins, and honest cider barrels. In a house sheltering one of these subterranean mysteries, a hard-working young woman was laboriously and discreetly washing clothes when surprised by the sheriff and his aids, who wisely invaded but fruitlessly searched the house. Nothing save the simplest

Ibid., pp. 388–393.

household belongings was found in that abode of domesticity; but in later years, after the gang was scattered, a trap-door and ladder were found leading to the sub-cellar, and with chagrin and mortification the sheriff remembered that the woman's washing tubs stood unharmed upon the trap-door during the fruitless search.

* * * * *

The leader of this band of thieves was an ingenious and delightful scamp —one George White. He was hard to catch, and harder to keep than to catch. Handcuffs were to him but pleasing toys. His wrists were large, his hands small; and when the right moment came, the steel bracelets were quickly empty. Locks and bolts were as easily thrust aside and left far, far behind him as were the handcuffs. At last he was branded on his fore-head H. T., which stands for horse thief; a mean trick of a stupid constable who had scant self-confidence or inventiveness. Curling lovelocks quickly grow, however, and are ill in no one's sight; indeed, they were in high fashion in similar circles in England at that time, when various letters of the alphabet might be seen on the cheeks and brow of many a gay traveller on the highway when the wind blew among the long locks.

Term after term in jail and prison were decreed to George White when luck turned against him. Yet still was he pardoned, as he deserved to be, for his decorous deportment when behind bars; and he had a habit of being taken out on a writ of *habeas corpus* or to be transferred; but he never seemed to reach his journey's end, and soon he would appear on the road, stealing and roistering. The last word which came from him to New England was a letter from the Ohio Penitentiary, saying he was dying, and asking some of his kin to visit him. They did not go, he had fooled them too often. Perhaps they feared they might put new life into him. But the one time they were sure he lied he told the truth—and his varied career thus ended.

Flying once along a Massachusetts highway on a stolen horse, George White was hotly pursued. At the first sharp turn in the road he dismounted in a flash, cut the horse a lash with his whip, altered the look of his garment with a turn of his hand, tore off his hat brim and thus had a jaunty cap, and started boldly back on foot. Meeting the sheriff and his men all in a heat, he fairly got under their horses' feet, and as they pulled up they bawled out to know whether he had seen a man riding fast on horseback. "Why, yes," he answered ingenuously, "I met a man riding as though the devil were after him." They found the horse in half an hour, but they never found George White.

He once stole a tavern-keeper's horse, trimmed the mane, thinned out the tail, and dyed the horse's white feet. He led the renovated animal in to the bereft landlord, saying innocently that he had heard his horse was stolen, and thought he might want to buy another. He actually sold this horse back to his owner, but in short time the horse's too evident familiarity with his wonted stable and yard and the fast-fading dye revealed the rascal's work. To another tavern-keeper he owed a bill for board and lodging, which, with the incongruity of ideals and morals which is often characteristic of great minds, he really wished to pay. The landlord had a fine black horse which he had displayed to his boarder with pride. This horse was kept temporarily in a distant pasture. White stole the horse one night, rode off a few miles, and sold it and was paid for it. He stole it again that night from the purchaser, sold it, and was paid. He stole it a third time and returned it to the pasture from whence it never had been missed. He then paid his boardbill as an honest man should.

Dexter's Profitable Blunders

ACCORDING to his own account, TIMOTHY DEXTER was born in Malden, Mass., Jan. 22, 1747. After having served as an apprentice to a leather dresser, he commenced business in Newburyport, where he also married a widow, who owned a house and a small piece of land, part of which, soon after the nuptials, was converted by him into a shop and tanyard for his own use.

By application to his business, his property increased, and the purchase of a large tract of land near Penobscot, together with an interest which he bought in the Ohio Company's purchase, eventually afforded him so much profit as to induce him to buy up public securities at forty cents for the pound, which securities soon after became worth twenty shillings on the pound. By these and other fortunate business transactions, he prospered so greatly, that property now was no longer the sole object of his pursuit; he exchanged this god of idolatry for that of *popularity*. He was charitable to the poor, gave liberal donations to religious societies, and handsomely rewarded those who wrote in his praise. His lordship—a self-conferred title—about this time acquired his peculiar taste for style and splendor, set up an elegant equipage, and, at great cost, adorned the front of his mansion with numerous figures of illustrious personages.

Some of his lordship's speculations in trade have become quite as celebrated for their oddity as those of Rothschild for their . . . cunning. He once anxiously inquired of some merchants, whom he knew, how he should dispose of a few hundred dollars. Wishing to hoax him, they answered, "Why, buy a cargo of warming pans, and send them to the West Indies, to be sure." Not suspecting the trick, he at once bought all the warming pans he could find, and sent them to a climate where—there was every reason to suppose—ice would be far more acceptable. But "Providence sometimes shows his contempt of wealth, by giving it to fools." The warming pans met with a ready sale—the tops being used for strainers, and the lower parts for dippers, in the manufacture of molasses.

With the proceeds of his cargo of warming pans, Dexter built a fine vessel; and being informed by the carpenter that *wales* were wanting, he called on an acquaintance. and said, "My head workman sends me word that he wants 'wales' for the vessel. What does he mean?" "Why, whale-bones, to be sure," answered the man, who, like everybody else, was tempted to improve the opportunity of imposing upon Dexter's stupidity. Whalebones were accordingly bought; but, finding that Boston could not furnish enough, he emptied New York and Philadelphia. The ship-carpenters, of course, had a hearty laugh at his expense; but, by a singular turn of fortune, this blunder was also the means of increasing his wealth. It soon after became fashionable for ladies to wear stays completely lined with whalebone; and as none was to be found in the country, on account of his having thus so completely swept the market, it brought a golden price. Thus his coffers were a second time filled by his odd transactions.[1]

How Did Dexter make his money Inw ye says bying whale bone for staing for ships in grosing three houndred & 40 tuns bort all in boston salum and all in Noue york under Cover oppenly told them for my ships thay all Lafed so I had at my one prise I had four Couning men for Rouners thay founed the horne as I told them to Act the fool I was foull of cash I had Nine tun of silver on hand at that time all that time the Creaters more or Less Lafing it spread very fast heare is the Rub in fifty Days thay smelt A Rat found whare it was gone to Nouebry Port speklaters swarmed Like hell houns to be short with it I made seventey five per sent one tun and halfe of silver and over one more spect Drole A Nouf I Dreamed of worming pans three Nits that thay would doue in the west inges I got not more than fortey two thousand put them in Nine vessels for difrent ports that tuck good hold——I cleared sevinty nine per sent——the pans thay mad yous of them for Coucking very good master for Coukey blessed good in Deade missey got Nise handel Now bourn my fase the best thing I Ever see in borne days I found I was very luckkey in spekkelation I Dreamed that the good book was Run Down in this Countrey Nine years gone so low as halfe prise and Dull at that the bibbel I means I had the Readey Cash by holl sale I bort twelve per sent under halfe prise thay Cost forty one sents Each bibels twenty one thousand I put them into twenty one vessels for the westinges and sent A text that all of them must have one bibel in Every familey or if not thay would goue to hell and if thay had Dun wiked flie to the bibel and on thare Neas and kiss the bibel three times and Look up to heaven Annest for giveness my Capttens all had Compleat orders heare coms the good Luck I made one hundred per sent & Littel over then I found I had made money A Nuf I hant speck A Lated sence old times by gouerment secourties I made or cleared forty

---

[1] From *Cyclopaedia of Commercial and Business Anecdotes* . . . , edited by Frazar Kirkland, Vol. I, pp. 20–21. Entered, according to Act of Congress, in the year 1864, by D. Appleton and Company, in the Clerk's Office of the District Court of the United States for the Southern District of New York. New York and London.

seven thosands Dolors that is the old A fare Now I toald the all the sekrett Now be still Let me A Lone Dont wonder Now more houe I got my money boaz [2]

T DEXTER

Sam Hyde, Proverbial Liar

THERE are few, we imagine, who have not heard of this personage; but; notwithstanding his great notoriety, we might not be thought *serious* in the rest of our work, were we to enter seriously into his biography; for the reason, that from his day to this, his name has been a by-word in all New England, and means as much as to say the *greatest of liars*. It is on account of the following anecdote that he is noticed.

Sam Hide was a notorious cider-drinker as well as liar, and used to travel the country to and fro begging it from door to door. At one time he happened in a region of country where cider was very hard to be procured, either from its scarcity, or from *Sam's* frequent visits. However, cider he was determined to have, if lying, in any shape or color, would gain it. Being not far from the house of an acquaintance, who he knew had cider, but he knew, or was well satisfied, that, in the ordinary way of begging, he could not get it, he set his wits at work to lay a plan to insure it. This did not occupy him long. On arriving at the house of the gentleman, instead of asking for cider, he inquired for the man of the house, whom, on appearing, *Sam* requested to go aside with him, as he had something of importance to communicate to him. When they were by themselves, *Sam* told him he had that morning shot a fine deer, and that, if he would give him a crown, he would tell him where it was. The gentleman did not incline to do this, but

---

[2] From *A Pickle for the Knowing Ones:* or Plain Truths in a Homespun Dress, by Timothy Dexter, Esq., pp. 20–21. Second Edition with Large Additions. Newburyport: Printed for the Author. 1805.

From *The Book of the Indians*, by Samuel G. Drake (Boston, 1841), Book I, pp. 21–22. Cited in *The Old Farmer and His Almanack*, by George Lyman Kittredge, pp. 241–243. Copyright, 1904, by Horace E. Ware. Boston: William Ware and Company. "To lie like Sam Hyde" is still a New England saying, though, like so many old saws, it is going out of use as the population becomes more mixed. He is said to have been an Indian, and here is his biography as it stands in S. G. Drake's Book of the Indians. If it is not true, it is all the more appropriate in view of Sam's talent for mendacity. . . . We must take this narrative for what it is worth. Drake cites no authority, and one regrets to find that the Dedham archives contain no record of Sam Hyde's death, whether in 1732 or in any other year. The deer story is told of "one Tom Hyde, an Indian famous for his cunning," in Freeman Hunt's anonymous book of American Anecdotes, which was published in 1830. Hunt dates it "some years anterior to the independence of the United States," and says that the white man whom Hyde tricked was an innkeeper at Brookfield, Massachusetts. Drake's account of Sam's ambition to kill twenty of his foes seems to be adapted from a passage in Hubbard's Indian Wars.—G. L. K., *ibid.*, pp. 241, 243.

offered half a crown. Finally, *Sam* said, as he had walked a great distance that morning, and was very dry, for a half crown and a mug of cider he would tell him. This was agreed upon, and the price paid. Now *Sam* was required to point out the spot where the deer was to be found, which he did in this manner. He said to his friend, *You know of such a meadow,* describing it—Yes—*You know a big ash tree, with a big top by the little brook*—Yes—*Well, under that tree lies the deer.* This was satisfactory, and Sam departed. It is unnecessary to mention that the meadow was found, and the tree by the brook, but no deer. The duped man could hardly contain himself on considering. what he had been doing. To look after *Sam* for satisfaction would be worse than looking after the deer, so the farmer concluded to go home contented. Some years after, he happened to fall in with the Indian; and he immediately began to rally him for deceiving him so; and demanded back his money and pay for his cider and trouble. *Why,* said *Sam, would you find fault if Indian told truth half the time?*—No—*Well,* says *Sam, you find him meadow?*—Yes— *You find him tree?*—Yes—*What for then you find fault* Sam Hide, *when he told you two truth to one lie?* The affair ended here. *Sam* heard no more from the farmer.

This is but one of the numerous anecdotes of *Sam Hide,* which, could they be collected, would fill many pages. He died in Dedham, 5 January, 1732, at the great age of 105 years. He was a great jester, and passed for an uncommon wit. In all the wars against the Indians during his lifetime, he served the English faithfully, and had the name of a brave soldier. He had himself killed 19 of the enemy, and tried hard to make up the 20th, but was unable.

The Old Darnman

OF ALL the eccentric characters New England has produced, none ever inspired such a feeling of sympathy and tenderness as the Old Darnman.

To the present generation he is quite as mythical a figure as the Wandering Jew or Rip Van Winkle; but, fortunately, there are a few octogenarians still living who either heard of him from their parents or who themselves recall him as a vivid personality, hurrying along Connecticut highways and byways. Then, too, many people whose lives touched his during his wanderings of much more than half a century have left behind them frequent allusions to the Darnman, in both letters and other documents.

By Louise E. Dew Watrous, Clinton, Connecticut. Manuscripts of the Federal Writers' Project of the Works Progress Administration for the State of Connecticut.

I first heard of the Darnman through an uncle of my husband, a Mr. Charles Dolph of Centerbrook, Conn., who passed away the summer of 1936, aged 94. As he used to see the Darnman when he was a boy, it must have been around 1850. All I know is what Mr. Dolph told me, and also an aged man in the town of Clinton—a man who now has paralysis and cannot see visitors.—L. E. D. W.

Apparently his real history was never fully known and with his passing in the late Eighteen Hundreds it was irrevocably lost. But piecing all these fragments together, one gleans that this pathetic old character had a regular itinerary in Massachusetts and Connecticut which lasted about six months and that those whom he honored by accepting their hospitality always looked forward to his coming around the time he was supposed to be due.

If he arrived in time for dinner, he remained over night, but was off before breakfast. If he was too late for dinner, he would accept no food until the morning meal. After morning prayers, through which he stood with bowed head, eyes closed, and hands folded reverently on his breast, he would express his thanks for the hospitality accorded him and take his departure. Nor could any amount of persuasion induce him to remain for another night or another meal.

While he did not say so, it was evident that he did not wish to impose on the hospitality of his friends, nor to wear out his welcome; hence his respect for the precedent he established.

His most outstanding eccentricity, which gave rise to his name as the Darn Coat, the Darned Man, or the Darnman, was his request for a needle and thread to mend his garments the moment he entered a house. Then he would slip off his coat or vest and sometimes his trousers, sit down quietly in an inconspicuous place, and proceed to make needed repairs. Now and then, where he was well acquainted, he would ask for a skillet and a little oil which he would heat and rub into his well-worn boots. There were never any holes in them, for he kept them patched and in as good condition as possible.

To describe the Darnman is difficult, for his personality was so elusive. He was tall and must have had a well-knit, fine physique in his youth. Even in his old age, when he had grown wan and spectral, he still carried himself with stately dignity.

It was apparent to every one from his bearing and attire that he was to the manner born. He wore a suit of the finest navy-blue broadcloth. The long coat was not unlike a swallow-tail or dress-coat of to-day and it was double-breasted. A long brocaded vest hung down below the coat in front, and from the old-fashioned watch pocket there dangled a gold fob which gave him the appearance of a dandy. His trousers were close-fitting and had straps at the bottom. Topping his long-limbed figure was a bell-crowned tall hat, probably once white, but metamorphosed by the elements, the dust of years, and time to a dingy smoke gray.

During all the sixty years or so he journeyed up and down the valley, from shore town to shore town, and back up through Windham County again, he wore the same garments, always scrupulously clean, but each year a little more threadbare and shabby. As the years passed, his shoulders became slightly bent, his eyes sunken and his cheeks pale and wan. But his blue eyes retained the same bright piercing look.

An old Connecticut Yankee of ninety, whose mind is still alert, recalls the Darnman distinctly. He says that when he was a boy of ten or thereabouts in Civil War times, an uncle in Windham County wrote his parents about the Darnman. He had appeared unexpectedly, so spring was almost there. He had asked for a needle and thread the moment of his arrival. Aunt Sarah had offered to mend the rent in his coat for him, but he had refused with a deprecatory "Thank you, Madame, but I must refuse. These are my wedding clothes and they are sacred. My bride will be here soon. . . ."

A few weeks later, the old gentleman says, he saw the Darnman hurrying along through the village. He knew him by his picturesque attire that was so reminiscent of Uncle Sam as depicted by so many artists. The small boy, curious to know more of the Darnman's movements, followed him for some distance. As always, he walked with head bent, and hands clasped in front of him, apparently oblivious to all else. Presently, he turned off at the shore-road and went down to the beach where the children were sailing their toy boats. They stopped playing and watched him, but there were no cat-calls or stones thrown as was sometimes done when odd characters passed through the town. There was something about the pathetic face and drooping shoulders that inspired them with a feeling of awe.

Without looking either to the right or the left, the Darnman paid no attention to the children, but walked past them down to the sands. Picking up a razor-back clam shell, he began digging in the sands. After a time, the children crept closer to watch him, but he kept right on at his task. Finally, the village boy ventured to ask him if he had lost something.

"Yes, my little man," was the low reply and the words came with stately courtesy, "I have had the great misfortune to lose a gold ring . . . a wedding ring . . . like the one I wear." He held up the third finger of his left hand where a gold ring gleamed brightly in the sunset, then went on: "Only the ring I have lost is tiny and beautiful. It belonged to my bride. If you should find the little gold band, will you not be so good as to take care of it until I come again?"

The boy, now much older than the Darnman was then, says that he promised to do so, and so convinced was he that the Darnman had actually lost a ring, long hours were spent digging in the sands for it.

The Darnman passed through this village-by-the-sea, many times after that, and the boy's family, like the uncle in Windham County, always kept a room ready for him. If it was not yet dark when the gentle old man had reverently finished mending his garments, he and the boy used to go and hunt for the bride's lost ring.

Years passed. The boy grew up. The old Darnman still paid his visit to the village wearing the same worn garments, asking for a needle and thread to mend them, the moment he arrived. But his fingers trembled now, and the pathetic look in his face and eyes had deepened. "My bride is so long in coming . . . ," he would whisper sadly to himself as he darned and mended, and oiled his ancient boots, now covered patch upon patch. But his manner still set him apart as a gentleman.

There was only one thing about which he was at all particular and that was his tea. He was a connoisseur. "Madame," he would begin with stately courtesy, "the bouquet is sadly lacking in this beverage. Would you mind if I show you how to brew me a cup, or better still, permit me to brew my own tea?"

Those who had become acquainted with him during all these years, whom he favored with his few confidences, gathered from the few remarks he made from time to time that he had passed through some great emotional shock and that it had upset his mental equilibrium. He was not crazy, but his mind was disordered and out of tune.

One evening he sat on the porch with a family where he had often accepted sanctuary. He was unusually quiet and abstracted. Presently, he rose and went out to sit in the moonlight under the tall elm he so loved, and where his sick spirit always seemed to find repose. A glorious June moon was shining through the branches of the tree. He kept glancing up at the glowing orb and whispering: "My bride will come tonight. Surely she will not disappoint me. . . . Come, my beloved little bride. . . ."

Suddenly, through the stillness there was the sound of carriage wheels on the hilltop. Voices. One was the rippling laughter of a girl. The old Darnman rose quickly and walked down to the picket-fence. At the gateway he paused for an instant. He rushed out to the road. Instead of stopping, the horse was urged on.

"Here I am, my little bride," the old Darnman cried in an agony of fear. "Long have I been waiting, do not pass me by. . . ." And he held out his arms.

At this instant, the horse became frightened at the sudden apparition, and lurched forward. Before the driver could control the animal, the carriage had knocked the old man down and passed over his body. Loving hands carried him into the house, but he died that night.

When they came to lay him away, instead of the shroud the undertaker brought, the women folk shook their heads, and said: "No, he wouldn't feel at home in that garment. We will clean, press, and mend his own."

The old Darnman was laid to rest in his own wedding clothes—the ones in which he'd wandered up and down Connecticut highways and byways for more than sixty years in search of his bride.

According to popular beliefs, the Darnman was Frank Howland, a direct descendant of John Howland, the Mayflower Pilgrim. Young Howland's father came from Cape Cod. When a young man, Frank had a strong physique and a brilliant, well-balanced mind. He planned to go to Yale and fit himself for the law. Owing to overstudy and carelessness, he was stricken down with a fever, which nearly proved fatal. His strong constitution pulled him through. After some months, when he had regained his strength, he accepted an offer to teach in a school near New London.

It was while there he met the daughter of a sea-captain who won his heart. They became betrothed and the girl went to New York for her trousseau. On her way back, the vessel she was on sank in a storm and Frank Howland never saw her again. A funeral service was held for her in her home-city, but young Howland was unable to attend. The shock of her drowning had been so great that reason was tottering.

When he finally regained his poise, his mind was a blank of all that had happened except that the lovely girl to whom he had plighted his troth had gone to the city for her wedding trousseau. When she failed to return, he donned his wedding suit and fared forth to find her, continuing his search until the day of his death sixty years or so later.

This in brief is the story of the old Darnman, one of Connecticut's most eccentric and beloved characters of an earlier day.

Crazy Lorenzo Dow

NOT many years since, there was a famous preacher of the old Puritan school in one of the New England States, who used to play such pranks in the pulpit as our Rowland Hill is said to have done, and as a contemporary now occasionally indulges in at the Tabernacle, only the Rev. Lorenzo Dow was the more daring performer of the three. On one occasion he took a text from Paul, *"I can do all things."* The preacher paused, took off his spectacles, laid them on the open Bible, and said, "No, Paul, you are mistaken for once; I'll bet you five dollars you can't, and stake the money." At the same time putting his hand into his pocket, he took out a five-dollar bill, laid it on the Bible, took up his spectacles again, and read, *"Through Jesus Christ our Lord."* "Ah, Paul!" exclaimed Dow, snatching up the five-dollar bill, and returning it to his pocket, "that's a very different matter; the bet's withdrawn." [1]

There was a story going the rounds of the papers in Vermont of Lorenzo Dow raising the devil. One day while he was at the dinner table at our house in Hardwick, mother asked him about it. Lorenzo replied that the circumstances were as follows: In traveling through the northern part of Vermont, he was belated one night in a blinding snow-storm. He went for the only light he could discover, and found it came from a small log-house. After repeated knockings at the door, a woman opened it. He asked accommodations for the night. She said her husband was gone, and she could not possibly accommodate a stranger. But he plead with so much earnestness, she concluded to take him in. He immediately went to bed, without removing his clothing, in a little corner, separated off from the room where the family lived by a partition of rough boards, with cracks between, covered with paper pasted over, which was torn off in many places, and anything going on in the opposite room could be easily seen. It soon appeared this woman was not alone, but had a paramour. Late in

---

[1] By John Camden Hotten. From Introduction to *The Complete Works of Charles F. Browne,* Better Known as "Artemus Ward," pp. 27–28. London: John Camden Hotten.

the night on came her husband, drunk as usual, and demanded admittance, hallooing and cursing at the top of his voice, his wife all the while trying to stop him, but before opening the door, she secreted her pal in a cask of tow in the room. When admitting her husband, she tried to silence him by telling him that Lorenzo Dow was in the other room, and if he was not still he would wake him up. Well, says the husband, I understand he can raise the devil, and now he has got to *do it*. Notwithstanding all the appeals of his wife, the husband pounded on the door, calling on Dow to come out. At last Dow pretended to be roused out of a sound sleep (although he had been awake all the time); rubbing his eyes and yawning, he came out. The man insisted on Dow's raising the devil, and would not take *no* for an answer. Well, if you insist on it, said Dow, I will do it, but when *he* comes, it will be in a flame of fire, and you must set the doors wide open, so he will have plenty of room. The man opened his door, and Dow, taking the candle, touched the tow in the cask. In an instant the cask was wrapped in flame, and the man inside jumping out, all on fire, ran up the street like the very devil, all of a light blaze, tearing through the snow at the rate of 2:40. The husband was so frightened, for once it made a sober man of him.[2]

In Vermont, in passing through a dense woods one day to fill an appointment, he saw two men chopping wood. He mounted on a large stump, and said "Crazy Dow will preach from this stump 6 months from to day, at 2 o'clock, P. M." Six months from that time an immense audience was assembled, and Dow in going to the place saw a man in great distress looking for something. Dow enquired what the matter was. The man replied that he was poor, and that some one had stolen his axe, and that he felt the loss very much. Lorenzo told him if he would go to the meeting he would find his axe. Before getting to the place of service, Dow picked up a stone and put it in his pocket. After the delivery of a powerful sermon, Dow said—"There is a man here who has had his axe stolen, and the thief is here in this audience, and I am going to throw this stone right to his head," —drawing back his hand as though in the act of throwing the stone. One

---

[2] By Lewis Joseph Bridgman (nephew of Lorenzo Dow), in "Montpelier," *Vermont Historical Gazetteer*, A Local History of All the Towns in the State, Civil, Educational, Biographical, Religious, and Military. Vol. IV, collated and published by Abby Maria Hemenway, p. 372. Copyright secured to Miss Hemenway. Montpelier, Vermont: Vermont Watchman and State Journal Press. 1882.

For the genealogy and geographical distribution of this story, which is common in European folklore and which is told of Lorenzo Dow with locales varying from New York and Delaware to the Oxfordshire border of Warwickshire, see Emelyn E. Gardner, *Folklore from the Schoharie Hills* (Ann Arbor, 1937), pp. 314–317.

The same story is told of Rev. Matthew Clark, of Londonderry, New Hampshire (*The Scotch-Irish in America*, Cincinnati, 1890, p. 143) and the English divine, Charles H. Spurgeon.

man ducked his head. Dow went up to him and said—"You have got this man's axe!" And so he had, and went and brought it and gave it to him.[3]

The most conspicuous of these [preachers and propagators of Methodism] was the noted Lorenzo Dow. He was a native of Connecticut, and at the period of my boyhood had begun to be talked about chiefly on account of his eccentricities—though he was also a man of some talent. About the time that Methodism began to spread itself in Connecticut, Dow appeared in Ridgefield, and taking a stand on Squire Nathan Smith's wood-pile, held forth to a few boys and other people that chanced to be in that quarter. I was returning from school, and stopped to hear his discourse. He was then about thirty years of age, but looked much older. He was thin and weather-beaten, and appeared haggard and ill-favored, partly on account of his reddish, dusty beard, some six inches long—then a singularity if not an enormity, as nobody among us but old Jagger the beggar cultivated such an appendage. I did not comprehend what he said, and only remember his general appearance. He was merely passing through Ridgefield, and soon departed, having produced an impression that he was an odd sort of person, and rather light-headed. I afterward heard him preach twice at camp-meetings, and will endeavor to give you some idea of his manner. The following is a passage, as nearly as I can recollect, his general discourse being aimed at those who accused the Methodists of being New Lights—a mere set of enthusiasts.

"Now, my friends, you all know we are called New Lights. It is said that we have in us a false fire which throws out a glare only to mislead and deceive the people. They say we are actuated by the spirit of the devil, instead of the spirit of religion. Well, no matter what they say; no matter what they call us: the question is, whether we have the real fire or the false fire? I say we have got the true fire, and the old Church-and-State Presbyterians have got the false fire. That's what I say, and I'll prove it.

"There is in nater, no doubt, as well as in religion, both false fire and true fire: the first is rotten-wood, which shines in the night. You often see it among the roots and trunks of old decayed trees. But you may pile it up as high as a haystack, and it won't make a pot boil. Now ain't that like the old, sleepy, decayed Presbyterians? But as to the true fire—if you take a few kindlings, and put 'em under a kittle, and put some water in the kittle, and then set the kindlings on fire, you'll see something, won't you? Well: what will you see? Why, the water begins to wallop and wallop and wallop! Well, suppose you had never seen water bile before— you'd say the devil was in it, wouldn't you? Of course you would. Now, it is just so with this carnal generation—the old school, the rotten-wood,

[3] *Ibid.*, p. 366.

the false-fire people—they see us moved with the true fire of religion, and they say the devil's in it—because they never saw it before, and don't understand it. Thus it is they call us New Lights. No wonder, for they have nothing but false fire in their hearts!"

Lorenzo was not only uncouth in his person and appearance, but his voice was harsh, his action hard and rectangular. It is scarcely possible to conceive of a person more entirely destitute of all natural eloquence. But he understood common life, and especially vulgar life—its tastes, prejudices, and weaknesses; and he possessed a cunning knack of adapting his discourses to such audiences. He told stories with considerable art, and his memory being stored with them, he could always point a moral or clinch a proposition by an anecdote. He knew that with simple people an illustration is better than logic, and when he ran short of Scripture, or argument failed, he usually resorted to some pertinent story or adapted allegory. He affected oddity in all things—in his mode of preaching as well as in dress. He took pains to appear suddenly and by surprise among the people where he proposed to hold forth; he frequently made his appointments a year before hand, and at the very minute set, he would come like an apparition. He often took scraps of texts, and extracted from them, by a play upon words, an unexpected argument or startling inference. His endeavor seemed to be to exercise an influence over the imagination by associating himself in the minds of the people with John the Baptist, preaching in the wilderness, and living on locusts and wild honey. . . .[4]

Exploits of Ethan Allen

HIS LEGEND [1]

ETHAN ALLEN was a legendary character long before his death, and the legends about him multiplied for the next half-century or so; then production dropped. All the legends now current have probably seen service for more than a century, and many of them go back to the times of the man himself.

Some legends, unquestionably, are historically true, and many others are elaborations on historical fact. And a few no doubt are pure invention, concocted for sheer amusement or for some reason in the mind of the inventor. In the latter category doubtless belongs the hardy old story of Ethan at the bedside of his dying daughter, one of those by his first wife.

---

[4] From *Recollections of a Lifetime,* or Men and Things I Have Seen; in a Series of Familiar Letters to a Friend, Historical, Biographical, Anecdotical, and Descriptive, by S. G. Goodrich, Vol. I, pp. 205–210. Entered according to Act of Congress, in the year 1856, in the Clerk's Office of the District Court of the United States for the Southern District of New York, by S. G. Goodrich. New York and Auburn: Miller, Orton & Co., 1857.

[1] From *Ethan Allen,* by Stewart H. Holbrook, pp. 266–269, 143. Copyright, 1940, by The Macmillan Company. New York.

It goes that the child *knew* that she was going to die, and further that she knew her profane father to be a gross Infidel. During her last gasps this precocious infant said to Ethan, "Father, now that I am going to leave you, in what should I put my faith—mamma's religion, or your Nature?" The Great Infidel is supposed to have cried gently a moment, then to have told daughter to die in the faith of her mother.

Better authenticated is another child story, told to Zadock Thompson, the Vermont historian, in 1841 by T. Bradley of Williston, Vermont, who had it direct from Dr. Baker, first president of the Vermont Medical Society. Dr. Baker had been called to a home where a child was suffering from worms. General Allen and two parsons were present. Ethan walked up and down the room. "I wish," he said, "all the worms which were ever permitted to torment an innocent being were in my body all at once."

"What would you do with so many?" inquired one of the parsons.

"Do?" cried Ethan. "Do? I'd take a dose of hellfire and destroy them."

Then, there is the famous white-horse story. In a discussion with St. John de Crèvecoeur, Ethan once said that if the transmigration of souls were a fact, he hoped to return to his Vermont hills in the form of a great white stallion, when he would snort, whinny, and range all over the claim. A Colonel Graham; who came to live in Rutland, Vermont, in 1785, has been quoted as saying, "I have often heard General Allen affirm that he should live again under the form of a large white horse." Just such an animal has been seen a number of times since 1789.

That Ethan could and did bite nails into bits and spit them out with the force of buckshot has never been doubted by any true Vermonter.

A signal used at night by the Green Mountain Boys was three mournful hoots of an owl. Ethan was so good at this call that on one or more occasions he was attacked by large male owls, jealous of some lady owl in the neighborhood. Another time when Ethan was hurrying through the woods a huge catamount leaped onto his back. It was the last time that catamount leaped anywhere. Reaching up and behind his head, Ethan grabbed the big animal around the neck, heaved it forward and to the ground, then strangled it where it lay, without once removing his hands. When he arrived at Cephas Kent's tavern in Dorset that night, he excused his delay. "The goddam Yorkers," he said, "have trained and set varmints against me, God damn their miserable Tory souls."

Not a legend but simply a favorite Big Story often told of Ethan Allen and Seth Warner, to illustrate their differences in character, is revealing. The two were fishing from a boat on Lake Champlain, when Seth's powderhorn fell into the water.

"What'll I do?" complained Seth.

Ethan didn't reply but dived overboard at once. The cautious Warner waited some minutes, then he too dived in. Down deep on the bottom he found Ethan. He was trying to pour Seth's powder into his own horn.[1]

---

[1] Cf. "Jonathan's Hunting Excursion," p. 141 above.

The straight hunting stories told on the man would make a sizeable monograph. A favorite has him shooting the horns off a buck deer at one hundred yards, with a smoothbore. Another has him killing a mean and wounded bear by ramming his powderhorn down the animal's throat.

The best of the real estate stories brings in Ira. The property at Charlotte, Vermont, of an exiled Yorker was to be sold for Vermont by the sheriff to the highest bidder. The speculating Allens had tried to keep the coming sale secret, but news leaked out and a number of speculators showed up. The Allen boys didn't like the look of so much potential competition, and the sheriff, at Ethan's order, and on some pretext, announced that the sale would be put off "until one o'clock tomorrow." The crowd went away, planning to return at one the next afternoon. But promptly at one o'clock next morning the sheriff and the two Allens were back on the ground. The sheriff asked for bids. Out of the dark came Ethan's bid—one dollar for house, barn, and a hundred acres. Ira bid two dollars. "Sold," said the sheriff, "to the short man in the coonskin cap."

It seems strange, or possibly it is significant, that no legendary tales concerning extramarital adventures have been told of Ethan Allen. Certainly it was not respect for the Seventh Commandment that kept him "moral" in the generally accepted sense; nor was it a case of inability, as witness eight children, the last of them posthumous. His contemporary enemies called him almost every name conceivable except that fine old English compound word used to describe a man of vast adulteries. He must have been essentially a monogamist.

But the stories of his drinking prowess are without end and, except for the rattlesnake incident, will not be repeated here. Ethan did not like rattlers, which in old times were found in certain regions of southern Vermont. On a hot day in August he was making a long trip afoot with Remember Baker. Up late the night before, the men became sleepy and lay down for a nap in a rocky glen. Sometime later Baker was roused by a noise and woke to gaze horrified at the spectacle of Colonel Allen asleep, while on his broad chest was coiled a huge rattler, all of five feet long. It struck Ethan again and again, on the neck, the arm, the hand, but did not rouse him. Baker jumped up, grabbed his gun and advanced to poke the snake away.

At his approach Baker was startled to see the snake glide off the man and onto the ground, its head weaving from side to side and its body making contortions strange even in a reptile. Baker held his blow, watching fascinated, while the snake stopped and turned to gaze at him, cross-eyed. The snake then gave forth a mighty "Burrp!" and collapsed into sound sleep. "Drunk, by Jesus!" exclaimed Remember Baker, who was an acute if not a pious man.

When Colonel Allen awoke he complained bitterly to Baker about "these eternal, damnable, bloodsucking mosquitoes" which had bitten him while he slept.

Long a favorite story, and dignified in print for more than a century, is the one about Ethan and the dentist of Sunderland. A woman, suffering terribly from toothache, had approached the dentist, then became frightened at his devilish gear used for extraction. Colonel Allen urged her to submit to the grim business. "I'll show you, madam," he said, "that losing a tooth is nothing." Thereupon he sat in a chair and had the dentist extract a perfectly sound tooth, by way of demonstration. "I didn't feel it," he lied gallantly, and the lady took courage.

* * * * *

. . . A man, too, had to mix a modicum of rum with his ink, and on a number of evenings, so legend has it, Ethan returned home from Bennington slightly under the weather.

Whether his wife Mary had a hand in it isn't known, but one night a group of his friends decided to frighten him into sobriety. Wrapping themselves in white sheets, they hid under a bridge on the outskirts of Arlington. Ethan came trotting along on his horse. Suddenly the horse snorted and shied at an army of ghosts in the road. Ethan reined the animal. "Hallo!" he shouted. "If you're angels of light, I'm glad to meet you. And if you're devils, then come along home with me. I married your sister."

WHAT HE SAID AT TICONDEROGA: A VARIANT [2]

An amusing illustration of one of these persistent and popularly cherished fictions has recently come to the knowledge of the writer. According to all histories of the United States, Ethan Allen demanded from the British commander the surrender of Ticonderoga "In the name of the Great Jehovah and the Continental Congress." Prof. James D. Butler, of Madison, Wisconsin, has informed me that his grandfather Israel Harris was present and had often told him that Ethan Allen's real language was, "Come out of here, you d——d old rat."

HUNTING EXPLOITS [3]

At Landlord Fay's in Bennington they said he could mix the best drinks and tell the best stories of anybody who came to town, and in the woods he had a reputation for traveling fast and killing many deer. There is a story, Brother Ira used to tell, beginning:

He was fond of hunting game in his youth, run after deer tired them down or turned them by often firing on them so as to kill them by night. I remember to have heard him tell that one day in Poultney he came across

---

[2] From *Lord Timothy Dexter*, by William Cleaves Todd, in *The New-England Historical and Genealogical Register,* Published Quarterly by the New-England Historical Genealogical Society for the year 1886, Vol. XL, p. 380 n. Boston: Published at the Society's House.

[3] From *Ethan Allen*, by John Pell, pp. 34–35. Copyright, 1929, by John Pell. Boston and New York: Houghton Mifflin Company.

a company of Deer and killed one which he dressed hung up the Skin and Meat then to preserve that from the Ravens hung his hat on it and went on. He soon killed another deer; with that he left a short hunting Jaccoat and went on; killed another deer—with that left his Frock and went on and killed another—with that left his Breeches then pursued the deer and killed another—took the skin about him and went to his camp.

Another time late in the fall after being much fatigued and raining in the after part of the day so that he had not a dry thread about him got bewildered and lay out all night; the weather cleared off extremely cold—it was out of his power to make any fire—his clothes began to freeze on him—he knew not what course to take—an extensive wilderness on one side—in this situation—he thought it most prudent to mark out a path in a circle in which he could keep himself awake by going round not daring to sit down lest he should fall asleep and perish this I have often heard him say was among the greatest hazards of his life and required the greatest exer ion both of body and mind to preserve life till day being much fatigued by travelling all day without victuals benumbed with the cold became sleepy . . . of Every exertion he repeatedly fell in the snow; this would so far bring him to his senses that he would spring on his feet in a few minutes fall again; when daylight came he came more to himself and after travelling a short time came fully to his senses—his clothes were froze except shirt to his skin—before noon he reached a house where he got some refreshment!

CHASTISING YORKERS [4]

He went about with a small band of followers (Yorkers called them rioters and the Bennington mob) stirring up the settlers to resist the encroachments of their unwelcome landlords. When he came upon surveyors running lines in the forest, he set up a "Judgment Seat" under some huge, old pine tree, tried them on the spot, and often had them stripped and whipped, calling the punishment "Chastisement with the Twigs of the Wilderness." Both the settlers and Yorkers respected him, and stories of his prowess and strength began to get about among the people. They said he could seize by his teeth, and throw over his head, bags containing each a bushel of salt, as fast as two men could bring them round to him; that he had grasped two enemies, one in each hand, and, lifting them off the ground, held them out at arms' length, and beat them together till they cried for mercy; and that he had engaged alone with a York sheriff and his posse of six men, leaving them all sprawling on the ground. Ethan probably invented stories and told them to the credulous settlers whom he visited in their solitary cabins, but others were based on the experiences of his victims. John Munro, an old offender, was taken, tried, and ordered to be whipped on his naked back. He was tied to a tree and flogged till

---

[4] *Ibid.*, pp. 35–37.

he fainted; on recovering, he was whipped again till he fainted; he revived and underwent a third lashing till he fainted; his wounds were then dressed and he was banished from the district of the New Hampshire Grants.

Once Ethan captured two New York sheriffs. He locked them in separate rooms on the same side of a house, and during the night tied an effigy to the limb of a tree outside their windows. At dawn he awakened one prisoner after the other, and told him to look out of the window to see his companion swinging from a tree. Each was allowed to escape believing he had just missed a terrible death, a conviction which lasted until he met the other on the streets of Albany.

Dr. Samuel Adams, of Arlington, openly declared himself a partisan of New York. His neighbors tried advice and warnings. The Doctor armed himself with a brace of pistols, and proclaimed his opinions more loudly and decidedly than ever. He announced his full determination to defend himself to the best of his ability against any person who should approach him with unfriendly design.

When the case was reported to Ethan, he sent a squad of Green Mountain Boys to capture the contumacious doctor. They caught him unawares as he was leaving his house. When the prisoner had been tried and convicted, Ethan sentenced him to be tied in a chair, hoisted up the sign-post of Stephen Fay's tavern at Bennington (a twenty-five-foot gallows surmounted by a stuffed catamount grinning toward New York), and left there for an hour. Afterwards, the Doctor returned to Arlington, but insisted on his opinion no more.

He Eats Iron [5]

I was confined in the manner I have related, on board the Gaspee schooner, about six weeks, during which time I was obliged to throw out plenty of extravagant language, which answered certain purposes (at that time), better than to grace a history.

To give an instance, upon being insulted, in a fit of anger I twisted off a nail with my teeth, which I took to be a ten-penny nail; it went through the mortise of the bar on my handcuff, and at the same time I swaggered over those who abused me; particularly a Doctor Dace, who told me that I was outlawed by New York, and deserved death for several years past; was at last fully ripened for the halter, and in a fair way to obtain it: When I challenged him, he excused himself in consequence, as he said, of my being a criminal; but I flung such a flood of language at him that it shocked him and the spectators, for my anger was very great. I heard one say, damn him, can he eat iron? After that a small padlock was fixed to

[5] From *A Narrative of Colonel Ethan Allen's Captivity* . . . containing his Voyages and Travels . . . , written by himself and now published for the information of the Curious in all Nations, p. 10. Philadelphia: Printed. Boston: Reprinted by Draper & Folsom. 1779.

the handcuff, instead of the nail, and as they were mean-spirited in their treatment to me; so it appeared to me, that they were equally timorous and cowardly.

A Conjurer by Passion [6]

Among the great numbers of people, who came to the castle to see the prisoners, some gentlemen told me that they had come 50 miles on purpose to see me, and desired to ask me a number of questions, and to make free with me in conversation. I gave for answer, that I chose freedom in every sense of the word: Then one of them asked me what my occupation in life had been? I answered him, that in my younger days I had studied divinity, but was a conjurer by passion. He replied that I conjured wrong at the time that I was taken; and I was obliged to own, that I mistook a figure at that time, but that I had conjured them out of Ticonderoga. This was a place of great notoriety in England, so that the joke seemed to go in my favour.

Ethan and Fanny Wall [7]

Stephen Bradley had built a house facing the street (there was only one street in Westminster: there still is), just north of the court-house. It was one of those fine, square, solid houses which has all the best furniture in a best room which nobody ever uses. It had in fact so many rooms that Stephen had to take in boarders.

Crean Brush, an Irish lawyer and adventurer, had accumulated sixty thousand acres of Vermont land before he committed suicide in Boston. His estate, divided in thirds, was left to his wife, his daughter (by a former marriage), and his stepdaughter. His wife (now married to Patrick Wall, her third husband and second Irishman) and Fanny, her daughter, came to Westminster to locate their lands, and lodged in some of Stephen Bradley's spare rooms.

Fanny's father, Captain Montresor, was a French officer of the British army. From him she had inherited delicate features, a sensitive, vivacious nature: from her stepfather, Brush, twenty thousand acres.

Fanny's mother was a forceful woman. I believe she survived all three husbands. She forced her child to marry, at sixteen, a British officer named Buchanan. It is said that he loved her tenderly, but that she was repelled by his affection. She bore him a son, but the child never saw its father, for he was killed in action before his son was born.

At twenty-four, Fanny was a widow, an heiress, and a beautiful girl. In the histories she is always referred to as "a dashing woman." With her

---

[6] *Ibid.*, p. 15.

[7] From *Ethan Allen,* by John Pell, pp. 242–245. Copyright, 1929, by John Pell. Boston and New York: Houghton Mifflin Company.

forceful mother and a wardrobe of New York clothes, she dashed into Westminster, into Brush's acres, into Stephen Bradley's spare rooms, and simply overwhelmed the natives. They talked about her "imperious manner," and waited, cold winter days, to see her dash by in a fresh-painted "pung."

The Assembly met. Ethan came to town. Stephen gave parties. Ethan did not serve on committees. The Yorkers kidnapped Luke Knoulton. Ethan put on his uniform, mounted his charger, looked ferocious, and frightened the Yorkers away.

There was in this town a tavern-keeper named John Norton, one of those unfathomable fellows who seem to understand people's secrets without being told and to attract customers by telling them the disparaging truth. To Fanny he said: "If you marry General Allen, you will be queen of a new state." And she replied: "If I should marry the devil, I'd be queen of Hell "

On the morning of the 9th of February, 1784, while Stephen Bradley was entertaining the judges of the Superior Court at breakfast, he heard the bells of a sleigh stopping at his door, and a moment later saw Ethan entering the room. The judges invited him to join them, but he replied that he had breakfasted at Norton's and, while they were finishing, would step across the hall and see the ladies.

Fanny, dressed in a morning gown, was standing on a chair arranging a china closet when Ethan opened the door. With a cracked decanter in her hand, she turned around on the chair and greeted the intruder by telling him that people didn't make calls so early in the morning. He explained that military duties had brought him to Westminster and that he was on his way to Sunderland. So, he added, "If we are to be married, now is the time." She put the decanter back on the shelf, descended from the chair, and then replied: "Very well, but give me time to put on my Joseph." *

A few minutes later, they crossed the hall and found the judges, still sitting at the breakfast table, smoking their long pipes. With Fanny on his arm, Ethan walked up to his old friend Moses Robinson and said: "Judge Robinson, this young woman and myself have concluded to marry each other and to have you perform the ceremony." "When?" asked Moses, somewhat surprised. "Now," replied Ethan; continuing: "For myself I have no great opinion of such formality, and from what I can discover, she thinks as little of it as I do. But as a decent respect for the opinions of mankind seems to require it, you will proceed." Moses said: "General, this is an important matter. Have you given it serious consideration?" "Certainly," Ethan replied, glancing at Fanny. "But I do not think it requires much consideration."

---

* A name given in the eighteenth century to a lady's riding habit or great-coat buttoned down the front, and with a broad cape. It is said to have been named in allusion to Joseph's coat of many colors.—Alice Morse Earle, *Costume of Colonial Times* (New York, 1894), p. 144.

The ceremony then proceeded until Moses asked Ethan whether he promised to live with Fanny "agreeable to the laws of God." At this Ethan stopped the proceedings. Then, looking out of the window, he exclaimed: "The law of God as written in the great book of nature? Yes. Go on." When the ceremony was completed and Fanny's trunk and guitar case were stowed in the back of the sleigh, Ethan wrapped his bride in the big bear rug and they drove off across the mountains.

DRUNK OR SOBER [8]

. . . One night, it seems, he came home tight. When Fanny rebuked him, he denied the charge. The next morning she remarked, "I will find out whether you come home drunk or sober." Thereupon she drove a nail—pretty well up—in the wall of the bedroom, saying: "When your watch is hanging on that nail in the morning, I shall know that you came home sober." Ethan agreed—of course—but he found it rather a difficult job to prove his good behavior by this severe test. Sometimes the nail would dodge him and the watch ring hit one side. When he tried again, the floor would give way or his knees get out of joint, but he would stick to it until the ring was hooked. If Fanny had anything to say in the morning, he would point his finger at the watch, saying: "You see, I came home sober last night."

MY NAME IS ALLEN [9]

. . . This was the same Ethan Allen who, a few years later, when New York had put a price on him dead or alive as leader of the Green Mountain Boys, rode into Albany alone, entered the tavern frequented by the politicians, ordered a bowl of punch, drank it all, set it down, faced the room, put his fists on his hips and said, "Now then, my name is Allen. Who wants that reward?" . . .

"Ave" Henry, Lumber Baron

J. E. HENRY is undoubtedly the most colorful character that Northern New Hampshire has ever produced. He was born in Littleton and was engaged in lumbering on an extensive scale and most successfully from a financial

---

[8] *Ibid.*, p. 261.

[9] From *The Housatonic, Puritan River,* by Chard Powers Smith, p. 260. Copyright, 1946, by Chard Powers Smith. New York and Toronto: Rinehart & Company, Incorporated.

By Ola G. Veazie. Manuscripts of the Federal Writers' Project of the Works Progress Administration for the State of New Hampshire.
Cf. Ernest Poole, *The Great White Hills of New Hampshire* (1946), pp. 36–43.

viewpoint. He came from a poor family but was a natural trader, and it is said of him that he was always ready to "sugar anything off" that could be sold at a profit. He firmly believed that the time to sell anything was when someone else wanted it. His advice to his boys, "Make money, honestly if possible, but make money," is a key to his character. He worked hard himself and brought his children up to work early and late, for he said that if he did not put them to work the devil would.

He frequently ran afoul of the law and was generally in a lawsuit. One time when a young man he saw the sheriff coming across the field and knew that the only thing he owned that could be attached was two hogs. The law allowed him one live one and one dressed; so he rushed out of the house with a butcher knife and stuck one of them and, when the sheriff arrived, looked up at him and said, "I beat you that time, didn't I?" This was during the time that he lived on a farm in Pattenville.

"Ave" Henry, as he was always called, bought out a small mill at Zealand (just above Twin Mountain village) with two other men as partners, but soon bought them out. They are reported to have logged much of the Zealand country before they purchased it and then paid only a nominal sum for the land.

When he decided to put in a log railroad seven miles in length, he ordered the rails to be delivered at a certain time in the early summer. The rails failed to arrive, but he had engaged a large crew to lay them and so set the crew to work in the woods. When the rails arrived, he sued the company for not getting them there in time and finally got $50,000 damages plus the rails for nothing. In the meantime the crew had piled up a great many logs beside the track while they were supposedly idle waiting for the rails.

There was quite a good-sized village at Zealand with a store, post-office, large barns, and a number of houses, school, and railroad station. To-day an old iron water tub beside the road is the sole remainder of a once prosperous settlement.

Mr. Henry was very strict about liquor and would not have any around a camp that belonged to him. It was in the days when it could be delivered through the mails. One night two men were expecting a case, and two other men had learned that it had been ordered and was expected on a certain train. The men went to the post-office for it and started down the track toward their quarters with it. The other two men dressed up as Mr. Henry and his son. Mr. Henry always wore a fur coat and the son a fur cap, and these two were seen coming toward the men with the case of whiskey. They started to run but were hampered by the weight of the liquor. The other two men took after them and soon they were forced to abandon their load and run so as not to be recognized. This was what the two men had wanted and so of course they got the case of liquor. Mr. Henry heard about it and said that if they were smart enough to work a trick like that he would make an exception and let them keep it.

One time the Henrys moved to Boston for an indefinite stay but returned in a few weeks. Asked why he returned, Mr. Henry said that he enjoyed being a big pig in a small puddle rather than competing with other big pigs in a big one.

He approved of keeping in debt, for he claimed that the only way to keep interested in making money was to buy something that you wanted before you could pay for it and then have to struggle to make enough to pay for it. When he moved to Lincoln and bought a large acreage and mill there, it cost a lot more than he had, but it seemed worthwhile to him to go into debt in order to get it.

He succeeded in buying all of the land around Lincoln except one small building lot which a man by the name of Pat McGuire owned and would not sell. One day Pat met Mr. Henry on the street, and it is reported that he had indulged in more than one drink before meeting him. He walked up to Mr. Henry and said, "You and I own the whole of Lincoln, don't we, Mr. Henry?"

One time a new stable boy was hired to take care of the team that Mr. Henry used personally and was an excellent team. The first day he worked they drove a long distance and were on the road many hours; so the man cared for them as quickly as possible and went directly to bed. The next day they did not use the team much, and the fellow again did not take very good care of them. About ten o'clock Mr. Henry went to his room and woke him up. He asked him if he liked his job, if the team was good, if they bit him, kicked him, or were at all vicious. The fellow answered by highly praising the team as there was a stranger present and he thought that perhaps the stranger was interested in buying them. Then Mr. Henry said, "Well, if it is as good a team as you claim it to be, you had better get up and go and take better care of them."

One day Mr. Henry saw a woodsman searching the snow for something and at once was all curiosity and asked him what he was looking for. The man answered, "A chain, but I can't seem to find it." When he went to the office to settle up in the spring, he found he was charged with the loss of a logging chain. He asked what that meant as he had never lost one. Mr. Henry reminded him of the time he was searching for one and could not find it. The man began to laugh and told him that it was a watch chain that he had been looking for.

Henry found a K. of P. charm and insisted on wearing it although he was not a member of that order. His son had sponsored the lodge and told him it was against the rules for him to have such a charm. He replied, "Haven't I paid for all of their paraphernalia? I guess I can wear this pin if I want to." A good many of the help belonged, and one day a man got fired and complained to Mr. Henry that he was fired because he had not seen fit to join. He then proceeded to lay off everyone who did belong and to hire those who did not.

A good many men were hired through an employment agency in Boston but had to make their own way to Lincoln. One day too many of them arrived for his needs, and so when another came into the office and asked for a job he said, "I'll give you a job. Count the ties from here to Boston."

He meant, of course, that he had no job open for him. The man, however, took him literally and counted the railroad ties to Boston. He reported back in due time with the number of ties. Mr. Henry checked with railroad officials and found that the man was approximately right and so paid him for his time.

A certain man who lived near Lincoln was a constant source of annoyance to Mr. Henry. He tried hard to get rid of the man by buying him out but did not succeed. One time he laid a deep plot to bother the poor man. He pretended to become friendly with him and asked him to keep a sickly shoat for him. The man owned a very good one and after a week or so he (Henry) sent the sheriff after his shoat which he claimed the man had taken without his permission. The sheriff took the big one as Mr. Henry claimed it was his. The other man had no proof and so lost the big one for a poor one.

A Frenchman down the valley sold him a pile of pulpwood, and he would only pay him for 50 cords, although both knew that there was considerable more there. The Frenchman had no other market for the wood; so had to take what was given. As soon as he bought it, he set it on fire and started by team for Plymouth to insure it. He insured and collected for 200 cords. Later the Frenchman heard of the amount that he had insured it for and went to him for pay for the other 150 cords. He protested, but, when the Frenchman threatened to tell the sheriff about it, had to come across with the amount demanded.

Driving out of the woods one spring day, Henry overtook one of his men and gave him a ride. The man was carrying a large bag which aroused Henry's curiosity. The man told him that it contained spruce gum which was worth $1.50 per pound. When they were settling up, he called for the bag and had it weighed and charged the man $1.50 per pound for the contents and also for the time it would take to pick it. The man had gathered it on Sundays, and as he had happened to run across it and not really spent any of the company's time on it at all, he was very indignant about it but could do nothing. This action was highly characteristic on Henry's part.

Another of his favorite tricks was to get the men going into the woods to leave their watches or jewelry with him in his office for safe-keeping. Then if they did not make good, and many of them would come out of the woods owing the company more than they had made, he would keep the watches, etc. It is even reported that he would sometimes claim he lost them, and one man back in the woods recognized his watch which another had bought on his way in and which Henry, claiming he did not know the owner, had sold.

A man sluiced a horse and Henry charged him $60.00 for the horse. He only had about $20.00 coming to him. His brother was present when he told Henry that he would quit and asked him if he would keep back his pay also. Henry got up close to the brother and grabbed his gold watch and said, "Yes, and this too."

Henry was often heard to brag that no one ever made a cent working for him. He forced all to trade at the company store where very high prices were charged for everything. For instance, if eggs were selling at 18¢, the company store would ask 28¢ for them.

A family came there with two horses and a cow. They were persuaded to leave the cow at Lincoln while they went back into the woods. In the spring they came out to settle up and then learned that they could not have the cow, for she had "dried up and eaten her head off" and so would have to be kept to pay for her board. They were in debt to the company after working hard all winter and were allowed to take only one of their pair of horses with them.

Hired girls at the Henry home were expected to work every minute and amongst other things had to split the dry wood for kindling, feed the pigs, milk cows, and in their spare time braid rugs and sew. They received $3.00 per week and the Henrys could never understand why they had difficulty in keeping help. One time they discovered that a girl had a pair of silk stockings and brought her into court as they were sure that she had stolen them from Mrs. Henry. She proved that her family, who were quite well to do, had given them to her. She also had to prove that some silver found in her trunk had also been given her by her family.

One time Henry had a warrant served on a certain woman for letting her hens out so that they got in a neighbor's garden. He was overly interested in the neighbor and was quite surprised when he found that they were the neighbor's own hens and she had been afraid to tell him they were hers.

He used to have potatoes planted on both sides of the road so close that teams could not pass and then watch and, if anyone turned out and touched a potato plant, have them arrested for trespassing.

There was an old cemetery beside the road which had been there before he came to Lincoln. When he started to put in some water works for the town, he started to go through the cemetery rather than go around it. Neighbors protested and stopped him but he could not see why it was not all right to go through as he said, "Why, they're all gone, aren't they?" referring to the bodies in the old graves.

Usually Mr. Henry was very meticulous in his dress and wore a white shirt and a diamond stud in his tie, but whenever he got up in the morning and put on a certain old faded blue cap and an old coat, everyone knew that he was on the war-path and that they had better not cross him that day or they would be fired.

When G. L. Johnson wanted to put the Elbow Lake branch of his railroad from Johnson Village into the end of the lake where he had another mill, he secured the money from Henry. Johnson had a certain number of years to return logs in lieu of money to Henry. The price of lumber dropped sharply and so he returned them all the first year, causing Henry to lose several dollars per thousand. Henry claimed that Johnson was the only man who ever got the best of him on a large deal.

"All I care about a dollar is to see it tick" was a frequent statement of "Ave" Henry.

In 1884 Henry bought a large ranch at Tintah, Minnesota, which is twelve hours' ride west of Minneapolis. Cattle and wheat were raised there and, as he started things on his usual scale, he soon had a small village with a post-office and school on his property. Many of his help came from New Hampshire. One time he was there and refused to pay the help. It was not that he did not have the money but that he got angry about something and was trying to punish the whole crowd. They seized him and strung him up. He promised to pay if they would let him down. They did and then he found some reason for not immediately complying. They strung him up again and left him until he was nearly dead. They finally let him down and he paid. They told him never to show himself in that community again under penalty of death. He never did. He gave the ranch to his daughters and never went there again.

The Enigma of Silent Cal

"You Got to be Mighty Careful" [1]

"How does it feel to be President of the United States?"

He weighed the question for nearly a quarter of a minute.

"Well," he said finally, "you got to be mighty careful."

He was a long way from Windsor County, Vermont, but . . . Cal Coolidge had expressed his entire philosophy in those six words—"You got to be mighty careful!"

* * * * *

It is only to be expected that an effort should have been made for political reasons to gloss over his peculiarities and picture him as a sort of Yankee Will Rogers with a dry wit that showed itself in pithy sayings. Well, I knew Cal for over half a century. I never heard him say anything that I regarded as witty, and many of the remarks that were heralded as examples of Coolidge humor he meant seriously. He had a perverse streak that led him to do and say eccentric things which he did not intend to be funny at all. I think the truth of the matter to be that he was a thin-lipped, cautious New Englander, and since the Americans as a whole did not understand him they had to invent another and somewhat more appealing figure. I sat near him that night at the Gridiron Club dinner and for two hours he neither cracked a smile nor uttered a word. He did not enjoy the jokes at his expense and on the way back to the White House he remarked that "all that tomfoolery" was a waste of money.

* * * * *

. . . These [White House] breakfasts were so notoriously dismal that those who were invited would resort to every imaginable excuse to avoid coming. In one instance eight senators declined in a row. I found out afterwards that a meal at which a public official had been a guest could be

---

[1] From *Yankee Lawyer*, The Autobiography of Ephraim Tutt, [by Arthur Train], pp. 306–309. Copyright, 1943, by Ephraim Tutt. New York: Charles Scribner's Sons.

charged to "public entertaining." Cal was certainly economical. During his incumbency the White House bought the supplies for its kitchen and pantry from the Piggly-Wiggly and Sanitary Grocery Chain.

I never could tell whether economy or eccentricity was the controlling element in some of his acts. For example, he never allowed any one to sit in the same automobile with him when he went to church. . . . Did Cal wish to savor his importance by riding in solitary state? It seems hardly likely. Did he consider that the White House chauffeurs had too easy a time? Possibly. Or did he regard the garage and its contents as something which he was entitled to use and wished to make the most of the privilege while it lasted? Probably a mixture of all three or some other mysterious factor of which he was unaware himself. Did he perhaps in small ways like to exercise power, as when, pointing to the Stuart portrait of John Adams which he could see from the state dining room as it hung on the wall of the Red Room, he said, according to Ike Hoover: "I'm tired of seeing that old bald head. Have some hair put on it." *

Ike told me that out in South Dakota near the presidential lodge among the Black Hills the local inhabitants released fifteen hundred trout in the stream nearby, keeping them within bounds with nets. Cal fished with worms, but he wore white gloves and the hook was baited and the fish grudgingly removed by the secret service men. Once a stranger caught some trout just in front of the Coolidge Camp. Cal sent one of the men to take them away from him, saying: "They are my fish." Grace made such fun of his wearing the white gloves that he eventually replaced them with a darker shade. Whether he fished because the trout were there and he thought he might as well have them, or because it seemed like good publicity, I don't know.

Cal may have been too careful. He had been president six years and there was the threat of a third term issue being raised if he ran in 1928, but he was canny enough to know, as William Allen White had said, that he represented "something definite in the American heart." I am aware of the strong evidence that has been adduced to prove that, when he issued his statement in August, 1927, "I do not choose to run for president in 1928," he had made up his mind not to do so.** But with my knowledge of his character I am personally of the opinion that he chose his words carefully to see what the reaction would be and never really intended his declaration to be taken as it was. It was in the nature of a "trial balloon." I believe that he was bitterly disappointed at the result, for he was the logical Republican candidate; and that in the end he was humiliated and angry

---

* In point of fact the picture was touched up with turpentine so that it did look as if it had some hair.—E. T.

** See Cyril Clemens and Athern P. Daggett, "Coolidge's 'I Do Not Choose to Run': Granite or Putty?", *The New England Quarterly*, Vol. XVIII (June, 1945), No. 2, pp. 147–163.

at not being re-nominated and would not have been disturbed had Hoover lost the election.

His Apparent Irrelevance [2]

. . . The Yankee is deeply appreciative of human shortcomings, but he often deceives the stranger by the apparent gravity of his remarks. Since the stranger does not understand the workings of the Yankee's mind, he fails to follow him, and hence does not recognize his apparently irrelevant remark as a humorous criticism. I believe President Coolidge to be a true Yankee in this respect. A recent writer in a popular magazine, I think, completely underestimates the humorous undercurrent of Mr. Coolidge's thinking. He certainly is not stupid, as this writer implies. You may recall the incident of the Pennsylvania senator and the "rubbers." After the senator's earnest and somewhat lengthy statement of a plea for some local cause, the President is reported to have observed his visitor's wet shoes, and instead of uttering the expected opinion on the issue to have remarked that he *ought not to be out without rubbers on a day like this.* From my own experience with New Englanders I should have taken this as my *answer.* Analyzed, the President's mind may have worked in this fashion: "This man is very amusing. He is asking my aid on a matter that is really trifling, quite beneath my attention. He hasn't even sense enough to wear rubbers. I can't do anything about his petition. His lack of judgment in coming to me is expressed by his failure to keep his feet dry." Hence the remark which the magazine editor explains as "slow" thinking. I think a Northern Yankee would have seen the point.

His Silence [3]

Known very favorably as Silent Cal, Coolidge said nothing publicly because of one of two possible reasons: Either he had no ideas on public affairs, which seems reasonable; or he was too timid to voice them. But in private Coolidge was garrulity itself. Philip Parrish, newspaperman of Portland, Oregon, once went to what he fondly thought would be an interview with President Coolidge, but for two hours Mr. Parrish was harangued on everything from trout fishing to the cost of cigars and, though he tried diligently, never once managed to get in a question.

His Laconic Style [4]

Now and then in our time the humor of New England will hint of some

[2] From "Maine Dialect," by E. K. Maxfield, *American Speech,* Vol. II (November, 1926), No. 2, p. 82.

[3] From *Lost Men of American History,* by Stewart H. Holbrook, p. 338 n. Copyright, 1946, by Stewart H. Holbrook. New York: The Macmillan Company.

[4] From *As Much As I Dare,* A Personal Recollection, by Burges Johnson, pp. 30–31. Copyright, 1944, by Ives Washburn, Inc. New York.

dour ancestral strain, when it becomes sharp and cold as a frost-etching on a window pane. Calvin Coolidge had more than a little of this harsh wit. During his governorship he spoke one day in a tent near Pittsfield, campaigning for Congressman Treadway. An old lady came up to him afterwards and said tremulously, "I came fifty miles to hear you, Mr. Coolidge, and I stood up all through your speech."

"So did I," said Mr. Coolidge.

Many anecdotes widely quoted as examples of New England humor were never humorously intended. They are bits of wisdom compressed into epigram, the fruit of solitary meditation behind the plow. Mr. Coolidge shared with other Vermonters this trick of condensation in clipt dialect. Dwight Morrow told me two such bits of Coolidgeana. He overheard his son-in-law urging the President to go up in a plane. "Why, Mr. President," urged Colonel Lindbergh, "it's the safest mode of passenger transportation! In two hundred thousand passenger miles only one casualty."

"Very little comfort for the casualty," said Mr. Coolidge.

Dwight said that he was spending a week end at the White House and on Sunday morning called across the hall from his bedroom, "Cal, what time is church?"

The answer came back, "E-leven o'clock."

"What time do we start?"

"Seven minutes to e-leven from upstairs."

One might pleasantly remember his reply, delivered in the [Massachusetts] House, to a colleague dissimilarly minded upon a bill under discussion, a colleague who spoke windily and at length, prefacing each period and each argument with the affirmative statement, "It is." Calvin, when he had risen to refute, had said, clearly but dejectedly, as though the talk had wearied him: "Mr. Speaker: It isn't"—and had sat down.[5]

A prominent Washington society woman was sitting next to the President at a smart party.

"Oh, Mr. President," she said gushingly, "you are so silent. I made a bet to-day that I could get more than two words out of you."

"You lose," the President replied.[6]

Mrs. Coolidge says that her husband presented her with an old brown bag when they returned from their wedding trip. In it were fifty-two pairs of socks with holes in them.

---

[5] From *The Legend of Calvin Coolidge,* by Cameron Rogers, p. 129. Copyright, 1928, by Doubleday, Doran & Company. Garden City, New York.

[6] From *Coolidge Wit and Wisdom,* 125 Short Stories about "Cal," compiled by John Hiram McKee, p. 43. Copyright, 1933, by John Hiram McKee. New York: Frederick A. Stokes Company.

"Calvin Coolidge!" she exclaimed. "Did you marry me to get your socks darned?"

"No—but I find it mighty handy," he said.

When they moved to a place of their own, Mrs. Coolidge bought a book called *Our Home Doctor*. It would be a good thing, she thought, to have around, with a new baby in the house. But she knew that she might be reproved for her extravagance, so she left it on the table in the sitting room, and waited for her husband to say something. A few days later she noticed a paper in it:

"Don't see any receipt here for curing suckers," she read. "C. C."

There are a hundred anecdotes that newspaper people tell about Coolidge and his mean ways. There is one about two reporters who went to his room in the Parker House, and found Tom W. there. Coolidge unlocked a bureau drawer, and produced a pint of rye, and poured them each a drink. Tom sat on the side of the bed, and didn't get one.

"You forgot Tom," said one of them.

"Tom's had his," said the Governor, and put the bottle back where it came from. . . . So, with much retelling, the legends live. But few tell the truth about the man, and all his grim and ancient virtues.

For fourteen years, Coolidge commuted in a day coach from Northampton to Boston, which is about a hundred miles. On Saturday nights when the Governor went home for supper, they had baked beans and brown bread, and Mrs. Coolidge often cooked a ham for Sunday.

Years later, Coolidge exclaimed, "Those White House hams! They worried me. A big one would be brought to the table. Mummer would have a slice, and I'd have a slice. Then the butler would take it away, and what happened to it after that, I never found out."

One night there was a State dinner at the White House, and the President went to the kitchen for a look around.

"Don't see why we have to have six hams," he said.

"But, Mr. President, there will be sixty people," explained the housekeeper. "And Virginia hams are so small! We can't serve more than ten people with one ham."

"Seems an awful lot of ham to me," muttered the President.

Shortly after this, the housekeeper departed. And the Coolidges sent to Boston for Ellen Riley—a New Englander.

"Wilful waste," said Miss Riley, "makes woeful want"—and she made a nice pea soup on a ham bone.[7]

———————

On a certain Sunday morning Mrs. Coolidge did not accompany her husband to church. Upon his return she asked:

[7] From *A New England Sampler*, by Eleanor Early, pp. 282–283, 292–293. Copyright, 1940, by Waverly House. Boston.

"Hear a good sermon?"

"Yes."

"What did the minister preach about?"

"Sin."

"What did he have to say about it?"

"He's agin it."

The story goes that on the occasion of his first meeting President Calvin Coolidge, Will Rogers offered to wager that he could make the President laugh. His friends were willing to let him try it, but were doubtful of his success.

"Mr. President, this is Mr. Rogers, Will Rogers."

Mr. Rogers took the hand of the President quietly, and looking him in the eye, said, "What is the name, please?"

One of the Washington correspondents attempted to sound President Coolidge on the subject of prohibition.

"Instead of answering your question, I'll tell you a story," countered the President.

"Frankie dropped in to tell his mother that he was going to his uncle's house for dinner.

" 'I suppose Mary is also going,' said his mother, referring to a grown-up cousin.

"Frankie evidently thought the question too personal, for, after a moment of deep thought, he replied: 'I don't know; I just go round minding my own business.' " [8]

He had been asked to plant a tree in honor of something-or-other. Surrounded by the general staff and the entire diplomatic corps, he perfunctorily turned over the sod with a golden trowel and stood back bored, while the seedling was imbedded. All looked towards the President, including the massed bands of the Army and Navy, waiting until he should make his speech of dedication. Nothing happened: Cal just stood there in stony silence. At length, when the situation had become awkward, Chief Justice Taft stepped to his side and whispered:

"Please say a few words, Mr. President!"

Cal puckered his mouth. Looking down his nose at the upturned earth he remarked solemnly:

"That's a good angleworm!" [9]

[8] From *Master Book of Humorous Illustrations,* Compiled and Edited by Leewin B. Williams, pp. 90–91. Copyright. 1938, by Whitmore & Smith. Nashville: Abingdon-Cokesbury Press.

[9] From *Yankee Lawyer,* The Autobiography of Ephraim Tutt (by Arthur Train), p. 7. Copyright, 1943, by Ephraim Tutt. New York: Charles Scribner's Sons.

At one of the White House press conferences various reporters were vainly firing their questions at Calvin Coolidge.

"Have you anything to say about Prohibition?"

"No."

"Have you anything to say about the World Court?"

"No."

"About the farm situation?"

"No."

"About the forthcoming senatorial campaign?"

"No."

The meeting broke up and the reporters began to file out of the room.

"And," called the President, "don't quote me." [10]

[10] From *Thesaurus of Anecdotes,* A New Classified Collection of the Best Anecdotes from Ancient Times to the Present Day, edited by Edmund Fuller, p. 25. Copyright, 1942, by Crown Publishers. New York.

PART THREE

BELIEFS AND CUSTOMS

New England was the child of a superstitious mother.
—SAMUEL ADAMS DRAKE

I stand by the old thought, the old thing, the old place, and the old friend.
—JAMES RUSSELL LOWELL

When questioned, they rarely go further than to say, that they do so because they have been taught that it is right to do it, or because their fathers did so before them: if they add anything to this, it is, that they expect blessings from the observance of the practice, and evils from the neglect.
—EDWARD AUGUSTUS KENDALL

I. THE POWER OF FAITH

Why do you conjure up a thousand frightful monsters to torment yourself, when there are enough of real evils? Some seem to think there is a ghost in every gust of wind. Away with such vain illusions of the imagination. Strange it is that a courage, that never startles at real dangers, should shrink at even the thought of an empty chimera! Signs and omens and prognostics continually fill the mind of some. . . . What power has superstition!
—ROBERT B. THOMAS, The Farmer's Almanack, 1830

Signs! Signs everywhere for the man who knew his acres and their heavens, and one must learn to read them all aright.
—MARION NICHOLL RAWSON

I beleave in ghosts,—only a little,—just enuff to keep up an assortment.—JOSH BILLINGS

There will be Weather this Week tho' I say nothing about it.
—NATHANIEL AMES, Almanack for 1731

1. EVANESCENT CLUES

ALTHOUGH the fairy faith is dead, as Whittier points out, and "never had much hold upon the Yankee mind," superstition will never die. Nor is it conceivable that, like the fairies, it will pack up and leave New England for a more congenial clime. We shall always have superstition because most superstition is the obsolete science of yesterday. Like children's games, which were once the pastimes of adults, signs, warnings, divination, taboos, charms, countercharms, and folk cures are part of the wreckage of culture, which has sunk from a higher to a lower level and been pushed to the periphery of society and to the back of our minds. In the process of downward transmission, superstition, like myth, has decayed, and survives chiefly in scraps of belief concerning good and bad luck.

More than the relics of an earlier stage of culture, superstition also represents a kind of empirical knowledge and prelogical or alogical thinking. While resting its case on faith, superstition likes to adduce evidence of its faith from experience—erroneous observation, hearsay, resemblances mistaken for causes—evidence that proves nothing except that superstition, like myth, sees what it wants to see and believes what it wants to believe.

The evidence of superstition consists of signs and warnings. Whether unusual natural phenomena, visions, or simply intuitions, signs and omens are forewarnings of something that is going to happen or (as in the case of wraiths) a telepathic signal that something has happened. All of us have hunches or a sixth sense, but only a few of us are gifted with "second sight."

The most common signs are weather signs, which survive in rural New England as in other rural areas as a traditional tool of the farmer; but the unpredictability of New England weather gives them special bearing and importance in this region. The weather also dominates the life of seafaring and fishing folk; and the hold of superstition upon sailors and fishermen is explainable in terms of their need of a superior kind of intelligence or wisdom to keep them safe.

> Knowledge and intelligence was theirs; and theirs also that extra sense . . . , call it intuition or instinct or even genius, that subconscious sense or faculty—whatever we care to call it—in sea-born men which makes it safe for them to do the thing that other men say cannot be done.[1]

On the sea intuition also takes the form of a "nose for fish," the "fisherman's greatest gift," according to Mary Heaton Vorse. Like a nose for fish, weather lore and folk medicine are a synthesis of empirical knowledge and "some evanescent clue" which some men are able to perceive before it is gone.

2. THE POWER OF SYMPATHY

Besides mystical faith—faith in intuition—superstition involves the "willing suspension of disbelief that constitutes poetic faith." Superstition is also poetic in its symbolism, its ability to see a pattern of analogy and sympathy in things apparently unrelated. Analogy—the principle that "like produces like"—is especially notable in folk cures, with its doctrines of "like cures like" and the "hair of the dog that bit you."

An aspect of analogy or sympathy which once played an important part in pseudo-medicine, and which survives in folk rhymes like the one beginning "Monday's child is fair of face," has to do with planetary influences, physiognomy, etc. Many almanacs (not including, however, Robert B. Thomas's *Old Farmer's Almanack*) featured prominently the Man of the Signs—the "figure of a man, surrounded by the twelve Signs of the Zodiac, each referred to some part of his body by means of a connecting line or a pointing dagger," indicating that "Each sign of the zodiac 'governed' an organ or part of the body, and, in selecting a day to treat any ailment, or to let blood, it was necessary to know whether the moon was or was not in that sign."[2]

The Man of the Signs, or the Moon's Man, is himself a perfect symbol of the Power of Superstition, which sees a man as determined by mystic influences and tied to the universe by thousands of imperceptible lines radiating this influence. This sympathetic relationship of man and the universe is the ultimate source of the faith, intuition, and analogy of superstition. One of the strongest influences on man is custom. And even among hard-

---

[1] James B. Connolly, *The Book of the Gloucester Fishermen* (New York, 1927), p. 286.

[2] George Lyman Kittredge, *The Old Farmer and His Almanack* (Boston, 1904), p. 54.

headed New Englanders, where superstition is made of sterner stuff than the poetry of fairy faith, folk beliefs survive as folkways or expedients, with a power of custom all the greater because of the strong hold of the past on New England.

B. A. B.

SIGNS AND WARNINGS

St. Elmo's Fire

. . . ABOUT 8 of the clock at night, a flame settled upon the main mast, it was about the bigness of a great Candle, and is called by our Seamen St. *Elmes* fire, it comes before a storm, and is commonly thought to be a Spirit; if two appear they prognosticate safety: These are known to the learned by the names of *Castor* and *Pollux,* to the *Italians* by St. *Nicholas* and St. *Hermes,* by the *Spaniards* called *Corpos Santos.*[1]

. . . Those pale flames that we beheld burning from the spikes of the lightning-rod, I suppose were identical with the St. Elmo's fire that I have since seen described as haunting the spars of ships in thunder-storms. And here I am reminded of a story told by some gentlemen visiting Appledore sixteen or eighteen years ago. They started from Portsmouth for the Shoals in a whaleboat, one evening in summer, with a native Star-Islander, Richard Randall by name, to manage the boat. They had sailed about half the distance, when they were surprised at seeing a large ball of fire, like a rising moon, rolling toward them over the sea from the south. They watched it eagerly as it bore down upon them, and, veering off, went east of them at some little distance, and then passed astern, and there, of course, they expected to lose sight of it; but while they were marvelling and speculating, it altered its course, and suddenly began to near them, coming back upon its track against the wind and steadily following in their wake. This was too much for the native Shoaler. He took off his jacket and turned it inside out to exorcise the fiend, and lo, the apparition most certainly disappeared! We heard the excited account of the strange gentlemen and witnessed the holy horror of the boatman on the occasion; but no one could imagine what had set the globe of fire rolling across the sea. Some one suggested that it might be an exhalation, a phosphorescent light, from the decaying body of some dead fish; but in that case it must have been taken in tow by some living finny creature, else how could

---

[1] From *An Account of Two Voyages to New-England,* Made during the years 1638, 1663, by John Josselyn, Gent., p. 8. Boston, Massachusetts: Published by William Veazie. 1865.

it have sailed straight "into the teeth of the wind"? It was never satisfactorily accounted for, and must remain a mystery.[2]

St. Elmo Sees Them Through

"I AIN'T the one to believe in no furriner's miracles. You know that. But
what I seen, I seen. And I say that vessel never should have stayed afloat
by rights, never *would* have, without it was just a plain and simple
miracle!"

They were yarning in the Master Mariners' clubrooms. While rubber-
shod feet kept up a constant shuffle through the metropolis-in-little that
was Gloucester's main street, the select group of skippers up here in "the
Rooms" spent their evenings ashore in the dignified piracy of cutthroat
whist or "swacker," and occasionally in making statements of "fact," plain
and fancy, which nobody dared question.

Just now Captain Frank Hall, Captain Joe Mesquita, and half a dozen
others had tilted back for a session, and old Captain Bob McEachern was
getting under way on the subject of St. Elmo's fire—those eerie lights that
sometimes appeared out of nowhere on a vessel's rigging.

Queer balls of fire, they were, which showed at the masthead or the
bowsprit or the tips of the booms; but only once in a great while, in the
worst part of the heaviest gales, and not always then. Sailors had given
them the name "corposant" (*corpo santo*—saint's body) but Captain Bob
added that professors and high-toned people like that said 'twas only
brush electricity that come to roost somehow on the ironwork of the rigging.

"P'r'aps so, p'r'aps so," Captain Bob conceded. "But in the gale of
'73, when we seen that Frenchman rolling in the trough, with everything
carried away but the split stump of her bowsprit, I watched two of them
lights dancing along the hull, and it didn't look like no electricity to me.

"I yelled down to the captain that we had a Frenchman afire almost
alongside. He come on deck, and a feller named Louis Veneau, which we'd
shipped in Judique, Nova Scotia, come up too when he heard it was a
French vessel.

"The minute the Judiquer looked at her, he give a laugh like he was
tickled to death. The skipper stared at him and said he didn't see nothing

[2] From *Among the Isles of Shoals,* by Celia Thaxter, pp. 136–138. Entered according
to Act of Congress, in the year 1873, by James R. Osgood & Co., in the Office of the
Librarian of Congress, at Washington. Boston.

From *In Great Waters,* The Story of the Portuguese Fishermen, by Jeremiah Digges,
pp. 171–173. Copyright, 1941, by Josef Berger. New York: The Macmillan Company.

funny in it—them poor devils with their vessel afire and in such a gale, and with their craft already the saddest-looking wreck you ever seen! And what kind of a man was he, to be laughing when it was a crew of Frenchmen—his own people—that was dying out there on the Queero? But the Judiquer just grinned.

" 'No fire, no fire!' he says. 'That vessel, she safe, Captain, she safer as we are!'

"Well, the Judiquer had always seemed to me like a good, level-headed sort of a feller, so when my watch was over I went below to see what 'twas that had throwed him off ballast like that. He told me the light I'd seen on that vessel was St. Elmo's fire. She was from Brittany, and St. Elmo is them fellers' patron saint. When that kind of fire shows on a vessel, they know their saint has come to watch over her, and they quit worrying then, no matter what shape she's in. St. Elmo will see her through.

"I told him I still didn't see no reason to laugh. Even if that craft wasn't afire, she was in such desperate bad shape that all the saints in the catalogue wasn't going to save her. I'd never seen a gale like this one, and that vessel was just about the completest wreck that ever had the nerve to show herself out of water on Queero bank.

"Through the night it blowed harder and harder. I didn't know whether we was going to see daylight ourselves, and we had one of the best sea boats out of Gloucester. For that other craft, there wasn't a chance in a thousand to keep afloat through them next twenty-odd hours of gale!

"But she did. Yes, sir, so help me God, we sighted her again the next night, and we took off her crew and towed the wreck to Canso! Eighteen of 'em, there was, and they was in pretty bad shape. But after he'd jabbered with 'em awhile, the Judiquer told me there wasn't none of 'em really worried through the worst of the blow, because when they seen that fire on their wreck, they knew St. Elmo was going to see 'em through. Their saint had hoisted his colors on their craft. They knew there was going to be a miracle, and—well, there was!"

The Wraith in the Storm

THE number of persons who have testified to having seen the apparitions or death wraiths of dying or deceased friends is already large, as the records of various societies for psychical research bear witness. These phenomena are not in their nature forewarnings of something that is about to happen, but announcements of something that already has happened. They therefore can have no relation to what was formerly known as "second sight."

In spite of all that our much-boasted civilization has done in the way

From *The Myths and Fables of To-Day*, by Samuel Adams Drake, pp. 224–228. Copyright, 1900, by Samuel Adams Drake. Boston: Lee and Shepard.

of freeing poor, fallible man from the thraldom of superstition, there is indubitable evidence that a great many people still put faith in direct revelations from the land of spirits. In the course of a quiet chat one evening, where the subject was under discussion, one of the company who had listened attentively, though silently all the while, to all manner of theories, spiced with ridicule, abruptly asked how we would account for the following incident which he went on to relate, and I have here set down word for word:—

"My grandparents," he began, "had a son whom they thought all the world of. From all accounts I guess Tom was about one of the likeliest young fellows that could be scared up in a day's journey. Everybody said Tom was bound to make his mark in the world, and at the time I speak of he seemed in a fair way of doing it, too, for at one and twenty he was first mate of the old *Argonaut* which had just sailed for Calcutta. This would make her tenth voyage. Well, as I am telling you, the very day after the *Argonaut* went to sea, a tremendous gale set in from the eastward. It blew great guns. Actually, now, it seemed as if that gale would never stop blowing.

"As day after day went by, and the storm raged on without intermission, you may judge if the hearts of those who had friends at sea in that ship did not sink down and down with the passing hours. Of course, the old folks could think of nothing else.

"Let me see; it was a good bit ago. Ah, yes; it was on the third or four night of the gale, I don't rightly remember which, and it don't matter much, that grandfather and grandmother were sitting together, as usual, in the old family sitting-room, he poring over the family Bible as he was wont to do in such cases, she knitting and rocking, or pretending to knit, but both full of the one ever present thought, which each was trying so hard to hide from the other.

"Dismally splashed the raindrops against the windowpanes, mournfully the wind whined in the chimney-top, while every now and then the fire would spit and sputter angrily on the hearth, or flare up fitfully when some big gust came roaring down the chimney to fan the embers into a fiercer flame. Then there would be a lull, during which, like an echo of the tempest, the dull and distant booming of the sea was borne to the affrighted listener's ears. But nothing I could say would begin to give you an idea of the great gale of 1817.

"Well, the old folks sat there as stiff as two statues, listening to every sound. When a big gust tore over the house and shook it till it rocked again, gran'ther would steal a look at grandmother over his specs, but say never a word. The old lady would give a start, let her hands fall idly upon her lap, sit for a moment as if dazed, and then go on with her knitting again as if her very life depended on it.

"Unable at length to control her feelings, grandmother got up out of her chair, with her work in her hand, went to the window, put aside the curtain, and looked out. I say looked out, for of course all was so pitchdark outside that nothing could be seen, yet there she stood with her white face pressed close to the wet panes, peering out into the night, as if questioning the storm itself of the absent one.

"All at once she drew back from the window with a low cry, saying in a broken voice: 'My God, father, it's Tom in his coffin! They're bringing him up here, to the house.' Then she covered her face with her hands, to shut out the horrid sight.

"'Set down 'Mandy!' sternly commanded the startled old man. 'Don't be making a fool of yourself. Don't ye know tain't no sech a thing what you're sayin'? Set down, I say, this minnit!'

"But no one could ever convince grandmother that she had not actually seen, with her own eyes, her dear boy Tom, the idol of her heart, lying cold in death. To her indeed it was a revelation from the tomb, for the ship in which Tom had sailed was never heard from."

The Cradle Will Rock

"My AUNT, Lois Toothacre, that lives down by Middle Bay," said Miss Ruey, "used to tell about a dreadful blow they had once in time of the equinoctial storm,—and what was remarkable, she insisted that she heard a baby cryin' out in the storm—she heard it just as plain as could be."

"Laws a-mercy," said Mrs. Pennel, nervously, "it was nothing but the wind,—it always screeches like a child crying; or maybe it was the seals; seals will cry just like babes."

"So they told her,—but no; she insisted she knew the difference,—it *was* a baby. Well, what do you think, when the storm cleared off, they found a baby's cradle washed ashore sure enough!"

"But they did n't find any baby," said Mrs. Pennel, nervously.

"No, they searched the beach far and near, and that cradle was all they found. Aunt Lois took it in—it was a very good cradle, and she took it to use, but every time there came up a gale, that ar cradle would rock, rock, jist as if somebody was a-sittin' by it; and you could stand across the room and see there wa' n't nobody there."

"You make me all of a shiver," said Mrs. Pennel.

This, of course, was just what Miss Ruey intended, and she went on:—

"Wal', you see they kind o' got used to it—they found there wa' n't no harm come of its rockin', and so they didn't mind; but Aunt Lois had a sister Cerinthy that was a weakly girl, and had the janders. Cerinthy was one of the sort that 's born with veils over their faces, and can see sperits; and one time Cerinthy was a-visitin' Lois after her second baby was born, and there came up a blow, and Cerinthy comes out of the keepin'-room, where the cradle was a-standin', and says, 'Sister,' says she, 'who's

From *The Pearl of Orr's Island, A Story of the Coast of Maine,* by Harriet Beecher Stowe, pp. 47–49. Copyright, 1862, and 1890, by Harriet Beecher Stowe. Boston and New York: Houghton, Mifflin and Company. 1891.

that woman sittin' rockin' the cradle?' and Aunt Lois says she, 'Why, there a'n't nobody. That ar cradle always will rock in a gale, but I've got used to it, and don't mind it.' 'Well,' says Cerinthy, 'jist as true as you live, I jist saw a woman with a silk gown on, and long black hair a-hangin' down, and her face was pale as a sheet, sittin' rockin' that ar cradle, and she looked round at me with her great black eyes kind o' mournful and wishful, and then she stooped down over the cradle.' 'Well,' says Lois, 'I a'n't goin' to have no such doin's in my house,' and she went right in and took up the baby, and the very next day she jist had the cradle split up for kindlin'; and that night, if you 'll believe, when they was a-burnin' of it, they heard, jist as plain as could be, a baby scream, scream, screamin' round the house; but after that they never heard it no more."

The Girl in the Fog

CAPTAIN COOK would tell stories of wrecks and rescues and legends. One was the story of the coast guard who, when on his rounds, saw a girl "loomin' out of the fog." He was surprised to see anyone so far from the town. The next night he was on patrol he met her once again. This time she seemed so beautiful he realized that he had fallen in love with her and begged her to meet him again. She smiled at him in a dubious fashion and answered,

"I'll meet you again, soon," and vanished in the fog.

Within a few nights there was a wreck of a Portuguese vessel from the Western Islands. There, on the deck, a child in her arms, was the girl whom he had met in the fog. She recognized him and waved to him.

As the surfboat came alongside "on the heave of the wave," she threw the child to him. Then she jumped, but missed the boat and was swirled away in the churning sea. Then he realized that it had been her spirit he had seen and that she had given him the child in trust. The child proved to be an orphan and he adopted the little girl and brought her up.

The Black Newfoundland Dog

FOG imperils the vessels as well as the dories. Most Provincetown trawl-fishermen can tell you the story of the black Newfoundland dog.

Old "Cheeny" Marshall, who was drowned on the banks when his dory

From *Time and the Town,* A Provincetown Chronicle, by Mary Heaton Vorse, p. 57. Copyright, 1942, by Mary Heaton Vorse. New York: The Dial Press.

From *Cape Cod Pilot,* by Jeremiah Digges, with Editorial and Research Assistance of the Members of the Federal Writers' Project, pp. 239–240. American Guide Series, Federal Writers' Project, Works Progress Administration for the State of Massachusetts. Copyright, 1937, by Poor Richard Associates. Provincetown and New York: Modern Pilgrim Press and the Viking Press.

capsized in April, 1937, told this story to me. Cheeny was just a boy, a "salt-passer" on one of the old hand-liners, when—so help him God! it happened.

The vessel is well out to sea, off Newfoundland. She has not sighted a sail all day, when suddenly, out of a sea calm and smooth as an oil slick, up pops the great black dog. Cheeny lifts him over the rail and lets him lie, half dead, on the deck. The dog has webbed feet.

"Heave him overboard!" shouts one old-timer. "He's the divil!"

But the lad pleads for him, keeps him, takes care of him, puts him in his own bunk. And finally comes the day when the "soup" settles thick over the Devil's Graveyard, in the Bay of Fundy. The helmsman is steering blindly. The dog, standing in the bow, suddenly barks a warning. The helmsman—Cheeny Marshall himself—puts her hard over. And the vessel veers in time to clear by inches the massive bows of a steamer looming out of the mist! It happened, Cheeny Marshall assured me over and over— so help him God!

The Telltale Seaweed

THIS IS THE story just as I heard it the other evening—a ghost story told me as true. It seems that one chilly October night in the first decade of the present century, two sisters were motoring along a Cape Cod road, when their car broke down just before midnight and would go no further. This was in an era when such mishaps were both commoner and more hopeless than they are today. For these two, there was no chance of help until another car might chance to come by in the morning and give them a tow. Of a lodging for the night there was no hope, except a gaunt, unlighted, frame house which, with a clump of pine trees beside it, stood black in the moonlight, across a neglected stretch of frost-hardened lawn.

They yanked at its ancient bell-pull, but only a faint tinkle within made answer. They banged despairingly on the door panel, only to awaken what at first they thought was an echo, and then identified as a shutter responding antiphonally with the help of a nipping wind. This shutter was around the corner, and the ground-floor window behind it was broken and unfastened. There was enough moonlight to show that the room within

From *The Portable Woollcott*, by Alexander Woollcott, selected by Joseph Hennessey, pp. 121–124. Copyright, 1934, by Alexander Woollcott; 1962, by Joseph P. Hennessey. New York: Viking Press, Inc. Reprinted by permission of the publisher.

More recently, the Curator of the Botanical Museum in St. Louis has assured me that this tale, whispered from neighbor to neighbor across the country, has become distorted in a manner offensive to students of submarine vegetation. According to him, the visitor from the sea was seen in a house in Woods Hole, Mass. He was a son of the house who had been drowned during his honeymoon off the coast of Australia. The seaweed picked up off the dusty floor of that New England mansion was of a variety which grows only off the Australian coast. The Curator even presented me with the actual seaweed. I regard it with mingled affection and skepticism, and keep it pressed between the pages of Bullfinch's *Mythology*.—A. W.

Cf. "Cap'n Santos' Leg," *A Treasury of American Folklore* (1944), pp. 713–714.

was a deserted library, with a few books left on the sagging shelves and a few pieces of dilapidated furniture still standing where some departing family had left them, long before. At least the sweep of the electric flash which one of the women had brought with her showed them that on the uncarpeted floor the dust lay thick and trackless, as if no one had trod there in many a day.

They decided to bring their blankets in from the car and stretch out there on the floor until daylight, none too comfortable, perhaps, but at least sheltered from that salt and cutting wind. It was while they were lying there, trying to get to sleep, while, indeed, they had drifted halfway across the borderland, that they saw—each confirming the other's fear by a convulsive grip of the hand—saw standing at the empty fireplace, as if trying to dry himself by a fire that was not there, the wraithlike figure of a sailor, come dripping from the sea.

After an endless moment, in which neither woman breathed, one of them somehow found the strength to call out, "Who's there?" The challenge shattered the intolerable silence, and at the sound, muttering a little—they said afterwards that it was something between a groan and a whimper— the misty figure seemed to dissolve. They strained their eyes, but could see nothing between themselves and the battered mantlepiece.

Then, telling themselves (and, as one does, half believing it) that they had been dreaming, they tried again to sleep, and, indeed, did sleep until a patch of shuttered sunlight striped the morning floor. As they sat up and blinked at the gritty realism of the forsaken room, they would, I think, have laughed at their shared illusion of the night before, had it not been for something at which one of the sisters pointed with a kind of gasp. There, in the still undisturbed dust, on the spot in front of the fireplace where the apparition had seemed to stand, was a patch of water, a little, circular pool that had issued from no crack in the floor nor, as far as they could see, fallen from any point in the innocent ceiling. Near it in the surrounding dust was no footprint—their own or any other's—and in it was a piece of green that looked like seaweed. One of the women bent down and put her finger to the water, then lifted it to her tongue. The water was salty.

After that the sisters scuttled out and sat in their car, until a passerby gave them a tow to the nearest village. In its tavern at breakfast they gossiped with the proprietress about the empty house among the pine trees down the road. Oh, yes, it had been just that way for a score of years or more. Folks did say the place was spooky, haunted by a son of the family who, driven out by his father, had shipped before the mast and been drowned at sea. Some said the family had moved away because they could not stand the things they heard and saw at night.

A year later, one of the sisters told the story at a dinner party in New York. In the pause that followed a man across the table leaned forward.

"My dear lady," he said, with a smile, "I happen to be the curator of a museum where they are doing a good deal of work on submarine vegetation. In your place, I never would have left that house without taking the bit of seaweed with me."

"Of course you wouldn't," she answered tartly, "and neither did I."

It seems she had lifted it out of the water and dried it a little by pressing it against a window pane. Then she had carried it off in her pocketbook, as a souvenir. As far as she knew, it was still in an envelope in a little drawer of her desk at home. If she could find it, would he like to see it? He would. Next morning she sent it around by messenger, and a few days later it came back with a note.

"You were right," the note said, "this is seaweed. Furthermore, it may interest you to learn that it is of a rare variety which, as far as we know, grows only on dead bodies."

Esau and the Gorbey

. . . Now, BEFORE I relate the story almost exactly as it was told to me, and this I am able to do because I wrote it down at its ending, I must digress a bit. . . . Since this bird is one of the principals in the tale, it is necessary to speak a little of the Canada Jay, or—as it was commonly called by the woodsmen—the gorbey or moose bird.

Years ago, when I first went into the woods north of Moosehead, these birds were very plentiful and very tame and fearless. Lunching alone on the trail, I have had them fly down and take crumbs from my fingers a number of times. Wherever there was food or a campground, there was sure to be a flock of the sooty-gray little thieves hanging around and nobody ever thought of harming them until in later years the sports found them easy targets for their twenty-twos. It was commonly believed among the older men that it was exceedingly bad luck for anyone to offer them harm or to drive them away, in spite of the fact that I have seen them around

From *Ridge Runner, The Story of a Maine Woodsman*, by Gerald Averill, pp. 120–126. Copyright, 1948, by J. B. Lippincott Company. Philadelphia and New York.

For the legend and lore of the gorbey see Edward Ives, "The Man Who Plucked the Gorbey," *Journal of American Folklore*, 74 (January–March, 1961), pp. 1–8. He notes that in Joseph Wright's *English Dialect Dictionary*," we find the word 'gorb' not only listed as Scots and Irish for 'glutton, a greedy person or animal,' but also as Scots and North-Country for 'an unfledged bird,' and figuratively, 'anything very young or bare.' . . . From Scotland or the North Country, the story came to New Brunswick, where it became associated with the Canada Jay (perhaps because this bird is easily caught). Through the story, the bird itself came to be called a 'gorbey.' New Brunswick woodsmen brought the term to Maine, where it flourished, partly because there was a well-known, utterly bald 'character' named Archie Stackhouse in the heart of the busiest lumbering country in the Northeast, [one of twenty-eight men of whom the story has been told in over a hundred versions collected by Ives]." Underlying the story, according to Ives, are beliefs that gorbies are the souls of dead woodsmen, that no woodsman will harm a gorbey, and that "Anything that you do to a garbie happens to you."

wangans and open camps so thick that they became a real nuisance. Margarine especially attracted them, and many times I have seen them swoop down and scoop a beakful from right under the noses of a feeding crew seated at an outdoor table. Sometimes when a man was recovering from a big drunk and hanging on the edge of the D.T.'s, this could be very disconcerting, but the ordinary run of oldtimers took it as a matter of course. The gorbeys are not nearly as numerous these days, and it has been a long while since I have seen one.

Rocky Emmons told [me] the story fully, and this is the way of it:

"In the old days, an' I will not say how long gone it was, Esau was a bold giant of a man. He took charge in the camps an' on the drives, an' a hard man he was on a crew. His temper was quick an' his hand heavy an' he would take no lip from no man great or small. He had a thick head of yeller hair an' a great silky beard of the same, an' he spent hours combin' both the beard and his head till they would glisten an' gleam like yeller gold. There was a great mat of hair upon his chest an' it was thick, too, upon his arms and legs, an' he was sinfully proud of it all. This hair was a sign to him of his strength an' manhood an', bein' who an' what he was, no man made light of it twice. He was a cruel man with the might of an ox an' the heart of a weasel. No man called him 'friend,' but he could drive a crew an' get out the timber.

" 'Twas in a camp on the north side of Pogy Mountain on a day in January that the thing happened—a day of bitter cold an' drivin' snow, dry ice that could peel the hide from a man's face. Esau was wild because the crew laid in an' he spent half the day goddamning them all for a bunch of old women, even though he knew no man, exceptin' perhaps himself, could live an' work outside the way it was. After the noon meal, he calmed down some and sat in a great chair he had made for himself an' began to comb his hair an' beard. Most of the men was tired an' napped, but Jean Ayette from across the line, meself an' two others got out a deck of cards, but it was too cold to play. The wind shrieked an' howled over an' around the roof, drivin' the dry snow in through the chinkin', an' every once in a while you could hear one of the cedar roof shakes loosen up and clatter. Half the time the stove wouldn't draw an' would puke great puffs of smoke an' ashes out into the room. It was one cruel, God-awful day, boy, the like of which I have never seen since.

"It must have been around two o'clock when the storm was at its worst that the bird come—the little half-froze gorbey. He come an' fluttered his wings ag'inst the winder an' the wind caught him an' blew him away like a wisp of paper. An' then in the space of a few breaths he was back ag'in, an' Esau looked up an' seen him there flutterin' an' beatin' his wings ag'inst the pane. The bird dropped to the sill an' huddled into the corner where the frame was let into the logs, an' Esau got onto his feet an' stepped quick as a cat to the winder.

"He pulled the pegs that held in the frame an' scooped up the bird in his fist, yellin' for one of us to put the winder back in. Jean an' me put it back an' Esau sat down by the stove. The little gray head, lookin' this way an' that, peeked up through his fist an' the comical black-rimmed beady eyes never so much as blinked. He held the bird up level with his eyes an' talked soft an' easy to it.

" 'Ha,' he says, 'ye have a familiar look about ye, me little gray crow. Ye look like Frenchy Aucoin with them two black eyes I gave him over on Black Brook two years gone, but Frenchy slipped on a jam an' went to hell.'

"He held the bird up closer an' looked an' looked, an' the bird looked back.

" 'Now,' Esau went on, 'they's some that believe men has souls an', when they die, the souls come back an' flitter around. You wouldn't be the little thievin' flutterin' soul of Frenchy Aucoin, would ye, now?'

"The bird turned his head this way and that an' then he pulled back his little neck an' gave a tiny peck at the hand that held him.

" 'Well now,' croons Esau, soft an' easy, 'well now, will ye look at that! I take him in an' warm him in me own soft hands an' he bites me. Right before me own crew in me own camp the little gray crumb of a thievin' bastard of a crow bites me! Well, me fine rooster, if ye don't like it here, back ye go outside where ye belong. But first, before ye become over-heated, leave us take off a few clothes.'

"An' then, whilst the whole caboodle of us stood by in shame an' fear, he opened his fist, spread an' clamped fast a wing with his thumb an' held the other open with a finger and, quick an' dainty as you please, he began to pluck the soft, short breast an' body feathers. The camp was deathly still, barrin' the howlin' o' the wind an' we could all hear the small rip-rip as the feathers came free. The gorbey squeaked once, an' then ag'in, an' was quiet.

" 'Twas but a minute he worked, for he was quick with his hands, an' then he let out a beller of laughter an' held up the bird by the tips of his two wings. Ah, me lad, 'twas a pitiful sight, all the feathers stripped clean from the body an' only the wing an' tail feathers left. Even the neck he had picked, but the little black eyes were bright an' glitterin' an', whilst we looked, the head turned an' dipped an' the small beak plucked at his fingers.

" 'An' now,' said Esau, an' there was the very devil in the tone of his voice, 'an' now, me little naked chicken, nobody asked ye here. Ye have been warmed an' entertained an' be damned to ye. Should ye turn out to be the black-eyed soul of Mister Aucoin, ye'll flutter back to hell an' be warm enough. An' if ye should be jest the little thievin' jay bird I think ye are, then ye'll freeze quick an' easy, so out ye go.'

"He folded the bird's wings close to its body, closed his fist around it, an' steppin' to the winder, he loosed the sash an' thrust forth the naked bird into the storm. It turned once an' spread itself ag'inst the glass like one crucified, an' then the wind whisked it away."

The old teamster paused for refreshment. His voice had taken on a slight burr, and his suspicion of a brogue was growing by the minute.

"There was little sleep amongst us that night," he went on. "We ate an' stretched on our bunks. Them was the days when we slept ten or a dozen under one long spread, an' when one turned in the night, all must do the same. The storm grew worse toward dark an' it tore at the camp until we thought surely the roof would leave her. Along towards mornin' the wind died an' we dozed off an' woke again when the bull-cook stoked the stove and lit the lanterns. I was half asleep when he rolled us out an' was rubbin' the sleep from me eyes an' gropin' for me stags, when I heard the noise— a queer sound it was, a kind of a cross between a bleat an' a groan. It came from over in the corner where the wooden sink an' the water barrel stood, but before I could turn meself for a look, there was a gabble of French an' I seen Ayette down on his knees crossin' hisself whilst others of the crew stood starin' an' stiff with fear.

" 'Twas Esau's habit—to toughen him, as he said—to strip naked in the morn an' splash the icy water over his head an' chest, an' there he stood in the corner by the sink, white an' naked an', by the Little Old White-Eye an' the Holy Old Mackinaw, there was no wisp of hair upon him at any place! The thick mane of hair, the glossy beard, his brows an' even his eye-winkers was gone. The hair from his body was gone, too, an' he stood, scared an' shiverin', as white an' smooth as one of them marble statues of a man.

"The place was like a madhouse. The Frenchman Ayette was half mad with fear, an' Neil Hart, a Black Irishman with a tongue as sharp as a new file, cursed Esau, the mother that bore him, the man that fathered him and that man's father before him. Up an' down an' over an' under an' before an' behind he cursed Esau, until the Irishman's eyes rolled in his head, the froth came from his mouth, an' we could no longer understand his gibberish. An' Esau did nothin' but stand there in his nakedness an' tremble, an' it come to us that with his hair the best or the worst of him was gone with it, an' after a time we covered his shame with his clothes, hung his turkey on his shoulders an' druv him out from among us with kicks an' blows.

"The storm had stopped an' he went flounderin' off down the mountain through the deep snow. No man knows where he went, but for a matter of two years he was seen by none of us. 'Twas agreed that we would not speak of the thing, but the Frenchman Ayette could not hold his tongue an' Hart had a loose mouth while in his cups. The tale went round, but 'twas told so many different ways an' so wildly that there seemed no truth to it at all, an' as those that were there at the camp on Pogy were killed off or died in their beds, the truth of the matter was lost entirely.

"They say that the Big Feller heard the tale an', believin' in neither good luck nor bad, put Esau on the office payroll as a hunter of stray horses, an' when ye see him now, he is at that work. He travels when an' where he pleases, an' he tells me sunthin' drives him from place to place. There is no rest anywheres for him, for men refuse to sit at table with him or sleep under the same roof. He comes an' he goes, an' if ye make note of it, ye'll see that the storms come wtih him. As for me I can take no harm from him, for no worse luck can come upon me than I have already borne."

Rooster Talk

IN ONE of the old New England towns there lived in days of yore a youth named William Smith. William lived at the lower end of the chief village street. Near the upper end of the same street lived a young woman with whose charms William was so smitten that his calls on her were not only frequent but protracted.

One night when he had made one of these calls, he sought his home at the magic hour when, in such towns as had steeple clocks, the bells tolled twelve. William had not gone down the street far when he was startled by the crow of a rooster. But the remarkable thing was that he clearly detected beneath its rough notes these words, "The woman rules here." There was no doubt about what the rooster said, for it immediately repeated the words, and even more clearly, "The woman rules here."

While William walked along pondering this strange statement, he heard the voice of a second rooster at the next house below. It said, "The man rules here. The man rules here."

It was plain to William that he was being let into some of the family secrets of the village. All through the street the roosters greeted him as he passed along. At some of the houses it was the man that was chief, at some the woman. William certainly had food for reflection, but it is not related that he ever made any use of this knowledge which came to him so strangely.

In this connection I may mention that some say if you listen to roosters calling back and forth you can hear this conversation.

Rooster at first house. "The women rule here."

Rooster at second house. "And so they do here."

Rooster at third house. "And so they do everywhere."

A grown person, when a rooster crows, will sometimes imitate its call, and work a child's name into the sound. Then he says to the child, "Didn't you hear the rooster calling you?"

From *What They Say in New England*, A Book of Signs, Sayings, and Superstitions, collected by Clifton Johnson, pp. 253–254. Copyright, 1896, by Lee and Shepard. Boston.

LUCK, DIVINATION, AND CONJURATION
The Dream Line

IT WAS the sun-cured salt-fish that was the favorite article of diet in the islanders' households, while very little account was made of the fresh. The young people had some merry customs of their own with it. They represented that if a certain particularly salt strip in the centre, called the "dream line," were eaten before going to bed, the girl or the young man one was to marry would be indicated by appearing in a vision and handing him or her a glass of water.

Flower Oracles

HERE we picked great bunches of yellow-eyed bird-foot violets, or made bouquets of dandelion "curls." Buttercups held under each other's chins usually cast a yellow shadow and proved that we "loved butter." Fortunes were told by means of "white weed" petals, but I could never decide whether "rich man, poor man, beggar man, thief, doctor, lawyer, merchant, chief," referred to four or eight possible husbands, and "chief" in my mind, was always associated with scalplock and tomahawk. When three puffs of breath failed to blow all the tufted seeds from a dandelion globe, the shout arose, "Your mother wants you!" If the drop of juice pressed with thumb nail to the top of one grass stalk "took off" the drop from the one held against it, then your "wish would come true." [1]

. . . There was a love divination by Lilacs which we children solemnly observed. There will occasionally appear a tiny Lilac flower, usually a white Lilac, with five divisions of the petal instead of four—this is a Luck Lilac. This must be solemnly swallowed. If it goes down smoothly, the dabbler in magic cries out, "He loves me"; if she chokes at her floral food, she must say sadly, "He loves me not." I remember once calling out, with gratification and pride, "He loves me!" "Who is he?" said my older companions. "Oh, I didn't know he had to be somebody," I answered in surprise, to be met by derisive laughter at my satisfaction with a lover in general and not in particular. It was a matter of Lilac-luck-etiquette that the lover's name should be pronounced mentally before the petal was swallowed. [2]

From "Fish and Men in the Maine Islands," by W. H. Bishop, in *Harper's New Monthly Magazine*, Vol. LXI, (August, 1880), No. 363, p. 351. Entered according to Act of Congress in the year 1880, by Harper and Brothers, in the Office of the Librarian of Congress at Washington. New York.

---

[1] From *In Dover on the Charles*, A Contribution to New England Folk-Lore, by Alice J. Jones, p. 37. Copyright, 1906, by Alice J. Jones. Newport, Rhode Island: The Milne Printery.

[2] From *Old Time Gardens*, Newly Set Forth, by Alice Morse Earle, pp. 150–151. Copyright, 1901, by The Macmillan Company. New York and London, 1902.

Apple Divinations

THE following rhyme, used in New England at the beginning of the present century, remains unchanged in a single word, except the omission of the last three lines.

Apples formerly were an essential part of every entertainment in the country; in the winter season, a dish of such always stood on the sideboard. As the hours went by, a foaming dish of eggnog would be brought in, always with a red-hot poker inserted, for the purpose of keeping up the proper temperature. It was then that the apple, having been properly named, with a fillip of the finger was divided, to decide the fate of the person concerned according to its number of seeds.

One, I love,
Two, I love,
Three, I love, I say,
Four, I love with all my heart,
And five, I cast away;
Six, he loves,
Seven, she loves,
Eight, they both love;
Nine, he comes,
Ten, he tarries,
Eleven, he courts,
Twelve, he marries;
Thirteen wishes,
Fourteen kisses,
All the rest little witches.[1]

It is interesting to note the folk customs of Old England which have lingered here, such as domestic love divinations. The poet Gay wrote:—

I pare this Pippin round and round again,
My shepherd's name to flourish on the plain.
I fling th' unbroken paring o'er my head,
Upon the grass a perfect L. is read.

I have seen New England schoolgirls, scores of times, thus toss an "unbroken paring." An ancient trial of my youth was done with Apple seeds; these were named for various swains, then slightly wetted and stuck on the cheek or forehead, while we chanted:—

"Pippin! Pippin! Paradise!
Tell me where my true love lies!"

The seed that remained longest in place indicated the favored and favoring lover.[2]

---

[1] From *Games and Songs of American Children,* collected and compared by William Wells Newell, p. 109. Copyright, 1883, 1903, by Harper & Brothers. New York and London.

[2] From *Old Time Gardens,* Newly Set Forth, by Alice Morse Earle, pp. 205–206. Copyright, 1901, by The Macmillan Company. New York and London. 1902.

A Fortune in a Stick

THERE WERE once three girls who were anxious as to the kind of husbands they should have.

At length the eldest said, "You know, sisters, there is a little wood back of the house. Let us all walk through it, and each pick a stick as we go along. The one that picks the handsomest stick will get the handsomest husband."

The others agreed, and off they all three went. They had not gone far when the youngest saw a stick that she thought would do well enough for her, and she forthwith picked it. Her sisters walked on and on until they came out of the wood on the other side, but not a stick did they find that was handsome enough to suit them. Then all three went home.

Not long after the youngest married; but the eldest two remained single all their lives.

The consequence of the general knowledge of this story was, that the old people used sometimes to say to a girl whom they thought over particular in her criticism of the marriageable young men, "You better look out, and not have to go through the woods to pick a stick."

If a woman married a man who was held in low esteem by the community, it was said, "Well, she went through the wood, and picked a crooked stick after all."

Sailors' Superstitions

ONE curious characteristic of the sailors is their faith in superstitions. In particular, they have an ineradicable belief in "Jonahs." A person or thing that causes a poor voyage is a Jonah. If a single new man joins a crew and there is a small catch of fish that cruise, he is a Jonah. One man is known to have hoodooed three schooners thus in a twelve-month. Very strange instances are related of ships "losing their luck" when a certain man sailed on them, and regaining it when he left.

If a cake of ice is accidentally dropped overboard when a vessel is preparing for a fishing trip the voyage will be fortunate; but if the hatch should fall into the hold there will result some dire disaster. Scarcely less serious is the trouble that will follow if, when the hatch is taken off, it is turned bottom up. In such a case there is sure to be a good deal of excitement and apprehension on board.

Clifton Johnson. *What They Say in New England,* A Book of Signs, Sayings, and Superstitions, pp. 254–256. Copyright, 1896, by Lee and Shepard. Boston.

From *Highways and Byways of New England,* including the States of Massachusetts, New Hampshire, Rhode Island, Connecticut, Vermont, and Maine, Written and Illustrated by Clifton Johnson, pp. 166–168. Copyright, 1915, by The Macmillan Company. New York and London. 1916.

If you watch a ship out of sight you will never see it again.

It is unlucky to have an umbrella brought on board.

It is unlucky to drive nails on Sunday.

Whistle for a breeze when it is calm; and if you would have the wind fair stick a knife in the after side of the main-mast.

If a bee or a small bird comes on board it brings good luck; but ill luck results when a hawk, owl, or crow alights in the rigging.

A horseshoe nailed to the mast is a protection against witches.

Have nothing to do with a man who comes on board with a black valise, and don't ship with him; for he is sure to be a Jonah.

> Sunday sail, never fail,
> Friday sail, ill luck and gale.

This last saying has lost much of its old-time influence, and Friday is a not unusual sailing-day if the weather is favorable.

Lucky and Unlucky Ships' Names

SHIPMASTERS are admittedly very superstitious folk. I once knew of a ship being named for a certain well-known cotton mill, because the said mill had always proved a lucky investment to its owners. Another instance came to my knowledge where a master, himself part owner, consulted a clairvoyant, about naming his new ship. When the applicant timidly suggested the name of *Pocahontas,* it was promptly rejected with the remark: "She was nothing but an old Indian woman. What do you want to name your vessel after her for? Call her the *Eagle Wing.*" And *Eagle Wing* it was.

By way of reënforcing beliefs of this particular kind, we find a newspaper writer saying, it is supposed in all sincerity, as otherwise his offence would be unpardonable: "Don't let us call any of the new ships for Uncle Sam's navy after the state of Maine. For my part, nothing would induce me to go aboard a new *Maine* or a new *Portland.* Like that watch of Captain Sigsbee, which has gone down into the ocean three times, the last plunge being caused by the explosion of the *Maine,* a superstitious person would prefer to be left at home." Whether or not the navy bureau shall listen to this plea, and change the name proposed for one of the new battleships, we fear that an ineffaceable stigma will hereafter rest upon these two names in the minds not alone of seafaring folk, but of the whole generation to whom the twin horrors which these names recall are so familiar.[1]

---

[1] From *The Myths and Fables of To-day,* by Samuel Adams Drake, pp. 82–83. Copyright, 1900, by Samuel Adams Drake. Boston: Lee and Shepard.

It would seem the most natural thing in the world that the vessels engaged in this [ice] traffic should bear such high-sounding and suggestive names as the *Ice-King*, or the *Ice-Monarch*, or even the *Iceberg*, instead of those of their owners, or their owners' wives and daughters, which seem so puerile and commonplace. Speaking of this to a large taker of marine risks, he replied, quite off-hand, that nobody would think of taking a risk on a ship having the word "ice" in any part of its name, because such names are considered unlucky.[2]

Ship Figureheads

You will wonder who was the most noted woodcarver. I should say that it was Joseph True, for his work, more than any of the others has been handed down. He was a particular friend of us both, and we were always welcome visitors with him. It was from him I learned many legends of the sea, many romantic tales which the quaint imagination of the old salts had woven around the relics of the past. He used to say that it was only natural that sailors during the long and tiresome voyages around the Horn or the Cape of Good Hope should attach undue importance to the influence which they believed the figureheads exerted on good and bad luck. Indeed some of them went so far as to attribute superhuman qualities to the wooden man or woman that adorned the prow, and woe betide the voyage if the figurehead received damage in any way.

One of the sailors had told him a story of what once happened in the Indian Ocean when the Captain of a full-rigged ship threatened a mutinous crew with a punishment he probably would never dare have inflicted. Those were the days of pirates and the crew, determining to become pirates themselves, had fastened the Captain and first mate into the cabin, but, armed only with knives, they could make little resistance to the fire of muskets opened on them from the cabin windows. Attracting the crew by a well-planned ruse to the starboard side of the vessel, the Captain, carrying a pail of black paint, and a paint brush, rushed from his hiding place toward the bowsprit. Quickly the crew darted after him with eyes blazing and knives uplifted in the sunlight, when, stopping in horror, they saw that the Captain was about to give the beautiful white-draped figure of a woman that surmounted the prow a coat of black paint. Dropping on their knees, they promised submission if only he would relinquish his fatal purpose.

To such tales of the sea we listened, our blood thrilling with excitement,

---

[2] From *The Pine-Tree Coast*, by Samuel Adams Drake, p. 193. Copyright, 1890, by Estes & Lauriat. Boston. 1891.

From *Memories of Old Salem*, Drawn from the Letters of a Great-Grandmother, by Mary Harrod Northend, pp. 86–88. Copyright, 1917, by Moffat, Yard and Company. New York.

till the old woodcarver, noting our disorder, would calm us by quiet talk. He showed us a bust of the Apostle Paul which he had been asked to make for the ship *St. Paul,* owned by one Stephen Phillips. This bust rode proudly on the prow for many years, when, for some unaccountable reason, probably because in need of repairs, it was removed just before the ship started for Manila. When the sailors discovered their loss they were very uneasy. John Hancock, the second mate, went as far as to say he refused to ship, giving as a reason his premonition that the vessel without its mascot would never return—which proved true. For many years I loved to look at this particular bust. It stood in front of an old shop, but it has recently been removed to other quarters.

Say "Minister"

THE man with the ear-rings had picked up a piece of shell and was attempting to drop it from the height of his shoulder through a crack in the wharf. He failed to accomplish his purpose though he tried again and again.

"Mr. Klunn, if you want to drop that shell through thar, just mention the minister," advised Cap'n Benson.

He had hardly spoken when Mr. Klunn let the shell fall, and it slipped straight through the crack. "I godfrey!" exclaimed the Cap'n, "I did it for you. I never known that to fail. When I been whaling, and we was cutting up the whale, you couldn't sometimes strike a j'int. You'd try and try and you couldn't strike it, and then you'd stop and say 'Minister!' and it was done already—you'd hit the j'int right off."

Why the Flounder Has a Wry Mouth and Two Colors

THE French fishermen account for the distorted mouth of the flounder by the following legend: St. Christopher, a martyr of the third century, one day took it into his head to bless the fishes and to preach to them. All the inhabitants of the deep came and listened with attention and respect except the flounder, who derided the holy man by making faces at him. The Saint, indignant at the insult, cursed the whole brood, and condemned them forever after to exhibit themselves with mouths awry.

In the course of ages the rebuke thus given by Saint Christopher seems to have wrought a change in the character of the flounder, for a Greek legend, still current at Constantinople, ascribes the discordant color of the

From *New England and Its Neighbors,* written and illustrated by Clifton Johnson, p. 328. Copyright, 1902, by The Macmillan Company. New York and London. 1912.

From *A Summer Cruise on the Coast of New England,* by Robert Carter, pp. 197–198. Copyright, 1864, by Crosby and Nichols; 1888, by Cupples and Hurd. Boston. Cupples and Hurd, Publishers.

two sides of the fish to the fact that when the Turks conquered Constantinople in 1453, some priests at a church near the Silivria gate were frying flounders for dinner just as the Infidels entered the city, and were among the first victims of the massacre. The fish, filled with pious respect for the Church, expressed their horror at the sacrilegious deed by jumping out of the frying-pan into a neighboring stream, whence they made their way to the sea, completely cooked on one side. In token of the miracle, the entire species has ever since exhibited the mark of the fire, generally on the right side; though, now and then, an eccentric individual displays it on the left side.

Snake Lore

"THE way a snake catches birds and frogs and things is not by chasing and grabbing them, but by charming them. It just gets its eyes on their eyes, and runs its tongue out and in, and then the bird can't move if it wanted to. The snake keeps that up a while, and then he can take his own time about doin' the swallorin'. You have to be kind o' careful yourself about not bein' charmed, specially by black snakes. I know there was some of the children out berrying one time, and Sarah Hill came near bein' charmed. They thought she was comin' along all right, when they noticed she warn't with 'em. They ran back then, and Sarah was standin' still lookin' right into a bush. They told her to come along, and she didn't say a word. Then they tried to pull her away; but she said, 'Don't,' because she saw such beautiful sights. Well, there was a black snake in that bush, and she was bein' charmed by it. Little more'n she might a got bit."

When a snake proposes to charm you, it looks you straight in the eye in such a sinister and unwinking way that you are fascinated and paralyzed.

I was told the story of a boy who was charmed one day. His companions found him looking at a snake and making a strange kind of noise. He did not come to himself until they killed the snake, and broke the spell.

An old farmer told me that one morning when he was out mowing his attention was attracted by a bird fluttering around a bush in a queer kind of way. "It was makin' sort of a mournful noise, and flutterin' round and round close to the bush. I went along up to the bush to see what the matter was. Then I see there was an adder in there watching of it, and its nest was in that bush. The snake was charming it; for I no sooner give the bush a little shake and took the snake's attention, than away the bird went as quick as a flash.

"I s'pose most any kind of a snake will charm birds and such things; but I don't s'pose these striped snakes are powerful enough to charm

From *What They Say in New England, A Book of Signs, Sayings, and Superstitions*, by Clifton Johnson, pp. 96–101, 102–103. Copyright, 1896, by Lee and Shepard. Boston.

people. Black snakes and rattlers will, though. My uncle got charmed once. He was goin' along through the woods with my father when he stopped and was gettin' left behind. My father called to him to come along; but he didn't pay no attention—just kep' lookin' at somethin'. My father see he was gettin' charmed by a snake. So he went back and give him a yank, and then they killed the snake. He said he wanted to come when father called him, but he couldn't. He said that he saw everything that was pretty,—all the colors he ever thought of and more too, and they seemed to be right in the snake's eyes."

Many still believe that in drinking from brooks one runs the risk of swallowing a young snake, which is liable to grow in the stomach, and become large and troublesome. In support of this idea, it is related that once there was a certain child that took large quantities of food, in particular a great deal of milk, yet became more and more emaciated. One night when the child was sitting at the table with a bowl of milk before it, of which it had not eaten, a great snake put its head out of the child's mouth. Apparently it was hungry, had scented the milk, and came up out of the child's stomach to get it. The child's father was by, and he gripped the snake by the neck, and pulled it out. It was four feet long.

Some say that instead of a bowl of milk on the table, it was a pailful on the kitchen-floor fresh from the cow.

Another telling of the story has it that a woman swallowed the snake. As it grew she was in great distress, so that finally she could not eat. At length her friends laid her down with her stomach on a chair, and put a basin of steaming hot food on the floor before her. That brought out the snake, and the woman got well.

It is bad enough to have a snake in your stomach, but you are even worse off if you meet with one of these hoop-snakes. Let one of those chase you, and you are a goner. They ain't afraid of a man no more'n nothin', and they can run faster'n any horse goin'. The way the snake does is to pick its tail up in its mouth, and then whirl over and over like a hoop. His tail is sharp-pointed and hard like a spike. When he catches up with you, he just takes his tail out of his mouth, and jabs it into you. Oh, I tell you, you'd better swallow a dozen snakes rather'n get one o' these hoop-snakes after you.

It is said that when a hoop-snake strikes a man it "blasts" him. I suppose that means he is paralyzed, turns black, shrivels up, and like enough blows away. When one of these hoop-snakes strikes its tail into anything wooden,—a hoe-handle, for instance,—it shivers the wood into splinters, just as if it had been struck by lightning.

Another snake you want to beware of is the "black racer snake." It is said that he has a bluish tinge, and that he will chase a man whenever he gets sight of one.

* * * * *

"I've hearn 'em tell about how that there was a little girl once that always used to eat her dinner out-doors when it was good weather. She'd get her plate full, and then she'd go off out back o' the barn somewhere, and nobody didn't know what she went off like that for. So after a while her folks followed her; and she went along out there by a stone wall and set down, and she rapped on her plate, and out there come a big rattlesnake, and went to eatin' off the plate with her. And when the snake got over on to her side of the plate too much, she'd rap him with her spoon, and push him away, and say, 'Keep back, Graycoat, on your own side.' Her folks didn't like to have her eatin' with a snake that way, and they sent her off to stay somewhere else. When she was gone, they went and killed the snake. Bimeby the little girl come home again, and then she found out her snake was killed. Arter that she kind o' pined away and died.

"I've hearn 'em tell about that a good many times, and I s'pose that's a pretty true story."

A Letter to the Rats

CONJURING RATS [1]

IN NEW ENGLAND, as well as in other parts of the United States, it is still believed, by certain persons, that if a house is infested with rats, these can be exiled by the simple process of writing them a letter, in which they are recommended to depart, and make their abode in another locality. The letter should indicate precisely the habitation to which they are assigned, and the road to be taken, and should contain such representations of the advantages of the change as may be supposed to affect the intelligence of the animal in question. This method of freeing a house from its domestic pests is well known, but is commonly regarded as a jest. As in most such cases, however, what is supposed to be mere humor is, in fact, the survival of a perfectly serious and very ancient usage. This custom, still existing in retired places, is illustrated by the following document, the genuineness of which may be relied on.

The country house of a gentleman, whose permanent home was in Boston, being infested by rats, the owner proposed to use poison; but the caretaker, who was in charge of the empty house, represented that there was a better way, namely, to address an epistle to the creatures; he prepared a letter, of which the following is a reproduction.

**** Maine, October 31, 1888

MESSRS. RATS AND Co.,—Having taken quite a deep interest in your welfare in regard to your winter quarters I thought I would drop you a few lines which might be of some considerable benefit to you in the future

[1] From "Conjuring Rats," by William Wells Newell, *The Journal of American Folk-Lore*, Vol. V (January–March, 1892), No. XVI, pp. 23–24. Copyright, 1892, by the American Folk-Lore Society. Boston and New York: Houghton, Mifflin and Company.

seeing that you have pitched your winter quarters at the summer residence of **** No. 1 Seaview Street, I wish to inform you that you will be very much disturbed during cold winter months as I am expecting to be at work through all parts of the house, shall take down ceilings, take up floors, and clean out every substance that would serve to make you comfortable, likewise there will be nothing left for you to feed on, as I shall remove every eatable substance; so you had better take up your abode elsewhere. I will here refer you to the farm of **** No. 6 Incubator Street, where you will find a splendid cellar well filled with vegetations of (all) kinds besides a shed leading to a barn, with a good supply of grain, where you can live snug and happy. Shall do you no harm if you heed to my advice; but if not, shall employ "Rough on Rats."

Yours,   ****

This letter was greased, rolled up, and thrust into the entrance of the rat-holes, in order that it might be duly read, marked, and inwardly digested; the result being, as the owner of the house was assured, that the number of the pests had been considerably diminished.

The reader cannot but admire the persuasive style of the Yankee farmer, and the judicious mixture of argument, blandishment, and terror, exhibited in the document; while in the choice of the barn of a neighbor, recommended as a desirable place of abode, is shown a shrewdness worthy of its reward.

AUNT WEED'S RAT LETTER [2]

It was found tucked away in a crevice in the cellar wall, after the old house in East Sandwich was "gone in ruins." It was a piece of paper, good old paper made from linen rags, or it would not have remained intact and the writing on it legible after long years in that interstice between granite block and granite block of the potato pit. It was damp, of course, even in that inner cellar far from the bulkhead door; it had been damp even before the roof leaked and the floors began to sag. The piece of paper, apparently a second sheet of a folded over note, had weathered successfully under those unfavorable conditions some forty years' immuration, the last ten of which the house was unoccupied.

Since it has come into possession of Mrs. Leon Currier, the great-great-niece of the Mrs. Abigail Weed who wrote it, it has had a certain local currency as "Emmy's Rat Letter." It now hangs, framed, in Mrs. Currier's parlor. It has for fellows there other relics of old times, an inlaid candle stand, fanback windsors, a Currier and Ives of Lincoln, the most generous flip glass I ever saw, a Washington and Lafayette pitcher in blue and white,

[2] From *New Hampshire Neighbors*, Country Folks and Things in the White Hills, by Cornelius Weygandt, pp. 191–194. Copyright, 1937, by Henry Holt and Company, Inc. New York.

a pewter wafer box and a sugar shaker in soft paste Staffordshire known in the family as "Mrs. Phillpotts." It has been widely copied, and it has been photographed, but I cannot discover that any one in recent years has tried the efficacy of its formula by inserting a copy in cellar or chamber or corn loft. Perhaps they feel that what banished, three generations ago, the gentle creatures of dark mole gray known as black rats, would fail in this day and generation with the predatory brown rats that have supplanted them.

Inasmuch as the exorcism is written with a dearth of punctuation and capitalization, and as it has a word or two of unfamiliar or uncertain meaning, I cannot reproduce it exactly as it was written. I must print it so that its meaning can be followed as it is read, and I must add a little exegesis. It is dated "Sandwich May the 9th 1845." It reads as follows:

"I have bourn with you till my patience is all gone. I cannot find words bad enough to express what I feel, you black devils you are, gnawing our trace corn while we are asleep! And even when we are awake you have the audacity to set your infernal jaws to going. Now, spirits of the bottomless pit, depart from this place with all speed! Look not back! Begone, or you are ruined! If you could know as much as I do, you never would take another thing from here. I will keep nothing to myself. You shall hear the whole. We are preparing water [to] drown you; fire to roast you; cats to catch you; and clubs to maul you. Unless you want your detested garments dyed in fire and brimstone, you satans, quit here and go to Ike Nute's! This is for cellar rats. Please give notice to those in the chamber. There are many of us in the garret plotting against you, when our eyes are open all but one poor female who is affraid of life. But the rest is not affraid I can tell you. There is our bill, and I leve if they get hold of you [you] would think you're in wire cage. A hint to the wise is sufficient. To the bigest and most inventive rat.

Mrs. Weed."

It is necessary, perhaps, to explain that "trace corn" is seed corn bound together in a long string by the plaiting together of the husks turned back from the ears. Twenty such strung ears make a "trace." "Leve" is the old word of the countryside for "believe." The chamber is the low attic over the ell of the one-story house, as the garret is the high attic over the main part of that house. One-story house proper and ell, together with garret and chamber, make the story-and-a-half house typical of New England.

A re-reading of the exorcism tells us the writer is playful as well as earnest. She is making game at the same time that she is half hoping the letter will rid her home of rats. She is laughing at herself for writing the charm and trusting there is enough power in it to induce her to feel the thrill of making magic. Light from her family on her personality and character make clearer, perhaps, certain of the letter's phrases. She was a prim and exact little person who was, as she says in the letter, "affraid of life."

Her great-grandniece says she was timorous about everything from mice to tramps. Mistress Abigail lost her husband and returned with her daughter to her childhood's home where she lived with her brothers William and Steven Cogan.

As I read it first I could not but wonder if the hocus-pocus of it was veiled language threatening reprisals against some one who was vilifying the old lady or some of her family. "To the bigest and most inventive rat" would so well suit a fabricator of lies. I have dismissed any such inter-pretation. I think it is a charm, an exorcism to rid the house of black rats. Written apparently on the back of a sheet from an old letter which was saved, no doubt, because it had little writing on it, for scrap paper, it has not the importance of a document written on unused paper. It is not to be taken too seriously. I say this, not because charms and incantations are taboo to Puritanism. They are not, as the world knows. There was witch-craft in Sandwich, New Hampshire, as well as in Salem, Massachusetts, plenty of it when witchcraft was in season. I say the exorcism is not to be taken too seriously because of the mockery with which it is written. The writer had a sense of humor. She was play-acting in writing it, but many a play-actor has convinced herself that her rôle was real life. I believe that she had by her in some old almanac, that repository of strange odds and ends, some sort of incantation against rats; or that she remembered the phrases of some evangelist tearing into the Devil. I believe she was half satiric, half serious in what she wrote, that it is a mock exorcism as well as an exorcism. It has affiliations with well-known charms, even to those in Anglo-Saxon days. Whatever your interpretation of Aunt Weed's Rat Letter, it drives you to own that there were complexities as well as sim-plicities in back-country life three generations ago.

It should perhaps be added that it is the tradition of the countryside that the rats did leave the cellar of the old lady's house after she put in it the letter to them, and that they did go, as she exorcised them, to Ike Nute's.

Driving a Witch Out of the Soap

IN LATER years two pounds of potash in dark-colored pieces were purchased at the store and put into the melted fat. This potash was dangerous stuff to handle. A man in Scituate, while breaking some pieces for his wife to use, made a piece fly into his eye and he lost his sight. Into the melted grease the lye was poured a little at a time, some one stirring the hot mass continuously for all one day and a part of the next with a long stick. The stick, usually of apple tree, was a sort of mascot, for good luck in soap

From *A Narrative History of the Town of Cohasset, Massachusetts,* by E. Victor Bigelow, p. 234. Copyright, 1898, by E. Victor Bigelow. Published under the Auspices of the Committee on Town History. 1898.

making was not at everybody's bidding. Too much or too little lye or some unknown defect would easily spoil the soap. This uncertain behavior gave rise to witch stories, and a certain woman in Beechwood was accused of bewitching people's soap. To drive her out of the soap a black-handled butcher knife was once stabbed into the soap, and the soap-maker claimed that it cut off the witch's ear, so that she wore a shawl over her head ever afterwards to conceal the wound.

The Fairies Who Didn't Stay

FAIRY faith is, we may safely say, now dead everywhere,—buried, indeed, —for the mad painter Blake saw the funeral of the last of the little people, and an irreverent English Bishop has sung their requiem. It never had much hold upon the Yankee mind, our superstititions being mostly of a sterner and less poetical kind. The Irish Presbyterians who settled in New Hampshire about the year 1720 brought indeed with them, among other strange matters, potatoes and fairies; but while the former took root and flourished among us, the latter died out, after lingering a few years in a very melancholy and disconsolate way, looking regretfully back to their green turf dances, moonlight revels, and cheerful nestling around the shealing fires of Ireland. The last that has been heard of them was some forty or fifty years ago in a tavern house in S——, New Hampshire. The landlord was a spiteful little man, whose sour, pinched look was a standing libel upon the state of his larder. He made his house so uncomfortable by his moroseness that travellers even at nightfall pushed by his door and drove to the next town. Teamsters and drovers, who in those days were apt to be very thirsty, learned, even before temperance societies were thought of, to practise total abstinence on that road, and cracked their whips and goaded on their teams in full view of a most tempting array of bottles and glasses, from behind which the surly little landlord glared out upon them with a look which seemed expressive of all sorts of evil wishes, broken legs, overturned carriages, spavined horses, sprained oxen, unsavory poultry, damaged butter, and bad markets. And if, as a matter of necessity, to "keep the cold out of his stomach," occasionally a way-farer stopped his team and ventured to call for "somethin' warmin'," the testy publican stirred up the beverage in such a spiteful way, that, on receiving it foaming from his hand, the poor customer was half afraid to open his mouth, lest the red-hot flip iron should be plunged down his gullet.

As a matter of course, poverty came upon the house and its tenants like an armed man. Loose clapboards rattled in the wind; rags fluttered from the broken windows; within doors were tattered children and scanty fare.

From *Prose Works of John Greenleaf Whittier*, Vol. II, pp. 237–240. Entered according to Act of Congress, in the year 1866, by John Greenleaf Whittier, in the Clerk's Office of the District Court of the District of Massachusetts. Boston: Ticknor and Fields.

The landlord's wife was a stout, buxom woman, of Irish lineage, and, what with scolding her husband and liberally patronizing his bar in his absence, managed to keep, as she said, her "own heart whole," although the same could scarcely be said of her children's trousers and her own frock of homespun. She confidently predicted that "a betther day was coming," being, in fact, the only thing hopeful about the premises. And it did come sure enough. Not only all the regular travellers on the road made a point of stopping at the tavern, but guests from all the adjacent towns filled its long-deserted rooms,—the secret of which was, that it had somehow got abroad that a company of fairies had taken up their abode in the hostelry and daily held conversation with each other in the capacious parlor. I have heard those who at the time visited the tavern say that it was literally thronged for several weeks. Small, squeaking voices spoke in a sort of Yankee-Irish dialect, in the haunted room, to the astonishment and admiration of hundreds. The inn, of course, was blessed by this fairy visitation; the clapboards ceased their racket, clear panes took the place of rags in the sashes, and the little till under the bar grew daily heavy with coin. The magical influence extended even farther; for it was observable that the landlord wore a good-natured face, and that the landlady's visits to the gin-bottle were less and less frequent. But the thing could not, in the nature of the case, continue long. It was too late in the day and on the wrong side of the water. As the novelty wore off, people began to doubt and reason about it. Had the place been traversed by a ghost or disturbed by a witch they could have acquiesced in it very quietly; but this outlandish belief in fairies was altogether an overtask for Yankee credulity. As might have been expected, the little strangers, unable to breathe in an atmosphere of doubt and suspicion, soon took their leave, shaking off the dust of their elfin feet as a testimony against an unbelieving generation. It was, indeed, said that certain rude fellows from the Bay State pulled away a board from the ceiling and disclosed to view the fairies in the shape of the landlady's three slatternly daughters. But the reader who has any degree of that charity which thinks no evil will rather credit the statement of the fairies themselves, as reported by the mistress of the house, "that they were tired of the new country, and had no pace of their lives among the Yankees, and were going back to Ould Ireland."

WEATHER LORE

Signs and Seasons

THE skunks were coming in early from the woods and renting houseroom under the barns for the winter. The coats of the foxes were heavy. Up under the walnut tree the nuts were falling by the bushel. Down along Warren's brook the muskrat homes were going up in great number and size, from three to seven feet long and from two to three feet high. There would be a long hard winter.

Out in the barnyard the hens were "curling up and picking," so it was soon going to rain. It was the end of the second quarter of the moon so tonight there would be a change in the weather. This line storm of March was clearing warm, so it would be warm in The Town for the next six months, or at least there would be an early spring. The last three days of January or June or August or any other month had been rainy, the next month then would be too rainy for much outdoor work. Dame Messer, the great hill east of the Pond, was wearing her nightcap of fog, it would be a long time before the storm was over. The Pond was roaring tonight, it would soon be yielding under a big thaw. Cobwebs on the morning grass meant a clear pleasant day, if one would but notice their ecstasy of lace. Sundogs were showing their broken rainbows over old Tory hill in Langdon, so the winter day would be very cold, or the summer day very hot. Signs! Signs everywhere for the man who knew his acres and their heavens, and one must learn to read them all aright.[1]

There are all sorts of ways to prophesy the weather when you go fishing. In Boston there was "Old Solitaire," a one-legged gull who frequented the wharves for years, and whose presence always meant a hard blow ahead. In Provincetown, when you see the gulls flying high over the harbor, be ready for a bad blow within a matter of hours. And if you look across the water, at the Truro shore, and the land looms high, you have another sure sign of heavy weather.

Your rheumatism should warn you of an easterly; but if it is hazy and a yeller-eyed sou'wester is in prospect, you may suffer no more than a wetting through the neck of your oil jacket.

There are ways, too, of looking still further ahead. When the oysters bed deep at Wellfleet, there will be a hard winter, and Provincetown Harbor will fill up with pack ice in February—floes so wide there won't be enough open water for a duck to light on, and so thick only the flatfish can navigate below. But if a chicken's gizzard comes away easily from the inner skin, look for an "open winter"; and if a school of herring is raised in January, stow your overcoat for another year—especially if the ducks start laying ahead of schedule and the willows on the swamp banks bud too soon.[2]

---

[1] From *New Hampshire Borns a Town*, by Marion Nicholl Rawson, pp. 138–139. Copyright, 1942, by E. P. Dutton & Co., Inc. New York.

[2] From *Cape Cod Pilot*, by Jeremiah Digges, with Editorial and Research Assistance of the Members of the Federal Writers' Project, pp. 240–241. American Guide Series, Federal Writers' Project, Works Progress Administration for the State of Massachusetts. Copyright, 1937, by Poor Richard Associates. Provincetown and New York: Modern Pilgrim Press and the Viking Press.

Prognostics of the Weather

ANIMALS, by some peculiar sensibility to electrical or other atmospheric influence, often indicate changes of the weather, by their uneasy motions and habits; for instance, asses bray more than ordinary, and shake their ears, before rain.

> When the ass begins to bray,
> We surely shall have rain that day.

Again,

> When the donkey blows his horn,
> 'Tis time to house your hay and corn.

Swine will be restless, grunt loudly, squeal and jerk up their heads, before high winds. Moles will cast up their hills before rain. Horses will stretch out their necks, sniff the air, and assemble in the corner of the field, before rain. Rats and mice will be restless and squeak much. Foxes and dogs will growl and bark more than usual, and dogs will grow sleepy and dull, and eat grass, before showery weather, and cats will lick their bodies and wash their faces. Cattle will leave off feeding, and chase each other in their pastures. Sheep will spring about the meadows, more than usual. The change from fair weather to foul makes all animated nature restless and uneasy.

ANTS.—Bustle and activity in the ant-hills may be regarded as a sign of rain. Before a storm, these curious insects appear all in motion together, and carry their eggs about from place to place. If they clear their holes and pile the dirt high before eleven in the morning, it seldom fails to be fair the rest of the day.

*   *   *   *   *

BATS flitting about late in the evening, in spring and autumn, foretell a fine day on the morrow.

BEES, when they remain in their hives, or fly but a short distance from them, foretell showers and rainy weather.

BEETLES flying about late at evening foretell a fine day on the morrow.

BIRDS are particularly sensitive as to changes of the weather. The gull, seemingly one of the most stupid of birds, will fly inland, on the approach of a storm, long before it appears, and will fly out to sea again when fair weather is coming. Swallows fly low before the approach of a storm, and high when fair weather is upon us. When the blue jay comes near the houses and screams, foul weather is at hand. The peacock will squall, the guinea-hen call "come back," the cock crow upon the fence less than usual, the quail call out "more wet," and be more noisy than he is wont. The crow will "caw," the owl screech, the water-fowl scream and plunge into the water, the thrush will sing loud and long, and most of the bird tribe will pick their feathers, plume themselves, and fly to their nests, before stormy weather, seeming anxious to avoid trouble.

BLUE SKY.—When there is a piece of blue sky seen on a rainy morning, big enough, as the proverb says, "to make a Dutchman a pair of breeches," we shall probably have a fine afternoon.[1]

* * * * *

BUTTERFLIES, when they appear early, are sometimes forerunners of fine weather. The first kind that appears in spring is called the Sulphur Butterfly,—his wings being yellow; the next, called the tortoise-shell butter-fly, appears later; and still later, the white, or cabbage butterfly.

* * * * *

CANDLEMAS DAY.—(Feb. 2d.)

> If Candlemas Day be fair and bright,
> Winter will have another flight;
> But if Candlemas Day be cloudy and rain,
> Winter has gone, not to come again.

CHICKENS, when they are more noisy than usual, are said by some to prognosticate rain.

CHICKWEED.—When open in the morning, fair weather may be expected; when closed, rain. It is called, like the pimpernell, the poor man's weather-glass, or barometer. As long as they continue to unfold and display themselves, the whole day may be depended on. If, however, the flowers withdraw into their green envelope, the pedestrian need wish no better hint to take his umbrella in his walk.

* * * * *

CHRISTMAS.—The clemency of the season at Christmas is a blessing to the poor, whatever it be to the coal-merchants. We may fear, however, for its effects on health, if there be truth in the old adage:

> When Christmas is white
> The graveyard is lean;
> But fat is the graveyard
> When Christmas is green.

* * * * *

COBWEBS.—If on the grass early in the morning, they indicate fair weather that day.

---

[1] From *The (Old) Farmer's Almanack,* Calculated on a New and Improved Plan for the Year of Our Lord 1855, by Robert B. Thomas, p. 46. Entered, according to Act of Congress, in the year 1854, by Jenks, Hickling & Swan, in the Clerk's Office of the District Court of the District of Massachusetts. Boston.

From Actual Observation—Alphabetically Arranged. Collected from Various Sources. and. Prepared for this Almanac.

Instead of repeating the Weather Table, inserted on this page for several years, and which may be referred to in previous numbers of the Almanac, we have thought it would be more acceptable to our readers to give an alphabetical list, to be continued from year to year, until completed, of Prognostics of the Weather, from the experience of actual observers. We should be very glad to have our farming friends aid us in this plan, by forwarding their own observations.—R. B. T.

CORN HUSKS.—If these adhere closely and are more difficult to pull apart than usual, it is a sign of a hard winter.[2]

COLORS of various shades in the sky and clouds are tokens of different phenomena, or changes. Much red, says Forster, always forbodes wind or rain. . . . Sometimes, however, much red indicates a fine day, if the morning be gray. The following lines of the poet are familiar to most of our readers.

> An evening red and a morning gray,
> Will set the traveller on his way;
> But an evening gray and a morning red,
> Will pour down rain on the pilgrim's head.

A greenish color of the sky near the horizon often shows that we may expect more wet weather. The most beautiful greenish tints are seen in autumn, and in that season the purple of the falling haze is often a sign of a continuation of fine weather.

* * * * *

CROWS.—These utter a peculiar cry before rain, different from their usual voice.

* * * * *

DANDELIONS.—When these blow out full, early in the morning, expect fair weather that day.

* * * * *

FISH.—When fish bite readily, and gambol near the surface of streams or ponds, it is an indication that foul or wet weather is near.[3]

FLIES.—These and various sorts of volatile insects, become more troublesome, and sting and bite more than usual, before, as well as in the intervals of, rainy weather, particularly in autumn. This remark applies to several kinds of flies. Horse-flies are more troublesome before the fall of rain.

FLOWERS.—Many of these are excellent indicators of approaching changes by their opening and shutting, and other motions. We wish some observing friend would note these, and give us the result. For instance, the evening primrose opens at sunset and closes at daybreak.

---

[2] From *The (Old) Farmer's Almanack,* Calculated on a New and Improved Plan, for the Year of Our Lord 1856, by Robert B. Thomas, p. 46. Entered, according to Act of Congress, in the year 1855, by Hickling, Swan & Brown, in the Clerk's Office of the District Court of the District of Massachusetts. Boston.

[3] From *The (Old) Farmer's Almanack,* Calculated on a New and Improved Plan, for the Year of Our Lord 1857, by Robert B. Thomas, p. 46. Entered, according to Act of Congress, in the year 1856, by Hickling, Swan & Brown, in the Clerk's Office of the District Court of the District of Massachusetts. Boston.

Linnaeus has enumerated forty-six flowers that possess sensibility to the weather. He divides them into three classes. 1. Meteoric flowers, which less accurately observe the hour of folding, but are expanded sooner or later, according to the cloudiness, moisture, or pressure of the air. 2. Tropical flowers, that open in the morning, and close before evening, every day; their hour of expanding becoming earlier or later, as the length of the day increases or decreases. 3. Equinoctial flowers, which open at an exact hour of the day, and, for the most part, close at another determinate hour.

*   *   *   *   *

FROGS, by their clamorous croaking, indicate rainy weather; as does, likewise, their coming abroad in great numbers of an evening; but this sign applies more obviously to toads.[4]

GEESE are not such "geese" as we think them; their movements are impelled and controlled by strong and almost unerring instincts. When washing, or taking wing with a clamorous noise and flying to water, they portend rain. Geese are excellent guards against fire or thieves, always watchful, and giving notice by their noise of any unusual movements about them. When wild geese are observed to migrate southward or westward in greater numbers than usual in autumn and winter, they are said to indicate hard weather; when to the northward, warmer weather. In general, the early appearance of flocks of geese or other wild fowls in the south foreshows a severe winter. A curious illustration of their instinct is seen in their flight, which is wedge-shaped, the leader cleaving the air for those who follow, and at stated intervals falling in the rear, and his place being supplied by another, who pursues the same course; which proceeding will at once be seen to facilitate as much as possible the flight and preserve the strength of the flock.

GENTIANELLA.—This dark and lovely plant is said to "open its blue eyes to greet the mid-day sun, but to close its petals against the approach of a shower."

GNATS.—When these bite keenly and fly near the ground, we look for wind or rain; when they fly in a vortex in the beams of the setting sun, they forebode fair weather; when they frisk about more widely in the open air at eve, they foreshow heat; and when they assemble under trees and bite more than usual, they indicate rain.

GOATS-BEARD.—This plant, called also salsify and oyster-plant, will not unclose its flowers in cloudy weather. From its habit of closing its flowers at noon it has received the common name of "Go-to-bed-at-noon,"

---

[4] From *The (Old) Farmer's Almanack*, Calculated on a New and Improved Plan, for the Year of Our Lord 1858, by Robert B. Thomas, p. 46. Entered, according to Act of Congress, in the year 1857, by Hickling, Swan & Brewer, in the Clerk's Office of the District Court of the District of Massachusetts. Boston.

and in many districts of England the farmers' boys are said to regulate their dinner-hour by the closing of the goats-beard.

GOSSAMER, as it is called, being the fine web of a certain species of spider, floating in the air in abundance and lodging on the trees or rigging of vessels, and on other objects, affords a sign of fine settled weather in autumn, as does the much covering of the ground and herbage by the woof of the spiders in general.

*　　*　　*　　*　　*

HAWKWEED.—Most plants of this tribe open their flowers at morning, but go to sleep, or close them, in the afternoon, especially if rain is near.[5]

Signs in the Sea's Rote

I HEAR the sea, very strong and loud at the North, which is not unusual after violent atmospheric agitations, and when the wind has lulled. They call this the "rote," or "rut," of the sea. Either expression is correct. The Latin *rota* is the root of both words. The "ruts" in the road are the result of rolling, or the repeated and successive pressure of blows of the wheel. Rotation means repetition as well as succession. To learn a thing by *rote*, is to possess the mind of it by repeated readings or hearings. The *rote* or *rut* of sea, therefore, means only the noise produced by the action of the surf, the successive breaking of wave after wave on the shore; and the beach means precisely the smooth shore, beaten by this eternal restlessness of the ocean. There is another expression for the same thing, sometimes used instead of "rut" or "rote"; I hear our people speak of the "cry of the sea," not an unapt phrase to signify the deep, hollow-sounding, half-groaning, or loud wailing voice of the ocean, uttered as if in resentment of its violent disturbance by the winds. As an indication of wind and weather, the rote of the sea is generally understood to signify either that the wind has recently left the quarter whence the rote is heard, or else is soon to spring up in that quarter.[1]

---

[5] From *The (Old) Farmer's Almanack,* Calculated on a New and Improved Plan, for the Year of Our Lord 1859, by Robert B. Thomas, p. 46. Entered according to Act of Congress, in the year 1858, by Hickling, Swan & Brewer, in the Clerk's Office of the District Court of the District of Massachusetts. Boston.

---

[1] Quoted from Daniel Webster. In *Marshfield, 70°–40′ W: 42°–5′ N, The Autobiography of a Pilgrim Town,* Being an Account of Three Hundred Years of a New England Town; Founded by the Pilgrims; Lived in and Developed by the Royalists; Adopted by Daniel Webster & Beloved by Many of the Ancestors of Those Who Today Make it Their Home, 1640–1940, p. 214. Copyright, 1940, by Marshfield Tercentenary Committee. Marshfield, Massachusetts.

Cf. Henry David Thoreau, *Cape Cod* (Boston, 1896). Vol. I, pp. 129–130.

The air here was tremulous with the steady roll of the surf. To an untrained ear, this sound of the sea is the sound of the sea. But to those who follow the sea, or live by its shores, the dash of the breakers against the rocks would never be mistaken for the long roll upon the beach. This noise of the rote is also an infallible sign of a change of wind or weather; for the quarter out of which it comes to your ears is that from which the wind will blow before many hours. In thick weather, pilots feel their way among the crookedest passages, safely guided only by the echo from the shores or sound of the surf. "I speak of pilots who know the wind by its scent, and the wave by its taste, and could steer to any port between Boston and Mount Desert, simply by listening to the peculiar sound of the surf on each island, beach, and line of rocks along the coast." [2]

CURES

Simples and Benefits

. . . THE young doctor learned about simples and benefits, the efficacy of herbs, that a plaster of onions would save a lung patient, that grease rubbed on the soles of the feet was sovereign for heading off colds in the head and the "prevailing distemper," that salt pork was sovereign for almost every disease, especially when a slab of it was worn about the throat, or over an infected part. A rush to the cobwebby cellar and the pork barrel saved many a life, the heavy brine killing all of the germs which might have accrued to barrel or pork during its cellar months. Tea was good for sore eyes, mashed-up potato or butter for burns, mud for bee stings, kerosene on a feather for a sore throat, a pin run through a wart would be its finish, whiskey with honey and butter for bronchial gruntings, cornmeal and honey for a sty, a brew of tobacco to deaden pain, and so on and on. What was good in The Town was just as good over in Marlow or Keene.

Roots and Herbs

AN OLD character, Chucky Reuben used to help Mother gather her roots

---

[2] From *The Pine-Tree Coast*, by Samuel Adams Drake, p. 116. Copyright, 1890, by Estes & Lauriat. Boston. 1891.

From *New Hampshire Borns a Town*, by Marion Nicholl Rawson, p. 140. Copyright, 1942, by E. P. Dutton & Co., Inc. New York.

From *Village Down East*, Sketches of Village Life on the Northeast Coast of New England before "Gas Buggies" Came, from Conversations with Zackery Adams, Duck Trap Cove, Maine, by John Wallace, p. 62. Copyright, 1943, by Stephen Daye Press, Inc. Brattleboro, Vermont.

and herbs. He wuz a Cobe, but there bein' two Charles Cobes—descent of Ed and Reuben; distant rel'tives—we diff'rentated 'em that way: Charles Ed and Chucky Reuben.

I dunno how Mother got to know so much about nature remidies, but she doctered all our fam'ly and half the neighbors of her time.

In helpin' her scour the fields and woods for medicine greejentses, Chucky took in (and made up), consid'able "root-'n-yarb l'arnin'," as he called it, and after Mother passed on, he confided to me, that if he had his rights, he'd have a shingle hung out and tote a docter's satchel 'round, "a-treatin' folks cons'itutions."

"Lis'n," he'd say, "I kin fix what ails ye! Rheumatiz? Chaw some Canady thistle root, like I do. Knocks the creaks an' aches right out-a ye! Never have no more toothache neither. Fever? Chaw the peth of March turnip root. Chills? Try the Thompsonian treatment: red-pepper tea an' dry pepper in yer stockin's."

"Fidgets? Steep some dried skullcap or archangel leaves fer a nerveen. A cold? Lobelia tea mixed with West Injie m'lasses will throw it off (a-vomitin' ye), an' fer a cough: take jingshang or spike-root tea, or a cough syrup made of the squeezin's of fir-balsom blisters, or jest water, syrupied with brake root peth."

(Dunno but I'd ought-a hang out a shingle myself—the way I'm reelin' this off.) But Chucky'd run on jest so: "A puffball mushroom to stop bleedin', yaller dock or burr dock b'iled in hard cider is good fer biles (modified with wicky-up),"—and so on, no end.

Mother took pains a-brewin' her herbs and roots, but Chucky—bein' shif'less—carried his 'round in his pockets, and jest chawed 'em raw—and lived to be nigh ninety.

Tonics and Family Rites

Sometimes instead of baskets they [the Indians] sold medicines, various salves and tonics. In the disposal of these I think they were more successful. Baskets were after all luxuries, whereas a beneficial mixture, made exclusively as they always averred from the herbs of the fields and tested as to its efficacy upon any number of Indians, might prove in the long run less dear than even infrequent doctor's bills. Moreover, since the nature of man is ever to seek release from major or minor bodily ills and likewise seldom to be averse to the delineation of them, these wandering herbalists did no little business especially among the outlying districts.

My mother stoutly set her face against their remedies. She felt that we, as more enlightened town dwellers, should not be led away by them. But my father grievously disappointed her by purchasing each spring from a very tall and old Indian, who claimed to be a Penobscot chief, a great

From *A Goodly Heritage*, by Mary Ellen Chase, pp. 78–80. Copyright, 1932, by Henry Holt and Company, Inc. New York.

bottle labeled "Kickapoo Indian Sagwaw." This concoction, which was black and syrupy, emitted a really delectable smell. With each yearly acquisition my father alternately sniffed the contents and read the ingredients, which with commendable if not complete honesty were printed upon the label beneath the feathered head of an Indian chief.

"Horehound, anise, checkerberry, sarsaparilla, camomile, wormwood"— thus he would enumerate to my mother as he laughed at her misgivings. "Herbs made for the service of man."

But she remained obdurate until three unopened bottles had collected on the shelf in the cellarway. What influence finally proved her undoing, I do not know. Perhaps it was her innate thrift, for my father's relative extravagance caused her no little anxiety. At all events, one March morning she began to alternate the Sagwaw with the sulphur and molasses, which with the coming of spring was always dealt out to us on the principle of three mornings in succession followed by a skipping of the three ensuing.

This consumption of sulphur and molasses was a rite familiar to rural New England and needs neither introduction nor description to middle-aged and elderly New England readers. The two ingredients were mixed in a large bowl to the consistency of a heavy paste. In our large family we ranged ourselves before breakfast in a line and received, each from the same big spoon, a mouthful, which in the phraseology of to-day would be termed "capacity." The taste was not unpleasant, although the double nature of the dose sometimes made swallowing a long and complicated process. Much easier and more agreeable in every way was the Sagwaw, which, though it was perhaps a trifle bitter, savored of spring woods and disappeared with ease.

Whether we received any benefits from either of these tonics beyond the sense of family solidarity which they engendered I cannot say. Certain it is that we received no harm. I am sure, too, that my nephews and nieces, who are beset by baby specialists, carrots, orange juice, and spinach, present no better appearance of health than did we in our day. It is at least a matter of some regret that they will never know that family rite, instituted by sulphur and molasses, alleviated by Kickapoo Indian Sagwaw, and carrying in its long wake such resultant humor in reminiscence.

Meetin' Seed

IN THE herb garden grew three free-growing plants, all three called indifferently in country tongue, "meetin' seed." They were Fennel, Dill, and Caraway, and similar in growth and seed. . . . Their name was given because, in summer days of years gone by, nearly every woman and child carried to "meeting" on Sundays bunches of the ripe seeds of one or all

From *Old Time Gardens,* Newly Set Forth, by Alice Morse Earle, pp. 341–343. Copyright, 1901, by The Macmillan Company. New York and London. 1902.

of these three plants, to nibble throughout the long prayers and sermon.

It is fancied that these herbs were anti-soporific, but I find no record of such power. On the contrary, Galen says Dill "procureth sleep, wherefore garlands of Dill are worn at feasts." A far more probable reason for its presence at church was the quality assigned to it by Pliny and other herbalists down to Gerarde, that of staving the "yeox or hicket or hicquet," otherwise the hiccough. If we can judge by the manifold remedies offered to allay this affliction, it was certainly very prevalent in ancient times. Cotton Mather wrote a bulky medical treatise entitled *The Angel of Bethesda*. It was never printed; the manuscript is owned by the American Antiquarian Society. The character of this medico-religious book may be judged by this opening sentence of his chapter on the hiccough:—

> The Hiccough or the Hicox rather, for it's a Teutonic word that signifies to sog, appears a Lively Emblem of the battle between the Flesh and the Spirit in the Life of Piety. The Conflict in the Pious Mind gives all the Trouble and same uneasiness as Hickox. Death puts an end to the Conflict.

Parson Mather gives Tansy and Caraway as remedies for the hiccough, but far better still—spiders, prepared in various odious ways; I prefer Dill.

Peter Parley said that "a sprig of Fennel was the theological smelling-bottle of the tender sex, and not unfrequently of the men, who from long sitting in the sanctuary, after a week of labor in the field, found themselves tempted to sleep, would sometimes borrow a sprig of Fennel, to exorcise the fiend that threatened their spiritual welfare."

Old-fashioned folk kept up a constant nibbling in church, not only of these three seeds, but of bits of Cinnamon or Lovage root, or, more commonly still, the roots of Sweet Flag. Many children went to brooksides and the banks of ponds to gather these roots. . . .

Plantain

A TOAD was seen fighting with a spider in Rhode-Island; and when the former was bit, it hopped to a plantain leaf, bit off a piece, and then engaged with the spider again. After this had been repeated sundry times, a spectator pulled up the plantain, and put it out of the way. The toad,

From *The Farmer's Almanack*, Calculated on a New and Improved Plan, for the Year of Our Lord, 1798, No. VI, by Robert B. Thomas. Boston: Printed by Manning & Loring, for John West, Proprietor of the Copy-Right.
The essential element in the story of the duel between the Toad and the Spider lies in the doctrine that animals know what is good for them, and in particular that they instinctively seek curative herbs when they have suffered an injury. This doctrine is universal.—George Lyman Kittredge, *The Old Farmer and His Almanack* (Boston, 1904), pp. 119–120.

on being bit again, jumped to where the plantain had stood; and as it was not to be found, she hopped round several times, turned over on her back swelled up, and died immediately. This is an evident demonstration that the juice of the plantain is an antidote against the bites of those venomous insects.

Snake Ball

SYLVESTER WOODBRIDGE, [Southampton] merchant, advertised in 1793, "Satin, West India rum, snake balls, etc." He closes with an invitation to all indebted to him "to make immediate payment, as the day of patience with them will soon expire, when the law will bite-and-sting."

A snake ball was a small piece of stone or bone or other substance which is placed on the bite of a poisonous snake to absorb or charm away the poison. The common people believed in this means of cure.

Skunk Oil and Other Remedies

(CONVERSATION of Mary and Walter Burroughs and Fred Mills, Alstead, New Hampshire)

Mary: There were a lot of weather signs as to what kind of winter you were going to have. What was the one about the first days of the year?

Walter: The first twelve days of Christmas—each day described the weather of each month of the year.

Mary: Was it your brother Charles who used to do that? Charles was a very wise man.

Walter: Charles would keep track of that.

Mary: Charles, he was really the oldest brother. Very tall, very handsome man. Terribly hampered by asthma all his life so that he couldn't live a full life. But he was a mighty man. He was strong, and could do things. He was absolutely honest. It is a law that you weren't to hunt on somebody's posted woodland, for instance. And a conscientious, ordinary man would think he was pretty virtuous if he just didn't shoot anything when he crossed it. And some would unload their guns. But Charles would walk around the boundaries—all the way around—to avoid trespassing. And the game warden used to cooperate with him and rely on him—bring him wild cats to skin and things like that.

From *Historic Hampshire in the Connecticut Valley*, Happenings in a Charming Old New England County from the Time of the Dinosaur Down to about 1900, by Clifton Johnson, p. 223. Copyright, 1932, by The Northampton Historical Society. Springfield, Massachusetts: Milton Bradley Company.

As told by Mary and Walter Burroughs and Fred Mills ("Uncle Freddie"), Alstead, New Hampshire, February 12, 1964. Recorded by B. A. Botkin.

He was the one everybody consulted. He was very shy. He and his next older brother, who was a little short man, lived together after their mother died. And it was told that once another—the youngest brother [and his wife] wanted to go somewhere, and they left the baby with Judd and Charles. They just couldn't take it on such a long trip that evening. And the baby began to cough—was quite croupy. The two old bachelors were rather worried. Finally Charles hunted up the skunk oil, wasn't it, and when they arrived he was rubbing the skunk oil on the baby's chest. I don't know much about remedies except skunk oil. There's still people who get a hold of it if they possibly can. It is for rheumatism—and what else? This baby had congestion in its chest.

Walter: We used to take sulphur and molasses as a spring tonic when we were children.

Fred: And have to wear a tansy bag all winter on our chest.

Mary: Tansy would be a good deal superior to asafoetida.

Walter: And balm of Gilead buds and alcohol was for any bruises or cuts and so forth.

Mary: They're delicious-smelling.

Fred: Balm of Gilead. I know that my mother used to swear by it. She used to have a lot of it then. And they used to use this sage and catnip for tea, you know. A lot of things that these old people used to use—pennyroyal and all that stuff, you know—they'd gather up every fall and they'd hang it up in the attic there and dry it out. Anything that was the matter with you, you'd have a cup of hot catnip tea. Well, I don't know. We were taken pretty good care of. We didn't have so much sickness them days.

Mary: What was thoroughwort for, Walter?

Walter: Well, whatever ails you. You'd just collect the herb and steep it, and take it for—well—spring tonic. Any time of year. It didn't have to be spring. That was an internal remedy.

II. THE FORCE OF CUSTOM

*. . . on the southern coast of Rhode Island, the fabled Atlantis
. . . the soft, balmy breezes from the Gulf Stream . . . impart
to the grain that genial softness, that tempting fragrance and delicious flavor, that caused the Greeks of old to bestow upon Narragansett corn meal the name of Ambrosia.*
        —THOMAS ROBINSON HAZARD

*How blessed are we to live in a more charitable and enlightened
age, to enjoy the comforts and conveniences of modern times,
and to realize that the world is continually growing wiser and
better.*—P. T. BARNUM

Many hands make light work.—OLD PROVERB

Reminiscences and not history is the intended basis of this book.
        —JOSEPH C. FARNHAM

1. THE GOOD OLD DAYS

ALICE MORSE EARLE'S unhappy experience with flip, made, as related below, according to Old Put's recipe, was sufficient to cure her of "any
overweening longing for the good old times." This atavistic yearning for
the past, especially the past of one's childhood, on which a "rare epic
glamor" is wont to rest, is one of the oldest and most persistent of old
New England customs. From the beginning Yankees have sought to perpetuate or cling to the past—in place-names sacred with historical or ancestral associations; in zealously cultivated family and local history and
traditions; in grandfather worship; and in countless survivals, symbols,
and shibboleths treasured for their emotional and association value. Not
the least powerful of these links and ties with a glorified past are local
and old-time customs, whose memory is preserved in antiquarian reminiscences and in nostalgic antique-collecting.

When Dorothy Canfield Fisher writes that "Vermont represents the
past, is a piece of the past in the midst of the present and future," [1] she is
testifying to the force of custom which binds one generation to another and
to the power of survival which the folklife of New England possesses
amidst change and decay.

A strong sense of the past as a Golden Age usually goes hand in hand
with strong local pride in a Land of Milk and Honey. And in one of the
most ardent and zestful of New England local patriots, "Shepherd Tom"
Hazard, contempt for the degeneracy of modern times is mingled with
praise of Narragansett dishes as the food of the gods. But if the *Jonny-
Cake Papers* are a delightful monument to the glory that was Narragansett and the grandeur that was Washington and Newport Counties, *Recol-*

---

[1] *Vermont: A Guide to the Green Mountain State* (Boston, 1937), p. 4.

lections of Olden Times proves that Thomas Robinson Hazard was also something of a social historian. And it is only by seeing lost arts and passing institutions in their social context and historical perspective that one can avoid the pitfalls of merely antiquarian and provincial enthusiasm.

2. CO-OPERATION AND RITUAL

When we examine the functional basis of old New England customs (some of which were local and others merely pioneer folkways), we see that they served the purposes mainly of co-operation and ritual—both characteristic of primitive and folk society. Mary Ellen Chase points out that chores —a foundation stone of Yankee household economy—are distinguished from jobs by their co-operative and voluntary character.

> One was paid for a job but never for a chore. The performance of the former connoted agreement and consent; the performance of the latter, participation and partnership.[1]

In the same way, bees and change-work were chores on a community or neighborhood basis; and in exchanging chores with one's neighbors, one not only proved the truth of the old adage that "Many hands make light work" but also laid oneself open to the danger (pointed out by Robert B. Thomas) that "many go more for the sport than to do any real good" and "it tends to lounging and idleness, and neglect of business; for we cannot always have our neighbours at work with us."[2]

When co-operative labor takes on the nature of a celebration, as in the case of "raisings," the element of ritual is added to that of sociability and amusement. The rhymes used at raisings ("Here is a fine house! It stands high on dry land") are reminiscent of Anglo-Saxon charms. Ritual and symbolism also enter into handicrafts and folk arts as an aesthetic element superimposed upon utility. Quilt patterns, even to their very names, preserve symbolic memories of personal experiences and historical events as well as memorials of the living and the dead. The old New Hampshire needlewoman who went in for basket patterns said that "When I'm making patchwork, I think of all the baskets I've had. . . . I do like baskets." Even local foods and food-making take on the aspect of a ritual, in the hands of a high priestess like Shepherd Tom's Phillis.

The addition of sociability and ritual to home and local industries is all the more inevitable and important in early New England and other pioneer societies in view of the sheer amount of labor and drudgery to be performed. And the adjustment of work to individual talent and skill increased not only the dignity but the virtuosity of labor so that whittling Yankees become not only inventive but creative Yankees. Life, in New England, however, was never wholly divorced from purpose, as illustrated by Samuel Goodrich's story of the Yankee in straits and the wealthy Quaker, who kept him busy pounding on a log with the head of an ax. The Yankee quit in disgust, saying: "I'll be hanged if I'll cut wood without seeing the chips fly!"[3]

---

[1] *A Goodly Heritage* (New York, 1932), p. 43.

[2] *The Old Farmer's Almanack,* October, 1808, and June, 1821, cited by George Lyman Kittredge, *The Old Farmer and His Almanack* (Boston, 1904), pp. 169, 179.

[3] *Recollections of a Lifetime* (New York and Auburn, 1857), Vol. I, pp. 96–97.

In games and pastimes, finally, ritual seems to be an end in itself. But in so far as children in their amusements inherit or imitate adult interests and activities, even playing at work may have a pedagogic as well as a symbolic value. And this may be the crowning achievement of folk culture and folk art—that whether at work or at play, the folk succeeds in combining the two in ingenious forms and fashions, especially in the far-from-simple good old days.

B. A. B.

OLD NEW ENGLAND DISHES

Narragansett Johnny-Cake

> White Indian meal is very nice, as all Rhode Islanders know, but we should like to ask Thomas R. Hazard how much his cost him in his farming days?—*Providence Journal*, January 16, 1879.

AND where, let me ask in turn, did the Journal learn that white Indian meal is very nice? Not certainly outside of Washington and Newport counties, for nowhere else on the globe was the real article ever to be found. The Southern epicures crack a good deal about hoe-cakes and hominy made from their white flint corn, the Pennsylvanians of their mush, the Boston folks of their Boston brown bread, whilst one Joel Barlow, of New Haven, or somewhere else in Connecticut, used to sing a long song in glorification of New England hasty pudding; but none of these reputed luxuries are worthy of holding a candle to an old-fashioned Narragansett jonny-cake made by an old-time Narragansett colored cook, from Indian corn meal raised on the southern coast of Rhode Island, the fabled Atlantis, where alone the soft, balmy breezes from the Gulf Stream ever fan the celestial plant in its growth, and impart to the grain that genial softness, that tempting fragrance and delicious flavor, that caused the Greeks of old to bestow upon Narragansett corn meal the name of Ambrosia, imagining it to be a food originally designed and set apart by the gods exclusively for their own delectation.

But alas, since the introduction of coal fires, cooking stoves, common schools, and French and Irish bedeviling cooks, the making and baking of a jonny-cake has become one of the lost arts. And yet I can remember when its preparation and completion deservedly stood at the very acme of the fine arts of Rhode Island. My grandfather used to have in his kitchen an old cook by the name of Phillis, originally from Senegambia, or Guinea, who probably made as good a jonny-cake in her day as any other

---

From *The Jonny-Cake Papers of "Shepherd Tom,"* together with Reminiscences of Narragansett Schools of Former Days, by Thomas Robinson Hazard, with a Biographical Sketch and Notes by Rowland Gibson Hazard, pp. 17–18, 28–30. Copyright, 1915, by Rowland G. Hazard. Boston: Printed for the Subscribers. 1915.

artist known, whether white or black, or in short, as was ever made outside of heaven. Her process, so far as I could gather from observation,
was as follows:—premising that she always insisted on having white
Narragansett corn, ground at what is now called Hammond's Mill, which
is situated on the site of the elder Gilbert Stuart's snuff mill, just above
the head of Pettaquamscutt pond or lake.

* * * * *

. . . after Phillis had sifted the meal for her jonny-cake, she proceeded
to carefully knead it in a wooden tray, having first scalded it with boiling
water, and added sufficient fluid, sometimes new milk, at other times pure
water, to make it of a proper consistence. It was then placed on the jonny-
cake board about three-quarters of an inch in thickness, and well dressed
on the surface with rich sweet cream to keep it from blistering when
placed before the fire. The red oak jonny-cake board was always the
middle portion of a flour barrel from five to six inches wide. This was
considered an indispensable requisite in the baking of a good jonny-cake.
All the old-time colored cooks, without exception, hold that the flour
barrel was first made for the express purpose of furnishing jonny-cake
boards, and that its subsequent application to the holding of flour was
merely the result of an afterthought. Be this as it may, no one I feel
certain ever saw a regular, first-rate, old-time jonny-cake that was not
baked on a red oak board taken from the middle part of the head of a
flour barrel. The cake was next placed upright on the hearth before a bright,
green hardwood fire. This kind of fire was indispensable also. And so too
was the heart-shaped flat-iron that supported it, which was shaped exactly to
meet every exigency. First the flat [iron]'s front smooth surface was placed
immediately against the back of the jonny-cake to hold it in a perpendicular position before the fire until the main part of the cake was sufficiently
baked. Then a slanting side of the flat-iron was turned so as to support
the board in a reclining position until the bottom and top extremities of
the cake were in turn baked, and lastly, the board was slewed round and
rested partly against the handle of the flat-iron, so as to bring the ends of
the cake in a better position to receive the heat from the fire. After a time
it was discovered that the flat-iron, first invented as a jonny-cake holder,
was a convenient thing to iron clothes with, and has since been used for
that purpose very extensively. When the jonny-cake was sufficiently done
on the first side, a knife was passed between it and the board, and it was
dextrously turned and anointed, as before, with sweet, golden-tinged
cream, previous to being placed again before the fire.

Such, as I have described, was the process of making and baking the
best article of farinaceous food that was ever partaken of by mortal man,
to wit, an old-fashioned jonny-cake made of white Rhode Island corn meal,
carefully and slowly ground with Rhode Island fine-grained granite mill-
stones, and baked and conscientiously tended before glowing coals of a
quick green hardwood fire, on a red oak barrel-head supported by a flat-
iron. With proper materials and care, a decent jonny-cake can be baked on

a coal stove, though by no means equal to the old-time genuine article, for the simple reason that wood fires in open fireplaces have become, as a general rule, things of the past, and good, careful, painstaking cooks extinct.

Corn Dishes

PEOPLE living in cities can know but little of the exquisite flavor of the early red-cobbed sweet-corn, or of the later white-cobbed evergreen, for the reason that the market is supplied with ears of corn gathered some hours before it is eaten. Old Phillis' method of boiling green-corn was first to set her pot of water boiling, drawn fresh and sparkling from the bubbling well, whilst she took the outside husks from the ears of corn just gathered by old mill-boy, fresh from the stalk in the green-corn patch, back of the barn, leaving a few of the inside husks on the outside of each ear, and then plunging them instanter into the boiling water before the sweetness had departed. How many ears of Phillis' corn, prepared after this fashion, a small boy could eat with a fair amount of sweet, fragrant, aromatic butter, I cannot say, for although Phillis always boiled a bushel pot full of green-corn at once, I could never manage to get enough fully to satisfy my appetite. As for the green sweet-corn, when nicely roasted before a green hardwood fragrant fire, I used to think when a small boy that I could have eaten at least two bushels of it could I have got all I wanted. So, too, with succotash, the Indian for dried sweet-corn and beans, which my grand-mother used to always caution me about eating too much of, as she had once known a naughty boy who burst asunder in the middle from having eaten too heartily of the tempting dish. . . .

* * * * *

Then again there was the Indian baked pudding made of ambrosia, milk, and eggs, with a trifle of Muscovado sugar or Portorique molasses. I can remember when I could eat near upon a six-quart pan of this delicious viand and then cry for more. Still again there was the huckleberry and blackberry baked and boiled pudding, and the green fox-grape boiled pudding, none of your tasteless catawba or Isabella insipids, all eaten with luscious brown sugar sauce. . . .

* * * * *

Then again, there was the hasty pudding, not the half-cooked knotty stuff of modern days, but nice faithfully stirred, well-boiled pudding without any two particles of ambrosia sticking together in it. Phillis used to say there was "nothing an airth she 'spised so as lumpy, half-raw, half-burned hasty pudding." People nowadays don't know how to eat hasty pudding and milk. A spoon should be dipped into the milk before it lifts the pudding, to keep it from sticking, which should then be dropped into the porringer of milk, so as each mouthful shall remain separate.

Ibid., pp. 50–51, 53–59 *passim*, 61–62.

When cold, Phillis used to fry her hasty pudding in the nicest fresh butter, which made it a dish, as she said, fit to set before a king. . . .

* * * * *

Then again, there was the never-absent dish in good families of old, milk porridge, a luxury of surpassing excellence when rightly concocted and cooked, that must be reckoned among the lost arts in these hurrying, money-getting and universal thievery, food-spoiling and food-bolting days. Many a time have I sat by when a boy, watching old Phillis as she made this delicious beverage. First, she boiled the water, always drawn fresh, buoyant, and sparkling from the well; none of your poison leaden pipe, or wooden pump, dead and alive wells, or water works, but a real old-fashioned well, every stone of which was coated with life-given green moss, with a frog or two seated near the bottom, which was ever vitalized and kept alive and fresh by the plunges and splashings of the old oaken bucket hanging at the end of the pole of a big, long well-sweep, balanced at the further end with a pile of stones. Into the boiling water she carefully sifted through the fingers of her left hand the flour of ambrosia, if for the sick, and if for common purposes the second sifting, which she stirred with a pudding-stick, held in her right hand, so artistically, that no two grains of the meal were ever known to adhere together. Phillis used to carry a magnifying glass of some twenty-five hundred or as many thousand horse-power, I disremember which, with which she from time to time surveyed the boiling compound, nor did she commence adding the rich new milk until every separate minute particle of the ambrosia had become transparent and sufficiently expanded in dimensions to enable her to discern the image of her own nose fully reflected therefrom. So exquisite was this compound that I have known one pint porringer of Phillis' milk porridge to work a complete and instant cure of the blues, and that of the worst kind. In fact, the old woman used to tell a story of Sol Smith, who once stopped in my grandfather's kitchen to warm, whilst on his way to hang himself on the limb of a sour apple tree in our lower orchard, about some love affair, just as she was finishing off a pot of porridge. Phillis said he looked so woe-begone-like that she gave him a porringer of her porridge, which was not more than half finished, when he took a rope with a noose braided on one end out of his pocket and threw it to Phillis to mend her clothes-line with as he said, accompanied with the remark that Almira might marry as many other fellows as she wanted to, and he wouldn't mind, so long as he could get "such porridge as them was." In such high esteem was the milk porridge of the olden time held by Narragansettees that since my memory they always spoke of it in the plural number. No ordinary man or woman in Narragansett ever said in those days, "Please give me a little more of that porridge," but, "Please give me a few more of them porridge."

Then again, there was the samp—coarse hominy pounded in a mortar— and the great and little hominy, all Indian dishes fit to be set before princes and gods. But what shall I say of the hulled corn of old? None of your modern tasteless western corn, hulled with potash, but the real, genuine ambrosia, hulled in the nice sweet lye made from fresh hard oak and maple-wood ashes. I remember when a bowl or porringer of hulled corn and milk was a thousand times more relished by me than any dish I can now find at any hotel in the United States. Narragansett hulled corn and beans was in those days ten thousand times as good, as I remember, as the best pork and beans ever cooked in Boston town of that day, or in Boston city of the present dishonest, defaulting age. Then again, there was the great Indian dish called no-cake, in which was concentrated such inexpressible sweetness and life-sustaining power that the aborigines of New England, when hunting or on the warpath, could carry forty days' provisions each on their backs without inconvenience.

The No-cake family, the last survivors of the famous Narragansett Indians, have recently, I think, with one exception, become extinct in Washington county, where the scanty remnants of the tribe were located, on the Indian reserve in Charlestown.

No-cake was made of pounded parched Indian corn. Curious enough, I can remember when the eating of no-cake and milk was considered somewhat a test in Narragansett of good breeding. To be eaten gracefully no-cake must be placed very carefully on the top of the milk, so as to float, and a novice, in taking a spoonful of it to his mouth, is very liable to draw his breath, when the semi-volatile substance enters his throat in advance of the milk and causes violent strangling or sneezing. An expert in the art places the spoonful of milk with the no-cake floating upon the top, carefully into his mouth, and mixes them together without drawing his breath until he swallows. I well remember the old no-cake mortar that used to stand in my grandfather's kitchen, upside down when not in use, so as to serve for a seat. I think it would hold half a gallon of parched corn, or more, which was pounded with a heavy double-headed pestle, for lack of one made of stone, as used by the Indians. This mortar was made of unsplittable wood, known as gumwood or horn-beam, the heart of which is absolutely without grain running in any direction. Old Tom Griswold once described horn-beam, after burying every wedge at the woodpile in a short log without cracking it, as being made of "double and twisted lignum vitae sawdust, spun cross-banded, wove kairsy, cussed at both ends, and damned in the middle."

* * * * *

Corn biscuit, or pound cake, another Indian meal luxury, used to be made with one pound of butter, one pound of sugar, ten eggs, and a pint of new milk, with enough ambrosia to mould it into thin cakes. Then there was the whitpot, differing but little from the common baked Indian pudding, except that it is mixed very thin, and baked very slowly and a great while, so that the milk, eggs, and molasses form a jelly throughout the whole pudding. . . .

Narragansett Fried Smelts and Broiled Eels

. . . PHILLIS, after taking from the chest her modicum of meal, proceeded to bolt it through her finest sieve, reserving the first teacupful that fell for the especial purpose of powdering fish before their being fried. This brings to my recollection the vast difference there was in the old-fashioned way of frying fish, especially smelts, from that now in vogue in Providence, Boston, and such like outlandish places, at least so far as hotels and restaurants are concerned. There smelts are nowadays, without preparation, simply thrown pell-mell into a pan with raw hog's lard of questionable purity, which they absorb before it is half cooked, imparting thereby a greasy, slippery savor to the dear little fish too horrible to mention or abide. On the contrary, Phillis used always to keep a kettle of pure leaf lard, from corn-fed hogs, thoroughly boiled, set apart for the especial purpose of frying smelts during their season. These were always obtained each morning from the Saucatucket smelt weir, and delivered to her alive and flipping, the kettle of lard being on the fire boiling all the time. Each delicate little fish was, after being washed, rolled carefully in the meal until every hair breadth of it from the tip of its head to the end of its tail was coated in the flour of ambrosia; then taking the caudal extremity of each smelt between her thumb and finger, she dropped it head foremost into the boiling kettle, and there left it until it was thoroughly done and crisp. No epicure who has never tasted smelts cooked by that method knows anything of what a smelt is, nor after having once tasted of such can he ever be induced to put into his mouth one of the vile things bearing the name, that has been, minus the meal, half fried in less than half-cooked hog's lard, thereafter.

It is said by some that the Narragansett smelt, cooked in the only proper way, was in pagan times one of the two relishes or condiments that the gods alone indulged in whilst reveling in jonny-cake made of Narragansett white corn meal, the other being Pettaquamscutt eels caught in the months of January and February with spears thrust into the mud beneath the ice, where they lie. The glorious excellence of these eels, prepared in the old-time way, I am sure no poet—not even Homer or Byron, with all their glowing powers of description—can portray, much less a simple writer of prose. The method was as follows: A basket of fat, yellow-breasted eels being brought fresh from the frozen river, were first saturated with a handful of live wood ashes. This loosened the coating of slime so that they were readily cleansed. Next the head was taken off, and the eel split down the entire length of the back. They were then washed in clean sea water and hung up the kitchen chimney, with its wide, open fireplace, for one night only. Next morning the eels were cut in short pieces and placed on a gridiron, flesh side next to sweet-smelling, glowing coals, made from green oak, walnut, or maple wood. When sufficiently broiled on that side, they were turned on the gridiron and a small slice of fragrant butter, made

Ibid., pp. 24–27.

from the milk of cows fed on honey-laden white clover and aromatic five-fingers, put on each piece of eel. By this time the family were seated at the breakfast table in the great-room, waiting impatiently for the all-but-divine luxury, the exquisite aroma of which penetrated every nook and cranny of the house. In due time it appears, on a China plate, you may say; by no means! but on the identical gridiron, hot and luscious, with little transparent globules of dew-like nectar sparkling on each piece. Every guest or member of the family helps himself from the hot gridiron, which is then returned to the glowing coals, and again and again replenished until the appetite is surfeited or the supply of eels exhausted; probably the latter, as I never heard of but one instance wherein a fatal surfeit was produced by the dainty dish, which was the case of one of the kings of England, who died from eating too enormously of broiled eels, speared under the ice at the mouth of the river Humber. I am aware that history charges his death to gormandizing on stewed lamprey eels—a transparent mistake—as no man could be tempted to indulge his appetite exorbitantly on eels of any kind—stewed or fried, but only on yellow-breasted eels, speared under the ice and prepared and cooked after the Narragansett mode.

There used to be an old man in Narragansett by the name of Scribbins, who was a great favorite of my grandfather because of his simplicity and honesty. When a small boy, I remember Scribbins's breakfasting at our house, one winter morning, when we had broiled eels. The old man helped himself from the gridiron seventeen times, a steady smile playing over his features every moment that passed between the first and last mouthful. He then looked my grandfather—Uncle Toby like—blandly and steadily in the face, and significantly nodding his head sideways in the direction of the kitchen door, remarked: "Them's eels, them is."

Nantucket Quahaugs

THE savory and hearty meal was further supplied, or we may say "topped off," with amazing quantities of a species of animal called by the islanders

---

From *Miriam Coffin*, or The Whale-Fishermen, by Joseph C. Hart, Chapter IV, in *Spun-Yarn from Old Nantucket,* edited and published by H. S. Wyer, pp. 16–18. Copyright, 1914, by Henry S. Wyer. Nantucket: The Inquirer and Mirror Press.

In the Cape vocabulary, as in the bright lexicon of youth, occur certain words that trap the stranger. Quahaug is the worst offender. Let us at once solve the mystery of its pronunciation by saying that if you call it "co-hog" you will be talking the language of the native fishermen. When the Government was about to purchase the Canal in 1926, it was necessary for the congressman from the Cape to turn tutor, and tell his colleagues in Washington about this nationally unknown bivalve and its relation to the waterway.

Of all this linguistic effort which it causes, the quahaug is sublimely ignorant, for it shuts itself out from the world in a fashion that few living creatures can command. If you think that a clam or an oyster has a retiring disposition, you should try to open

the "Pooquaw," and sometimes by the other Indian name of "Quohog." These are found in great numbers on the sandy shores of the island; and, but for their great plenty in the northern parts of America, they would be esteemed a delicious luxury.

Lest we may not be well understood while we speak of the inimitable quohog, and, by our obscurity, engender doubts of its inexhaustible abundance, it may be well to inform the gentle reader and enlighten his understanding. Its aboriginal name, and that which it still holds in the oldest parts of America, is just as we have written it down. Nevertheless, the *quo-hog* hath neither bristles nor tail, nor is it a quadruped, as its name would seem to import; but it is in truth a species of shell-fish, which naturalists, in the plenitude of their lore, denominate *bivalvular.* It is grievous further to say, in explanation, that its original and sonorous name, and that by which it is still known in Nantucket, has been made to yield, by the pestilent spirit of innovation in the middle states, to the flat, insipid, and unsounding title of—the clam! Spirit of the erudite Barnes, the conchologist—spirits of Sir Joseph Banks, and Sir Humphrey Davy— spirit of the learned Mitchell—could you not, in the course of your long and well-spent lives, hit upon a more expressive and euphonious jaw- cracker for the persecuted quohog, than the abominable name of *clam?*

The manner of cooking the quohog in the most palatable way at the *Squantums* of Nantucket, as oracularly given out by the knowing Peleg Folger, was resorted to on this occasion [of the sheep-shearing], to eke out the foregoing meal. Even unto this day, some of the eastern people adopt the same method to "stap the vitals" of the quohog at their "roast-outs" or forest junketings. As to the peculiar mode of cooking, we adopt the argu- ment of Peleg, even as he learnedly discussed the matter while arranging a bed of the aforesaid bivalvular shell-fish on the morning of the shearing. Imprimis—The quohogs were placed upon the bare ground, side by side, with their mouths biting the dust. The burning coals of the camp-fires, which had done the office of boiling and broiling, were removed from

---

one of the mollusks with which we are for the moment concerned. Almost adamantine is its refusal to yield entrance to its abode. The shell is extraordinarily hard, and all doors are bolted to any amateurish approach. Only an expert knows the trick of admission. It was the blue portion of the interior of this shell from which the Indians made their "suckanhock," or black money, worth twice the white wampum that passed with them as coin of the realm.

While it is true that the adult quahaug is scarcely known away from the Massa- chusetts coast, its children are widely famous on metropolitan menus as "little neck" clams. The man who reaches down into the sea to harvest them uses a still different name, "cherrystones." . . . Wellfleet Harbor is commonly regarded as the largest quahaug grounds in the country, 2500 acres being devoted to this industry, with a yearly shipment of 2,000 barrels. A group of Finns do most of the dredging, with a fleet of about thirty converted catboats, powered with gasoline engines. They steer the same course in and out of the bay that a picturesque predecessor of theirs once steered, Captain Baker of Wellfleet and the West Indies. . . .—Arthur Wilson Tarbell, *Cape Cod Ahoy!* (Boston, 1932), pp. 181–183.

under the cross-trees, where hung the pot and tea-water kettle, and applied plentifully to the backs of the quohogs. In a few minutes after the application of the fire, the cooking was declared to be at an end, and the roasting of the quohogs complete. The steam of the savory liquor, which escaped in part without putting out the fire, preserved the meat in a parboiled state, and prevented it from scorching, or drying to a cinder, and the whole virtue of the fish from being lost. The ashes of the fire were effectually excluded by the position in which the animal was placed at the beginning; and the heat as completely destroyed the tenacity of the hinge which connected the shells.

"And now," said Peleg, "take a few on thy platter; remove the upper shell, and apply a lump of fresh butter and a sprinkling of pepper and salt." Our blessings on thee, Peleg Folger. The morsel, if taken hot, might be envied by an eastern emperor, whose palate is pampered by bird-nest delicacies; or by the exquisite gourmand of any nation. But in America, who eats a clam or a quohog? None but the wise—and that includes a majority of the people;—the fashionable, never—more's the pity.

New England *versus* Manhattan Clam Chowder

THERE is a terrible pink mixture (with tomatoes in it, and herbs) called Manhattan Clam Chowder, that is only a vegetable soup, and not to be confused with New England Clam Chowder, nor spoken of in the same breath. Tomatoes and clams have no more affinity than ice cream and horse radish. It is sacrilege to wed bivalves with bay leaves, and only a degraded cook would do such a thing.

Representative Cleveland Sleeper of Maine recently introduced a bill in the State legislature, to make it an illegal as well as a culinary offense to introduce tomatoes to clam chowder. And immediately a chowder battle ensued—with high-class chefs asserting that a tomato and clam should never meet, and the low maestros of Manhattan advocating their unholy union.

Anyone who wants tomato soup can have it; but Manhattan Clam Chowder is a kind of thin minestrone, or dish water, and fit only for foreigners. In Boston we like our chowders rich and creamy, and this is how we make them:

First you must have:

A quart of clams (from Duxury, if possible)
A quarter of a pound of salt pork
Four potatoes
Two onions

From *a New England Sampler*, by Eleanor Early, pp. 349–351. Copyright, 1940 by Waverly House. Boston.

A quart of milk
A quarter of a pound of butter
Plenty of Common Crackers
Salt and pepper
A kernel of garlic (if you like garlic)
And a jar of cream (if you want a very rich chowder)

Cut the pork up in small pieces and try it out. Strain the fat, and sauté the chopped onions gently, until they are golden-yellow. Fried onions won't give people indigestion, unless they (the onions) are brown or black. Heat the clams in their own juice until the edges turn up (this will take only a couple of minutes). Dice and parboil the potatoes. When the clams are cool enough to handle, some people squeeze the dark part from their little bellies. This is done with the thumb and forefinger, and is not as surgical as it sounds. The necks are of no value except to the clam, and might as well be removed. Personally, I eat clams *as is*. But for company, I pinch their bellies and cut off their necks.

Pour everything together and add the milk and butter. Split half a dozen Common Crackers and float on the top, with a spot of butter on each. Spear the garlic on a toothpick, and let that float too. The toothpick will locate it, when you want to take it out.

*   *   *   *   *

A proper chowder should marinate on the back of the stove for an hour or more while the ingredients become thoroughly familiar with one another. The cream should be added at the last.

Daniel Webster's Fish Chowder

TAKE a cod of ten pounds, well cleaned, leaving on the skin. Cut into pieces one and a half pounds thick, preserving the head whole. Take one and a half pounds of clear, fat salt pork, cut in thin slices. Do the same with twelve potatoes. Take the largest pot you have. Try out the pork first, then take out the pieces of pork, leaving in the drippings. Add to that three parts of water, a layer of fish, so as to cover the bottom of the pot; next a layer of potatoes, then two tablespoons of salt, 1 teaspoon of pepper, then the pork, another layer of fish, and the remainder of the potatoes.

Fill the pot with water to cover the ingredients. Put over a good fire. Let the chowder boil twenty-five minutes. When this is done have a quart of boiling milk ready, and ten hard crackers split and dipped in cold water. Add milk and crackers. Let the whole boil five minutes. The chowder is then ready to be first-rate if you have followed the directions. An onion may be added if you like the flavor.

From *The Yankee Cook Book*, by Imogene Wolcott, pp. 8–9. Copyright, 1939, by Coward-McCann, Inc. New York.

Herring Sticks

THE Herring Brook attracted us youngsters throughout three quarters of the year, but it was in May or early June that it became of general interest to all, grownups as well as children. Then the herring run was on.

The Cape Cod herring is, as every one knows, an alewife.[1] According to the dictionary, the name was "perhaps jocularly given or, perhaps, derived from the Indian." It, the same dictionary, also adds that the alewife is "a poor food fish." Well, maybe, but Cape Codders did not use to think so. Either that, or they were accustomed to poor food, an alternative which, I am sure, no Codder will admit. In at least one of the towns—and no doubt in many others—each child born within township limits was entitled to so many herring—alewifes of course—each year. This was an old law dating back to early Colonial times. Herring was an accepted part of the community food supply.

When the run was on, the brook was literally packed with herring. . . .

About a hundred feet from the foot of the fall, where the brook ran between boulders and the channel was narrowest, was a section with plank gates which raised and lowered in grooves. Ordinarily, in the herring season these gates were kept closed and the water forced to flow through another and wider section, walled and floored with plank and also fitted with gates at each end. Once daily, at "shut-down" time, these latter gates were closed and those of the regular channel opened. The surplus water in the artificial channel drained away through holes in the lower gate and the herring were left high and dry, trapped in a wooden box.·

* * * * *

There were far more herring taken during the running season than the townspeople could use, of course, and many were shipped to the city. But a surprising number were taken care of locally. Some were eaten fresh— Grandmother used to say, "I do relish a nice fresh herring with my breakfast"—but many more were salted and smoked. Before salting or smoking, they were strung on sticks.

The sticks were for the most part whittled from cedar—we are quite sure cedar was the wood used. Made from the old split-cedar rail fences that used to be so common. You see very few of these old rail fences nowadays. In our boyhood they were plenty. We used to make our bows and arrows from cedar rails. The herring sticks were pointed at both ends and whittled thin enough to pass through the gills of the fish. A dozen were strung on a stick. All along the Cape roads the lettered signs on the

---

---

[1] And you pronounce it "ell-y," in case you don't know.—Robert P. Tristram Coffin, *Kennebec, Cradle of Americans* (New York, 1937), p. 202.

fences used to read, "Herring 10 Cents a Stick." Occasionally we see those signs now, but not very often.

Against the rafters of practically every barn, and in many sheds and outbuildings, those sticks of herring used to hang. You could smell them before you opened the door. During the summer they were often hung out of doors in the sunshine, festooning the eaves of barns and sheds. You could smell them there, too. That is one characteristic of a herring which salting or drying does not remove, but rather accentuates—the smell. The memory of an old-time Cape Cod kitchen at breakfast hour would not be complete without the odor of fried herring. Call him an alewife if you will, but, like the rose by another name, it does not change his aroma.

*   *   *   *   *

But when I state, as I did earlier in this chapter, that the herring used to be a regular and important part of Cape Cod's food supply, I do not exaggerate. They not only ate them on land but carried them on fishing vessels as part of the regular rations. A good friend of ours, now dead, more is the pity—a comrade with whom we camped and fished and sailed times without number—was an old sea captain. In his youth, however, he had gone "mackereling" aboard Captain Ote Young's little fore-and-aft schooner. . . .

This Captain Young, so our friend said, had the reputation, spread by the unlucky foremost hands who had sailed with him, of being a "poor provider." He was a first-rate skipper and fisherman, but he fed his crews in meager fashion. . . .

*   *   *   *   *

According to our friend, an acquaintance of his sailed with the Captain on another trip in the same schooner. On this cruise, so the narrator avowed, the sole supply of "hearty" on board were three sticks of salt herring. If you are a confirmed Cape Codder, you know that "hearty" means, or used to mean, "meat victuals."

The herring lasted four days and the schooner did not return to port until the afternoon of the sixth day. When the yarn was sprung upon its innocent victim, there was always a pause at this point. And then the said victim, having been allowed time to think it over, was supposed to, and usually did, ask this question:

"But if there were no more herring, what did you and the rest of the crew eat during those last two days?"

"Oh," with sad solemnity, "we chewed the sticks."

Lobster Stew

SAVE every part of the hot lobsters you have taken apart, except the shells, the colon, and the sack of the stomach with its "lady." Take all the clotted

From *Mainstays of Maine,* by Robert P. Tristram Coffin, egged on by Ruth P. Coffin, pp. 11–12. Copyright, 1944, by the Macmillan Company. New York. Originally printed in *Gourmet,* May, 1943.

blood. And especially every drop of the liquid spared by the shellers. The proportion of solid to liquid will be about 50–50. For this is no ordinary stew, no curtain-raiser to a feast. It is the whole business. The man who gets outside of two bowls of this pottage is through with eating for some hours, and he is a nobler man. Perhaps two sour pickles. Maybe two rounds of pilot bread. But no other fringes to this feast. This stew is all in all.

Begin with the tomally [liver]. Sauté it in about an equal quantity of new butter, and in an old-fashioned thick iron kettle, for seven minutes, say. Then add the lobster meat, the blood, the juice. Add no salt, no pepper. There is the whole sea full of salt this lobster has drawn on artistically, and all the spices of the deep are in him. He is all-spice already. Add not a drop of water, on peril of your soul. But add more melted butter. At the end, this stew is pure gold on top and Kingdom Come below. Leave the kettle on a very hot fire. Say, ten minutes. Then push it back on the stove, let it cool down slightly. Then gently—O, gently, gently!— pour in milk, a trickle poured continuously, and stir as you do. About a cupful of rich cream can go in to advantage, at great risk I say it, for this is one of my helpmate's little nuances that I do not mean to let slip out. Stir constantly, for you do not want to have a curdled ruin to your masterpiece. When the stew blossoms out suddenly into a rich salmon pink under your spoon, you can know you have achieved fame. You are done. Why green tomally blossoms out pink I do not know. But it does. That is the last hallmark of excellence.

Set the kettle off the stove to cool. The cooling is as important as everything else. For every hour that passes increases the flavor, not in arithmetic, but in geometric progression. But once the fragrance of the dish goes through the house, there is little likelihood of there being many hours or even minutes to the aging. Short of standing over the kettle with a shotgun, my wife has found it practically impossible to age her nectar for more than five or six hours. That is enough, though, to give her the reputation of being the artist in lobsters she so deservedly is.

My wife always heats the stew up when she finally has to serve it, of course.

Scootin'-'long-the-Shore

MRS. MAE BANGS TWITE, Oak Bluffs, Martha's Vineyard, Mass., says this plain but appetizing combination of potatoes and onions rejoices in the name of Scootin'-'long-the-Shore because for years upon years Cape Cod fishermen prepared this meal while at their work. Mrs. Twite has often heard her grandmother ask her "granddad" what they should have for lunch. Always his comeback was, "Well, Mother, make it Scootin'-'long-the-Shore."

Down in Maine a similar recipe is popular. Potatoes are sliced as thin as possible, and thrown into cold water while salt pork is tried out. Pork is removed from pan and potatoes fried slowly for about 30 minutes, stirring frequently. Sometimes an onion is added. When the potatoes are done, the salt pork is placed on top. This dish is known as Very Poor Man's Dinner.

New England Boiled Dinner

THE "boiled dinner" to which, on hotel menus, the descriptive words "New England" are still universally appended, was, as a matter of fact, the universal *pièce de résistance* of the comfortable but uncultivated householder of olden times. It was prepared in a single great pot, the meat being put in first, and then—at intervals properly calculated to turn the whole thing out cooked, just as it should be, the minute the big clock in the corner should strike the hour of noon—were added potatoes, beets, squash, turnip, and cabbage, with very likely a bag of Indian pudding into the bargain. Such a dish was a meal of itself, neither dessert nor bread being regarded as necessary to its completeness.

Muslin Toast

MUSLIN toast was a favorite supper dish, prepared with nicety and precision. A rye short cake, the full size of the griddle iron, was browned to a delicate crisp, on each side, the thin crust deftly flayed from the hot side, the denuded surface returned to the griddle, and the crust placed in the waiting basin of hot, thickened and salted milk. This process was repeated until the upper crust of the cake was reached and ready to be "dipped."

Nantucket Wonders

. . . WHAT were they? Simply doughnuts made in a certain prescribed regulation form—cut out round, jagged across and separated at the center two or three times, but not cut through to the edge; made in that way the fat, while they were frying, passed between those jagged cuts, with the

From *Social Life in Old New England,* by Mary Caroline Crawford, pp. 260–261. Copyright, 1914, by Little, Brown and Company. Boston. 1915.

From *In Dover on the Charles,* A Contribution to New England Folk-Lore, by Alice J. Jones, pp. 50–51. Copyright, 1906, by Alice J. Jones. Newport, Rhode Island: The Milne Printery.

From *Brief Historical Data and Memories of My Boyhood Days in Nantucket,* by Joseph E. C. Farnham, pp. 180–181. Providence: Joseph E. C. Farnham. 1923.

result of crisp, deliciously browned cross-pieces, so that the "wonder" easily broke into such separate sections, or bars, and was peculiarly appetizing.

. . . The ordinary ring doughnut, with hole in the center, in lusciousness could in no wise approximate unto them. Surely the "wonder" was—may I not say is?—the king of doughnuts. I have often in these later years "wondered" if the "wonder" was known as a "wonder" anywhere but at Nantucket. I am inclined to think that it is a name for a doughnut solely indigenous to my native town. Here in my adopted city of Providence I have produced occasional merriment by calling a doughnut, no matter the form in which it was made, a "wonder." The name is a "quaint" belonging exclusively to the town where it is used, is a "laconic" of its inhabitants, and is of "lore" exclusively their own—at least, I believe so.

Skully-Jo

. . . PROVINCETOWN youngsters used to carry around bits of a delicacy known as "skully-jo," which was a kind of dried fish, cured until it was very hard, and . . . they munched on this as children of other places ate candy—only it was said of skully-jo that the longer you chewed on it, the more you had. And if you ever lost or mislaid it, you could buy a new piece almost anywhere in town—including the hardware store.

"Biled Cider Apple Sass"

IN NEW ENGLAND what the "hired man" on the farm called "biled cider apple sass" took the place of apple butter. Preferably this was made in the "summer kitchen," where three kettles, usually of graduated sizes, could be set over the fire; the three kettles could be hung from a crane, or trammels. All were filled with cider, and as the liquid boiled away in the largest kettle it was filled from the second and that from the third. The fresh cider was always poured into the third kettle, thus the large kettle was never checked in its boiling. This continued till the cider was as thick as molasses. Apples (preferably Pound Sweets or Pumpkin Sweets) had been chosen with care, pared, cored, and quartered, and heated in a small kettle. These were slowly added to the thickened cider, in small quantities, in order not to check the boiling. The rule was to cook them till so softened that a rye straw could be run into them, and yet they must retain their shape. This was truly a critical time; the slightest scorched flavor would ruin the whole kettleful. A great wooden, long-handled, shovel-like ladle was used to stir the sauce fiercely until it was finished in triumph. Often

From *In Great Waters, The Story of the Portuguese Fishermen,* by Jeremiah Digges, pp. 56–57. Copyright, 1941, by Josef Berger. New York: The Macmillan Company.

From *Old Time Gardens,* Newly Set Forth by Alice Morse Earle, pp. 213–214. Copyright, 1901, by the Macmillan Company. New York and London. 1902.

a barrel of this was made by our grandmothers, and frozen solid for winter use. The farmer and "hired men" ate it clear as a relish with meats; and it was suited to appetites and digestions which had been formed by a diet of salted meats, fried breads, many pickles, and the drinking of hot cider sprinkled with pepper.

Salt Horse

THE cabin fare was the same as ours except that they had sugar for coffee and butter on their white bread (soft-tack) with a few delicacies thrown in. We had salt beef and pork, good of the kind, but the cabin was furnished with the choice cuts. The beef came in three-hundred-pound casks and was soaked in brine well saturated with saltpeter. When taken from the cask it was as red as a flannel shirt. It was put into a wooden oval cask, holding about forty gallons, larger at the bottom than the top to keep it from capsizing. The wood was usually scraped and oiled on the outside and bound with brass hoops, which were polished bright, and this piece of deck furniture, called a "harness-cask," was used exclusively for soaking out salt meat by covering it with salt water. The meat was allowed to soak for a day or so before it was fresh enough to cook.

It was customary at this time, when a cask of salt beef was opened, to let the steward first pick out the choice pieces, for the cabin, and leave the lean pieces for the crew. These were called by the sailors "old horse" and were thrown into the "harness-cask" only as the cook needed them. The name of "old horse" is ancient history. Richard H. Dana in his "Two Years before the Mast" says, "There is a story current among seamen that a beef-dealer was convicted, at Boston, of having sold an old horse for ship's stores, instead of beef, and had been sentenced to be confined in jail until he should eat the whole of it, and that he is now lying in Boston jail." He also quotes the rhyme all sailors knew in my time, "Old horse! Old horse! what brought you here?" This would seem to show that the name is purely American.

Another writer claims the words to be of Welsh extraction of years ago. The fact that Dana mentions the "harness-cask" would indicate that it was used years before he went to sea and he sailed from Boston, around the Horn to California in the brig *Pilgrim,* in the year 1834.

The "harness-cask" no doubt obtained its name from throwing the scraps of the old salt beef to be soaked out in a tub and it is easily understood how these scraps could have been called the horse's harness. Even in my day I have heard some old sailor with a grouch, when the evening

From *The Making of a Sailor* or Sea Life Aboard a Yankee Square-Rigger, by Frederick Pease Harlow, pp. 147–149. Publication Number Seventeen of The Marine Research Society. Copyright, 1928, by The Marine Research Society. Salem, Massachusetts.

meal was brought in, stab at a particularly uninviting dry piece of salt beef, with his fork or sheath-knife, in a vicious manner and with an oath that would arrest the attention of us all, hold it above the pan and reverently proceed to recite the well-known rhyme:

> Old horse! old horse! what brought you here?
> From. Sacarap' to Portland pier
> I carted stone for many a year.
> I labored long and well, alack,
> Till I fell down and broke my back.
> They picked me up with sore abuse
> And salted me down for sailor's use.
> The sailors they do me despise,
> They pick me up and damn my eyes,
> They eat my flesh and gnaw my bones
> And throw the rest to Davy Jones.

. . . The salt beef is not noted for its moisture and usually was as dry as a chip; but with salt pork, which we were allowed three times per week and is quite a delicacy, the beef was eatable. It takes a little time to get used to salt beef and at first it takes the skin off the roof of your mouth, but as with your hands in hauling ropes, your mouth soon becomes calloused and the sailor can digest anything he can swallow.

Whaleship's Menu

It would be a mistake to fail to preserve here the menu known to whalemen in the early days. It will intensify our respect for our forbears, who as lads were eager to risk the loss of all the comforts of home to sail on long voyages, knowing full well what conditions they would be compelled to meet. The mess table of those days was in strong contrast to what is served Jack in these days of tinned food-stuffs, and the "tar" of to-day is better looked after in every particular, through better national and international laws bearing upon his protection.

In the old days *Lobscouse* was a prominent feature of the menu of a whaleship. It was a stew of soaked hard-tack, pork fat, or "top o' the pot" (grease left after boiling "salt horse"—beef), or any sort of "slush" (sailor's term for grease), boiled with molasses and water.

Potato scouse was the same as above, excepting that potatoes were substituted for hard-tack.

Dandy junk. This appears to have been a dish of class on shipboard, made of powdered hard-tack, molasses, and water and baked in the oven —evidently a sort of pudding.

Salt horse (salted beef) was served twice a week, as was boiled salt pork.

Duff, boiled in a cloth, was on the menu twice weekly, and one day of the seven gingerbread was served.

Scalded yellow meal with molasses was served daily, and occasionally salt fish and potatoes.

Whale scraps were occasionally eaten, and porpoise meat, and sometimes fresh fish found place on the festive board; and when they were trying out a whale, advantage was taken of the abundance of hot fat to do more or less frying in the try-pots.[1]

To the whaleman, salt beef was always "meat," while pork was pork. As some preferred one and some the other, a sailor would frequently offer to swap his "meat" for his mess-mate's pork, or vice versa. Whalemen used to say they varied their diet by having salt horse and hard-tack one meal, and hard-tack and salt horse the next, and so on.

LOST ARTS AND PASSING INSTITUTIONS

Barnum Recalls the Good Old Days

MY FRIENDS: Among all the varied scenes of an active and eventful life, crowded with strange incidents of struggle and excitement, of joy and sorrow, taking me often through foreign lands and bringing me face to face with the king in his palace and the peasant in his turf-covered hut, I have invariably cherished with the most affectionate remembrance the place of my birth, the old village meeting house, without steeple or bell, where in its square family pew I sweltered in summer and shivered through my Sunday-school lessons in winter, and the old school-house where the ferule, the birchen rod and rattan did active duty, and which I deserved and received a liberal share [of]. I am surprised to find that I can distinctly re-

From *The Nantucket Scrap Basket*, Being a Collection of Characteristic Stories and Sayings of the People of the Town and Island of Nantucket, Massachusetts, Second Edition, Revised, Expanded, and Rearranged by William F. Macy, pp. 146–148. Copyright, 1916, by William F. Macy and Roland B. Hussey; 1930, by William F. Macy. Boston and New York: Houghton Mifflin Company. 1930.

[1] If a whaling man is lucky, he gets aboard a ship where the captain's wife is aboard. When the blubber is being "tried out," she often gives the crew a treat by frying a batch of doughnuts in the hot fat of the tried-out blubber.—Imogene Wolcott, *The Yankee Cook Book* (New York, 1939), p. 143.

From *Barnum*, by M. R. Werner, pp. 10–13. Copyright, 1923, by Harcourt, Brace and Company, Inc. Garden City, New York.
The character of his early environment in Bethel, Connecticut, was admirably summed up by Barnum when he was seventy-one years old. He presented a bronze fountain eighteen feet high, "the design a Triton of heroic size, spouting water from an uplifted horn," to the inhabitants of his birthplace. The town was decorated with flags and bunting, and the police and fire companies, with apparatus and bands of music, greeted their native son, their returned hero, the conqueror of Success. Barnum made this speech, which is inserted here because it tells with characteristic altiloquence more of his early life than anything he ever wrote, or which ever could be written by another.—M. R. W., *ibid.*, p. 10.

member events which occurred before I was four years old.

I can see as if but yesterday our hard-working mothers hetcheling their flax, carding their tow and wool, spinning, reeling, and weaving it into fabrics for bedding and clothing for all the family of both sexes. The same good mothers did the knitting, darning, mending, washing, ironing, cooking, soap and candle making, picked the geese, milked the cows, made butter and cheese, and did many other things for the support of the family.

We babies of 1810, when at home, were dressed in tow frocks, and the garments of our elders were not much superior, except on Sunday, when they wore their "go-to-meeting clothes" of homespun and linsey-woolsey.

Rain water was caught and used for washing, while that for drinking and cooking was drawn from wells with their "old oaken bucket" and long poles and well sweeps.

Fire was kept over night by banking up the brands in ashes in the fireplace, and if it went out one neighbor would visit another about daylight the next morning with a pair of tongs to borrow a coal of fire to kindle with. Our candles were tallow, home-made, with dark tow wicks. In summer nearly all retired to rest at early dark without lighting a candle except on extraordinary occasions. Home-made soft soap was used for washing hands, faces, and everything else. The children in families of ordinary circumstances ate their meals on trenchers, wooden plates. As I grew older our family and others got an extravagant streak, discarded the trenchers and rose to the dignity of pewter plates and leaden spoons. Tin peddlers who traveled through the country with their wagons supplied these and other luxuries. Our food consisted chiefly of boiled and baked beans, bean porridge, coarse rye bread, apple sauce, hasty pudding beaten in milk, of which we all had plenty. The elder portion of the family ate meat twice a day—had plenty of vegetables, fish of their own catching, and occasionally big clams, which were cheap in those days, and shad in their season. . . .

Our dinners several times each week consisted of "pot luck," which was corned beef, salt pork and vegetables, all boiled together in the same big iron pot hanging from the crane which was supplied with iron hooks and trammels and swung in and out of the huge fireplace. In the same pot with the salt pork, potatoes, turnips, parsnips, beets, carrots, cabbage, and sometimes onions, was placed an Indian pudding, consisting of plain Indian meal mixed in water, pretty thick, salted and poured into a home-made brown linen bag which was tied at the top. When dinner was ready the Indian pudding was *first* taken from the pot, slipped out of the bag and eaten with molasses. Then followed the "pot luck." . . .

There were but few wagons or carriages in Bethel when I was a boy. Our grists of grain were taken to the mill in bags on horseback, and the women rode to church on Sundays and around the country on week days on horseback, usually on a cushion called a pillion fastened behind the saddle, the husband, father, brother, or lover riding in front on the saddle. The country doctor visited his patients on horseback, carrying his saddle-bags, containing calomel, jalap, Epsom salts, lancet, and a turnkey, those being the principal aids in relieving the sick. Nearly every person sick or well was bled every spring.

Teeth were pulled with a turnkey, and a dreadful instrument it was in looks, and terrible in execution. . . .

I remember seeing my father and our neighbors put through military drill every day by Capt. Noah Ferry in 1814, for the war with Great Britain of 1812–15. . . .

My uncles, aunts, and others, when I was a child, often spoke about ravages of Indians from which their ancestors had suffered, and numbers of them remembered and described the burning of Danbury by the British in 1777. . . .

Esquire Tom Taylor sometimes wore white-topped boots. He was a large, majestic-looking man, of great will-force, and was considered the richest man in Bethel. Mr. Eli Judd was marked second in point of wealth. Every year I took twelve dollars to Esquire Tom Taylor to pay the interest on a two hundred dollar note which my father owed him. I also annually carried four dollars and fifty cents to Eli Judd for interest on a seventy-five dollar note which he held against my father. As these wealthy men quietly turned over each note filed away in a small package till they found the note of my father, and then indorsed the interest thereon, I trembled with awe to think I stood in the presence of such wonderfully rich men. It was estimated that the richer of them was actually worth three thousand dollars!

Esquire Tom Taylor made quite a revolution here by one act. He got two yards of figured carpet to put down in front of his bed in the winter, because the bare board floor was too cold for his feet, while he was dressing. This was a big event in the social life of that day, and Esquire Tom was thought to be putting on airs which his great wealth alone permitted.

When I was but ten years old, newspapers came only once a week. The man who brought us the week's papers came up from Norwalk, and drove through this section with newspapers for subscribers and pins and needles for customers. He was called Uncle Silliman. I can remember well his weekly visit through Bethel, and his queer cry. On coming to a house or village he would shout, "News! News! The Lord reigns!" One time he pass·d our schoolhouse when a snow storm was prevailing. He shouted: "News! News! The Lord reigns—and snows a little."

Everybody had barrels of cider in their cellars and drank cider-spirits called "gumption." Professors of religion and the clergy all drank liquor. They drank it in all the hat and comb shops, and the farmers had it at hay and harvest times. Every sort of excuse was made for being treated. A new journeyman must give a pint or quart of rum to pay his footing. If a man had a new coat he must "sponge" it by treating. Even at funerals the clergy, mourners, and friends drank liquor. At public vendues the auctioneer held a bottle of liquor in his hand and when bidding lagged he would cry "a dram to the next bidder," the bid would be raised a cent, and the bidder would take his boldly and be the envy of most of the others.

The public whipping post and imprisonment for debt both flourished in Bethel in my youthful days. Suicides were buried at crossroads. How blessed are we to live in a more charitable and enlightened age, to enjoy the comforts and conveniences of modern times, and to realize that the world is continually growing wiser and better.

I sincerely congratulate my native village on her character for temperance, industry, and other good qualities.

And now, my friends, I take very great pleasure in presenting this fountain to the town and borough of Bethel as a small evidence of the love which I bear them and the respect which I feel for my successors, the present and future citizens of my native village.

Some Public Land Record Lore of Vermont and New Hampshire

I

Many hints of early rural life, character and customs in New England can be found in the public land records.

For a long time New England was made up of communities, people who knew each other, cooperated with one another for reasons of necessity if not from real brotherliness, knew each other's business, and, in rural regions anyhow, each other's lands as well. In buying and selling such properties, they often wrote out their own descriptions for deeds themselves, from memory, with no help from surveyors or the technical terms, measurements, and so on, such professionals would use, thus saving money at the time. It is perfectly evident that they never imagined a day when the identity of their own or their neighbors' "calf pasture," "Smith lot," "Jones lot," "Wilson mowing," or other area, would not be publicly and generally known. This lack of imagination is reflected in many terms used and locations mentioned.

Here are some of the humorous or peculiar ways these people used to describe rural property corners or lines:

1. Manchester, Vt. "Beginning at a corner near a stump where Bill Robinson used to skin bears."

2. Sunapee, N.H. "Beginning at a point on the shore of Lake Sunapee near the Cherry tree where they build the steam boat."

3. Somewhere in Cheshire County, N.H. "A corner at the shore of the pond, marked by a hole in the ice." (This is recalled by several men in

---

Contributed by Heman Chase, Alstead, New Hampshire.

Cheshire County, N.H., but I cannot find where the land or the pond are. Such a description is not as indefinite as it sounds at first, because often a spring in the bottom of a pond will regularly keep a hole open, always in the same place within a few feet.)

4. Weston, Vt. "A corner marked by a tumblin weed."

5. Putney, Vt. "Beginning at a road fork, located 250 north of a grave yard and 200 feet northwest of the Baptist Dipping Hole."

6. Cheshire County, N.H. "Beginning at the point where you and I stood talking yesterday."

7. "Thence westerly about 20 rods to a white maple tree." (Following this instruction brought the survey party into a whole grove of white maple trees, none of which was ever marked by man.)

8. Cheshire County, N.H. "Thence along the west and north sides of the corncrib to the barn. Then along the north and east sides of the barn and running to the wall on the lane to the pasture," etc.

A typical complete land description might run like this:

Beginning at the southwest corner of the farm, this being Capt. Davis's Corner; thence northerly on land of said Davis to land of Eliphalet Jones; thence east on said Jones's land to his southeast corner and north to his northeast corner at land of Increase Johnson; thence east 50 rods and 12 links to the foot of the ledges; thence south and east along the ledges and land of the Widow Desire Gore French to her southeast corner; thence south and a little east as the old fence ran on land of Prosper Hardy to his southwest corner, marked by an old shot-gun barrel set in the ground; thence east on said Hardy's land to an oak staddle [small oak] on the east side of the swamp; thence south to the road; thence to the place beginning. Containing 190 acres, be the same more or less.

II

There were many such strange "deals" to be found among public land records. There was, too, one fairly standardized way of "taking care of the aged" (and administering medical care to them); namely, the deeding of the farm to a younger couple, for which they—the grantees—agreed to render complete basic care, usually enumerating—taking "shelter" for granted—the several necessities, food, clothing, nursing, medicine and tobacco. This sort of arrangement was very common. One exceptional case, in Cheshire County, New Hampshire, had an additional element of "consideration"; to wit, "and four barrels of cider each year." This deal lasted but one week, for by a following deed, the younger couple deeded the place right back to the old man. Though the records are silent as to who desired to back out, one valid hypothesis is—many old New England men being what they were—that the delivery of the first barrel so impaired the tranquility of the home, and the health of the old man was so good, that the young people saw that they could not stand the possible duration of the arrangement.

Two men, long keeping house together on a farm in Windham County, Vermont, had, it would seem, an acrimonious falling out, for not only did they divide the property "by a line passing easterly through the center of the front door step, the front door, the hall, the kitchen, the back door, and continuing to the east line of the farm," but in the two quit claim deeds (or boundary agreements) by which the property was distributed, each grantor agreed, further, thus: "And I agree never to lay no claim to nothing laying to the north (or south) of the herein described line."

Bees, Change-Work, and Whangs

. . . SOMETIMES a logging-bee was made to clear a special lot for a neighbor, and a band of wood-choppers worked all day together. It was cheerful work, though the men had to stand all day in the snow, and the thermometer was below zero. But there was no cutting wind in the forest, and the exercise kept the blood warm. Many a time a hearty man would drop his axe to wipe the sweat from his brow. Loose woolen frocks, or long-shorts, two or three over each other, were warm as are the overlapping feathers of a bird; a few had buckskin or sheepskin waistcoats; their hands were warmly covered with home-knit mittens. In later days all had heavy well-greased boots, but in the early years of such pioneer settlements, as the towns of New Hampshire and Vermont, all could not afford to wear boots. Their place was well supplied by heavy woolen stockings, shoes, and an over-covering of old stockings, or cloth soaked in neat's-foot oil; this was deemed a positive preventive of frozen feet.

It was the custom both among men and women to join forces on a smaller scale and have a little neighborly visiting by what was called "change-work." For instance, if two neighbors both were to make soap, or both to make apple-butter, or both to make up a rag carpet, instead of each woman sitting at home alone sewing and fitting the carpet, one would take her thimble and go to spend the day, and the two would sew all day long, finish and lay the carpet at one house. In a few days the visit would be returned, and the second carpet be finished. Sometimes the work was easier when two worked together. One man could load logs and sled them down to the sawmill alone, but two by "change-work" could accomplish the task much more rapidly and with less strain.

Even those evil days of New England households, the annual house-cleaning, were robbed of some of their dismal terrors by what was known as a "whang," a gathering of a few friendly women neighbors to assist one another in that dire time, and thus speed and shorten the hours of misery.

From *Home Life in Colonial Days,* by Alice Morse Earle, pp. 416–417. Copyright, 1898, by The Macmillan Company. New York and London. 1919.

Raisings

> "Here is a fine house! It stands high on dry land.
> The owner is rich, and a very fine man.
> At home he is honored, and abroad it's the same;
> May he still keep increasing in honor and fame.
> This house it stands square, and in a fair view
> Of a river, fine meadows and neighbors a few.
> The timber is square, and is well put together;
> May God bless the owner, forever and ever!"

THIS was the toast proposed by Kimball Fletcher in 1835, when Parker Tabor's frame house was raised near the river in old Indian Stream Republic, now the town of Pittsburg, which lies just under the Canadian border.

In New Hampshire, as elsewhere in pioneer America, a "raising" brought out all the neighbors for miles around. Every available able-bodied man came to lift the heavy timbers when the master-builder gave the signal and cried, "Heave O heave!" The women gathered to serve the mammoth noon meal and early supper; the boys, accompanied by their dogs, scampered around everywhere, carrying tools and water to the workmen and running errands for the women.

Unless there was a bad accident like the one which happened in 1773 when the Wilton meetinghouse was raised and one of the center beams supporting the frame broke and pitched timber, axes, board saws, and fifty men to the ground, raisings were gala occasions for the whole countryside. During the day there were intervals of relaxation from the hard work of lifting the great sills, plates, posts, and beams, when the young men held races and wrestled while their elders smoked and gossiped and watched the fun. Everybody had access to the hard cider and to the West India rum, which was furnished by the town if a public building was raised or by the host when a house was put up.

Liquid refreshments usually helped out even in the raisings of meeting-houses. In Mont Vernon, when the church was framed in the late eighteenth century, the building committee was instructed to provide one barrel of rum, two barrels of cider, and "one quarter of sugar" for the workmen. Tradition also tells us that the lack of rum at the raising of the Sandown meetinghouse, completed in 1774, was responsible for the first labor strike in New Hampshire. The supply ran out just as the workmen were about to put on the roof; so the men refused to work for half a day while a messenger was sent down to Newburyport for another half-barrel.

But in some communities there was opposition to so much drinking at raisings. The master builder, William Abbot of Boscawen, framer of

From *Hands That Built New Hampshire,* The Story of Granite State Craftsmen Past & Present, compiled by Workers of the Writers' Program of the Work Projects Administration in the State of New Hampshire, pp. 25–27. Copyright, 1940, by Francis P. Murphy, Governor of New Hampshire. Brattleboro, Vermont: Stephen Daye Press.

churches at Somersworth, Cornish, Wentworth, Unity, Thornton, Henniker, and West Concord, took an active part in temperance reform. When the question of buying liquor for the raising of the West Concord meeting-house came up in 1820, Mr. Abbot opposed it vigorously. He was told that there was always drinking at raisings and that it would be impossible to get workmen without rum.

"If there are not enough temperance men in Concord, I'll try and get them elsewhere," answered. "Send me down twelve good men," he told Thomas Coffin of Boscawen. There were so many volunteers that nearly one hundred men arrived to raise the meetinghouse, without rum.

The high point of a raising came after the body of the frame was actually up, the beams put in place, and the rafters placed in position, a pair at a time. Then the final task of pinning the ribs, to which the shingles were to be fastened, was divided between two crews, both ready for a merry contest to see which team would get its allotment of ribs placed first. The honor of setting the ridgepole and naming the building went to the victors, so the rivalry between the teams was great. When the last nail had been pounded down, two men from the winning team, each one with a bottle in his hand, clambered out on the ridgepole. Reaching the center of their high perch, up they stood, one of them facing the south, and the other, the north.

"This is a fine frame and deserves a good name!" one man cried, following a recognized custom of the North Country.

"Oh, yes! Oh, yes!" chanted the crowd below him. "What shall we call it?"

The man facing the north answered by giving a very humorous or elaborate name; and when his companion sang out "Oh, yes!", each of them took a long drink from his bottle.

An eye-witness of a barn-raising held in Coös County in the mid-nineteenth century says that, in this particular instance, one of the pseudo godparents was a sailor who added an original note to the customary procedure by reciting at the top of his lungs:

> "The owner is a cooper, a jolly old soul,
> We'll drink all his rum, but leave the ridgepole."

Sailors were particularly popular at raisings, for they dared to climb to and height and to perform all kinds of daring feats. They stood on the ridgepole or hung down by their heels as they drank the toast and christened the building, according to their own doggerel:

> "Some oak and some pine,
> Some coarse and some fine,
> Some old and some new,
> Hand on the bottle and that will do."

Country Auctions

ONE OF THE interesting features of our early life in the country was going
to auctions. Hartley Dennett, my stepfather, loved to go to auctions and
he bought a great many antiques and old tools. In fact, during his lifetime
and that of my mother, they collected about four housefuls of antique
furniture and other equipment. Our favorite auctioneer was the renowned
James A. Hall, who died only recently at a very great age.

I can well remember the first time I ever as a child got up the courage
to bid on anything at an auction. It was down at the Old Brick House a
little west of Roundy's Corner in Gilsum, which has long since burnt. Mr.
Hall had the habit of setting aside some article on which there had not
been a bid, planning to throw it in with whatever he sold next. As a child I
had failed to notice what was about to befall me when I bid ten cents for
a large checkerboard. When it was knocked down to me for ten cents,
there being no other bids, just before he handed it to me he placed upon
it two large white chamber pots—an item which always drew much
humor at country auctions. I was pretty red in the face as he said, "Sold
to the young man, and the pots go with it." I remember I carefully put
those pots out behind the house and never took them home.

I remember there were two humorous incidents that occurred at the
Wood auction. The Wood house is the house just southeast of the church
in East Alstead. Mr. Hall had that auction. Many people were gathered
in seats under Mr. Hall's tent in readiness for the auction. Two old ladies
came up the aisle between the seats looking for a place to sit down, and
Mr. Hall saw them and he said, "Step right up front, ladies. There are
plenty of seats up here. There's a couple of young men sitting here but
I'm sure they'll be glad to give their seats to you." And then he turned to
Joe, his assistant, and he said, "I betcha they won't move."

The other incident was this. Just before the auction was to begin two
people begged to be let into the house for a preliminary glance at what
was to be sold. The Wood family heirs had not wanted any one to come in
the house, but finally they did accede to Mr. Hall's request, which was
put in these words. He said, "Here are some people that would just like
to glance into the house before the sale starts. They're very good friends
of mine. I'm sure they're absolutely honest. Of course, we'll search 'em
when they come out."

I remember at Westmoreland at the sale of a lot of farm implements
and wagons and carriages the next thing to be sold was a one-seated buggy
with a very long dark cover over it. And when Mr. Hall finally said—oh,
I forgot to say there was an old man with a full beard just sitting in the
shade of the cover in the seat of the carriage—it was somebody Jim knew—
and when he finally said "Sold"—for whatever the bid had been—he said,

As told by Heman Chase, Alstead, New Hampshire, February 13, 1964. Recorded
by B. A. Botkin.

"And the bird cage goes with it." And then he added, "Oh, Fred, I didn't know that was you."

At Acworth, I remember going to an auction with Hartley—mostly of farm tools. It was a terribly, terribly cold day, and the thermometer must have been way below zero, but still they held the sale. One item to be sold was a very large crowbar, and I remember Mr. Hall looking it over before asking for bids. He said, "Why, that's a fine crowbar. It would be very useful to pry frozen cows up with in the morning." Some time after that they brought a small crowbar and he said, "Well, here's a nice little crowbar. It must be awfully good for something—oh, will probably be very good to pry calves up with."

Hartley Dennett never minded being the butt of quite a number of jokes at auctions and his good nature was always indicated by Mr. Hall's confidence in him, which was reflected in this: Very often if there wasn't a bid on some article, Mr. Hall would say, "Are you all done? All done? Sold to Hartley Dennett for five cents," even though Hartley hadn't bid at all.

Mrs. Spurr—Sophie Spurr—was always going to auctions. I remember on one occasion Mr. Hall sold her a large-print Bible, and he ended up the sale with these words, "Sold to Mrs. Spurr for seventy-five cents. I warrant it will never be opened."

Mr. Hall was not so good in his set stories as he was at his incidental remarks made on the spur of the moment. Mr. Hall knew just about how far he could go with the summer people and the year-round people. I remember one time he said to a Polish woman who had said that a bed sheet which he'd just sold her wasn't wide enough—why, he said, "Well, when Fred ain't awake you can pull it over on your side." He wouldn't have said that to the summer people.

Sugaring Science

LIKE I said, they generally start sugaring operations along the first week in March; they begin to wash the buckets. Nowadays they get the buckets out of the sugarhouse and scald them. In grandpa's time they didn't have sugarhouses, to begin with, and at first they didn't even keep buckets from year to year, but made wooden trenchers.

They would cut down a white birch or some other tree with soft wood, and split the tree in half. They would adz out a hollow in the flat side and chop off that section, and then adz out another hollow and chop that off. So the trenchers was a sort of rough oblong chopping bowls, as you might say. They didn't hang them on the trees, but just propped them up on the ground where the sap was handy.

From "Grandpa Was Quite a Fellow," by Walter Needham, as recorded by Barrows Mussey, *Saturday Evening Post*, Vol. 219 (Nov. 9, 1946), No. 19, pp. 93–94, 96. Copyright, 1946, by The Curtis Publishing Company. Philadelphia.

When they got their trenchers made or their buckets tightened up and cleaned and distributed around by the trees, they could start tapping. The Indians used to cut a gash in the tree just as if they was making turpentine. Gramp had got a little beyond that; he used a tapping iron.

A tapping iron looks like a big gouge chisel, and it was used the same way—you simply drove it into the tree at a right angle. Then you put in a steel sap spout. They've come back to metal spouts again now; the oldest and the newest spouts is metal, and the wooden ones that you occasionally see come from the time in between.

The auger to bore a hole for tapping is newer, too; the old-time blacksmiths couldn't make an auger, where they could make a tapping iron. The big old three-quarter-inch augers with a wooden cross handle go along with the wooden spouts. You will find a great many old trees around here that have been bored with an old T-handled three-quarter-inch auger. Now, of course, they only use a half or three-eighths bit, with the small metal spout.

The old steel spouts was made by the blacksmith out of worn-out scythe blades. The blacksmith would cut off the heavy rim on the back to make nails with, and bend the thin part into spouts. That was just one sign of how precious metal was in gramp's time. That was why the blacksmith was such a big man in the community.

The steel spouts they drove into the cut made by the tapping iron. The wooden spouts was whittled out of staghorn shoemake. I've made them myself. You take a piece that is about right for size, and whittle it around to fit a hole the size of your auger. You cut away half of the spout on top, and just left the end that went into the tree round. Then you run a hot iron through the pith and burned out a hole for the sap to flow through.

The science of tapping a tree is something that not many people know. The only results you get from tapping comes from the sap growth, the outer growth. You could bore a hole clear to the center of the tree, and you wouldn't get no more sap than if you just bored two inches under the bark. There is only two inches' depth of sapwood on a tree. You can bore as much deeper as you're a mind to, and all you will do is hurt the tree.

The trees don't seem to be damaged any by tapping. Some of the old holes in a big tree will be ten inches under the bark. Wherever you bore, it makes a kind of an elliptical dead place, and that spot always stays in the tree forever, and the hole doesn't fill up; it grows over, but it won't fill up. You cut any old maple, and you will find the holes far underneath the bark.

In deciding where to tap a tree, you pick out a place that has new growth. It's very hard to tell without you study it, but if you look at the tree, there will be new cracks or openings in the bark. As the tree expands, the bark doesn't expand with it, but keeps splitting open; that is why they are shaggy. If you look around carefully, you will find where the new growth shows on the bark.

The next part of the science is to set your buckets on the side where there is the most limbs or the biggest limbs. The sap goes to the limbs, so you always look up a tree as well as at the bark. You look for the new growth on the side where the limbs will draw the sap. The ideal is to get more or less on the southeasterly exposure, but you tap on any side if the new growth and limbs is right.

Once a tree has been tapped, you mustn't tap directly in line with the old hole, above it or below it. If you tap below it, you will get sap, but it's injurious to the tree. If you tap above it, you won't get any sap. Just move out of line to one side, and it won't matter. The height doesn't matter in itself; you just want a convenient level for handling the buckets.

Well, you tap your trees and you hand your buckets. Then you come back to the weather and the season, the same as gramp done every day of his life. They've got their evaporators and their central-reservoir gathering systems and their state grading nowadays, but the weather is still the only thing that will make the sap run.

To get a good run of sap, it should freeze hard at night and thaw daytimes. For a good sap day there must be a west wind and bright sunshine; It is unusual that sap will run on a south wind.

When the snow goes and the frost gets out of the ground, the minute the buds begin to swell on the tree, the sirup starts to take on a leathery taste. It's like the difference between Scotch and straight whisky. What little sap runs after that is called the bud run; that sugar is generally just sold for tobacco sweetening. The quality of the sap varies from year to year too. Some years it's good and some years it's quite sandy. And some years it's sweeter than other years, so you get more sirup for the same amount of sap.

In a bad year, the sap won't hardly run at all, to do you any good; in a very good year, it may run as long as four weeks. It isn't usually steady. It will run a day or two, and you'll have a freeze-up and it will stop entirely. Then it will start again and run two or three days more. As long as it freezes at night, you're all right; you don't get the buddy taste. During some of these extra runs, the sap may even run all night, and the buckets will be full again in the morning. Then the buckets may start to sour, and instead of drawing sap away, you have to draw water to the buckets and wash them.

Gramp would go around and collect in the morning, and again in the afternoon. Nowadays they use a big gathering tub on a sledge or even run the sap straight from the trees down metal gutters to a reservoir. In gramp's time, you just lugged the buckets in by hand, and they got pretty heavy along toward night, especially if the snow was deep. The modern buckets hold around fourteen to fifteen quarts. The old ones was a lot more awkward, but they had two of the staves on opposite sides prolonged at the top, with a stick running between them for a handle. A lot of people in gramp's time used wooden sap yokes—pieces of wood hollowed out to fit over your shoulders, with a semicircle cut out for the neck and a piece sticking out from the shoulder at each end. You would take two of your wide-bottomed wooden buckets, and hang them by cords on the ends of the yoke, and go to a tree. You could collect from one tree to another until your two buckets was full or, if the ones on the tree was full, you would just swap buckets and go back. In those days you wouldn't pretend to gather a great ways off. Sometimes you see a sap yoke made of two bows fastened together at the ends, with two straps across in between for your shoulders, but I think those mostly come from Canada.

Before the time of the gathering tub, they would just go around and collect the sap, come back and pour it in a big kettle over a fire of maple chunks, and leave it to boil while they went back for more sap. When things got more permanent, they used what they called a sap pan—just an ordinary big iron pan maybe eight feet long and two or three feet wide. That's all I ever knew of gramp's using. After that come the evaporator. There's different kinds of evaporators, but the idea is about the same in all of them. The Bellows Falls evaporator, for example, is a sap pan with crosswise partitions. Each partition connects at one end with the wall of the pan, and at the other end it doesn't. The openings are at alternate ends, so that the cold sap flows in over the fire on the front end, and zigzags through these partitions until it gets to the back end, which has a partition with a gate. You lift up the gate and fill the back end. You shut the gate and start watching your thermometer; the back end boils slowly because it's so far away from the fire, and when you get to the temperature of sirup or sugar—the sugar temperature is higher, of course—you draw the liquid off through a felt strainer into your cans or tubs or whatever you're putting it up in.

In the old days they used to use part of the run to make sap beer. They put the sap in a barrel and let it ferment, just the same as you make cider. I never knew of grandpa's making sap beer, which may be why I never cared much for it. I don't think it's a very appetizing drink myself, but if you go back into the hills around Wardsboro at the right time, you will still get some sap beer, in case you want to try it.

Gramp's sirup was a black molasses, of course, but like I said, he would boil it on down to sugar, and pour it into crocks or tubs. He made wooden sugar tubs specially, and he would pour the liquid sugar right in and let it harden in the tub. When they wanted some sugar, they'd just go in there and crack some out. Sometimes they might melt it. If they wanted it fine, they would pound it up. Ordinarily, they used it in lumps just as they pounded it out, for cooking or in their tea. They didn't drink coffee much in those days, anyway. For sweetening, they put it on the stove and heated it, because when it was melted you could measure it. They melted it for pancakes, too.

Sugaring off is a big occasion around here. The young folks will come in for a party, with doughnuts and coffee and sour pickles. They bring in tubs of snow. They boil the sirup down until it will wax—a little past what the cookbook calls the soft-ball stage—and then they pour it on the snow. It cools right away into sheets or strips, not particularly sticky, and you can pick it straight off the snow with a fork and eat it. The pickles is to cut the sweetness, so as you can eat more sugar.

In the old days they used to sugar off sometimes on the kitchen stove, and they would hang a piece of fat salt pork from the stove shelf. When the sirup got to boiling up, it would hit that salt pork and would flatten right out.

After white sugar got to be common, and maple sugar was something special, it was mostly sold as cake sugar. I remember when they sold a five-pound box of cake sugar for a dollar. That box would probably cost you around six dollars now, if you could find it. I helped put the cakes up in nice clean white basswood boxes with pinked paper. My job was pinking the paper with a toothed iron.

When I was in Indiana I met a girl at Huntington who had what she called maple sugar and pecan nuts, a kind of black stuff. I told her she didn't know what maple sugar was, and I sent her out a box of the best maple sugar I could find. She wouldn't give in, though; she said that was maple candy.

Late years they think they have to have stirred sugar—a very recent invention. You cook it to the temperature marked for stirred sugar on your sugar thermometer, and while it's cooling you beat it with a wooden paddle. It's like warm butter, and never hardens; it grains, but the grains are very fine from being beaten, and that makes it white. It makes a pretty good spread or a frosting, but it don't taste much like maple to me.

Another thing they do in making these little candy hearts and leaves and shapes like that, they dip them in hot sirup while they're fresh. That glazes them and keeps the inside from ever hardening.

Building a Stone Wall

GRAMP was really more of a hand with the cobblestones that come up out of the field. They was something the seasons brought out on the farm. The land hereabouts is strewed with these round, smooth stones left by the ice sheets, supposedly. They are various kinds but mostly a granite formation that was rolled in here.

They would plow once the best they could to free the stones some. They would just dig out the small ones with a spade. For the big ones they would have to use the oxen and a stoneboat. They would dig around them, and then flip a chain over the stone with what they called a rolling hitch. It was quite a trick to make the hitch stay on various different shapes of stone, because no two were alike. It looked simple, but I can't even tell you what a rolling hitch is like without I see the stone you're going to hitch on to. Anyway, with a proper rolling hitch, the oxen could pull the stone right out of the ground and onto the stoneboat.

A stoneboat is merely a large plank toboggan, except the front end is not turned up so high. The planks was sawed special, nosed up at the

Ibid., p. 99.

end, so that the front would run three inches or so from the ground. At the sawmill the planks was sawed straight to a certain point, and then put on the carriage at a diagonal and sawed the rest of the way, so the nose turned up.

The stone walls both fenced in the fields and cleared them out. In preparation for the wall, they would plow the loam where the wall was going, and shovel it out more or less to the subsoil. Then they would draw the stoneboat along beside this trench, and roll the big ones in for foundation stones. Quite often they would wall off a ten-acre lot, forty rods one way and forty rods the other. Sometimes it was only haphazard.

After gramp had rolled the big stones off into the ditch and placed them to suit him, he would draw the boat beside of it. As fast as the boat comes along he would take off the small stones that a man could pick up, and he'd throw them right on the wall, and build it straight ahead just as easy as you please. He worked so fast you might have thought he was just throwing them in at random, yet when he got through, the wall was as solid as if it was one rock.

Samplers

THE word sampler, the "ensempler" of Chaucer's day, referred originally to the fact that these pieces were a means of recording needlework stitches for future reference. All seventeenth-century samplers, both English and American, had this purpose. They were made by experienced needle-workers, and the stitches worked on them were elaborate and intricate in design. Like English samplers of the period, American specimens were rich with drawnwork, cutwork, and lace stitches which the owners intended to use in the adornment of bed curtains, petticoats, and other household and personal finery. Few of them are in existence today. An exhaustive search conducted by the Society of the Colonial Dames of Massachusetts in 1921 revealed only seven American samplers of the years of 1600–1700. One of these is the well-known Anne Gower sampler (actually made in England), embroidered by the first wife of Governor John Endicott of

---

From *Hands That Built New Hampshire*, The Story of Granite State Craftsmen Past and Present, compiled by Workers of the Writers' Program of the Work Project Administration in the State of New Hampshire, pp. 176–179, 180–181. Copyright, 1940, by Francis P. Murphy, Governor of New Hampshire. Brattleboro, Vermont: Stephen Daye Press.

The oldest sampler I have ever seen is in the collection of antique articles now in Pilgrim Hall at Plymouth. It was made by a daughter of the Pilgrims. The verse embroidered on it reads:—

> Lorea Standish is My Name.
> Lord Guide my Heart that I may do thy Will,
> And fill my Hands with such convenient skill
> As will conduce to Virtue void of Shame,
> And I will give the Glory to thy Name.

—Alice Morse Earle, *Home Life in Colonial Days* (New York and London, 1919), p. 266.

Massachusetts Bay Colony. None of the seven was of New Hampshire origin.

These early samplers were worked on the narrow, coarse linens produced on the hand looms used at the time. The embroidery threads were linen or loosely woven silk strands, usually no coarser than present-day sewing silks. "Sam-cloths," as they were called, could be easily rolled up, tucked into a bag or an apron pocket, and then brought out at an instant's notice when the needleworker wished to study a stitch or to add a new one to her collection. Sometimes they were a yard long and only eight to twelve inches wide. Even after wider linen became available, they held to this convenient, longer-than-wide form during the years when samplers were used simply for pattern purposes.

The oldest New Hampshire sampler of which we have record was worked by Mary Wingate of Hampton, probably in 1719, and is nearly twice as long as it is wide. Besides the pattern stitches, it is ornamented with designs of animals and birds and has two sets of alphabets. Another example of these longer-than-wide samplers is one made in 1731 by Lydia Hart. It is owned by the New Hampshire Historical Society.

Besides the rows of stitches with colorful names, like trellis stitch, holly stitch, fern stitch, queen stitch, and fisher stitch, all of which John Taylor immortalized in verse in 1640, samplers were adorned with alphabets and numerals, as patterns to mark household linens and to keep track of the number of pieces turned out. They were also embellished with embroidered portrayals of "Flowers, Plants, and Fishes, Beasts, Birds, Flyes, and Bees," as Taylor, in "Needle's Excellency," pointed out three hundred years ago:

> There's nothing near at hand, or farthest sought,
> But with the needle may be shaped and wrought.

Many of the motifs were executed in that oldest form of needlework decoration, the cross-stitch, which is still one of the best liked of stitches. Arranged in double lines, blocks, and borders, the tiny crosses make perfect frames to enclose embroidered verses and pictures. After 1740 few samplers were made which did not include such frames.

On a sampler embroidered in 1729 by Polly Eppes of Francestown, and now owned by Mrs. Orpha Durgin of Manchester, the border appears only as a frame around the verse, but it anticipates the general use of borders by a number of years. This piece of New Hampshire needlework, next

---

Other sampler rhymes:

Mary Jackson is my name,
America my nation,
Boston is my dwelling place,
And Christ is my salvation.

Dorothy Lynde is my Name
And this Work is mine
My Friends may have
When I am Dead and laid in Grave
This Needlework of mine can tell
That in my youth I learned well
And by my elders also taught
Not to spend my time for naught.
(In Old South Church, Boston)

—Alice Morse Earle, *Child Life in Colonial Days* (New York, 1899), pp. 332, 333.

in age to the Wingate sampler, is worked on two layers of linen. On it Polly inscribed this couplet:

> This needle work of mine doth tell
> That the child hath learned well.

When the sampler advanced from the sam-cloth stage to a status where it was displayed as a certificate of merit for ability in needlecraft, the name of the work, the date it was finished, and an inscription, became part of the design. Many of the inscriptions of eighteenth and nineteenth century work were moral mottoes, often designed to instruct the young needlewoman in the precepts of daily living. Mrs. Mary Thompson of Troy says she was brought up on the principle expressed in a verse on her grandmother's sampler, and that she, in turn, impressed the thought upon her own children. When one of them started to complain of another's wrongdoing, Mrs. Thompson quoted the first line and asked the child to complete the quatrain which little Ruth Aked embroidered in 1811:

> How soon our watchful eyes can view
> The smallest faults which others do
> Yet to our own we're ever blind
> And very few or none we find.

The stanza worked by Sarah K. Little in 1827 is more sombre in its feeling and quite similar to the melancholy lines which were inscribed on samplers made during the years when the followers of Jonathan Edwards were hurling their threats of damnation at the New England people. Fourteen-year-old Sarah embroidered a design of pink roses and green leaves with feathery edges on her sampler, but she enclosed in a black-bordered frame the following verse:

> As summer flowers fall to rise no more
> As billows rise and die upon the shore
> So generations live and pass away
> They sleep in silence till the Judgement Day.

This sampler hangs in the Manchester Historic Association Building.
Even more lugubrious is the inscription on a sampler owned by Mrs. Eaton Sargent of Nashua:

> Let me in life prepare to die
>   That I may live with God on high,
> With Saints and Angels let me be
>   And dwell with them eternally.

The saddest note of all the words enclosed in the beautifully embroidered border is found in these words: "Elizabeth Gage wrought this in 1822 in the 10th year of her age."

Among the definite changes which took place in the evolution of the

American sampler during the eighteenth century was the decrease in the ages of their makers. The samplers of the seventeenth century were embroidered by mature women; by the 1780's they had become the prerogative of girls around thirteen years of age and younger. Every well-brought up daughter of the family made at least one, to show that she had served her apprenticeship in an important branch of work which for centuries has been allotted to womankind.

* * * * *

The period between the close of the Revolutionary War and the beginning of the Civil War was the great era of American sampler-making. Nineteenth-century samplers are distinguished for their original designs, which include birds of a coloring and shape Audubon never catalogued, and animals of strangely mixed characteristics. Pictorial samplers portraying Biblical scenes, like the tempting of Adam and Eve, and the spies returning from the Land of Canaan, or showing representations of patriotic symbols, public buildings, and dwelling houses, were all popular.

Death, never far distant from the minds of early New England settlers, left a definite imprint on needlework designs. Memorial samplers,

> Each with its urn and stiffly-weeping tree
> Devoted to some memory long ago
> More faded than their lines of worsted woe, [1]

often were worked at girls' schools as a part of the assigned courses in needlework for all young gentlewomen. . . .

* * * * *

Genealogical samplers, which appeared just before the Revolutionary War, read like pages from the family Bible, and provide a valuable historic record of births, marriages, and deaths. . . .

Quilting

FOR many years patchwork, like sampler-making, was part of every young girl's education. According to Lucy Larcom, almost every New England girl learned to make patchwork at school while she was learning the alphabet.

Patchwork bedcovers were divided into two groups: the "comforter," made with a thick interlining, and the quilt, in which the interlining was much lighter. The top and under covers of the "comforter" were held together by strands of worsted pulled through them and the interlining and then tied or "tacked" together, while the coverings of quilts were

---

[1] James Russell Lowell.

Ibid., pp. 183–185, 186, 187–189.

fastened by means of fine patterns done in running stitches.

Quilting was an art in itself, and needleworkers were proud of their ability in this line. Sometimes they "quilted by the eye"; again they used the edge of a saucer or pan to make patterns of scallops or circles. Sometimes a string was chalked and stretched tautly across the quilt top. It was then snapped to impress the lines of the design on the fabric. A Nashua woman says that one of her earliest recollections was watching her grandmother mark a quilt in this manner. "Snap it again, Grannie!" she always cried as her grandmother completed each step of the marking process.

Another method of marking patterns was by means of carved wooden blocks which were heavily chalked and then pressed firmly against the upper side of the coverlet. Mrs. R. P. Peabody, a native of the Androscoggin valley town of Shelburne, wrote in 1882 that in her girlhood pressed quilts were part of every bride's marriage outfit. She recalled a number of pressed quilts of unusual beauty made by her mother's friends. One was bright green, lined with straw color, and quilted in inch squares with blue thread; another was blue, quilted in little fans; a third was quilted in feather work with a border of sunflower leaves, and then cross-quilted in straight lines. The patterns for these, like most others made in this vicinity, were pressed and marked by Mrs. Ezekiel Evans, who was famous in those days for her designs.

In the nineteenth century, needlewomen who were expert quilters were the queens of the quilting bees. All the women in the neighborhood were invited to these social gatherings, which combined business and pleasure, to quilt or tack the patchwork tops made by the hostess during the winter. Probably no other festival is more fundamentally a part of early American folklore than is the quilting bee. Customary thrift and industry imposed traditional restrictions on gaiety unless it was for a practical purpose, but a day busily spent over a quilting frame provided that justification. The men folks came to the bee, the village parson rendered thanks for all material benefits, and then merriment reigned. The hostess prepared stewed chicken, smoked hams, beans and Indian pudding baked in brick ovens, pies, cakes, jams, preserves, and pickles. After the evening meal, in communities where such amusement was permitted, the floor was cleared for games and dancing.

* * * * *

The terms "pieced" quilt and "patchwork" quilt have become synonymous through common usage, despite the fact that to *piece* means to *join by seams* and to *patch* means to *sew a smaller piece of goods onto a larger one*. Strictly speaking, the appliquéd quilt belongs in the latter category.

The pieced variety is the more common, and nearly all the quilts made in America before 1750 were of this type. The pieced squares of geometrical figures, based on the square, the rectangle, the diamond, the circle, and the hexagon, were made by sewing together vari-colored pieces of cloth, usually combining an equal number of light and dark pieces. Quiltmakers were proud of the fine stitches they used in joining these myriad bits of fabric. A quilt of this kind, composed of four triangular pieces in the inch block pattern, the whole containing 42,568 pieces, was completed by a young girl of Bow when she was only ten years of age. It, too, was displayed at the New Hampshire Historical Society exhibition of 1939.

In making appliquéd or laid-on quilts, flowers, leaves, wreaths, and similar motifs were cut from colored fabrics and sewed with small stitches to a neutral background. The one well-known deviation from these two standard groups is the crazy quilt, in which odds and ends of cloth were put together hit-or-miss "crazy fashion," and which was probably the earliest type of American-made quilt. In its simplest form it was designed to use up scraps of worn-out clothing; the more elaborate type, which was very popular in the late nineteenth century, consisted of "boughten" pieces of cloth and was adorned with featherstitching, herringbone, and other examples of line stitches.

* * * * *

Every quilt block, from the simple pieced-up "four-square" and "nine-square" to the intricate laid-on "Rising Sun," has its own individual name. To the imagination of our feminine ancestors, we are indebted for the variety given the designs of their handicraft. Living experiences, involving history, religion, politics, romance, and nature, were reproduced through the creations of their fingers, and christened "Log Cabin," "Star of Bethlehem," "Tree of Life," "Jacob's Ladder," "Rose of Sharon," "Whig Rose," "Yankee Pride," "Fifty-Four Forty or Fight," "Lincoln's Platform," "Air Castle," "Lovers' Links," "Orange Peel," and other picturesque names.

Variations of the "Log Cabin," "Star," and "Basket" designs are perhaps the most popular with modern quiltmakers. One elderly New Hampshire needlewoman confided to a visitor that there was "an awful lot of sameness" in her quilts because she loved the basket pattern. She said: "When I'm making patchwork, I think of all the baskets I've had. One I used to put apples in, shiny red Mackintoshes, one for flowers, and then my old work basket—I sort of miss my old work basket, it got lost someway. But I do like baskets."

One of the most ornate designs ever used by American quiltmakers is the "American Eagle," which was applied to many forms of arts and crafts during the first part of the last century. Mrs. Mabel F. Ames of Somersworth displayed a quilt decorated with this symbol at the Rochester Fair in 1939. The quilt was made approximately one hundred and fifty years ago. In the center, narrow red, green, and gold bands, shaped like elongated leaves, form a circle. These are enclosed in a narrow band of crosswise stitches, arranged to form a sort of frame to the first picture. Around this circle are placed four eagles with heads and tails of green, bodies of deep gold color, and spreading red wings. A four-inch band of needle scrollwork, finished with a band of red, encircles the four eagles. The quilt is finished with a narrow band of green.

Like the sampler, a quilt was often used as a memorial piece. Friends and neighbors of the deceased would reverently open her scrap bag and stitch together bits of dress materials she had worn into a "Memory Quilt," reminiscent of her life and the qualities which endeared her to them.

A near relative to the "Memory Quilt" is the "Memorial" coverlet. At first the names were interchangeable, but later the term "Memorial" came to mean the work of living persons to perpetuate their memory for posterity. An illustration of this type of bedcovering is found in the rooms of the Milford Historical Society at "Lullwood," ancestral home of Colonel Oliver W. Lull. It is made of unbleached cotton, each block bearing the embroidered name of some person prominent in the life of the community. The writing was all done in the same fine hand, that of the late Mrs. Arthur W. Howison, during the first World War. The embroidery is beautifully executed, and the brilliant colors of the material make the quilt a valuable memento of which the town is very proud.

Out of the autograph album with its varying sentiments both wise and maudlin, emerged the "Album" quilt, each block bearing an embroidered text or verse and signed by the donor. Sometimes the inscription, written in indelible ink in a bold masculine hand, gave evidence that men were not averse to joining in these testimonial tokens. To be the recipient of an "Album" quilt was considered a distinguished honor.

Similar to the "Album" was the "Friendship" coverlet, often more interesting than beautiful because of the latitude allowed in both design and coloring. The finished product was a medley of patterns and fabrics, since each block, including material and workmanship, was the contribution of some friend.

*   *   *   *   *

The names of New Hampshire quiltmakers are legion. Many of them are elderly women who, as a pastime for unaccustomed leisure, revert to a form of handicraft which they learned in their childhood. One of them said recently, "Yes, indeed, I sewed patchwork from the time I was five years old. Used to have to piece so many blocks as a stint before I could play. And I couldn't hurry it either for if it wasn't done just so, I had to rip it out and do it all over again. . . .

Coast Traders

WE KNEW and cherished with no little covetousness the stories of the "traders," which had gladdened the hearts of children of an earlier generation. A trader was a vessel from Boston or New York which earned the livelihood of its captain, or perchance of its owner, by carrying annually into the smaller harbors of the coast every kind of ware imaginable and selling its multifarious cargo at prices which the village stores could not meet. Blue Hill children of the sixties and seventies had waited months

From *A Goodly Heritage,* by Mary Ellen Chase, pp. 163–166. Copyright, 1932, by Henry Holt and Company, Inc. New York.

for the arrival of this floating junk-shop, scanning the sea from every hill
and headland for an unfamiliar sail. According to the older people among
us, its captain was invariably an accommodating soul, who was not in the
least averse to interpreting as coin of the realm any stray bits of old iron,
in exchange for which he would proffer oranges and great Boston apples,
gorgeously striped candies, dates, figs, and nuts. Moreover, he carried in
his hold, for those who had been most thrifty and parsimonious of their
small savings, doll buggies and pop-guns, and for the despair of fathers and
mothers, who could be lured to the wharf, bolts of cloth and shiny new
shoes with voluptuous and alluring tassels.

Sometimes in those days, we understood, still with envy that progress
had cheated us of so much greater excitement, Blue Hill had supplied her
own traders. An obliging captain, with a weather eye out for his own pocket,
sailing light from Boston or New York, Philadelphia or Norfolk, would
gladly undertake the filling of commissions in those centers and bring
home a sundry cargo. . . .

These shopping sea-captains must, indeed, have been men of gregarious
instincts and of great good nature. A slip of paper much torn and obviously incomplete, dated in 1859, gives a partial list of commissions to be
fulfilled and suggests the arduous undertaking of the purchaser:

For J. Candage, a hoss harness

For Messrs. Holt, Horton, Candage, & 3 Hinckleys tobaco, both
chewing & smoking

For J. C.—a new hat, my own size with 2 cravats & ties

For the minister, one cane, snake's head prefered, not to cost over $1

For Sylvester C., a good quantity nails, all sizes, & 12 brass handles

For Coggin family, to invest $20 in white flour and raisins, also nuts
of sorts, also toys such as marbles, tops, & a book of pictures

For Miss Clara Wood, stuff for weding dress with threads & silks for
sewing same & white lace for triming

For Mrs. Duffy, 1 bolt flowered calico at lowest price, blue & white
prefered, also buttons, also wools for kniting socks in bright shades,
also pink roses for bonet brims

For Horton boys, 2 large pocket knives

For H. Henderson, 6 steel traps suitable for rabits or foxes

For little Osgood girl, a doll with black hair, blue eyes, big as possible
for $1

For Mrs. Grindle, one singing bird in cage, for the church gift.

Even we in the nineties knew at first hand something of this sort of
supply and demand. When I was in the neighborhood of twelve, my father,
together with three other men of the village, bought a quarter share in a
two-masted schooner called *The Gold Hunter*. Rumor had it that their
act was largely one of charity since the captain and owner had fallen on
evil days by the decline of the coast trade. But whatever its cause, the
effect brought delighted satisfaction to four large families. . . .

Ride and Tie

THIS was a clever, economical mode of journeying in good old times, when we could boast of rigid honesty among men. It was done after this wise. If John and James, two young farmers, both wanted to go to Boston at the same time—having but one horse between them, and neither chaise nor buggy, John would first mount the saddle and ride on, while James set off on foot. Having rode a few miles, John made fast the bridle to a post or tree, and then became the pedestrian in his turn. James coming up, took his turn to ride a bit, and in this way of *ride* and *tie* they effected their journey with ease and safety. Dobbin stood perfectly safe and secure with the saddle-bags across him, holding the cold junk and bread and cheese on one side, and a stone to balance on the other. Such a thing as thieving was not thought of, any more than in the famous good moral reign of the excellent King Alfred of England. Say, my friend, how would such a project answer now, when a man must watch his coat hanging up in his own entry, to have it safe against pilferers! Alas, for the degeneracy of the times!

Chebobbins

AFTER there had been a heavy fall of snow and the roads were well broken, the time was always chosen where any logging was done to haul logs to the sawmill on ox-sleds. An interesting sled was used which had an interesting name—chebobbin. One writer called it a cross between a tree and a bobsled. It was made by a close and ingenious adaptation of natural forms of wood, which made excellent runners, cross-bars, etc.; they were fastened together so loosely that they readily adjusted themselves to the inequalities of the wood-roads. The word and article are now almost obsolete. In some localities chebobbin became tebobbin and tarboggin, all three being adaptations in nomenclature, as they were in form, of the Indian toboggan or moose-sled,—a sledge with runners or flat bottom of wood or bark, upon which the red men drew heavy loads over the snow. This sledge has become familiar to us in the light and strong Canadian form now used for the delightful winter sport of tobogganing.

On these chebobbins great logs were hitched together by chains, and dragged down from the upland wood-lots. Under these mighty loads the

From *The Old Farmer's Almanack*, Calculated on a New and Improved Plan, for the Year of Our Lord 1855, by Robert B. Thomas, p. 23, September. Entered, according to Act of Congress, in the year 1854, by Jenks, Hickling & Swan, in the Clerk's Office of the District Court of the District of Massachusetts. Boston.

From *Home Life in Colonial Days*, by Alice Morse Earle, pp. 415–416. Copyright, 1898, by The Macmillan Company. New York and London. 1919.

snow-tracks got an almost icy polish, prime sledding for country sleighing parties. . . .

Stranger's Fire

THE distance from village to town was so great before the railway entered five years ago, and in spring the mud of the rude, rutty roads so heavy, that Rehobothites with good old-fashioned hospitality kept a "Stranger's fire." An old lady, now of Providence, said:

"I was often aroused at night by the clicking of the latch and whispers of weary, chilled farmers with loads of woods. My hospitable uncle would call out 'Open the fire,' and, after refreshing themselves from the great mug of cider which stood by the andirons, the unseen visitors would cover the fire and away they'd go, and presently others would appear and open the fire."

Pillow Bears and Feather Voyages

LIVE-GEESE feather-beds were an object of considerable emulation, and moved the social barometer much as would now a solid silver service. The frequent visits of the fishermen to Belle Isle and Labrador (pronounced by the fishermen Larbadore) afforded excellent opportunity to secure the genuine article. The sack that left home filled with straw, returned with the downy store for bed-pillows, the latter called pillow bears, and apostrophized by the old people as pille'bers. Fifty years ago or less, high beds were as fashionable as now the other extreme. The boys used to joke about rigging a jury-mast and rattle down the shrouds to climb into bed.[1]

Josiah and Edward [Childs] bought the small estate of John Logge, (a part of Elder Cobb's great lot), which they divided, and each had a house thereon. Both were coopers and small farmers, and displayed more taste for horticultural and floricultural pursuits than was common in those days. Both, in early life, went on *feather voyages*, a term which few, at the present time, will understand. About a century ago, vessels were fitted out for the coast of Labrador to collect feathers and eider down. At a certain season of the year some species of wild fowl shed a part of their wing

---

feathers, and either cannot fly, or only for a short distance. On some of the barren islands on that coast, thousands of those birds congregated. The crews of the vessels would drive them together, kill them with a short club or a broom made of spruce branches, and strip off their feathers. Millions of wild fowl were thus destroyed, and in a few years, their haunts were broken up by this wholesale slaughter, and their numbers so greatly diminished that feather voyages became unprofitable and were discontinued.[2]

Filling Boots with Flaxseed

THIS was in the days when shoddy was unknown, and cloth was made to wear rather than to sell, and when "go-to-meeting" boots passed from generation to generation in the same way. It was a custom with many farmers, as soon as they returned from "meeting," to fill these last named expensive articles of wear with beans or flax-seed and hang them up on pegs until some extraordinary occasion or "meetin' day" called for their use again. The use of flax-seed was finally pretty much abandoned, because of a mischievous boy, on occasion of his father's whipping him one day, hitting the old man's suspended boots now and then a sly rap with the broom-handle for several days in succession, in consequence of which, when his father took them down on the next Sunday, he found both split at the toes, through the pressure of the slippery flax-seed.

Powder-Horns

ON HIS powder-horn the rustic carver bestowed his best and daintiest work. Emblem both of war and of sport, it seemed worthy of being shaped into the highest expression of his artistic longing. A chapter, even a book, might be filled with the romantic history and representations of American powder-horns; patriotism, sentiment, and adventure shed equal halos over

From *Recollections of Olden Times:* Rowland Robinson of Narragansett and His Unfortunate Daughter, with Genealogies of the Robinson and Hazard Families of Rhode Island, by Thomas R. Hazard, "Shepherd Tom," in His Eighty-First and Eighty-Second Years, Also Genealogical Sketch of the Hazards of the Middle States, by Willis P. Hazard, of Westchester, Pa., p. 60. Entered according to Act of Congress, in the year 1879, by John P. Sanborn, in the Office of the Librarian of Congress, at Washington, D. C. Newport, Rhode Island.

From *Home Life in Colonial Days*, by Alice Morse Earle, pp. 320–321. Copyright, 1898, by The Macmillan Company. New York and London. 1919.

them. Months of the patient work of every spare moment was spent in beautifying them, and their quaintness, variety, and individuality are a never-ceasing delight to the antiquary. Maps, plans, legends, verses, portraits, landscapes, family history, crests, dates of births, marriages, and deaths, lists of battles, patriotic and religious sentiments, all may be found on powder-horns. They have in many cases proved valuable historical records, and have sometimes been the only records of events.

Jagger-Knives

THE "jagger-knife" by which those [Nantucket] "wonders" were scored may be more or less known; but such as was used, and are used in my native town, I think, are exclusive to localities from whence hailed and sailed the whale ship. Unique in construction they surely are. They were made "aboard-ship" from ivory, and were deftly wrought from the tooth of the sperm whale. Each consisted of a revolving wheel set into a slot or groove at the end of a handle. The handle, sometimes made straight, sometimes slightly circular in form, was about four or five inches in length, and the wheel about an inch or an inch and a half in diameter.

Those wheels, fashioned smooth and round, had an edge cut like a "frill" so as to get the jagged effect when used for scoring dough. Each section or part of this peculiar knife, "made at sea," was artistically executed. The wheel revolved on a metal pin, fastened at each end outside of the slot in the handle to hold it in place. With much time on their hands while at sea, no whales in sight, sailors were nevertheless busy, and many articles made by them on ship-board manifested rare skill and workmanship, and these "jagger-knives" represent such to a marked degree, for the varying genius of the "sailor-mechanic" was aptly shown in their construction.[1]

In different artistic shapes have I seen them, and I could minutely describe the make of many of them. Just one by way of illustration. The handle of one I have in mind was delicately smoothed, concaved from the center to represent the arm of a child, the end finished in a closed hand or closed fist, and the fingers were delicately and perfectly formed; drilled in slightly from each side of that closed hand a hole was made in which was placed a neatly made ring, also of ivory, sprung in, which swung a little rigidly in its place. I have tried to minutely describe the sailor-made "jagger-knife," not that native Nantucketers required any such description, but rather because some eyes may read this sketch who never heard of such an affair.

From *Brief Historical Data and Memories of My Boyhood Days in Nantucket,* by Joseph E. C. Farnham, pp. 181–182. Providence: Joseph E. C. Farnham. 1923.

[1] Jagger-knives were an ingenious and beautiful form of scrimshaw, or "carving or decorating whales' teeth, walrus' tusks or bones," etc., especially engraving teeth. See A. Hyatt Verrill, *The Real Story of the Whaler* (New York, 1923), pp. 191–194.

Noggin and Piggin

. . . No HOME in central New Hampshire in old days was considered completely equipped if it had not "a noggin for milk and a piggin for soap." A piggin is a small piece of cooperage with one stave left high for a handle, a miniature in short of that sort of sap bucket that has one stave left high, with a hole in that stave so the bucket may be hung on the tap inserted in the auger hole bored into the tree. Through this tap the maple sap seeps through and drops into the bucket The piggin has sometimes, too, a hole in its high stave, so that it may be hung above the sink in a place handy for use.

A noggin I have is of two-quart size. It is six inches in diameter. Its staves are four and a half inches high. It would, perhaps, be more exact to speak of its stave, for all its twenty-one and a half inches of circumference seem of one piece of wood save where the piece carrying the handle is inserted. If you call this handle's base a stave, there are two staves. To get the pitch necessary to the diminishing diameter of the noggin from top to bottom, the lower end of the broad stave has had narrow gores cut out of it by a very sharp knife. This gives its lower sides a shivered effect. All the noggin is so brown with the use of years it is difficult to say of what wood it is made. The wide stave, I shall venture to guess, is of brown ash, as are the hoops, two at top and two at bottom, and each a half an inch wide. The bottom and handle seem to be of pine.

Its lightness is a part of the noggin's efficiency. One of its uses, according to the talk of the countryside, was to carry out to barn or pasture, or wherever the cow happened to be, when milk fell short in the house. The woman of the house would run out with the noggin, and crouch down by bossy. With the noggin held in one hand she would use the other to milk the sup she wanted for this or that into the noggin.

Cat Holes

. . . OF THE hardiest of Tom Fool stories is that of the two holes at the bottom of the barn door, the larger one for the old cat, the smaller for the kitten. My own eyes have seen two instances of the two holes side by side in a door that admitted to an undivided interior.

. . . One wondered were there occasions when it would be desirable to keep the old cat out, but to let the kitten in. . . .

From *New Hampshire Neighbors,* Country Folks and Things in the White Hills, by Cornelius Weygandt, pp. 111–112. Copyright, 1937, by Henry Holt and Company, Inc. New York.

Ibid., pp. 259, 260–262.

\- * * * * *

. . . A more plausible explanation of the two cat holes, but one that hardly accounts for their difference in size, is suggested by a story Mrs. Robert Frost loves to tell. Asked why he had five cat holes cut at the bottom of his barn door for his five cats, all grown tabbies and toms, the old farmer replied: "When I says 'scat,' I means 'scat!'"

The single cat hole is, of course, in instances a necessity, but I have known it to be made in barn doors when there were other easy ways of entrance for puss into the barn, an open space between the timbers of the overshot second story, a pane of glass out of a low window, a slit for ventilation in the stone end of the barn. The cat hole, though, is, I think, in a sense an institution, a something dictated by tradition to be made in the doors of well-conducted barns, at least in places of not too severe winters.

The farther north you go, the fewer cat holes there are in barn and stable doors. . . .

* * * * *

There are, though, in our section of New Hampshire, indoor cat holes to compensate in a measure for the dearth of the commoner variety in barn doors. Such indoor cat holes are rare, but not unique, as I thought when I saw the first series of them. This series is in the attic of a farmhouse under the west scarp of the Ossipees. The cat holes are thought to be part of the original equipment of the house, the three of them in the floor of the chamber and the one between the chamber and the grain loft of the barn. Here, of course, house and woodshed and barn are all one building. Two of the cat holes in the floor still have in place the caps to cover them. The cat holes, circular and of six-inch diameter, were designed to let puss into the spaces between four great floor timbers that ran the whole width of the house. The three are in a row, about four feet apart. Each had been cut out with a compass saw, and a square piece of wood nailed to the circular piece cut out of the floor. When in place, the upper layer of the cap projected above the floor. That top part was beveled on its edges, but there must be, even at that, many a stumble over the caps. If they were left out an ankle sprained might easily have been the result. The fourth cat hole, between this chamber and the corn loft, was very necessary to give puss access to this granary so sought by mice and rats.

Boarding Around

It was the custom in those days [in Suffield, Connecticut,] for the teacher to "board around." The arguments for the practice were two and conclu-

From "Old Slave Days in Connecticut," by Judge Martin H. Smith, in *The Connecticut Magazine*, Vol. X (January–March, 1906), No. 1, pp. 113–114. Copyright, 1906, by The Connecticut Magazine Company, Hartford, Conn.

sive. It was cheaper than any other plan. It enabled the teacher to get acquainted with the home life of his pupils. Whatever a man might have thought of it at the time, it is certainly a pleasant thing to look back on.

If the session was to be ninety days and there were thirty pupils, of course it meant three days for each. It was quite an event to have the teacher to board and suitable preparations must be made. So it was customary for him to send word a day or two beforehand that he was coming. Very often word came back for him "to wait a few days as they had not killed their hogs yet." He was reasonably sure of a plenty of fresh pork, sausage, and feather beds. Once when the teacher was up quite late helping one of his pupils, a seventeen year old lass, to solve some problems in the double "Rule of Three," he suddenly realized how late and how cold it was. He hurried to his room and undressing as quickly as possible jumped into bed. Here he made the acquaintance of a warming pan full of live coals. There was not room enough for both of them in bed, and as a result, quicker than can be told, they were sprawling on the floor. The kind hostess had tried to warm his bed, but forgot to tell him of it. As a result she warmed both the bed and the teacher. After all there were some very pleasant features in this "boarding-round," and many a life-long friendship came of it. But woe to the bashful man that tried it. If it did not cure him of bashfulness his case was past hope.

Letter Writing

LETTER writing was a very serious affair to many folks in The Town, especially the "backing" of the double-fold sheets which were simply folded and sealed with a red wax wafer, with no thought yet of an envelope. Three sides could be covered with writing but the fourth must be left empty for the address, which was called the "backing."

"Uncle says when you back your letters you should put the town's name in a large fair hand."

Even after the 1860's had brought envelopes the old expression was still in use. "George, this is the last envelope you backed for me before you left for the war."

Because postage was so high and the earlier letters must be confined to the one sheet, many letters were dizzy affairs with the first part written over crisscross by the latter part, and again some letters were so little more than "I take my pen in hand," and inquiry after the health of each member of the addressed family, that the complaint would come back: "Don't send so much clean paper," or ". . . so much waste space paid for!" Secret missives were written in old Bossy's milk to be scorched into visibility in front of the receiver's hearthfire. Gaiety began to enter the

---

From *New Hampshire Borns a Town*, by Marion Nicholl Rawson, p. 232. Copyright, 1942, by E. P. Dutton & Co., Inc. New York.

postal ranks when tiny paper wafers of glossy black, carrying some message from Cupid, were affixed to the heated wax wafer. "When this you see remember me, though many a mile we distant be." One would have a picture of a broken gate: "I'm quite unhinged."

Visiting and Advertising Cards

"HERE's somethin' else." Mr. Botsford reaches into the bookcase, brings forth a small box, from which he removes the cover. "Visitin' cards," says he. "It used to be an old habit to swap these cards with your friends. Not leave 'em when you called at someone's home, understand, just swap 'em." He takes the cards out, one by one, recalling old friends whose names are printed, or in some cases handwritten. "Papers used to be full of advertisements for these cards. Here's one should interest you. Used to be the custom to hand one of these to a girl when she was comin' out of church."

The card bore this message: "Escort card Fair Lady, will you allow me the pleasure of escorting you home? If so, keep this card, if not return it. Yours respectfully," with a space for the gallant's signature.

"Used to have lozenges, too," says Mr. Botsford, "with some sentimental message printed on 'em. You'd hand one to a girl you was sweet on. Another great thing was advertisin' cards. Did I mention them before? Kids used to collect 'em and paste 'em in big books, like scrap books. It was a great fad back in the seventies. Older people used to collect 'em too. You go in any drug store, in them days, and the counters would be piled high with these big books. You got the cards from the merchants. Come on out in the woodshed and I'll show you some."

We repair to the woodshed, where Mr. Botsford digs out two old books, turns the pages. "See what I mean?" The cards are an interesting sidelight on the vast changes in advertising methods coincident with the dawn of the motor age. Every conceivable subject was covered by them. They ran the gamut from the sublime to the ridiculous, dwelt on matters political and matters amorous, touched such widely diversified subjects as religion and warfare—advocated temperance and advertised liquor. In virtually no instance was the sponsor's product, or goods, prominently mentioned, and on some of them the merchant's name was in such small print as to almost escape attention.

"There's a good story about them advertising cards. You remember how old Mr. Lemmon, the druggist, used to stutter. When he first came to town here and went to work in the drug store, there was another fellow used to stutter just as bad, name was Fred Birch.

"Birch went into the store one day, and he says, 'G-g-g-g-imme, s-s-s-

---

From "Connecticut Clockmaker," as told by Arthur Botsford, Thomaston, Connecticut, to Francis Donovan, in *Living Lore of New England*. Manuscripts of the Federal Writers' Project of the Works Progress Administration for the State of Connecticut.

some advertisin' c-c-c-ards.' Lemon says, "You g-g-g-get the h-h-hell outa here.' Thought he was mockin' him, you see.

"All the merchants handled them cards. Sometimes they'd give you one or two, sometimes, if they was in a good humor, they'd give you a whole stack of 'em.

"Cards came in cigarette packages later, the kids took to collectin' them. And some of them gave out printed flags of all countries. Idea was to get as many different flags as you could, and then the girls would make sofa pillows out of them.

"Times change. In the old days, there was so little to do, now it's all different. The kids now have a million things they can do."

Deaconing the Psalm

IT WAS customary with our early ancestors to appoint an individual from the church to read the psalm, two lines at a time; after which reading, the whole congregation sang the two lines. The reading was so commonly done by a deacon, that this mode of announcing the psalm was called "deaconing" it. The scarcity of psalm-books was the origin of this custom; and, when they became so common as to be left in the meeting-house through the week, the proposition to discontinue the "deaconing" of the psalm was made, and it met with quick opposition from the deacons and readers. The habit continued till the Revolution. . . .

The Meetinghouse Bell

THE meetinghouse was nearly square, with a turret for a bell rising from the center of the roof. A small bell was bought and paid for with wheat the same year that the building was finished. The bell rope hung down in the broad aisle.

Henry Clarke, who died in 1675, left in his will money "for a bigger bell that may be heard generally by the inhabitants." The next year the town voted that the new bell should be rung each night at nine o'clock This "nine o'clock bell" was long a regular institution in the New England towns. It was universally understood to be the signal for bedtime.

From *History of the Town of Medford, Middlesex County, Massachusetts,* from Its First Settlement, in 1630, to the Present Time, 1855, by Charles Brooks, pp. 259–260. Boston: Published by James M. Usher. 1855.

For the origin and abolition of the custom of "lining out" (fought by musicians), see Alice Morse Earle, *The Sabbath in Puritan New England* (New York, 1893), pp. 213–217. Cf. "Lining Out the Hymn," p. 184 above.

From *Historic Hampshire in the Connecticut Valley,* Happenings in a Charming Old New England County from the Time of the Dinosaur Down to about 1900, by Clifton Johnson, pp. 89–91. Copyright, 1932, by The Northampton Historical Society, Northampton, Mass. Springfield, Massachusetts: Milton Bradley Company.

Custom and courtesy alike demanded that any visitors who had dropped in to call should prepare immediately to depart; and the comment often was made, "It is nine o'clock—time for honest men to go home, and for rogues to go about their business."

Of course, in the case of a ball or an evening party, or of young couples who were "sitting up," the participants did not feel obliged to be "tied to the bell-rope." The ringing ended with a number of light, quick taps to show the day of the month. For some reason or other the sound of the Hadley nine o'clock bell was very disturbing to Dr. Reuben Bell's dog. He began howling at its first stroke and kept up his dismal protest until the ringing ceased.

During the summer, the bell was rung in the middle of the day at 12 o'clock. This was largely for the benefit of workers on the meadows, and the sound was joyful music to man and beast, for it meant an hour of rest after a long morning of laborious toil.

It used to be the custom to ring what was known as the "passing bell" when a person died in the community. Nine strokes at half-minute intervals announced the death of a man; six that of a woman; and three that of a child. After a short pause, a series of rapid strokes gave the age of the deceased in years. All activities of people within hearing of the bell stopped at its first peal, and everybody waited to get the full announcement. It usually revealed to them, without the need of any questioning, what family was bereaved and where kindly help was needed.

Stove and Anti-Stove Factions

. . . FELT, in his *Annals of Salem*, asserts that the First Church of Boston was the first New England congregation to have a stove for heating the meeting-house at the time of public worship; this was in 1773. This statement is incorrect. Mr. Judd says the Hadley church had an iron stove in their meeting-house as early as 1734—the Hadley people were such sybarites and novelty-lovers in those early days! The Old South Church of Boston followed in the luxurious fashion in 1783, and the *Evening Post* of January 25, 1783, contained a poem of which these four lines show the criticising and deprecating spirit:—

> Extinct the sacred fire of love,
>   Our zeal grown cold and dead,
> In the house of God we fix a stove
>   To warm us in their stead.

Other New England congregations piously froze during service-time well into this century. The Longmeadow church, early in the field, had a stove in 1810; the Salem people in 1815; and the Medford meeting in

1820. The church in Brimfield in 1819 refused to pay for a stove, but ordered, as some sacrifice to the desire for comfort, two extra doors placed on the gallery-stairs to keep out draughts; but when in that town, a few years later, a subscription was made to buy a church stove, one old member refused to contribute, saying, "good preaching kept him hot enough without stoves."

As all the church edifices were built without any thought of the possibility of such comfortable furniture, they had to be adapted as best they might to the ungainly and unsightly great stoves which were usually placed in the central aisle of the building. From these cast-iron monsters, there extended to the nearest windows and projected through them hideous stove-pipes that too often spread, from every leaky and ill-fastened joint, smoke and sooty vapors, and sometimes pyroligneous drippings on the congregation. Often tin pails to catch the drippings were hung under the stove-pipes, forming a further chaste and elegant church-decoration. Many serious objections were made to the stoves besides the aesthetic ones. It was alleged that they would be the means of starting many destructive conflagrations; that they caused severe headaches in the church attendants; and worst of all, that the *heat warped the ladies' tortoise-shell back-combs.*

The church reformers contended, on the other hand, that no one could properly receive spiritual comfort while enduring such decided bodily discomfort. They hoped that with increased physical warmth, fervor in religion would be equally augmented—that, as Cowper wrote,—

> The churches warmed, they would no longer hold
> Such frozen figures, stiff as they are cold.

Many were the quarrels and discussions that arose in New England communities over the purchase and use of stoves, and many were the meetings held and votes taken upon the important subject.

"Peter Parley"—Mr. Samuel Goodrich—gave, in his *Recollections,* a very amusing account of the sufferings endured by the wife of an anti-stove deacon. She came to church with a look of perfect resignation on the Sabbath of the stove's introduction, and swept past the unwelcome intruder with averted head, and into her pew. She sat there through the service, growing paler with the unaccustomed heat, until the minister's words about "heaping coals of fire" brought too keen a sense of the overwhelming and unhealthful stove-heat to her mind, and she fainted. She was carried out of church, and upon recovering said languidly that it "was the heat from the stove." A most complete and sudden resuscitation was effected, however, when she was informed of the fact that no fire had as yet been lighted in the new church-furnishing.

Similar chronicles exist about other New England churches, and bear a striking resemblance to each other. Rev. Henry Ward Beecher in an address delivered in New York on December 20, 1853, the anniversary of the Landing of the Pilgrims, referred to the opposition made to the introduction of stoves in the old meeting-house in Litchfield, Connecticut, during the ministry of his father, and gave an amusing account of the results of the introgression. This allusion called up many reminiscences of anti-stove wars, and a writer in the *New York Enquirer* told the same story of the fainting woman in Litchfield meeting, who began to fan herself and at length swooned, saying when she recovered "that the heat of the horrid stove had caused her to faint." A correspondent of the *Cleveland Herald* confirmed the fact that the fainting episode occurred in the Litchfield meeting house. The editor of the *Hartford Daily Courant* thus added his testimony:—

Violent opposition had been made to the introduction of a stove in the old meeting-house, and an attempt made in vain to induce the society to purchase one. The writer was one of seven young men who finally purchased a stove and requested permission to put it up in the meeting-house on trial. After much difficulty the committee consented. It was all arranged on Saturday afternoon, and on Sunday we took our seats in the Bass, rather earlier than usual, to see the fun. It was a warm November Sunday, in which the sun shone cheerfully and warmly on the old south steps and into the naked windows. The stove stood in the middle aisle, rather in front of the Tenor Gallery. People came in and stared. Good old Deacon Trowbridge, one of the most simple-hearted and worthy men of that generation, had, as Mr. Beecher says, been induced to give up his opposition. He shook his head, however, as he felt the heat reflected from it, and gathered up the skirts of his great coat as he passed up the broad aisle to the deacon's seat. Old Uncle Noah Stone, a wealthy farmer of the West End, who sat near, scowled and muttered at the effects of the heat, but waited until noon to utter his maledictions over his nut-cakes and cheese at the intermission. There had in fact been *no fire in the stove,* the day being too warm. We were too much upon the broad grin to be very devotional, and smiled rather loudly at the funny things we saw. But when the editor of the village paper, Mr. Bunce, came in (who was a believer in stoves in churches) and with a most satisfactory air warmed his hands by the stove, keeping the skirts of his great-coat carefully between his knees, we could stand it no longer but dropped invisible behind the breastwork. But the climax of the whole was (as the Cleveland man says) when Mrs. Peck went out in the middle of the service. It was, however, the means of reconciling the whole society; for after that first day we heard no more opposition to the warm stove in the meeting-house.

With all this corroborative evidence I think it is fully proved that the event really happened in Litchfield, and that the honor was stolen for other towns by unveracious chroniclers; otherwise we must believe in an amazing unanimity of church-joking and sham-fainting all over New England.

Disciplining the Congregation

A RATHER unconventional and eccentric preacher in Newbury awoke one sleeper in a most novel manner. The first name of the sleeping man was Mark, and the preacher in his sermon made use of these Biblical words: "I say unto you, mark the perfect man and behold the upright." But in the midst of his low, monotonous sermon-voice he roared out the word "mark" in a loud shout that brought the dozing Mark to his feet, bewildered but wide awake.

Mr. Moody, of York, Maine, employed a similar device to awaken and mortify the sleepers in meeting. He shouted "Fire, fire, fire!" and when the startled and blinking men jumped up, calling out "Where?" he roared back in turn, "In hell, for sleeping sinners." Rev. Mr. Phillips, of Andover, in 1755, openly rebuked his congregation for "sleeping away a great part of the sermon"; and on the Sunday following an earthquake shock which was felt throughout New England, he said he hoped the "Glorious Lord of the Sabbath had given them such a shaking as would keep them awake through one sermon-time." Other and more autocratic parsons did not hesitate to call out their sleeping parishioners plainly by name, sternly telling them also to "Wake up!" A minister in Brunswick, Maine, thus pointedly wakened one of his sweet-sleeping church-attendants, a man of some dignity and standing in the community, and received the shocking and tautological answer, "Mind your own business, and go on with your sermon."

The women would sometimes nap a little without being discovered. "Ye women may sometimes sleepe and none know by reason of their enormous bonnets. Mr. Whiting doth pleasantlie say from ye pulpit hee doth seeme to be preaching to stacks of straw with men among them."

* * * * *

A minister about to preach in a neighboring parish was told of a custom which prevailed there of persons who lived at a distance rising and leaving the house ere the sermon was ended. He determined to teach them a lesson, and announced that he would preach the first part of his sermon to the sinners, and the latter part to the saints, and that the sinners would of course all leave as soon as their portion had been delivered. Every soul remained until the end of the service.

* * * * *

Another clergyman was irritated beyond endurance by the stamping, clattering feet, a *supplosio pedis* that he regarded as an irreverent protest and complaint against the severity of the weather, rather than as a hint to him to conclude his long sermon. He suddenly and noisily closed his sermon-book, leaned forward out of his high pulpit, and thundered out

From *The Sabbath in Puritan New England*, by Alice Morse Earle, pp. 70–71, 83, 87–88, 314–315. Copyright, 1891, by Charles Scribner's Sons. New York. 1893.

these Biblical words of rebuke at his freezing congregation, whose startled faces stared up at him through dense clouds of vapor. "Out of whose womb came the ice? And the hoary frost of heaven, who hath gendered it? The waters are hid as with a stone, and the face of the deep is frozen. Knowest thou the ordinance of heaven? Canst thou set the dominion thereof on the earth? Great things doth God which we cannot comprehend. He saith to the snow, Be thou on the earth. By the breath of God frost is given. He causeth it to come, whether for correction, or for his land, or for mercy. Hearken unto this. *Stand still*, and consider the wondrous works of God." We can believe that he roared out the words "stand still," and that there was no more noise in that meeting-house on cold Sundays during the remainder of that winter.

* * * * *

Another arbitrary clergyman, having had an altercation with some unruly singers in the choir, gave out with much vehemence on the following Sunday the hymn beginning,—

> "And are you wretches yet alive
> And do you yet rebel?"

with a very significant glower towards the singers' gallery. In a similar situation another minister gave out to the rebellious choir the hymn commencing,—

> "Let those refuse to sing
> Who never knew our God."

A visiting clergyman, preaching in a small and shabby church built in a parish of barren and stony farm-land, very spitefully and sneeringly read out to be sung the hymn of Watts' beginning,—

> "Lord, what a wretched land is this,
> That yields us no supplies!"

But his malicious intent was frustrated and the tables were adroitly turned by the quick-witted choirmaster, who bawled out in a loud voice as if in answer, "Northfield,"—the name of the minister's own home and parish, —while he was really giving out to the choir as was his wont, the name of the tune to which the hymn was to be sung.

Bundling

. . . IF YOU inquired into the business, you are pretty sure to be told, inquire where you may, that bundling is not known *there*, but somewhere further back in the woods, or further "down east."

By John Neal, *Yankee* (1829), reprinted in Robb Sagendorph, ed., *Robb's Cabinet of Curiosities* (Dublin, New Hampshire, Yankee, Inc.), Vol. I (1951), pp. 40–41.

I, myself, though I have taken trouble enough to learn the truth, have never yet been able to meet with a case of bundling—of bundling proper, I should say, in the United-States, nor with but one trustworthy individual who had ever met with so much as one case—and he had met with *but* one, for which he would give his word.

They bundle in Wales; but bundling there is a serious matter. A lady— a Welsh-woman, whose word is truth itself, assured me, not long ago, that in her country they do not think a bit the worse of a girl for anticipating her duties, or in other words, for being a mother before she has been a wife.

That which is called bundling here, though bad enough—is not a twentieth part so bad. Here it is only a mode of courtship. The parties instead of sitting up, together, go to bed together; but go to bed with their clothes on. This would appear to be a perilous fashion; but I have been assured by the individual above, that he had proof to the contrary; or in the particular case alluded to, the only case I ever heard of on good authority, although he was invited by the parents of a pretty girl who stood near him, to bundle with her, and although he did bundle with her, he had every reason to believe that, if he had been very free—or more free than he might have been, at a country frolic, after they had invited him to escort her, to sit up with her, to dance with her, he would have been treated as a traitor by all parties. He had a fair opportunity of knowing the truth; and he spoke of the matter, as if he would prefer the etiquette of sitting up, to the etiquette of going to bed, with a girl who had been so brought up. He complained of her as a prude. The following communication however, appears to be one that may be depended on.

If you wish to know the *truth* about bundling, I am inclined to think that your correspondent V. could tell you all about it—it seems, by his confession, that he has practised it upon a large scale. I never heard of the thing till about three years ago; an acquaintance of mine had gone to spend the summer with an aunt, who lived somewhere near Sandy-River. The following is a copy of one of her letters while there:

If you go walk with a young man here, instead of offering you his arm, as the young men do up our way, he either takes your hand in his, or passes one arm around your waist; and this he does with such a provoking careless honesty, that you cannot, for your life, be offended with him. Well, I had walked with my Jonathan several times in this kind of style. I confess that there was something in him that I could not but like—he does not lack for wit, and has a good share of common sense; his language is never studied—he always seems to speak from the heart. So when he asked what sort of a companion I thought he would make, I very candidly answered, that I thought he would make a very agreeable one. I think just so of you, said he, and it shall not be my fault, he continued, if we are not companions for life. We shall surely make a bargain, said he, after sitting silent a few moments, so we'll *bundle* tonight. *Bundle* what? I asked. *We* will bundle together, said he; you surely know what I mean.

I know that our farmers bundle *wheat, corn-stalks* and *hay;* do you mean that you want me to help you bundle any of these: enquired I. I mean that I want you to stay with me tonight! It is the custom in this place, when a man stays with a girl—if it is warm weather, for them to throw themselves on the bed, outside of the bed-clothes; if the weather is cold, they crawl under the clothes, then if they have anything to *say,* they say it—when they get tired of talking, they can go to sleep; this is what we call bundling—now what do you call it in your part of the world? We have no such words, answered I; not amongst respectable people, nor do I think that any people would that either thought themselves respectable, or wished to be thought so.

I have since made enquiries about *bundling,* and have learned that it is *really* the custom here, and that they think no more harm of it, than we do our way of a young couple's sitting up together. I have known an instance, since I have been here, of a girl's taking her sweet-heart to a neighbor's house, and asking for a bed for two to lodge in, or rather to *bundle* in. They happened to have company at her father's, so that their beds were all occupied; she thought no harm of it. She and her family are respectable.

Grandmother says, that bundling was a very common thing in our part of the country, in old times; that most of the first settlers lived in log-houses; that these log-houses seldom had more than one room that had a fire-place,—in this room the old people slept—so if one of their girls had a sweet-heart in the winter, she must either sit with him in the room where her father and mother slept, or take him into her sleeping room—she would choose the latter for the sake of being alone with him; but sometimes when the cold was very severe, rather than freeze to death, they would crawl under the bed-clothes; and this, after a while, became a habit, a custom, or a fashion.

Tarrying

SINGULAR situations and manners will be productive of singular customs; but frequently such as upon slight examination may appear to be the effects of mere grossness of character, will, upon deeper research, be found to proceed from simplicity and innocence. A very extraordinary method of courtship, which is sometimes practised amongst the lower people of this province, and is called Tarrying, has given occasion to this reflection. When a man is enamoured of a young woman, and wishes to marry her, he proposes the affair to her parents, (without whose consent no marriage in this colony can take place); if they have no objection, they allow him to

Rev. Andrew Burnaby, A.M., Vicar of Greenwich, *Travels through the Middle Settlements in North-America.* In the Years 1759 and 1760. With Observations upon the State of the Colonies. The Second Edition (Ithaca, New York: Cornell University Press, 1960), pp. 102–103.

tarry with her one night, in order to make his court to her. At their usual time the old couple retire to bed, leaving the young ones to settle matters as they can; who, after having sat up as long as they think proper, get into bed together also, but without pulling off their undergarments, in order to prevent scandal. If the parties agree, it is all very well; the banns are published, and they are married without delay. If not, they part, and possibly never see each other again; unless, which is an accident that seldom happens, the forsaken fair-one prove pregnant, and then the man is obliged to marry her, under pain of excommunication.

Courting-Sticks

LUKE MONTAGUE, a stalwart bachelor of 27, brought to South Hadley one of the famous courting-sticks. It was very useful on winter nights when there was only the single fire in the house and the whole family must be present at the wooing. The lovers heeded the conventions by sitting primly apart from each other, yet by means of the courting-stick, which was a hollow tube about five feet long, could whisper back and forth without their conversation being audible to those about them.

Courting with Stones

VERY ancient tradition says that the method of courtship at the Isles of Shoals was after this fashion: If a youth fell in love with a maid, he lay in wait till she passed by, and then pelted her with stones, after the manner of our friends of Marblehead; so that if a fair Shoaler found herself the centre of a volley of missiles, she might be sure that an ardent admirer was expressing himself with decision certainly, if not with tact! If she turned, and exhibited any curiosity as to the point of the compass whence the bombardment proceeded, her doubts were dispelled by another shower; but if she went on her way in maiden meditation, then was her swain in despair, and life, as is usual in such cases, became a burden to him.

Bride Stealing

THE sport of stealing "Mistress Bride," a curious survival of the old

From *Historic Hampshire in the Connecticut Valley,* Happenings in a Charming Old New England County from the Time of the Dinosaur Down to About 1900, by Clifton Johnson, pp. 165–166. Copyright, 1932, by The Northampton Historical Society. Springfield, Massachusetts: Milton Bradley Company.

From *Among the Isles of Shoals,* by Čelia Thaxter, p. 58. Entered according to Act of Congress, in the year 1873, by James R. Osgood & Co., in the Office of the Librarian of Congress, at Washington. Boston.

From *Customs and Fashions in Old New England,* by Alice Morse Earle, p. 77. Copyright, 1893, by Charles Scribner's Sons. New York.

savage bridals of many peoples, lingered long in the Connecticut valley. A company of young men, usually composed of slighted ones who had not been invited to the wedding, rushed in after the marriage ceremony, seized the bride, carried her to a waiting carriage, or lifted her up on a pillion, and rode to the country tavern. The groom with his friends followed, and usually redeemed the bride by furnishing a supper to the stealers. The last bride stolen in Hadley was Mrs. Job Marsh, in the year 1783. To this day, however, in certain localities in Rhode Island, the young men of the neighborhood invade the bridal chamber and pull the bride downstairs, and even out-of-doors, thus forcing the husband to follow to her rescue. If the room or house-door be locked against their invasion, the rough visitors break the lock.

The Devil's Fiddle

. . . [THE horning or skimmerton] generally comes upon the midnight clear, this still-virile welcome home of the bride and groom, and along with the jugs of cider which are shoved up on the hayrick along with the neighbors, or horners, is the Devil's Fiddle, famous in one town in New Hampshire, where it has driven out all humbler efforts at noise. The originator of this agent of torment, a man beloved in his village, gives us his own version of the hornings which he has enjoyed, and always to the accompaniment of plenty of good cider.

"We used to hitch up my old white horse and another in a team, hitch em to a haybody, put the old Devil's Fiddle on and go to let the young couple know we were glad for them and wanted to pay them some attention. You could hear the old fiddle for miles. They'd invite us in and treat us on cider and cigars. Sometimes we took along an old circular saw. They'd run a stick through it and two men hold the ends and then somebody'd begin to hammer it, and it certain did make an uncommon awful noise. Some folks thought they could make more noise on an old plough share, but give me an old circular saw.

"Then I got thinkin' it would be nicer for the bride if we took some of the girls along. Of course I said always I wouldn't take the fiddle out at all if they didn't behave good—like gentlemen, you know, not get drunk. And so now sometimes more girls than men go long."

There was a difference between the fiddle of the pre-girl era and that in use today. The "old fiddle" was a huge wooden box, six feet long and three across and deep, with its edges resined. The bow was a "two by four" sixteen feet long. One man stood in the box to keep it steady and the others drew the bow across the edges, and the noise which came forth "would shake a house, honest." The "new" fiddle is an improved product, needing even more cider to make it work musically, harboring a still more

From *Little Old Mills*, by Marion Nicholl Rawson, pp. 322–324. Copyright, 1935, by E. P. Dutton & Co., Inc. New York.

raucous sound, especially when it begins its music without warning at the door of a neighbor just across the mowing. This box is only four feet four long, two deep and three across. The edges are resined but the bow is a mere stripling of some six feet and one by two inches in thickness. Here the changes occur. Two telephone wires run through two holes in each end, and two movable boards—like bridges on a violin—pull the wires taut and make it howl. Upon this double taut wire hang two banged-up but still voluble tin oil cans with stones in them, which, when the bow begins to saw across resined edge and wires, dance up and down and along the strings, rattling their stones and groaning in chorus with the rest.

Shift Marriages

THESE ungallant and extremely inconvenient ceremonies are not American inventions or Yankee notions, but an old English custom, being in brief the marriage of a woman, usually a widow, clad only in her shift, to avoid hampering her newly made husband with her old debts. All through New England, in New York and Pennsylvania, this custom was known until this century. In Narragansett it was comparatively common. The exact form of the *sacrifice* (for sacrifice it was of modesty to the new husband's cupidity) and notions about it varied in localities. Let me give a marriage-certificate of a shift-marriage which took place on this very cross-roads where the three towns meet: [1]

> On March 11th, 1717, did Philip Shearman Take the Widow Hannah Clarke in her Shift, without any other Apparel, and led her across the Highway, as the Law directs in such Cases and was then married according to law by me.
>
> WILLIAM HALL, *Justice.*

It is not specified in this certificate that this grotesque proceeding took place at night, but, out of some regard for decency, and to avoid notoriety, such was usually the case.

There is an ancient registration book of births, deaths, and marriages at the handsome new Town Hall at South Kingston, R. I. There is an entry within it of a shift-marriage:

> Thomas Calverwell was joyned in marriage to Abigail Calverwell his wife the 22. February, 1719–20. He took her in marriage after she had gone four times across the highway in only her shift and hair-lace and no other clothing. Joyned together in marriage by me.
>
> GEORGE HAZARD, *Justice.*

This was but two years after the marriage of Widow Clarke, and the

---

From *In Old Narragansett*, Romances and Realities, by Alice Morse Earle, pp. 54–58, 59. Copyright, 1898, by Charles Scribner's Sons. New York.
[1] North Kingston, South Kingston, and Exeter, Rhode Island.

public parade may have taken place on the same spot, but there is a slight variation, in that the fair Abigail's ordeal was prolonged to four times crossing the road. The naming of the hair-lace seems trivial and superfluous with such other complete disrobing, but it was more significant than may appear to a careless reader. At that date women wore caps even in early girlhood, and were never seen in public without them. To be capless indicated complete dishabille. A court record still exists wherein is an entry of a great insult offered to the town constables by an angry and contemptuous woman. She threatened to pull off her head-gear and go before them, "only in her hair-lace and hair, like a parcel of pitiful, beggarly curs that they were." So the abandon of only a hair-lace comported well with Abigail Calverwell's only a shift.

Hopkinton is another Narragansett town, in the same county. In 1780 David Lewis married at Hopkinton, Widow Jemima Hill, "where four roads meet," at midnight, she being dressed only in her shift. This was to avoid payment of Husband Hill's debts. Ten years later, in a neighboring town, Richmond, still in the South County, Widow Sarah Collins appeared in the twilight in a long shift, a special wedding-shift covering her to her feet, and was then and thus married to Thomas Kenyon.

Westerly, still in the same Naragansett county, had the same custom and the same belief.

To all People whom It May Concern. This Certifies that Nathanell Bundy of Westerly took ye Widdow Mary Parmenter of sd. town on ye highway with no other clothing but shifting or smock on ye Evening of ye 20 day of April, 1724, and was joined together in that honorable Estate of matrimony in ye presence of

JOHN SANDERS, *Justice.*

JOHN COREY.	MARY HILL.
GEORGE COREY.	PETER CRANDALL.
	MARY CRANDALL.

The use of the word smock recalls the fact that in England these marriages were always called smock-marriages.

* * * * *

Another husband who thus formally lent wedding-garments to a widow-bride was Major Moses Joy, who married Widow Hannah Ward in Newfane, Vt., in 1789. The widow stood in her shift, within a closet, and held out her hand through a diamond-shaped hole in the door to the Major, who had gallantly deposited the garments for Madam to don before appearing as a bride. In Vermont many similar marriages are recorded, the bride not being required to cross the highway. One of these unclad brides left the room by a window, and dressed on the upper rounds of a ladder, a somewhat difficult feat even for a "lightning-change artist." In Maine the custom also prevailed. One half-frozen bride, on a winter's night in February, was saved for a long and happy life by having the pitying minister, who was about to marry her, throw a coat over her as she stood in her shift on the king's highway. In early New York, in Holland, in ancient Rhynland, this avoidance of debt-paying was accomplished in less annoying fashion by a widow's appearing in borrowed clothing at her husband's funeral, or laying a straw or key on the coffin and kicking it off.

* * * * *

It has been asserted that these shift-marriages were but an ignorant folk-custom, and that there never was any law or reason for the belief that the observance procured immunity from payment of past debts. But it is plainly stated in many of these Narragansett certificates that it was "according to the law in such cases." The marriages were certainly degrading in character, and were gone through with only for the express purpose of debt evasion, and they must have been successful. The chief actors in these Narragansett comedies were, from scant negative testimony of their life and the social position of their families, not necessarily of limited means. Any man of wealth might not, however, wish to pay the debts of his matrimonial "predecessor," as the first husband is termed in one case.

CALENDAR CUSTOMS

Thanksgiving

Its History [1]

THANKSGIVING, commonly regarded as being from its earliest beginning a distinctive New England festival, and an equally characteristic Puritan holiday, was originally neither.

The first New England Thanksgiving was not observed by either Plymouth Pilgrim or Boston Puritan. "Gyving God thanks" for safe arrival and many other liberal blessings was first heard on New England shores from the lips of the Popham colonists at Monhegan, in the Thanksgiving service of the Church of England.

Days set apart for thanksgiving were known in Europe before the Reformation, and were in frequent use by Protestants afterward, especially in the Church of England, where they were a fixed custom long before they were in New England. One wonders that the Puritans, hating so fiercely the customs and set days and holy days of the Established Church,* should so quickly have appointed a Thanksgiving Day. But the first New England Thanksgiving was not a day of religious observance, it was a day of recreation. Those who fancy all Puritans, and especially all Pilgrims, to

---

[1] From *Customs and Fashions in Old New England*, by Alice Morse Earle, pp. 216–220, 221, 222. Copyright, 1893, by Charles Scribner's Sons. New York.

* The Churchmen derisively referred to Thanksgiving Day as St. Pompion's (Pumpkin's) Day.

have been sour, morose, and gloomy men should read this account of the first Thanksgiving week (not day) in Plymouth. It was written on December 11, 1621, by Edward Winslow to a friend in England:

Our harvest being gotten in our governor sent four men on fowling that so we might after a special manner rejoice together after we had gathered the fruits of our labors. They four killed as much fowl as with a little help beside served the company about a week. At which times among other recreations we exercised our arms, many of the Indians coming amongst us, and among the rest their greatest king Massasoyt with some ninety men, whom for three days we entertained and feasted, and they went out and killed five deer which they brought and bestow'd on our governor, and upon the captains and others.

As Governor Bradford specified that during that autumn "beside waterfoule ther was great store of wild turkies," we can have the satisfaction of feeling sure that at that first Pilgrim Thanksgiving our forefathers and foremothers had turkeys.

Thus fared the Pilgrims better at their Thanksgiving than did their English brothers, for turkeys were far from plentiful in England at that date.

Though there were but fifty-five English to eat the Pilgrim Thanksgiving feast, there were "partakers in plenty," and the ninety sociable Indian visitors did not come empty-handed, but joined fraternally in provision for the feast, and probably also in the games.

These recreations were, without doubt, competitions in running, leaping, jumping, and perhaps stool-ball, a popular game played by both sexes, in which a ball was driven from stool to stool or wicket to wicket.

During that chilly November week in Plymouth, Priscilla Mullins and John Alden may have "recreated" themselves with this ancient form of croquet—if any recreation were possible for the four women of the colony, who, with the help of one servant and a few young girls or maidekins, had to prepare and cook food for three days for one hundred and twenty hungry men, ninety-one of them being Indians, with an unbounded capacity for gluttonous gorging unsurpassed by any other race. Doubtless the deer, and possibly the great turkeys, were roasted in the open air. The picture of that Thanksgiving Day, the block-house with its few cannon, the Pilgrim men in buff breeches, red waistcoats, and green or sad-colored mandillions; * the great company of Indians, gay in holiday paint and feathers and furs; the few sad, overworked, homesick women, in worn

---

* A man's garment something of the nature of a doublet and also spelt mandilian. It was first worn in France in the sixteenth century, and was for many years a soldier's wear, and was frequently sleeveless. . . . Mandillions were among the articles of clothing given to each Bay and Piscataway planter. The mandillions of the New England colonists were fastened with hooks and eyes, and lined with cotton.—Alice Morse Earle, *Costume of Colonial Times* (New York, 1894), pp. 154–155.

and simple gowns, with plain coifs and kerchiefs, and the pathetic handful of little children, forms a keen contrast to the prosperous, cheerful Thanksgivings of a century later.

There is no record of any special religious service during this week of feasting. The Pilgrims had good courage, stanch faith, to thus celebrate and give thanks, for they apparently had but little cause to rejoice. They had been lost in the woods, where they had wandered surbated,* and been terrified by the roar of "Lyons," and had met wolves that "sat on thier tayles and grinned" at them; they had been half frozen in their poorly built houses; had been famished, or sickened with unwonted and unpalatable food; their common house had burned down, half their company was dead—they had borne sore sorrows, and equal trials were to come. They were in dire distress for the next two years. In the spring of 1623 a drought scorched the corn and stunted the beans, and in July a fast day of nine hours of prayer was followed by a rain that revived their "withered corn and their drooping affections." In testimony of their gratitude for the rain, which would not have been vouchsafed for private prayer, and thinking they would "show great ingratitude if they smothered up the same," the second Pilgrim Thanksgiving was ordered and observed.

In 1630, on February 22d, the first public thanksgiving was held in Boston by the Bay Colony, in gratitude for the safe arrival of food-bearing and friend-bringing ships. On November 4, 1631, Winthrop wrote again: "We kept thanksgiving day in Boston." From that time till 1684 there were at least twenty-two public thanksgiving days appointed in Massachusetts—about one in two years; but it was not a regular biennial festival. In 1675, a time of deep gloom through the many and widely separated attacks from the fierce savages, there was no public thanksgiving celebrated in either Massachusetts or Connecticut. It is difficult to state when the feast became a fixed annual observance in New England. In the year 1742 were two Thanksgiving Days.

* * * * *

The early Thanksgivings were not always set upon Thursday. It is said that that day was chosen on account of its reflected glory as lecture day. Judge Sewall told the governor and his council, in 1697, that he "desir'd the same day of the week might be for Thanksgiving and Fasts," and that "Boston and Ipswich Lectures led us to Thorsday." The feast of thanks was for many years appointed with equal frequency upon "Tusday com seuen-night," or "vppon Wensday com fort-nit." Nor was any special season of the year chosen: in 1716 it was appointed in August; in 1713, in January; in 1718, in December; in 1719, in October. The frequent appointments in gratitude for bountiful harvests finally made the autumn the customary time.**

---

* Sore-footed.

** [In 1680] the form of recommendation indicates that the autumnal Thanksgiving had gained recognition as an annual festival. . . . During the Revolution Thanksgiv-

* * * * *

Though in the mind of the Puritan, Christmas smelled to heaven of idolatry, when his own festival, Thanksgiving, became annual, it assumed many of the features of the old English Christmas; it was simply a day of family reunion in November instead of December, on which Puritans ate turkey and Indian pudding and pumpkin-pie, instead of "superstitious meats" such as a baron of beef, boar's head, and plum-pudding.

Many funny stories are told of the early Thanksgiving Days, such as the town of Colchester calmly ignoring the governor's appointed day and observing their own festival a week later in order to allow time for the arrival, by sloop from New York, of a hogshead of molasses for pies. . . .

Its Customs [2]

It was the practice of some of this class to knock at the doors of those thought to be better off, on the evening before, begging "something for Thanksgiving"; and, by way of a joke, the children of comfortable neighbors and friends would often array themselves in cast-off bizarre habiliments, and come in bands of three or four to the houses of those whom they knew, preferring the same request. Ordinarily, the disguise was readily detected. Sometimes the little mimics would come in, and keep up the show and the fun for a while; but for the most part their courage failed them at the threshold, and they skurried away, shouting for glee, almost before they got any answer to their mock petitions. It was a queer fancy, thus to simulate poverty; but kings have sometimes done so. Did not James of Scotland find amusement in roaming through a portion of his domain, as a "gaberlunzieman?" Yes—and even composed a famous ballad to celebrate his exploits in this humble way. In the evening, we had a lively company, regaled with nuts, apples, and cider; and my grandmother, who indulged in the old-fashioned practice, that is for females, of smoking a pipe, sat in the chimney-corner, where a genial wood-fire was brightly blazing, for coal was then a thing unknown in family consumption, duly furnished with the implement, and sometimes called out to us,— "A-done, children, a-done," when in anywise annoyed by us, and occasionally would sing us an old song, of which I remember only "Robert Kid" and "A galliant ship, launched off the stocks, from Old England she

---

ing became national, the Congress annually recommending a day to be set apart for this purpose. In 1862-3, President Lincoln recommended special days for Thanksgiving, and since the Civil War the practice has assumed the regularity of official routine, and may be regarded as a national institution.—Charles Ledyard Norton, "Thanksgiving Day, Past and Present," *The Magazine of American History,* Vol. 14 (December, 1885), No. 6, pp. 560–561.

[2] From *Old New England Traits,* edited by George Lunt, pp. 105–107. Entered, according to Act of Congress, in the year 1873, by George Lunt, in the Office of the Librarian of Congress, at Washington. New York: Hurd and Houghton. Cambridge: The Riverside Press.

came," etc.; and, often when a storm was raging without, repeating to us the rhymes,—

"How little do" (pronounced doe) "we think, or know,
What *the* poor sailors undergo."

Christmas Eve on Beacon Hill

EVERY Christmas Eve Boston's Beacon Hill turns back the pages of history and offers an enchanting scene.

From the brilliantly illuminated State House to Charles Street, from aristocratic Beacon Street right over the Hill into the slum districts, old houses beam holiday tidings to all and hospitality reigns.

Caroling groups stream up and down the Hill past Bullfinch mansion fronts which are gaily illuminated with vari-colored lights. Good fellowship flourishes as luxuriantly as Yuletide greetings. At Louisburg Square, the focal point of the celebration, guests toast each other with eggnog.

Householders come to their doors as the carolers halt outside. With them, as a gesture of democracy, the servants are permitted to stand. A few homes invite small groups of carolers to enter and warm themselves before the open fire. The custom of Beacon Hill carols was originated by Frederick W. Briggs, of Newtonville, Mass., in 1895 after spending a merry and musical evening in an English town. In recent years some 150,000 Christmas Eve celebrators have joined the wandering minstrels in celebrating Joyous Yuletide on the Hill.

Menin Jesu in Provincetown

CHRISTMAS to New Year's is our great moment, and the loveliest of all local customs was *Menin Jesu,* the little Jesus, brought by the Portuguese from the Western Islands. The older Portuguese people once kept open house from Christmas to New Year's. Every window in their houses had a candle behind it. A home ablaze with lights meant that everyone was welcome, whether or not he knew the host. Indeed, the most welcome and honored guests were the strangers.

In the front room was a pyramid of graduated shelves. One candle on top, on the next shelf two saucers of sprouted wheat; on the next, two candles; on the next, four saucers of sprouted wheat, and so on. These represented the Resurrection and the Light. At the bottom was a crèche of little figures brought from the Western Islands. To everyone who came was given a tiny cordial glass of homemade wine—beach plum, elderberry, or dandelion—and a tiny cake.

From *The Yankee Cook Book,* edited by Imogene Wolcott, pp. 328–329. Copyright, 1939, by Coward-McCann, Inc. New York.

From *Time and the Town,* A Provincetown Chronicle, by Mary Heaton Vorse, p. 51. Copyright, 1942, by Mary Heaton Vorse. New York: The Dial Press.

The Avellars and ourselves used to go at Christmas through the western part of town, seeing down a dark lane, under willow trees, houses brilliant with light. In the distance there was the sound of music and singing. The ships' bands of Portuguese instruments, from the great vessels, went from house to house, saluting the *Menin Jesu*. In some houses they would have both the *Menin Jesu* and a Christmas tree—the Christmas tree, with its presents, looking materialistic and Teutonic beside the sprouted wheat and the lights. Little by little the custom of *Menin Jesu* has vanished. Only a few very old people still celebrate it.

Hallowe'en

. . . HALLOWE'EN was not much remembered in Boston at this time, outside of a few English families associated with Christ Church.

These families had loved to keep the remembrance of the old superstitions, and to pretend to believe that the dead return to their late habitations on that one night of the year, and mingle with the people as they used to do. They filled great tubs with water and floating apples, and tried to secure the apples with their teeth, and so bobbed their heads into the water. They hung sticks from the ceiling, with a burning candle on one end of them and an apple on the other, and twisted them, and tried to catch the apple in their teeth, and received smutches from the candle. They threw apple parings over their shoulders that these might form the initial letters of their lovers' names. They combed their hair before lookingglasses in lonely chambers that their future husbands might appear and look over their shoulders. They told ghost stories of castle life in old England, and sang ballads, the same as people now read Burns's Hallowe'en, or Poe's Black Cat, or William Morris's tale of the Northern knight who visited Elsie with "his coffin on his back." The gift of pieces of cake on which were rings or sibyl-like poems and prophecies ended the merriment at midnight.

The Fourth of July

ON THE Fourth of July here the boys fired the old cannon which for immemorial years had voiced the patriotism of the eager lads of the town. It was a primitive cannon cast by farmers in a sand mould of their own and guiltless of art. It was usually fired by touching the red-hot end of a scythe to the powder at the vent. In order to make it "speak" it was the custom to follow the powder with dry paper and then "ram home" wet paper and fill the cannon to the muzzle with green grass or soaked rags. When such a charge was touched off, the charge went one way, the cannon another and the boys another.

From *In Old New England, The Romance of a Colonial Fireside*, by Hezekiah Butterworth, p. 89. Copyright, 1895, by D. Appleton and Company. New York.

In the passing of the years the touch-hole, or vent, had become worn and enlarged so that occasionally there was a back fire and most of the powder went out at the vent. It was therefore necessary that the vent should be tightly covered. It was an important and distinguished task to be allowed to thumb the vent. If this was carefully done the danger of a premature discharge was reduced to the minimum. On one never-to-be-forgotten Fourth of July morning, Bill undertook to thumb that hole. The iron was so hot that he moved his thumb a little, when off went the cannon. This time the boy and the cannon went the same way. When his comrades picked Bill up his face was as black as a negro's and he was blind. They took him to our barn and called the doctor. The powder had imbedded itself in his face, his eyebrows and lashes were gone, and it seemed a miracle that he was ever able to see. But for years the powder marks were plain upon his face and a certain amount of respect was accorded by his comrades, and by myself to this day, to one who had survived being shot by a cannon!

All raids against the peace and order of the town were planned in dark hours on The Common or in the horse shed bordering it. The glorious Fourth was rung in at midnight by Church and Academy bell, and when every boy had satisfactorily blistered his hands at the rope there was a lull in the tintinnabulation and the boys made ready for strategy and war. An ancient strong man is said to have borne off the gates of Gaza and our boys emulated his example by removing every gate in town that could be broken or torn from its place. There was a tradition that a certain itinerant pastor's rooster would walk into the house on the morning of April first and roll on his back, sticking up his legs to be tied and ready for the journey to the next appointment. The gates around town must have had the same state of mind on the Fourth of July. However faithfully they had swung back and forth to welcome the coming and speed the parting guest, off they went themselves in the darkness of Independence Day. Most of them would be hidden in the tall grasses of the meadow not to be discovered until the mower struck them with his scythe in late July or August.[1]

The worst day in the year for horses was the Fourth of July. No one who could help it drove a horse in town on that day. . . .

Frightening horses by tossing lighted firecrackers near them was considered legitimate sport. If your horse bolted in consequence of a firecracker exploding under its feet, you got little sympathy. You should have known better than to take your horse out on the Fourth. So most people stayed home and ate watermelon and ice cream, and if they wanted to hear the Independence Day oration and witness the balloon ascension, or if in the evening they wished to attend the band concert and fireworks exhibition in the park, they went in public conveyances or walked.

---

[1] From *Black Tavern Tales, Stories of Old New England*, by Charles L. Goodell, pp. 44–46. Copyright, 1932, by Charles L. Goodell. Brooklyn: Willis McDonald & Co.

How milkmen hated the day! There was no better kind of wagon to figure in a runaway than a milk cart filled with cans and bottles. Daring indeed was the milkman who drove his route on the Fourth of July without a helper to hold his horse while he ran round to back doors to deliver milk. . . .[2]

Guy Fawkes' Day

GUY FAWKES' DAY, or "Pope's Day," was observed with much noise throughout New England for many years by burning of bonfires, preceded by parades of young men and boys dressed in fantastic costumes and carrying "guys" or "popes" of straw. Fires are still lighted on the 5th of November in New England towns by boys, who know not what they commemorate. In Newburyport, Mass., and Portsmouth, N. H., Guy Fawkes' Day is still celebrated. In Newcastle, N. H., it is called "Pork Night." In New York and Brooklyn, the bonfires on the night of election, and the importunate begging on Thanksgiving Day of ragged fantastics, usually children of Roman Catholic parents, are both direct survivals of the ancient celebration of "Pope's Day." [1]

. . . Portsmouth, N. H. . . . enjoys, I think, the special distinction of being the only place in this hemisphere where Guy Fawkes and the Gunpowder Plot are still appropriately celebrated.

The anniversary is known as "Pope Night," and the observances have dwindled to hornblowing and the carrying about of pumpkin-lanterns by the boys. The origin of the celebration is quite forgotten.[2]

Nantucket Sheep Shearing

. . . THE moors, or "commons," as they are popularly called, are especially adapted for sheep-grazing, both in a positive and negative sense— the short, dry herbage making particularly fine mutton, and the soil seeming incapable of raising anything else. Hence, from the earliest days, sheep

[2] From *The Horse & Buggy Age in New England*, by Edwin Valentine Mitchell, p. 174. Copyright, 1937, by Coward-McCann, Inc. New York.

[1] From *Customs and Fashions in Old New England*, by Alice Morse Earle, p. 229. Copyright, 1893, by Charles Scribner's Sons. New York.

[2] From "Contributions to the New England Vocabulary," by Frederic D. Allen, in *Dialect Notes*, Vol. I (Part I, 1890), p. 18 and note. Boston: Published by the American Dialect Society.

From *Nantucket Scraps*, Being the Experiences of an Off-Islander, in Season and out of Season, among a Passing People, by Jane G. Austin, pp. 233–236. Copyright, 1882, by James R. Osgood and Company. Boston. 1883.

have been a specialty of Nantucket, and a source of wealth rivaling the whale. To thoroughly elucidate the sheep question is reserved for some Macaulay, Carlyle, or Mackenzie of the future, for it involves not only the chief land-industry of this remarkable island, but its chief political economy, its municipal struggles, its angry passions, its still smoldering feuds, its family quarrel decently guarded from the stranger's eye. Suffice it to say that the moors were once owned in common, any man using them for grazing ground as he would; and subsequently they were nominally divided into shares, each shareholder having the right to graze a fixed number of sheep without boundaries. There were several favorite pastures for these flocks, one of them lying just outside the part of the village called Newtown; and here a gate was placed across the road to keep what was called the Town Flock from coming in and devastating the gardens by night. Beside this gate also stood the only gallows ever erected in Nantucket, and here the solitary execution took place; the culprit was an Indian, taken red-handed in the act of murder, and whether the gallows was a salutary terror to the sheep as well as the Indians is not mentioned in history.

The Indians soon died out, but the sheep increased and multiplied until they were counted by thousands; and for a century or so an idyllic and pastoral Shearing Feast was kept by the entire population, who, on the first Monday in June, migrated to the ponds near the western end of the island, where the sheep had been previously driven up and penned. Miacomet Plain, with its chain of ponds—one of them still called Washing Pond—then became for three days an encampment of tents and booths, where busy matrons and merry girls cooked such savory dishes as were at that time dear to the island epicure, or set forth those daintier viands prepared at home. The fathers, husbands, brothers, and sweethearts meantime washed the sheep, lightening their labor with a great deal of rough play and many practical jokes among themselves, and returned them to the pens to dry until next day, when the shearing began; and let us be glad Mr. Bergh was not obliged to watch its progress, since seldom did a sheep escape his shearer's hands without one or more patches of tar to show where the scissors had gone deeper than the fleece. The next thing was to rebrand each animal with its owner's initial or emblem; and then the shearing was over, and the encampment broke up, the lads and lasses finishing out the holiday with a surreptitious dance in town—for these were the days of Quaker supremacy, when dancing, music, cards, and most modes of amusement were strictly forbidden. But like most efforts to suppress human nature, these laws were only fully honored by those who had no longer the temptation to break them; and the young Quakers danced, sang, and frolicked in their generation very much as their too-liberal descendants do to-day.

Town Meeting Day

THAT second Tuesday in March was and still is the Big Red Letter Day of the old New England towns—Town Meetin' Day! To the children of the early 1800's it meant a gift of gingerbread in the homecoming pockets of their fathers; to the older folks it meant the great expression of democracy where each man might have his say on town affairs, make his vote in his own voice, and if on the wrong side of the question learn to take his defeat like a man, quite sold to the idea that the greater number should win. . . .

* * * * *

In 1845 Angelina Kidder of Mill Hollow, in the East Part, wrote to her brother: "Father is as merry as possible. I wish they would have town meeting every week if it would always have such a good effect on his spirits. He is moderator." So it was then and so it has been ever since, Town Meeting an event of fair import and a raiser of the spirits of every one, from the youngest to the oldest. And if one might but be "Moderator" —there was nothing more for which to long.

Then, after our forefathers had found that the beautiful red but poisonous Love Apple was a perfectly edible tomato, it became the custom to see that the saved and dried tomato seeds from the summer before were planted in their seed box on the window sill—always on Town Meetin' Day!

Muster or Training Day

THIS MUSTER, or "training day," as it was more often called, was their best holiday, when the militia was drilled in a vacant lot of some fortunate town. What child ever forgot that show when once seen? As an early experience or a remembered picture, what could surpass it? How real the soldiers were with their muskets and bright uniforms! What a great man the captain was! And the drum-major, who ever saw his like? What a marvel of discipline the soldiers showed! what uniformity of step! what skill in evolution! what success of officers in horsemanship! All day long they went through their drills, and the gaping crowd stared and marveled, half taking this play for a real thing and these men for true soldiers.

From *New Hampshire Borns a Town*, by Marion Nicholl Rawson, pp. 54, 67. Copyright, 1942, by E. P. Dutton & Co., Inc. New York.

For accounts of the present-day Town Meeting, see Charles Edward Crane, *Winter in Vermont* (New York, 1941), pp. 292–296; Louise Dickinson Rich, *We Took to the Woods* (Philadelphia, 1942), pp. 298–306; and Clarence M. Webster, *Town Meeting Country* (New York, 1945), pp. 228–235.

From *New England Bygones*, by E. H. Arr, pp. 56–58. Copyright, 1880, by J. B. Lippincott & Co. Philadelphia.

Before daylight, from the country miles around, wagons full of living freight began to pour into the field, until it was half packed with sight-seers. These wagons were drawn close up by the wall as a safe place for the girls and younger children. The unharnessed horses, to be kept quiet with hay, were tied close by, and the larger boys got astride the wall or climbed into neighboring trees. Booths were put up, and peddlers' carts stood thick in an inner ring. Gingerbread and candy were the staple articles of trade, with such bright gauds as would be likely to catch an uncritical eye. It was the custom for lasses to receive presents on this day, and because of this many a hard-earned penny was foolishly spent. It was amusing to see the plain farmers going about with their red bandanna handkerchiefs (show things) full of gingerbread, the extent of their day's dissipation. It was good gingerbread, with a sort of training flavor, which died out with the giving up of the custom of the day. At noon, when the soldiers dispersed for dinner, the most adventurous boys followed the great officers to the tavern, and looked in at the windows to see them eat, whispering to each other of the prowess of these dangerous men. It was not considered respectable for young girls to wander about among the crowd, so they lunched in the wagons, or on the greensward by them, and their nooning was the harvest of the dealers in gingerbread.

The climax of the drill was the firing off of the guns, which brought many an urchin down from his perch as quickly as if he had been shot in the head. Unbred horses did not relish the day, and were constantly making little side stampedes, no less exciting than the drill itself. A shower took all the feather and glory out of the show, and sent soldiers flying in front of the crowd. Before nightfall parties got mixed. Soldiers mistook themselves for citizens, and citizens forgot the deference due to soldiers. It was generally growing to be truly warlike, when at order of the great captain the trainers, led by music of bugle and drum, marched magnificently from the field. The crowd waited. Men, women, and children seemed to devour with their eyes this departing glory; this toy pageant, which had given them a merry day; this mock soldiery, which had simulated patriotic virtue; this thing, which was not foolish because it was so real to them. When it had fairly passed out of sight each went his and her own way, and, almost before the drum had stopped playing its marching tune, the field was deserted.

PASTIMES AND GAMES

Chimney-Corner Story-Telling

IN THOSE days we had no magazines and daily papers, each reeling off a

From *Oldtown Fireside Stories*, by Harriet Beecher Stowe, pp. 1–3. Entered, according to Act of Congress, in the year 1871, by James R. Osgood & Co., in the Office of the Librarian of Congress, at Washington. Boston: James R. Osgood & Company. 1872.

serial story. Once a week, "The Columbian Sentinel" came from Boston with its slender stock of news and editorial; but all the multiform devices —pictorial, narrative, and poetical—which keep the mind of the present generation ablaze with excitement, had not then even an existence. There was no theatre, no opera; there were in Oldtown no parties or balls, except, perhaps, the annual election, or Thanksgiving festival; and when winter came, and the sun went down at half-past four o'clock, and left the long, dark hours of evening to be provided for, the necessity of amusement became urgent. Hence, in those days, chimney-corner story-telling became an art and an accomplishment. Society then was full of traditions and narratives which had all the uncertain glow and shifting mystery of the firelit hearth upon them. They were told to sympathetic audiences, by the rising and falling light of the solemn embers, with the hearth-crickets filling up every pause. Then the aged told their stories to the young,—tales of early life; tales of war and adventure, of forest-days, of Indian captivities and escapes, of bears and wild-cats, and panthers, of rattlesnakes, of witches and wizards, and strange and wonderful dreams and appearances and ·providences.

In those days of early Massachusetts, faith and credence were in the very air. Two-thirds of New England was then dark, unbroken forests, through whose tangled paths the mysterious winter wind groaned and shrieked and howled with weird noises and unaccountable clamors. Along the iron-bound shore, the stormful Atlantic raved and thundered, and dashed its moaning waters, as if to deaden and deafen any voice that might tell of the settled life of the old civilized world, and shut us forever into the wilderness. A good story-teller, in those days, was always sure of a warm seat at the hearthstone, and the delighted homage of children. . . .

The Debating Society

PERHAPS chief among our most pleasurable concerns was a debating club, known as the Webster-Hayne Society. Throughout the academy and even throughout the village the loyalty accorded to this organization was intense. Debates were held once a fortnight between opposing teams of two each; and since it was the aim of the club to be inclusive rather than selective in the choice of its speakers, opportunity was widespread for this legitimate means of self-expression. Our subjects were many and varied, and it was an unalterable rule that we should *draw* both for them and for the side we were to support. Thus it was conceivable that I, who would have liked to defend the heroism of the American Indian, or the pre-eminence of sailing vessels over steamships, might be compelled to denounce the Monroe Doctrine or the Assassination of Julius Caesar. The preceptor of my day, who was responsible for this rule as well as for the list of suggested sub-

From *A Goodly Heritage,* by Mary Ellen Chase, pp. 268–270. Copyright, 1932, by Henry Holt and Company, Inc. New York.

jects, maintained that by this method of assignment we were trained in the necessary virtue of adaptability; and my father, who was for years a patron of the society, entirely agreed with him.

We usually wrote our arguments and then committed them to memory, although gifted ones among us might prefer to speak "off-hand." The rebuttal which followed the debate proper always called for some spontaneous denouncing of our rivals, which, in the heat of the controversy, we found not too difficult in spite of a large and interested audience. A letter of commendation from my father, written from Augusta a few days following my spirited denunication of Napoleon as a monster to civilization, is one of my treasured possessions as is also a notebook which lists our subjects of one winter term:

> Resolved, that the American Indian was, on the whole, an heroic rather than a dastardly figure in history.
>
> Resolved, that the system of taxation under the Roman Empire was unjust to the provinces.
>
> Resolved, that the study of Greek is valuable to the student in Blue Hill Academy.
>
> Resolved, that the Annexation of Texas was unjustifiable.
>
> Resolved, that the rural life of Maine affords advantages above that of the urban.
>
> Resolved, that *Ivanhoe* is a greater and a more interesting novel than *The Last of the Mohicans*.

Sleigh Riding

AMONG the amusements of New England, sleigh-riding has always held a distinguished place. It is one of the principal winter pastimes; is entered into with a great deal of zest; and is altogether a social amusement. Sleigh-riders are generally divided into two classes—the married and the single. These form separate companies. The young do not choose to be restrained by the gravity of the old; and the old do not like to be annoyed by the flirtations of the young. Such is the natural conclusion; but it is shrewdly hinted by the single ones that gravity, on these occasions, finds little place even among married people; that, in fact, they carry their merriment to a pitch never ventured upon by the single; and that it is the old who dread the restraints of the young, rather than the young of the old.

* * * * *

The mere business of riding in a sleigh is not the sole object on these

From *The Life and Adventures of Dr. Dodimus Duckworth,* A.N.Q., to which is added, The History of a Steam Doctor, by The Author of "A Yankee among the Nullifiers" (Asa Greene), Vol. II, pp. 157–158, 159–160. Entered, according to Act of Congress, in the year 1833, by Asa Greene, in the Office of the Clerk of the District Court of the United States for the Southern District of New York. New York: Published by Peter Hill.

occasions; but a dance, or frolic of some kind, is connected with it. If the party consists of young persons, dancing is usually the order of the night; if of married ones, some other amusement—such as blindman's buff, changing partners, forfeits, and the like—is not unfrequently substituted; and grave papas and mamas, throwing aside their sober parental character, for the time being, assume that of frolicsome children.

The order of a sleigh-ride is this: All the members of the party convene at some given point, from whence they start in company, and drive in a sort of procession, or long line of vehicles, to some other point at a convenient distance—usually some tavern out of town, provided with a large hall, where dancing, or other amusements may be carried on. A supper is bespoken, and wines and other liquors are expected to be forthcoming, if called for. Here all is joy, sport, and hilarity. Dull care is given to the winds; and life and merriment succeed. Sambo has his fiddle new strung, and his bow new rosined for the occasion; and sitting on a platform in one corner, while he makes all feet obedient to the motion of his elbow, fancies himself a greater man than Solomon in all his glory. Or if some other amusement take the place of dancing, then mirth, life, and frolic, move round the circle; and the infliction of sportive penalties, the redemption of forfeits, and the romping and playing of grown-up children occupy the festive hours.

The amusements being over, the party return in the same regular order in which they went forth. It is not to be supposed, however, because they move in a line, that their procession is slow and solemn, like that of a funeral; or stately and exact, like that of a regiment on the line of march. On the contrary, they move briskly and merrily along at a swift trot— the sleighs gliding one after another, as though they slid upon nothing— and the bells musically chiming, to the great animation both of steed and rider. But there is, nevertheless, an order even here—a rule, enacted for the preservation of the property, the life, and character of those concerned. The enactment is this—that there shall be no running of horses during the ride; and that whoever drives his steed faster than a trot, shall forfeit and pay a certain sum of money, to be expended for the benefit of the party; and moreover shall be held and deemed to have drunk more than becomes a respectable man, or than the occasion itself requires.

Husking Bees or Frolics

HUSKING. The act of stripping off husks from Indian corn. In New England it is the custom for farmers to invite their friends to assist them in this task. The ceremonies on these occasions are well described by Joel Barlow, in his poem on Hasty Pudding:

From *Dictionary of Americanisms*, by John Russell Bartlett, p. 186. New York: Bartlett and Welford, 1848.

For now, the cow-house fill'd, the harvest home,
Th' invited neighbors to the *Husking* come;
A frolic scene, where work, and mirth, and play,
Unite their charms, to chase the hours away.

* * * * *

The laws of *husking* every wight can tell;
And sure no laws he ever keeps so well:
For each red ear a gen'ral kiss he gains,
With each smut ear, she smuts the luckless swains;
But when to some sweet maid a prize is cast,
Red as her lips, and taper as her waist,
She walks around, and culls one favor'd beau,
Who leaps, the luscious tribute to bestow.
Various the sport, as are the wits and brains
Of well-pleas'd lasses and contending swains;
Till the vast mound of corn is swept away,
And he that gains the last ear, wins the day.—Canto 3.

Cattle Show

Now for the cattle-show and the premiums! At daybreak all are on the move, and wide awake for the grand exhibition. Fat beeves and working cattle, fill-pail milkers, Ayrshire bulls, bellowing calves, snorting grunters, with wagon-loads of fat cheeses, and boxes of rich butter, bearing the stamp of super-excellence, carefully put on by my honest aunt Tabitha. See what mammoth squashes, and other fruits in abundance! Here come the groups of fair damsels, crowding into the hall, to see the various handi-work. Carpets, mats, rugs, bedspreads, needle-work and knitting-work, of every kind and description! But come; let us away to the ploughing match; that is what takes the rag off, and is something to the purpose. Twelve teams,—no drivers. Keep steady helm, boys, and mind your eye! How true they lay the sod! The committee will have their match to settle who does the best. Off yonder are the working cattle, drawing their ponderous loads of stone; hard and heavy they tug and tug. See how they haw, gee, go ahead, and back astern! no lashing, no bawling, and their teams move as regular as a platoon of soldiers!

County Fair

THE best place to see neo-Puritans really at play was at the county fairs

From *The Old Farmer's Almanack*, Calculated on a New and Improved Plan, for the Year of Our Lord 1852, p. 25, October. Entered, according to Act of Congress, in the year 1851, by Jenks, Hickling & Swan, in the Clerk's Office of the District Court of the District of Massachusetts. Boston.

From *Town Meeting Country*, by Clarence M. Webster, pp. 159–161. Copyright, 1945, by Clarence M. Webster. New York: Duell, Sloan & Pearce.

held every fall. The fair-going addict had plenty of attractions to choose from. I've forgotten which one opened the season in early September, but the Stafford Springs event in the middle of October was the last. Sturbridge, Oxford, Willimantic, Norwich, Putnam, Rockville, Palmer, Woodstock, and other towns had at one time or another a fair of their own. But the oldest and most typical of all was the one at Brooklyn, Connecticut.

There was the place where you best caught the real Yankee land as it completely relaxed for one day in the year. Over in Massachusetts there was the famous Brockton Fair where prizes were magnificent and the exhibits awe-inspiring. At Hartford in Charter Oak Park famous harness racing could be enjoyed, the Willimantic track was a sporty half-mile, and Sturbridge had its noted drivers. Brooklyn could not match such attractions; nevertheless, people seemed to feel that it had something the other fairs lacked. For one thing, it was a nice home affair that respected the old ways and exhibited a mode of life that was sound even while it pleased. You met everybody at Brooklyn Fair. You heard a woman say, "Why, I ain't seen her since last Fair day." And a man remark, "When I run into him at th' Fair he told me. . . ." Plenty of people went to the other fairs, but they never seemed to meet old friends the way they did at Brooklyn. As far as I can figure out, that Fair was a sort of catalytic which helped bring to a fine, satisfying blend all the sedate pleasures of a quiet, sensible people, who, nevertheless, could take a day off in the fall and spend a dollar or two and perhaps win a few blue ribbons and the accompanying cash prize.

There were three days to the Fair, Opening, Cattle, and Horse. The first was more or less given over to arranging exhibits in the buildings, although the Midway had started, and there were harness races in the afternoon. The second day was the big one, for then the cattle were on exhibit and were judged. On the third, the horses were shown, and there were some good races. Schools were let out for the Big Day, and only the sternest fathers dared to keep their families home. Even Sam Hunt, famous among thrifty men for his more-than-thrift, bestowed one-half of a dollar on each of his seven children, sorrowfully accepting the fact that, as he said, "There goes a lot of damned good money I've worked hard for, but th' little cusses sorta look forward t' Brooklyn Fair."

By ten o'clock in the morning every one was there, even Lester Gull, who walked the eight miles barefoot and put on his shoes at the gates. Up against the rails of the half-mile track were hitched the teams. Fancy rubber-tired buggies and black pacers, smart spans of horses and the canopy-topped surrey, farm horses hitched to lumber wagons with boards for seats. Ever since dawn the farmers had been driving their cattle toward Brooklyn, and now the long sheds were filled with calves, bulls, milch cows, hogs, and sheep. A man could spend quite a while, happily wandering from one stall or pen to another, commenting freely on each exhibit and telling a friend that he had a boar or yearling heifer better than any he'd seen yet. Over in the Main Exhibition or the Food and Fancy Work buildings the women folks were happy. Over the hum of voices rose the cry of the sideshow barker, the crack of the buggy whip wielded by the sporty vendor, and the occasional roar of the Wild Man from Borneo down in his pit.

In the afternoon the grandstand was full, and the crowd stood three deep against the rails. Next to the judges' stand was the platform where a band played when acrobats were not performing. The races were gallantly listed as 2/05 pace and trot, 2/13 trot, but if any horse made 2/20 he was very suspect indeed. This was the time when the young bloods had their big moment of the year, and the fellow who entered a horse and even drove it himself was a real hero.

When the last heat was trotted, tired celebrators piled into their carriages and express wagons and started home. Brooklyn Fair was over for the year, and there were chores to do. Most families in my town went to at least one or other fair during the fall, and a few reckless men took in four or five, but on the whole it was considered very bad form to waste too much time in this way. For in pleasure-seeking, as in other habits, the Yankees I knew were men of "measured merriment" and could not enjoy themselves if they broke the bonds of decorum. To them life was not an adventure; rather, it was a nice comfortable affair in which one day a year at Brooklyn Fair fitted neatly, a pleasant, almost gay eight hours, with just a touch of the sportive, even the exotic, but never unrestrained. For in the Indian Summer of a civilization, it is not coltish and wild; its joys are quiet ones.

Cockroach and Bedbug Match

OH, YES! The cook gave me a lot of insect powder and a squirt-gun to blow into the cracks. I used it once but the bugs ate it all up and came out of their holes licking their chops and looking for more, so I gave up in disgust. You ought to see the arena the cook has on his table. He has made a frame which slips over the edges of his cake-board and placing this on the table, he goes behind the range and catches a cockroach; then, taking a straw from the broom, he runs it up and down in the cracks of the bulkhead, back of your bunk, chasing out the bugs until he secures a lively one. Then placing the two in the center of the board, with their heads together, he sics 'em on. You'd naturally think that the cockroach would eat the bug up, but believe me! the bug is there with bells.

The first time I saw the fight I nearly laughed my head off. I was talking to the cook one Sunday afternoon when I saw him with a straw in his hands poking the bugs about the board. "What have you got there?" I asked. "Come down and see," said he. "How much will you bet on the

From *The Making of a Sailor* or Sea Life Aboard a Yankee Square-Rigger, by Frederick Pease Harlow, pp. 51–52. Publication Number Seventeen of The Marine Research Society. Copyright, 1928, by The Marine Research Society. Salem, Massachusetts.

bed-bug that he can lick the cockroach?" "Oh, I'll bet the cockroach can lick the bed-bug," said I. "All right! It'll cost you twenty-five cents to come in," said the cook. I put up the money and the cook said, "Ready! Go!" keeping their noses pointed together with the straw. The roach finally got mad and jumped on the bug and stuck his beak in, but the bug rolled over on his back and caught a leg of the roach and working himself up under his breast, tried to get a half-Nelson on him. The roach would draw up first one leg and then another in an effort to pry the bug loose and sometimes all his legs would be working at the same time. It was sure a comical sight. His legs seemed too long and there was no way in which he could bring two feet in a position at the same time so as to shake off the bug which held to it like a bulldog holding a shaggy cur by the throat. Finally, getting a vulnerable spot on the roach, he fairly sucked the life out of him and I lost my quarter. If it wasn't so late we'd ask the cook to give us an entertainment this afternoon.

The Gam

IF TWO strangers crossing the Pine Barrens in New York State, or the equally desolate Salisbury Plain in England; if casually encountering each other in such inhospitable wilds, these twain, for the life of them, cannot well avoid a mutual salutation; and stopping for a moment to interchange the news; and, perhaps, sitting down for a while and resting in concert; then, how much more natural that upon the illimitable Pine Barrens and Salisbury Plains of the sea, two whaling vessels descrying each other at the ends of the earth—off lone Fanning's Island, or the far away King's Mills; how much more natural, I say, that under such circumstances these ships should not only interchange hails, but come into still closer, more friendly and sociable contact? And especially would this seem to be a matter of course, in the case of vessels owned in one seaport, and whose captains, officers, and not a few of the men are personally known to each other; and consequently, have all sorts of dear domestic things to talk about.

For the long absent ship, the outward-bounder, perhaps, has letters on board; at any rate, she will be sure to let her have some papers of a date a year or two later than the last one on her blurred and thumb-worn files. And in return for that courtesy, the outward-bound ship would receive the latest whaling intelligence from the cruising-ground to which she may be destined, a thing of the utmost importance to her. And in degree, all this will hold true concerning whaling vessels crossing each other's track on the

From *Moby-Dick: or The Whale,* by Herman Melville, Chapter LIII, *The Works of Herman Melville,* Standard Edition, Vol. VII, pp. 301–304. London, Bombay, Sydney: Constable and Company, Ltd. 1922.

cruising-ground itself, even though they are equally long absent from home. For one of them may have received a transfer of letters from some third, and now far remote vessel; and some of those letters may be for the people of the ship she now meets. Besides, they would exchange the whaling news, and have an agreeable chat. For not only would they meet with all the sympathies of sailors, but likewise with all the peculiar congenialities arising from a common pursuit and mutually shared privations and perils.

Nor would difference of country make any very essential difference; that is, so long as both parties speak one language, as is the case with Americans and English. . . .

So, then, we see that of all ships separately sailing the sea, whalers have most reason to be sociable—and they are so. . . .

. . . What does the whaler do when she meets another whaler in any sort of decent weather? She has a *"Gam,"* a thing so utterly unknown to all other ships that they never heard of the name even; and if by chance they should hear of it, they only grin at it, and repeat gamesome stuff about "spouters," "blubber-boilers," and such like pretty exclamations. . . .

But what is a *Gam?* You might wear out your index-finger running up and down the columns of dictionaries, and never find the word. Dr. Johnson never attained to that erudition; Noah Webster's ark does not hold it. Nevertheless, this same expressive word has now for many years been in constant use among some fifteen thousand true born Yankees. Certainly, it needs a definition, and should be incorporated into the Lexicon. With that view, let me learnedly define it.

GAM. NOUN—*A social meeting of two (or more) Whaleships, generally on a cruising-ground; when, after exchanging hails, they exchange visits by boats' crews: the two captains remaining, for the time, on board of one ship, and the two chief mates on the other.*

A Childish Pastime

I MIGHT have mentioned, as one of the amusements of childhood, the throwing of a piece of paper upon the embers of our wood-fire, for we had no coal in those days, and watching the gradual extinguishment of the sparks, likening it to a congregation entering the meeting-house. "There they go in," we would say. "There's the ministers"; and as the final spark disappeared,—"Now, the sexton has gone in and shut the door." I speak of this only as a curious illustration of English ways traditionally surviving in New England. Thus Cowper tells us:—

From *Old New England Traits*, edited by George Lunt, pp. 225–226. Entered, according to Act of Congress, in the year 1873, by George Lunt, in the Office of the Librarian of Congress, at Washington. New York: Hurd and Houghton. Cambridge: The Riverside Press.

So when a child, as playful children use,
Has burnt to tinder a stale last year's news,
The flame extinct, he views the roving fire,—
There goes my lady, and there goes the squire;
There goes the parson, O illustrious spark!
And there, scarce less illustrious, goes the clerk!

Horse Chestnut Men

. . . THE small boy of the family brought a cup of boiled chestnuts, and while we munched them, explained how he had picked up eighty-one quarts of nuts so far that year. In his pocket the boy had other treasures. He pulled forth a handful of horse-chestnuts, and told me they grew on a little tree down by the burying-ground.

"The boys up at our school make men of 'em," he said. "They take one chestnut and cut a face on it like you do on a pumpkin for a jack-o'-lantern. That's the head. Then they take a bigger one and cut two or three places in front for buttons, and make holes to stick in toothpicks for legs, and they stick in more for arms, and with a little short piece fasten the head on the body. Then they put 'em up on the stovepipe where the teacher can't get 'em, and they stay there all day. Sometimes they make caps for 'em." He got out his jack-knife and spent the rest of the evening manufacturing these queer little men for my benefit.

Fly Away, Jack

A TRICK to amuse children. A person sticks pieces of white paper to the nails of his forefingers. He places his forefingers on the edge of a table with the other fingers closed. He raises his right hand and brings it back, with the middle finger substituted for the forefinger, crying *fly away, Jack.* He does the same with the left and cries *fly away, Gill.* He then restores his forefingers in the same way crying *come again, Jack; come again, Gill.*

Smell Brimstone

A CHILD is asked if he wishes to smell brimstone. He naturally does. He

From *The New England Country,* by Clifton Johnson, pp. 61–62. Copyright, 1892, by Clifton Johnson. Boston: Lee and Shepard. 1893.

From "Cape Cod Dialect Addenda," by George Davis Chase, in *Dialect Notes,* Vol. III (Part V, 1909), p. 420. Publication of the American Dialect Society. New Haven, Connecticut.

Ibid., p. 422.

is asked to double his fists and hold them in front of his face. The person then seizes his wrists, rubs his knuckles briskly together to make the brimstone and suddenly hits him in the nose with his own fist.

I Languish

A FEW years later, we forced our mother in a moment of weakness to admit that she too had played kissing games in her youth. She described one called "I Languish"—a game in which two straight chairs were placed back to back, in the center of the room. A boy knelt in one of them and announced, "I languish."

"Who do you languish for?" inquired the encircling company.

"I languish for Susan."

Susan then knelt in the other chair and they kissed. The young man retired and Susan proceeded to languish in her turn. My mother's mother was of pure New England stock, and her father three-quarters Yankee, so my first Puritans must accept seven-eighths of the responsibility for that unpuritanic pastime.

Hailey Over

PERHAPS a corruption for hail ye! over! A children's game of ball played as follows: The players choose sides and take positions on opposite sides of a barn. One player throws the ball over the barn, crying out, *hailey over*. Some one of the opposing players tries to catch it, and then tags one of his opponents with the ball. The player tagged has to change sides. The side wins which gains all of the players.

Violet Fights

THE recorder, Mrs. Fanny D. Bergen, writes:

"Armies of blue violets are annually sacrificed by little people in the 'Violet Fights.' Two children provide themselves with a goodly pile of

From *As Much As I Dare*, A Personal Recollection, by Burges Johnson, p. 11. Copyright, 1944, by Ives Washburn, Inc. New York.

From "A Word-List from Aroostook," by J. W. Carr and G. D. Chase, in *Dialect Notes*, Vol. III (Part V, 1909), p. 412. Publication of the American Dialect Society. New Haven, Connecticut.

From *Games and Songs of American Children*, collected and compared by William Wells Newell, pp. 251–252. New and Enlarged Edition. Copyright, 1883, 1903, by Harper & Brothers. New York and London.

these flowers, which they have purposely plucked with long stems. Each combatant holds his posy by the stem; the two spurs are interlocked; then the children simultaneously jerk the stems, and off comes one or the other violet head. Once in a great while the two heads fall, so evenly matched in resistance are they. Usually, however, one conquers the other; the flowerless stem is replaced by a fresh one from the pile, and the flower battle goes on. Occasionally a soldier is so valiant and successful as to lay low the heads of as many as a hundred or two of his enemies, but sooner or later he, too, is numbered with the beautiful slain. I am glad to have known of a few little girls who were too humane to take part in this ruthless play. The pastime is not only common among children throughout the United States and Canada, but is a familiar childish amusement in Japan, and a friend found that the same play was known to Indian children in the summer encampment at York Beach, Maine. The little red children say that the one whose violet conquers will be a great man. The Onandagas have a name for violets which, interpreted, means 'two heads entangled,' referring to the flower game."

Statues

DURING the long summer evenings until our bedtime at eight or eight-thirty we played with others of the neighborhood in all manner of merry-makings, usually the noisier the better. But there was one diversion which never palled, serious and silent as it was by contrast. This was the making of ourselves into *statues*. A judge was chosen, usually by counting out, and he thereupon at once retired from the scene while we decided by individuals or by groups what we should personify. The odd thing about this amusement lay in its abstract nature. There was nothing to prevent our choosing to make our forms and our faces into images of well-known persons or representative of famous events. Rather we decided to typify various emotions or states of mind—Joy, Fear, Pity, Hatred, Jealousy, Faith, Rage, Pride, Cruelty, Melancholy, and Grief. Sometimes one strove singly to make oneself into the outward and visible sign of some mental or spiritual mood; sometimes we functioned in small groups, our aim to present an ensemble like the Niobe in one of our history books. When we had finally decided what we were to represent, for which task we were allowed but a few minutes, we communicated this information to the judge, who if material was at hand wrote down the emotion or the state of mind opposite the name of the actor. If no pencil, paper, or slate were easily procurable, the judge relinquished his position in favor of mere guesswork.

Whence this game sprang it is impossible to say. Perhaps, indeed, it was born from gazing upon the reproductions of famous statuary in school-books. It seems to have been of relatively new growth; my mother had

From *A Goodly Heritage*, by Mary Ellen Chase, pp. 66–68. Copyright, 1932, by Henry Holt and Company, Inc. New York.

never played it. But it was dear to the children of my generation and environment. We always entered upon it with high seriousness, perhaps vaguely realizing that the emotions and passions we attempted to portray were the very stuff and pattern of human life. Melancholy, clasping his knees, his head sunk upon his flannel blouse, remained for long, solemn minutes while the judge criticized, appraised, or attempted to guess what his posture indicated; Faith, gazing heavenward in a blue gingham apron, was too rapt in her contemplation of eternal verities to laugh; Jealousy, called to bed in the very act of stabbing his rival, preferred to incur punishment rather than to abandon his studied, awful formation until all chance of getting first place had been well lost.

Old Witch

A.—Ten girls, a mother, a witch, and eight children—namely, Sunday, Monday, Tuesday, Wednesday, Thursday, Friday, Saturday, and the eldest daughter Sue. The mother, preparing to go out, addresses her children:

> Now all you children stay at home,
> And be good girls while I am gone;
> Let no one in [1]
> *   *   *   *   *   •
> Especially you, my daughter Sue,
> Or else I'll beat you black and blue. [2]

The witch knocks at the door, and is refused entrance by the children. She beguiles them by promises to admit her, which they finally do. She then holds out her pipe (a bit of stick), which she carries between her teeth, saying to Sue, "Light my pipe!" Sue refusing, she makes the same demand to each child, in the order of the days of the week in which they are ranged. All refuse till she reaches the last, who consents and touches her pipe, whereupon the witch seizes her hand, and drags her out of the house to her "den."

The mother then returns, counts the children, and Sue is questioned and punished. This is played over until each child is taken, Sue last.

From *Games and Songs of American Children*, collected and compared by William Wells Newell, pp. 215–216, 217–218. New and Enlarged Edition. Copyright, 1883, 1903, by Harper & Brothers. New York and London.

[1] A line and a half are wanting.—W. W. N.

[2]
> "I charge my daughters every one,
> To keep good house while I am gone.
> *You* and *you* [points] but especially *Sue*,
> Or else I'll beat you black and blue."

From "Nursery Rhymes of England," where it is said to be a game of the Gypsy, who "during the mother's absence comes in, entices a child away, and hides her. This process is repeated till all the children are hidden, when the mother has to find them." —W. W. N.

When the mother has lost all her children, the witch calls, and invites her to dinner. Upon going to the witch's door, she finds a table set for the meal, and the witch asks her to order a dish to suit her taste. She does so, whereupon the witch produces Sunday, and lays her upon the table, with considerable assistance from Sunday.

A very amusing dialogue now ensues between the witch and the mother. The former urges the mother to eat, with many blandishments, and the mother (recognizing her child) declines, with such excuses as any ingenious child can devise.

The mother, upon pretence of inability to eat the food, calls for another dish, and when the witch leaves the room, hurries the child from the table and places her behind the chair. When the witch returns, she says that she found the dish so good that she ate it all, and calls for another.

Each child is produced in turn, with the same result. When all are arranged behind their mother, she calls for another dish, and when the witch leaves the room to get it, runs home with all her children.

Hartford, Conn.

* * * * *

C.—The name of the witch in this variation is "Old Mother Cripsy-crops," and the game begins by playing No. 89 [*Old Mother Tipsy-toe*]. When the mother goes out, the children call after her, "Old mother, the kettle boils." She answers, "Take a spoon and stir it." "We haven't got any." "Buy one." "We have no money." "Borrow," says the mother. "People won't lend," reply the children.

The witch come in, and entices Sunday away by fine promises. When the mother comes back, she inquires, "Where's my Sunday?" The children make some excuse, as, "Perhaps he has gone down cellar," etc. She tells Tuesday to take care of Monday, as she had previously placed Monday in charge of Sunday, and goes out again, when the same scene is repeated, until all the children have been carried off.

The mother now calls at the witch's house, and asks to be let in. The witch refuses, saying, "No, your shoes are too dirty." "But I will take off my shoes." "Your stockings are too dirty." "Then I will take off my stockings." "Your feet are too dirty." "I will cut off my feet." "That would make the carpet all bloody." "But I must see my children, and you have got them." "What should I know about your children? But if you like you may call to-morrow at twelve."

The mother departs, and as soon as she is gone the witch goes to the children and renames them all. One she calls Mustard, another Pepper, another Salt, another Vinegar, etc. Then she turns their faces to the wall; and tells them to give these names if they are asked who they are. The mother calls again at the house of the witch, and this time is admitted. She asks the children what their names are, and they all answer as they were instructed by the witch. She then asks the first child to let her feel his toe. He puts up his foot, and when the mother feels it she says, "This is my Sunday! let your big toe carry you home;" whereupon he runs off.

The same process is gone through with all the other children.

D.—To the mother (this time present), in the midst of her children, approaches the witch, who comes limping, leaning on a cane. The dialogue is between mother and witch.

> "There's old mother Hippletyhop; I wonder what she wants to-day?"
> "I want one of your children."
> "Which one do you want?"

The witch names any child of the row.

> "What will you give her to eat?"
> "Plum-cake" (a different delicacy for each child).

The witch carries off the child, and observes: "Walk as I do, or else I'll kill you." She takes the child home and kills her, then returns for another. When all are gone the mother goes out to look for her children. She goes to the witch's house, and finds all the children (presumed to be dead) against the wall, making the most horrible faces. She points to a child, and asks, "What did [Mary] die of?" "She died of sucking her thumbs" (naming the child's gesture). Suddenly all the children come to themselves, and cry out, "Oh, mother, we are not dead!"

Portsmouth, N. H.

Tiddledewinks

DURING SCHOOL recesses, when the ice began to break up, we enjoyed the sport of "tiddledewinks," or "running tiddly," on the Public Garden Pond. This meant crossing the pond by running over floating ice cakes and jumping from one to another. At such times, the Public Garden rang with cries of "Hey, tiddely!" as the boys dared each other; and hardly a day passed wherein one hero did not fall in, to be sent home, wet through and shivering, or to be dried out by kind Mrs. Trower, the school housekeeper. Our elders never seemed to mind these escapades; there was a saying that no Boston boy was a real boy until he had fallen into the Frog or the Garden pond, but that none ever drowned there.

From *One Boy's Boston: 1887–1901,* by Samuel Eliot Morison, p. 35. Copyright, 1962, by Samuel Eliot Morison. Boston: Houghton Mifflin Company.

Games of Boston Boys

PUNK

THE games played by the boys of Chestnut and the adjacent streets are most pleasantly recalled; among which "I Spy," "The Red Lion," and "Punk" stand out prominently. This last was always popular, the only requisite being a soft ball,—not too soft, however, for obvious reasons, when it is known that the first boy holding it plugged, or "punked," the boy that suited him as a mark. A general scrimmage then ensued for the possession of the ball, and the one securing it promptly "punked" another victim selected from the rapidly scattering boys.

THE LOCUST

The American boy is nothing if not inventive, and anything that can be produced which will make a noise is dear to his heart. One of the earliest of such inventions which I recall was named the "locust," a harmless production, and one that no doubt paved the way for the later abomination known as the "Devil's fiddle." The locust was made of an old-fashioned, round wooden match-box, over the open end of which a piece of kid was tightly stretched; a strand or two of horse hair was then passed in and out of this improvised drumhead, and the long ends were made into a loop which ran around in a groove, with a little resin in it, made at the end of a stick. The box was then whirled around rapidly, the result being a sound which almost exactly resembled the note of the insect from which it received its name.

COASTING

Of course the winter sport *par excellence* was coasting, and those Boston boys whose boyhood was at the zenith in the fifties include coasting, as it was then practised, among the lost arts. If any of the youngsters of to-day are inclined to laugh at this statement, let any one of them, athlete though he may be, take a running start of from three to ten yards at full speed with the sled following at the end of its cord, and when sufficient impetus has been acquired, throw it ahead, letting the line fall along the seat, at the same time launching his body, curved bow-wise, forward through the air, alighting breast first, with no apparent effort, jar, or retardment of speed as softly as a falling snowflake, upon the flying sled as it shoots underneath. This would be called a pretty, acrobatic feat to-day, but was

From *Old Boston Boys and the Games They Played*, by James D'Wolf Lovett, pp. 10, 18–19; 29–32, 36–37; 41–47, 137–138. Copyright, 1906, by James D'Wolf Lovett. Boston: Privately printed at the Riverside Press.

too common then to attract special notice. That's the difference.

All coasting in those days was racing, pure and simple. Prominent sleds were as well known among the boys as race horses and yachts are to-day, and on any Saturday afternoon hundreds of spectators might be seen hedging in the "Long Coast," which ran from the corner of Park and Beacon streets to the West Street entrance and as much farther along Tremont Street Mall as one's impetus would carry him. A squad of coasters would be bunched together at the top of this coast, holding their sleds like dogs in leash, waiting for some "crack" to lead off. As he straightened himself and started on his run with the cry of "Lullah!" to clear the way, it was the signal for all to follow, and one after another would string out from the bunch after him, in rapid succession, each keen to pass as many of those ahead as possible, the lesser lights being careful not to start until the "heavyweights" had sped on their way.

The walk back uphill was made interesting by discussing the merits, faults, lines, etc., of the noted sleds, and if, as often happened, invidious comparisons were made between a "South End" and a "West End" sled, a lively and not altogether unwelcome scrap, then and there, was usually the logical outcome.

Sleds (the first-class ones) were made with much care and skill, and cost proportionately. Natural black walnut was a favorite material, finished either with a fine dead polish or a bright surface, varnished with as much care as a coach; the name, if it bore one, was usually a fine specimen of lettering in gold or bright colors. The model was carefully planned, and the lines were graceful and a delight to the eye of a connoisseur. Black enameled leather, bordered by gold or silver headed tacks, made a popular seat, and the "irons," as they were called, were made of the best "silver steel," whatever that meant. They were kept burnished like glass, with constant care and fine emery and oil, and a streak of ashes or a bare spot was avoided as a yacht steers clear of rocks.

The amount of "spring" given to the irons was also a matter of moment, and a nice gradation of the same was thought to have influence on the speed; it certainly added greatly to one's bodily comfort.

"Let's see your irons" was a common request, and the owner thus honored would jerk his sled up on its hind legs, so to speak, wipe off the steel with mitten or handkerchief, and show off the bright surface with much pride.

* * * * *

Steering a first-class sled in those days was not accomplished by sticking out one's leg and digging gullies in the snow with the toe of the boot. Heaven forbid! Those who owned crack sleds knew how to handle and get all the speed possible out of them, and would no more have retarded the speed by employing the above method than a yachtsman would think of steering his boat by towing a spar overboard. The correct form for a coaster who knew the game was to lie on the sled with head well down, feet firmly crossed and knees flexed as far over the back as possible, both hands resting easily upon the same runner near its point; the steering was done by "pulling her head round" in the desired direction, by little short jerks of the runner upon which the hands rested.

Dan Sargent conceived the idea of steering by holding out in front of his sled a second one of diminutive proportions. This, however, could only be done on a steep coast, where no running start was necessary. I saw him try it several times, but it was never adopted. The first step to the "double runner" was two sleds hitched together tandem, and then the long connecting board quickly followed.

MARBLES

In the spring, as soon as the frost was out of the ground, many games stood waiting for us. Probably to the boys of to-day "marbles" sounds rather weak, and "Go and play marbles" is a phrase which one often hears hurled at the head of some unsuccessful competitor in field sports. It is true that it cannot be classed among athletics, but it was a much more serious business then than it is to-day, and was played with a good deal of skill. To shoot an "alley" with force and precision, "knuckling down," that is, with the knuckles resting upon the ground, is not so easy and requires much practice.

A boy's stock of marbles was usually carried in a bag with a running string, and consisted of "Alleys," "Jaspers," "Chinees," "Peewees," "Agates," "Bull's Eyes," and several other kinds. A special marble was kept for long shots, which might perhaps have been six feet, and it was remarkable how many times a small marble would be struck at this distance, with only the snap of the thumb.

I wonder if Mr. Rogers, a most courteous and dignified gentleman, whom I often see, remembers his skill at this sport! He was as expert as any boy of whom I can think. He, among many others, used to run a "bank," as we called it,—which consisted of a strip of wood, perhaps twelve or fifteen inches long, with six or eight little arches cut in it, each somewhat wider than a marble, and numbered from one up. This row of arches was held upright upon the ground, and the marksman, a few feet away, would shoot his marble with the object of entering one of the arches; if he succeeded, he was given the number of marbles which corresponded with the number over the arch, while, if he failed, the marble was appropriated by the banker.

Then there was "ring taw" and "three holes," and lots of other names which have been forgotten. These games were good fun, and kept boys out of doors as well as out of mischief.

KITE-FLYING

Kite-flying had and always will have a fascination for boys. Few "grown-ups," however, give it any attention at the present day, except in the interest of science. Formerly many gentlemen used to make kites for their children, and meet upon the Common to fly them. The late Dr. Nathaniel B. Shurtleff, once mayor of Boston, the writer's father, and several others made fine kites. Dr. Shurtleff was very skilful in making Chinese kites; I remember several which resembled owls, with large, blinking eyes, and which were most effective in the air. My father once made a bow-kite seven feet high, a piece of rattan forming the bow. It had a "pull" which would have delighted the heart of a politician; one afternoon I was allowed to hold the cross-bar to which the string was attached, but I did not hold it long, as, although I dug both heels into the ground, it drew me along with the utmost ease. Stout gloves were required in letting out and pulling in the string of this kite.

Tops

Tops, of course, had their innings, and some of the older boys used to get theirs turned to order, from hard, fancy woods, such as lignum vitae, rose, box, tulip, leopard, and many other woods. These had long and sharp steel spikes fixed in them, with which we would try to split each other's tops while spinning. Since then I have never seen boys, playing at this sport, throw the tops with their utmost strength, as we used to do.

Stilting

Stilting, too, was a fad for a time, and some got to be quite expert at the game, hopping upon one stilt and shouldering the other. We would in this fashion have jousts, necessarily short-lived, handling the unused stilt as a lance. Games of tag, too, were played upon stilts, and in fact we got to feel pretty much at home upon them.

Tip-Cat

"Tip-cat"[1] was also a popular game. One occasionally sees it played to-day, but not to the extent that it was then. Not content with small soft wood cats, two or three inches in length, we made them of a section of broom handle and about six or eight inches long, using the remainder of the handle for the cat-stick. With the three strokes which were allowed in this game, I have seen a cat of the latter kind sent from the Spruce Street path on the Common over the Public Garden fence. Charlie Troupe, who was a fine player at the old "Massachusetts" game of baseball, made these three strokes; they held the record, and I very much doubt if any cat has ever jumped as far since.

Choosing Sides

The mode of choosing sides was about as follows: one of the two captains would sharply toss a bat, held in perpendicular position, to the other,

---

[1] Also known as "peggy."

who would catch it wherever he could. The one who tossed it would then place one of his hands above and touching that of the other, and so on, alternately, until the knob on the end was reached, when the last one would endeavor, by digging his thumb and finger nails down inside the other's grip, to get such a hold upon it as would enable him to swing the bat three times around his head. Failing to do this, the other had his first choice of the players for his side, and then the choosing proceeded alternately and rapidly.

The reader will, no doubt, wonder why a coin was not "flipped" up and the first choice decided in a jiffy. Well, it was a boy's way of deciding; and it afforded some sort of fun, mingled with a mild excitement, as the two neared the top of the bat, to watch the last one try to get a hold upon the rounded knob and with clenched teeth swing the bat around his head.

Games of Nantucket Boys

CRACKS AND SQUARES

IN MY native town, when a boy, we had but few stone sidewalks,—laid in squares, we knew them as "flagstone" sidewalks. The cracks between those squares of stone we children always avoided by stepping over them, as we, in our innocent, honest belief, used to say if we "step on the cracks" we will "miss our lessons." . . .

PITCHING PENNY SHELLS AND LEADIES

"Pitching penny shells" I think is distinctly peculiar and entirely original to Nantucket. Possibly it may have been a practice elsewhere, but if so, I never heard of it. . . . "Penny shells" were, and presumably now are, abundant about the ocean-washed shores of Nantucket. Many a day in boyhood have I roamed about the south shore gathering and filling my pockets with them. They are simply the shells of a small sea animal, similar in shape to the quahaug or little-neck, varying in size from about the dimensions of one of the old-fashioned copper cents and graduating down to about half that size. . . . They are washed, scoured and bleached by the waves and sand, only a slight black or brownish discoloration appearing on the outer side of some of them. Such were our "penny shells." With a knife-blade stuck in the ground at a fence, or similar background, we used to pitch those shells at that knife as a goal, after the manner of pitching pennies. We also employed them by tossing in the air and letting them fall to the ground on the "heads I win and tails you lose" order. "Heads" was the outside of the shell; "tails" the inner side. . . .

Another of our long-ago games was pitching "leadies." I know not

From *Brief Historical Data and Memories of My Boyhood Days in Nantucket*, by Joseph E. C. Farnham, pp. 65–66, 124–125, 249, 250. Providence: Joseph E. C. Farnham. 1923.

whether this was distinctively and absolutely a Nantucket creation, but I am morally sure that it was far from being universal, and I am quite as certain that it was closely allied to my native heath. Leadies were of our own manufacture. Scores of these I have made in my father's shop, where I had the privilege of using his tools for my boyish pleasures. First was the construction of a mould. This we made from a piece of pine or other soft wood. We carefully fashioned two pieces of wood, each of a size of three or four inches long, perhaps two or two and one-half inches wide and a half or three-quarters of an inch thick. The frame for the mould made ready we would then throw an old-fashioned copper cent into the fire in the little cast-iron cylinder stove, leaving it to become red hot. Removing it we would place it on one side of the mould, about a quarter of an inch from the top, place the other side carefully and evenly over it, then holding it firm in position we would place it in a vise and gradually close it until the two sides of the mould came together. This done we removed the cent, and we had a perfect mould for casting our leadies. In other words we could make the old-fashioned cent, except that it was cast in lead, and was of no use except as a plaything. Then we cut on the inside at the top of each portion of the mould a slight opening which made the run into which we poured the lead. In moulding we held the mould firmly in place by again using the vise. These we pitched up against a knife or other object set up for the purpose the same as we did for the penny-shells. It was a crude process and an equally crude product. I am inclined to the belief that this was quite a Nantucket institution.

KICK POKE

While it was most decidedly more crude, yet the now popular collegiate game of football is not more enthusiastically appreciated than such a game was by us associated boys more than fifty years ago, albeit it was with us not only a more limited enthusiasm, but it was, perforce, a more unique and quite original pastime. Our sport was, as we called it, to "kick poke." With us it certainly was a great game. We did not have the regulation ball, but most essentially a far different one, because we used a hog's bladder. So many hogs were killed in the town, especially in the fall, for numerous citizens, that a plea for a bladder by a boy at the slaughter house was usually graciously granted. Thus many of the boys each had such an unseemly football which, with his fellows, all enjoyed kicking. One of those bladders obtained, we would break the stem from an ordinary clay pipe, insert it into the orifice at the neck of the bladder, and "blow it up." In that homely way we got a prodigious ball, as to size and lightness, and with it in the open had many hours of exhilarating pastime. . . .

* * * * *

A number of the more deft of the boys made from thin leather a quite nicely finished covering within which the bladder was inserted and laced, thus preserving it for more extended active service. . . .

Round Ball

THIS [Dudley Common] was the place where old-fashioned round ball came into its own, before baseball was heard of. Round ball was of the same athletic family as "barn-tick," "three-old-cat" and "four-old-cat" and synchronous [*sic*] with them. It was played with a soft ball—reasonably soft, if it was thrown with moderate speed. The bases were at the corners of a parallelogram instead of a diamond and it was allowable to hit the base runner with the ball; in which case he was out. There were no fouls behind the catcher. Indeed the most expert stroke was a back-hand hit driving the ball behind the catcher and so opening the whole field to the runner. So it happened that one of the fielders was placed behind the catcher when a back-handed hitter was at the bat. The catcher stood close to the batter and caught off the bat—and—tell it not in Gath— sometimes caught the *bat*.

From *Black Tavern Tales, Stories of Old New England,* by Charles L. Goodell, p. 43. Copyright, 1932, by Charles L. Goodell. Brooklyn: Willis McDonald & Co.

PART FOUR

WORD LORE

It is only from its roots in the living generations of men that a language can be reinforced with fresh vigor for its needs. . . . True vigor and heartiness of phrase do not pass from page to page, but from man to man. . . .
— JAMES RUSSELL LOWELL

The metaphorical and other odd expressions . . . often originate in some curious anecdote or event, which is transmitted from mouth to mouth, and soon made the property of all.
— JOHN RUSSELL BARTLETT

We were talking about names, one day. Was there ever anything, I said, like the Yankee for inventing the most uncouth, pretentious, detestable appellations, inventing or finding them, since the time of Praise God Barebones?
— OLIVER WENDELL HOLMES

It is curious how we are attracted by the wise, pithy sayings of an unlettered man. It is the contrast between his mind and his culture. We like contrasts and we like metaphors and striking comparisons. The more they are according to nature and everyday life, the better they please the masses. . . . It is an old thought that has been dressed up for centuries, and suddenly appears in everyday clothes.
— CHARLES HENRY SMITH ("Bill Arp")
on Josh Billings

I. YANKEEISMS

. . . country New Englanders use the dialect in all stages of its gradual disintegration, from those who use still a pure "Biglow" vocabulary and pronunciation, to those whose dictionary English is tinged by the mere dying twang of Yankeedom.

— PERCY MACKAYE

. . . the geographic variations in American English are the result of the history of the settlement and of the influence of trade areas and culture areas on the speech of the American people.

— HANS KURATH

Boston has enough of England about it to make a good English dictionary. — OLIVER WENDELL HOLMES

Though this native speech was felt to be vigorously expressive, may even have been felt to be the real speech of New England, yet it was always used with a reluctant admission that the reality was not good enough for the highest purposes. . . . This sense for double personality has existed nowhere else in the country so completely as in New England. — GEORGE PHILIP KRAPP

1. REGIONALISM IN YANKEE SPEECH

FROM the beginning the gen-u-ine Yankee has been tagged with clichés like *snum, tarnal, plaguey, nation, tarnation.*[1] Even the dialect of *The Biglow Papers,* which has the authentic Yankee ring and flavor, contains a maximum of colloquialism and a minimum of localism, with a generous proportion of "eye dialect," or humorous misspelling. Because of the long association of Yankee dialect (like all dialect) with humor and caricature, Lowell's discovery and investigation of the linguistic and literary riches of rural New England speech came as a revelation—the revelation that dialect is a matter of character as well as custom, of sense as well as sound.

> An' yit I love th' unhighschooled way
> Ol' farmers hed when I wuz younger;

---

[1] For more vigorous and elaborate Yankee oaths, compare "Dod blast ye to Helsi-bub," which, Burges Johnson says, "seems to avoid both hell and Beelzebub, but gains strength from each"; (*As Much as I Dare,* New York, p. 29) also: "Goshfrey mighty dorman," "Flush-to-bung-town," and "Jumped-up flat-footed Sabriny," reported by Ola G. Veazie from New Hampshire (Manuscripts of the Federal Writers' Project). As Johnson explains, "upon the farms of Vermont and New Hampshire, and along the coast and in the forests of Maine, there has been since the days of Ethan Allen an easy fluency in cussing that never sought the least disguise" because "All of that northern territory was first peopled by folk who had fled the Massachusetts and Connecticut clergy and their dour god."

Their talk wuz meatier, an' 'ould stay,
  While book-froth seems to whet your hunger;
For puttin' in a downright lick
  'twixt Humbug's eyes, ther' 's few can metch it,
An' then it helves my thoughts ez slick
  Ez stret-grained hickory does a hetchet.[1]

Lowell's mastery of the speech enabled him to explain as well as demonstrate its uses skilfully. While it was well known that Yankees are distinguished from speakers from other parts of the country by their flat, drawling nasal tone (which Whitman, in *An American Primer,* called "offensive") and by their tortuous vowel-twisting and juggling of *r,*[2] less was known about differences between one Yankee and another and variations in the pronunciation of the same word according to the emphasis. Lowell distinguishes five ways of pronouncing *well* and two ways each of pronouncing *for, too,* and *to.*

A friend of mine . . . told me that he once heard five "wells," like pioneers, precede the answer to an inquiry about the price of land. The first was the ordinary *wul,* in deference to custom; the second, the long, perpending *ooahl,* with a falling inflection of the voice; the third, the same, but with the voice rising, as if in despair of a conclusion, into a plaintively nasal whine; the fourth, *wulh,* ending in the aspirate of a sigh; and then, fifth, came a short, sharp *wal,* showing that a conclusion had been reached.[3]

. . . *for* is commonly *fer* (a shorter sound than *fur* for *far*), but when emphatic it always becomes *for,* as "wut *for!*" So *too* is pronounced like *to* (as it was anciently spelt), and *to* like *ta* (the sound as in the *tou* of *touch*), but *too,* when emphatic, changes into *tue,* and *to,* sometimes, in similar cases, into *toe,* as "I did n' hardly know wut *toe* du!"[4]

The peculiarities and variations of Yankee speech are a matter not only of custom but also of linguistic geography, which is in turn patterned after population history.[5] So Vermont is linguistically as well as historically and geographically split in two by the Green Mountains, its two major speech divisions corresponding to the two major speech areas of New England— roughly, a westward-expanding coastal region and a northward-pushing

---

[1] *The Biglow Papers, Second Series, The Poetical Works of James Russell Lowell* (Boston, 1885), p. 286.

[2] It is said that one of Calvin Coolidge's remarkable achievements was the pronunciation of "cow" in four syllables.—Charles Edward Crane, *Let Me Show You Vermont* (New York, 1937), p. 30.

. . . the Southern English and Eastern American habit of adding superfluous [r], as in *the idear of it,* is frequently misunderstood. This is subject to the same law,— the superfluous [r] is added only when a vowel quickly follows. The Bostonian or Englishman is apt to say *Americar and France,* though he says *France and America* as Westerners do. I recently heard from a native of Boston, "No, this is not the piazza; the piazzar is here."—John S. Kenyon, "Some Notes on American R," *American Speech,* Vol. 1 (March, 1926), No. 6, p. 333.

[3] Lowell, *op. cit.,* p. 221.

[4] *Ibid.,* p. 227.

[5] Cf. Hans Kurath and others, *Linguistic Atlas of New England* and *Handbook of the Linguistic Geography of New England* (Providence, 1939).

trans-Connecticut River hill region. And since the original colonists brought with them the speech habits of their mother provinces (chiefly in the South of England), many typical Yankeeisms may be traced to British sources, such as *ben* (been), *eend* (end), and *yender* (yonder).[1] The following Cornish survivals have been noted on Cape Cod:

> We instance *housen,* for house, quite common among a few of the old people less than fifty years ago; *banger* for very large; *million* for melon; *sheer* for share, as half a sheer; *sight* for a good many, as a sight of 'em; *bagnet* for bayonet; *puss, nuss,* and *wuss,* for purse, nurse, and worse; *chaney* for china; *chimbley* for chimney, and many kindred expressions, some of which still linger, all of which are in use in some parts of Cornwall.[2]

2. Folk Speech and Speech Folklore

The linguistic geography of New England involves not only regionalism of speech but also the curious rivalry between the speech of Boston and that of the hinterland—essentially a conflict between Boston as a state of mind and the Yankee as a type of character. On the one hand, in attempting to set itself up as a national standard, Boston has fought the provinciality of the back country; and, on the other, the back country has clung to many of its vernacular and provincial speech forms as a badge of defiance against the artificial and polite standards of Boston.[3]

The struggle between Biglowese and Bostonese was thus a struggle between idiom and diction, between a living language and a dead language, between folk speech and "talking like a book" (whether schoolmarm English, journalese, or Websterian rhetoric). In spite of its limitations as a literary language, folk speech, as Lowell recognized, contains within itself the power of reviving and invigorating language. Just as dialect links the past with the present of language, so folk speech relates language to the experience of ordinary men—folk words, like proverbs and proverbial phrases, being symbols or signs that bind man to man and that evoke the very "influences of place and kinship and common emotion" that gave them birth.

Not only does folk speech take on something of the time-hallowed, ritualistic quality of the traditional mindskills and handskills of the folk, but local customs, characters, and events are enshrined in many local words and bywords, names and nicknames. The origin of these terms is transmitted in anecdotes and stories that are likewise part of the folklore of speech, as folk speech is part of folklore.

Perhaps the most fertile source of speech folklore is the process of playing upon words, one form of which is folk etymology (previously illustrated in place-names). This consists in the "changing of a strange or more or less learned term into a familiar or partly familiar one, often by substituting,

---

[1] Lowell, *op. cit.,* pp. 214–218 *passim.*

[2] Shebnah Rich, *Truro—Cape Cod* (Boston, 1884), pp. 128–129.

[3] Cf. George Philip Krapp, *The English Language in America* (New York, 1925), Vol. I, pp. 19–45. On page 44, he writers: "Boston is the only city in America in which *boots* is a common equivalent for *shoes, calico* for *unbleached muslin,* and *shop* a common name for *store."*

adding, or omitting a sound or two." [1] Sometimes the change is only a change in spelling. Thus *jonny-cake* (from journey-cake) is commonly spelt *Johnny-cake*—a spelling which arouses the violent denunciation of "Shepherd Tom" Hazard, who attempts to rationalize *jonny* by deriving it from "Brother Jonathan" Trumbull. Other examples of Yankee folk etymology are *kill-er-cure* (killcow), and *intervale* (interval).

Around words with disputed etymologies and fluctuating favorable and unfavorable connotations (like the word *Yankee*) or with changed applications (like *mooncussin'* in its original London slang use and in its various Cape Cod uses) has grown up another species of speech folklore. This consists of the myths, legends, and traditions surrounding words with a folk history if not a folk origin.

B. A. B.

PROVINCIAL SPEECH
Vermont Dialect Areas

VERMONT . . . is divided linguistically as well as historically and geographically into two major sections by the Green Mountains. The western section, which derives its population largely from western Connecticut and has always had fairly intimate contacts with New York State, contrasts in several respects with the eastern, whose settlement is much more diverse, comprising elements from the lower Connecticut valley, eastern and central Massachusetts, and New Hampshire, as well as colonies of Scotch and Scotch-Irish. For instance, the *r* in words like *work, first, father, hammer, bar, beard,* which is pronounced by speakers in western Connecticut and in the entire northern United States west of New England, but is silent in the greater part of eastern New England, is correspondingly present in the speech of western Vermont, but absent from that of eastern Vermont (except for the Scotch and Scotch-Irish sections and a few other communities). The vowel in *calf, glass, pasture, afternoon, bath* is universally pronounced with a flat *a* in western Vermont, while eastern Vermont has many cases of the broad *a*. The so-called "New England short o" in words like *home, stone, coat, road, toad, whole* (pronounced almost like *hum, stun,* etc.) is rather rare in western Vermont, but very common in eastern Vermont; the second syllable of *towel* is pronounced in western Vermont with a short, obscure second vowel or with no vowel at all, but in eastern Vermont has *ill* with a clear vowel.

As for vocabulary, the two sections again show interesting differences. The seesaw is called *seesaw* in all parts of the state, but the word *teeter-totter* (imported from southwestern Connecticut) occurs twice and the

---

[1] Harold Wentworth, *American Dialect Dictionary* (New York, 1944), p. 225.

From *Let Me Show You Vermont,* by Charles Edward Crane, pp. 34–35. Copyright, 1937, by Alfred A. Knopf, Inc. New York and London.

word *tinter* (from central Connecticut) occurs once in western Vermont, while *tilt* (a Cape Cod word) occurs once in eastern Vermont. The earthworm is called *angleworm*, but several cases of angledog (a central Connecticut word) occur in western Vermont, and several cases of *mud-worm* (a northeastern Massachusetts word) in eastern Vermont. Sour milk is called *lobbered* or *loppered* milk throughout Vermont, but in eastern Vermont the term *bonnyclabber* (originally an Irish word, but now found in many parts of eastern New England) is equally common. The horizontal rain-gutter along the edge of the roof is usually called *eaves trough* in western Vermont, but *eaves spout* in eastern Vermont. The funnel used when pouring liquids into a narrow-necked bottle is called either *funnel* or *tunnel* in western Vermont, but nearly always *tunnel* in eastern Vermont. When a boy slides downhill lying flat on his sled, western Vermonters say he is sliding downhill *belly-bunt* or *belly-bunk,* while eastern Vermonters say he is sliding *belly-bump*. It is clear that in many respects the eastern part of the state is more old-fashioned or more conservative than the western part, but it is interesting to observe that natives of each side of the Green Mountains profess to be greatly amused by the "flatness" of the dialect spoken by the natives on the other side.

The Yankee Twang

THE NASAL TONE [1]

THE nasal tone in New England, it is said, was caused by the severe climate and the prevalent catarrh; but those were not the sole causes. Catarrh debases speech, both in quality of tone and in distinctness of articulation; but the disease is more prevalent now than formerly, while the general speech is probably less nasal. Australians are said to have nasal voices, and they are not afflicted with catarrh. The New England drawl and the nasal tone were probably derived originally from the meeting-house and the prayer-meetings; both defects became fixed by habit, and, of course, have been greatly heightened by climatic conditions.

The virtue constantly insisted upon in the old times by parents and religious teachers was humility, self-abnegation. In repeating passages of Scripture, or of the Catechism, the tone was subdued. The religious spirit was manifested in awe and reverence, seldom in cheerfulness, and never in exaltation—except in such exaltation as was accompanied with moistened eyes and "tears in the voice." It was "a dying world" in which our fathers lived; the expression of their ideas and feelings would not require the expansive lungs, nor heave the deep chest, of a vigorous and well-developed

---

[1] From *Quabbin, The Story of a Small Town, with Outlooks Upon Puritan Life,* by Francis H. Underwood, pp. 71–73. Copyright, 1892, by Lee and Shepard. Boston. 1893.

man. The *noise,* no less than the manner, of a burly fox-hunter and athlete, would be abhorrent to one whose soul was melted in penitence, and who in his daily devotions *intoned* in dragging minor intervals the prayers that he dared not address to the Dread Majesty of Heaven with steady eyes and manly voice. There was a good deacon in Quabbin whose words, when he prayed, were joined, as by a singer's *portamento,* with *ah* and *er,* and with indescribable sounds, like the final hum of a nasal *m* and *n.* The words were hyphenated, and each sentence was a close-linked, long-drawn chain. Let such usages of speech go on for generations, and the infection will pervade the community. The child will be soothed by a nasal lullaby, and will drawl from the time he leaves his cradle. He will drawl at his lessons, and make catarrhal yells in the playground. As a lover he will drawl to his mistress, and repeat love's litany through the nose. When his duet with her is finished, and his snuffy voice extinct, he will be drawn (slowly) to his grave, to drawl no more.

It appears to be certain that the nasal and drawling tone is in a large measure the result of two and a half centuries of Puritan training; just as the peculiarities of language, including local and obsolete terms, half-articulated contractions, and clipping of words, are the result of the fusion of many illiterate British dialects. The bucolic speech is dying out, for school-teachers are uprooting it, as farmers do thistles, but the tone hangs on, like the scent of musk in Hosea Biglow's "draw."

AN ODD MIXTURE [2]

The American Reader lay open on the teacher's desk. "Hiram, read on page 11, and read good with Expression."

"Little Torm walked along the raw'd through the ha'dwood trees. Yender came marster preacher a'horseback. The poine trees was hidin' b'ar in Torm's young mind and he so laded daown he could not run away. He was not motch afeared of b'ar but he was afeared of Preacher Weatherby."

"Say *much,* not *motch.* Dan'l, you read the next." Tom sat down and Daniel began: "Last Sabbath a week Torm had larfed out loud in Meetin' when a black crow come in the window and the tythin' man had wropped him on the head with his stick. He cal'lated as how the preacher would be worser to meet nor a b'ar nor even a Injin, for larfin' was no manners for chorch. But bein' as how Torm was afoot he must go on and meet the preacher. 'If he don't be layin' on with the switch I'll git me this solather home to Paw come candlelight. Mebbe if I slip behind this here big poplar he will not be a'seein' of me.' But a pa'tridge flew up in Torm's face and he yowled out good and the Preacher seen him. Moral: Good little boys do not larf out in Meetin' and so love to meet their good Preachers."

"You got the sense oncommon good, Dan'l, but you fetched in some of

---

[2] From *New Hampshire Borns a Town,* by Marion Nicholl Rawson, pp. 264–265. Copyright, 1942, by E. P. Dutton & Co., Inc. New York.

your own words. Say *church,* not *chorch,* and go put that houn'dawg out
in the raw'd. He's got fleas."

When the next class came to recite they ranged themselves along the
back wall, for now *The North American Spelling Book* was open on the
desk. Said Teacher: "Caow," and the first child spelled c o w. Teacher
said: "Caounty," and the next child spelled: c o u n t y. The Teacher
said: "Collar, what you wear round your neck, not the person who comes
to see you in the evening." There was no chance to spell phonetically here.
An odd mixture of flat *ow* slipped in where no *ow's* should be, and *A's* were
broadened and darkened where they stood alone, and lightened where they
shouldered with an *R.* Yankee twang mated kindly with a most extreme
Harvard accent, a combination which would in days ahead lose somewhat
of the former, and, oddly enough among the most backroad folks, retain
the latter.

Ancient Pronunciation

IN A certain class, the ancient pronunciation of many English words was
maintained, doubtless brought by the ancestors of New England families
from "home," and transmitted to their descendants; such as *airth* for earth,
fairm for firm, *sartain* for certain, *pint* for point, en*vy* for envy, *ax* with the
broad *â* for ask, *housen* for houses, *his'n* and *her'n* for his and hers, *rare* for
rear; as, for instance, the horse *rares* up; and sounding the *l* in would.
Common enough names, too, were clipped or contracted in English fashion.
Thus, the names of Norwood and Harwood became Norrod in sound and
Harrod in spelling; and the name of Currier, whether with any reference
or not to the French *Cuir,* for leather, was not long since uniformly pronounced *Kiah,* with the long *i;* Thurlow was strangely transformed into
Thurrill; and Pierpont, often formerly spelled Pierpoint, with entire neglect
of its derivation, was pronounced *Pearpint,* by old-fashioned people, the
first syllable approximating to the original formation of *pierre.*

Kentish Provincialisms in New England

. . . WE RECOGNIZE our old Yankee friends, slick, for sleek or smooth;
swath, swarth, a row of grass left on the ground by the mower; grub, for

---

From *Old New England Traits,* edited by George Lunt, pp. 144–145. Entered,
according to Act of Congress, in the year 1873, by George Lunt, in the Office of the
Librarian of Congress, at Washington. New York: Hurd and Houghton. Cambridge: The Riverside Press.

From *The Obligations of New England to the County of Kent,* A Paper Read
before the American Antiquarian Society as a Part of the Report of the Council,
April 29, 1885, by George F. Hoar, pp. 26–27. Worcester, Massachusetts: Press of
Charles Hamilton. 1885.

food; bail, the handle of a pail; agen, for against; argufy, for argue; along used as in the phrase, all along of you; bar-way, the passage into a field where the bars are removed; bat, a large stick; biddy, a chicken; bay, the space between two beams; by-gorries and by-gollies, a sort of oath; botch, to do any thing badly; bodily, for entire; bolt, to swallow whole, and fast; bolt-upright; booby-hatch, a clumsy carriage; boosy, drunk; brand-new; buck, the body of a cart or wagon; cess, a tax, cess-pool; cheeses, the seed of the mullen; moonshine, for illicit spirits. . . .

Nantucket Pronunciation of the Points of the Compass

WE HAVE our own names for the points of the compass. Many writers persist in making the sailorman say "nor'east" and "sou'east." None such ever used the words. He does say "nor'west" and "sou'west," but north is "no'the," with a long "o" and a soft "th." Northeast is "no'theast," pronounced the same way (the "no'the" like the verb "loathe"). South is pronounced with the same soft "th" (like "mouth" when used as a verb).

When either north or south is used as an adjective before the noun, however, each takes its ordinary dictionary pronunciation, as a "north wind," or the "south shore." It is only when used without the noun that the long "o" sound in "no'the" and the soft "th" in both words are heard. Thus we say the wind is "out southe," or "about no'the"—never a "no'the wind" or the "southe shore." It is a curious distinction, for which there seems to be no reason except custom itself. Then we have "no-no'theast," and "sou'-southeast," but always "nor'nor'west" and "sou'sou'west." Writers who wish to apply the local color correctly are urged to study these forms carefully, and not slip up, as most of them do, on such simple matters. "Southe" is sometimes used as a verb, when speaking of the moon, as "when the moon southes"; and the word "easting" is sometimes heard.

Contributions to the New England Vocabulary and Idiom

FROM LOWELL'S LEXICON [1]

I SUBJOIN a few phrases not in Mr. Bartlett's book which I have heard. *Baldheaded:* "to go it bald-headed"; in great haste, as where one rushes

From *The Nantucket Scrap Basket*, Second Edition, Revised, Expanded, and Re-arranged by William F. Macy, pp. 145–146. Copyright, 1916, by William F. Macy and Roland B. Hussey; 1930, by William F. Macy. Boston and New York: Houghton Mifflin Co. 1930.

[1] From Introduction to *The Biglow Papers*, Second Series, in *The Poetical Works of James Russell Lowell*, pp. 223–224. Copyright, 1848, 1857, 1866, 1868, 1869, 1876, and 1885, by James Russell Lowell. Boston and New York: Houghton Mifflin Co.

out without his hat. *Bogue:* "I don't git much done 'thout I *bogue* right in along 'th my men." *Carry:* a *portage.* *Cat-nap:* a short doze. *Cat-stick:* a small stick. *Chowder-head:* a muddle-brain. *Cling-john:* a soft cake of rye. *Cocoa-nut:* the head. *Cohees:* applied to the people of certain settlements in Western Pennsylvania, from their use of the archaic form *Quo' he.* *Dunnow'z I know:* the nearest your true Yankee ever comes to acknowledging ignorance. *Essence-pedlar:* a skunk. *First-rate and a half.* *Fish-flakes,* for drying fish: O. E.: *fleck (cratis).* *Gander-party:* a social gathering of men only. *Gawnicus:* a dolt. *Hawkins's whetstone:* rum; in derision of one Hawkins, a well-known temperance-lecturer. *Hyper:* to bustle: "I mus' *hyper* about an' git tea." *Keeler-tub:* one in which dishes are washed. ("And Greasy Joan doth *keel* the pot.") *Lap-tea:* where the guests are too many to sit at table. *Last of pea-time:* to be hard-up. *Lōse-laid (loose-laid):* a weaver's term, and probably English; weak-willed. *Malahak:* to cut up hastily or awkwardly. *Moonglade:* a beautiful word: for the track of moonlight on the water. *Off-ox:* an unmanageable, cross-grained fellow. *Old Driver, Old Splitfoot:* the Devil. *Onhitch:* to pull trigger (cf. Spanish *disparar*). *Popular:* conceited. *Rote:* sound of surf before a storm. *Rot-gut:* cheap whiskey; the word occurs in Heywood's "English Traveller" and Addison's "Drummer," for a poor kind of drink. *Seem:* it is habitual with the New-Englander to put this verb to strange uses, as, "I can't *seem* to be suited," "I could n't *seem* to know him." *Sidehill,* for *hillside.* *State-house:* this seems an Americanism, whether invented or derived from the Dutch *Stadhuys,* I know not. *Strike* and *string:* from the game of ninepins; to make a *strike* is to knock down all the pins with one ball, hence it has come to mean fortunate, successful. *Swampers:* men who break out roads for lumberers. *Tormented:* euphemism for damned, as, "not a tormented cent." *Virginia fence, to make a:* to walk like a drunken man.

Chiefly from Portsmouth [2]

caught: milk is "caught" when it is slightly burned.

claw out: make excuses, get out of an embarrassment, and the like. [Portsmouth, N. H.] Elsewhere (in New England) "claw off" is said.

fresh: in the phrase "a fresh cook," that is, one who uses little salt. [Portsmouth, N. H.]

heavy-handed (or *heavy*): said of a cook. "She's heavy-handed with salt"—uses much salt. [Portsmouth, N. H.]

light and shut: of the weather. "It lights and shuts," that is, the sun peeps out at intervals. The common New England maxim is "Open and shet's a sign of wet." [Portsmouth, N. H.]

---

[2] From "Contributions to the New England Vocabulary," by Frederic D. Allen, in *Dialect Notes,* Vol. I (Part I, 1890), pp. 18–20. Boston: American Dialect Society.

on the mending hand: convalescent. A common New England phrase.

out: of the wind. Along the seaboard, the wind "is out" or "has got out" when it blows from the sea. The expression is known in Portsmouth, Salem, and Plymouth. I do not think it is common in Boston.

primlico: in the phrase "in primlico order," of furniture, etc. [Portsmouth, N. H.] The opposite of this is:

ride-out: "The chairs are riding out." "The room looks like ride-out." [Portsmouth, N. H.] *

rub the time close: allow little time. "Aren't you rubbing the time too close?" [Portsmouth, N. H.]

rubbers: misfortune, ill-luck. The phrase is, "to meet with the rubbers." [Portsmouth, N. H.]

scooch: crouch. "To scooch down in the corner." In New York City *scouch* . . . is said to be used.

scoocher: to "take a scoocher" is to slide down a snowslope in a squatting position. [Portsmouth, N. H.]

spandy: clean, spick-span, of linen. "Spandy" alone is used; elsewhere "spandy-clean," or "spandy-dandy."

sprawl: life, animation, vigor. "He has no sprawl." Portsmouth and Lowell.

stand in hand: behoove, beseem. "It stands you in hand to be careful." Widely used.

thatchy: said of milk. The milk tastes "thatchy" because the cows eat "thatch." A long, coarse grass, growing in the salt marshes, is known as "thatch" on the New Hampshire and Massachusetts seacoast. If it was ever used for roofing, it is no longer so used. The "thatch" which the New Hampshire cows eat seems to be different from this. It is described as a sort of weed, growing in low places. [Portsmouth, N. H.]

trappatch (trap-hatch): trap-door; rent in clothes. "You've torn a trap-patch in your dress." [Portsmouth, N. H.]

FROM MAINE AND NEW HAMPSHIRE [3]

Able to set up an' eat a few porriges, adj. phr. Convalescent. Or, in good health. Usually the latter. A common answer to any inquiry regarding a person's health.

accommodatin' as a hog on ice, adj. phr. Extremely disagreeable or unobliging.

---

* This use is explained by the saying common fifty years ago on Cape Cod: "The room looks as if it was ready to ride out; every chair saddled and bridled"; used of a room in great disorder.—George Lyman Kittredge, *ibid.*, p. 79.

---

[3] From "Rural Locutions of Maine and Northern New Hampshire," by George Allen England, in *Dialect Notes,* Vol. IV (Part II, 1914), pp. 67–83. Publication of The American Dialect Society. New Haven, Connecticut: Published by the Society.

bag yer head, v. phr. Retire; pull in one's horns; be more modest. "I cal'late he better *bag his head!*"

bean-water, up on one's, adv. phr. Feeling very lively, strong, frisky. "Gosh! I'm right *up on* my *bean-water* this mornin'!"

big fer y'r boots, gittin' too, v. phr. Getting uppish, self-assertive.

black as zip, or *sip,* adj. phr. Extremely black.

bluer 'n a whetstone, adj. phr. Extremely dejected.

boil-thickened, adj. Referring to a kind of gravy, thickened, while boiling, by flour stirred in.

boozefuddle, n. Liquor.

buffle-brained, adj. Stupid.

bug-bite an' moonshine, interj. Expressive of incredulity or disgust.

bust yer haslet [*harslet*] * *out,* v. phr. A violent threat involving complete evisceration.

carry guts to a bear, he ain't got sense enough to, v. phr. Equivalent of "He doesn't know enough to come in when it rains."

cheeky as a man on the town, adj. phr. Overbearing, "nervy."

choppin'-block, n. In the phrase, "Bate ye two fingers on the *choppin'-block,* an' resk it." A common form of laying a wager.

dead clear to y'r navel, adj. phr. Lifeless.

devil an' Tom Walker. Same as desprit. "He wukked like the *Devil an' Tom Walker.*"

dingclicker, n. An unusually fine or pleasing person or thing. . . .

dingmaul, n. Mythical animal in lumber-camp.

dish, in yer own, prep. phr. Happening to your own self. "How'd ye like t' hev that *in yer own dish?*"

doctor ordered, what the. Something very pleasing, useful, or necessary. "She thought Ezry was jest *what the Doctor ordered.*"

dull, v. i. To make a mistake, miscalculation, or stupid blunder. "When she married that 'ar Bud Hayes, she shore *dulled.*"

dust yer back, v. phr. Wrestle; throw a man. "Fer two cents I'll *dust yer back!*"

fallin' out, him an' wuk has had a. Said of a lazy, shiftless man.

fiddlers in Hell, thick as, adj. phr. Very plentiful.

flamigigs, n. pl. Airs and graces: affectations.

go bag yer head! Angry, scornful, or sarcastic advice.

God's amint, any, or *Any God's immense,* n. phr. A large quantity. "They're *any God's amint* [amount?] o' woodchucks in them woods!"

goolthrite, n. Any small, wizened, puckered object. "She was all puckered up to a *goolthrite,* with the cold."

gormin', adj. Clumsy, stupid.

harker, n. A fine, strong person or thing.

haulin' a hog out'n a scaldin' tub, like, adv. phr. Comparison to denote difficulty.

---

* Viscera.

heaven, as long as John Brown stayed in, adv. phr. No time at all.

hell-bent an' crooked, adv. phr. In a swift, disorderly, excited manner.
"He lit out fer hum, *hell-bent an' crooked.*"

Herrin'-choker, n. A Prince Edward's Islander, or native of any of the
Provinces "down east."

higher'n his head, don't look no, etc., *fer my Saviour,* v. phr. He fills
all the world, for me; satisfies every aspiration and longing.

hook an' bendum, a little, n. phr. Any small, gripping tool.

hotter'n a skunk, hotter'n love in hayin'-time, adj. phr. Extremely intoxicated.

hyker, hyper, [*hiker, hiper*], v. i. To go quickly, to run. *"Hyper out-a
thar, now!"* "He more than *hikered!*"

jeeroosely, adj. Mighty, big, enormous.

jill-poke, n. A log stuck in the mud or along the banks of a lake or
stream. [*Jell-poke.*]

jorum, n Jug of liquor.

keezer's ghost! Great keezer's ghost! Ejaculations.

kicked to death by cripples, to be, v. phr. An expression of supreme contempt. "Huh! You'd oughta *be kicked to death by cripples,* you varmint!"

kill-er-cure,[1] *no gret,* n. phr. No great importance. "It hain't *no gret
kill-er-cure* ef he comes or don't."

lap salt, know enough to, v. phr. To have common sense. "He don't
know enough to lap salt." He is thoroughly stupid.

livin' laws! by the. Form of affirmation.

lollygags, n. pl. Airs, affectations, love-making. "Him an' her was
lollygaggin' the hull 'tarnal time."

long arms, make, v phr. To help one's self, at table. *"Make long arms,*
everybody!"

longer'n [*taller'n*] *the moral law,* adj. phr. Very long [tall].

lucivee, n. The loup-cervier, or "Injun devil," apparently a half-mythical
"specie" of wild-cat.

mad as hops, also *madder'n snakes in hayin',* adj. phr. Very angry.

make a touse, v. phr. To make a row, or fight; "take on."

make brags, v. phr. To brag, boast. "You've allus *made yer brags* you'd
go."

make one's haslet curl, v. phr. To surprise or injure one.

mill tail o' thunder, like the, adv. phr. See "Hell-bent an' crooked."

mingie, n. A gnat. Corruption of midge [?].

'mongst the missin', come up, v. phr. To die; to be lost. "Some day he'll
come up *'mongst the missin'.*"

mooner, n. Mythical creature in logging-woods.

naked bed, in one's, prep. phr. Down sick.

nimshy, n. A human being, creature, girl, young girl. "She was a smart
young *nimshy.*" Rather a laudatory sense.

---

[1] See "Killcow" below.

no bigger'n a pint o' cider; a goolthrite, adj. phr. Very small.

oh-be-joyful. Also, *oh-be-rich-an'-happy.* Hard liquor. "They come home plumb full of," etc.

P.I., abbrev. A Prince Edward's Islander.

pale's dishwater, adj. phr. Very pale.

peg out, v. phr. To get ill; die. "He's all *pegged out.*" "He'll *peg out* 'fore snow flies." Also, very tired; same as "beat."

pell-mell fer a cat-race! Also, *pell-mell fer Kitt'ry.* Very fast.

pile out, v. phr. To get up and go to work. "Hank's quite a feller to *pile out.*"

poor's pooduc, also, *poor's poverty in a gale o' wind,* or *poorer'n skimmed whey,* adj. phr. Extremely poor.

prayer-handles, n. pl. Knees.

pumple-footed, adj. Club-footed.

rackergaited, adj. Loose-jointed.

red wagon, hot's a, adj. phr. Very drunk.

salter'n the briny ocean, adj. phr. Very salt.

sand in a rat-hole, don't know enough to pound, v. phr. Very stupid.

settled minister, fatter'n a, adj. phr. Very fat; in good condition.

shirt on a beanpole, n. phr. A bad fit. "It looks like, etc."

shoe taps, up on yer, prep. phr. Feeling fit and fine.

sick abed in the wood-box, adv. phr. In good health. A common answer to any inquiry after one's condition.

side-hill ranger, n. phr. Mythical animal in lumber-woods.

sight by suthin' to see ef he's movin', v. phr. Said of a lazy, indolent person.

slacker'n dishwater, adj. phr. Untidy, dirty, slovenly.

slick's a ram-cat, or *greased pig,* or *school-marm's leg,* adj. phr. Very pleasing, successful, pretty, etc.

slower'n a jill-poke, or *slower'n stock-still,* adj. phr. Extremely slow.

spin a thread, can't, v. phr. Powerless to act. "He *can't spin a thread,* nohow!"

spoon victuals, n. phr. Invalid diet.

starved fit to eat the Lord's supper, or *the Lamb o' God,* adj. phr. Very hungry.

still ez mouse wuk, adj. phr. Extremely quiet.

taller'n a stackpole, adj. phr. Very tall.

thin's vanity, adj. phr. Very thin, said of persons, fabrics, etc.

thinner'n a hayrake, adj. phr. Same as "thin's vanity."

throw up Jonah, also, *throw up yer shoe-taps,* v. i. To be extremely nauseated.

tight's ye can jump fer luck, adv. phr. As fast or hard as you can go, work.

tip-toe Nancy, n. phr. Affected girl, putting on airs.

tunket, n. Hell. "Madder'n *tunket.*"

twitch, v. i. To drag timber from the forest into a road, clearing or "yard."

warm it to anybody or *anything,* v. phr. To strike or work hard. "Warm it to him, Bill!"

wee-waw, adj. Shaky, loose, rickety. "The ole waggin was *wee-wawin'* all over the road."

white hen's chickens, n. phr. Extremely pleasant or desirable persons. "Sue thought Hy was one o' the *white hen's chickens.*"

witherlick, n. Mythical animal, in lumber-camps.

withy, adj. Wiry, tough, strong. "A withy feller."

wroppin' round yer finger, n. phr. Anything of slight value. "Tain't wuth a wroppin' round my finger."

y'r Uncle Dud, n. phr. The narrator. "Y'r *Uncle Dud* [contraction of *Dudley*] seen it, himself!"

STORIES IN WORDS

The Baldwin Apple

SURVEYING one day for the Middlesex Canal near "Butters Row" in Wilmington, Colonel Baldwin was attracted by woodpeckers drilling circles about the trunk of a tree, red with apples. He set a dish of the delectable fruit before his guests at dinner. "What is the name, Colonel?" "It is an unknown species hereabouts," answered their host. "Then a toast to the Baldwin apple!"

The Bofat

ONE of the most unique of these [names] is "the Bofat," the name of a section of the township. Constable Benjamin Bryant had been sent over to this section to collect certain unpaid taxes. Being asked on his return how the settlers in that region were prospering, he replied that they were "as poor as the devil's bofat." Hence the name. A bofat, I need hardly say, is a little corner closet where the family rum was generally kept. The word is evidently a corruption of buffet, to which our ancestors did not give the

From *Old Paths and Legends of New England,* Saunterings Over Historic Roads with Glimpses of Picturesque Fields and Old Homesteads in Massachusetts, Rhode Island, and New Hampshire, by Katharine M. Abbott, pp. 93–94. Copyright, 1903, by Katharine M. Abbott. New York and London: G. P. Putnam's Sons. 1904.

From "In Western Massachusetts," by John W. Chadwick, in *Harper's New Monthly Magazine,* Vol. LXI (November, 1880), No. 366, p 879. Entered according to Act of Congress in the year 1880, by Harper and Brothers, in the Office of the Librarian of Congress at Washington. New York.

French pronunciation. Indeed, this word buffet seems to tend easily to corruption, the king's "beef-eaters," the yeomen of the guard, being the king's buffetiers, the keepers of the king's buffet.

The Cape Cod Cat

THE Rev. Thomas Crosby came to New England with his father Simon in the ship Susan & Ellen in 1685. Jesse Crosby, a descendant, was born in 1732 and grew up with a family named Lewis in Centerville. He had eleven children, one of whom, Daniel, settled in Osterville. Andrew, a son, lived a short distance along the shore from the Hinckley shipyard in or near Kokachoise, and built small craft with his two sons, Worthington and Horace. As he grew older, Andrew became, with a number of others, interested in Spiritualism. The group spent much time together, and his wife Tirza became a "medium."

At that time most of the small boats used along the Cape were called sharpies, being about twenty feet long and sharp at both ends. Andrew, from his experience and as he claimed, with the help of "spirits," began working on a very different type. He was much scoffed at by other boatmen, who said no boat would sail with the mast up in the eye, with no keel, and that with only one sail it would have no speed. Before he could complete his plan Andrew died and the boys were left to carry on. When difficulties arose on which they needed advice, Tirza, their mother, would hold a "seance" and bring them from their father their mistakes and how to remedy them. In 1850 the "Little Eva," as the new craft was called, was finished, launched, and a curious crowd gathered for her trial trip. Many boats were also waiting to test her speed and found, as an old sea captain remarked, that "She would sail three inches to their one." Another man exclaimed: "She comes about as quick as a cat." That is the story of the origin and naming of the "Cape Cod Cat." Its design remains the same to this day and as a popular pleasure boat it is seen everywhere along our shores.

Cape Cod Turkey

THE origin of the name "Cape Cod turkey" is obscure. It has come to mean cooked fish; what kind doesn't matter unless you are literal. If you are, it means baked stuffed codfish well-larded with salt pork.

From *Barnstable: Three Centuries of a Cape Cod Town*, by Donald G. Trayser, with Articles by Phyllis Bearse, Sarah H. Boult, Louisa Cobb, Richard Cobb, Alfred Crocker, Chester A. Crocker, Ora Hinckley, Elizabeth C. Jenkins, Henry C. Kittredge, A. Lawrence Lowell, Nathaniel B. H. Parker, p. 433. Copyright, 1939, by Donald G. Trayser. Hyannis, Massachusetts: F. B. & F. P. Goss.

From *The Yankee Cook Book*, by Imogene Wolcott, p. 41. Copyright, 1939, by Coward-McCann, Inc. New York.

One explanation of the term centers about Thanksgiving. The traditional food for that day was, and still is, turkey. Turkey meant thankfulness to God for his bounty. However, without the fishing industry the colonists would have had very little to be thankful for. No doubt the term "Cape Cod turkey" was started by some wit, which shows that even in early times life was not all drab.

* * * * *

Then, too, the Irish in and around Boston used the term "Cape Cod turkey" to refer to their Friday meal of fish. Fish, and particularly salt fish, seemed to taste better if it bore the more aristocratic name "Cape Cod turkey."

"Cat" Words

I SHALL never forget . . . in Dublin, New Hampshire, driving through what our delightful Yankee charioteer and guide called "only a cat-road."
This was to me a new use of the word cat as a praenomen, though I knew, as did Dr. Holmes and Hosea Biglow, and every good New Englander, that "cat-sticks" were poor spindling sticks, either growing or in a load of cut wood. I heard a country parson say as he regarded ruefully a gift of a sled load of firewood, "The deacon's load is all cat-sticks." Of course a cat-stick was also the stick used in the game of ball called tip-cat. Myself when young did much practise another loved ball game, "one old cat," a local favorite, perhaps a local name. "Cat-ice," too, is a good old New England word and thing; it is the thin layer of brittle ice formed over puddles, from under which the water has afterward receded. . . .

Comfort Powders

FOR several successive summers a tall thin man with a long beard called at our house. He was the purveyor of what he called "Comfort Powders." These were tiny bits of white paper, folded like medicinal powders. Opened, each revealed a verse of Scripture of a distinctly comforting nature. I remember him, perhaps not so much because of his quieting doses as because of my grandmother's terrible anger when one day we so far forgot ourselves as to laugh at him and to call our taunts behind his attenuated back. . . .

From *Old Time Gardens*, Newly Set Forth, by Alice Morse Earle, pp. 452–453. Copyright, 1901, by The Macmillan Company. New York and London.

From *A Goodly Heritage*, by Mary Ellen Chase, pp. 82–83. Copyright, 1932, by Henry Holt and Company, Inc. New York.

A Dead Horse

A DEAD horse was work you got paid for before you finished it. Say you had a half a case done at the end of the week. Well, you could have the whole case put on the books as done, and you'd get your money for it. But then on the next Monday morning you'd have that empty case to do, and no pay for it. A dead horse sure looked dead on Monday morning.

The foreman would be the one responsible for getting the dead horses done, for he was the one that let the help give them in, often unbeknownst to the owner.

And sometimes a worker, especially a cutter, would skin out, quit his job, and the foreman would be left with a whopper of a dead horse to explain. And say if that dead horse was eight or ten cases, it would be considerable to explain.

If the foreman was the right kind of fellow, though, we always pitched in and done that dead horse for him. That was a help to us too for if we didn't do that, the boss would likely come along and say:

"There'll be no more dead horses in this shop from now on."

We'd do a lot to prevent that 'cause dead horses would be durn handy, when you wanted to buy something special some week and you was short of cash.

But among the cutters there come to be so durn many that skun out on their dead horses, that they come to be pretty hard to get. For cutters in the old days was like the old class of printers. Kind of hoboes. Here today and gone tomorrow. They had the kind of trade that made it easy for them to get a job quick, so they didn't have to stick to one place any longer than it suited them. That made kind of tramps of them.

If your reputation was reliable, though, you could always give in a dead horse. Many is the time I done that when I was short of change some week.

Drail

WHY it is a "drail," we know not. It is, and on Cape Cod it has always been, so far as I can learn. The troller from a boat uses one of those

---

From "The Lynn Shoe Worker," as told by John Healey to Jane K. Leary, in *Living Lore of New England*. Manuscripts of the Federal Writers' Project of the Works Progress Administration for the State of Massachusetts.

From *Cape Cod Yesterdays*, by Joseph C. Lincoln, pp. 188–189. Copyright, 1935, by Joseph C. Lincoln and Harold Brett. Boston: Little, Brown & Company.

Japanese feather baits—the lure with a metal head set with glass eyes and a feathered tail covering the hook—but the genuine heaver and hauler still sticks to his drail. It—the drail—is made of some heavy metal, is bright and shiny and has the hook rigidly set in its after end. I mention the "rigidly" because the hook attached to the feather bait usually swings loose from a ring. Pulled—or "hauled"—through the water, it looks like a rapidly swimming sand eel or "shiner" and the bluefish darts to snap at it. This is an error of judgment on his part.

In former days, the heaver and hauler often covered his drail with an eelskin. The dried skin was pulled over the metal with the tail flopping loosely about the hook. Some old-timers still cover their drails in this way. It is a good bait, especially for striped bass.

Ear-Timers

AN EAR-TIMER named "Buddy" Keen or Kerr had a fetish of some kind tacked above his bench. Whether it was a small statue, a doll, or a kind of billiken he had won some place, Mr. Potter wasn't sure. But Kerr was obsessed with the idea that the thing was his lucky piece. He thought it had some definite bearing on his work. Somebody stole it one day and never brought it back, and Kerr became a nervous wreck. He resigned his job a few weeks later and went elsewhere to work, though Mr. Potter says he is still working at his trade and has apparently forgotten the incident.

Ear-timing is a process which seems to be on the way out in clock manufacture. It has been abolished at Seth Thomas, though still a part of the clock-making routine at Ingraham's. Ear-timers must regulate a clock with the use of a metronome, depending, as the name implies, upon their sense of hearing to synchronize the movement with the metronome beat. There seems to be a prevalent impression among clockmakers that ear-timing is likely to develop eccentricities. Because of the tension under which ear-timers work day in and day out, many of them become hard drinkers, according to popular belief. This impression is the nearest approach to a superstition brought to light during the conversation with Mr. Richmond. It may have basis in fact, or it may be that its widespread acceptance has in some cases actually been an evil influence upon credulous ear-timers. Because of the difficulty of training men for this phase of clock-making ear-timing has been one of the highest paid jobs in the industry, with wages reported authentically of as high as one dollar per hour piecework.

From "Connecticut Clockmakers," by Francis Donovan, in *Living Lore in New England*. Manuscripts of the Federal Writers' Project of the Works Progress Administration for the State of Connecticut.

Gallbuster

ONE morning when a head wind had us at full disadvantage, and common sailing vessels were passing us like steam boats, I ventured out of the gangway and said, "Mr. Hatch, how does she go along?" He promptly replied, "By the Prophets' nippers, Skipper, when you can see her wake out of the weather hawse-hole, I call it a gallbuster!"

Heave and Haul

HERE are two good Cape Cod words for you. Brought ashore from the deep sea, of course. The fo'mast hands on the old "wind-jammers" heaved —or "hove"—the anchor or the lead and hauled the sheet or the bowline.

> Haul on the bowline,
> The *Polly* is a-rollin',
> Haul on the bowline,
> The bowline HAUL.

So the old chantey goes. Surely it is not necessary to tell you that "bowline" is pronounced "bo-lin." I should not mention it if I had not heard a landlubber—and he was a college professor, at that—pronounce it "bow line," "bow," like the bough of a tree, and "line" like something to catch fish with. It may have been a bow line in the beginning, but it has been a bo-lin since Noah hove short on the Ark's cable—shortly after that, anyhow. If it were not "bo-lin" how could it rhyme with "rollin'?" I ask you.

But down on the Cape, we heave and haul on land, as well as on water. Our small boys "heave" a baseball or a stone. Our horses "haul" a buggy or truck-wagon, or did in the days when there were truck-wagons and buggies. A summer neighbor noticed that a neighbor of his—a retired mackerel seiner—was at work with hammer and saw on the roof of his dwelling. Naturally, being a neighbor, our friend stopped to ask questions. The old mackerelman explained.

"Goin' to put in one of them dormer windows," he said. "Cal'latin' to see if I can't heave a little sunshine into the front upstairs bedroom."

And when we asked a Cape acquaintance as to the professional ability of a dentist who had recently begun practice in the community, the answer was informative and characteristic.

From *Truro—Cape Cod, or Land Marks and Sea Marks,* by Shebnah Rich, p. 433. Second Edition, Revised and Corrected. Copyright, 1883, by D. Lothrop and Company. Boston. 1884.

From *Cape Cod Yesterdays,* by Joseph C. Lincoln, pp. 181–183. Copyright, 1935, by Joseph C. Lincoln and Harold Brett. Boston: Little, Brown & Company.

"They say he's first-rate at his job. Fixes your teeth up fine and don't charge all outdoors for it. But," by way of warning, "you understand he don't do no haulin'."

Meaning that the dentist did not extract teeth.

Yes, we heave and haul almost everything on Cape Cod, but when, early in August, we notice men walking along the edge of the surf at Monomoy Point or on the beach below the lighthouse, men who whirl their right hands in circles above their heads, we know that they are both heaving *and* hauling. We know that the bluefish have "struck on."

For, down our way, in August and September and early October, to "heave and haul" means to cast for bluefish from the beach with a hand line and it does not mean anything else.

Herb Tea

ON THE corner of Winchester Road (Mystic Street) the troops knocked roughly at the village shoemaker's, asking why the candles burned at this unseemly hour. The gudewife replied that she was making herb tea. The shoemaker's "herb tea" was a concoction afterwards absorbed by the red-coats in the form of solid material, sometimes known as "Yankee bullets," made from the household pewter.

Hubbub

SKULL HEAD was the scene of aboriginal battles, and Nantasket Beach the play-ground of Indian tribes. Three centuries ago, where yonder children are now playing leap-frog, stood a pole hung with beaver skins and wampum; fantastic, swarthy figures are running and playing football to win these trophies; their wild shouts may be heard above the *sawkiss* (great panting) of the ocean. Chiefs who have seen eighty snows look on stoically while the young men strike on the beach a wooden bowl containing five flat pieces of bone, black on one side and white on the other; as the bones bound and fall, white or black, the game is decided; the players sit in a circle making a deafening noise,—*hub, hub,* "come, come," from which it was called hubbub. Their council fires were lighted on Sagamore Hill.

From *Old Paths and Legends of New England,* Saunterings Over Historic Roads with Glimpses of Picturesque Fields and Old Homesteads in Massachusetts, Rhode Island, and New Hampshire, by Katharine M. Abbott, p. 56. Copyright, 1903, by Katharine M. Abbott. New York and London: G. P. Putnam's Sons. 1904.

Ibid., p. 329.

Interval(e)

. . . THE term *interval,* though originating with the colonists themselves, has almost ceased to be understood by writers in the United States, and even in New England itself. They are at one time perplexed as to its etymology, and at another as to its application.

One of them, translating Mr. Volney's work on the soil and climate of the United States, is careful to present the word *interval* under a peculiar form:—"The *inter-vales* and banks of rivers"; a refinement of which the intention appears to be, that of refreshing the reader's memory as to a supposed derivation of the word from *inter* and *vallis,* meaning a space between valleys. This etymology I have heard assigned by word of mouth, and it appears to be adopted in the passage cited, because, had the writer supposed the word to come from *inter* and *vallum,* he would certainly have left it *interval,* in the ordinary form. Meanwhile, a moment's reflection will suggest, that a space *between valleys* must necessarily be filled only with mountains.

Again: as to the signification of the term, we find it confounded with the term meadow:—"The lands west of the last mentioned range of mountains," says a native geographer, "boarding on Connecticut River, are interspersed with extensive *meadows* or *intervals,* rich and well watered." [1]

But, if the word *interval* were synonymous with *meadow,* it ought upon no occasion to be employed; and it is only because it is not synonymous that [it] is useful, and deserves to be retained. The elder colonists resorted to it on account of the peculiar disposition of a very great proportion of the surface, over all the country which they colonized.

The *interval,* intended in New England geography, is the *interval* or *space between a river and the mountains* which on both sides uniformly accompany its course, at a greater or less distance from the margin. Hence, *interval-lands* include meadow and uplands, and in general the whole of the narrow valley, through which, in these regions, the rivers flow. Where rivers flow through extensive plains; where, in short, the eye is not constantly tempted to measure the distance between the river and the adjacent mountains, there is no mention of *interval-lands.* Among the interval-lands are to be reckoned the *swales,* or rich hollows, lying behind the uplands, by which latter they are separated from the meadows. These hollows are on levels greatly raised above the meadows, and have not been visited by the floods for ages, but are composed of bog-earth, formed by the long growth and repeated decay of timber, together with their aptness for collecting and detaining water on their surface.

From *Travels Through the Northern Parts of the United States,* in the Years 1807 and 1808, by Edward Augustus Kendall, Esq., Vol. III, pp. 191–194. New York: Printed and published by I. Riley. 1809.

[1] American Universal Geography.—E. A. K.

Johnny-Cake

. . . To DESECRATE the name of Rhode Island's chiefest luxury with an "h" sticking up in the middle of it! This proves Old Cove's entire ignorance of the patriotic derivation of the Christian name Jonny as applied to the far-famed cake, made only in perfection in the South counties of Rhode Island, of soft-feeling, fine, flat meal, ground from pure white floury Rhode Island corn, in Rhode Island granite stone mills. Old Cove, if to the manor of Rhode Island and Providence Plantations born, should have known that the original spelling of the name of the favorite food of the gods was journey-cake, so called, because of the facility with which it could be prepared, to gratify the impatient appetites of those heathen deities, on their annual arrival at the delightful summer resorts or watering-places on the southern shores of the Atlantic, the chief of which were situated where the Narragansett Pier and Newport now stand. This name journey-cake was retained until the close of the War of Independence, about which time, in compliance with the prayers of memorials from the women of Connecticut and Rhode Island to the respective Legislatures of these commonwealths— the term journey, as applied to the favorite food of the gods and of the Yankee nation, was abrogated by sovereign authority, and that of jonny substituted in its place, in honor of Gov. Jonathan Trumbull, the honored and trusted friend of General Washington, who always addressed the sterling patriot with the affectionate pet name of *Brother Jonathan.* . . .

Kennebec Turkey

KENNEBEC turkey! To me and any Kennebec man those words are pure music. I know there is a Yankee joke in this name for herring. It is all of a piece with wind-pudding, which is a word for a dinner consisting of tightening the belt. But there is substance and truth behind the joke. For any Kennebec man would rather have a slab of that dark meat that grows in the sea than one off the best speckled and bearded bird that ever blushed and gobbled on a Vermont hill. And herring is a foundation stone of Maine life and character.

From *The Jonny-Cake Papers of "Shepherd Tom,"* Together with Reminiscences of Narragansett Schools of Former Days, by Thomas Robinson Hazard, with a Biographical Sketch and Notes by Rowland Gibson Hazard, pp. 31–32. Copyright, 1915, by Rowland G. Hazard. Boston: Printed for the Subscribers.

From *Kennebec,* Cradle of Americans, by Robert P. Tristram Coffin, p. 202. Copyright, 1937, by Farrar & Rinehart, Inc. New York and Toronto.

Killcow

IN OLD-FASHIONED use on Cape Cod and in Cheshire County, N. H., in the phrases: "That's no great killcow," *i.e., that's of no great account, that's no matter;* and "He's no great killcow," *i.e., he doesn't amount to much* (of a person who thinks himself somebody). The word was common in the Elizabethan age. ·Thus,—"The killcow champion of the three brethren," Nashe, ed. Grosart, II, 184; "This vaine of kilcowe vanitie," Id., III, 37; "It is the kill-cow Dorilaus," Fletcher, Lovers' Progress, iii, 3, *ad fin.;* "the kill-cow Caratach," Fletcher, Bonduca, ii, 3 (where see Weber). In these places it seems to mean a bully, a madcap fighter with a touch of Drawcansir about him. Weber is no doubt right in referring its origin to Guy of Warwick's exploit with the Dun Cow. (Two or three further citations in Nares and in Halliwell. The latter gives "kill-cow: a matter of consequence; a terrible fellow" as a Northumberland word.)

The Minister's Rib Factory

. . . MOUNT HOLYOKE College, when it was Mount Holyoke Seminary, used to be called "The Minister's Rib Factory" because it turned out so many wives for ministers and missionaries.

Mooncussin'

> The Moon Curser is generally taken for any Link-Boy; but particularly he is one that waits at some Corner of Lincolns-Inn-Fields with a Link in his hand, who under the pretence of Lighting you over the Fields, being late and few stiring, shall Light you into a Pack of Rogues that wait for the comming of this Setter, and so they will all joyne in the Robbery.
>
> Richard Head's *Canting Academy*, 1673, p. 101.

At haggard sea-corners of old Cape Cod men held lanthorns high in the black nights of the Seventeenth and Eighteenth Centuries. They swung the discs in a wide arc as though directing pilotless ships over Nauset Sea. Many an hemp-and-salt shipmaster mistook these swaying signals for

From "Various Contributions," in *Dialect Notes*, Vol. I (Part I, 1890), p. 22. Boston: Published by the American Dialect Society.

From *The Yankee Cook Book*, by Imogene Wolcott, p. 202. Copyright, 1933, by Coward-McCann, Inc. New York.

From *The Narrow Land, Folk Chronicles of Old Cape Cod*, by Elizabeth Reynard, pp. 237–238. Copyright, 1934, by Elizabeth Reynard. Boston and New York: Houghton Mifflin Company.

mastlights of other craft, turned to follow them, and ran on hidden bars. Such misfortune only occurred when no moon whitened the dunes that loom along that water-line, when no decisive starlight sharpened the shadow between tall Clay Pounds to the northward and the foam-spreckled edges of the sea. 'Mooncussers' was the name bestowed on these human harpies who fed on the spoils of such moonless disaster, who filched a lucrative plunder from the unchartable, shifting shoals of Race Point, Nauset, and Monomoy.

A few wise inhabitants put their hands into their pockets to contribute toward 'Government Beacons,' whereupon certain God-fearing puritans advanced sharp arguments against the 'policy of beaconing,' a device designed to 'injure the wrecking business.' Yet these same puritans risked their lives again and again to rescue sailors as well as cargoes and ribbed hulls and wreck-iron from fishing sloops, snows, pinks, bermudas boats, broad-winged Eastindia Men, deeply laden yawls and ketches that were 'Poundin' up' on the offshore bars. After initial salvage had been completed and flotsam had been gathered from spume-wet beaches, the goodmen buried drowned sailorboys while churchbells rang and prayer-books lay open and salt tears glazed the eyes.

In up-Cape towns such as Sandwich and Barnstable, whose harbours face Baywater, freemen expressed disgust at the 'dirty doings' down Nauset way, to which the wreckmasters of Monomoy and Nauset replied by mentioning 'green grape cankers itchin' the tongues' of envious 'upCapers.'

With the growing trade of a young nation, so many ships perished along that 'White Graveyard of the Atlantic' that link-boys were not necessary to lure unwary wanderers into a Pack of Rogues. The term *mooncursing* gradually lost its older connotation. With no implication of false lights it was used, in the Nineteenth Century, to indicate all those who practised beachcombing or salvage. But in 1717 the old derisive, condemnatory aspect of the word still clung to it, though without the precise implication of 'luring lights.' So a hostile Cape took pleasure in bestowing the title 'King of the Mooncursers' on Captain Cyprian Southack, brave mariner, skilled map-maker, when he came at the behest of the Royal Governor to court 'fickell salvedge,' after word had reached Boston of the Black Bellamy's death.

Mud Time

ONE old lady wrote that the roads were the "terabilist" after the spring rains, and today The Town still has her annual spring "mud time"—but now only on the old dirt roads. It is not many years since the schools let

From *New Hampshire Borns a Town*, by Marion Nicholl Rawson, p. 96. Copyright, 1942, by E. P. Dutton & Co., Inc. New York.

out for three weeks in March because the "bottoms of the roads had fell out." The children were always jubilant at mud time, shrilling their yearly cry of "Mud time! Six weeks to bare feet."

Munching Drawer

. . . MRS. MAUD ELLIOT remembers the munching drawer in the cabin of her father's vessel, the Independent. Captain Willis L. Case kept in his munching drawer all sorts of good things, fruits, nuts, candy, and various sweets, to which he went when he felt like eating.

The Pilgrims

. . . IN THE history and the saga of the Pilgrims, both curiously tangled tales, surely nothing is more curious than this—that their very name, "the Pilgrims," is little more than a century old, having come into common usage since 1840. Heterogeneous in origin, split even by religious differences, the Pilgrims had no name for themselves as a group. For generations they were known to their descendants merely as the Forefathers, a name preserved in the only holiday officially dedicated to their memory, Forefathers' Day, tardily instituted by Massachusetts in 1895.

* * * * *

To the end of the Revolutionary War the plain people of Plymouth celebrated Forefathers' Day with fitting ceremony each year in Town Square, renamed Liberty Pole Square, but not again till 1793 when the Reverend Chandler Robbins preached a memorial sermon. It was in no way remarkable but for one fact—thumbing through the old church records, particularly those yellowed pages on which Nathaniel Morton had copied long passages from Bradford's now "lost" manuscript,[1] Robbins

---

From *Barnstable: Three Centuries of a Cape Cod Town*, with Articles by Phyllis Bearse, Sarah H. Boult, Louisa Cobb, Richard Cobb, Alfred Crocker, Chester A. Crocker, Ora Hinckley, Elizabeth C. Jenkins, Henry C. Kittredge, A. Lawrence Lowell, Nathaniel B. H. Parker, edited by Donald G. Trayser, p. 320. Hyannis, Massachusetts: F. B. & F. P. Goss. Copyright, 1939, by Donald G. Trayser.

From *Saints and Strangers*, by George F. Willison, pp. 2, 421. Copyright, 1945, by George F. Willison. New York: Reynal & Hitchcock.

[1] It was in 1630, as he himself tells us, that Governor Bradford sat down amid the distractions and burdens of office to begin what he called his "scribled Writings." These were necessarily "peeced up at times of leesure afterwards," for to the day of his death some thirty years later Bradford led a busy and usually bedevilled life at the center of affairs. By 1650, when he laid down his pen, he had piled up a manuscript of 270 folio pages, all patiently inscribed in his own neat hand. His chronicle, simply and modestly entitled *Of Plimoth Plantation*, related in graphic detail the story of the Pilgrims from 1606 to 1647, through the most critical and eventful period of their always eventful career.

* * * * *

came upon the phrase, "they knew they were pilgrimes," [1] and happily so named them. But not until the 1840's did the phrase begin to make its way into print and become the generally accepted designation of the heterogeneous group long known merely as the First Comers.

But for two hundred years the world was little the wiser for anything that Bradford had written, for his history had a curious history of its own. As Bradford had not written for publication, his manuscript was handed down from father to son for several generations, with little or no appreciation of its unique worth. Some passages were copied into the church records by Nathaniel Morton, Bradford's nephew and secretary of the Old Colony, who also consulted it in compiling his rather dull and sketchy annals of the Forefathers, *New England's Memorial* (1669). Many years later Bradford's history passed into the hands of another early New England chronicler, the Reverend Thomas Prince, who published a few excerpts from it and then placed it on the shelves of the library he had fitted up for himself in the tower of the renowned Old South Church, Boston. Here the manuscript presumably remained until the American Revolution.

During the early years of that conflict the Old South was turned into a stable and a riding academy by the British, and after their evacuation of Boston an inventory of Prince's library revealed that Bradford's chronicle and other priceless old documents were missing. A search for them was made, and hopes of recovering them bounded up in 1793 when a manuscript volume of Bradford's letters suddenly came to light in a grocer's shop at Halifax, Nova Scotia, where its large folio pages were being used to wrap up pickles, soap, cheese, butter, and other small purchases. What little remained of it was rescued and published at Boston the next year, which stimulated more determined search for the other missing treasures. But when decade after decade passed without the discovery of a single clue, they were given up as irretrievably lost and written off as casualties of the Revolution.

But here, as often in the Pilgrim story, chance had yet to speak the last word. In 1855, while thumbing through a book borrowed from a friend, a dull ecclesiastical work published in England almost ten years before, a student of Massachusetts history suddenly came upon several quoted passages attributed to an anonymous manuscript and instantly recognized that they could have been written only by Bradford. This promising lead was quickly followed up, and the long-lost manuscript was soon traced to its dusty hiding place. It was found—of all places—in the library of Fulham Palace, beside the Thames on the outskirts of London, one of the episcopal seats and long the favored summer residence of the bishops of London. How this loot from the Old South came into their possession has never been explained, and delicacy has precluded any too pressing inquiry. In any case, his then Lordship graciously allowed a transcript of *Plimoth Plantation* to be made, and with its publication at Boston early the next year the mists that had so long enshrouded the Pilgrims, blurring their features both as a group and as individuals, began to lift for the first time.

The year 1856 marks, in a real sense, the beginning of Pilgrim history.—G. F. W. *ibid.*, pp. 3, 4–5.

[1] . . . "that goodly & pleasante citie which had been their resting place for near 12 years; but they knew they were pilgrimes, & looked not much on those things, but lift[ed] up their eyes to ye heavens, their dearest cuntrie, and quieted their spirits." —G. F. W. *ibid.*, p. 120.

P. I.'s and Frenchmen

. . . STRICTLY speaking, a P. I. is one who hails originally from Prince Edward's Island; but around here it has come to be used loosely to refer to any Canadian who isn't a Frenchman. A Canadian Frenchman is just a Frenchman. If you mean a man from France—and you very seldom do —you say a French Frenchman.

Pot Luck

FROM East Lee is said to have come the phrase "pot luck" as applied to a delectable New England boiled dinner. A town historian, the Reverend L. S. Rowland, speaks of it as . . . the most satisfying dish for the men who spent long hours in outside labor. It is interesting to note that corned beef and cabbage is not, as generally supposed, a dish brought from Ireland by early immigrants. They did not arrive here until about 1850 and "pot luck" was well-known in 1791, in the town of Lee which was settled by Cape Cod people mostly.

This homely dish is still a favorite in Lee. In 1938 the Corned Beef and Cabbage Club was organized in the town for the purpose of "sociability and the enjoyment of good food." The founder has moved away, but if you should lift the lid of the iron pot bubbling on many a range in Lee, you'd sniff the appetizing smell of "pot luck."

Pumpkin-Heads

NEW HAVEN is celebrated for having given the name of "pumpkin-heads" to all the New Englanders. It originated from the "Blue Laws," which enjoined every male to have his hair cut round by a cap. When caps were not to be had, they substituted the hard shell of a pumpkin, which being put on the head every Saturday, the hair is cut by the shell all round the head. Whatever religious virtue is supposed to be derived from the custom,

I know not; but there is much prudence in it: first, it prevents the hair from snarling; secondly, it saves the use of combs, bags, and ribbons; thirdly, the hair cannot incommode the eyes by falling over them; and fourthly, such persons as have lost their ears for heresy, and other wickedness, cannot conceal their misfortune and disgrace.

The Sacred Cod

IT is said that fishermen originally believed the cod became "the sacred cod" because it was the fish that Christ used when He multiplied the fish and fed the multitude, and even to-day the marks of His thumbs and forefingers are plainly visible on the codfish. His Satanic majesty stood by and said he, too, could multiply fish and feed multitudes. Reaching for one of the fish it wriggled and slid through his red-hot fingers, burning two black stripes down its side and thus clearly differentiating the haddock with its stripes from the sacred cod. These markings, in actual practice, do distinguish one variety from the other.

Schooner

THESE were genuine New England vessels. It is stated in the Journal of Moses Prince, a brother of the annalist, under date of 1721, at which time he visited Gloucester, that the first vessel of the class called schooner was built at Gloucester about eight years before, by Andrew Robinson; and late in the same century one Cotton Tufts gives us the tradition with some particulars, which he learned on a visit to the same place. According to the latter, Robinson having constructed a vessel which he masted and rigged in a peculiar manner, on her going off the stocks a by-stander cried out, *"Oh, how she scoons!"* whereat Robinson replied, *"A schooner let her be!"* "From which time," says Tufts, "vessels thus masted and rigged have gone by the name of schooners; before which, vessels of this description were not known in Europe." [1] Yet I can hardly believe this, for a schooner has always seemed to me the typical vessel.

According to C. E. Potter of Manchester, New Hampshire, the very word schooner is of New England origin, being from the Indian *schoon* or *scoot,* meaning to rush, as Schoodic, from *scoot* and *auke,* a place where water rushes. N. B. Somebody of Gloucester was to read a paper on this matter before a genealogical society in Boston, March 3, 1859, according to the Boston Journal, q.v.

From *The Yankee Cook Book,* by Imogene Wolcott, p. 36. Copyright, 1939, by Coward-McCann, Inc. New York.

From *Cape Cod,* by Henry David Thoreau, pp. 239–240. Copyright, 1864, by Ticknor and Fields; 1893, by Houghton, Mifflin & Co. Boston and New York.

[1] See *Mass. Hist. Coll.* vol. ix, 1st series, and vol. i, 4th series.—H. D. T.

Shun-Pikes

A CENTURY ago there were a score of turnpikes in Vermont, and when they were in their prime, taking tolls at frequent intervals, the back roads were called "shun-pikes" because, by the use of them, one might shun the use of turnpikes and thus shun the shelling-out of the toll. Some of these back roads were built with this very purpose in view, to circumvent the tollkeeper—a trick which became so prevalent in some places that penalties were provided to prohibit the building of roads parallel to the turnpikes.

Today, though the shun-pike doesn't offer the old-time thrill of tax-dodging, it does dodge traffic, and as the back road offers certain delights peculiar to itself, shun-pike exploring is a game to be recommended. . . .

Thank'ee Ma'ams

To PREVENT a hill-road from being washed in time of heavy rain, it was the custom to make across it, at intervals, a series of barriers or dams that would turn off any sudden current. These dams, built obliquely, gave an emphatic "jounce" and a twist to a wagon descending—a jounce of which the driver had his share in a jerk that threatened to dislocate his neck. From the involuntary motion of the head in going over these dams, they were popularly known as "thank'ee ma'ams," although the motion was scarcely conducive to a grateful state of mind.

Towner

MR. RICHARD PAINE told the writer that he could remember when there were lookouts at the Pond Landing for whale, and a man was kept constantly on them. When a whale was discovered, the alarm was given by shouting from the lookout, *Towner!* which was quickly taken up, and repeated and repeated with might of lung. And that he had heard on calm days the shout at his father's house, quite two miles distant. I inquired what was the meaning of Towner; he could not tell, but afterwards, when reading Walter Folger's description of Nantucket I found it was an Indian word, and signifies that they have seen the whale twice. I have referred to a similar practice in Cornwall during the pilchard season.

From *Let Me Show You Vermont,* by Charles Edward Crane, p. 248. Copyright, 1937, by Alfred A. Knopf, Inc. New York and London.

From *Quabbin,* The Story of a Small Town, with Outlooks upon Puritan Life, by Francis E. Underwood, p. 119. Copyright, 1892, by Lee and Shepard. Boston. 1893.

From *Truro—Cape Cod, or Land Marks and Sea Marks,* by Shebnah Rich, pp. 111–112. Second Edition, Revised and Corrected. Copyright, 1883, by D. Lothrop and Company. Boston. 1884.

Twitches

. . . A YARDING crew consists of three men and a twitch horse. One of the men cuts down the trees and limbs them, one drives the twitch horse, dragging—or "twitching"—the entire trunk of the tree to a cleared space called a yard, where the third man saws it up with a buck saw and piles it.

* * * * *

. . . He was finally discovered about five hundred yards from the tar paper shack where the horses are taken to eat their noon-day meals; or as the man who found him said, "About two and a half good twitches." A good twitch is the distance a horse can drag a full-length pulp log without resting. Distances are frequently measured in twitches or fractions thereof by woodsmen. It's a habit I've got into myself.

Twizzles

EVERY now and then the men would come across a snarl in their nets that they called a twizzle, and often a good deal of time and patience were required to pick and shake it out. "All sorts of fish make twizzles," Dan said. "Sometimes a little alewife will make one of the meanest sort."

Wangan

I SHOULD explain "wangan." It is an Indian word, and can mean almost anything, like the Latin *res.* It can mean a camp or building. Pond-in-the-River wangan—or Pondy wangan, as the drivers call it—is a long, low shack a third of a mile above us, where the Rapid River crew lives during the drive. There is a sign in the bunk-house that reads, "Wangan open an hour after supper." That refers to the store where the cook sells candy, tobacco, snuff, and clothing. (It really is a big box in the kitchen, and the reason it isn't open all the time is that the cook doesn't want to be bothered in the middle of his baking to hand out and charge against wages a nickel's worth of makings.) The cook may say, "I lost my wangan when the work boat swamped," and that means that his dishes are at the bottom of the lake. Or he may complain, "The wangan's runnin' low," meaning this time that he's short of food. Or a man may take his wangan and fly —leave the job with his little bundle of personal belongings. You can tell only by the context what the word means, and it's a very convenient word to know. I use it myself a lot, in non-[log]driving connections.

Yankee

ACCORDING TO REVEREND GORDON [1]

You may wish to know the origin of the term Yankee. Take the best account of it which your friend can procure. It was a cant, favorite word with farmer Jonathan Hastings, of Cambridge, about 1713. Two aged ministers, who were at the college in that town, have told me they remembered it to have been then in use among the students, but had no recollection of it before that period. The inventor used it to express excellency. A *Yankee* good horse, or *Yankee* cider and the like, were an excellent good horse and excellent cider.

ACCORDING TO MENCKEN [2]

Perhaps the most notable of all the contributions of Knickerbocker Dutch to American is the word *Yankee*. The earlier etymologists, all of them amateurs, sought an Indian origin for it. Thomas Anbury, a British officer who served in the Revolution with Burgoyne, argued in his "Travels" (1789, Ch. II) that it came from a Cherokee word, *eankke,* meaning a coward or slave; Washington Irving, in "Knickerbocker's History of New York" (1809, Ch. VII) derived it (probably only humorously) from *yano-kies,* "which in the Mais-Tschusaeg or Massachusetts language signifies silent men"; and the Rev. John Gottlieb Ernestus Heckewelder, a learned Moravian missionary who published "An Account of the History, Manners and Customs of the Indian Nations Who Once Inhabited Pennsylvania and the Neighboring States" in 1822, maintained therein that it was simply a product of the Indians' unhappy effort to pronounce the word *English,* which they converted, he said, into *Yengees.* Noah Webster ac-

---

[1] From *The History of the Rise, Progress and Establishment of Independence in the United States of America,* by William Gordon, Vol. I, p. 324. London. 1789.

---

[2] From *The American Language,* An Inquiry into the Development of English in the United States, by H. L. Mencken, Fourth Edition, corrected, enlarged, and rewritten, pp. 110–111. Copyright, 1919, 1921, 1923, 1936 by Alfred A. Knopf. New York.
   Also *The American Language: Supplement I,* by H. L. Mencken, pp. 192–194. Copyright, 1945, by Alfred A. Knopf, Inc. New York.

cepted this guess, but other contemporary authorities held that the word the Indians were trying to pronounce was not *English* but the French *Anglais*. There were, however, difficulties in the way of all forms of this theory, for investigation showed that *Yankee* was apparently first applied, not to the English but to the Dutch. So early as 1683, it was discovered, *Yankey* was a common nickname among the buccaneers who then raged along the Spanish Main, and always the men who bore it were Dutchmen. Apparently it was derived either from *Janke*, a diminutive of the common Dutch given name *Jan*, or from *Jankees* (pronounced *Yoncase*), a blend of *Jan* and *Cornelis*, two Dutch names which often appear in combination. Analogues in support of the former hypothesis are to be found in the use of *dago (Diego)* to indicate any Spaniard (and now, by extension, any Italian), and of *Heinie* or *Fritz*, *Sandy* and *Pat* to indicate any German, Scotsman or Irishman, respectively; and for the latter there is reinforcement in such familiar back-formations as *Chinee* from *Chinese*, *Portugee* from *Portuguese*, *tactic* from *tactics*, and *specie* from *species*. But how did this nickname for Dutchmen ever come to be applied to Englishmen, and particularly to the people of New England, male and female alike? To this day no satisfactory answer has been made. All that may be said with any certainty is that it was already in use by 1765 as a term of derision, and that by 1775 the Yankees began to take pride in it. In the latter year, in fact, John Turnbull spoke of it in his "McFingal" as connoting "distinction." But he neglected to explain its transfer from Dutch pirates to New England Puritans, and no one has done so to this day. During the Civil War, as everyone knows, Yankee became a term of disparagement again, applied by the people of the South to all Northerners. But its evil significance began to wear off after the turn of the century, and when in 1917 the English began applying it to the men of the A.E.F., Southerners and Northerners alike, the former seem to have borne the affliction philosophically. At that time a characteristic clipped form, *Yank*, came into popularity at home, launched by its use in George M. Cohan's war song, "Over There." But *Yank* was not invented by Cohan, for it has been traced back to 1778, and the Confederates often used it during the Civil War. . . .

* * * * *

The etymology . . . adopted in AL4,[1] to wit, that *Yankee* comes from *Jan* and *kees*, signifying *John Cheese*, is not approved by the DAE,[2] but it has the support of Dr. Henri Logeman of the University of Ghent, and it seems likely to stand. In its original form the term was *Jan Kaas*, and in that form it has been a nickname for a Hollander, in Flanders and Germany, for a great many years. In the days of the buccaneers the English sailors began to use it to designate a Dutch freebooter, and in this sense it became familiar in New York. Presently the New York Dutch, apparently seizing upon its opprobrious significance, began to apply it to the

---

[1] *The American Language,* Fourth Edition.
[2] Craigie and Hulbert, *A Dictionary of American English.*

English settlers of Connecticut, who were regarded at the time as persons whose commercial enterprise ran far beyond their moral scruples. A little while later it came into general use in the colonies to designate a disliked neighbor to the northward, and there was a time when the Virginians applied it to Marylanders. In the end the New Englanders saw in it a flattering tribute to their cunning, and so not only adopted it themselves, but converted it into an adjective signifying excellence. The DAE's first printed example of *Yankee*, then spelled *Yankey*, is dated 1683, at which time the term still meant a pirate, and was applied as a proper name to one of the Dutch commanders in the West Indies. By the middle of the Eighteenth Century it had come to mean a New Englander, and by the Revolutionary period the English were using it to designate any American. During the Civil War, as everyone knows, the Southerners used it, usually contemptuously, of all Northerners, and in consequence its widened meaning became restricted again, but in World War I it underwent another change, and since then, though they objected at first, even Southerners have got used to being called *Yankees*, *e.g.*, by the English. The shortened form *Yank* is traced by the DAE to 1778. The adjective *yankee*, signifying good or superior, had a vogue in the Boston area at the beginning of the Eighteenth Century, but soon passed out of use, and has not been found in print for many years. To *yankee*, a verb signifying to cheat, followed a century later, but is also now obsolete. So is *yankee*, as the name of a drink made of whiskey sweetened with molasses, recorded for 1804, but forgotten by the Civil War era.

Many derivatives are listed by the DAE, *e.g.*, *Yankee-trick*, traced to 1776; *-land*, to 1788; *-ism*, to 1792; *-like*, to 1799; *-phrase*, to 1803; *-notions*, to c. 1851; *-ish*, to 1830; *-dialect*, to 1832; *-peddler*, to 1834; *-made* and *-clock*, to 1839; *-dom*, to 1843; *-grit*, to 1865; *-twang*, to 1866; to *catch a Yankee* (to catch a tartar), to 1811, and *to play Yankee* (to reply to a question by asking one), to 1896. *Yankee Doodle* as the name of a song is traced to 1767. . . .

NAMES AND NICKNAMES

Old Testament Names in New England

IN DISCOURSES and exhortations, references were constantly made to the favor shown by the Creator of all men to "His chosen people." It is not to be supposed that the disciples and apostles were not reverenced, but there was far more heard of Moses, David, and the prophets. The bush that burned and was not consumed was as often in mind as the pathetic symbol of Christ's death and man's redemption. The sonorous names of Semitic warriors and kings were familiar to the lips of the early ministers; the syllables of Ze-rub-ba-bel gurgled like water falling over stones; Jehoiada, Jeroboam, Ahasuerus, Ahab, Hezekiah and Sennacherib, how well they were known! But Augustine, Ambrose, Chrysostom, Clement, Ignatius, Irenaeus, and Polycarp, were never mentioned except once a year, in the course of a thundering attack upon the Scarlet Woman of the Apocalypse.

Baptismal names showed a similar drift. Of course, a few old English names were represented; but most children wore appellations laboriously sought out from the Bible; and they were often ponderous enough to make the toddling wearers top-heavy. The names were not necessarily Hebrew; they might be Greek or Roman; but they had become hallowed by being imbedded in a biblical text. Aquila, Epaphras, and Theophilus flourished, though less frequently than Abijah, Eliphaz, and Ichabod. A father who had been christened Moses had three sons, Moses, Aaron, and Josiah. In Webster's Dictionary there is a list of Scripture names, and, in running them over, about one hundred and eighty were found that were well known in Quabbin and vicinity. Many were beautiful, but more were inharmonious. Ridiculous associations came to be attached to some that were originally noble. In hearing the names Hosea and Ezekiel, one seldom thinks of the majestic prophets, but of "Hosy" the shrewd and comic hero of the Biglow Papers, and of "Zekle" of the Yankee idyl. What young lady in modern society would willingly own to the name of Jemima, Jerusha, or Tabitha? There were twin sisters not many miles from Quabbin named Tryphena and Tryphosa. One bright-eyed matron was named Tirzah; another, fair and delicate, had been called Zeruiah. What angelic patience must have been required to bear such burdens for life!

In common speech all names were clipped and vulgarized; and among school-boys and young men the actual designations were "Eph," "Bije," "Ez," "Hi," "Rast," "Josh," "Lije," etc. Poets must find it hard to fit these docked and ill-used names into pastoral verse; and even when the line is made, the reader is apt to be disgusted by some unromantic association. Lowell's ballad of "The Courtin'" is almost perfect in beauty; and yet, in some moods, at the mention of "Zekle" and "Huldy" a sense of vulgar comedy comes in to overbear the poetic feeling.

Oddly enough, there was never a man or boy named Paul in Quabbin, or in the region. Was there some half-conscious sympathy with the Judaistic distrust and dislike of the great apostle to the artistic and lettered world? [1]

The names in those old burying grounds are interesting—to me, at least. There is one critic who has objected to the Christian names in my Cape Cod novels and stories. He insists that those names are, for the most part, the author's own invention. There never were, so he maintains, such names on the Cape or anywhere else.

---

[1] From *Quabbin, The Story of a Small Town, with Outlooks upon Puritan Life*, by Francis H. Underwood, LL.D., pp. 63–64. Copyright, 1892, by Lee and Shepard. Boston. 1893.

Well, I wish I might conduct that critic through a few of these grave-yards. In one—and I was not "name hunting" either, but merely seeking unusual inscriptions—I casually picked up the following in something less than ten minutes:

"Bashua, widow of Jeptha." "Theophilus, son of Veranus." "Levi and Asenath." "Tamisen." "Diadama." "Bathsheba." "Tryphenia." "Sabra." "Aruna." "Shubel." "Susa."

These, beside the usual assortment of Jedidiahs and Sophronias and Jeremiahs and Calebs and Solomons and Elkanahs and the like.[2]

Providential Names

LIKE the old Jews, the Pilgrims and Puritans had a providential way of naming their children from local surroundings, or events of time and place. Thus "Peregrine" [White], travelling from one country; "Oceanus," a boy born to Stephen Hopkins, on the ocean. "Reliance," Governor Hinckley's daughter, the wife of Nathaniel Stone, second minister of Boston, born on the day when the English whipped the Narragansetts, was so named by Rev. Mr. Russell as a token of divine favor, and became a popular name not extinct to this day on the Cape. "Love," "Fear," "Patience," and "Wrestling" were some of the names of Elder Brewster's children.

"Seaborn" was a son of Rev. John Cotton, born on the passage. He married a daughter of Governor Bradford. "Resolved," "Humility," "Remember," "Shining," "Desire," and "Faith" were other female names.

"Armemaryvetta," born 1714, was the name of an accomplished daughter of the schoolmaster, Mr. John Rogers, of Sandwich. Scripture names were their delight and duty: the longer and harder, the more religious. "Mahershallalhashbaz (Isaiah viii I), son of William Dyar, born in Newport, 1661.

An old lady who lived in Provincetown, born in Truro, used to thank the Lord that all her family had Scripture names. This was the way she told them:—

Hezekiah, Jedediah, Shebnah, and Eliakim,
Sarah and Mary, Hannah and Penina,

Girls' Names

AN INTERESTING subject of thought is found in the Christian names which have been given to children, borne through longer or shorter lives, and

[2] From *Cape Cod Yesterdays*, by Joseph C. Lincoln, p. 124. Copyright, 1935, by Joseph C. Lincoln and Harold Brett. Boston: Little, Brown & Company.

From *Truro—Cape Cod, or Land Marks and Sea Marks,* by Shebnah Rich, pp. 75–76. Second Edition, Revised and Corrected. Copyright, 1883, by D. Lothrop and Company. Boston. 1884.

From *Along New England Roads,* by W. C. Prime, pp. 114–115. Copyright, 1892, by Harper & Brothers. New York and London.

finally carved on gravestones. Whence came some of these names, especially as names given to female children? Here are a few out of many which I have copied in various burial-places along the roads. Some are Scriptural, varied in spelling, some noteworthy only for the spelling:

Vesta	Smilinda	Bezaleed
Madona	Theodate	Phileena
Imagene	Mitty	Asenath
Sabrisal	Rozill	Resolved
Alanette	Lima	Comfort
Rocksena	Orlo	Romanzo
Ora	Elmon	Theda
Phene	Ede	Diademia
Arozina	Irena	Coral

While on this subject of names of the dead, here is an illustration of names now in use by the living. In a village inn in New Hampshire I found the printed catalogue of a school located there, and copied in my notebook the following Christian names of young lady students:

Myrtie Ioline	Mary Etta
Una Gertrude	Margaret Marilla
Mary Adella	Lora Eliza
Lois Ella	Franca Lydia
Corrie Elbra	Fannie Mae
Daisy Sarah	Minnie Etta
Hattie Rose Pearl	Lizzie Estelle
Myrtie Kate	Mary Loraine
Florence Genevra	Bernette Samantha

Double Christian Names

THERE is one thing more. By the natural expansion of a few families, whole neighborhoods often exhibit a single surname, like that of Wildes or Huff. There may be half a dozen persons of the same Christian name. The surname being dropped among themselves, it has an odd effect to hear them speaking of each other as Miss Mary Clem, Aunt Sally Josh, Aunt Hannah Eben, Aunt Sam Paulina, and so on, all being of one surname. Then the archaic words or idioms in everyday use, of vagrant or unknown origin, would set a college of comparative philology wild with delight.

Portuguese American Names and Nicknames

MANY Portuguese families have American names. A cabin boy would be brought over by some old sea captain and raised as a son of the family. First he would be known, perhaps, as "Snow's Manell," and then he would

From *The Pine-Tree Coast*, by Samuel Adams Drake, p. 109. Copyright, 1890, by Estes & Lauriat. Boston. 1891.

From *Time and the Town, A Provincetown Chronicle,* by Mary Heaton Vorse, pp. 163, 164, 178. Copyright, 1942, by Mary Heaton Vorse. New York: The Dial Press.

become known as "Manny Snow," his old name forgotten but his religion kept. Other names became Anglicized. Perriaras or Perez became Perrys, Diaz became Deers.

* * * * *

Almost everyone in Provincetown has a nickname. This custom is said to have come from São Miguel. The nickname often descends from father to son. So Louis Chocolate, whose tan was doubled by tarring nets, has a flock of little Chocolates. Captain Gaspy, one of the highliners of the great fresh fishermen, was known as "Vadee." Mr. Silva of the fish market was called "Begunna." And there is Mrs. Jazz Garters who lives to the westward. John Bull, Tony Fall River, Manny Bigfeet—there is no end to the nicknames. There is the Goddamn family, with Tony Goddamn and Manny Goddamn.

* * * * *

Captain Antoine Joaquin Sousa, who became captain of the *Jessie Costa* in 1911, one of the great Provincetown vessels of that day, was among the famous captains. He was generally known as "Joe King," because when he first came to America in the whaling vessel he was asked by the mate what his name was.

"Joaquin," he answered.

"Oh yes, Joe King," said the mate, and he was Joe King all his days.

Ships' Names

THE very names of their ships stir the imagination: the Light Foot, the Chariot of Fame, the Chispa, the Rosario, named for the wife of an owner who had been a captain in his day and had loved and won a Spanish beauty. The Whirlwind and Challenger were famous clipper ships; and one man commanded successively the Undaunted, the Kingfisher, the Monsoon and Mogul and Ocean King, and the steamers Zenobia and Palmyra—and Edward Everett. There was the Young Turk and Santa Claus, the Tally Ho, the Expounder and Centaur and Cape Cod; the Agenor and Charmer and Vahalla, the Shooting Star and the Flying Dragon, the Altof Oak, and, quaintly, the Rice Plant; the Oxenbridge and Kedar. Some ships were so famous that when their day was done, they passed down their names to ships of a younger generation than theirs. Masters changed from one ship to another, and discussion as to how this captain and that handled the Expounder or Monsoon on such or such a voyage filled many a long evening of their old age at home.

* * * * *

From *Old Cape Cod: The Land, The Men, The Sea*, by Mary Rogers Bangs, pp. 243–244, 275–276. Copyright, 1920 and 1931, by Mary Rogers Bangs. Boston and New York: Houghton Mifflin Company.

The captains of these packets that ran out of every town on the north shore of the Cape had their fun racing one another from port to port; it is probable some money was lost or won on the results. Barnstable, even, produced a ballad to immortalize some of the contestants:

> "The Commodore Hull she sails so dull
> She makes her crew look sour;
> The Eagle Flight she is out of sight
> In less than half an hour,
> But the bold old Emerald takes delight
> To beat the Commodore and the Flight."

Other packets had the romantic names of Winged Hunter and Leading Wind; the Sarah of Brewster was as familiar to her people as "old Mis' Paine" or "Squire Freeman." Truro had the Young Tell, the Post Boy and the Modena. . . .

Ships' Names on Old Barns

ON THE way to the Atwood house, watch on the left for the white barn that says HORATIO HALL in great big letters. It is an ancient custom on Cape Cod to place the name of an old boat on the front of a barn.[1] The *Horatio Hall* was a steam vessel, but some of the loveliest clippers ended the same way—their beautiful names on old barns, their figure-heads over the doors. Of the great ships that sailed so proudly, that fought typhoons and knew the doldrums, the monsoons, and the roaring forties, there is nothing left but names on barn doors. Once I saw the name of the *Magdalena,* and I thought she must have been a ship of great beauty and a strange doom. And I have seen the *Wanderer*—a black name on a gray board—on an old red barn.

'Sconset House Names

UNIQUE, catchy, original and forcefully cute titles have been given by present owners and occupants to many of the old houses once possessed and occupied as homes by a hardy farmer and fisherman people of days

---

From *And This is Cape Cod!* by Eleanor Early, p. 150. Copyright, 1936, by Eleanor Early. Boston and New York: Houghton Mifflin Company.

[1] This statement of "an innocent lady observer" amuses Jeremiah Digges (*Cape Cod Pilot,* p. 309). For the Cape Cod custom of salvaging ships' quarterboards, wheels, etc., for souvenirs and ornaments, see Henry C. Kittredge, *Mooncussers of Cape Cod* (Boston, 1937), pp. 96–121.

From *Brief Historical Data and Memories of My Boyhood Days in Nantucket,* by Joseph E. C. Farnham, pp. 28–29. Published by the author. Providence. 1923.

long agone. Similar titles, by inviting, dainty lettering, also grace the exterior of many of the modern built dwellings. All are scrupulously neat and pretty, and the names given to them add alluring charm.

Of those appellations I have record of the following: Takitezie, In and Out, Hatetoquitit, Bigenough, Nonetoobig, High Tide, House of Lords, Seldomin, Castle Bandbox, Ocean Spray, Come Aboard, Loafalot, Solid Comfort, The Pilot House, The Deck House, The After Cabin, Mizzen Top, Nipantucket, Cap'n's Cabin, Fo'castle, Doubledecker, The Breezes, Daisy Cot, Nauticon Lodge, Whick Whack, Waldorf Astoria, Jr., The Anchorage, Flagship, Cosey Corner, Sea Shell, Cap'n's Gig, Thimble Castle, Big Sunflower, Beehive, Vale of Rest, Castle William, Liberty Hall, Hill Top, Martin Box, Columbia Cottage, Blue Bird, Rosemary, The Manor, Bluff View, Eagle Cottage.

That many of these titles are aptly apropos is strikingly evident on perusal; the old island and its once hardy dwellers. in days agone so closely dependent upon marine affairs, are, in that line of service, notably memorialized by several of them.

Names of Apples

ON A WINTER's evening now I think of those days of thirty-odd years ago. When it got late, along about eight-thirty, and we children had finished our homework, Father had read the journals and worked on his sermon, and Mother had had enough of the never-ending darning, mending, and knitting, I would take a hand lamp and a big wooden bowl and go down cellar for a half dozen big Northern Spies. We would sit and eat, and if Father was in the mood he would tell us about the history of apples and the story of Johnny Appleseed. It was good to listen to the names of old-time apples: Workaroe, Victuals and Drink, Wandering Spy, Sweet and Sour, Titus Pippin, Tom Putt, Nodhead, Sops-of-Wine, Smokehouse, Shiawassee, Savewell, Arkansas Beauty, Bailey Spice, Bunker Hill, Cabashea, Beauty of Kent, Belborodooskoe, Blushing Bride, Genesee Flower, Egg Top, Fallawater, Evening Party, Disharoon, Crow Egg, Chenango, Devonshire Duke, Lady Finger, Kentish Fillbasket, Iowa Beauty, King David, Kansas Keeper, Hartford Rose, Gloria Mundi, Good Peasant, Grandmother, Great Mogul, Missing Link, Old Garden, Mountain Sweet, Longevity, Legal Tender, Long Stem of Penn, Lowland Raspberry, Malinda, Pine Stump, Plumb Cider, Red Wine, Pumpkin Russet, Seek-No-Further, Tolman Sweet, and Hubbardston Nonesuch.

Poor Old Country Railroad

THE Portland & Oxford Central Railroad, running out of Minot, was built in 1850. It had a hard time to meet running expenses. There were no water stops, and the crew had to fill the tender with buckets from brooks, and stump fences furnished the fuel. One cold, sleety winter's day ice formed over the rails and had to be picked off by hand. They were six days in running thirteen miles. One day the engineer was sick and the superintendent tried running the engine. He threw the lever back in the engine house. It kicked and threw the super through the cab window, and then rushed through the engine house wall and out into the pasture. Because of these mechanical escapades and the suggestive initial letters on the cars, the road was nicknamed "Poor Old Country Railroad."

The Hub

A JAUNTY-LOOKING person, who had come in with the young fellow they call John—evidently a stranger—said there was one more wise man's say-ing that he had heard: it was about our place, but he didn't know who said it. A civil curiosity was manifested by the company to hear the fourth wise saying. I heard him distinctly whispering to the young fellow who brought him to dinner, *Shall I tell it?* To which the answer was, *Go ahead!* Well—he said—this is what I heard:

"Boston State-House is the hub of the solar system. You couldn't pry that out of a Boston man, if you had the tire of all creation straightened out for a crowbar."

Sir—said I—I am gratified with your remark. It expresses with pleas-ing vivacity that which I have sometimes heard uttered with malignant dulness. The satire of the remark is essentially true of Boston, and of all other considerable and inconsiderable places with which I have had the privilege of being acquainted. Cockneys think London is the only place in the world. Frenchmen—you remember the line about Paris, the Court, the World, etc. I recollect well, by the way, a sign in that city which ran thus: "Hôtel de l'Univers et des États Unis"; and, as Paris *is* the universe to a Frenchman, of course the United States are outside of it. "See Naples and then die." It is quite as bad with smaller places. I have been about lecturing, you know, and have found the following propositions to hold true of all of them:—

From Minot, Maine. Manuscripts of the Federal Writers' Project of the Works Progress Administration for the State of Maine.

From *The Autocrat of the Breakfast-Table*, VI, in *The Writings of Oliver Wendell Holmes*, Vol. I, pp. 125–126. Copyright 1858, 1882, 1886, 1891, by Oliver Wendell Holmes. Cambridge: The Riverside Press. 1891.

1. The axis of the earth sticks out visibly through the center of each and every town or city.

2. If more than fifty years have passed since its foundation, it is affectionately styled by the inhabitants the "*good old* town of"—(whatever its name may happen to be).

3. Every collection of its inhabitants that comes together to listen to a stranger is invariably declared to be a "remarkably intelligent audience."

4. The climate of the place is particularly favorable to longevity.

5. It contains several persons of vast talent little known to the world. (One or two of them, you may perhaps chance to remember, sent short pieces to the *Pactolian* some time since, which were "respectfully declined.")

Boston is just like other places of its size—only, perhaps, considering its excellent fish-market, paid fire-department, superior monthly publications, and correct habit of spelling the English language, it has some right to look down on the mob of cities. . . .

Back Side and Bay Side

"BACK SIDE" and "Bay Side" . . . are terms to remember when you visit Cape Cod. A prim Wellfleet housewife who rents rooms to summer people once confessed to me that she had somehow shocked her guests by a "perfectly civil answer" she had given them. They wanted to know the best place to take a sunbath. And, of course, she told them the best place was on the Back Side.

II. FOLK-SAY

Dialect speech as the embodiment of living, many-sided human nature is perhaps nowhere so closely seen as in a collection of the figurative terms and phrases applied to people and things.
—ELIZABETH MARY WRIGHT

Proverbs are not merely decorations on life. They have life itself in them. They are the bedrock substance of living, built up by many people and many years. They are the beginnings of all literature, the first metaphors and similes, the first comedies and tragedies. They are the first poetry we have. The Kennebec valley is rich in such poetry, a poetry of Yankeedom, tart, sparkling, and full of meat.—ROBERT P. TRISTRAM COFFIN.

From *Cape Cod Pilot*, by Jeremiah Digges, with Editorial and Research Assistance of the Members of the Federal Writers' Project, p. 6. American Guide Series, Federal Writers' Project, Works Progress Administration for the State of Massachusetts. Copyright, 1937, by Poor Richard Associates. Provincetown and New York: Modern Pilgrim Press and the Viking Press.

Ginowine proverbs ar like good kambric needles—short, sharp, and shiny.—Josh Billings.

1. Mythology in Folk Speech

Lowell was impressed by two aspects of New England folk speech, which, at first seemingly contradictory, are reciprocal parts of the same process— the process, that is, by which literature and folklore are constantly passing into each other, to their mutual enrichment. On the one hand, Yankee speech usage has behind it the sanction of "antiquity and very respectable literary authority." On the other hand, the "ordinary talk of unlettered men among us is fuller of metaphor and of phrases that suggest lively images than that of any other people I have seen." Folk speech is thus both conservative and creative; and the "germinal element" in language, which gives life to poetry and slang as well as folk speech, is metaphor, including proverbial comparisons.

Among the attributes of this proverbial lore of trope and comparison are two which folk speech shares with poetry and mythology: the "power of rapidly dramatizing a dry fact into flesh and blood," and the "quality of the mind which delights in finding an element of identity in things seem- ingly the most incongruous." The process by which language interchanges inanimate, animal, and human qualities, in the attempt to explain nature and human nature, is essentially a mythopoeic process.

This process is nowhere better illustrated than in "those comparisons wherein the moods, habits, and actions of men are likened to those of birds, beasts, fishes, and even insects in real or imaginary situations,"[1] as well as to things. Such comparisons are too familiar to need citing, but partic- ularly characteristic (it would seem) of New England are "crazy as a coot," "deader than a pelcher [pilchard]," "happy as a clam," "pious as a barn rat," and (of a mawkish sentimentalist) "softer'n stewed punkin." Among metaphors are "no see 'ems" (the Indian's words for midges), the "old seedfolks" (ancestors), and "soft sawder [solder]" (smooth talk, deception). Examples of irony and hyperbole are: "A pushing individual was 'not backward in going forward' and a disagreeable one had 'winning ways to make himself hated.' . . . A poor marriage was described as 'nothing marrying nothing.' A futile act or speech was '*to* nothing and *for* nothing.' "[2]

For another kind of speech mythology involving folk metaphor we turn to the "odd custom" noted by Jeremiah Digges among the Portuguese fishermen of Cape Cod—"of bestowing nicknames on one another—not in a spirit of levity, but in dead earnest"—so earnestly, in fact, that the nick- name replaces the surname of the entire family and "Some have been in use so long that in the course of generations the real family names have become obscured, and legal problems have arisen." "There is the 'Rat

---

[1] Elizabeth Mary Wright, *Rustic Speech and Folklore* (London, 1913), p. 158.

[2] For most of these expressions, see Annie E. Perkins, "Vanishing Expressions of the Maine Coast," *American Speech*, Vol. III. (December, 1927), No. 2, pp. 134–141. "No- see-ems" is also cited by Thoreau in *The Maine Woods* (Boston, 1893), p. 2; while "soft sawder" was made popular by Sam Slick.

family,' for instance; there are the 'Codfishes'—Manuel Codfish, Maria Codfish, and the little Codfishes. . . ."[1] Perhaps the most famous example of this type of surname is the "Goddams," which Captain Joseph Captiva explains thus:

> That's 'cause the old lady she couldn't speak English so good and she'd call the children when they was little: "You come here, goddam," "Don't you do that, goddam." So they call 'em the "Goddams."[2]

Nomenclature descriptive of local and group traits, both depreciatory and affectionate, has given rise to an extensive mythology of nicknames of states, towns, neighborhoods, sections of the population, etc.; *e. g.*, the Nutmeg State; Pudding Town and Puddingers (Northampton and its residents, from the custom of eating hasty pudding and milk for Saturday evening supper);[3] Scrabbletown (the lower end of Chatham); Bluenoses (Nova Scotians or New Brunswickers); lard-eaters (Canucks);[4] chowderheads; mooncussers (Cape Codders); codfish aristocracy ("an opprobrious name for persons who have made money in trade," according to Thornton); Boston Brahmins; bean-eaters; lace-curtain Irish; Hoot, Toot, & Whistle, the Hot Tea & Whisky, and the Hog-Tied & Weary (the Hoosac Tunnel & Wilmington R. R., among short line fans).[5]

2. LOCAL BYWORDS AND PROVERBS

Local bywords are clearly mythological when they involve a mythical character like Sock Saunders, the "guy who hangs around and makes life complicated" for Maine loggers. But the mythology of local characters and customs enters into other bywords which originate in an old story or for which an explanatory story has been invented—it is often difficult to tell which. Sometimes the story has been forgotten and all that is left is the proverb. In this way every community has its proverbial characters as well as its "character" proverbs, of which Ola G. Veazie reports the following examples from New Hampshire:

> Any one around Bath who makes a strong and rather queer statement is said to be "equal to Priest Sutherland," as he was a man who made many such statements and who influenced the town greatly during his fifty years as minister there.
> "Going back like John Northey's lamb": equivalent to backsliding. (John Northey was an early resident on Sugar Hill.)
> "Leaning toward Sawyer's" was said when some one went out of a house sur-

---

[1] *Cape Cod Pilot* (Provincetown and New York, 1937), pp. 232–233.

[2] As told to Alice Douglas Kelly, *Living Lore of New England*, Manuscripts of the Federal Writers' Project of the Works Progress Administration for the State of Massachusetts.

[3] Clifton Johnson, *Historic Hampshire in the Connecticut Valley* (Springfield, 1932), p. 36.

[4] Robert P. Tristram Coffin, *Kennebec, Cradle of Americans* (New York, 1937), p. 193.

[5] Archie Robertson, *Slow Train to Yesterday* (Boston, 1945), p. 24.

reptitiously or as though going for a drink when he should not. A family by the name of Sawyer kept a store where drinks could be purchased many years ago on Sugar Hill.[1]

Other local sayings allude to the character of the place and the people, with jests and gibes about weather, seasons, landmarks, towns, customs, and similar features.

We have two seasons: winter and Fourth of July.[2]
. . . the New England climate consists of "nine months winter and three months late in the fall."[3]
Fogs so thick you could cut 'em up into junks with your jack-knife.[4]
Boston folks are full of notions.
"Go to Poodic!" (An Indian name for a point of land on the Maine coast; equivalent to "Go jump in the bay!".)[5]
Here is to the Nutmeg State—who can produce a grater? (A toast.)
A rib was taken off Billerica to make Bedford.[6]
They call a house a house, but a house with a shed is a village. (Of Cape Cod, as observed by travelers.)[7]
Put a bag of coffee in the mouth of hell, and a Yankee will be sure to go after it.[8]

In addition to proverbial characters and local proverbs, New England has its local phrase-makers and folk-sayers. Out of Poor Richard, by way of the comic almanacs, the Yankee aphorism flowers in Josh Billings.

B. A. B.

---

[1] Manuscripts of the Federal Writers' Project of the Works Progress Administration for the State of New Hampshire.

[2] Louise Dickinson Rich, *Happy the Land* (Philadelphia, 1946), p. 251.

[3] Arthur G. Crandall, *New England Joke Lore* (Philadelphia, 1922), p. 15.

[4] "My Summer with Dr. Singletary," *Prose Works of John Greenleaf Whittier* (Boston, 1886), Vol. II, p. 226.

[5] George R. Stewart, *Names on the Land* (New York, 1945), p. 338.

[6] Katharine M. Abbot, *Old Paths and Legends of New England* (New York, 1904), p. 70.

[7] *Massachusetts: A Guide to Its Places and People* (Boston, 1937), p. 326.

[8] George Lunt, *Old New England Traits* (New York, 1873), p. 61. As attributed to Emperor Christophe of Haiti: "Hang up a bag of coffee in hell, and a Yankee would go down and bring it up without being singed." (Samuel S. Cox, *Why We Laugh*, New York, 1876, p. 325.)

SALT OF THE SEA

Nantucket Nauticalisms

THEY never pull, they always "haul"; they do not tie or fasten anything, they "splice" or "belay" it; they do not arrange a thing, they "rig it"; they do not throw anything away, but "heave it overboard"; they "back and fill," they "luff," "tack," "come about" and "square away" on any and all occasions. Before engaging in any venture they first "see if the coast is clear," then, as they proceed, they "keep the weather eye peeled" and always "look out for squalls." Then they "sound it out" until they "fathom" it. If they don't like "the lay of the land" they "give it a wide berth." To be prudent is "to keep an eye to windward," but to be over-prudent to the point of timidity is to be "always reefed down and standing on the inshore tack." To be reckless and take too many chances is to "sail too close to the wind," and to be caught off one's guard is to be "taken aback," meaning to catch the wind on the wrong side of the sails—an exasperating and sometimes perilous experience for a mariner. Anything put by for a rainy day, or any provision against adversity or disaster is "an anchor to windward," while to be gay or foolish is to "carry on" as an inexperienced or reckless navigator may carry on (sail). A telling rebuke of extravagance is the phrase "two lamps burning and no ship at sea." To overcome or to best an opponent is to "take the wind out of his sails." To be ready for anything is to be "always on deck," and so on *ad infinitum*.

Some day, perhaps, if you are an old-time Nantucketer, you "tackle up" the horse and "all rigged out" you "cruise down along." A "mate" recognizes you by "the cut of your jib," and you are "hailed" with the query, "where you bound?" Replying that you are "bound to the south'ard" or to the "east'ard," as the case may be, you are urged to "heave to" or to "come alongside." Complying with the request, you are urged to "drop anchor," and to "come aboard and have a gam"; so you "make fast" and visit for a while, till it's time to "heave your anchor short" and "get under way" for the next "port."

So the conversation goes, not always with the nauticalisms as thick as in the samples given, but always with the salty flavor of the sea. Less now than formerly, perhaps, for the times are changing; but much of it lingers yet in the speech of the older generation. Some of the old expressions are rarely heard nowadays. In former times a Nantucket mother told her children to "splice their patience," and if she went out, one of the older ones had to "tend the kitchen halyards" in her absence.

From *The Nantucket Scrap Basket,* Being a Collection of Characteristic Stories and Sayings of the People of the Town and Island of Nantucket, Massachusetts, Second Edition, revised, expanded, and rearranged by William F. Macy, pp. 6–11. Copyright, 1916, by William F. Macy and Roland B. Hussey and 1930, by William F. Macy. Boston and New York: Houghton Mifflin Company.

Of a light-minded person or one who didn't amount to much they would say, "Well, I guess he'd come over the bar without camels," while the expression applied to an absolutely useless fellow, "he ain't good enough even to take in slack," explains itself. An ill-fitting garment was said to "fit like a purser's shirt on a hand-spike." "God made the food, but the devil made the cook" is a sailor's phrase, often borrowed to describe a poor cook ashore; and the expression "we must take it as it comes from the cook" is, perhaps, another form of the same idea.

A certain Nantucket Quaker mother once denied that she ever used these nautical phrases, and told her children to remind her if they ever caught her doing it. The very next morning she gave one of them some eggs to leave at the house of a relative on the way to school with the words: "Take these into Cousin Phebe's, and tell her I think this squares the yards with us; and thee must scud, for it's almost school time."

Of course not all these expressions are peculiar to Nantucket. Many of them are heard elsewhere along the coast, and even far inland, and many of them, indeed, have become so much a part of the language that they are not recognized as nautical phrases at all.[1] Of such are several already given—notably such terms as "taken aback," to "carry on" or "the lay of the land" and many others, such as mainstay, bulwark, chock full, etc.; but even of these, when their sense is grasped and understood, it must be admitted that their origin is obvious. Even the very common word "landmark," is a sailor's term, meaning a mark on the land by which to steer or lay a course. "Landfall" was land sighted from a ship. Others not recognizable at all, except by the initiated, are constantly used. "A1" or "A No. 1" originated in the classification of wooden ships, being the highest grade in Lloyd's register. "First rate" was originally a naval term, applied to the old wooden line-of-battle ships. "Skyscraper," long before the day of high buildings, was the sailor's name for a ship with very tall masts. Even more surprising, perhaps, will be the statement that the term "bitter end" is a very technical nautical phrase, that being the sailor's name for that part of the cable which is abaft the windlass bitts; so when the cable is let out to the bitter end, that is as far as it is possible for it to go, and it is only in very deep water or when riding out a gale at anchor that this occurs

"To know the ropes" is obviously of nautical origin. It is said there are only seven "ropes" on a full-rigged ship. Everything else which might be taken for a rope by a land-lubber goes by some other name, as halyards, clewlines, earrings, garnets, sheets, tacks, stays, buntlines, gaskets, etc., to mention only a few. So that to pick the seven "ropes" from all this confusion of nomenclature requires an "A.B." degree in seamanship.

Another common expression, "fagged out," or the "fag end," is undoubtedly of nautical origin, that being the sailor's term for a rope which is untwisted and frayed at the end.

---

[1] Cf. Joanna Carver Colcord, *Sea Language Comes Ashore* (New York; 1945).

A "fake" in its original meaning was a turn in a rope or a cable. Hence to "fake" a rope is to lay it down in coils.

Examples of this nature might be multiplied indefinitely, and it is a fascinating study; but further discussion of the subject is hardly within the scope of this work, even if space permitted. Our language undoubtedly owes much to the sailors, who, while they may not have actually coined many of the words in question, have probably preserved many very old ones which would otherwise have passed into disuse and been forgotten.

"Give a woman all the advice in the world and then she'll go ashore with both anchors on the bows" expresses the contempt of an old Nantucket captain for feminine judgment and capacity.

"The devil would have made a sailor if he'd ever looked aloft" is said of or to a man who gets things snarled aloft by not looking to see that everything is clear; and the first thing he knows everything is "mops and brooms."

"Nothing but hot water and ashes can be thrown to windward" is told to the green-horn, who needs only to try it once to learn the lesson.

Said of a gale off Cape Horn: "It blows so hard it takes two men to hold one man's hair on."

Of a captain in a tight place, from which it would seem next to impossible to extricate himself, the sailors were wont to say: "The old man's 'twixt Heaven and hell without halyard or downhaul."

Of an incredible story: "That yarn doesn't square by its lifts and braces."

Of an over-dressed woman, displaying flounce, ruffle and furbelow: "Here she comes, stud'n's'ls set alow and aloft."

Similarly, of a sailor home from sea, with his pockets full of money rolling down Main street on his sea-legs, with a girl on each arm: "There goes Jack, rolling down to St. Helena, eighteen cloths in the lower stud'n's'l, and no change out of a dollar!"

An old skipper, still hale and hearty, being asked why he quit going to sea, replied: "Well, I thought when I got to the north'ard o' sixty, 'twas time to heave to."

Another, being invited out to dinner, announced on his arrival that he was "ready to fall to any time," as he had "come with a swep' hold."

Still another old salt spoke of "bending on a new necktie."

Captain Stephen Bailey, partaking of an oyster stew at a church supper, called the waitress with, "See here, my lass, can't ye get me some more oysters? These here are a day's sail apart."

It was Captain Bailey who said, "Once you start the standing rigging of a five-dollar bill, there's d——n little left."

Varieties of Nantucket Wind and Weather

THE varieties of weather known to Nantucketers often surprise the inland visitor, who recognizes only two kinds, good and bad. We have fair, good, fine, foul, dirty, nasty, bad, thick, rough, heavy, and several other sorts, including "owlish" and "mirogenous," whatever that may mean. Wind conditions are described as dead calm, stark calm, calm, light, puffy, squally, heavy, single-reef, two-, three-, and close-reef breezes, half-a-gale, gale, hurricane, etc.; or a wind may be described as a six- or eight-knot breeze, and so on. Among those to the manner born, a "tempest" means a thunderstorm.

Nantucketisms

WHEN an old whaleman was asked after his health, his reply was *"Bung up and bilge-free,"* referring to the way casks are stowed in the hold of a ship; but if you happen to hear one say that he was *"pretty nigh fin out,"* you can know that he has been very sick, or that he thought he was, for that expresses the condition of a dying whale when he rolls over on his side, showing a fin above water. The nearest counterpart to this expression we have now is "about all in."

Bungy—"Where you going?" "I'm going to Bungy." What and where is Bungy? The impression seems to be that the reply is a rather saucy one—almost as if to say, "None of your business."

Clip—A Nantucketer would say, "I'll just 'clip' in to Mary's on the way back." One meaning of the verb clip is to move quickly, and as our use of this term implies haste, or a hurried call, it is doubtless derived from that meaning.

Coof, the Century defines as "a lout, a coward." (Scotch.) Originally, the word was without doubt used in a somewhat contemptuous sense, and to the resident of a prosperous urban community of ten thousand people, such as Nantucket was seventy or eighty years ago, visitors from Cape

From *The Nantucket Scrap Basket*, Being a Collection of Characteristic Stories and Sayings of the People of the Town and Island of Nantucket, Massachusetts, Second Edition, Revised, Expanded, and Rearranged by William F. Macy, pp. 144–145. Copyright, 1916, by William F. Macy and Roland B. Hussey; 1930, by William F. Macy. Boston and New York: Houghton Mifflin Company. 1930.

From *The Nantucket Scrap Basket*, Being a Collection of Characteristic Stories and Sayings of the People of the Town and Island of Nantucket, Massachusett, Compiled, Edited, and Arranged by William F. Macy and Roland B. Hussey, and Published for the Benefit of "The Sons and Daughters of Nantucket," pp. 17–19, 129–151 *passim*, and 160–169 *passim*. Copyright, 1916, by William F. Macy and Roland B. Hussey. Nantucket: The Inquirer and Mirror Press.

The material has been rearranged and alphabetized in a single word list.

Cod (to whom the term was originally applied) might well have seemed loutish. Gradually the word came to be applied to any off-islander, and lost most of its contemptuous significance, implying only a slight inferiority by reason of the accident of birth [or residence] elsewhere than on the island. It is a good English word, which is the main point.

Diddledees—A curious old word used for pine-needles. This has always been something of a puzzle, but the Century again helps us out: "Diddledees—a shrub in the Falkland Islands and other Antarctic regions used for fuel." As pine-needles have been used as "kindlings" by the Nantucket people for generations past, may it not be that the word was brought from the Antarctic by the whalers? In the absence of any better explanation of the origin of the term, this theory is advanced for what it may be worth.

Down Along—Many Nantucketers, when asked as to where they are bound, reply, "Oh, jest down along." No one has ever been able to locate just where this popular destination is located. The North Shorer, the Upper Main Streeter, or the Chicken Hiller means when he uses it, that he is going down town. The Newtowner gives it the same meaning, but he also uses it to express a port in the opposite direction, as when he heads for home. The Under-the-Banker also uses it to indicate both up town and down town. We have always heard of people who were going there but we never knew any one to arrive. "Up-along" is sometimes heard, but much less frequently.

Flink—"I'm going out on a flink," meaning a good time. May it be a corruption of "fling" sometimes used in a similar sense?

Another common term was *foopaw*. This is said to have been a corruption of the French *faux pas,* and is believed to have been borrowed from the French whalers. To "make a foopaw" of anything was to make a mess of it, to bungle it—as when a harpooner missed his whale, or having succeeded in "getting an iron in," to have the line foul or snarl. That was a dangerous "foopaw to make, as unless the line was cut quickly before the whale "ran" or "sounded," it might mean death to one or more men in the boat.

The expression *gallied* is still current to some extent among the older generation of Nantucketers. It was a whaling term, meaning primarily frightened and excited, and withal uncertain what to do next. Its nearest synonym, perhaps, is the modern word "rattled," though it implies more of fear and fright than the latter term. If a whale became "gallied" before being struck, it required much more skill and caution in the attack than would otherwise be the case.

Gam—A social visit and talk. Originally this term was applied to a school of whales, and its use by the whalemen is doubtless derived from that source. Whaleships meeting at sea often hove to, and the captains would visit back and forth during the time the ships were in company. Under certain conditions the crews were allowed the privilege also. The word was used both as a noun and as a verb, and it is still very frequently heard among Nantucketers. One says, "I met so-and-so today, and we had a grand gam together," or "we gammed for an hour or more."

Greasy Luck—To wish a whaleman greasy luck meant to wish him a good voyage with plenty of oil; hence the Nantucketer uses it in well-wishes to his friends in any proposed venture. To say on parting, "Well, greasy luck to you!" is to say "Bon voyage!"

Huddle—An old-time name for a dance or ball. All the old-timers will recall "Handy's huddles."

It Takes a Voyage to Learn—Equivalent to "experience is the best teacher." This is often quoted as an excuse for mistakes or inefficiency due to inexperience.

Tradition has it that no whaleman was expected to ask the girl of his choice for her hand until he had *killed his whale,* and if she were of the better class of the island maidens, the wedding day was not fixed until he had won a command. *"She married him before he had a ship"* was a reproach which no high-born damsel of spirit would venture to endure.

Meeching—Is another word often noted. The dictionary gives "skulking, sneaking, mean," which is just the sense we give it in Nantucket.

Off—An abbreviation of "off-island," is very frequently heard. One often hears such a remark as "I haven't seen you lately. Have you been Off?" Still more odd is the expression, "When did you come On from Off?"

Old Town Turkey—The Nantucketer's name for any resident of Martha s Vineyard; from the town of Edgartown, which was formerly known as Old Town.

Porch—Applied to an ell kitchen. A summer cottager who instructed the native man-of-all-work to sweep and clean the porch accused him of stupidity when she returned an hour or two later to find her kitchen nicely cleaned, while the veranda remained in the same disorder as when she went out. Each knew what a porch was, but each had something quite different in mind. The word porch is defined as "a covered way or entrance, whether enclosed or unenclosed." In ecclesiastical architecture, where it presumably originated, it describes the covered and usually enclosed entrance built on to a church or cathedral—for all the world, in general outline and appearance, like the ell kitchen of a typical old Nantucket house, succeeding the "lean-to" in the very old ones. The use of the word as applied to a veranda is modern U. S., and more or less local at that. So the Nantucketer may have been nearer right than his employer. The room over this style of kitchen was always "the porch chamber."

"Put that butter within darting distance, will you?" was the request of an old whaleman at the table, bread in one hand and knife in the other, as he scanned the intervening distance.

Rantum Scoot [1]—A term, we believe, peculiar to Nantucket, and very old. It means a day's "cruise" or picnic about the island, usually a drive,

---

[1] Also reported from New York state by Harold W. Thompson in *Body, Boots & Britches* (Philadelphia, 1940), p. 287.

but it might be on foot. The distinctive feature of such an excursion is that the party has no definite destination, but rather a roving commission, in which respect such a trip differs from a "squantum" (which see later). "Rantum" is probably a corruption of random.

Scrap Islander—The name applied to a Nantucketer by the people of Martha's Vineyard.

Scrimshont—A curious word, of which the original is said to have been scrimshaw. The dictionary defines it in effect as any fine or delicate mechanical work, especially the carving on shells or ivory done by sailors. Many fine examples of "scrimshonting" may still be seen in some of the old Nantucket homes, and the Historical Association has some excellent specimens in its collection.

Serve—If a Nantucket woman breaks her broomstick or mop-handle, she fits the pieces together and asks her husband or some other man to "serve" it. If he is a sailor he knows what she means, and he does a wonderfully neat job. He does not need to look in the dictionary, where he might learn that it means "to bind or wind tightly with small cord or marline"; but unless he is a sailor, or has been taught by a sailor, he cannot do it without having at least one of the ends, if not both, showing when the work is finished. It is a fine art when properly done.

Of a particularly fine young woman it was said: *"She deserves an East India cap'n,"* the popular impression being that such worthies were likely to be more than ordinarily prosperous and successful.

Shool—according to the dictionary, means "to saunter about, to loiter idly"—a favorite pastime with the "shooler," who is a well-known character in the local vernacular.

Skimming Slicks—Securing the full limit of return from any effort. A "slick," as used by the islanders, refers to the smooth, oily patches often seen on the sea over a school of blue-fish, mackerel or other surface-feeding fish, and which exudes from the small fish or "bait" on which the school are feeding. The full significance of this term will be recognized if one stops to think of the labor necessary to skim the slick and get all there is in it.

Slatch—A word still in quite common use on the island among the older people. It means "a short gleam of fine weather, an interval in a storm." When caught away from home in a heavy rain, we plan, if possible, to "wait for a slatch" before starting to return. The term is also sometimes used in the sense of a respite from labor, as "I had a slatch in my work, and I thought I'd run over and see you."

Sliver—(pronounced with a long "i")—Ask your city fish man to sliver a flounder, a plaice fish or a scup for you, and there's one chance in ten, if he's not an old fisherman himself, that he will know what you mean; yet the dictionary defines it exactly: "to cut each side of a fish away in one piece from the head to the tail," which is the only proper way to clean either of the fish mentioned, as every Nantucketer knows.

Snivver—Here's a queer word, still used occasionally. One says "I'll be over to your house snivver dinner." The presumption is that the speaker means "as soon as ever I have had my dinner." A good definition would be: immediately after. We have been unable to find any record of the use of this odd term off-island.

Squantum—Doubtless of Indian origin; the Nantucketer's name for a party outing or picnic—differing from a "rantum scoot" (see before) in that a squantum usually implies some definite destination for the cruise.

To *throw a tub to a whale* is to offer a sop to keep any one quiet, said to be a survival of a very ancient custom when approaching a sperm whale suspected of being ugly, or perhaps only "gallied," to throw a cask overboard so it would drift toward the whale to distract its attention while the boat was approaching.

Tivis—To wander aimlessly about.

Top up your boom—Get ready to go; from the custom of hoisting on the topping-lift of a fore and aft sail, before hoisting the sail itself.

Nantucketers never sit at the window or by the window, but always *"under" the window*. There is perhaps no phrase, which is more often noted in our speech than this, and we who use it are often asked to explain or even to demonstrate just how we sit under the window. The answer is, obviously, that as Nantucket windows are usually rather high from the floor, as we sit by or at one of them, we are under them, just as the wall paper or the baseboard, or even the floor, for that matter, is under them—which only goes to prove that whatever may be said of us, we are never in the wrong. Let him who can prove the contrary.

Wadgetty—Fidgety; nervous.

Whittle—There seems to be no good authority for our use of this word, meaning to fuss, to get uneasy; also, sometimes, to tease, to pester. One says, "Well, it's time to go. Mother'll be whittling." What child of a Nantucket mother hasn't been told, when he had exhausted her patience to the point of exasperation by teasing for something, "Oh, stop your whittling!"

Wilcox—Much used in Nantucket formerly, to describe an uneasy, sleepless night. To this day the old folks (and some of the young ones) say: "I couldn't sleep. I wilcoxed all night long." It has been suggested that the term originated with a story of some family named Wilcox who, having an overplus of company one night, slept four or five in a bed, with the natural result that no one slept at all.

Wild as a Tuckernuck Steer—Wild, harum-scarum. Many beef cattle were formerly raised on Tuckernuck, and their antics, when brought into the gay metropolis of Nantucket town, probably gave rise to this expression.

Nantucket Similes and Sayings

THE speech of the older generation of Nantucketers is full of quaint similes, most of which refer to some old story. In some cases the story has been

Ibid., pp. 75–77.

forgotten, while the expression still remains. We have succeeded in collecting a number of these odd sayings with the accompanying stories:

"As Mad as Tucker."

Tucker was one of those gentle souls whose heart was bigger than his brains. His only relation and caretaker was a grandmother to whom he was as deeply attached as his feeble mental capacity would permit. When this poor innocent was seen on the street one day, crying bitterly, the compassionate neighbor hastened to inquire the cause. "I'm so mad," he sobbed. "I'm so mad. Granny's dead and I'm so mad I don't know what to do." The poor fellow could not even distinguish between his emotions, and although not wholly unsympathetic, the Nantucketers could not refrain from their inalienable right to seize upon a joke by using the simile, "As mad as Tucker when his granny died."

"As Weak as Annie Burrill's Tea."

Annie Burrill was so flustered when she entertained the minister that she forgot to put any tea in the teapot, serving him with a nice cup of freshly-boiled water. When asked if his tea was satisfactory, his reply was: "It has no bad taste, madam." Thus the expression became a simile for weakness in her day.

"As Bad as Old Skitzy."

Skitzy remarked one day, "Now, wife, that cheese is all gone, and I've had none of it." "Well, why didn't you eat some?" she asked. "Why, I don't like cheese," answered Skitzy.

"As Handy as Caleb's Cheese."

It is said that Caleb Macy was (unlike Skitzy) so fond of cheese that he kept one hanging by a string in his sitting room, "so's to have it handy"; hence the expression.

"A Poor Gamaliel."

Gamaliel, a poor good-for-nothing, coming home one night, said to his long-suffering wife: "Well, I've sold my horse." "Have you? What did you get for it?" "Why—a cart!" Hence, the expression, "a poor Gamaliel" has a deep significance to the Nantucketer.

"You Haven't Got Dinah Paddock to Deal with."

Dinah Paddock was a weak-minded woman whom the boys delighted to tease, when playing around her door. After she moved away, they began playing the same tricks on her successor, but she soon scattered them, saying: "I'll let you know you haven't got Dinah Paddock to deal with." This became a simile for efficiency for that day and generation.

"Keeping Still like Uncle Jimmy." [1]

In the old days when families laid in the winter's supply of beef and pork in barrels, Uncle Jimmy missed, little by little, the pork from the barrel which stood in the yard. He suspected a certain man, but said nothing.

Fourteen years went by, and one day, in talking of losses, the man whom he had suspected, said: "Uncle Jimmy, you never found out who took that pork, did you?" "No," said Uncle Jimmy, *"not till this day."* Out of this incident grew the well-known expression, "keeping still like Uncle Jimmy."

"No More Use for Them than Meader Had for His Teeth."

A man named Meader, living during the war of 1812, applied to his neighbor for the loan of a hammer. Being asked why he wished it, he replied: "To knock out my teeth. I have no need of them, for I can get nothing to eat." Hence the saying among old Nantucketers, "I have no more use for it than Nick Meader had for his teeth."

YANKEE ELOQUENCE

Wit in Yankee Speech

Prosaic as American life seems in many of its aspects to a European, bleak and bare as it is on the side of tradition, and utterly orphaned of the solemn inspiration of antiquity, I cannot help thinking that the ordinary talk of unlettered men among us is fuller of metaphor and of phrases that suggest lively images than that of any other people I have seen. Very many such will be found in Mr. Bartlett's book,[2] though his short list of proverbs at the end seem to me, with one or two exceptions, as un-American as possible. Most of them have no character at all but coarseness, and are quite too long-skirted for working proverbs, in which language always "takes off its coat to it," as a Yankee would say. There are plenty that have a more native and puckery flavor, seedlings from the old stock often, and yet new

---

[1] See "Who Stole the Pork?", p. 39 above.

From Introduction to *The Biglow Papers*, Second Series, in *The Poetical Works of James Russell Lowell*, pp. 224–225. Copyright, 1848, 1857, 1866, 1868, 1869, 1876, and 1885, by James Russell Lowell. Boston and New York: Houghton, Mifflin and Company.

[2] John Russell Bartlett, *Dictionary of Americanisms* (New York, 1848), the 1859 edition of which Lowell reviewed.

varieties. One hears such not seldom among us Easteners, and the West would yield many more. "Mean enough to steal acorns from a blind hog"; "Cold as the north side of a Jenooary gravestone by starlight"; "Hungry as a graven image"; "Pop'lar as a hen with one chicken"; "A hen's time ain't much"; "Quicker'n greased lightnin' "; "Ther's sech a thing ez bein' *tu*" . . .; hence the phrase *tooin' round,* meaning a supererogatory activity like that of flies; "Stingy enough to skim his milk at both eends"; "Hot as the Devil's kitchen"; "Handy as a pocket in a shirt"; "He's a whole team and the dog under the wagon"; "All deacons are good, but there's odds in deacons" (to *deacon* berries is to put the largest atop); "So thievish they hev to take in their stone walls nights"; [1] may serve as specimens. "I take my tea *barfoot*," said a backwoodsman when asked if he would have cream and sugar. (I find *barfoot,* by the way, in the Coventry Plays.) A man speaking to me once of a very rocky clearing said, "Stone's got a pretty heavy mortgage on that land," and I overheard a guide in the woods say to his companions who were urging him to sing, "Wal, I *did* sing once, but toons gut invented, an' thet spilt my trade." Whoever has driven over a stream by a bridge made of *slabs* will feel the picturesque force of the epithet *slab-bridged* applied to a fellow of shaky character. Almost every county has some good die-sinker in phrase, whose mintage passes into the currency of the whole neighborhood. Such a one described the county jail (the one stone building where all the dwellings are of wood) as "the house whose underpinnin' come up to the eaves," and called hell "the place where they didn't rake up their fires nights." I once asked a stage-driver if the other side of a hill were as steep as the one we were climbing: "Steep? chain-lightnin' couldn' go down it 'thout puttin' the shoe on!" And this brings me back to the exaggeration of which I spoke before. To me there is something very taking in the Negro "so black that charcoal made a chalk-mark on him," and the wooden shingle "painted so like marble that it sank in water," as if its very consciousness or its vanity had been overpersuaded by the cunning of the painter. I heard a man, in order to give a notion of some very cold weather, say to another that a certain Joe, who had been taking mercury, found a lump of quick-silver in each boot, when he went home to dinner. This power of rapidly dramatizing a dry fact into flesh and blood, and the vivid conception of Joe as a human thermometer, strike me as showing a poetic sense that may be refined into faculty. At any rate, there is humor here, and not mere quickness of wit,—the deeper and not the shallower quality. The *tendency* of humor is always towards overplus of expression, while the very essence of wit is its logical precision. Captain Basil Hall denied that our people had any humor, deceived, perhaps, by their gravity of manner. But this very seriousness is often the outward sign of that humorous quality of the mind which delights in finding an element of identity in things seemingly the most incongruous, and then again in forcing an incongruity upon things identical. . . .

[1] And, by the way, the Yankee never says "o'nights," but uses the older adverbial form, analogous to the German *nachts.*—J. R. L.

Humor in Yankee Speech

I REMEMBER a remark made to one of our local merchants by a pert "summer boarder." "I don't see what you people do in the winter when *we* are gone." "Oh," said he, "we jest hibernate." [1] I don't suppose that reply would appear the least funny outside of the locality, but it was chuckled over at many a social function. The laugh was on the "boarder," for her "airs" do not impress the "rubes" as much as she supposes. The real life of the village never begins until cold weather has driven these aliens away. The merchant "tacks on" his prices and "makes" all he can out of their patronage, but is secretly amused at their "duds" and their "goings-on." They wouldn't feel quite so superior if they knew that behind their backs they are "summer complaints."

You may have heard the more apocryphal anecdote of the resident who was asked this same question, implying stagnation in the winter. This native is reported to have said, "Oh, I jest sets and thinks, an' sometimes I jest sets." It at least illustrates the Maine type of humor. Another story is told of an old bachelor who at length "made up to" and "up and married" the village "old maid." "I hear you've taken on a wife, Jed, sence I ben gone," remarks an acquaintance just returned from a "cousining" ("cousining" means a visit to distant relatives). "Ye-es," is the tolerant reply, "a *kind* uv one."

Speaking of old maids, they are usually regarded as jokes in most Maine towns, a reminiscence of the old-time feeling that girls are disgraced if they can't "land" a man. If she behaves herself and "quits strugglin'" she will probably escape notice, but if she attempts to prolong her youth by "running with" the "young fry," she will probably win the title of "the youth's companion," which is the name of a literary "stand-by" in New England.

The lazy man is also a joke. Yankee humor describes him as "bottoming chairs" for an occupation. A man who is too lavish with his energy may be cautioned not to "bust his biler." Your humorist will answer your conventional greeting regarding his health with "Oh, jest staggerin' around." I remember I sprang this unthinkingly upon a western Pennsylvanian once and got an indignant reproof. Another reply is, "Sick abed." A person much given to practical joking is a "case." The term equally applies to a clever child. Either may be said to "act up," also. You get a real slant on the psychology of Maine humor, in the statement, "He ken knock a haouse

From "Maine Dialect," by E. K. Maxfield, *American Speech,* Vol. II (November, 1926), No. 2, pp. 82–83. Copyright, 1926, by Williams & Wilkins Company. Baltimore.
[1] The question, "What on earth do you do here after the summer people leave?" drew the following reply from Shavy Noyes, of Norway, Maine: "Oh, we jest fumigate." See Arthur Bartlett, "Maine," in *Holiday,* Vol. 2 (August, 1947), No. 8, p. 44.

daoun!" It expresses an amused contempt for the "upstart" braggart, the pronunciation being deliberately exaggerated to contribute to the effect.*

Miscellany

A LADY summoned a jack-of-all-trades to repair her fence. After contemplation he enquired, "Well, marm, will you hev it hen-tight or cow-tight?" "As we haven't any hens, I think cow-tight will do." [Guilford, Conn.]

A dweller on Old Street [Deerfield,] many years before his death had a copper coffin built for himself, declaring emphatically, "I'll be d——d if I go snappin' raound hell in a hemlock coffin."

At Shelburne Falls—formerly Deerfield Northwest—some one remarked that the water in the river was very low. "Yaas," drawled a bystander, "it lacks a quart of being any water in it."[1]

The city fellow was discussing the general wild state of spending and nobody paying with a resident of a small Cape Cod town. The old man listened, agreed and then opined—"Nossir, I don't hold with all these new ideas. I've allus made it a point to never wash more'n I can hang out!"

* * * * *

"He pries up the sun with a crowbar"—said of a man who gets up early in the morning.

"The wind blew straight up and down"—a gale.

"Looking for salt pork and sundown"—when a hired man shirks.

"Slower than a hop toad in hot tar."

"Faster than a cat lapping chain lightning."

"Safe as in God's pocket."[2]

"I wish I had a neck as long as a cart-rut." (New Hampshire.) Praise for good drink.

"He's always a-stern of the lighter." (Nantucket.) Behind the last one.

"There was no more heat in the sun than a yellow dog." (Maine.)

"It's tougher where there's none." (Nantucket.) Upon hearing complaints about a tough steak.

---

* I suppose this vowel-twisting was a direct inheritance from certain counties in England where it can still be noted; but I think to some extent our twisting has been deliberate—a sort of contemptuous effort of the Yankee to show he was not of the aristocracy, but good common folk.—Charles Edward Crane, *Let Me Show You Vermont* (New York, 1937), p. 30.

---

[1] From *Old Paths and Legends of the New England Border:* Connecticut, Deerfield, Berkshire, by Katharine M. Abbott, pp. 111, 193. Copyright, 1907, by Katharine M. Abbott. New York and London: G. P. Putnam's Sons.

[2] From *The (Old) Farmer's Almanack*, Calculated on a New and Improved Plan for the Year of Our Lord 1946, No. 154, by Robert B. Thomas, pp. 44, 45. Copyright, 1945, by Mabel M. Swan. Dublin, New Hampshire: Yankee, Inc.

"He had no more suavity than a swine." (Maine.)

"I just ate chagrin." (Maine.) Embarrassment over a faux pas.[3]

When two Marbleheaders meet, they say to each other, "Down bucket!" or else they say, "To hell I pitch it!" Why they say it, or how they began, the Marbleheaders themselves can't tell you.[4]

. . . I like descriptions of how the smelt ran in Mill Brook, spring before last—"You never see nawthin' like it. Looked like a big snake swimming up the current, they was so thick. Every dip, you'd net half a water-pail full"—and of the stately dance of a male spruce-partridge observed in a little sunny clearing, courting his demure brown hen—"She sat there like a bump on a log, never letting on she see him at all till he got disgusted and moseyed off into the bushes. She come to life then all right and ske-daddled right along after him. Just like any woman." . . .[5]

Fog's so durn thick this mornin' you kin hardly spit.

It wuz cold enough to freeze two dry rags together. . . .

. . . 'twould break a snake's back to foller that last furrer.

. . . so homely, 'twould gag ye.

He could sell a fiddle to a one-arm deef an' dumber.

. . . the cussed critter was so tough then, ye c'd hardly stick a fork in his gravy!

Somebody declared once that Will Frisbie must-a been the last one in the back row when the faces wuz handed out.[6]

A keen sense of the humorous, with aptness in illustration, drawn from observation in their own sphere, is another distinguishing trait. I was present at a discussion among some village philosophers, about a wedding

---

[3] From *From Here to Yender*, Early Trails and Highway Life, by Marion Nicholl Rawson, pp. 285, 294, 296, 305. Copyright, 1932, by E. P. Dutton and Company, Inc. New York.

[4] From *Cape Cod Pilot*, by Jeremiah Digges, with Editorial and Research Assistance of the Members of the Federal Writers' Project, p. 311. American Guide Series, Federal Writers' Project, Works Progress Administration for the State of Massachusetts. Copyright, 1937, by Poor Richard Associates. Provincetown and New York: Modern Pilgrim Press and the Viking Press.

[5] From *Happy the Land*, by Louise Dickinson Rich, p. 246. Copyright, 1946, by Louise Dickinson Rich. Philadelphia and New York: J. B. Lippincott Company.

[6] From *Village Down East*, Sketches of Village Life on the Northeast Coast of New England before "Gas-Buggies" Came, by John Wallace, from Conversations with Zackary Adams, Duck Trap Cove, Maine, pp. 12, 18, 46, 52, 92, 114, 182. Copyright, 1943, by Stephen Daye Press, Inc. Brattleboro, Vermont.

recently solemnized in the neighborhood. The groom was described as being as poor as a church-mouse; so that the union of hearts did not promise a golden future. "Oh, never mind," said one of these graybeards; "tew pigs allers doos better'n one." [7]

"THE hill farmer," one wisecracker said, "got up so early that often he met himself going to bed."

"There ain't much of any winter here," one of our wisecrackers declared, "except from September to June, but we have dog-gone good sleddin' the rest of the year." [8]

A Vermont "Idioticon"

I HAVE my own "idioticon"—a little privately compiled dictionary of words and phrases used by Vermonters I know, all the way from the Supreme Court bench to the backwoods farm. In a few radio talks I asked my fellow Vermonters what were their favorite expressions and I was surprised at the number of contributions from towns all over northern Vermont. I recognize many that are common to all New England, some that may have become familiar farther west or south, but the fact remains they are relished by Vermonters and therefore part and parcel of our way of speech.

Justice Leighton P. Slack of the Vermont Supreme Court, venerable, but sly in his humor, is a rich mine for the good old phrases. "Slipper-toe" is one of the Judge's old-time expressions for a no-account, and an "old pelter" is his way of describing an old Tartar. And I heard him one day say somebody was "homely enough to stop a down train," and that's a phrase which, if you stop to think of it, has much more significance than "homely enough to stop a clock," "homely as a hedge fence," or "homely as hell is wicked."

To "pestle around," a phrase plucked from the mortar-and-pestle days, was a common expression which I recall from the Black River Valley to describe a hasty, puttering activity. But for being "busy" there are many other phrases which my radio helpers sent in to me. The ironic line "as busy as a man on the town" indicates relief workers were always that way. Several persons sent this: "I've trotted around all day in a bushel," meaning a busy day, evidently, without getting anywhere.

---

[7] From *The Pine-Tree Coast*, by Samuel Adams Drake, p. 74. Copyright, 1890, by Estes & Lauriat. Boston. 1891.

[8] From *The Great White Hills of New Hampshire*, by Ernest Poole, pp. 82, 84. Copyright, 1946, by Ernest Poole. Garden City, New York: Doubleday & Company, Inc.

From *Let Me Show You Vermont*, by Charles Edward Crane, pp. 31–32. Copyright, 1937, by Alfred A. Knopf, Inc. New York and London.

The Vermonter would seem to have a hearty contempt for ignorance, especially of the kind that lacks even common sense, for many expressions are of this run of shad: "Don't know enough to pound sand in a rat-hole," "to go in when it rains," to "pour water out of a boot," to "suck alum and drool." To have rendered any of the foregoing with *doesn't* instead of *don't* would have spoiled it all, for this use of *don't* is the most common grammatical error current in Vermont, possibly defensible as it was sanctioned by the highest classes in the eighteenth century.

I can think of some of my friends who find the future "darker'n a wolf's mouth," "blacker'n a stack of black cats," or "dark as a pocket," and "feel bluer'n a whetstone." There are those who are often found to be "fixing for a spell of sickness" or "enjoying dretful poor health," or "just feeling peakéd."

Vermonters' contempt for a lack of common sense is matched by their contempt for lack of thrift, as reflected in such expressions as: "He don't need it any more than a pig needs a wallet," or "He has no more use for it than for water in his boots," or "He don't need it any more than a dog needs two tails."

I'll turn on a few of the expressions sent in:
"It's a poor back that can't press its own shirt."
"Stands out like a blackberry in a pan of milk."
"He's the whole team and the little dog under the wagon."
"Her house was a regular hurrah's nest."
"Jumped like a cat out of the wood-box."
"He's as straight as a yard of pump-water."
"Her head looks as if it had worn out two bodies."
"Twice around a toothpick and half-way back."

A lady up in Craftsbury Common said of a poor, tired, hungry hired man:—"looking for salt pork and sundown."

A Montpelier woman sent me a list in which was that classic phrase: "independent as a hog on ice" (it ought to go on our state seal), and added: "slow as a hog on ice with his tail froze in."

A woman turned to me in a theater to contribute this as her favorite: "Twenty tailors around a buttonhole."

Seamen's Sermon

THE only preacher I heard in Boston was Mr. Taylor, who addresses himself peculiarly to seamen, and who was once a mariner himself. I found his chapel down among the shipping, in one of the narrow, old, water-side streets, with a gay blue flag waving freely from its roof. In the gallery opposite to the pulpit were a little choir of male and female singers, a

From *American Notes*, for General Circulation, by Charles Dickens, pp. 39–41. London: Chapman and Hall. 1850.

violoncello, and a violin. The preacher already sat in the pulpit, which was raised on pillars, and ornamented behind him with painted drapery of a lively and somewhat theatrical appearance. He looked a weather-beaten hard-featured man, of about six or eight and fifty; with deep lines graven as it were into his face, dark hair, and a stern, keen eye. Yet the general character of his countenance was pleasant and agreeable.

The service commenced with a hymn, to which succeeded an extemporary prayer. It had the fault of frequent repetition, incidental to all such prayers; but it was plain and comprehensive in its doctrines, and breathed a tone of general sympathy and charity, which is not so commonly a characteristic of this form of address to the Deity as it might be. That done he opened his discourse, taking for his text a passage from the Songs of Solomon, laid upon the desk before the commencement of the service by some unknown member of the congregation: "Who is this coming up from the wilderness, leaning on the arm of her beloved!"

He handled his text in all kinds of ways, and twisted it into all manner of shapes; but always ingeniously, and with a rude eloquence, well adapted to the comprehension of his hearers. Indeed if I be not mistaken, he studied their sympathies and understandings much more than the display of his own powers. His imagery was all drawn from the sea, and from the incidents of a seaman's life; and was often remarkably good. He spoke to them of "that glorious man, Lord Nelson," and of Collingwood; and drew nothing in, as the saying is, by the head and shoulders, but brought it to bear upon his purpose, naturally, and with a sharp mind to its effect. Sometimes, when much excited with his subject, he had an odd way—compounded of John Bunyan, and Balfour of Burley—of taking his great quarto bible under his arm and pacing up and down the pulpit with it; looking steadily down, meantime, into the midst of the congregation. Thus, when he applied his text to the first assemblage of his hearers, and pictured the wonder of the church at their presumption in forming a congregation among themselves, he stopped short with his bible under his arm in the manner I have described, and pursued his discourse after this manner:

"Who are these—who are they—who are these fellows? where do they come from? Where are they going to?—Come from! What's the answer?" —leaning out of the pulpit, and pointing downward with his right hand: "From below!"—starting back again, and looking at the sailors before him: "From below, my brethren. From under the hatches of sin, battened down above you by the evil one. That's where you came from!"—a walk up and down the pulpit: "and where are you going"—stopping abruptly: "where are you going? Aloft!"—very softly, and pointing upward: "Aloft!"—louder: "aloft!"—louder still: "That's where you are going— with a fair wind,—all taut and trim, steering direct for Heaven in its glory, where there are no storms or foul weather, and where the wicked cease from troubling, and the weary are at rest."—Another walk: "That's where you're going to, my friends. That's it. That's the place. That's the port. That's the haven. It's a blessed harbour—still water there, in all changes of the winds and tides; no driving ashore upon the rocks, or slipping your cables and running out to sea, there: Peace—Peace—Peace—all peace!"—Another walk, and patting the bible under his left arm: "What! These fellows are coming from the wilderness, are they? Yes. From the dreary, blighted wilderness of Iniquity, whose only crop is Death. But do they lean upon anything—do they lean upon nothing, these poor seamen?"—Three raps upon the bible: "Oh yes.—Yes.—They lean upon the arm of their Beloved"—three more raps: "upon the arm of their Beloved"—three more, and a walk: "Pilot, guiding star, and compass, all in one, to all hands—here it is"—three more: "Here it is. They can do their seaman's duty manfully, and be easy in their minds in the utmost peril and danger, with this"—two more: "They can come, even these poor fellows can come, from the wilderness leaning on the arm of their Beloved, and go up—up—up!"—raising his hand higher, and higher, at every repetition of the word, so that he stood with it at last stretched above his head, regarding them in a strange, rapt manner, and pressing the book triumphantly to his breast, until he gradually subsided into some other portion of his discourse.

I have cited this, rather as an instance of the preacher's eccentricities than his merits, though taken in connection with his look and manner, and the character of his audience, even this was striking. It is possible, however, that my favourable impression of him may have been greatly influenced and strengthened, firstly, by his impressing upon his hearers that the true observance of religion was not inconsistent with a cheerful deportment and an exact discharge of the duties of their station, which, indeed, it scrupulously required of them; and secondly, by his cautioning them not to set up any monopoly in Paradise and its mercies. I never heard these two points so wisely touched (if indeed I have ever heard them touched at all), by any preacher of that kind, before.

A 'Sconseter's Will

Siasconset, May 30th, 1841

I, OBED GARDNER, master mariner, now living at 'Sconset, write down this will.

From *The Nantucket Scrap Basket,* Being a Collection of Characteristic Stories and Sayings of the People of the Town and Island of Nantucket, Massachusetts, revised, expanded, and rearranged by William F. Macy, pp. 158–160. Copyright, 1916, by William F. Macy and Roland B. Hussey, and 1930, by William F. Macy. Boston and New York: Houghton Mifflin Company.

This manuscript will was found in an old sea-chest in a house in Siasconset some years ago.

The will was never presented in court for probate, because the turn of events made it unnecessary. The Nancy Rotch returned and was sold for a good price. Belindy's husband was drowned by the upsetting of his dory on Miacomet Rip. Ezra returned from China, prosperous and anxious to make amends for past shortcomings, and no one was more delighted to see him than Cap'n Obed. When the latter died, it was

Item. I have cruised with my wife, Huldy Jane, since 1811. We signed articles in town before the preacher on Independence Day. I want her and my oldest boy Jotham to be Captain and Mate in bringing to port whatever I leave and to see that every one of the crew gets the lay as writ down on this paper. I put mother in command. I know sheel be Captain anyway, for six months after we started on our life cruise I found out that I was mate and she was master. I don't mean that she ever mutinied, but I no that whenever we didn't agree she always manoovred to work to windward. May be it is all right for she could sail closer to wind than I could and could manage the crew of little ones that she had as much to do with shipping as I did. She always wanted me to do the swearin' when there was any trouble. I no that when she and Jotham break bulk the cargo will be got out as well as I could do it myself.

Item. In 1838 Captain Ichabod Worth got tired of the old Nancy Rotch and wanted to get rid of her so he got me to take a piece of her. When I saw her last she was lyin' at the wharf in Valparaiso more'n half full. I mean she was more'n half full of oil. Mother never liked her. I want Jotham to have that piece as extra pay for what he does in settlin' up my affairs for heel have to steer things while mother is takin' observations, watchin the weather and lookin over things below deck.

Item. I want mother to have the house on Union street until she goes aloft. Then I want it to go to the children in equal lays and if any child dies I want the lay of the parent to go to the parent's young ones. But I don't want my daughter Belindy to have anythin as long as her husband is livin. He is a lubber, but she has been cruisin with him for years. I haven't got anything agin him, but he doesn't no how to navigate the sea of life. I do believe if he wanted to stop a leak board ship it would be just like him to go into the hold with an auger and bore a hole threw the plankin to let the bilge water out into the sea. But Belindy likes him. Thas just like a woman. If I should give the lay out and out to her, I am afraid her husband would manoover to get hold of it. So I want mother and Jotham to put it out at interest, and give what comes out of it to her until her husband ships for a corpse below decks in the grave yard. Then she can take the lay and do what she wants with it.

Item. I dont want my son Ezry to have anything from what I leave. All the children except him was good ones. They looked out for their mother and me. He didn't take after either of us except the time he took after me with a fid and hit me over the starboard eye. He new what was to come and was smart enough to jump into Johnny Gibbs catboat, hawl in the sheet and steer for the continent. When he got to Bedford he shipped as a boat steerer on the old Falcon. I was glad he did. I don't no where he is now but I herd he was master of a steamboat runnin between Canton and

at Ezra's suggestion that the whole estate was given to the widow during her lifetime. After her death, at the age of 92, it was divided among the children, but Ezry gave his "lay" to Belindy's oldest boy, who had been named after him.—W. F. M.

Whampoa. I havent got any use for him and I guess he hasnt any use for me. The black eye he gave me is outlawed and I dont now lay anythin up agin him for that.

Item. I want mother and Jotham to settle up things as soon as they can break bulk, and make a fair divide between the children. But don't forget what I have writ down about mother and Belindy. I don't think Belindy's husband will make any fuss about the way I have taken care of her unless she runs head on the shoals of a lawyers office. Then look out for squalls. I hope sheel stand off if she sees a lawyer comin thort her bows.

Item. I want mother to have half of what comes from what is left of my property besides the house in Union street. She deserves it. Every time I was around the Horn she did her duty to the young ones and I want her to have enough to live on until she goes aloft. Then I want her lay to go to the children in equal pieces except that Belindy shall only have what comes from it until her husband dies. If mother wants to marry again thats her business. I never did like to cruise without a mate, and I guess she wouldn't like to either.

OBED GARDNER
Master Mariner

Captain Obed Gardner ast us into his porch and opened his locker. He then ast us to take a drink of rum that was fetched to him from Boston by Captain George Swain in his schooner. We done so. It was a masterly warmin to our insides. Then he pulled this paper out of his pea jacket and signed it and said it was his will and he ast us to sign it as witnesses. We done so, then he ast one of us to write down what took place and as they said I was more of a skoller than they, I did so.

JETHRO COFFIN, 2ND,
ELEASUR PADDOCK,
SHUBAEL STARBUCK.

PROVERBS AND SAYINGS

Old English Proverbs

ALL truths must not be told at all times. A handsaw is a good thing, but not to shave with. A stumble may prevent a fall. Be patient and you shall have patient children. Fair and softly goes far in a day. He who loses money loses much; he who loses a friend loses more; but he who loses his spirits loses all. At a good bargain pause a while. Good words cost nothing, but are worth much. He who says what he likes, hears what he does not like.[1]

---

[1] From *The (Old) Farmer's Almanack,* Calculated on a New and Improved Plan, for the Year of Our Lord 1871, by Robert B. Thomas, p. 40. Entered, according to Act of Congress, in the year 1870, by Brewer & Tileston, in the Office of the Librarian of Congress, at Washington. Boston.

The frost hurts not weeds.
He that goes barefoot must not plant thorns.
Get thy spindle and thy distaff ready, and God will send the flax.
Wise men are like timber trees in a hedge: here and there one.
There is small choice in rotten apples.
He that handles a nettle tenderly is soonest stung.
There's no tree but bears some fruit.
He that would have the fruit must climb the tree.
He who plants trees loves others besides himself.
If you would enjoy the fruit, pluck not the flower.[2]

The Sayings of Poor Ned

POOR Ned says, He that makes himself an ass, must not take it ill, if men ride him.

A customary railer is the devil's bagpipe, which the world danceth after.
Good dancers have mostly better heels than heads.
Half-witted people speak much and say little.
It is not a sign of humility to declaim against pride.
Man's best fortune, or his worst, is a wife.
One cannot live by selling goods for words.
When poverty comes in at the door, love creeps out at the window.

Aphorisms of Manners

IN THE lower school the morning religious instruction and exercise were followed by the recital of what we called "Manners." We even used the word in its singular form: The aphorism or injunction for which each was responsible we termed a "manner." For the searching out and the composition of his daily "manner" each child was a law unto himself; perhaps, indeed, it was the one part of the day's inflexible program which can be called entirely self-directing. We culled these "manners" from books, from parents, from memory, or in cases of the eleventh hour from our own heads; there was no rule against reasonable repetition provided the same

---

[2] From *The (Old) Farmer's Almanack,* Calculated on a New and Improved Plan, for the Year of Our Lord 1890, by Robert B. Thomas, p. 39. Entered, according to Act of Congress, in the year 1889, by William Ware, in the Office of the Librarian of Congress, at Washington. Boston.

From *The Old Farmer's Almanac,* 1795. Reprinted in *The (Old) Farmer's Almanack,* Calculated on a New and Improved Plan for the Year of Our Lord 1935, by Robert B. Thomas, p. 49. Copyright, 1934, by Carroll J. Swan. Boston.

From *A Goodly Heritage,* by Mary Ellen Chase, p. 253–254. Copyright, 1932, by Henry Holt and Company, Inc. New York.

child did not too frequently recite the same "manner" or that the same "manner" were not proffered twice on the same morning by two different children.

The philosopher, Epictetus, who objected to the laying down of rules, particularly rules of etiquette, would have been sadly annoyed at the enjoyment we derived and the glibness we displayed in this peculiar exercise. As the teacher called the roll, each child rose, stood by his seat in the prescribed position, and delivered himself of his "manner." Even the littlest were not excused. The subjects of the "manners" varied from the high affairs of ethics to the more practical concerns of decent and decorous living. A few examples will suffice to suggest their limitless scope and range. A serious, frail little girl, whose general make-up denied an ounce of drama, was given to crying out in impassioned tones, "In case of shipwreck, save the women and children first!" A fat little boy in very tight trousers, who has since become one of the financial props of Boston, furnished proof for the once popular contention concerning the New England morning meal by his reminder, repeated as often as possible and always with a suggestion of regret: "Never ask for two pieces of pie at breakfast." The most popular "manner" of a drab, prosy child, who usually remained for weeks on end at the foot of the spelling-class, echoed her mother's widespread talents as a housewife: "In sweeping a room, never forget the corners."

Hi's Got Some Great Sayings

"Yes, there used to be some great sayin's, if I could remember them all. You know Hi Minor don't you, owns the farm up off Two Mile Bridge? Hi's got some great sayin's. One of his favorites is "Just 'cause I say it's so don't make it so."

Then there was the lad who asked could he go fishin' in Hi's trout stream. "Sure you can go," says Hi, "but don't let me catch you."

Famous Sayings and Allusions

"A dead whale or a stove boat."—Motto of old Yankee whalemen.

"After their arrival, they thankfully fell upon their knees, and then fell upon the aborigines."—Ancient writer.

From "Connecticut Clockmaker," as told by Arthur Botsford, Thomaston, Connecticut, to Francis Donovan, in *Living Lore of New England*. Manuscripts of the Federal Writers' Project of the Works Progress Administration for the State of Connecticut.

For many of these sayings see Henry F. Woods, *American Sayings, Famous Phrases, Slogans and Aphorisms* (New York, 1945).

"And this is good old Boston,
   The home of the bean and the cod,
Where the Lowells talk to the Cabots,
   And the Cabots talk only to God."
                                        —John Collins Bossidy
              (Toast, Midwinter Dinner, Holy Cross Alumni, 1910)
   "As Maine goes, so goes the country."—Political maxim, 1888.
   "Boston is a state of mind."
   "Don't fire until you see the whites of their eyes."—Col. William Prescott, 1775.
   "Every one talks about the weather, but no one does anything about it."
—Charles Dudley Warner (generally attributed to Mark Twain).
   "He comes of the Brahmin caste of New England. This is the harmless, inoffensive, untitled Aristocracy."—Oliver Wendell Holmes ("The Brahmin Caste of New England," *Atlantic Monthly*, January, 1860).
   "Hitch your wagon to a star."—Ralph Waldo Emerson, "Civilization and Solitude."
   "I do not choose to run for President in 1928."—Calvin Coolidge, 1927.
   "I only regret that I have but one life to lose for my country."—Nathan Hale, 1776.
   "If you don't like the weather, wait a minute."—Mark Twain.
   "In the name of the great Jehovah and the Continental Congress."—Ethan Allen, 1775.
   "Keep cool with Coolidge."—Campaign slogan, 1924.
   "Massachusetts, there she stands."
   "No taxation without representation."—James Otis, 1765.
   "One, if by land, and two, if by sea;
And I on the opposite shore will be."
              —Henry Wadsworth Longfellow, "Paul Revere's Ride."
   "Politics makes strange bedfellows."—Charles Dudley Warner.
   "There, my boys, are your enemies, redcoats and tories. You must beat them—or Molly Stark is a widow tonight."—John Stark, 1777.
   "There's a sucker born every minute."—P. T. Barnum.

Cold Roast Boston

. . . Tom Appleton * ("the first conversationalist in America," Emerson

---

   * Thomas G. Appleton, the brother of Longfellow's wife and the son of a notable manufacturer . . . with large means and expansive tastes, was a gourmet and also a spiritualist, and a lover of purple and gold and all things edible, visible, touchable, including Persian rugs and downy sofas. A bachelor and a globe-trotter, a yachtsman and a book collector, "Tom" Appleton was the only man who could ride over Holmes and Lowell and talk them down.—Van Wyck Brooks, *New England: Indian Summer* (New York, 1940), p. 17.

testified * was famous for his "cold roast Boston," "mutual admiration society," and "good Americans when they die go to Paris"—a sentence appropriated by Holmes for his Autocrat, and still later by Wilde. . . .[1]

During the years of the Second Empire, Paris had had all the prestige. Americans had praised everything French and were rather inclined to slight everything English. . . . This was the moment of T. G. Appleton's phrase, "All good Americans, when they die, go to Paris." [2]

It was Appleton who said of the [Boston art] museum—the building replaced in 1908—that, if architecture was "frozen music," this was "frozen Yankee Doodle." [3]

Appleton said if it was true God tempers the wind [to the shorn lamb], he wished somebody would tether a shorn lamb on the steps of Park Street Church.[4]

STORIES IN BYWORDS

Better Have Paid Your Washwoman

. . . I REMEMBER that even when the danger was worst, we found room for joking and one of our men cried out, "Better have paid your washwoman!" That is the usual gibe when a man is caught in a stoven boat, for there is a belief among whalers that if you don't pay your washwoman you'll suffer the penalty of getting your boat smashed.

Boston Folks Are Full of Notions

THIS saying, now world-wide, came around in this way. The Narragansett Indians were many of them mechanics. Many are good stone masons and

---

* Julia Ward Howe, *Reminiscences* (Boston, 1889), p. 432.

[1] From *Amy Lowell*, by S. Foster Damon, p. 101. Copyright, 1935, by S. Foster Damon. Boston and New York: Houghton Mifflin Co.

[2] From *New England: Indian Summer, 1865–1915*, by Van Wyck Brooks, p. 286 and note. Copyright, 1940, by Van Wyck Brooks. New York: E. P. Dutton & Co., Inc.

[3] *Ibid.*, p. 164 n.

[4] From *Yankee from Olympus*, by Catherine Drinker Bowen, p. 191. Copyright, 1943, 1944, by Catherine Drinker Bowen. Boston: Little, Brown and Company.

From *The Gam*, Being a Group of Whaling Stories, by Capt. Charles Henry Robbins, Who Gratefully Acknowledges the Editorial Suggestions of his Friend, Mr. Rollin Lynde Hartt, p. 67. Copyright, 1899, by Lizzie Pope Robbins. New Bedford: H. S. Hutchinson & Company.

From "Notes on Narragansett," by Joseph P. Hazard, in *The Narragansett Historical Register*, A Magazine Devoted to the Antiquities, Genealogy and Historical Matter Illustrating the History of the Narragansett Country, or Southern Rhode Island, Vol. I (January, 1883), No. 3, edited by James N. Arnold, pp. 225–226. Entered according to Act of Congress, in the year 1882, by the Narragansett Historical Publishing Company, in the Office of the Librarian of Congress, at Washington. Hamilton, Rhode Island.

stone cutters. One whose name was pronounced "Bosum sided" was a watch maker, and after he married he set up business at Indiantown, Charlestown. He died about 1830. One was a tinker and used to make annual excursions to Boston in the spring for the purpose of plying his vocation. He went down one spring and returned after a very brief visit. He was silent as to why he did not stay longer. Another of the tribe, happening in Boston, learned that he had been caught stealing, and had been whipped at the cart's tail through the town, and a polite and emphatic invitation given him to leave, which he had thankfully received. Of course when he came home he told his story and the tribe became eager to learn the facts from the culprit himself. On being asked about it he gave no other information than "Boston folks are full of notions."

Ethan Allen's Saying

[ETHAN ALLEN] DELIGHTED in words. His use of the vernacular was the joy of those who in his lifetime heard him, is still the joy of those who hear his spoken words repeated. . . .

* * * * *

Ethan Allen had built a cow-shed, so the story goes. Nobody in Sunderland was surprised when it turned out a foot or more too short. A neighbor asked him, "Did you mean to make it that way?" Allen inquired, "What's the matter with it?" The neighbor explained that a considerable part of the animal's anatomy would be exposed to the weather. Allen, with a wave of his big hand, said, good-naturedly:

> "What's a drop of water
> On a damn cow's rump?"

When I was young it was not nice to say "damn" or "rump," so the story was not quoted in general company. Yet it was often used. When an irritable housewife scolded about mud brought in on the kitchen floor, when a fussy grandfather was disagreeable about an ax left on the damp ground instead of struck into the chopping block, someone asked with the deceptively naïve intonation which in Vermont is often used for irony, "What's a drop of water—" and needed to say no more.

From *Vermont Tradition,* The Biography of an Outlook on Life, by Dorothy Canfield Fisher, pp. 140–141, 143. Copyright, 1953, by Dorothy Canfield Fisher. Boston: Reprinted by permission of Little, Brown and Company.

Kilroy Was Here

On Dec. 5, 1941, I started to work for Bethlehem Steel Company, Fore River Ship Yard, Quincy, Mass., as a rate-setter. . . . I started my new job with enthusiasm, carefully surveying every inner bottom and tank before issuing a contract. I was thoroughly upset to find that practically every test leader I met wanted me to go down and look over his job with him, and when I explained to him that I had seen the job and could not spare the time to crawl through one of these tanks again with him, he would accuse me of not having looked the job over.

I was getting sick of being accused of not looking the jobs over and one day, as I came through the manhole of a tank I had just surveyed, I angrily marked with yellow crayon on the tank top, where the testers could see it, "KILROY WAS HERE." The following day a test gang leader approached me with a grin on his face and said, "I see you looked my job over."

Mind Your Orts

In the vocabulary of this Billerica of ours, and in secluded farming districts of New England, the casual visitor marks occasional quaint phrases now obsolete in England. At the old homestead farm on Thanksgiving day the white-haired house-mother—gentlewoman to her finger-tips—having heaped some twenty plates with turkey and "fixins," seizes the golden opportunity to inculcate a bit of thrift and table manners into the lively mind of her youngest grandson with her mother's early precept: "Look out for your *orts,* sonny, look out for your *orts,* then Grandma'll give you a piece of mince-pie!" The city boy's mother has to translate the queer word to her little son telling him that it means that the *odds and ends* left upon his plate must be duly swallowed. The expressive Yankee exclamation, "Oh dear me, suz!" is, in the original, "Oh dear me, sorrows!"

By James J. Kilroy, Halifax, Mass., in *The New York Times Magazine,* Jan. 12, 1947, p. 30.

Oh, Rinehart!

"HEADS out!" was the cry in Walker's day; "Oh, Rineheart!" began later, after a student of that name had repeatedly been shouted to by noisy friends. In course of time it has become a sort of Harvard battle-cry, and the word is now used to describe any Yard uproar, in which the calling of Mr. Rineheart's undying name is an inevitable feature. The story is told that a Harvard graduate, pestered by touts in the courtyard of Shepheard's Hotel, Cairo, called "Oh, Rineheart!" and was presently answered in the same kind from four or five windows, whose occupants then helped him to disperse the beggars.

Pick Up Your Feet

A VERY common admonition from one sawyer to another in this country is, "Pick up your feet, will you?" That is probably meaningless to the uninitiate, but a good sawyer resents it very much. It means that his partner is saying that he doesn't mind riding him back and forth with every stroke of the saw, but he does consider it unnecessary to have to drag his feet along the ground, too. It's the obscure local way of telling a man he's bearing down on his end of the saw and it's an implication that he doesn't know his trade.

From *Old Paths and Legends of New England,* Saunterings Over Historic Roads with Glimpses of Picturesque Fields and Old Homesteads in Massachusetts, Rhode Island, and New Hampshire, by Katharine M. Abbott, p. 123. Copyright, 1903, by Katharine M. Abbott. New York and London: G. P. Putnam's Sons. 1904.

From *Three Centuries of Harvard,* 1636–1936, by Samuel Eliot Morison, p. 300 n. Copyright, 1936, by the President and Fellows of Harvard College. Cambridge, Massachusetts. Harvard University Press.
I am indebted to Jane E. Howard, Assistant to the Editor of the *Harvard Alumni Bulletin,* for the following note on Rinehart: "Although the *Bulletin* did print a story on Rinehart, that particular card disappeared some time ago and we have been unable to trace it, even by thumbing through back volumes. At the time the story was printed I made a note in my own handbook. The correct spelling is 'Rinehart.' The man for whom it was first called is John Brice Gordon Rinehart, '00, LL.B. '03, c/o Jesse Rinehart, RFD 62, Waynesburg, Pa. The [Harvard] Archives have a clipping from the Boston *Sunday Journal* of June 24, 1900, telling of the original episode. . . . We also have a clipping from the New York *Sun,* 9-24-36, naming this same man. I know at the time we made our research we verified it carefully." For a similar battle-cry of University of California students, see "Pedro! Pedro!", by Archer Taylor, *Western Folklore,* Vol. VI (July, 1947), No. 3, pp. 228–231.

From *We Took to the Woods,* by Louise Dickinson Rich, pp. 73–74. Copyright, 1942, by Louise Dickinson Rich. Philadelphia and New York: J. B. Lippincott Company.

"Sock Saunders" Sayings

THE only stories that are told are woods gossip. Nobody ever heard of Paul Bunyan. The nearest thing to him is Sock Saunders, who is more of a poltergeist than a hero. If a man drops a picaroon into the river he says, "Well, take it, Sock Saunders!" If he slips on a log, but catches himself in time, he says, "Foxed you that time, Sock Saunders." If he cuts his foot, he explains, "Sock Saunders got me." There are no stories about Sock Saunders. He's just the guy who hangs around and makes life complicated.

Ibid., p. 197.

PART FIVE

SONGS AND RHYMES

*There were popular ballads and folk songs . . .
sailors' chanties along the coast, ballads of village
murders, rockaby songs, sugar-makers' songs, sung
by weavers and carpenters, by farm-wives and wandering fiddlers, by hunters, trappers, guides, and
lumbermen, snatches and refrains and longer pieces,
brought over from the old world or natural out-
growths of the American soil. . . . Catch a "real,
green, live Yankee," as Father Taylor liked to say,
and you always caught a man who could sing a song,
especially on the seacoast.*
—VAN WYCK BROOKS

*All over New England, from Cape Cod to the Green
Hills, the youngsters have kept in their singing
games the craft songs and country dances of a forgotten background of the New England colonist.*
—ELOISE HUBBARD LINSCOTT

*. . . here are tinkling fiddle tunes that have sent
thousands of merry feet dancing down the rough
pioneering paths of New England—despite lurking
Redskin or Puritan divine.*
—JAMES M. CARPENTER

*The tradition of a folk song begins when some one,
for pleasure's sake, sings a song from memory . . .
whoever sings a song from memory, let it be Child
ballad or Tin Pan Alley ditty, it matters not, becomes a folk-singer. . . . Changes in the text and
air of a ballad, often infinitesimal, but at times
appreciable even to the layman, will emerge as expressions of the singer's mood for the time being.
Some may be permanent, others evanescent. . . .
Yet not alone of the solitary type of singer is folk
song the possession. Its social aspects appear
wherever a group are gathered together, conserving
the elements of the primitive "folk"—congeniality,
freedom from care, and light-heartedness—hunters
and trappers around a camp-fire, it may be, or railway laborers in a box-car on a wet night.*
—PHILLIPS BARRY

I. BALLADS AND SONGS

"I'm not what you'd call a regular singer, you know, for I never learned by book nor never saw nothin' writ down, But . . . I've allus sung just 'cause I can't help it. My father was the same way and my grandfather too. Guess you'd call us of the old school of singing."—JAMES ATWOOD to EDITH B. STURGIS

. . . here are songs to suit almost every palate: semipopular songs treasured up by past generations; comical songs; songs of the read-'em-and-weep variety; quaint old minstrels; lumbermen's songs; sea chanteys; songs with a strictly New England flavor—one can all but hear the Yankee nasal twang; and finally, a fair number of child ballads, "the aristrocrats of folk song."
—JAMES M. CARPENTER

1. YANKEE SONGS AND SINGERS

IT IS told of a Yankee singing master that he " 'set up' in a town way down east as a cobbler! On his sign, under the announcement of his profession, as a provider for the wants of the bodily understanding, was the following choice couplet, setting forth [that], as a musician, he did not neglect to provide also for the wants of the mental.

> Delightful task! to mend the tender boot,
> And teach the young idea how to flute!" [1]

This musical cobbler was typical of the New England singing craftsmen who worked with both hand and brain. The folk music tradition—homespun and rural—fitted into the Yankee pattern of neighborly work and useful pleasure. And wherever the Yankee went, New Englandizing the country, he carried with him, not only the little red schoolhouse and the white meeting-house, but also the old-time songs and the old-time singing that were so closely identified with them. New England psalmody and hymnody were the foundation of our musical culture. But it took the Yankee singing master to break a psalm-singing folk of the "Bay Psalm Book" rote practice of lining-out or deaconing (reading a line before singing it) and to teach rural folk everywhere the art of singing not only by rule but for enjoyment and entertainment as well as for prayer.

At first, it is true, the singing school and society set themselves sternly, with Cotton Mather, against the "foolish Songs and Ballads, which the

---

[1] Augusta Brown, Cincinnati *Musician and Intelligencer*, Vol. II (1848), No. 1, pp. 21 ff. Cited by George Pullen Jackson in *White Spirituals of the Southern Uplands* (Chapel Hill, 1933), p. 20.

Hawkers and Pedlars carry into all parts of the Countrye." [1] But it was not long before singing masters like "Father" Robert Kemp, the retired shoe-dealer of Wellfleet and organizer of the Reading Old Folks Musical Society and the Old Folks Concert Troupe, yielded to the demands of popular taste and gave ballad concerts. It was Father Kemp, too, who included in *Father Kemp's Old Folks Concert Tunes* the "devil's ditty" of "Captain Kidd," thus forging another link in the chain of ballad diffusion.

But the folk song tradition is nothing if not catholic, and there has always been much borrowing back and forth between sacred and secular music. In accordance with the realization of revivalists and hymn-writers like Wesley that "It is a pity that the Devil has all the good tunes," "Captain Kidd" became a favorite hymn tune. By the same token, the folk did not forget their hymnals when they looked for tunes for their ballads; and "Springfield Mountain" was originally sung to "Old Hundred."

Ballad concerts, in which Father Kemp had been preceded by the Hutchinson family and in which the latter had many imitators, such as the Baker family, thus became an important medium of folk song transmission along with the singing school and society; along with the despised book-peddler and his song-sheets and garlands; and along with print and performance generally. For folk song lives not by the oral tradition alone; the folk memory is preserved in carefully compiled and treasured manuscript books and newspaper-clipping scrapbooks of old songs, of which the vest-pocket songster is the commercial equivalent.

The Hutchinsons and other singing families and troupes performed another important service for New England (and American) folk song and folklore. They helped to diffuse, as well as to create, the tradition of the "Yankee song." This was the comic, fabulous, and slightly nostalgic tradition of "Away Down East"—

> a land of notions, of apple sauce and greens
> A paradise of pumpkin pies, a land of pork and beans.

"Yankee land" is our first regional myth of a land of milk and honey, just as the fabulous Yankee is our first hero-legend. And because "Yankee land" combined the Yankee zest for the good earth and its abundance (which includes the ambrosia of Narragansett corn-meal and the nectar of Maine lobster stew) with the golden age of childhood ("I wish I was in Yankee land, And was a boy again, sirs: I'd suck sweet cider thro' a straw, And fish in ev'ry rain, sirs"), and somehow got mixed up with the American "go-ahead" spirit of whittling Yankee "bo-hoys" and spinning Yankee "gals," of Yankee skill and perseverance and "Yankee manufactures," it has been basic to our whole national tradition. To Yankees up and down the land Yankee songs (sung with the "Yankee" Hill nasal twang) were like a letter from the folks back home and a letter to the world, testifying more eloquently than perhaps any other type of folk song or folklore to New England's legacy to the rest of the country, just as the old English and Scottish ballads and ballad-speech testified to the

---

[1] *Reasonableness of Regular Singing, or Singing by Note* (1720). Cited by Williard Hallam Bonner, *Private Laureate: the Life and Legends of Captain Kidd* (New Brunswick, 1947), p. 100; which also see (pp. 107–109) for Father Kemp.

British heritage. The tradition of a land where "the girls are pretty and the cattle very fat" also served to offset the tradition of a hard land of snow and mountains and

> the land of Blue Laws where deacons cut their hair
> For fear their locks and tenants [tenets?] will not exactly square,

(in the twitting words of "Michigania").

Curiously, the Yankee peddler does not figure prominently in Yankee songs. The song of "The Connecticut Peddler" is of the imitative street-cry variety, cataloguing the peddler's wares:

> Here are pins,
> Papers and needles and pins,
> Tracts upon popular sins,
> Any of which I will sell you.
>
> And here are the seeds of asparagus,
> Lettuce, beets, onions, and peppergrass
> From the Limited Society,
> Seeds of all kinds and variety.[1]

Somehow all this sounds bookish and spurious and un-comic. The Yankee peddler seems to have flourished not in songs but in anecdotes and yarns, perhaps because Yankee stories are at home on a journey and in the gossipy environment of the village store and tavern; and perhaps also because the cheating miller had already beat the peddler to it as the favorite folk-song rogue.

2. Songs of the Sea and the Woods

The vogue of the sea song (thanks to Charles Dibdin) had already established itself in British popular tradition before the China and India trade, whaling, the War of 1812, the packet-ship and the clipper made the Yankee and the Bostonian synonymous with sea daring and adventure and naval strength. But the Yankee gave the chantey his characteristic stamp of "wooden ships and iron men," of the humor and protest of "Boston":

> We poor sailors standing on the deck,
> With the blasted rain all a-pouring down our necks;
> Not a drop of grog would he to us afford,
> But he damns our eyes with every other word.
>
> And one thing which we have to crave
> Is that he may have a watery grave,
> So we'll heave him into some dark hole,
> Where the sharks'll have his body and the
>   devil have his soul.[2]

---

[1] John A. Lomax and Alan Lomax, *American Ballads and Folk Songs* (New York, 1934), pp. 317–318.

[2] *A Treasury of American Folklore* (New York, 1944), pp. 831–832.

The sea and the War of 1812 gave us some of our best songs of freedom, like the swaggering *"Constitution and the Guerrière"* and "Ye Parliament of England," the latter with its ringing defiance:

Ye Parliament of England,   You're now to fight with Yankees,
   You lords and commons, too,   I'm sure you'll rue the day
Consider well what you're about,   You roused the sons of liberty
   And what you're going to do;   In North America.

In these two naval ballads, the Yankee sounded the two characteristic notes of his patriotic songs; the droll bravura of "Yankee Doodle" and the noble challenge of "Chester" (William Billings' song, which, according to John Tasker Howard, "became the 'Over There' of the Revolution" [1]).

The naval songs of the War of 1812 became part of the repertoire of the singing sailor as "forecastle" (recreational) songs and even of the singing lumberjack, whose songs differed from the sailor's in that they were all recreational (bunkhouse) songs. And like the sailor in his forecastle songs, the shanty-boy derived many of his tunes from Irish-come-all-ye's, which suited the double common metre of his verse.

As the shanty-boy followed the lumber industry, his songs traveled from Maine to the Northwest, with resultant changes, adaptations, and additions paralleling the development of imported English and Irish songs. So the history of the Yankee's western migration may be traced in his song history. In New Englandizing the country the Yankee Americanized his songs.

                                             B. A. B.

OLD AND NEW ENGLAND

Cape Ann

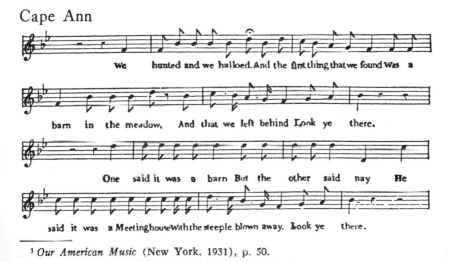

We hunted and we halloed. And the first thing that we found Was a barn in the meadow, And that we left behind Look ye there. One said it was a barn But the other said nay He said it was a Meetinghouse with the steeple blown away. Look ye there.

---

[1] *Our American Music* (New York, 1931), p. 50.

From *Songs of the Hutchinson Family*, No. 4. New York: Published by Firth & Hall

We hunted and we halloed,
And the first thing that we found,
Was a barn in the meadow,
And that we left behind.
    Look ye there!
One said it was a barn,
But the other said nay;
He said it was a Meetinghouse,
With the steeple blown away.
    Look ye there!

So we hunted and we halloed,
And the next thing we did find,
Was the Moon in the element,
And that we left behind.
    Look ye there!
One said it was the Moon,
But the other said nay;
He said it was a Yankee cheese,
With the one half cut away.
    Look ye there!

So we hunted and we halloed,
And the next thing we did find,
Was a frog in the Mill pond;
And that we left behind.
    Look ye there!

One said it was a frog,
But the other said nay;
He said it was a canary bird,
With its feathers washed away.
    Look ye there!

So we hunted and we halloed,
And the next thing we did find,
Was the light house in Cape Ann;
And that we left behind.
    Look ye there!
One said it was the light house,
But the other said nay,
He said it was a sugar loaf;
With the paper blown away.
    Look ye there!

So we hunted and we halloed,
And the last thing we did find,
Was the owl in the olive bush;
And that we left behind.
    Look ye there!
One said it was an owl;
But the other said nay,
He said it was the Evil One;
And we all three ran away.
    Look ye there!

---

and J. L. Hewitt & Co. [1843.] In *Series of Old American Songs,* Reproduced in Facsimile from Original or Early Editions in the Harris Collection of American Poetry and Plays, with Brief Annotations, by S. Foster Damon, Curator, No. 33. Providence, Rhode Island: Brown University Library. 1936.

The first recorded singing of "Cape Ann" occurred in a play of which Shakespeare himself wrote a part. In Act III, scene 5 of *The Two Noble Kinsman,* the crazed daughter of the jailor sings:

> "There was three fools, fell out about an howlet:
>   The one sed it was an owl
>   The other he sed nay,
> The third he sed it was a hawk, and her bels were cut away."

Evidently it was already a familiar ballad.

Between the time when Ann of Denmark was the British queen, and the time when the song localized itself about the North Shore cape in Massachusetts, which bore her name, the ballad travelled far and wide. The *Journal of American Folk Lore* (XXVII, 72) in 1908 said that seventy years before, it was an old circus song sung by Alabama negroes. To the Flanders and Brown *Vermont Folk Songs and Ballads* Dorothy Canfield Fisher contributed the version her mother sang.

"Cape Ann" was published in 1843, the year that the Hutchinson Family first sang in New York. This famous family was the leading exemplar of the quartets and quintets that soon were touring the States. Revivers of ballads and composers, as well as vocalists, they did much to spread Yankee culture.—S. F. D.

Old Colony Times

In good old Col-o-ny times When we were under the
king Three roguish chaps fell in-to mishaps, Because they could not sing Be - - cause they could not
sing Be - - cause they could not sing Three
roguish chaps, fell in-to mishaps, Be-cause they could not sing.

In good old Colony times,
  When we were under the king,
Three roguish chaps fell into mishaps,
  Because they could not sing,
  Because they could not sing,
  Because they could not sing.
Three roguish chaps, fell into mishaps,
  Because they could not sing.

The first he was a Miller,
  And the second he was a Weaver,
And the third he was, a little Tailor,
  Three roguish chaps together.

Now the Miller he stole corn,
  And the Weaver he stole yarn,
And the little Tailor, stole broadcloth for,
  To keep these three rogues warm.

The Miller got drown'd in his dam,
  The Weaver got hung in his yarn,
And the devil clapp'd his claw on the little Tailor,
  With the broadcloth under his arm.

Boston: Published by Parker & Ditson. In *Series of Old American Songs*, Reproduced in Facsimile from Original or Early Editions in the Harris Collection of American Poetry and Plays, with Brief Annotations, by S. Foster Damon, Curator, No. 6. Providence, Rhode Island: Brown University Library. 1936.

This ballad may have preceded even the first attempts at colonization in our country; but the opening lines of this version, sung from Maine to Georgia, and at least as far west as Nebraska, were probably shaped about 1800, when "old colony times" began to seem very remote.

When John Lothrop Motley studied at Göttingen in 1832, he taught this song, one of his favorites, to his fellow student, Bismarck. Over fifty years later, in a speech before the Reichstag on February 6, 1888, Bismarck quoted "Old Colony Times," which he had learned from his "dear deceased friend," Motley. (Orie William Long: *Literary Pioneers,* Cambridge, 1935). This song is sung by the archbishop in Agnes Repplier's *In Our Convent Days;* and in Hardy's *Under the Greenwood Tree* (Pt. IV, ch. 2) it is also to be found, beginning, however, "When Arthur first his court began."

Over There

Oh! po-ta-toes they grow small O-ver there! Oh! po-

ta-toes they grow small O ver there! Oh! po-

ta-toes they grow small 'Cause they plant 'em in the fall, And then

eats 'em tops and all O-ver there.____

Oh! potatoes they grow small
  Over there!
Oh! potatoes they grow small
  Over there!
Oh! potatoes they grow small,
'Cause they plant 'em in the fall,
And then eats 'em tops and all
  Over there!
	Oh! the candles they are small
	  Over there!
	Oh! the candles they are small
	  Over there!
	Oh! the candles they are small,
	For they dips 'em lean and tall,
	And then burns 'em sticks and all,
	  Over there!

Where sheep were raised, the "miller" ran a carding mill (see Flanders & Brown's *Vermont Folk Songs*, "The Farmer's Three Sons"). In the colleges, the tune was once much used for less familiar texts (*Journal Am. Folk-Lore*, XXIX, 167; see also XXXV, 350; XLV, 47).—S. F. D.

From *In Old New England*, The Romance of a Colonial Fireside, by Hezekiah Butterworth, pp. 233–234. Copyright, 1895, by D. Appleton and Company. New York. Tune from *"The Wonderful Song of Over There,"* Entered according to Act of Congress in the Year 1844, by J. F. Atwill in the Clerk's Office of the Southern District of New York, in *Series of Old American Songs*, Reproduced in Facsimile from Original or Early Editions in the Harris Collection of American Poetry and Plays, with Brief Annotations, by S. Foster Damon, Curator, No. 42. Providence, Rhode Island: Brown University Library. 1936.

This "wonderful song" is the prototype of "The Cows Fly High" and many another fantasia. How it originated remains a mystery as yet. It will be noted that the tune is not the insidious "Captain Kyd," which has come to replace it too often.—S. F. D.

Oh! I wish I was a geese,
  All forlorn!
Oh! I wish I was a geese,
  All forlorn!
Oh! I wish I was a geese,
'Cause they lives and dies in peace,
And accumulates much grease
  Eating corn!

Oh! they had a clam pie
  Over there!
Oh! they had a clam pie
  Over there!
Oh! they had a clam pie,
And the crust was made of rye—
You must eat it, or must die,
  Over there!

Away Down East

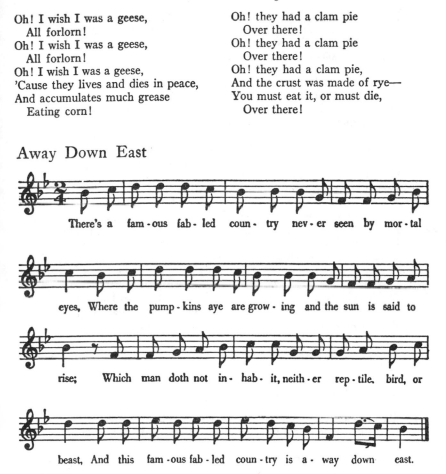

There's a fam-ous fab-led coun-try nev-er seen by mor-tal
eyes, Where the pump-kins aye are grow-ing and the sun is said to
rise; Which man doth not in-hab-it, neith-er rep-tile, bird, or
beast, And this fam-ous fab-led coun-try is a-way down east.

From *Songs of Yesterday*, A Song Anthology of American Life, by Philip D. Jordan and Lillian Kessler, pp. 185–188. Copyright, 1941, by Philip D. Jordan and Lillian Kessler. Garden City, New York: Doubleday, Doran & Co., Inc.

"Down east" is variously interpreted as New England, eastern or northeastern New England, Maine, the easternmost part of Maine, Nova Scotia, and New Brunswick. The following comment is almost a paraphrase of the song:

"The first-comers into New England waters were not more puzzled to find the ancient city of Norumbega than I to reach the fabulous Down East of the moderns. In San Francisco the name is vaguely applied to the territory east of the Mississippi, though more frequently the rest of the republic is alluded to as 'The States.' South of the obliterated Mason and Dixon's line, the region east of the Alleghanies and north of the Potomac is Down East, and no mistake about it. In New York you are as far as ever from this *terra incognita*. In Connecticut they shrug their shoulders and point you about north-north-east. Down East, say Massachusetts people, is just across our eastern border. Arrived on the Penobscot, I fancied myself there at last.

'Whither bound?' I asked of a fisherman, getting up his foresail before loosing from the wharf.

There's a famous fabled country never seen by mortal eyes,
Where the pumpkins aye are growing and the sun is said to rise;
Which man doth not inhabit, neither reptile, bird, or beast,
And this famous fabled country is away down [1] east.

It is called a land of notions, of apple sauce and greens,
A paradise of pumpkin pies, a land of pork and beans;
But where it is, who knoweth? neither mortal man nor beast,
But one thing we're assured of 'tis away down east.

Once a man in Indiana took his bundle in his hand,
And he came to New York city to seek this fabled land;
But how he stares on learning what is new to him at least
That this famous fabled country is farther down east.

Then away he posts for Boston with all his main and might,
And he puts up at the Tremont house, quite sure that all is right;
But they tell him in the morning a curious fact at least,
That he hasn't yet begun to get away down east.

Then he hurries off to Portland with his bundle in his hand,
And he sees Mount-joy, great joy for him for this must be the land;
Poh, nonsense, man, you're crazy, for doubt not in the least,
You'll go a long chalk farther e'er you find down east.

Then away through mud to Bangor, by which he soils his drabs,
The first that greets his vision is a pyramid of slabs;
Why this, says he, is Egypt, here's a pyramid at least,
And he thought that with a vengeance he has found down east.

My gracious, yes, he's found it, see how he cuts his pranks,
He's sure he can't get farther for the piles of boards and planks;
So pompously he questions a Pat of humble caste
Who tells him he was never yet away down east.

But soon he spies a native who was up to snuff I ween,
Who pointing o'er a precipice says don't you see something green.
Then off he jump'd to rise no more except he lives on yeast,
And this I think should be his drink away down east.

'Sir, to you. Down East.'
The evident determination to shift the responsibility forbade further pursuit of this fictitious land. Besides, Maine people are indisposed to accept without challenge the name so universally applied to them of Down Easters. We do not say down to the North Pole, and we do say down South. The higher latitude we make northwardly the farther down we get. Nevertheless, disposed as I avow myself to present the case fairly, the people of Maine uniformly say 'up to the westward,' when speaking of Massachusetts. Of one thing I am persuaded—Down East is nowhere in New England."
(Samuel Adams Drake, *Nooks and Corners of the New England Coast*, New York, 1875, pp. 85–86.)
[1] Sometimes pronounced daown.—P. D. J.

And now his anxious mother, whose tears will ever run,
Is ever on the look out to see her rising son;
But she may strain her eyes in vain, I calculate at least,
Her son has set in regions wet away down east.

Yankee Manufactures

I wish I was in Yankee land,
  And was a boy again, sirs:
I'd suck sweet cider thro' a straw,
  And fish in ev'ry rain, sirs.
I'd never wander from my home
  To visit other lands, sure,
But stay at home, eat pumpkin pie
  Of Yankee manufacture.

Chorus:
  Oh, diddle, daddle, diddle,
  Diddle, daddle, diddle, daddle,
  Dad di do.

The people there all go ahead,
  They never turn about, sirs,
And when the bo-hoys go on a spree,
  Their Mammies know they're out,
    sirs.

The gals can read and write and spin,
  Are modest, chaste, and fair, sure.
No other land has got such gals
  As of Yankee manufacture.

I love the Yankees for their skill,
  Their perseverance too, sirs.
Their railroads and their telegraphs,
  Show what their sons can do, sirs;
And Oregon, like Texas,
  The Yankees they will have, sure,
Or Johnny Bull will get some pills,
  Of Yankee manufacture.

Now Johnny Bull a lesson got,
  Which I hope he has not forgotten,
For Jackson brave at New Orleans
  Showed him the use of Yankee cot-
    ton.

Ibid., pp. 192–194.

Their Packenham he did brag,
  And his army they did blow, sure,
But British balls could not penetrate,
  The walls of Yankee manufacture.

There is a spot near Boston town,
  They call it Bunker Hill, sir,

Where Johnny Bull with Yankee lead.
  Did get his stomach filled, sir.
'Twas there brave General Warren
  fell,
  In freedom's glorious cause, sure,
Yet we had left Great Washington,
  Who was of Yankee manufacture.

HYMNS OF FAITH AND FREEDOM

Chester

Let tyrants shake their iron rod,
  And Slav'ry clank her galling chains,
We fear them not, we trust in God,
  New England's God for ever reigns.

Howe and Burgoyne and Clinton,
  too,
  With Prescott and Cornwallis join'd,
Together plot our overthrow,
  In one Infernal league combin'd.

When God inspir'd us for the fight,
  Their ranks were broke, their lines
  were forc'd,
Their Ships were shatter'd in our sight,
  Or swiftly driven from our Coast.

The Foe comes on with haughty Stride,
  Our troops advance with martial
  noise

From *The Singing Master's Assistant: or Key to Practical Music:* Being an abridgment from "The New England-Psalm Singer," together with several other tunes never before published, composed by William Billings, author of "The New-England Psalm-Singer," p. 12. Boston: Draper and Folsom. 1778.

Their Vet'rans flee before our Youth,
And Gen'rals yield to beardless
Boys.

What grateful Off'ring shall we bring,
What shall we render to the Lord?
Loud Hallelujahs let us Sing,
And praise his name on ev'ry Chord.

Free America

That seat of science, Athens,
And earth's proud mistress, Rome;
Where now are all their glories?
We scarce can find a tomb.
Then guard your rights, Americans,
Nor stoop to lawless sway,
Oppose, oppose, oppose,
For North America.

We led fair Franklin hither,
And, lo! the desert smiled;
A paradise of pleasure
Was opened to the world!
Your harvest, bold Americans,
No power shall snatch away!
Huzza, huzza, huzza,
For free America.

From *Heart Songs*, Dear to the American People and by Them Contributed in the Search for Treasured Songs Initiated by the *National Magazine*, pp. 44–45. Copyright, 1909, by The Chapple Publishing Company, Ltd. Boston.

By voice, sword and pen, Joseph Warren contributed to the cause of Independence. In 1772 and 1775, he delivered orations on the Boston Massacre. During the delivery of the second oration, the British soldiery lined the pulpit stairs, but nevertheless it

Torn from a world of tyrants,
　Beneath this western sky,
We formed a new dominion,
　A land of liberty.
The world shall own we're masters
　　here;
　Then hasten on the day:
Huzza, huzza, huzza,
　For free America.

Proud Albion bowed to Caesar,
　And numerous lords before;
To Picts, to Danes, to Normans,
　And many masters more;
But we can boast, Americans,
　We've never fallen a prey;
Huzza, huzza, huzza,
　For free America.

God bless this maiden climate,
　And through its vast domain
May hosts of heroes cluster,
　Who scorn to wear a chain:

And blast the venal sycophant
　That dares our rights betray;
Huzza, huzza, huzza,
　For free America.

Lift up your heads, ye heroes,
　And swear with proud disdain
The wretch that would ensnare you
　Shall lay his snares in vain;
Should Europe empty all her force,
　We'll meet her in array,
And fight and shout, and fight
　For free America.

Some future day shall crown us
　The masters of the main.
Our fleets shall speak in thunder
　To England, France and Spain;
And the nations o'er the oceans spread
　Shall tremble and obey
The sons, the sons, the sons,
　Of brave America.

Ballad of the Tea Party

Tea-ships near to Boston lying,
　On the wharf a numerous crew,
Sons of Freedom, never dying,
　Then appeared in view!
With a rinktum, dinktum, fa la link-
　　tum,
　Then appeared in view!

Armed with hammers, axes, chisels,
　Weapons new for warlike deed,
Toward the taxéd, freighted vessels,
　On they came with speed.

Deep into the sea descended
　Curséd weed of China's coast,
Thus at once our fears were ended,
　Rights shall ne'er be lost!

---

was pronounced in defiance of their threats. Not long, it is thought, before his lamented
death, he wrote the above ballad.—Joe Mitchell Chapple.
　The tune is that of "The British Grenadiers" (16th century).

From *Early American Ballads*, sung by John and Lucy Allison, with Chorus, Key-
note Album K-102, Record 535-B, 1. New York: Keynote Recordings, Inc. Leaflet
Copyright, 1943, by Keynote Recordings, Inc. Transcribed by Frances Kurland.
　Colonial folk turned out many jingles commemorating the so-called Boston Tea
Party. This one truly belonged to the people.—J. A.

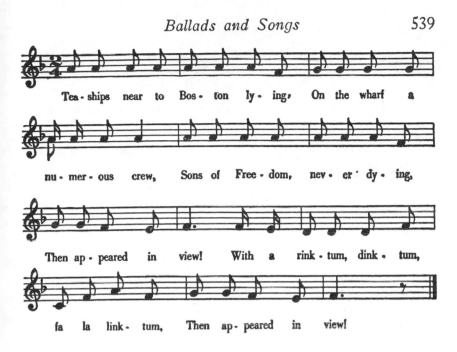

Tea-ships near to Bos-ton ly-ing, On the wharf a
nu-mer-ous crew, Sons of Free-dom, nev-er dy-ing,
Then ap-peared in view! With a rink-tum, dink-tum,
fa la link-tum, Then ap-peared in view!

The Boston Tea Tax

I snum [1] I am a Yankee lad,
   And I guess I'll sing a ditty;
And if you do not relish it,
   There more 'twill be the pity;
That is, I think I should have been
   A plaguey sight more finished man
If I'd been born in Boston town,
   But I warn't 'cause I'm a country-
   man.
Tol-le-lol-de-riddle, tol-le-lol-de-ray,
   But I warn't 'cause I'm a country-
   man.

And t'other day the Yankee folks
   Were mad about the taxes,
And so we went like Injuns dressed
   To split tea chests with axes.
It was the year of seventy-three,
   And we felt really gritty.
The Mayor he would have led the
   gang,
   But Boston warn't a city!

[You see we Yankees didn't care
   A pin for wealth or booty,

From *Ballads of the American Revolution and the War of 1812*, A Program of Early American Songs Taken from the Collection of John Allison, sung by John and Lucy Allison with Sawyer's Minuteman, Victor Album P-11, Record 26458-B, 2. Camden, New Jersey: RCA Victor Division, RCA Manufacturing Company, Inc. Transcribed by Frances Kurland.
   Written "in the style of a Yankee colonial wit," this song dates from the 1830's.
   Cf. George Stuyvesant Jackson, *Early Songs of Uncle Sam* (Boston, 1933), p. 46: Any character who said "tarnal," "snum," and "plaguey" was a true blue Yankee.
   The words of this song have been set by Mr. Allison to a traditional tune. The additional stanzas (in brackets) are from Burton L. Stevenson's *Poems of American History* (Boston, 1908).
   [1] Swear, declare, vow; *vum, swow, swan.*—Harold Wentworth, *American Dialect Dictionary* (New York, 1944), p. 575.

I—— snum I am a—— Yan-kee lad, And I
guess I'll sing a dit-ty; And—— if you do not
re-lish it, The more 'twill be the pi-ty; That——
is, I think I should have been A pla-guey sight more
fin-ished man If——I'd been born in Bos-ton town, But I
warn't 'cause I'm a coun-try-man. Tol-le-lol-de-rid-dle, Tol-le-
lol-de-ray, But I warn't 'cause I'm a coun-try-man.

And so in State Street we agreed
  We'd never pay the duty;
That is, in State Street 'twould have
    been,
  But 'twas King Street they called it
    then,
And tax on tea, it was so bad,
  The women wouldn't scald it then.
Tol-le-lol, etc.

To Charleston Bridge we all went
    down
  To see the thing corrected;
That is, we would have gone there,
  But the bridge it warn't erected.
The tea perhaps was very good,
  Bohea, Souchong, or Hyson,
But drinking tea it warn't the rage,
  The duty made it poison.
Tol-le-lol, etc.]

And then aboard the ships we went
 Our vengeance to administer,
And we didn't care one tarnal bit
 For any king or minister.
We made a plaguey mess of tea
 In one of the biggest dishes;
I mean we steeped it in the sea
 And treated all the fishes.
Tol-le-lol, etc.

[And then you see we were all found
 out,
 A thing we hadn't dreaded.
The leaders were to London sent
 And instantly beheaded;

That is, I mean they would have been
 If ever they'd been taken.
But the leaders they were never
 cotch'd,
 And so they saved their bacon.
Tol-le-lol, etc.

Now heaven bless the president
 And all this goodly nation.
And doubly bless our Boston mayor
 And all the corporation;
And may all those who are our foes,
 Or at our praise have falter'd,
Soon have a change—that is, I mean
 May all of them get halter'd.
Tol-le-lol, etc.]

The Ballad of Bunker Hill

The soldiers from town to the foot of the hill,
 In barges and rowboats, some great and some small,
They pottered and dawdled and twaddled until
 We feared there would be no attack after all.
Let the foeman draw nigh till the white of his eye
Comes in range with your rifles, and then let it fly,
And show to Columbia, to Britain and fame,
How justice smiles aweful when freemen take aim!

The redcoats were ready and all came along,
 The way they marched up the hillside wasn't slow;
We were not a-feared and we welcomed 'em strong,
 Held fire till the word and then laid the lads low.
But who shall declare the end of the affair?
At sundown there wasn't a man of us there;
We didn't depart till we'd given 'em some,
We used up our powder and had to go home!

Ibid., Record 26460-A, 1. Transcribed by Frances Kurland.

On a bright sunny day in June, 1775, three thousand Redcoats were advancing in parade formation up Bunker and Breed's hills to "rout out the peasants." Commanded by General Howe, they came forward steadily, but were met by so terrific a fire that they gave way, retreating in disorder.

Charlestown was set ablaze by cannon fire from the British fleet, and a second time the Redcoats advanced to be driven back. After the third assault, their last charge of powder and ball being spent, the Americans were forced to "go home" as the ballad depicts it, while the battle proved an expensive victory for the British.—J. A.

The words of this song have been set by Mr. Allison to a traditional tune.

Attributed to Edward Everett Hale by Burton L. Stevenson, *Poems of American History* (Boston, 1908), p. 162.

The sol-diers from town to the foot of the hill, In
bar-ges and row-boats, some great and some small, They
pot-tered and daw-dled and twad-dled un-til We
feared there would be no at-tack af-ter all, Let the
foe-man draw nigh till the white of his eye Comes in
range with your ri-fles, and then let it fly, And
show to Co-lum-bia, to Bri-tain and fame, How
jus-tice smiles awe-ful when free-men take aim!

Riflemen's Song at Bennington

Why come ye hith-er, Red-coats? Your____ mind what mad-ness fills? In our val-leys there is dan-ger, And there's dan-ger on our hills! Oh, hear ye not the sing-ing Of the bug-le wild and free? Full____ soon ye'll know the ring-ing Of the rif-le from the tree! For the rif-le (clap, clap, clap, clap, clap) - the rif-le (clap, clap, clap, clap) In our hands will prove no trif-le!

Ibid., Record 26460-B, **2.** Transcribed by Frances Kurland.

When "Gentleman Johnny" Burgoyne advanced on the colonies from Canada, he sent a foraging detachment with a view to raiding the village of Bennington, Vermont, where the Americans had collected horses and stores.

As news of the approaching raiders reached the town, Colonel John Stark organized eight hundred yeomen from the locality. Making their way through a driving rain, "Old Man Stark's Boys" set out to meet the enemy. [On August 16, 1777] Burgoyne's detachment was surrounded on all sides, and within two hours his men were either

Why come ye hither, Redcoats?
　Your mind what madness fills?
In our valleys there is danger,
　And there is danger on our hills!
Oh, hear ye not the singing
　Of the bugle wild and free?
Full soon ye'll know the ringing
　Of the rifle from the tree!
　　For the rifle (clap, clap, clap, clap,
　　　clap)—the rifle (clap, clap,
　　　clap, clap)
　　In our hands will prove no trifle!

Ye ride a goodly steed;
　Ye may know another master.

Ye forward come with speed,
　But ye'll learn to back much faster,
When ye meet our mountain boys
　And their leader, Johnny Stark!
Lads who make but little noise,
　Lads who always hit the mark!

Had ye no graves at home
　Across the briny water
That hither ye must come
　Like bullocks to the slaughter?
If we the work must do,
　Why, the sooner 'tis begun,
If flint and trigger hold but true,
　The quicker 'twill be done.

The *Constitution* and the *Guerrière*

I often have been told
That the British seamen bold
Could beat the tars of France neat and handy, oh!
　But they never found their match
　Till the Yankees did them catch,
For the Yankee boys at fighting are the dandy, oh!

Chorus:
　With a heave ho
　And a hey away!

Now the *Guerrière* so bold
On the foaming ocean rolled,
Commanded by Dacres, the grandee, oh!
　With a choice of British crew [1]
　As a rammer ever drew,
They could beat the French two to one so handy, oh!

---

killed or captured. The buoyant "Riflemen's Song at Bennington," of unknown authorship, depicts the sturdy spirit of the time and place.—J. A.

The words of this song have been set by Mr. Allison to a traditional tune.

Ibid., Record 26462-A, 1. Transcribed by Frances Kurland.

The bragging ballad, "The *Constitution* and the *Guerrière*," is known also by old sailormen as a sea-chanty. The melody is an alteration of the ancient English drinking-song, "A Good Old Glass of Brandy, Oh."—J. A.

This famous single-ship engagement took place on August 19, 1812, off the coast of Nova Scotia. Captain Isaac Hull, commanding the *Constitution,* 44 guns, had sailed from Boston without orders, in the hope of meeting some of the British frigates reported off the coast. In twenty-five minutes the *Guerrière,* 38 guns, Captain R. Dacres, was reduced to a perfect wreck, 78 of her crew being killed and wounded. The *Constitution* had only 7 killed and 7 wounded.—Robert W. Neeser, *American Naval Songs & Ballads* (New Haven, 1938), p. 95 n.

[1] As choice a British crew.

I of-ten have been told That the Bri-tish sea-men bold Could beat the tars of France neat and han-dy, oh! But they nev-er found their match Till the Yan-kees aia them catch, For the Yan-kee boys at fight-ing are the dan-dy, oh!

Fine

Chorus

D.C.

With a heave ho And a hey a-way!

This boasting Briton cries,
"Make that Yankee ship your prize,
You can in thirty minutes do it handy, oh!
Or in twenty-five, I'm sure—
If you'll do it in a score,
I will give to you a double share of brandy, oh!"

Cries Hull unto his crew,
"We will try what we can do,
And if we beat the Britons, we're the dandy, oh!"
With that our cannon roared,
Brought the mizzen by the board,
Which doused the royal ensign very handy, oh!

Our gunners aimed so well
That the fore and mainmast fell,
Which made this royal frigate look abandoned, oh!
Dacres says, "We're undone,"
And he fires a lee gun.
Our drummer struck up Yankee Doodle Dandy, oh!

Then Dacres he did sigh,
To his officers did cry,
"I didn't think the Yankees were so handy, oh!"
But when he came on board
To deliver up his sword,
He was loth to part with it, it looked so dandy, oh!

"You may keep it," says brave Hull.
"What makes you look so dull?
Cheer up and take a glass of good old brandy, oh!
Johnny Bull may boast his fill,
Let the world say what it will,
But the Yankee boys at fighting are the dandy, oh!

BALLADS

The Miller's Three Sons

There was a mil - ler who lived in shire, He
had three sons as you shall hear. He had a mind to
make his will All for to give a - way his mill. Sing
tra la la day, Sing tra la la day, Sing tra le la le day.

From *The New Green Mountain Songster*, Traditional Folk Songs of Vermont, Collected, Transcribed, and Edited by Helen Hartness Flanders, Elizabeth Flanders Ballard, George Brown, and Phillips Barry, pp. 11-13. Copyright, 1939, by Helen Hartness Flanders. New Haven: Yale University Press; London: Oxford University Press.

From Mrs. Florence Waters, Brattleboro, Vermont, as sung by her cousin. Mr. Henry Leland, Brownington, Vermont. Melody recorded on the dictaphone by H. H. F. Transcribed by Miss Marguerite Olney.

"Beginning with fibbing but coming speedily to downright lying and peculation, stealing corn from sacks and yielding short measure of adulterated flour, the millers in all ages were accused of licentious freedom or betrayal toward the superabundant sex, and too frequently resorted to murder" (Ebsworth, *Roxburghe Ballads*, VIII, 610).

There was a miller who lived in shire,
He had three sons as you shall hear.
He had a mind to make his will
All for to give away his mill.

Chorus:
  Sing tra la la day,
  Sing tra la la day,
  Sing tra le la le day.

The old man called his oldest son,
Saying, "My son, my glass is run,
And if to you my will I'll make,
Come tell me how much toll you'll
    take."

"Father, O father, my name is Dick,
From every bushel I'll take one peck,
From every bushel that I grind,
That I may a good living find."

"You are a fool," the old man said,
"You have not learned the miller's
    trade.
The mill to you I'll never give,
For by such toll no man can live."

The old man called his second son,
Saying, "My son, my glass is run,
And if to you my will I'll make,

Come tell me how much toll you'll
    take."

"Father, O father, my name is Ralph,
From every bushel I'll take one half,
From every bushel that I grind,
That I may a good living find."

"You are a fool," the old man said,
"You have not learned the miller's
    trade.
My mill to you I'll never give,
For by such toll no man can live."

The old man called his youngest son.
Saying, "My son, my glass is run.
And if to you my will I'll make,
Come tell me how much toll you'll
    take."

"Father, O father, I'm your bonnie
    boy,
And stealing corn is all my joy,
And if I should a living lack,
I'll take the whole and steal the sack."

"The mill is yours," the old man said,
"You have learned the miller's trade.
The mill is yours," the old man cried,
And closed his sinful eyes and died.

"The Miller's Advice to his Three Sons, in Taking of Toll," to quote the title from a London broadside of *ca.* 1730 reprinted by Ebsworth (*op. cit.*, p. 611), is the oldest, perhaps the original, version of our ballad. There is a ring of reality to the story; we very much suspect the knavish miller was a real person. Probably the song came to this country at an early date; a text printed by Newell, *Games and Songs of American Children* (2d ed., pp. 103–104), locates him in Gosport, presumably the English town of that name. Be that as it may, a closely similar text, sung by an old Shoaler, is printed in Celia Thaxter's *Among the Isles of Shoals,* pp. 81–82. One of the early settlements on the Shoals, now abandoned, was named Gosport.

The ballad is known from both Northern and Southern tradition: Ohio (*JAFL*, XXXV, 391); West Virginia (Cox, *Folk Songs of the South,* pp. 450–454); Kentucky and North Carolina (Sharp, Karpeles, *English Folk Songs from the Southern Appalachians,* II, 221–223). Ebsworth quotes from the broadside: "Tune of the Oxfordshire Tragedy" (cf. Chappell, *Popular Music of the Olden Time,* I, 191). The Ohio melody and the three from the South, printed by Cox and Sharp, Karpeles, are all sets of a single air.—P. B.

Mary of the Wild Moor

One night when the wind it blew cold,
　Blew bitter across the wild moor,
Young Mary she came with her child
　Wand'ring home to her own father's
　　door,
Saying, "Father, O pray let me in!
　Have pity on me, I implore;
Or the child on my bosom will die
　From the winds that blow 'cross the
　　wild moor!

"O why did I leave my lone cot,
　Where once I was happy and free?
Doomed to roam without friends or a
　home,
　O, Father, have pity on me!"

But her father was deaf to her cry;
　Not a voice nor a sound reached his
　　ear.
But the watchdog did howl and the
　village bell tolled
　From the winds that blew 'cross the
　　wild moor.

O what must the father have felt
　When he came to the door in the
　　morn?
There he found Mary dead and her
　child
　Fondly clasped in its dead mother's
　　arms.

From *Songs from the Hills of Vermont,* Sung by James and Mary Atwood and Aunt
Jenny Knapp, Texts Collected and Edited by Edith B. Sturgis, Tunes Collected and
Piano Accompaniments Arranged with Historical Notes by Robert Hughes, pp. 36–39.
Copyright, 1919, by G. Schirmer, Inc. New York.
"Mary of the Wild Moor" (sung by Mary Atwood), evidently a very popular
ballad, has been published with quite a different tune in Barrett's *English Folksongs*
(p. 76) and in Kidson's *Traditional Tunes* (p. 77). A version with a tune similar to
the present one is found in Helen K. Johnson's *Our Familiar Songs* (pp. 303–304). See
also *The Journal of American Folklore,* vol. xxvi, p. 355; and vol. xxix, p. 185. The
song has been printed in other song-books and in broadsides.—R. H.

The villagers point out the spot
  Where a willow droops over the door,
Saying, "There Mary perished and
  died

From the winds that blew 'cross the
  wild moor."

The Shining Dagger

"A-wake, a-wake, you drow-sy sleep-er, A-wake and lis-ten un-to me! There's some-one at your bed-room win-dow, A-weep-ing there most bit-ter-ly."

"Awake, awake, you drowsy sleeper,
  Awake and listen unto me!
There's some one at your bedroom
  window,
  A-weeping there most bitterly."

Mary raised her head from her drowsy
  pillow
  To see who calling her might be.
Whom did she spy but her own true
  lover
  A-weeping there most bitterly.

He said, "Mary dear, go ask your
  father
  If you my wedded bride may be.
If he says 'No,' love, return and tell
  me,
  And I no more will trouble thee."

"It is no use to ask my father,
  For he is on his bed of rest,

And by his side is a shining dagger
  To pierce the heart that I love best."

He said, "Mary dear, go ask your
  mother
  If you my wedded bride may be;
If she says, 'No,' love, return and tell
  me,
  And I no more will trouble thee."

"It is no use to ask my mother,
  She too intends to set us free.
So go, my dear, and court some other,
  And I no more will trouble thee."

Then did he seize his own bright dag-
  ger
  And pierced it through his aching
  heart.
"Adieu, adieu, my darling Mary;
  Adieu, adieu, we now must part!"

Ibid., pp. 30–31.
"The Shining Dagger" (sung by James Atwood) shows the admixture of the two ballads, "The Drowsy Sleeper" and "The Silver Dagger." See *The Journal of American Folk-Lore*, vol. xx p. 260; vol. xxx, pp. 338–343, 361–363; Campbell and Sharp, No. 47, pp. 173–175.—R. H.

Then Mary seized the blood-stained dagger
And pierced it through her lily breast.
"Adieu, adieu, both father and mother,
My love and I are now at rest.

"Oh, I can climb the tallest tree, love,
And I can reach the highest nest,
And I can pluck the sweetest rose, love,
But not the heart that I love best."

Jim Fisk

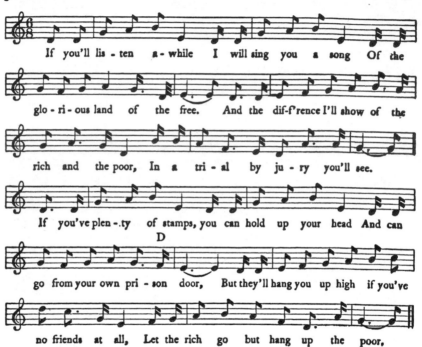

If you'll lis-ten a-while I will sing you a song Of the glo-ri-ous land of the free. And the dif-f'rence I'll show of the rich and the poor, In a tri-al by ju-ry you'll see. If you've plen-.ty of stamps, you can hold up your head And can go from your own pri-son door, But they'll hang you up high if you've no friends at all, Let the rich go but hang up the poor.

From *The New Green Mountain Songster,* Traditional Folk Songs of Vermont, Collected, Transcribed, and Edited by Helen Hartness Flanders, Elizabeth Flanders Ballard, George Brown, and Phillips Barry, pp. 213–215. Copyright, 1939, by Helen Hartness Flanders. New Haven: Yale University Press. London: Humphrey Milford, Oxford University Press.

Mr. Josiah S. Kennison of Townshend, Vermont, sang this version of "Jim Fisk" to H. H. F., which was later transcribed by G. B.

Three ballads of James Fisk, Jr., the already semilegendary Prince of Erie, are known. Of the three, the most popular is the one sung by Mr. Kennison. A sheet-music copy, "Jim Fisk, or He Never Went Back on the Poor," published by F. W. Helmick (Cincinnati, Ohio, copyright 1874), is inscribed "written and sung by William J. Scanlon."

A picture, truthful in the main if overvividly drawn, of the real Fisk, may be had in *Jubilee Jim,* by R. H. Fuller [New York, 1928]. Fisk was shot by Edward S. Stokes, and died January 7, 1872. The humor of the myth is that Stokes was actually penniless, subsisting on blackmail, and did murder when court action had cut off his

If you'll listen a while, I will sing you a song
  Of the glorious land of the free,
And the difference I'll show of the rich and the poor
  In a trial by jury, you'll see.
If you've plenty of stamps, you can hold up your head
  And can go from your own prison door;
But they'll hang you up high if you've no friends at all:
  Let the rich go, but hang up the poor.

Let me speak of a man who is now in his grave,
  A better man never was born.
Jim Fisk he was called, and his money he gave
  To the outcast, the poor and forlorn.
We all know he loved both women and wine,
  But his heart it was right, I am sure.
[Though he lived like a prince in his palace so fine,
  Yet he never went back on the poor.] [1]

Jim Fisk was a man with his heart in his hand,
  No matter what people would say.
He done all his deeds, both the good and the bad,
  In the broad open light of tho day.
With his grand six-in-hand of the Beach of Long Branch
  He cut a big gash, to be sure,
But Chicago's great fire showed the world that Jim Fisk
  And his wealth still remembered the poor.

---

last source of support. He was tried three times and finally convicted of manslaughter, for which he served four years in the New York State Prison.

Fisk sinned much, both publicly and privately; the song names only his love of women and wine, unconcerned with the social consequences, direct and indirect, of his love for playing with other people's money. Perhaps he saw the value of publicity; at any rate, his dispatch of a trainload of foodstuffs for the relief of the Chicago fire sufferers was a magnificent gesture which the folk imputed to him for goodness. It is a far cry from the hard-hitting and straight-shooting outlaws of romance to the luxury-loving money-changer, yet the way of the folk has placed Fisk in company with Robin Hood, the "good outlaws, who did pore men moch good"; with the Irish Willie Brennan, who "never robbed a poor man upon the king's highway," but gave to the needy what he took from the rich; with Jesse James, "friend to the poor," one who "never would see a man suffer pain." For the "Boston Burglar," on the other hand, the folk has but contemptuous pity; he did nothing great, even of evil. Yet the same folk applauds the pirate Ward, who vows to be king at sea, let who will reign on land. Perhaps the root of it all is grounded in our own infantilism: the outlaw and rebel which, we are told, is latent in all of us, approves successful outlawry, then sheepishly tries to cheat conscience by feigning to discover that such and such a great sinner had his good side; he was, forsooth, "a friend to the poor."

Scanlon's melody has little to recommend it. The ballad is sung in Maine to a different air.—P. B.

[1] These lines from the version given by Carl Sandburg in *The American Songbag* (New York, 1927), p. 419, are substituted for the following here sung by Mr. Kennison:

  He'd done all his deeds, both the good and the bad,
    In the broad open light of the day.

When the telegram came that the humble that night
    Were starving to death slow but sure,
Then the Lightning Express nobly flew from Jim Fisk
    To feed all the hungry and poor.
Now what do you think of the trials of Stokes
    Who murdered the friend of the poor?
If such men get free, is there any one safe
    To step outside their own door?

Is there one law for the rich and one for the poor?
    It seems so, at least so they say.
If they'd hang up the poor, why shouldn't the rich
    Ought to swing up the very same way?
Never show any favor to friend or to foe,
    To a beggar or prince at your door,
But the millionaire you must hang up also.
    Never go back on the poor.[1]

The Brookfield Murder

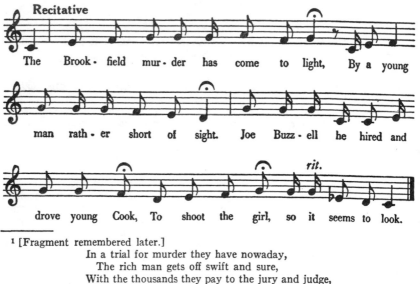

Recitative

The Brook-field mur-der has come to light, By a young man rath-er short of sight. Joe Buzz-ell he hired and drove young Cook, To shoot the girl, so it seems to look.

[1] [Fragment remembered later.]
    In a trial for murder they have nowaday,
    The rich man gets off swift and sure,
    With the thousands they pay to the jury and judge,
    But you bet they'll go back on the poor.
                        —P. B.

From *Folk Songs of Old New England*, collected and edited by Eloise Hubbard Linscott, pp. 175–177. Copyright, 1939, by The Macmillan Company. New York.
This song records a local New Hampshire tragedy. It was sung by Mrs. Winifred Allard Piper of Wolfeboro, New Hampshire, which adjoins Brookfield. The third

The Brookfield murder has come to light,
By a young man rather short of sight.
Joe Buzzell he hired and drove young Cook
To shoot the girl, so it seems to look.

She sued for damage which if he'd paid
Would have saved the time while in jail he laid.
But he with murder born in his heart
Soon caused young Susan to depart.

On Monday evening as we tell,
Miss Susan Hanson was known full well,
Sat at her table doing some work,
She little thought death so near did lurk.

The thief and murderer with gun in hand
Beside the house outside did stand.
Discharged his gun through windowpane,
And thus the promised bride was slain.

It was a dreadful shock to the aged mother,
The lamp was lit by the son and brother.
There lay the daughter once so fair
In death cold arms and bloodstained hair.

No farewell words to her friends could say,
But shot dead on the floor did lay.
So young and fair and in life's bloom,
To be hurried away so soon to the tomb.

Come, all young ladies, a warning take,
And shun such reptiles for Susan's sake.
For he who shot this lady gay
Would burn your home while in bed you lay.

---

verse was supplied by Dana Cate of Sanbornville, New Hampshire, who remembers hearing the song as a boy from Warren Stevens, an old man of ninety.

The crime was committed in 1847. According to the story, "Old Pike," a local character, urged Susan Hanson to sue Joseph Buzzell for heart balm when he jilted her. Buzzell was so angry that he hired the half-wit, Charles Cook, to kill his former sweetheart. While at work on the Henry Jones house in Wolfeboro, the wrath of Mr. Buzzell had cooled enough for him to be seized with a change of mind and he thereupon leaped on his horse and galloped for dear life to Miss Hanson's home in Brookfield. It was a matter of some ten miles over "the back road." He arrived too late; Miss Hanson had been done away with.

The case dragged on in the courts for five years before the law finally caught up with the murderer and his accomplice. Only a charge of arson on another case against Cook brought matters to an end. Buzzell was hanged and his accomplice, Cook, imprisoned for life.—E. H. L.

The Pesky Sarpent

On Springfield mountain there did dwell, A comely youth I knew full well, Ri ta ri nh ri ta di na, Ri ta di na ri ta di na.

On Springfield mountain there did
   dwell,
A comely youth I knew full well,

Chorus:
   Ri tu di nu, ri tu di na,
   Ri tu di nu, ri tu di na,

One Monday morning he did go,
Down in the meadow for to mow,

He scarce had mowed half the field,
When a Pesky Sarpent bit his heel,

He took his scythe and with a blow,
He laid the Pesky Sarpent low.

He took the Sarpent in his hand,
And straitway went to Molly Bland,

Oh Molly, Molly here you see,
The Pesky Sarpent what bit me,

Now Molly had a ruby lip,
With which the pizen she did sip.

But Molly had a rotten tooth,
Which the Pizen struck and kill'd 'em
   both,

From *The Pesky Sarpent,* A Pathetic Ballad, as sung by Mr. Spear. Arranged for the Piano-Forte and respectfully dedicated to the C. B. C.'s by the author. Boston: Published by George P. Reed. [1840.] In *Series of Old American Songs,* Reproduced in Facsimile from Original or Early Editions in Harris Collection of American Poetry and Plays, with Brief Annotations, by S. Foster Damon, Curator, No. 26. Providence, Rhode Island: Brown University Library. 1936.

This ballad is perhaps unique in that the circumstances which inspired it are fully known. (The best account is that by Phillips Barry, running in the *Bulletin of the Folk-Song Society of the Northeast.*)

Mr. Timothy Myrick, son of Lieut. Thomas Myrick of Springfield Mountain (now Wilbraham), Mass., was bitten by a rattlesnake on Friday, August 7, 1761, at Farmington, Mass., and died before he could reach home. He was twenty-two years, two months, and three days old, and "very near the point of marridg" to Sarah Blake. His gravestone is still in existence.

The original ballad was an elegy over this tragic death, which may have been sung at his funeral to the tune of "Old Hundred," in accordance with a custom in western Massachusetts. The author has been named as Nathan Torrey, or Daniel or Jesse Carpenter.

The song succeeded, and traveled far and wide, changing names, dates, and places, and acquiring a number of different tunes. The *Journal of American Folk Lore* is full of variants. About 1836 it began to be sung on the stage; the vogue of the Yankee was then in its prime; and the ancient tragedy became excellent comedy, when stammered or nasalized by George Gaines Spear, Yankee Hill, or Judson Hutchinson—S. F. D.

For a Vermont version of the original ballad, "On Springfield Mountain," see *A Treasury of American Folklore* (New York, 1944), pp. 828–829,

The neighbors found that they were dead,
So laid them both upon one bed,

And all their friends both far and near,
Did cry and howl they were so dear.

Now all you maids a warning take,
From Molly Bland and Tommy Blake.

And mind when you're in love don't pass,
Too near to patches of high grass.

Michigania

Come, all ye Yankee farmer boys who would like to change your lot
And spunk enough to travel beyond your native spot
And leave behind the village where pa and ma doth stay,
Come, go with me and settle in Michigania.[1]
For there's your Penobscot way down in parts of Maine
Where timber grows in plenty but not a bit of grain,
And there is your Quaddy and your Piscataqua,
But these can't hold a candle to Michigania.

And there's the state of Vermont, but what a place is that?
To be sure the girls are pretty and the cattle very fat,
But who among her mountains and clouds of snow would stay
While he can buy a section in Michigania?
And there is Massachusetts, once good enough, be sure,
But now she is always lying in taxation and manure.
She'll cause a peck of trouble but deal a peck will pay,
While all is scripture measure in Michigania.

And there's the land of Blue Laws where deacons cut their hair
For fear their locks and tenants [tenets?] will not exactly square,
Where beer that works on Sunday a penalty must pay,
While all is free and easy in Michigania.
And there's the state of New York, the people's very rich;
Among themselves and others have dug a mighty ditch
Which renders it more easy for us to find the way
And sail upon the waters of Michigania.

From the Gernsey Manuscript, in *Ballads and Songs of Southern Michigan*, collected and edited by Emelyn Elizabeth Gardner and Geraldine Jencks Chickering, pp. 5–6. Copyright, 1939, by The University of Michigan. Ann Arbor.

The facts revealed by historical research are stated as follows by George Newman Fuller, *Economic and Social Beginnings of Michigan* (Lansing, Michigan, 1916), p. 469: "It was exceptional for a settler to emigrate directly from his place of birth to Michigan. He was much more likely to have a number of intermediate stopping places; for example, he might be born in England, migrate with his parents to Connecticut, be educated in Vermont, engage in business in New York, and then spend some years on the frontier in Ohio and perhaps return to New York before finally settling in Michigan."—E. E. G., *ibid.*, pp. 4–5 and note. [No tune.]

[1] Pronounced Michiganiay.

What country ever grew up so great in little time,
Just popping from a nursery right into life its prime?
When Uncle Sam did wean her, 'twas but the other day,
And now she's quite a lady, this Michigania.
And if you want to go to a place called Washtenaw,
You'll first upon the Huron; such land you never saw,
Where ship come to Ann Arbor right through a pleasant bay
And touch at Ypsilanti in Michigania.

And if you want to go a little farther back,
You'll find the shire of Oakland, the town of Pontiac,
Which springing up so sudden scared the wolves and bears away
That used to roam about there in Michigania.
And if you want to go where Rochester is there,
And farther still Mt. Clemens looks out upon St. Clair,
Besides some other places within McCombia
That promise population to Michigania.

And if you want to travel a little farther on,
I guess you'll touch St. Joseph where everybody's gone,
Where everything like Jack's bean grows monstrous fast, they say,
And beats the rest all hollow in Michigania.
Come, all ye Yankee farmer boys with metal hearts like me
And elbow grease in plenty to bow the forest tree,
Come, buy a quarter section, and I'll be bound you'll say
This country takes the rag off, this Michigania.

No, Never, No

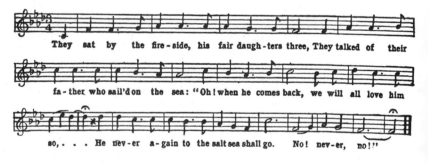

They sat by the fireside, his fair daughters three,
They talked of their father who sail'd on the sea:
"Oh! when he comes back, we will all love him so,
He never again to the salt sea shall go.
No! never, no!"

Written from memory by Edna Dean Proctor. From *Heart Songs*, Dear to the American People and by Them Contributed in the Search for Treasured Songs Initiated by the *National Magazine*, p. 147. Copyright, 1909, by The Chapple Publishing Company, Ltd. Boston.

"I'll give him this vest all of satin so fine";
"And I'll be his carver when he sits to dine";
"And I'll climb his knee and such kisses bestow
He never again to the salt sea shall go.
No! never, no!"

"O did ye not hear it?" the sisters declare,
"There's surely a spirit that talks in the air;
And whether we speak either loudly or low,
It answers in accents all mournful and slow,
'No! never, no!'"

"It is but the tempest that rages so strong;
The gale will itself waft our father along;
Go look at the vane and see how the winds blow:
He'll bring us gay things for he promised us so."
"No! never, no!"

Prepare ye, fair maidens, prepare ye to weep!
Your father lies cold in the dark-rolling deep;
Look not at the vane nor ask how the winds blow,
His ghost in the storm whispers mournful and slow:
"No! never, no!"

SEA SONGS AND CHANTEYS

The Boston Come-All-Ye

Come, all ye young sailormen, listen to me,
I'll sing you a song of the fish of the sea.

Chorus:
Then blow ye winds westerly, westerly blow,
We're bound to the south'ard, so steady she goes!

Oh, first come the whale, the biggest of all;
He clumb up aloft and let every sail fall.

From *Songs of American Sailormen*, by Joanna C. Colcord, pp. 187–188. Copyright, 1938, by W. W. Norton & Company.

There can be little doubt that the . . . song, although it was sung throughout the merchant service, began life with the fishing fleet. We have the testimony of Kipling in *Captain's Courageous* that it was a favorite within recent years of the Banks fishermen. It is known as "The Fishes" and also by its more American title of "The Boston Come-all-ye." The chorus finds its origin in a Scotch fishing song, "Blaw the Wind Southerly." A curious fact is that Captain Whall, a Scotchman himself, prints this song with an entirely different tune, and one that has no connection with the air of the Tyneside keelmen to which our own Gloucester fishermen sing it. The version given here was sung by Captain Frank Seeley.—J. C. C.

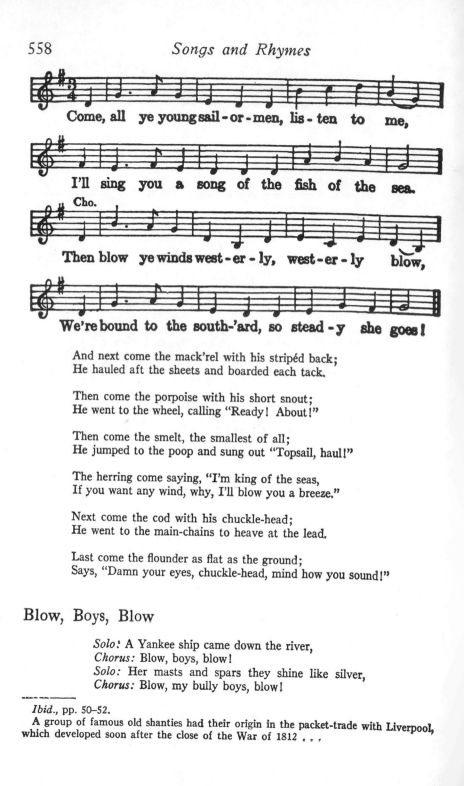

Come, all ye young sail-or-men, lis-ten to me,

I'll sing you a song of the fish of the sea.

Cho.

Then blow ye winds west-er-ly, west-er-ly blow,

We're bound to the south-'ard, so stead-y she goes!

And next come the mack'rel with his stripéd back;
He hauled aft the sheets and boarded each tack.

Then come the porpoise with his short snout;
He went to the wheel, calling "Ready! About!"

Then come the smelt, the smallest of all;
He jumped to the poop and sung out "Topsail, haul!"

The herring come saying, "I'm king of the seas,
If you want any wind, why, I'll blow you a breeze."

Next come the cod with his chuckle-head;
He went to the main-chains to heave at the lead.

Last come the flounder as flat as the ground;
Says, "Damn your eyes, chuckle-head, mind how you sound!"

Blow, Boys, Blow

Solo: A Yankee ship came down the river,
Chorus: Blow, boys, blow!
Solo: Her masts and spars they shine like silver,
Chorus: Blow, my bully boys, blow!

Ibid., pp. 50–52.

A group of famous old shanties had their origin in the packet-trade with Liverpool, which developed soon after the close of the War of 1812 . . .

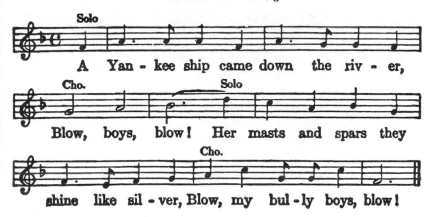

A Yan - kee ship came down the riv - er,

Blow, boys, blow! Her masts and spars they

shine like sil - ver, Blow, my bul - ly boys, blow!

How do you know she's a Yankee liner?
The Stars and Stripes float out behind her.

(*Or,* How do you know she's a Yankee packet?
They fired a gun, I heard the racket.)

And who d'you think is the captain of her?
Why, Bully Hayes is the captain of her.

'Oh, Bully Hayes, he loves us sailors;
Yes, he does like hell and blazes!

"Blow, Boys, Blow" started life as a slaving song, the opening couplet being

A Yankee ship on the Congo River,
Her masts they bend and her sails they shiver.

In this version, the captain is "Holy Joe, the nigger lover," and the mate "a big mulatta come from Antigua." Somewhat later, it was taken over by the "packet-rats" of the Western Ocean, and celebrated the brutalities aboard the Atlantic liners. Doubtless all the well-known masters and mates in that trade have heard themselves picturesquely described in this shanty; but it is Captain Hayes, who was lost in the *Rainbow* in 1848, whose name seems to have survived.

In other versions, the master is said to be "one-eyed Kelly, the Bowery runner," and the ship is recognized as a Yankee clipper "because the blood runs from her scuppers." One couplet, dating evidently from Civil War days, inquires:

What do you think she's got for cargo?
Old shot and shell, she breaks the embargo.

Still another tells of her fate:

Her sails were old, her timbers rotten,
His charts the skipper had forgotten.
She sailed away for London city;
Never got there, what a pity!

But the wildest flights of fancy concerned the bill of fare, which was variously stated to consist of "belaying-pin soup and monkey's liver," "mosquito's heart and sandfly's liver," "hot water soup, but slightly thinner," etc. I have never seen in print the menu here given; but it is what I heard sung aboard ship in the '90's.—J. C. C.

And who d'you think is the mate aboard her?
Santander James is the mate aboard her.

Santander James, he's a rocket from hell, boys,
He'll ride you down as you ride the spanker.

And what d'you think they've got for dinner?
Pickled eels' feet and bullock's liver.

Then blow, my bullies, all together,
Blow, my boys, for better weather.

Blow, boys, blow, the sun's drawing water;
Three cheers for the cook and one for his daughter.

Reuben Renzo

Rov-ing Reub-en Ren zo,   Ren-zo, boys,   Ren-zo;

Rov-ing Reub-en Ren- zo,   Ren-zo, boys,   Ren-zo!

Solo: Roving Reuben Renzo,   Renzo was no sailor,
Chorus: Renzo, boys, Renzo;   He might have been a tailor.
Solo: Roving Reuben Renzo,
Chorus: Renzo, boys, Renzo.   Renzo took a notion,
                                    That he would plough the ocean.

From *Folk Songs of Old New England*, Collected and Edited by Eloise Hubbard Linscott, pp. 144–146. Copyright, 1939, by The Macmillan Company. New York.
Captain Charlton L. Smith of Marblehead, Massachusetts, recalls this chantey from his many years at sea in the sailing ships of the mahogany trade. These ships went out of Liverpool to South America, in the middle of the nineteenth century.

It is a halyard chantey that was popular about fifty years ago and is thought originally to have been one of the songs of the whaling fleet. Whether the name of the hero is a corruption of the Portuguese "Lorenzo" is not definitely established, though it is generally known that the Yankee whalers carried a large number of "Portygee" sailors on their long and dangerous but profitable voyages.

It is probable too that Lorenzo may be a mythical hero, for his rise to the captaincy gave chance for sly digs at officers. No amount of book learning was ever known to make a sailor.

The "limejuice whaler" refers to the custom of rationing lime juice to prevent scurvy on the whaling ships that were so long out of port.—E. H. L.

So he sold his plough and harrow,
And likewise sold his barrow.

And Renzo had a pony,
And sold him to a loidy.

He went to London city,
Where the barmaids are so pretty.

He joined a limejuice whaler,
And tried to be a sailor.

The mate he was a bad man,
He took him to the gangway.

He gave him five and twenty,[1]
And that was a plenty!

But the skipper he was a fine old man,
He took him to his cabin.

And taught him navigation,
And now he ploughs the ocean.

Cape Cod Shanty

Oh, Cape Cod girls they have no combs,
Heave away, heave away!

They comb their hair with codfish bones,
Heave away, heave away!

---

[1] Refers to the number of lashes of the cat-o'-nine-tails, an instrument commonly used for punishing the refractory.—E. H. L.

Cf. the following variant:

O, Johnny was no sailor,
(Renso, boys, Renso.)
Still he shipped on a Yankee whaler,
(Renso, boys, Renso.)
He could not do his duty,
(Renso, boys, Renso.)
And he tried to run away then,
(Renso, boys, Renso.)
They caught and brought him back again,
(Renso, boys, Renso.)
And he said he never would go again,
(Renso, boys, Renso.)

They put him pounding cable,
(Renso, boys, Renso.)
And found him very able,
(Renso, boys, Renso.)
He said he'd run away no more,
(Renso, boys, Renso.)
He only waited to get on shore,
(Renso, boys, Renso.)
So when he put his feet on shore,
(Renso, boys, Renso.)
A-whaling he would go no more,
(Renso, boys, Renso.)

—Capt. Charles Henry Robbins, *The Gam* (New Bedford, 1899), p. 140.

From *The Folk Songs of New England*, sung by Earl Rogers, Musicraft Album 68, Record 334-A, 2. New York: Musicraft Corporation. Transcribed by Frances Kurland.

For a Gloucester version, see Joanna C. Colcord, *Songs of American Sailormen* (New York, 1938), p. 91, who notes of this windlass or capstan shanty: "A 'down-East' variant of this song goes to a simplified and livelier version of the same tune. The words are a rough jest at the expense of sailors who might hail from the fishing towns, and any such towns, from Cape Cod to St. John, were substituted."

For an additional Cape Cod stanza, see Arthur Loesser, *Humor in American Song* (New York, 1942), p. 211:

Oh, Cape Cod roosters never crow,
And crowing hens are all the go.

Oh, Cape Cod girls they have no combs, Heave a-way, Heave a-way! They comb their hair with cod-fish bones, Heave a-way, heave a-way!

Chorus

Heave a-way,—— you bul-ly, bul-ly boys! Heave a-way,—— heave a-way!——Heave a-way,—— and don't you make a noise, For we're bound for—— Aus-tral-ia.

Chorus:

Heave away, you bully, bully boys!
Heave away, heave away!
Heave away, and don't you make a
noise,
For we're bound for Australia!

Oh, Cape Cod boys they have no sleds,
They slide down hill on codfish heads.

Oh, Cape Cod cats they have no tails,
They blew away in heavy gales.

The Mermaid

'Twas Friday morn when we set sail,
And we were not far from the land,
When the captain spied a lovely mermaid,
With a comb and a glass in her hand.

Chorus:

Oh! the ocean waves may roll,
And the stormy winds may blow,
While we poor sailors go skipping to the tops,
And the landlubbers lie down below, below, below,
And the landlubbers lie down below.

From *The Most Popular Home Songs*, selected and arranged by Gilbert Clifford Noble, pp. 60–61. Copyright, 1906, 1908, by Hinds, Noble & Eldredge. New York.

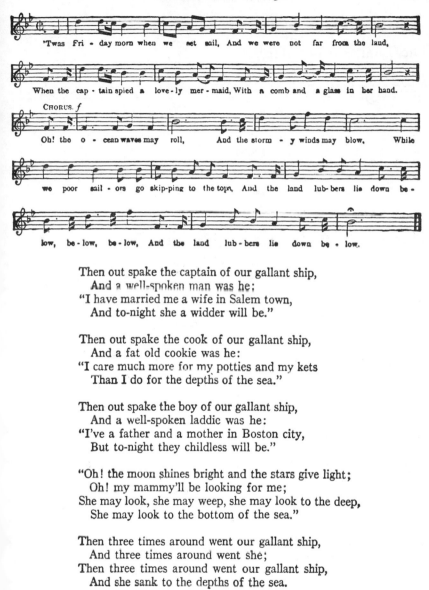

'Twas Fri-day morn when we set sail, And we were not far from the land,

When the cap-tain spied a love-ly mer-maid, With a comb and a glass in her hand.

CHORUS. *f*

Oh! the o-cean waves may roll, And the storm-y winds may blow, While

we poor sail-ors go skip-ping to the top, And the land lub-bers lie down be-

low, be-low, be-low, And the land lub-bers lie down be-low.

Then out spake the captain of our gallant ship,
    And a well-spoken man was he;
"I have married me a wife in Salem town,
    And to-night she a widder will be."

Then out spake the cook of our gallant ship,
    And a fat old cookie was he:
"I care much more for my potties and my kets
    Than I do for the depths of the sea."

Then out spake the boy of our gallant ship,
    And a well-spoken laddic was he:
"I've a father and a mother in Boston city,
    But to-night they childless will be."

"Oh! the moon shines bright and the stars give light;
    Oh! my mammy'll be looking for me;
She may look, she may weep, she may look to the deep,
    She may look to the bottom of the sea."

Then three times around went our gallant ship,
    And three times around went she;
Then three times around went our gallant ship,
    And she sank to the depths of the sea.

LUMBERJACK SONGS AND BALLADS

The Lumberman's Alphabet

A is for Ax, as you ver- y well know;

B is for the Boys—— that use them just so.

C is for the Chop- ping that soon will be- gin, And

D is for the Dan- ger we al- ways stand in.

Chorus

Sing Hi, der- ry- o, so mer- ry are we, There's

no one one- half—— as hap- py as we. With a

Hi, der- ry- o, Hi, der- ry- dong, At the

wood- man's shan- ty there's noth- ing goes wrong.

From *Folk Songs of Old New England,* collected and edited by Eloise Hubbard Linscott, pp. 235-237. Copyright, 1939, by The Macmillan Company. New York.

A is for Ax, as you very well know;
B is for the Boys that use them just so.
C is for the Chopping that soon will begin,
And D is for the Danger we always stand in.

Chorus:

    Sing hi, derry-o, so merry are we,
    There's no one one-half as happy as we.
    With a hi, derry-o, hi, derry-dong,
    At the woodman's shanty there's nothing goes wrong.

E is for the Echoes that through the woods ring;
F is for the Foreman, the head of the gang,
G is for the Grindstone that swiftly goes round,
And H is for the Handle so smooth and so round.

I is for Iron, with which we mark pine,
And J is for Jolly Boys, all in a line. *
K is for the Keen edge our axes we keep,
And L is for the Lice that over us creep.

M is for the Moss that we chink into our camps,
N is for the Needle which mendeth our pants,
O is for Owls that hoot in the night,
And P is for the Pines that we always fall right.

Q is for Quarrels, which we don't have round,
R is for River, where we drive our logs down;
S is for Sled, so stout and so strong,
And T is for the Team to draw it along.

U is for Use, which we put our teams to,
And V is the Valley which we draw our sleds through,
And W is for Woods that we leave in the spring,
And now I have sung all I'm going to sing.
    That's all.

While Charles Young of Moultonboro, New Hampshire, was river-driving on the Penobscot River, he learned this song in the lumber camp. In that region he was guide and woodsman for over ten years.

It is said that nearly all the really good tunes and woodsmen's songs were made up by Larry Gorman, one of the most famous fighting lumberjacks of Maine. He was supposed to have come from Prince Edward Island and to have lived near the headwaters of the Penobscot. Many of the men from the provinces were attracted by the good wages paid in the New England woods and crossed and recrossed the border.

There are several variations of this song, the most popular ones unprintable; the earliest known printed version appeared in the *Maine Sportsman*, in February, 1904.

As Charles Young sang the song, the chorus was used after the first, second, third, and last stanzas only; but he remarked that in the woods he'd probably sing the chorus after every verse, to pass the time.—E. H. L.

Jack Haggerty, or the Flat River Girl

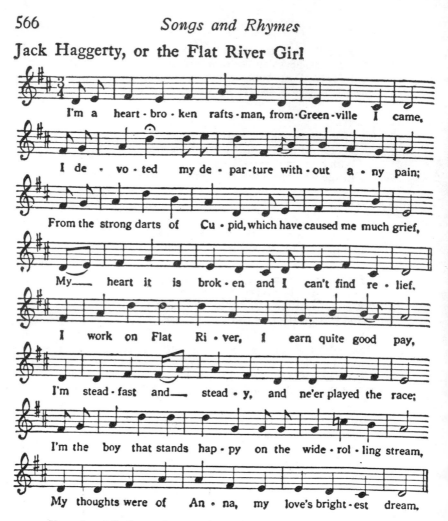

I'm a heart-bro-ken rafts-man, from Green-ville I came,

I de-vo-ted my de-par-ture with-out a-ny pain;

From the strong darts of Cu-pid, which have caused me much grief,

My— heart it is brok-en and I can't find re-lief.

I work on Flat Ri-ver, I earn quite good pay,

I'm stead-fast and— stead-y, and ne'er played the race;

I'm the boy that stands hap-py on the wide-rol-ling stream,

My thoughts were of An-na, my love's bright-est dream.

I'm a heart-broken raftsman, from Greenville I came;
I devoted my departure without any pain;
From the strong darts of Cupid, which have caused me much grief,
My heart it is broken, and I can't find relief.

From *The Maine Woods Songster,* edited by Phillips Barry, pp. 74–75. Copyright, 1939, by Kate Puffer Barry. The Powell Printing Company. Cambridge, Massachusetts.

For the origin of this song see Geraldine Chickering, "The Origin of a Ballad," *Modern Language Notes,* Vol. L, pp. 465–468. Eloise Hubbard Linscott in *Folk Songs of Old New England,* p. 214, locates Flat River near Greenville, Maine, at the foot of Moosehead Lake. According to Franz Rickaby in *Ballads and Songs of the Shanty-Boy* (Cambridge, 1926) p. 191, "This ballad . . . is native to the Flat River in southern Michigan," which flows through Greenville, Michigan.

I work on Flat Fiver, I earn quite good pay;
I'm steadfast and steady, and ne'er played the race;
I'm the boy that stands happy on the wide-rolling stream;
My thoughts were of Anna, my love's brightest dream.

I'll tell you my troubles without much delay,
'Twas of a fair schoolgirl my heart stole away;
She was a blacksmith's daughter by the Flat River side,
And I always intended to make her my bride.

I dressed her in muslins and the finest of lace,
In the costly linens I did her embrace;
I gave her my wages to keep for me safe;
I refused her nothing I could get in the place.

One day on Flat River a note I received;
She said from her promise herself she'd relieve,
For another true lover, who had long been delayed,
And the next time I saw her, she'd no more be a maid.

To her mother, Jane Tucker, I lay all the blame;
She caused her to desert me and hurt my good name;
She cast off the rigging that I would soon tie,
And left me a wanderer till the day that I died.

Farewell to Flat River, for me there's no rest;
I'll shoulder my peavey [1] and I'll go out West;
I'll start for Baskahegan, some pleasure to find,
And I'll leave my false love on Flat River behind.

Now, come all you young fellows with hearts strong and true,
Don't depend on a woman one bit, or you'll rue;
But if you should meet one with bright chestnut curls,
Just think of Jack Haggerty and the Flat River girl.

The Lumberman's Life

A lumberman's life is a wearisome life,
　　Although some say it's free from all care;
'Tis a-wielding of an ax from morning until night,
　　In the middle of the forests drear.

---

[1] The peavey, a short pole with an adjustable hook used in driving logs, was invented in 1858, by Joseph Peavey, a blacksmith of Stillwater Village, Maine.—Eloise Hubbard Linscott.

Ibid., p. 60.
Text and tune from Lamont Forbuss, Monson, Me. Tune transcribed from dictaphone record by Samuel P. Bayard.—P. B., *ibid.*, p. 100.
Also known as "The Shanty-Man's Life." Roland P. Gray, in *Songs and Ballads of the Maine Lumberjacks* (Cambridge, 1924), pp. 55–57, gives a broadside version, "composed and written by Geo. W. Stace, La Crosse Valley, Wis."

A——lum ber- man's life is a wea- ri- some life, Al-though

some say it's free—from all care; 'Tis a -wield-ing of an axe from——

morn-ing un- til night, In the mid-dle of the for-ests drear.

At four in the morning, the cook he rises up,
　　Saying, "Come boys, it is the break of day."
And through broken slumbers, we pass back
　　All the long, weary night away.

Sleeping in a shanty so bleak and cold,
　　Where the cold winter's winds they do blow,
As soon as the morning stars do appear,
　　To the wild woods we must go.

Transported we are from the haunts of all men,
　　On the banks of the Bonne Chere stream,
Where the wolves and the owls with their terrifying growls
　　Disturb our troubled nightly dream.

Transported from the glass and the charming little lass,
　　All enjoyment we've left so far behind,
There is no one here for to wipe away a tear
　　When sorrow fills our troubled mind.

When spring has come, then our troubles begin,
　　When the water is piercing and cold,
Dripping wet is our clothes, and our limbs are froze,
　　And the peavies we can scarcely hold.

The rocky shoals and sands give employment to our hands,
　　With a well-bounded raft for to steer,
Every rapid that we run, O we call it the fun,
　　We are free from all slavish fear.

The lumbering I'll give o'er, and I'll anchor safe on shore,
　　There to lead a quiet, sober life,
No more for to roam, but, contented, stay at home,
　　With a kind and loving little WIFE!

Canada I O

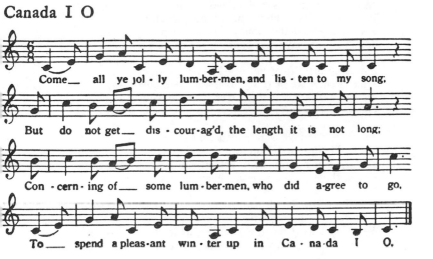

Come__ all ye jol-ly lum-ber-men, and lis-ten to my song;

But do not get__ dis-cour-ag'd, the length it is not long;

Con-cern-ing of__ some lum-ber-men, who did a-gree to go,

To__ spend a pleas-ant win-ter up in Ca-na-da I O.

Come all ye jolly lumbermen, and listen to my song,
But do not get discouraged, the length it is not long,
Concerning of some lumbermen, who did agree to go
To spend one pleasant winter up in Canada [1] I O.

It happened late one season in the fall of Fifty-three,
A preacher of the gospel one morning came to me;
Said he, "My jolly fellow, how would you like to go
To spend one pleasant winter up in Canada I O."

To him I quickly made reply, and unto him did say,
"In going out to Canada depends upon the pay.
If you will pay good wages, my passage to and fro,
I think I'll go along with you to Canada I O."

"Yes, we will pay good wages, and will pay your passage out,
Provided you sign papers that you will stay the route;
But if you do get homesick and swear that home you'll go,
We never can your passage pay from Canada I O.

Ibid., pp. 76–77.
The words are by Ephraim Braley, Charlestown, Me., 1854. Tune is "Lord Randall," Type II, come-all-ye variant. Text [previously printed in Eckstorm and Smyth, *Minstrelsy of Maine*, 22–23; *Bulletin of the Folk Song Society of the Northeast*, 6: 11]. Tune [previously printed in FSSNE, 6: 10] from Mrs. Annie Marston, Charlestown, Me. For the history of this song, of which "The Buffalo Skinners" [Lomax, *Cowboy Songs*, pp. 158–161] is an adaptation, see Fannie H. Eckstorm, "Canada I O," in FSSNE, 6: 11–13.—P. B., *ibid.*, p. 101.
[1] Pronounced Canaday.

"And if you get dissatisfied, and do not wish to stay,
We do not wish to bind you, no, not one single day;
You just refund the money we had to pay, you know,
Then you can leave that bonny place called Canada I O."

It was by his gift of flattery he enlisted quite a train,
Some twenty-five or thirty, both well and able men;
We had a pleasant journey o'er the road we had to go,
Till we landed at Three Rivers, up in Canada I O.

But there our joys were ended, and our sorrows did begin;
Fields, Phillips, and Norcross they then came marching in;
They sent us all directions, somewhere I do not know,
Among those jabbering Frenchmen up in Canada I O.

After we had suffered there some eight or ten long weeks,
We arrived at headquarters up among the lakes;
We thought we'd found a paradise, at least they told us so—
God grant there may be no worse hell than Canada I O.

To describe what we have suffered is past the art of man,
But to give a fair description, I will do the best I can.
Our food the dogs would snarl at, our beds were on the snow;
We suffered worse than murderers up in Canada I O.

Our hearts were made of iron and our souls were cased in steel,
The hardships of that winter could never make us yield;
Field, Phillips, and Norcross they found their match, I know,
Among the boys that went from Maine to Canada I O.

But now our lumbering is over and we are returning home,
To greet our wives and sweethearts and never more to roam,
To greet our wives and sweethearts and never more to roam,
Unto that God-forsaken place, called Canada I O.

NURSERY AND HUMOROUS SONGS

Nantucket Lullaby

Hm ———————————— Hush, the waves are
roll - ing in, White with foam, white with foam,
Fa - ther toils a - mid the din, While ba - by sleeps at home.

Hush, the waves are rolling in,
White with foam, white with foam,
Father toils amid the din,
While baby sleeps at home.

Hush, the ship rides in the gale,
Where they roam, where they roam,

Father seeks the roving whale,
But baby sleeps at home.

Hush, the wind sweeps o'er the deep.
All alone, all alone,
Mother now the watch will keep,
Till father's ship comes home.

The Frog in the Spring

There was a frog lived in a spring,
Singsong paddy woncha kymeo.
He had such a cold that he couldn't
sing.
Singsong paddy woncha kymeo.

Chorus:
Kymo, karo, delto, karo,
Kymo, karo, kymo.
Strimstrum, popadiddle,
There by the rigdum,
Rigdum bottom in the kymeo!

From *Early American Ballads,* sung by John and Lucy Allison, with Chorus, Keynote Album K-102, Record 533-B, 2. New York: Keynote Recordings, Inc. Leaflet copyright, 1943, by Keynote Recordings, Inc. Transcribed by Frances Kurland.

To words of unknown origin, Lucy Allison made this setting in 1924, and for many years used the song in the folk ballad programs of the Allisons.—J. A.

From *Songs from the Hills of Vermont,* Sung by James and Mary Atwood and Aunt Jenny Knapp, Texts Collected and Edited by Edith B. Sturgis, Tunes Collected and Piano Accompaniments Arranged with Historical Notes by Robert Hughes, pp. 18–21. Copyright, 1919, by G. Schirmer. New York and Boston.

The oldest extant version of "The Frog in the Spring" (sung by Mary Atwood) is "The Marriage of the Frogge and the Mouse," printed with music among the

There was a frog lived in a spring, Sing-song pad-dy won-cha ky-me-o. He had such a cold that he could-n't sing. Sing-song pad-dy won-cha ky-me-o. Ky-mo, ka-ro, del-to, ka-ro, Ky-mo, ka-ro, ky-_____mo, Strim-strum, pop-a-did-le, There by the rig-dum, Rig-dum bot-tom in the ky-me-o!

They took him out and put him on the ground,
And he jumped up and bounded around.

"O, Missis Mouse, are you within?"
"O yes, kind sir, I sit and spin.

"There has been here a fine young man,
And I will have him if I can."

He took the mouse where he did dwell.
'Twas in the bottom of the well.

She waded in up to her chin,
And wished she was a maid again.

"Country Passtimes" in Ravenscroft's _Melismata,_ 1611. In 1580 a ballad entitled "A Most Strange Wedding of the Frog and the Mouse" was licensed to Edward White at Stationers' Hall; and a song, "The Frog Came to the Myl Dur" (mill door) was sung in Wedderburn's "Complaint of Scotland" as early as 1549. (See Chappell's _Popular Music of the Olden Time,_ 1855, vol. i, p. 88.) For a group of related Scottish texts see Maidment's _Scottish Ballads and Songs,_ 1859, pp. 153–157; C. K. Sharp's _A Ballad Book,_ No. 30; _Journal of the Folksong Society,_ vol. ii, p. 225. For English traditional versions see Halliwell's _Nursery Rhymes_ (1st ed.), No. 93, pp. 70–72; Rimbault's _Collection of Old Nursery Rhymes,_ pp. 26–27; Miss Mason's _Nursery_

Birds' Courting Song

"Hi!" said the black-bird, sit-ting on a chair, "Once I court-ed a la-dy fair,

She proved fick-le and turned her back, And ev-er since then I've dressed in black."

Tow-dy, ow-dy, dil-do-dum, Tow-dy, ow-dy, dil-do-day,

Tow-dy, ow-dy, dil-do-dum, Tol-lol-li-dy, dil-do-day!

"Hi!" said the blackbird, sitting on a chair,
"Once I courted a lady fair;
She proved fickle and turned her back,
And ever since then I've dressed in black."

Chorus:

Towdy, owdy, dildodum,
  Towdy, owdy, dildoday,
Towdy, owdy, dildodum,
  Tollollidy, dildoday!

"Hi!" said the little leather-winged bat,
"I will tell you the reason that,
The reason that I fly in the night
Is because I've lost my heart's delight."

Rhymes and Country Songs, pp. 8–9; Rimbault's *A Little Book of Old Songs and Ballads,* p. 87; Baring-Gould's *A Book of Nursery Songs and Rhymes,* No. 17, p. 27. There is an Irish version printed in *Notes and Queries,* 1st series, vol. ii, p. 75. American versions have been printed in *The Journal of American Folk-Lore,* vol. xxvi, pp. 134–135; Brockway and Wyman, *Lonesome Tunes,* vol. i, pp. 25–29; Campbell and Sharp, *English Folksongs from the Appalachians,* Nos. 119–120, pp. 317–319. For the version sung by Liston see Davidson's *Universal Melodist,* 1847, vol. i, pp. 166–167. —R. H.

For further notes on the history of the song and British and American variants, see Albert H. Tolman and Mary O. Eddy, "Traditional Texts and Tunes," *The Journal of American Folk-Lore,* Vol. 35 (October–December, 1922), No. 138, pp. 394–399. For the "kymo" type of refrain, see Grace Partridge Smith, "A Vermont Variant of 'The Frog's Courting,'" *ibid.,* vol. 52 (January–March, 1939), No. 203, pp. 125–127.

Ibid., pp. 40–45.

For other versions of *The Birds' Courting Song* (sung by James Atwood) see Campbell and Sharp, pp. 310–311.—R. H.

"Hi!" said the little mourning dove,
"I'll tell you how to regain her love:
Court her night and court her day,
Never give her time to say 'O nay!' "

"Hi!" said the woodpecker. sitting on a fence,
"Once I courted a handsome wench;
She got scary and from me fled,
And ever since then my head's been red."

"Hi!" said the blue-jay, as she flew,
"If I was a young man I'd have two.
If one proved faithless and chanced for to go,
I'd have a new string to my bow."

The Little Pig

There was an old woman and she had a little pig,
   Um————,
There was an old woman and she had a little pig,
   Um————,
There was an old woman and she had a little pig,
He didn't cost much 'cause he wasn't very big,
   Um————,

Ibid., 46–49.

For other versions of *The Little Pig* see Halliwell's "Nursery Rhymes," 1st ed., No. 27, p. 18 (6th ed., No. 542, p. 266); M. H. Mason's "Nursery Rhymes and Country Songs," pp. 32–33; Rimbault's "A Collection of Old Nursery Rhymes," No. 34, p. 42. —R. H.

This little old woman kept the pig in the barn,
The prettiest thing she had on the farm.

This little woman fed the pig on clover,
And he laid down and died all over.

The little piggy died 'cause he could n't get his breath,
Now wasn't that a horrible death?

The little old woman she died of grief,
Now wasn't that a great relief.

The little old man laid down and died,
ONE, TWO, THREE laid side by side.

Johnny Sands

A man whose name was Johnny Sands, Had married Betty Hague. And though she brought him gold and lands. She prov'd a terrible plague. For Oh' she was a scolding wife. Full of caprice and whim. He said, that he was tired of life, And she was tired of him. And she was tired of him, And she was tired of him. Says he "then I will drown myself—The river runs below." Says she, "pray do you silly elf I wished it long a - go," Says he, "upon the brink I'll stand, Do you run down the hill, And push me in with all your might," Says she "my love I will," Says she "my love I will." Says she "my love I will."

From *Series of Old American Songs,* Reproduced in Facsimile from Original or Early Editions in the Harris Collection of American Poetry and Plays, with Brief Annotations by S. Foster Damon, Curator, No. 30. Providence, Rhode Island: Brown University Library. 1936.

This song was founded on a folk tale and in turn has become a folk song, collected by ballad experts. It was written, however, by John Sinclair, who was born in 1790 (probably in Scotland), and began his American career about 1830, singing in operas

A man whose name was Johnny Sands
  Had married Betty Hague,
And though she brought him gold and
    lands,
  She prov'd a terrible plague,
For oh! she was a scolding wife,
  Full of caprice and whim,
He said, that he was tired of life,
  And she was tired of him,
  And she was tired of him,
  And she was tired of him.

Says he, "Then I will drown myself—
  The river runs below,"
Says she, "Pray do you silly elf
  I wished it long ago,"
Says he, "Upon the brink I'll stand,
  Do you run down the hill,
And push me in with all your might,
  Says she, "My love, I will,"
  Says she, "My love, I will,"
  Says she, "My love, I will."

"For fear that I should courage lack
  And try to save my life,
Pray tie my hands behind my back."
  "I will," replied his wife.
She tied them fast as you may think,
  And when securely done,
"Now stand," she says, "upon the brink
  And I'll prepare to run,
  And I'll prepare to run,
  And I'll prepare to run."

All down the hill his loving bride
  Now ran with all her force
To push him in—he stepped aside,
  And she fell in, of course,
Now splashing, dashing, like a fish.
  "Oh, save me, Johnny Sands."
"I can't, my dear, tho' much I wish,
  For you have tied my hands,
  For you have tied my hands,
  For you have tied my hands."

Old Grimes

Air: "Auld Lang Syne."

Old Grimes is dead, that good old man,
  We ne'er shall see him more;
He wore a single-breasted coat,
  That buttoned down before.
His heart was open as the day,
  His feelings all were true;
His hair it was inclined to grey,
  He wore it in a queue.

Whene'er was heard the voice of pain,
  His breast with pity burned;
The large, round head upon his cane,
  From ivory was turned.
Thus ever prompt at pity's call,
  He knew no base design;
His eyes were dark, and rather small,
  His nose was aquiline.

---

and concerts for some twenty years. He specialized in Scotch ballads. The original sheet-music is copyrighted 1842. This, the most successful of his compositions, was a favorite in the repertory of the Hutchinson family.—S. F. D.

Ibid., No. 12.

The Hon. Albert Gorton Greene (1802–1868—for his career, see the Dictionary of American Biography), whose collection of American poetry became the nucleus of the Harris Collection, was the author of this ballad, which added a beloved figure to American folklore.

Greene is said to have written the song when only sixteen (at which time he was a sophomore at Brown); another tradition delays the composition until he was studying at the famous Lichfield Law School (1820–22). It was first published anonymously in the *Providence Gazette*, January 16, 1822; Greene acknowledged his authorship of all but the first stanza in a letter to the *Manufacturers' and Farmers' Journal* (Providence) May 16, 1833. He contributed a revised version to Anne Lynch's *Rhode Island*

He lived at peace with all mankind,
  In friendship he was true;
His coat had pocketholes behind,
  His pantaloons were blue,
But poor old Grimes is now at rest,
  Nor fears misfortune's frown;
He had a double-breasted vest,
  The stripes ran up and down.

He modest merit sought to find,
  And pay it its desert;
He had no malice in his mind,
  No ruffle on his shirt.

His neighbors he did not abuse,
  Was sociable and gay;
He wore not rights and lefts for shoes,
  But changed them every day.

His knowledge, hid from public gaze,
  He never brought to view;
He made a noise town-meeting days,
  As many people do.

Thus, undisturbed by anxious care,
  His peaceful moments ran;
And everybody said he was
  A fine old gentleman.

Derby Ram

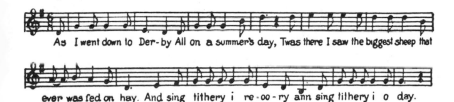

As I went down to Der-by All on a summer's day, Twas there I saw the biggest sheep that ever was fed on hay. And sing tithery i re-oo-ry ann sing tithery i o day.

As I went down to Derby,
  All on a summer's day,
'Twas there I saw the biggest sheep
  'Twas ever fed on hay.

Chorus:
  And sing tithery i reoory ann,
  Sing tithery i o day.

- ———

Book (1841). It was published separately, with illustrations by Augustus Hoppin, in 1867.

The many claimants to authorship while it was still anonymous have been forgotten. There were also several who claimed to be the original Grimes; but as Greene did not write the opening quatrain (it is said to have been an old epitaph), and Goldsmith's "Elegy on Madame Blaize" was obviously its other parent, these claimants also may be dismissed.

A host of imitations at once sprang into existence; Old Grimes was furnished with wives, children, parents, and live-stock, to a surprising extent. One of these, "Young Grimes," was written by Walter (not yet "Walt") Whitman.

The ballad was sung to the tune of "Auld Lang Syne."—S. F. D.

———

From *A Garland of Green Mountain Song*, edited by Helen Hartness Flanders, piano settings by Helen Norfleet, pp. 24-26. Copyright, 1934, by Helen Hartness Flanders. Number One, Green Mountain Pamphlets. Published as part of the publication program of the Committee for the Conservation of Vermont Traditions and Ideals of the Vermont Commission on Country Life, Arthur Wallace Peach, Agent. Northfield, Vermont.

We have many versions of this spirited song in Vermont. This is transcribed by E. F. as sung by Mr. Eugene Hall (deceased) of Ludlow. The fourth verse was supplied by Mr. E. M. Burdett, formerly of the same lumber camp where it had been learned.—H. H. F.

The wool on the sheep bag, sir,
    It reached unto the sky.
The eagles built their nests there,
    And I heard the young ones cry.

The wool on that sheep belly, sir,
    It dragged unto the ground,
Was sold there in Derby
    For forty thousand pounds.

The horns on this sheep's head, sir,
    They reached unto the moon.
A man went up in February
    And never came down till June.

He had four feet to walk, sir,
    He had four feet to stand;

And every foot he had, sir,
    It covered an acre of land.

When they killed this sheep, sir,
    It caused an awful flood;
And the man that killed the sheep,
    sir,
    Was drowned in his blood.

The man that owned this sheep, sir,
    He was immensely rich;
And the man that composed this
    song, sir,
    Was the lying son of a gun.

The wool on this sheep tail, sir,
    I've heard the weaver say,
It spun full forty yards, sir,
    And she wove it in a day.

The Herring Song

As I was walking down by the sea side,
I saw an old herring floating up with the tide;
He was forty feet long and fifty feet square,
If this ain't a great lie I will sing no more here.

And what do you think I made of his head?
'Twas forty fine ovens as ever baked bread,
Some shovels and pokers and other fine things,—
Don't you think I made well of my jovial herring?

And what do you think I made of his eyes?
'Twas forty great puddings and fifty great pies,
Some mustards and custards and other fine things,—
Don't you think I made well of my jovial herring?

And what do you think I made of his tail?
'Twas forty fine shipping as ever sot sail,
Some long-boats and barges and other fine things,—
Don't you think I made well of my jovial herring?

From "Cape Cod Dialect," by George Davis Chase, in *Dialect Notes*, Vol. II (Part V, 1903), pp. 302–303. Publication of the American Dialect Society. New Haven, Connecticut. Published by the Society.

The . . . *Herring Song* was sometimes used by the men as a cradle song.—G. D. C.

No tune. For a Somerset version, with tune, see "The Red Herring," Charles H. Farnsworth and Cecil J. Sharp, *Folk-Songs, Chanteys and Singing Games* (New York, [n.d.]), pp. 46–47.

And what do you think I made of his scales?
'Twas forty fine blacksmiths as ever made nails,
Some carpenters and masons and other fine things,—
Don't you think I made well of my jovial herring?

And what do you think I made of his guts?
Some forty pretty maidens and fifty great sluts,
Some kitchen maids and chamber maids and other fine things,—
Don't you think I made well of my jovial herring?

The Old Man Who Lived in the Wood

There was an old man that lived in a wood, As you can plain-ly see, Who said he could do more work in a day Than his wife could do in three. "If that be so," the old wom-an said, "Why, this you must al-low, That you shall do my work for a day, While I go drive the plough!"

From *Folk Songs of Old New England*, collected and edited by Eloise Hubbard Linscott, with an Introduction by James M. Carpenter, pp. 248–250. Copyright, 1939, by The Macmillan Company. New York.
Contributed by Phillips Barry, Cambridge, Massachusetts. This ballad is of Scotch origin and is based on a well-known theme in folklore. The oldest version of the story in English goes back to the late fifteenth century. It appeared in James Johnson's *Scots Musical Museum* in 1787. The song is widely known throughout New England.
—E. H. L.

There was an old man that lived in a wood,
  As you can plainly see,
Who said he could do more work in a day
  Than his wife could do in three.
"If that be so," the old woman said,
  "Why, this you must allow,
That you shall do my work for a day,
  While I go drive the plough!

"But you must milk the tiny cow,
  For fear she should go dry;
And you must feed the little pigs
  That are within the sty;
And you must watch the bracket hen,
  Lest she should lay astray;
And you must wind the reel of yarn
  That I spun yesterday."

The old woman took the staff in her hand,
  And went to drive the plough;
The old man took the pail in his hand,
  And went to milk the cow;

But Tiny hinched and Tiny flinched,
  And Tiny cocked her nose;
And Tiny hit the old man such a kick
  That the blood ran down his nose.

'T was, "Hey, my good cow," and "Ho, my good cow,"
  And "Now, my good cow, stand still.
If ever I milk this cow again,
  'T will be against my will."
And when he'd milked the Tiny cow,
  For fear she should go dry,
Why, then he fed the little pigs,
  That were within the sty.

And then he watched the bracket hen
  Lest she should lay astray;
But he forgot the reel of yarn
  His wife spun yesterday.
He swore by all the leaves on the tree
  And all the stars in heaven
That his wife could do more work in a day
  Than he could do in seven!

The Lone Fish-Ball

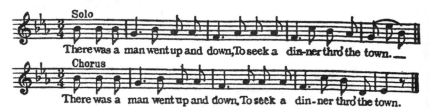

There was a man went up and down, To seek a din-ner thro' the town.

THE COLLEGE VERSION [1]

Solo: There was a man went up and down,
To seek a dinner thro' the town.

Chorus: There was a man went up and down,
To seek a dinner thro' the town.

---

[1] From *Carmina Collegensia*, edited by H. R. Waite, p. 15. Boston: Oliver Ditson & Company. 1876. Cited in *Read 'Em and Weep*, The Songs You Forgot to Remember, by Sigmund Spaeth, pp. 84–85. Copyright, 1926, by Doubleday, Page & Co. Garden City. 1927.

This song has been adapted by Hy Zaret and Lou Silver under the title "One Meat Ball."

It was one of the earliest and best of those immensely handy community songs in which a soloist presents two short lines, which are immediately repeated after him by the crowd."—S. S.

What wretch is he who wife forsakes,
Who best of jam and waffles makes!

He feels his cash to know his pence,
And finds he has but just six cents.

He finds at last a right cheap place,
And enters in with modest face.

The bill of fare he searches through,
To see what his six cents will do.

The cheapest viand of them all
Is "Twelve and a half cents for two
  Fish-balls."

The waiter he to him doth call,
And gently whispers—"One Fish-
  ball."

The waiter roars it through the hall,
The guests they start. at "One Fish-
  ball!"

The guest then says, quite ill at
  ease,
"A piece of bread, sir, if you please."

The waiter roars it through the hall,
"We don't give bread with one Fish-
  ball."

Moral

Who would have bread with his Fish-
  ball
Must get it first, or not at all.

Who would Fish-ball with fixin's eat
Must get some friend to stand a treat.

THE HISTORY OF THE SONG [2]

In the Boston area, especially among the Harvard elect, American humor in the late fifties, and beyond, centered about a Dr. Holmes-like "Skit" entitled "The Lay of the One Fishball." So fundamentally Harvard was it that as late as 1888, in the college song book of that year, it was the second song in the collection, following "Fair Harvard." Its author was George Martin Lane, Ph.D., Göttingen, 1851; Professor of Latin, Harvard, 1851-1894. That this seeming trifle should outlive all its author's scholarly volumes which for years were of international significance is one of the anomalies of literature.

The poem was first published in 1857, where I do not know. The authentic text, which differs from the song-book version, has been supplied by Charles Eliot Norton, as follows:

THE LAY OF THE ONE FISHBALL

1. There was a man went round the
     town,
   To hunt a supper up and down;
   There was a man, etc.

2. For he had been right far away,
   And nothing had to eat all day.

3. He feels his cash to count his
     pence,
   And all he had was just six cents.

4. "Wretch that I am, it happens
     meet,
   Why did I leave my Kirkland
     Street!

---

[2] From *The Feminine Fifties*, by Fred Lewis Pattee, pp. 217–220, 221–223. Copyright, 1940, by D. Appleton-Century Company, Inc. New York and London.

5. "None but a fool a wife forsakes,
Who raspberry jam and waffles
makes.

6. "If I were now safe out of town,
I'd give my bran-new dressing-
gown.

7. "But yet I'll make a start and
try
To see . what my six cents will
buy."

8. He finds at last a right cheap place,
And stealeth in with bashful face.

9. The bill of fare he runneth
through,
To see what his six cents will do.

10. The cheapest of the viands all,
Was 12½ for two fishball.

11. The waiter he to him doth call,

And whispers softly, "One fish-
ball."

12. The waiter roars it through the
hall,
The guests they start at *"One fish-
ball!"*

13. The waiter brings one fishball on,
The guest he looks abashéd down.

14. The scantness of the fare he sees:
"A piece of bread, now, if you
please."

15. The waiter roars it through the
hall,
*"We don't give bread with one
fishball!"*

16. Then whoso orders one fishball
Must get bread first or not at all.

17. And who would two with fixins eat,
Should get some friend to stand a
treat.

Few facetiae of equal caliber have had such distinguished treatment as
this Harvard *jeu d'esprit*. In the opening days of the Civil War it was
thrown into the form of an elaborate opera score in Italian by Professor
Francis James Child: *Il Pesceballo. Opera Seria: In Un Atto. Musica del
Maestro Rossibelli-Donimozarti.* Cambridge, 1862. On the verso of each
page was the Italian text and on the recto the poetic translation by James
Russell Lowell. The version, made for the Sanitary Commission, was performed several times in Cambridge and Boston, and a goodly sum of money
was realized for the use of the soldiers. In 1899 the Caxton Club reissued
the little volume in an edition limited to 210 copies with an introduction
written by Charles Eliot Norton. Concerning the origin of the ballad he
wrote this:

> The theme of the Pesceballo was suggested to him by a local ballad
> which had had great vogue, written not many years before by his class-
> mate and lifelong friend Lane, the genial and eminent professor of Latin
> at Harvard. I send you its genuine text. The account of its origin is
> given in a recent memoir of Mr. Lane by Professor Morgan. He says:
> "Many fables about the origin of this song have been told, and one was
> even printed with the song itself; but I know from Professor Lane's lips
> that it was based upon an adventure of his own. Arriving in Boston one
> day after a journey, he found himself hungry and with only twenty-five

cents in his pocket. Half that sum he had to reserve to pay his carfare to Cambridge. With the rest he entered a restaurant, "with modest face," and ordered a half portion of macaroni. What followed is described, doubtless with humorous exaggeration, in the ballad itself. During the late Civil War it was worked over into a mock Italian operetta, Il Pesceballo, by Professor Child, with an English version by Professor Lowell!"

Child's Italian version is a rare bit of humor. In a footnote, he explains to mythical Italians who may read the opera the mysteries of the Boston fishball:

Il Pesceballo *(corruzione della voce inglese Fish-ball)* è un *prodotto della cucina americana, consistente in una combinazione di stoccofisso con patate, fatta nella forma di pallottole, simili alle nostre polpette, e poi fritta. Msgr. Bedini, nel suo* Viaggio negli Stati Uniti, c' insegna *che la detta pietanza si usa massimamente nella Nuova-Inghilterra, ove, secondo quel venerabile, viene specialmente mangiato a colazione nelle domeniche.*

* * * * *

Few have known that Lowell, following Child's Italian with extravagant variations, ever wrote a complete opera like this. It must have been done with the pen, somewhat blunted, that had written the *Fable for Critics.* This, for instance, at the crisis moment of the tragedy:

THE STRANGER *in a rich tenor:*
Now, waiter, bring to me the bill of fare.
(*aside*) Ye pangs within, what will not hunger dare?

THE WAITER *in basso profundo:*
Here is the bill of fare, sir,
Of what there is for supper,
Long as the Proverbs of Tupper,—
Command, then, *s'il vous plait*!

Soup, with nothing, twenty coppers,
Roast spring-chicken, three and nime [*sic*],
Ditto biled (but then they're whoppers!)
Fish-balls, luscious, two a dime,
Two a dime, sir, hot and prime, sir,
Fried codfish-balls, two a dime!
There's the bill, and cash procures ye
Any viand that allures ye. . . .
Best of all, though, 's the fish-ball, though,
We have made 'em all the fashion.
Come to try 'em as we fry 'em,—
Presto! liking turns to passion!
There we carry off the banner,
'Taint so easy, neither, that ain't,—

But, you see, we've got a patent,—
Do 'em in the Cape Cod manner,—
That's the way to make 'em flavorous!
Fried in butter, tongue can't utter
How they're brown, and crisp, and savorous!

S. Peace, waiter, for I starve meanwhile,—but hold:
Bring me onè fish-ball, *one*,—(*aside*) curst lack of gold!
Moment of horror! crisis of my doom!
Led by the dreadful Shape, I sought this room
With half a dime! A slender sum, and yet
'Twill buy one fish-ball! Down, weak pride, forget
Thy happier—but what prate I? Thought of dread
If, with one fish-ball, they should *not* give bread!

W. Here's your *one* fish-ball, sir—(*sarcastically*) you ordered *one*?

S. Thanks,—and with bread to match, 'twere not ill done.

W. (*with fury*) With one single fish-ball, is't bread ye are after?
So wild a presumption provokes me to laughter!
So mad a suggestion proves, out of all question,
Howe'er the test shun, you're mad as a hornet!
I trample it, scorn it, so mad a suggestion!
It fills me with fury, it dumbs me with rage!

S. With one dainty fish-ball do *you* bread refuse me?
It's *you* are the madman yourself, sir, excuse me!
My wish was immodest? Of men you're the oddest!
In straight-waistcoat bodiced, go hide ye in Bedlam!
Your fish-balls, *there* peddle 'em! learn to be modest,
And tempt not a stranger half-starving to rage!

CHORUS. O'er one paltry fish-ball d'ye make such a rumpus?
For gracious sake, neighbors, we'd rather you'd thump us!

The entrance of the landlady calms the tumult. The opera ends in pure slapstick. . . .

GAME AND DANCE SONGS

Pompey

Pom - pey was dead and laid in his grave,

Laid in his grave, laid in his grave;

Pom - pey was dead and laid in his grave,—

Oh! oh! oh!

Pompey was dead, and laid in his grave,
  Laid in his grave, laid in his grave;
Pompey was dead, and laid in his
      grave,—
Oh! Oh! Oh!

An apple-tree grew over his head,
Over his head, over his head, etc.

The apples were ripe, beginning to
  fall.

There came an old woman a-picking
  them up.

Pompey jumped up and gave her a
  thump.

It made the old woman go hipple de
  hop.

If you want any more, then sing it
  yourself.

From "'Pompey!' A Famous End Song," Words by Mrs. K. B.—Music by W. R. Dehnoff, Arranged by J. J. Freeman. Copyright, 1876, by W. R. Dehnoff. In *Series of Old American Songs*, Reproduced in Facsimile from Original or Early Editions in the Harris Collection of American Poetry and Plays, with Brief Annotations by S. Foster Damon, Curator, No. 50. Providence, Rhode Island: Brown University Library. 1936.

"Pompey" is a child's game of considerable antiquity. The children sing it while enacting the parts of the dead boy, the apple-tree, and the little old woman. The terminal vocalizing is delightfully dramatic.

The ballad experts have found versions all over the United States, the name "Pompey" being variously given as "Old Grimes" (New York and Kentucky), "Old Cromwell" (Cambridge, Mass.), "Old Grampus" (North Carolina and Mississippi), also "Poor Robin," "Old Rover," "Poor Roger," "Poor Johnny," "Poor Tommy," "Sir Roger," "Cock Robin," "Old Tommy," "Old Granddaddy," "Old Pompey," and "Old Kramer." It is said that the song is known as a chantey.

The sheet-music, with "words by Mrs. K. B." and "music by W. R. Dehnoff," is dated 1876.

For references, see W. W. Newell's *Games and Songs of American Children*, p. 100; Louise Pound's *American Ballads and Songs*, pp. 232–233 and 256; Flanders and Brown's *Vermont Folk Songs and Ballads*, p. 182; Louise Pound's *Folk Songs of Nebraska*, p. 57; Mellinger E. Henry's *More Songs of American Southern Highlands*, pp. 94–95;

Old Woman All Skin and Bone.

There was an old wom-an all skin—and bone. M - M M . . . M

There was an old woman all skin and bone. M-M M---M.

She went to the churchyard all alone. Oo-oo-oo.

She looked up and looked down. Oo-oo-oo.

She saw a corpse lie on the ground. Oo-oo-oo.

"Father, Father," so she said. Oo-oo-oo.

"Shall I look so when I am dead?" Oo-oo-oo.

The sexton to her made reply. Oo-oo-oo.

"Yes, my darling, by and by." *Boo!*

---

and the *Journal of American Folk Lore,* Vols. XIII, XXVI, XXXIV, XXXV, XXXIX, XL.—S. F. D.

From *Folk Songs of Old New England,* Collected and Edited by Eloise Hubbard Linscott, With an Introduction by James M. Carpenter, pp. 44–46. Copyright, 1939, by The Macmillan Company. New York.

The children of Dr. and Mrs. Frank Allen Hubbard of Taunton, Massachusetts, who sang and played this game, sometimes reserved it to initiate visiting playmates and newcomers.

The most highly imaginative player usually was chosen for the corpse, for after one really fine screech the game was quite likely to end abruptly with the appearance of a grown-up bringing emphatic requests for less disturbance during the doctor's office hours.

This weird game originally came from Somersetshire and is a dramatization of the belief that the dead return for vengeance on those that disturb them.

Each object and person in the verses is represented by a player chosen by counting out. The one taking the part of the old woman approaches the corpse, which lies at the feet of the sexton. All the players sing as the old woman walks slowly toward the "churchyard," and the eerie, half-moaning chant is broken by the shrill scream of the corpse as it arises suddenly and gives chase to the other players, who add to the effect with shrill cries. If the corpse can catch another player, that one becomes the old woman, the first old woman becomes the sexton, and the game continues.—E. H. L.

Quaker's Courtship

Mad-am, I am come a-courting, Hum, hum, heigh-o hum! 'Tis for pleasure,

not for sport-ing, Hum, hum, heigh-o hum! Sir, it suits me to re-tire, Teedle link tum

D. C.

teedle tum a tee; You may sit and court the fire, Teedle link tum, teedle tum a tee.

"Madam, I am come a courting—
Hum, hum, heigho hum!
'Tis for pleasure, not for sporting—
Hum, hum, heigho hum!"

"Sir, it suits me to retire,
Teedle link tum, teedle tum a tee;
You may sit and court the fire,
Teedle link tum, teedle tum a tee."

"Madam, here's a ring worth forty
shilling,
Thou may'st have it if thou art willing."

"What care I for rings or money?
I'll have a man who will call me
honey."

"Madam, thou art tall and slender;
Madam, I know thy heart is tender."

"Sir, I see you are a flatterer,
And I never loved a Quaker."

"Must I give up my religion?
Must I be a Presbyterian?"

"Cheer up, cheer up, loving brother,
If you can't catch one fish catch another."

Hey, Betty Martin!

Hey, Betty Martin, tip-toe, tip-toe,
Hey, Betty Martin, tip-toe fine!

Johnny, get your hair cut, hair cut, hair cut,
Johnny, get your hair cut, hair cut short!

From *Games and Songs of American Children*, collected and compared by William
Wells Newell, pp. 94–95. New and Enlarged Edition. Copyright, 1883, 1903, by Harper
& Brothers. New York and London.

In this piece, two children (in costume or otherwise) impersonate a Quaker paying
his addresses to a young lady of the world.—W. W. N.

From *Ballads of the American Revolution and the War of 1812*, A Program of Early
American Songs Taken from the Collection of John Allison, sung by John and Lucy
Allison, with Sawyer's Minute Men, Victor Album P-11, Record 26462-A, 2. Camden,

Johnny, get your gun and your sword and pistol,
Johnny, get your gun and come with me!

Hey, Betty Martin, tip-toe, tip-toe,
Hey, Betty Martin, tip-toe fine!

Devil's Dream

New Jersey: RCA Victor Division, RCA Manufacturing Company, Inc. Transcribed by Frances Kurland.

. . . this ditty goes back to the War of 1812, and for over a century it has been a favorite march tune with the fifers and drummers of the American army. Iowa pioneers had a version of it as a play-party and dance tune under the title of "Old Brass Wagon."—J. A.

For a different version, from Howe's *Songs and Ballads of ye Olden Times*, describing a Yorkshireman's first visit to London, see Edward Arthur Dolph, *"Sound Off!"* (New York, 1942), pp. 437–439.

Played by Dennis McClure, Willimantic, Connecticut. Dance changes called by Happy Hale, Hinsdale, New Hampshire.

From *Folk Songs of Old New England*, collected and edited by Eloise Hubbard Linscott, with an Introduction by James M. Carpenter, pp. 72–74. Copyright, 1939, by The Macmillan Company. New York.

Square Formation   *Four Couples in a Set*

Balance partners eight hands around	8 bars
Swing to the corners	4 "
Head lady swings gentleman on her right.	
Head gentleman swings lady on his left.	
Join hands and circle eight hands around	8 "
Back to place	
First lady leads to the right and swings to the corner	4 "
First lady swings to the third gentleman at the same time the first gentleman swings the lady of the second couple	4 "
Dos-a-dos to the corners	4 "
Allemande left. Then right hand to the partner, and swing	8 "

Repeat, with the second couple progressing through the set as did the first couple.

This is the way Happy Hale sings it:

Here we go eight hands around
First lady leads to the right
Grab that gent and hold him up tight
Up to the next and on your toes
Swing that gent with the big long nose
Up to the next who's standing there
Swing that gent with the curly red hair
Up to the next and swing your own
Now—everybody swing
Dosey dos to the corners all
Dosey dos with your own little doll
Allemande left with the lady on your left
Give right hand to your own little doll
                    (*Grand right and left*)
Right foot up and left foot down
Hand over hand or you'll never get around
And when you meet her pass her by
Wink at the next as you go by
Kiss the next right on the sly
And swing your own by and by.

The Merry Dance

From *The Country Dance Book,* The Old-Fashioned Square Dance, Its History, Lore, Variations, & Its Callers, Complete & Joyful Instructions, written by Beth

PERHAPS one of the happiest numbers of this [contry] group is the Merry Dance. Everyone seems to like this one no matter which way he believes it should be danced. Of the several versions, we like the one which originated with the Holmes brothers in Stoddard, New Hampshire. They wrote the music for it, too. These boys are contemporary Yankees, and their dance is loyally done in all the surrounding towns. On one occasion not many years ago, the Merry ·Dance became part of Stoddard's history. It was the night of the "Great Blizzard" (not the Great Blizzard of '88). The snow began to swirl off Pitcher Mountain, and the dancers· were forced to stay the night in the town hall. The dance went on as the snow piled up against the windows. Nobody could get home. At the turn of dawn, when the oil lamps were blown out, the orchestra struck up the Holmes brothers' Merry Dance. The dancers stepped this one out until finally the cornetist rebelled. Putting down his instrument, he shouted, "What the hell is this anyway, a dance or a blank-blank overture?" Thereafter the dance was nicknamed the Stoddard Overture. And now, when someone suggests a Stoddard Overture, why don't you ask him if he remembers the night when . . . ?

Contry Formation   *Six or Eight Couples in a Set*

First couple cross over, first lady down outside and back with second gent; first gent down the outside and back with second lady at same time	8 bars
Same four join hands, down center four and back	8 "
Cast off, ladies chain	8 "
Half promenade	4 "
Half right and left	4 "

Third and fifth couples start the dance at the same time.

Wild Goose Chase

Contry Formation   *Six or Eight Couples in a Set*

First couple cross over before music starts
First and third couples join hands with partners and balance in center toward each other. (Second couple stand like lighthouses)   4 bars

Tolman & Ralph Page, pp. 95–96. Copyright, 1937, by The Countryman Press, Inc. New York: A. S. Barnes and Company.

Ibid., pp. 93, 167, 168.

Contry Formation   *Six or Eight Couples in a Set*

First couple walk behind second lady and take third couple's
place. At the same time third couple walks behind second gent
and takes first couple's place. (Second couple still stand like
lighthouses)   4 "
These two couples balance again   4 "
First and third couples return in same way to original places   4 "
First couple down center and back   8 "
Cast off, right and left   8 "
(Remember gent is on lady's side, from original crossing over
before music began.)
Head couple continue, dancing with fourth, fifth, sixth, etc.,
couples.
Each head couple cross over before they begin their performance.
When they reach the foot of the set they cross over to their
respective sides.

* * * * *

Mr. Barrett scoffs at the idea that the dance Wild Goose Chase was so
named by Federal soldiers floundering vainly after Jeb Stuart. "Why, old
Sewall Page has told me about playing that tune a good many years before
the Civil War. Called it Wild Goose Chase, too. Goes something like
this . . . ," and after one or two flourishes of the bow, he played it for
us. First a simple, direct melody, and then a bow-twisting variation, probably his own, although he didn't say so.

II. RHYMES AND JINGLES

*I trust, my friend, you will not gather from this that I condemn
rhymes for children. I know that there is a certain music in them
that delights the ear of children. Nor am I insensible to the fact
that in Mother Goose's Melodies, there is frequently a sort of
humor in the odd jingle of sound and sense. There is, furthermore, in many of them, an historical significance, which may
please the profound student who puzzles it out; but what I affirm
is, that many of these pieces are coarse, vulgar, offensive, and it is
precisely these portions that are apt to stick in the minds of children.*—SAMUEL G. GOODRICH

*. . . the old-fashioned idea was to put into rhyme anything that
should be committed to memory; in Yorkshire "nominy" is the
name given to this class of verse, an appellation very likely
derived from the church formula "in nominee Patris" (in the
name of the Father, etc.).*—JOURNAL OF AMERICAN FOLKLORE

*There is a nationality in districts as well as in countries. . . .
This has given rise . . . to an infinite number of phrases expres-*

sive of vituperation, obloquy, or contempt, which are applied to the inhabitants of various places by those whose lot it is to reside in the immediate vicinity.—ROBERT CHAMBERS

1. CHILDREN'S RHYMES

FOR all his moralistic objections to their content, or lack of it, Samuel G. Goodrich, the creator of "Peter Parley," hit upon the precise reasons for the appeal of children's rhymes—their jingle and nonsense, their odd humor and bantering wit, and their very impropriety. So even though Boston could not justly claim Elizabeth Vergoose to be the original of that "eponomyous preceptress" of nursery rhymes and tales, as William A. Wheeler attempted to prove in 1870,[1] the New England conscience could not completely ignore the low taste of Yankee youngsters for nursery rhymes any more than it could stamp out the taste of their elders for "devil's ditties." Thus even the rather dreary alphabet in the *New England Primer* surprises us, in the midst of pious and moral platitudes, with a lilting roster of Scriptural names:

> Young *Obadias*
> David, *Josias*,
> All were pious.

And the conclusion—

> Zaccheus he
> Did climb the tree
> His Lord to see—

was such good nursery-rhyme material that it eventually became incorporated into Negro folk song as "Zaccheus climbed the sycamo' tree[2] and into "Old Dan Tucker":

> Old Dan Tucker climbed a tree
> Just for his Lord to see.
> Limb did break and he did fall,
> And he didn't see his Lord at all.[3]

In the same irreverent vein is

> Where was Moses when the light went out?
> Down in the cellar with his shirt-tail out.[4]

At the same time, since even folk tradition has its didactic side, New England children's rhymes satisfied the demands of morality and faith, or at least of worldly wisdom, in such copybook mottoes as

---

[1] *Mother Goose's Melodies, or Songs for the Nursery* (New York, 1870). See Vincent Starrett, "Much Ado about Mother Goose," in Bookman's Holiday (New York, 1942), pp. 146–166.

[2] See Dorothy Scarborough, *On the Trail of Negro Folk-Songs* (Cambridge, 1925), pp. 200, 286.

[3] See B. A. Botkin, *The American Play-Party Song* (Lincoln, Nebraska, 1937), p. 263.

[4] Melville Johnson, Gorham, Maine, Manuscripts of the Federal Writers' Project of the Works Progress Administration, reports this as a dialogue spoken when a light is blown out by a breeze, with the ending:
> He was in the dark with his shirt-tail out.

> God is great,
> God is good.
> So always do
> What He thinks you should,

and in such gentle cynicisms as

> Needles and pins, needles and pins,
> When a man gets married, his trouble begins.

2. LOCAL RHYMES

Mary Heaton Vorse records an interesting example of local adaptation of a children's game in the Provincetown version of "Ring-around-a-rosy," which "has been translated into sea terms."

> Ring a ring a rounder,
> Daddy caught a flounder,
> Oysters, Oysters, Hooray! [1]

Although adaptation is an important part of the process of formula and variation in the transmission of folk rhymes, as in folk sayings, an even more fertile source of local rhymes is the spirit of local rivalry and satire. Local gibes and taunts belong to the class of popular reproaches, which also includes children's teasing and taunting rhymes. The children's taunt and the local gibe are combined in the Newport ditty whose various combinations served to incite the various boys' quarters—the "up-town boys," the "over-to-The-Point boys," the "Long-wharf boys," and the "down-town boys"—against one another.

Here, too, we encounter traditional formulae. Thus, after the pattern of the rhyme about Weymouth and its herring, we find:

> Amherst for beauty,
> Hadley for pride,
> But if it hadn't been for huckleberries,
> Shutesbury would have died. [2]

And the lines used by Truro and Wellfleet boys and girls to taunt Provincetown youngsters (already given under "The Codfish Shanty") turn up in Gloucester and Bahaman adaptations, the latter reading:

> Those Nassau girls ain't got no comb,
> O they comb they head with a whipper back bone. [3]

A similar formula is seen in:

> The Montague girls are pretty,
> And the Howland girls are sweet,

---

[1] *Time and the Town* (New York, 1942), p. 153.

[2] Mrs. Clifton Johnson, South Hadley, Mass., in a letter of July 24, 1947.

[3] "Round the Bay of Mexico," recorded for the Library of Congress by Alan Lomax and Mary Elizabeth Barnicle, *Folk Music of the United States, 1942* (Washington, D. C.), Album V, No. AFFS 21 A, 2.

But the Passadumkeag girls
Have big feet.[1]

Many nursery rhymes originate in local or historical rhymes, adding a
touch of nonsense and word-play to the jest.

As I was dashing down Cutting Hill,
A-cutting through the air,
I saw Charlie Cutting setting
In Oscar Cutting's chair;
And Oscar Cutting was a-cutting
Charlie Cutting's hair.[2]

Finally, the spirit of the nursery rhyme and the local rhyme combined
pervades the epitaph, a form of folk rhyme in which New England seems
to have excelled. Although the serious epitaph sometimes reaches the level
of folk poetry, the humorous (or unconsciously humorous) and the mock
epitaph rarely rise above the level of the limerick. Perhaps the most
frequently quoted is the following punning epitaph:

Under the sod and under the trees,
Here lies the body of Solomon Pease.
The Pease are not here, there's only the pod—
The Pease shelled out and went to God.[3]

Epitaph humor also includes such stories as the one based on the most
common of the traditional epitaphs:

Pause, stranger, ere you pass by—
As you are now, so once was I.
As I am now, soon you will be.
Prepare for death, and follow me.—

It is said of one Cape Cod widow, who had not got on too well with
her late husband, that she refused to let the minister spread one of these
tributes upon his stone. But something had to be written there, so the
usual stock verse was chiseled on it, this too, against her wishes—

As I am now, so you will be,
Prepare for death and follow me.

She went out one dark night and scratched beneath it:

To follow you I'll not consent
Because I know which way you went.[4]

B. A. B.

---

[1] Mrs. Catherine McGinn, Enfield, Me., Manuscripts of the Federal Writers' Project
of the Works Progress Administration for the State of Maine, who notes: "Montague
was an early name for Enfield."

[2] Bessie Powers Stevens, Georgetown, Me. *ibid.*

[3] Edwin Valentine Mitchell, *It's an Old New England Custom* (New York, 1946),
p. 145, who notes: "The descendants of a man at Searsport, Maine, are said to have
had so much fun poked at them on account of the . . . epitaph that they had it
effaced."

[4] Jeremiah Digges, *Cape Cod Pilot* (Provincetown and New York, 1937), p. 92.

PLAY RHYMES

Counting-Out Rhymes

FROM VERMONT [1]

Inty, minty, dibity fig
Dilah, dalah, dominig,
Ikah, pikah, dominika,
Elika, belika, boo—
Out goes Y O U.

Eenie, meenie, miney mo,
Crack a fenney, finey fo,
Ommanuga, poppatuga,
Rick, stick, dan do.

Entry, mentry, cutery corn,
Apple seed and apple thorn,

Wire, brier, limber lock,
Six geese in a flock.

One zaw, two zaw, zig, zaw, zan,
Bobtail, vinegar, ticklum tan,
Harum, scarum, virgum, marum,
Stringlum, stranglum, back and John.

Eenie, meenie, monie my,
Bassaloney, boney, stry,
Hair, ware, crown, nack,
Alko, balko, we wo wack.

FROM MASSACHUSETTS AND NEW HAMPSHIRE [2]

Eena, meena, mona my,
Tuscalona, bona stry,
Tin pan, maska, dary,
Highly, pigly, pig snout,
Crinkly, cranky, you are out.
 (New Hampshire.)

One is all, two is all, Zick is all zan,
Bobtail, vinegar, little tol tan,
Harum, scarum, Virginia merum,
Zee, tan, buck.
 (New Hampshire.)

Fe, fi, fo, fum,
I smell the blood of an Englishman,
Be he live, or be he dead,
I'll have his bones to make my bread.
 (Plymouth.)

Eggs, cheese, butter, bread,
Stick, stock, stone, dead,
Hang him up, lay him down,
On his father's living ground.
 (Plymouth.)

Een, teen, feather pip,
Sargo, larko, bump.
 (Plymouth.)

Inditie, Mentitie, Petitee, Dee,
Delia, Delia, Dominee,
Oacha, Poacha, Domminnicher,
Hing, Ping, Chee.
 (Plymouth.)

Henry, pennery, pit for gold,
Had a louse in his head,
Seven years old.
Seventy, seventy on to that,
This old logy will grow fat,
Hinchiman, pinchiman, make his back
 smart,
If ever I catch him, I'll sling him to
 my heart;
Sling, slang, chattery bang—out.
 (Plymouth.)

Up on yonder hill,
There's where my father dwells.
He has jewels, he has rings,
He has many pretty things,

---

[1] By Mrs. Rebecca M. Halley, West Newbury, Vermont. Manuscripts of the Federal Writers' Project of the Works Progress Administration for the State of Vermont.
[2] From *Plymouth Memories of an Octogenarian*, by William T. Davis, pp. 208–212. Copyright, 1906, by Bittinger Brothers. Plymouth, Massachusetts.

He has a hammer with two nails,
He has a cat with two tails.
Strike Jack, lick Tom,
Blow the bellows, old man.
  (New England.)

Ink, mink, pepper stink,
Sarko, Larko, Bump.
  (Plymouth.)

One-ery, two-ery, eckeery Ann,
Phillisy, phollisy, Nicholas John,
Queebe, quarby, Irish Mary,
Sinkum, sankum, Johnny go buck.
  (Cambridge.)

Ball-Bouncing Rhymes

Bounce-y bounce-y ball-y,
I called on pretty Polly!
But she's in love with Cholly,
And hasn't time for me!

Teacher, teacher, made a mistake—
She sat down on a chocolate cake!
  The cake was soft,
  Teacher fell off—
Teacher, teacher, made a mistake!

Gene, Gene, made a machine;
Joe, Joe, made it go;
Frank, Frank, turned the crank,
And his mother came out and gave him
    a spank
That sent him over the railroad bank!

Red, white, and green!
My father is a machine,
My mother is the steering wheel,
And I'm the gasoline!

Rope-Skipping Rhymes

My father has a horse to shoe,
How many nails do you thing will do?
One, two, three, four, etc.

Fudge, fudge, tell the judge,
  Mama's got a baby,
Not a girl, not a boy,
  Just a little lady.

Apples, peaches, pumpkin pie,
How many years before I die?

Andy Gump sat on a stump.
He fell off and got a bump.

Susan, Susan, thought she was losin',
  So she gave the whole thing up.

Martin, Martin, was only startin',
  But he finished and won the cup!

Charlie Chaplin sat on a pin.
How many inches did it go in?
One, two, three, four, etc.

Where are you going, Bill?
Down town, Bill?
What for, Bill?
To pay my gas bill.
How much, Bill?
Ten-dollar bill.

Last night, and the night before,
Twenty-four robbers came to my door.
When I went down to let them in,

From Willimantic, Connecticut. Manuscripts of the Federal Writers' Project of the Works Progress Administration for the State of Connecticut.

Ibid.

They knocked me down with the rolling pin.
Ten ran east, and ten ran west,
And four jumped over the cuckoo's
nest.

Shirley Temple walks like this;
Shirley Temple talks like this;
Shirley Temple smiles like this;
Shirley Temple throws a kiss.

Oldsmobile, Chevrolet, Studebaker,
Ford—
Now I jump my shining cord.

Ella, Ella, dressed in yellow,
Went downstairs to meet her fellow.
How many kisses did he give?
One, two, three, four, etc.

I come from Chink-a-China,
    My home is 'cross the sea.
I send my laundry over,
    For fifty cents a week.
So, over, over, over,
    You ought to be ashamed
To marry, marry, marry
    A boy without a name!

Mississippi lives on shore,
She has children three or four.
Which one shall I marry,
Rich man, poor man, beggar-man,
    thief,
Doctor, lawyer, merchant, chief.
[*The last two lines are repeated over
and over until the jumper misses.*]

Butterfly, butterfly, turn around,
Butterfly, butterfly, touch the ground,
Butterfly, butterfly, show your shoe,
Butterfly, butterfly, twenty-three to
do.

Johnny said to Tommy, "How much
    are your geese?"
Tommy said to Johnny, "Fifty cents
    apiece."
Johnny said to Tommy, "That's too
    dear."
Tommy said to Johnny, "Get out of
    here!"

Lady, lady, turn around.
Lady, lady, touch the ground.
Lady, lady, show your shoe.
Lady, lady, please skidoo!

Mother, mother, I am sick,
Send for the doctor, quick, quick,
    quick.
How many days shall I live?
One, two, three, etc.

Tenement to let,
Inquire within.
I'll jump out,
And let you jump in.

House for rent,
Furniture in.
As —— moves out,
—— moves in!

Tickling Rhymes

Tickle-y tickle-y
On the knee;
If you laugh,
You don't love me.

If you are an honest girl(boy),
As I suppose you be,
You will neither laugh nor cry
When I tickle you on the knee.

Ibid.

Children's Taunts

—— 's It,
And has a fit,
And doesn't know how to get out of it!

Tattle-tale, teacher's pet!
Tell it quick or you'll forget!

Mamma's little condensed-milk baby!

Can't catch me!
Can't catch a flea!

Liar, liar, your pants are on fire,
Your nose is as long as a telephone
    wire!

Run, Fatty, run! Run for your life!
Here comes Skinny with a butcher
    knife!
[*Names interchangeable.*]

You think you're cute
With a pimple on your snoot,
A five-cent collar
And a ten-cent suit!

RHYMES FOR OCCASIONS

Incantations and Formulae

Boys try to catch a bat by throwing up the hat and calling:——

> Bat, bat, come down my hat,
> And when I brew and when I bake,
> I'll give you a piece of bat-cake.
>
> *Massachusetts.*

> A swarm of bees in May
> Is worth a load of hay.
> A swarm of bees in June
> Is worth a silver spoon.
> A swarm of bees in July
> Is not worth a fly.
>
> *Westport, Mass.*

> One crow, sorrow,
> Two crows, mirth,
> Three crows, a wedding,
> Four crows, birth.
>
> *Maine.*

Children catch a butterfly and hold it in the hand, saying:

> Butterfly, butterfly, give me some butter,
> And I'll let you go away!
>
> *North Cambridge, Mass.*

————
Ibid.
————

From *Animal and Plant Lore,* Collected from the Oral Tradition of English Speaking Folk, edited and annotated by Fanny D. Bergen, with an Introduction by Joseph Y. Bergen, pp. 56, 57, 58, 59, 60. Copyright, 1899 by The American Folk-Lore Society. Boston and New York: Published for the Society by Houghton Mifflin and Company.

Boys often say while fishing:—

> Fishy, fishy,
> Come bite my hook,
> I'll go captain
> And you'll go cook(-ed in the pan).
>
>

Maine.

> Grasshopper, grasshopper, grasshopper gray,
> Give me some molasses to-day I pray,
> Or I'll kill you to-day
> And bury you to-morrow.
>
>

Auburn, Me.

> Grasshopper, grasshopper gray,
> Give me some molasses
> And then fly away.
>
>

Central Maine.

> Grasshopper, grasshopper green,
> Give me some molasses
> Or you'll never be seen.
>
>

Salem, Mass.

> Pick the first brake,
> Kill the first snake,
> And you will accomplish
> What you undertake.
>
>

Vermont, 1860.

> If you wish to live and thrive,
> Let the spider run alive.
>
>

Eastern Massachusetts.

On seeing a spider:—

> Black, sad,
> Brown, glad,
> White, good luck attend you.
>
>

Guilford, Conn.

The Weather

Rain before seven,
Clear before 'leven.

Red at night,
Sailors delight.

Red in the morning,
Sailors take warning;

Rainbow in the morning;
Sailors take warning;

From *What They Say in New England,* A Book of Signs, Sayings, and Superstitions, collected by Clifton Johnson, pp. 17, 18, 19, 20, 21, 22, 23, 24, 26, 27, 28, 29, 30, 38, 49–50, 51–52, 58, 60, 61, 63, 64, 65, 90, 101, 107, 108, 109, 124, 125, 126, 129, 130, 131, 135, 136, 144, 145–146, 151, 154. Copyright, 1896, by Lee and Shepard. Boston.

Rainbow at night,
Sailors delight;
Rainbow at noon,
Rain very soon.

Fog on the hills,
More water for the mills.

Between twelve and two
You can tell what the day will do.

A sunshiny shower
Won't last half an hour.

When the fog goes up the mountain
hoppin',
Then the rain comes down the mountain droppin'.

If the rooster crows when he goes to
bed,
He will get up with a wet head.

A mackerel sky
Won't leave the ground dry.

Mackerel scales and mares' tails
Make lofty ships to carry low sails.

A cold, wet May,
A barn full of hay.

When the wind is in the east,
Then the sap will run the least.
When the wind is in the west,
Then the sap will run the best.

Open and shet
Sign of wet.
(That is, you can expect rain
when the clouds open and shut.)

When the wind is in the east,
'Tis neither good for man nor beast.

Sun at seven,
Rain at 'leven.

As far as the sun shines in on Candle-
mas Day,
So far the snow blows in before May
Day.

If Candlemas Day be fair and bright,
Winter will take another flight;
If chance to fall a shower of rain,
Winter will not come again.

If Candlemas Day be bright and clear,
Be sure you will have two winters that
year.

On Candlemas Day
Half the wood and half the hay.

The old farmer at this time takes a critical survey of his woodpile and haymow; and if there is not in them half what there was at the beginning of winter, he lays plans for their replenishing before the opening of the new season.

Others say,—

Half the pork and half the hay
On Christmas Day.

The Winds

Wind from the east,—bad for man and for beast;
Wind from the south is too hot for them both;
Wind from the north is of very little worth;
Wind from the west is the softest and the best.[1]

---

[1] From *The Old Farmer's Almanack*, Calculated on a New and Improved Plan, for the Year of Our Lord 1851, by Robert B. Thomas, p. 46. Entered, according to Act

. . . The proverb quoted by Sewall is still current. I have heard the following traditional rhyme on Cape Cod:

> When the wind is to the north,
> The fisherman he goes not forth;
> When the wind is to the east,
> 'Tis neither good for man nor beast,
> When the wind is to the south,
> It blows the bait in the fish's mouth;
> When the wind is to the west,
> Then 'tis at the very best.[2]

Campaign Rhymes

> ——'s a patriot, noble and true;
> —— we never could trust;
> —— will guard well the red-white-and-blue;
> With —— it will drag in the dust!

(This was a campaign rhyme of the pre-Civil War period, and was given by Mr. Wilbur Davis of Sound Beach, whose ancestors for generations lived in northern Connecticut.)

> Coffee and gingerbread hot from the pans
> We'll serve to good Republicans.
> Fried rats and pickled cats
> Are good enough for Democrats.

> Shame, shame! Oh, what a shame!
> ——'s got a baby without any name!

(Back in the good old days, it seems anything went in the heat of a presidential campaign, and it was common to charge the head of the opposition party with at least one illegitmate child!)

> —— rides a white horse,
> —— rides a mule.
> —— is a gentleman,
> —— is a fool!

---

of Congress, in the year 1850, by J. H. Jenks and G. W. Palmer, in the Clerk's Office of the District Court of the District of Massachusetts. Boston: Jenks, Palmer & Co.

[2] By George Lyman Kittredge. From *Letters of Samuel Lee and Samuel Sewall Relating to New England and the Indians*, edited by George Lyman Kittredge, p. 177. Reprinted from *The Publications of the Colonial Society of Massachusetts*, Vol. XIV. Cambridge: John Wilson and Son, University Press. 1912.

From Willimantic, Connecticut. Manuscripts of the Federal Writers' Project of the Works Progress Administration for the State of Connecticut.

> One, two, three, four, five, six, seven!
> All good ——s go to Heaven!
> When they get there they will yell,
> "All bad ——s go to Hell!"

(One's own party being named in the first blank, of course, and the opposition party in the last.)

> One, two, three, four!
> Who are we for?
> ——, ——, ——,
> Five, six, seven, eight!
> Who do we hate?
> ——, ——, ——,

(The first row of blanks to be filled in with the name of the shouter's favorite candidate, the last row with the name of his candidate's opponent.)

Sailors' Rhymes

For Occasions [1]

There were his weather rhymes in great store:

> Winds that change against the sun
> Are always sure to backward run.

And of the barometer:

> First rise after a low,
> Squalls expect and more blow.

* * * * *

Of winds and clouds:

> First the rain and then the wind,
> Topsail sheets and halliards mind;
> First the wind and then the rain,
> Hoist your topsails up again.

> Mackerel skies and mares' tails
> Make tall ships carry low sails.

> When the sun sets behind a cloud
> A westerly wind will you enshroud.
> When the sun sets clear as a bell,
> An easterly wind as sure as hell.

---

[1] From *Songs of American Sailormen*, by Joanna C. Colcord, pp. 205–207. Copyrigh, 1938, by W. W. Norton & Company, Inc. New York.

Of hurricanes:

> June, too soon.
> July, stand by.
> August, look out you must.
> September, remember.
> October, all over.

There was his grace before meat, when the beef-kids came in from the alley:

> Old horse! old horse! how came you here?
> —From Sacarap' to Portland Pier,
> I carted stone this many a year,
> Until, worn out by sore abuse,
> They salted me down for sailors' use.
> The sailors they do me despise;
> They turn me over and damn my eyes,
> Cut off my meat and pick my bones,
> And heave the rest to Davy Jones.

And these were the rhymes for turning out the watch, which were sometimes chanted at the forecastle door:

> Awake, awake, you weary sleepers,
>   Know you not 'tis almost day?
> Here while thus you're sleeping,
>   God's best hours will pass away.
>
> Show a leg! Show a leg!

In the second rhyme, the terms "larbowlin" and "starbowlin" are old names for the port and starboard watches respectively.

> Larbowlins stout, you must turn out
>   And sleep no more within;
> For if you do we'll cut your clew,
>   And let starbowlins in.

RULES OF THE ROAD, AT SEA [2]

> Two close-hauled ships upon the sea
> To one safe rule must each agree:
> The starboard tack must keep his luff,
>   The port bear off.

---

[2] From *American Naval Songs & Ballads*, edited by Robert W. Neeser, p. 305. Copyright, 1938, by Yale University Press. New Haven.
Printed in Stephen B. Luce's *Naval Songs* (New York, 1902) pp. 74–76.—R. W. N.

Two steamships meeting:

When both side-lights I see ahead,
I port my helm and show my red.

Two steamships passing:

Green to green, and red to red,
Perfect safety, go ahead.

Two steamships crossing:

If to my starboard red appear,
It is my duty to keep clear,
To act as judgment says is proper,
To port, or starboard, back, or stop her;
But when upon my port is seen
A steamer's starboard light of green,
There's less for me to do or say,
The green is bound to keep away.
All ships must keep a good lookout!
And steamships must stop and go astern;
    If necessary;
Both in safety and in doubt,
Always keep a sharp lookout,
In danger with no room to turn
Ease her, stop her, go astern!

INDEX OF AUTHORS, COLLECTORS, INFORMANTS, TITLES, AND FIRST LINES OF SONGS

Abbott, Katharine M., 31, 399, 465, 471, 508, 522
Abraham Underhill's Wife, 107
A is for Ax, as you very well know, 565
Aldrich, Thomas Bailey, 57
Allen, Ethan, 299, 300, 518, 520
Allen, Frederic D., 425, 460
Allen, Joseph C.; 89, 122
Allis, Marguerite, 108
Allison, John, 538, 539, 541, 543, 544, 571, 587
Allison, Lucy, 538, 539, 541, 543, 544, 571, 587
A lumberman's life is a wearisome life, 567
A man whose name was Johnny Sands, 567
Ames, Nathaniel, 316
Amory, Cleveland, 254
Ancient Pronunciation, 458
Andrews, John, 143, 273
Anecdote Characteristic of Sailors, 95
Angel of Hadley, The, 268
Answering One Question by Asking Another, 82
Answering the Reproof, 123
Aphorisms of Manners, 516
Apple Cider, 69
Apple Divinations, 332
Archer, Gabriel, 241
Arnold, James N., 268
Arnold, Noah J., 268
Arr, E. H., 427
As Good as His Word, 33
Ashley, Clifford W., 88
As I was walking down by the sea side, 578
As I went down to Derby, 577
Atwood, James, 526, 549, 573
Atwood, Mary, 548, 571
Austin, Jane G., 425
Austin, John Osborne, 131
"Ave" Henry, Lumber Baron, 302
Averill, Gerald, 326
Awake, awake, you drowsy sleeper, 549
Away Down East, 533
A Yankee ship came down the river, 558

Back Side and Bay Side, 492
Bacon, Edward M., 279 n.
Baker, Mary Eva, 261
Baldwin Apple, The, 465
Ballad of Bunker Hill, The, 541
Ballad of the Tea Party, 538

Ballads and Songs, 526-591
Ballard, Elizabeth Flanders, 546, 550
Ball-Bouncing Rhymes, 596
Bangs, Mary Rogers, 488
Barber, John Warner, 102, 105, 107, 180, 183, 267, 268
Barnicle, Mary Elizabeth, 593
Barnum, Phineas T., 14, 15, 27, 28, 32, 376, 518
Barnum Recalls the Good Old Days, 357, 376
Barry, Phillips, 525, 546, 547 n., 550, 566, 567, 569
Bartlett, Arthur, 82
Bartlett, John Russell, 431, 451
Bates, Hon. William G., 39, 98
Beam, Lura, 25
Bees, Change-Work and Whangs, 381
Beliefs and Customs, 315-449
Bergen, Fanny D., 438, 598
Bernard, Mrs. Bayle, 10, 13
Bernard, John, 10, 13
Better Have Paid Your Washwoman, 519
Bigelow, Ella A., 108
Bigelow, E. Victor, 342
Biglow, William, 107
"Biled Cider Apple Sass," 373
Billings, Josh, 2, 316, 493
Billings, William, 536
Birds' Courting Song, 573
Bishop, W. H., 209, 331
Blackington, Alton H., 166
Black Newfoundland Dog, The, 323
Bliss, William Root, 100, 227
Blow, Boys, Blow, 558
Boarding Around, 403
Bofat, The, 465
Boots and Shoes, 42
Bossidy, John Collins, 518
Boston Come-All-Ye, The, 557
Boston Folks Are Full of Notions, 519
Boston Tea Tax, The, 539
Botkin, B. A., 44, 53, 61, 62, 63, 64, 65, 66, 67, 68, 69, 70, 71, 72, 73, 74, 76, 85, 142, 262, 355, 384
Botsford, Arthur, 405, 517
Bowen, Catherine Drinker, 519
Bowles, Ella Shannon, 390, 393
Braley, Ephraim, 569
Brayman, Charlie, 94
Breaking Steers, 64
Breaking the Pitcher, 110
Brewster, Charles, W., 38, 39
Bride Brook, 250

Bride Stealing, 414
Bridgman, Lewis Joseph, 292, 293
Bringing in the Log, 86
Brookfield Murder, The, 552
Brooks, Charles, 406
Brooks, Van Wyck, 1, 518, 519, 525
Brown, George, 546, 550
Browne, Irving, 100
Building a Stone Wall, 389
Building Wall, 82
Bundling, 411
Burnaby, Rev. Andrew, 413
Burroughs, Mary, 262, 355
Burroughs, Walter, 355
Butterworth, Hezekiah, 423, 532
Byword, A, 67

Caldera Dick, 199
Calm Man, A, 68
Camp, Raymond R., 132
Campaign Rhymes, 601
Canada I O, 569
Cape Ann, 529
Cape Cod Cat, The, 466
Cape Cod Rivalries, 256
Cape Cod Shanty, 561
Cape Cod Turkey, 466
Cap'n Tibbett and the Body, 93
Captain Basil Hall and the Countryman, 9
Captain Eleazer's Bulldog, 90
Captain Kidd Legends in New England, 280
Captain Paddock's Whale Iron, 142
Captain Peleg's Letter, 89
Captain Putnam and the British Major, 270
Captain's Hat, The, 88
Captain's Prescription, The, 90
Captain's Pudding, The, 125
Careless, Cuss, A, 122
Carmer, Carl, 202
Carpenter, James M., 525, 526
Carr, J. W., 104, 438
Carter, Robert, 336
Cassidy, Frederic G., 232
Catching Trout by Tickling, 154
Cat Holes, 402
Cattle Show, 432
"Cat" Words, 467
Chadwick, John W., 465
Chambers, Robert, 592
Chapple, Joe Mitchell, 538 n., 556
Characters, 84
Chase, Edith Newlin, 85
Chase, George Davis, 104, 437, 438, 578
Chase, George H., 255
Chase, Heman, 44, 71, 72, 73, 379, 384
Chase, Mary Ellen, 352, 358, 396, 429, 439, 467, 516
Cheating the Devil, 220
Chebobbins, 398

Chester, 536
Chestnut Mare, The, 23
Chickering, Geraldine Jencks, 555
Childish Pastime, 436
Children's Taunts, 598
Chimney-Corner Story-Telling, 428
Christening of Vermont, The, 243
Christmas Eve on Beacon Hill, 422
Clever Blacksmith, The, 41
Coast Traders, 396
Coatsworth, Elizabeth, 260
Cockroach and Bedbug Match, 434
Coffin, Robert P. Tristram, 369 n., 370, 473, 492
Colcord, Joanna C., 91, 557, 558, 602
Cold Roast Boston, 518
Collyer, Rev. Robert, 14
Come, all ye jolly lumbermen and listen to my song, 569
Come, all ye Yankee farmer boys who would like to change your lot, 555
Come, all ye young sailormen, listen to me, 557
Come-at-a-Body, The, 173
Comfort Powders, 467
Comic Yankee Servants, 11
Coming of Age, 67
Congdon, Benjamin, 189
Connolly, James B., 317
Constitution and the Guerrière, The, 544
Contributions to the New England Vocabulary and Idiom, 459
Converse, Parker Lindall, 31
Coolidge, Calvin, 518
Cordwood, 30
Corn Cobs Twist Your Hair, 7
Corn Dishes, 361
Cotton Mather's Snake Stories, 193
Counting-Out Rhymes, 595
Counting the Children, 89
Country Auctions, 384
Country Squire, 79
County Fair, 432
Couple of Reasons Too Many, A, 125
Courting-Sticks, 414
Courting with Stones, 414
Cox, William T., 171
Cradle Will Rock, The, 322
Crandall, Arthur G., 81, 83
Crane, Charles Edward, 60, 455, 480, 508 n., 510
Crawford, Mary Caroline, 372
Crazy Lorenzo Dow, 291
Creel of Big Ones, A, 155
Critic, The, 71
Crosberry, L., 137
Crothers, Samuel McChord, 1, 265 n.

Damaging the Engine, 126
Dame, Lawrence, 255
Damnation Alley, 255
Damon, S. Foster, 7, 519, 530, 531, 554,

575, 576, 585
Dana, Richard Henry, 374
Daniel Webster's Fish Chowder, 368
Davis, Hank, 21
Davis, Robert, 117, 118
Davis, William T., 595
Day's Pay, A, 44
Deaconing, 32
Deaconing the Psalm, 406
Dead Horse, A, 468
Deal in Oxen, A, 64
Deal in Timberland, A, 21
Debating Society, The, 429
Dehnoff, W. R., 585
Denison, Frederic, 110, 276
Dependable Horse, A, 25
Derby Ram, 577
De Vere, M. Schele, 240
Devil and the Card-Players, The, 220
Devil and the Loups-Garous, The, 222
Devil and the Wind in Boston, The, 255
Devil's Ash Heap, The, 252
Devil's Dream, 588
Devil's Fiddle, The, 415
Dexter's Profitable Blunders, 284
Dexter, Timothy, 286
Dickens, Charles, 511
Digges, Jeremiah, 87, 88, 89, 90, 205, 319,
  323, 345, 373, 492, 509
Diploma Digging, 126
Disciplining the Congregation, 410
Doane, Benjamin D., 199
Doane, Capt. Benjamin, 199
Dobie, J. Frank, 263
Dominie and the Horse, The, 103
Donovan, Francis, 405, 469, 517
Don't Hit That Post Again, 110
Double-Barreled Shotgun, The, 144
Double Christian Names, 487
Double Hitch, The, 115
Downing, Major Jack, 16, 34
Drail, 468
Drake, Samuel Adams, 1, 168, 175, 213,
  216, 241, 251, 315, 320, 334, 335, 351,
  487, 510, 534 n.
Drake, Samuel G., 286
Dream Line, The, 331
Driving a Witch Out of the Soap, 342
Drummer and the Stagecoach, The, 53
Duck Hunting Yarn, 147

Earle, Alice Morse, 281, 282, 301 n., 331,
  332, 353, 357, 373, 381, 390-391 n., 398,
  400, 407, 410, 414, 416, 418, 419 n., 425,
  467
Early, Eleanor, 119, 311, 367, 489
Ear-Timers, 469
Eaton, Gov., 35
Edwards, Agnes, 251
*Egg, the Darning-Needle, and the Treat,
  The*, 35

Eggs is Eggs, 123
Electric Fence, The, 73
Emerson, Ralph Waldo, 518
Emery, Sarah Anna, 41
England, George Allen, 461
Englishman with Two Heads, The, 106
Enigma of Silent Cal, The, 307
*Ephraim Wright and the Underground
  Railroad*, 261
Esau and the Gorbey, 326
Ethan Allen's Saying, 520
Exhuming the Remains, 85
Exploits of Ethan Allen, 294

Fabulous Yankees, 1-173
Fagan, James O., 255
Fairies Who Didn't Stay, The, 343
Famous Sayings and Allusions, 517
Fanny Kemble and the Yankee Farmer,
  10
Farnham, Joseph E. C., 357, 372, 401, 447,
  489
Farquhar, Samuel T., 152
Federal Writers' Project, Connecticut,
  117, 126, 273, 287, 405, 469, 517, 596,
  597, 598, 601; Maine, 115, 123, 133, 137,
  145, 259, 269 n., 491, 592, 594; Massa-
  chusetts, 51, 87, 88, 89, 90, 97, 101, 103,
  110, 245, 257, 274, 277, 323, 345, 468,
  478, 492, 494, 495, 509; New Hampshire,
  20, 30, 43, 82, 110, 116, 123, 147, 302,
  382, 390, 452 n.; Rhode Island, 222, 224;
  Vermont, 21, 140, 250, 357 n., 595
Filling Boots with Flaxseed, 400
Fire, The, 73
First-Rate Setter, A, 28
Fisher, Dorothy Canfield, 520
Fisherman's Reward, 96
Fishermen's Races, 258
Fishhouse Stories, 258
Flanders, Harry E., 147
Flanders, Helen Hartness, 546, 550, 577
Flower Oracles, 331
Fly Away, Jack, 437
Fog Yarn, 168
Following the Wrong Gulls, 87
Forbuss, Lamont, 567
For Knowing How, 43
Fortune in a Stick, A, 333
Fourth of July, The, 423
Franklin Forestalling Inquiry, 75
Free America, 537
Frog in the Spring, The, 571
From Nags to Riches, 22
Frozen Death, 164
Fuller, Edmund, 313

Gallbuster, 470
Games of Boston Boys, 443
Games of Nantucket Boys, 447
Gam, The, 435
Gardner, Emelyn Elizabeth, 555

Gazerium and Snydae, 172
George White, Horse Thief, 282
Getting More for His Money, 114
Ghost in the Attic, The, 61
Ghosts, 61
Ghosts of Georges Bank, The, 205
Gilbreth, Frank B., 118
Girl in the Fog, The, 323
Girls' Names, 486
God and the New Hampshire Farmer, 82
Gone Coon, A, 143
Gone Fish, A, 158
Goodell, Charles L., 32, 103, 112, 247
Goodenow, Elsie, 53 n., 71, 142
Goodrich, Samuel G., 294, 591
Goodspeed, Charles E., 159, 160
Gordon, William, 482
Gore, Mrs. Moody P., 98
Gough, John B., 12
Gould, R. E., 2, 23, 38, 39, 54, 113
Gould, Lieut.-Commander R. T., 194
Grandma Willey's Chair, 20
Grant's Tame Trout, 152
Graves, Merle Dixon, 99 n.
Great Ipswich Fright, The, 185
Green, Horace, 43, 60 n.
Green Duck Hunter and the Live Decoy, The, 148
Greenbie, Marjorie Barstow, 4
Greene, Hon. Albert Gorton, 576
Greene, Asa, 430
Grindstone Out of Cheese, 40
Guy Fawkes' Day, 425
Gyascutus, 172
Gyles, John, 242

Hailey Over, 438
Hale, Happy, 588
Hale, Nathan, 518
Haliburton, Thomas C., 74
Halley, Mrs. Rebecca M., 595
Hallowe'en, 423
Hallowe'en Prank, 62
Hard Lying, 132
Hard, Margaret, 107
Hard, Walter, 107
Harlow, Frederick Pease, 374, 434
Hart, Mrs. J., 137
Hart, Joseph C., 365
Hawk Feather That Ate the Chicken Feathers, The, 161
Hawthorne, Nathaniel, 175
Hazard, Joseph P., 519
Hazard, Rowland Gibson, 158
Hazard, Thomas Robinson ("Shepherd Tom"), 41, 116, 119, 127, 136, 154, 158, 188, 250, 357, 359, 361, 364, 473, 593
Hazard, Willis P., 136, 188
Hazing New Clerks, 39
Head Work, 104
Healey, John, 468
Heath, William H., 172

Heave and Haul, 470
Hemenway, Abby Maria, 35, 135, 292, 293
He Might as Well Have Et, 126
He Might as Well Have Stayed, 75
Herb Tea, 471
Herring Song, The, 578
Herring Sticks, 369
Hey, Betty Martin!, 587
Hey, Betty Martin, tip-toe, tip-toe, 587
Hine, C. G., 252
Hingston, E. P., 60 n.
"Hi!" said the blackbird, sitting on a chair, 573
His Father's Horse, 27
Hi's Got Some Great Sayings, 517
Historical Traditions, 263-313
Hoar, George F., 458
Holbrook, Stewart H., 263, 294, 309
Holmes, Oliver Wendell, 451, 452, 491, 518
Honest Man, An, 117
Horse Chestnut Men, 437
Hosmer, Rev. Mr., 181
Hotten, John Camden, 291
Howard, Jane E., 522 n.
How Long From Port?, 88
How Old Betty Booker Rode Skipper Perkins Down to York, 225
How the Cranberry Came to Cape Cod, 257
How the Old Lady Beat John, 120
Hubbard, Rev. William, 241 n.
Hubbub, 471
Hub, The, 491
Hughes, Robert, 548, 549, 571, 573, 574
Human Hibernation: The Mystery Solved, 166
Humor in Yankee Speech, 507
Humphrey, Zephine, 107
Humphreys, Col. David, 271
Hush, the waves are rolling in, 571
Husking Bees or Frolics, 431
Hussey, Roland B., 40, 90, 92, 113, 127, 135, 142, 375, 459, 496, 499, 503, 513
Hutton, Laurence, 10, 13

If you'll listen a while, I will sing you a song, 551
I Languish, 438
I'm a heart-broken raftsman, from Greenville I came, 566
Incantations and Formulae, 598
Independent Vermonters, 80
Indian Justice, 105
In good old Colony times, 531
Interval (e), 472
I often have been told, 544
I snum I am a Yankee lad, 539
I wish I was in Yankee land, 535

Jack and Hudson, 68
Jack Haggerty, or the Flat River Girl, 566

Jagger-Knives, 401
James, Henry, 233
Jennes, Fred, 160
Jennison, Keith W., 80
Jigger Johnson, River Boss, 138
Jim Eldredge's Old Mill, 84
Jim Fisk, 550
Johnny Sands, 575
Johnson, Burges, 85, 92, 93, 112, 309, 438
Johnson, Clifton, 2, 87, 97, 101, 183, 220, 230, 250, 274, 280, 330, 333, 336, 337, 355, 406, 414, 437, 481, 599
John Strong and the Bear, 135
Jonas Lord, 137
Jonathan Moulton and the Devil, 216
Jonathan's Hunting Excursion, 141
Jones, Alice J., 331, 372
Jonny-Cake, 473
Jonny-Cake under the Stove, 103
Jordan, Philip D., 533, 535
Josselyn, John, Gent., 176, 318
Jotham Stories, 149
Joy, Howard H., 42
Justice Waban, 107

Keen, Elsie, 115
Kempt, Robert, 92, 121, 125, 126, 130, 132, 169, 274
Kendall, Edward Augustus, Esq., 11, 235, 243, 315, 472
Kennebec Turkey, 473
Kennison, Josiah S., 550
Kentish Provincialisms in New England, 458
Kessler, Lillian, 533, 535
Kicking the Pig, 62
Killcow, 474
Kilroy, James J., 521
Kilroy Was Here, 521
King, Thomas Starr, 242
Kingsbury, William W., 63, 67, 68, 69, 70
Kirke, Edmund, 18
Kirkland, Frazar, 17, 32, 285
Kittredge, George Lyman, 106, 129, 193, 286 n., 317, 354 n., 461 n., 601
Kittredge, Henry C., 256
Knapp, Aunt Jenny, 548, 571
Krapp, George Philip, 190, 452, 454 n.
Kurath, Hans, 452

Lake Charcogg-Etc.-Maugg, 247
Lane, George Martin, 581
Lawrence, Robert Means, 255
Laziest Man in Vermont, The, 118
Lazy Shopkeeper, The, 40
Leach, Maria, 199
Leary, Jane K., 468
Lee, Samuel, 193
Leland, Henry, 546
Lemon Fair River, 250
Letter to the Rats, A, 339

Letter Writing, 404
Let tyrants shake their iron rod, 536
Levermore, Charles Herbert, 241
Lincoln, Joseph C., 58, 84, 148, 369, 468, 470
Linscott, Eloise Hubbard, 525, 552, 560, 564, 567 n., 579, 586, 588
Little Pig, The, 574
Lobster Stew, 370
Local Characters, 57-129
Lomax, Alan, 528, 593
Lomax, John A., 528
Lone Fish-Ball, The, 580
Longfellow, Henry Wadsworth, 518
Long Wreck Hook for the Preacher, A, 94
Lost Child, The, 262
Loup-Garou, The, 221
Lovel and the Indians, 269
Lovett, James D'Wolf, 443
Lowell, James Russell, 9, 58, 175, 315, 451, 459, 505
Loyal Tory of Hancock, A, 334
Lucky and Unlucky Ships' Names, 334
Lumberman's Alphabet, The, 564
Lumberman's Life, The, 567
Lunt, George, 98 n., 421, 436, 458

Ma'am Hackett's Garden, 87
MacKaye, Percy, 452
Macy, William F., 40, 90, 92, 113, 127, 135, 142, 375, 459, 496, 499, 503, 513
Madam, I am come a-courting, 587
Maine's Woodland Terrors, 169
"Make a Job or Take a Job": A Yankee Work Saga, 44
Man from Monkton, The, 83
Man That Cut Bread So Fast with the Shoe-Knife, The, 134
Man That Liked to Fish, The, 157
Man Who Bottled Up the Thunder, The, 133
Man Who Could Send Rats, The, 230
Man Who Made Weather, The, 231
Marryat, Capt. Frederick, 143
Marrying Late, 74
Martineau, Harriet, 11
Martin Richardson Stayed, 72
Mary of the Wild Moor, 548
Mason, Chester C., 61, 62, 64, 65, 66, 76
Masterson, James R., 131
Mather, Cotton, 96, 179, 193, 212, 354
Mather, Increase, 176
Matthews, Brander, 10, 13
Maule, Francis I., 152
Maxfield, E. K., 309, 507
McClure, Dennis, 588
McCormick, Samuel Jarvis, 190, 478
McGinn, Catherine, 594
McKee, John Hiram, 310
Meetinghouse Bell, The, 406
Meetin' Seed, 353
Melville, Herman, 175, 435

Mencken, H. L., 172, 482
Menin Jesu *in Provincetown*, 422
Mermaid, The, 562
Merry Dance, The, 589
Michigania, 555
Migratory Birds, 85
Miller, Clarence, 53, 64, 73, 74
Miller's Three Sons, The, 546
Mills, Fred ("Uncle Freddie"), 44, 61, 62, 355
Mind Your Orts, 521
Mingo Beach, 251
Minister and Fish, 100
Minister's Rib Factory, The, 474
Mink Story, The, 159
Miscellany, 508
Misfits, 114
Mrs. Bailey's Petticoat, 279
Mitchell, Edwin Valentine, 22, 115, 247, 425, 594
Mitchell, Joseph, 94
Model T, 70
Moodus Noises, The, 180
Mooncussin', 474
Morison, Samuel Eliot, 442, 522
Morrill, W., 137
Mosquitoes with the Canvas Britches, The, 164
Moving a Town down a Hill, 261
Mud Time, 475
Munching Drawer, 476
Muslin Toast, 372
Mussey, Barrows, 144, 261, 385, 389
Muster or Training Day, 427
Myths, Legends, and Traditions, 175-313

Names in the White Mountains, 242
Names of Apples, 490
Names of the New England States, 239
Naming of Auburn, The, 245
Naming of Cape Cod, The, 241
Nantucketisms, 499
Nantucket Lullaby, 571
Nantucket Nauticalisms, 496
Nantucket Pronunciation of the Points of the Compass, 459
Nantucket Quahaugs, 365
Nantucket Sheep Shearing, 425
Nantucket Similes and Sayings, 503
Nantucket "Sleigh Ride," 135
Nantucket Wonders, 372
Narragansett Fried Smelts and Broiled Eels, 364
Narragansett Jonny-Cake, 359
Nason, Emma Huntington, 231
Neal, John, 411
Needham, Walter, 144, 261, 385, 389
Neeser, Robert W., 603
Newell, William Wells, 332, 339, 438, 440, 587
New England Boiled Dinner, 372
New England Sea-Serpent, The, 194

New England versus *Manhattan Clam Chowder*, 367
New Haven Specter Ship, The, 179
New Way to Make People Happy, A, 105
Nicknames of the New England States, 240
Noble, Gilbert Clifford, 562
Noggin and Piggin, 402
No, Never, No, 556
Norfleet, Helen, 577
Northend, Mary Harrod, 335
Norton, Charles Ledyard, 421 n.
No Store for Him, 39
Not Bright, 116

Ocean-Born Mary, 202
Off Ox, The, 64
Oh, Cape Cod girls they have no combs, 561
Oh! Potatoes they grow small, 532
Oh! Rinehart!, 522
Old Colony Times, 531
Old Couple and the Bear, The, 111
Old Darnman, The, 287
Old Deb and Other Old Colony Witches, 227
Old English Proverbs, 515
Old Grimes, 576
Old Grimes is dead, that good old man, 576
Old Man Who Lived in the Wood, The, 579
Old Put's Wolf, 271
Old Sam Hewes, River Man, 140
Old Testament Names in New England, 484
Old Town Tall Tales, 145
Old Trickey, the Devil-Doomed Sandman, 215
Old Witch, 440
Old Woman All Skin and Bone, 586
One night when the wind it blew cold, 548
On Springfield mountain there did dwell, 554
Order of Their Going, The, 124
Ordway, Carrie, 98
Oren Wilder and the White Stones, 72
Original Brother Jonathan, The, 274
Origin of "Hoosic"—A Satire, The, 248
Otis, James, 518
Our Town, 74
Over There, 532

Packard, Winthrop, 149
Page, Ralph, 589, 590
Painting the Meeting House, 124
Palatine Light, The, 188
Parsimonious Widower, The, 112
Pattee, Fred Lewis, 581
Paying for the Cider, 34
Paying for the Stolen Butter, 35

Peach, Arthur Wallace, 155
Pearson, Haydn S., 25, 490
Pease, Zephaniah, 91
Peddler Humor, 16
Pelletier, Mike, 145
Pell, John, 297, 298, 300, 302
Perkins, George R., 164
Pesky Sarpent, The, 554
Peters, Reverend Samuel, 190, 244, 478
Pick Up Your Feet, 522
Pierpont, James, 180
Pilgrims, The, 476
Pillow Bears and Feather Voyages, 399
Piper, Winifred Allard, 552
P. I.'s and Frenchmen, 478
Place Lore, 232-263
Plantain, 354
Playing the Game, 25
Point Judith, 249
Pompey, 585
Pompey was dead and laid in his grave, 585
Poole, Ernest, 99, 120 n., 138, 213, 510
Poor Butter, 113
Poor Old Country Railroad, 491
Portuguese American Names and Nicknames, 487
Pot Luck, 478
Powder-Horns, 400
Power of Faith, The, 316-356
Powers of Darkness, The, 212-232
Prayer for Rain, 97
Prayer for Wind, 99
Prescott, Col. William, 518
Prime, W. C., 120, 486
Priscilla and John Alden,* 267
Proctor, Edna Dean, 556
Prognostics of the Weather, 346
"Proper Bostonians," 253
Providential Names, 486
Provincetown and the Devil, 257
Provincial Phraseology and Hospitality, 11
Pulling the Rope, 109
Pumpkin-Heads, 478
Purchas, Samuel, 241

Quaker's Courtship, 587
Quilting, 393
Quite a Storm, 126

Raisings, 382
Rat or Mouse, 111
Rawson, Marion Nicholl, 316, 345, 351, 404, 415, 427, 457, 475, 509
Razor-Strop Trade, 17
Recognizing the Broom, 115
Reed, Thomas, 10
Reformed Wife, The, 107
Return of the Native, The, 77
Reuben Renzo, 560
Rev. Mr. Bulkley's Advice, The, 102

Reverend Samuel Peters' Contributions to the Natural History of Connecticut, The, 190
Reynard, Elizabeth, 257 n., 474
Rich, Louise Dickinson, 53 n., 478, 481, 509, 522
Rich, Shebnah, 99, 101, 129, 399, 470, 480, 486
Richards, W., 137
Richmond, Roaldus, 21
Ride and Tie, 398
Riflemen's Song at Bennington, 543
Roads, Samuel, Jr., 277
Road to Walpole, The, 10
Robbins, Capt. Charles Henry, 519, 561 n.
Roberts, Kenneth L., 77
Robinson, Rowland E., 111, 114, 134, 146, 157, 161, 221
Rock Farm, 82
Rogers, Cameron, 310
Rogers, Earl, 561
Roosevelt, Franklin D., 117
Rooster Talk, 330
Roots and Herbs, 351
Rope-Skipping Rhymes, 596
Rosenman, Samuel, 117
Round Ball, 449
Rousseau, Edward, 222
Roving Reuben Renzo, 560
Rush, Nixon Orwin, 82
Russell, George R., 57

Sacred Cod, The, 479
Sagendorph, Robb, 411
Sailors' Rhymes, 602
Sailors' Superstitions, 333
St. Elmo Sees Them Through, 319
St. Elmo's Fire, 318
Salmon or Cod?, 122
Salt Horse, 374
Sam Hyde, Proverbial Liar, 286
Samplers, 390
Sam Temple's Store: A Rhyming Advertisement, 29
Sargent, Winthrop, 143
Satisfied Redemptioner, The, 276
Save the Peavies, 51
Saving a Fuss, 127
Sayings of Poor Ned, The, 516
Say "Minister," 336
Schooner, 479
"Schooner Ashore!", 100
'Sconseter's Will, A, 513
'Sconset House Names, 189
Scootin'-'Long-the-Shore, 371
Seagoing Coffin, The, 92
Sea-Gull Cliffs, 251
Seamen's Sermon, 511
Secret of True Economy, The, 113
Selling the Dog, 113
Sewall, Samuel, 193
Sharp Shooting, 143

Sheriff and the Shoes, The, 69
She Sleeps Six, 93
Shift Marriages, 416
Shingling Out onto the Fog, 169
Shining Dagger, The, 549
Ship Figureheads, 335
Ships' Names, 488
Ships' Names on Old Barns, 489
Shovel for "Uncle Ed," A, 117
Shower, The, 65
Shun-Pikes, 480
Shutting the Old Man Up, 67
Signs and Seasons, 344
Signs in the Sea's Rote, 350
Simples and Benefits, 351
Skinner, Charles M., 169, 249, 269
Skipper Ireson's Ride, 277
Skully-Jo, 373
Skunk Oil and Other Remedies, 355
Sleigh Riding, 430
Slow Powder, 142
Smell Brimstone, 437
Smith, Chard Powers, 109, 302
Smith, Charles Henry, 451
Smith, Fred, 133
Smith, Grace Partridge, 33
Smith, Judge Martin H., 403
Snake Ball, 355
Snake Lore, 337
Snowman, M. S. (Boob), 40, 116, 162
Snows of Yesteryear, The, 81
Soap Cure, The, 38
"Sock Saunders" Sayings, 523
Some Public Land Record Lore of Vermont and New Hampshire, 379
Songs and Rhymes, 525-604
Sorting the Pigs, 63
Spaeth, Sigmund, 580
Speare, Mrs. Guy E., 98
Spelling His Name, 116
S. S. Pierce Pung, The, 255
Stammering Sailor, The, 92
Stark, General John, 518
Statues, 439
Stevens, Bessie Powers, 594
Stevenson, Burton L., 539
Stewart, George R., 236, 239 n., 240 n., 250
Stolen Cheese, The, 38
Stolle, John William, 40, 116, 162
Stout Fellows and Hard Liars, 212-280
Stout Jeffrey, 136
Stove and Anti-Stove Factions, 407
Stowe, Harriet Beecher, 1, 29, 322, 428
Stranger's Fire, 399
Strong, Hon. John, 135
Stupid Hired Man, The, 153
Sturgis, Edith B., 526, 548, 549, 571, 573, 574
Sugaring Science, 385
Swift, C. F., 109, 113
Sylvester, Herbert Milton, 215, 225
Sylvester and John, 119

Tall Tales from the Maine Woods, 162
Tarbell, Arthur Wilson, 84, 93, 356 n.
Tarrying, 413
Taunton's Seasons, 83
Taylor, Isaac, 232
Tea-ships near to Boston lying, 538
Telltale Seaweed, The, 324
Thank'ee Ma'ams, 480
Thanksgiving, 418
Thar She Blows!, 91
That seat of science Athens, 537
Thaxter, Celia, 96, 319, 414
The Brookfield murder has come to light, 553
There are No Peruvians in Peru, 235
There's a famous fabled country never seen by mortal eyes, 534
There's Odds in Deacons, 31
There was a frog lived in a spring, 571
There was a man in our town, 7
There was a man went around the town, 581
There was a man went up and down, 580
There was a miller who lived in shire, 547
There was an old man that lived in a wood, 580
There was an old woman all skin and bone, 586
There was an old woman and she had a little pig, 574
These Haddams, 246
The soldiers from town to the foot of the hill, 541
They sat by the fireside, his fair daughters three, 556
Thief's Defense, The, 116
Thomas Hatch's Courtship, 109
Thomas, Robert B., 34, 75, 126, 141, 164, 316, 347, 348, 349, 350, 354, 398, 432, 508, 515, 516, 600
Thompson, Ellery Franklin, 94
Thompson, Zadock, 237
Thoreau, Henry David, 264, 479
Thwing, Annie Haven, 256
Tickling Rhymes, 597
Tiddledewinks, 442
Tiffany, Rev. O. H., 12
Timely Text, A, 101
Timothy Crumb's Courtship, 127
Tinker and the Fencing-Master, The, 268
Todd, Charles Burr, 279
Todd, William Cleaves, 297
Tolman, Beth, 589, 590
Tolman, Newton F., 78, 79
Tom Cook, the Leveler, 281
Tonics and Family Rites, 352
Too Good to Spoil, 41
Tote-Road Shagamaw, The, 171
Town Divided, A, 259
Towner, 480
Town Meeting Day, 427
Train, Arthur, 307, 312

Trayser, Donald G., 466, 476
Tryon, Henry H., 173
Turning Water into Grog, 33
Tutt, Ephraim, 307, 312
Twain, Mark, 246
'Twas Friday morn when we set sail, 562
Twitches, 481
Twizzles, 481
Two Round Trips, 119
Tying a Knot in a Panther's Tail, 146

Uncle Jed, 117
Underwood, Francis H., 456, 480, 485
Ungallant Sailor, The, 125

Valentine, Dr. W., 86
Varieties of Nantucket Wind and Weather, 499
Veazie, Ola G., 30, 43, 82, 110, 116, 123, 302, 494
Vermont Dialect Areas, 455
Vermont "Idioticon," A, 510
Vermont Summer, 74
Violet Fights, 438
Visiting and Advertising Cards, 405
Vorse, Mary Heaton, 89, 257, 258, 323, 422, 487, 593

Waite, H. R., 580
Walker, Mrs. Elva Kimball, 33
Wallace, John, 30, 351, 509
Wangan, 481
Warner, Charles Dudley, 518
Warren, Joseph, 537
Watch Trade, A, 16
Waters, Florence, 546
Watrous, Louise E. Drew, 287
Webster, Clarence M., 432
Webster, Daniel, 350
Weeden, William B., 83
Wehman, Henry J., 35, 248
We hunted and we halloed, 530
Wells, S., 137
Werner, M. R., 376
Weygandt, Cornelius, 340, 402
Whalers' Bastards, 89
Whaleship's Menu, 375
When the Powder Grows, 104
Which Dover?, 247
White, Rev. Henry, 104, 105, 213 n., 239
Whittier, John Greenleaf, 185, 279 n., 343
Whittling without a Purpose, 124

Who Stole the Pork?, 39
Why Ansel Rawson Never Joined the Grange, 71
Why Boston Streets Are Crooked, 256
Why come ye hither, Redcoats?, 544
Why I Never Shoot Bears, 160
Why Purgatory Was Made, 224
Why the Flounder Has a Wry Mouth and Two Colors, 336
Why the White Mountains Are Called "White," 241
Wickhegan, 104
Wife Sitter, 118
Wild Blueberries, 66
Wilder, Robert, 51
Wild Goose Chase, 590
Willard, Joseph A., 122
Williams, Leewin B., 312
Willison, George F., 476
Will of the Lord, The, 108
Wilson, Robert, 164
Windham Frogs, The, 183
Winds, The, 600
Wit in Yankee Speech, 505
Wolcott, Imogene, 368, 371, 375 n., 422, 466, 474, 479
Woman Who Sold Winds, The, 260
Wonders of the Invisible World, 176-212
Wooden Clocks and Wooden Oats, 18
Woodhull, Frost, 264
Woollcott, Alexander, 324
Word Lore, 451-522
World, the Flesh, and the Devil, The, 101
Wraith in the Storm, The, 320
Wreck's a Wreck, A, 94
Wright, Elizabeth Mary, 3 n, 492

Yankee, 482
Yankee Diligence, 112
Yankee Doodle, 273
Yankee Drummer Stories, 54
Yankee Flavor, 236
Yankee in Georgia, A, 76
Yankee in London: Buying Gape-Seed, A, 12
Yankeeisms, 452-492
Yankee Manufactures, 535
Yankee's Reputation, The, 2-57
Yankee Twang, The, 456
Yarn-Beam Cannon, The, 277
Yorkshireman of America, The, 13
Yorkshire Stories, 14
Young Rebels, The, 273

INDEX OF SUBJECTS AND NAMES

Adams, John, 266, 308
Alden, John, 264, 267, 419
Alden, Reverend Timothy, 101

Aldrich, Thomas Bailey, 58
Alewives, 369
Allen, Ethan, 266, 294-302, 520

Allen, Ira, 296, 297
Almanacs, 3, 233, 317, 495
Anecdotes, 9-129, 253-263, 265, 267-313
Animal comparisons, 493
Animals, 141-152, 158-163, 346. *See also* individual species.
Apples, 32, 69, 228, 332, 465, 490
Appleton, Thomas, 518
Auctions, 384
Ayers, Reverend Braman, 103

Bailey, Anna, 279
Baker, Remember, 296
Barlow, Joel, 359, 431
Barns, 169, 220, 402, 489
Barnum, P. T., 6, 266
Barrett, Forrest, 591
Bartlett, John Russell, 459, 505
Bay Psalm Book, 526
Bay State, 240
Beacon Hill, 255, 422, 444
Beans, 51, 311, 494, 518
Bears, 135, 145, 160, 162
Bees (gatherings), 358, 381, 394, 431
Beliefs, 316-356
Bells, 406
Benét, Stephen Vincent, 214
Bennington, Battle of, 543
Bible, 139, 233, 237, 484
Biglow, Hosea, 59, 467
Biglow Papers, The, 452
Billings, Josh, 60 n., 451, 495
Billings, William, 529
Birds and fowl, 87, 147-152, 161, 190, 326, 330, 346, 347, 573
Blackfish, 101
Blacksmiths, 41, 138
Blueberries, 65, 66
Bluefish, 100, 471
Blue laws, 240, 478
Blue Law State, 240
Bofat, 465
Booker, Betty, 225
Borden (Burden), Deborah (Old Deb), 227
Boston Common, 143, 273, 442, 444, 446
Boston Tea Party, 538, 539
Botkin, B. A., 592 n.
Bradford, Governor William, 419, 476 n.
Bradley, Stephen, 300
Brahmins, 494, 518
Bride stealing, 414
Brooks, Reverend Charles T., 279 n.
Brother Jonathan, 274, 455
Brown bread, 234, 311, 359, 364
Brush, Crean, 300
Bulkley, Rev. Mr., 102
Bulls, 127, 228
Bundling, 411, 413
Bunker Hill, Battle of, 518, 541
Buried treasure, 281
Butler, James D., 297
Buzzell, Joseph, 553

Cady, Jacob, 262
Canada, 10, 111, 161, 221, 222, 230. *See also* French Canadians.
Candlemas Day, 347
Cards, 220, 224
Carey, Parson, 185
Cats, 145, 346, 402, 467
Cattle, 64, 73, 346, 432, 433
Chester, 529
Child, Francis James, 582
Chores, 358
Chowder, 494; clam, 234, 367; fish, 368
Christmas, 421, 422
Churches, 124, 353, 406, 407, 410, 511
Cider, 34, 69, 137
Circus, 51
Civil War, 5, 16, 289, 393, 483, 582, 591
Clams, 227, 365, 493

Clergy, 94-103, 115, 126, 410
Clever and the Foolish, The, 113-129
Clockmaker, The, 5
Clocks, clock peddlers, and clockmakers, 16, 18, 469
Cod, 87, 207, 241, 368, 479, 494, 518
Codfish aristocracy, 494
Colcord, Joanna Carver, 497 n.
Conjuration, 337-342
"Connecticut Clockmakers," 469
Connecticut Peddler, The, 528
Coolidge, Calvin, 43, 60, 307-313
Coolidge, Grace, 310, 311
Corn dishes, 361
Cornish survivals in Cape Cod speech, 454
Courtship, 109, 127, 258, 267, 414
Courtship of Miles Standish, The, 267
Cranberry, 257
Crockett, Davy, 4, 5, 131
Crosby, Andrew, 466
Crothers, Samuel McChord, 233
Crumb, Timothy, 127
Crystal Hills, 241, 243
Cures, 351-356
Curtis, Captain Clifford, 207
Customs, 357-449

Dago, Joe, 49
Dancing, 584-591
Darnman, the old, 287
Davenport, Reverend Mr., 179
Deaconing, 32, 406
Death warnings and omens, 320-324
de Crèvecoeur, St. John, 295
Dennett, Hartley, 384, 385
Depression, 48
Devil, 212-225
Dexter, Timothy, 266, 284
Digges, Jeremiah, 493
Divination, 331-334
Doctors, 85, 120, 124
Dogs, 15, 61, 113, 323, 346
Dorson, Richard M., 132 n.
Dow, Lorenzo, 264, 291
Down East, 4, 533 n.
Downing, Jack, 4, 5, 266
Drummers, 53, 54, 75
Dudley, Gov. Joseph, 104

Earle, Alice Morse, 357, 406 n.
Eccentrics, 59, 287
Eels, 364
Ellis, Moll, 229
Enos, Joe, 207
Enos, Manuel, 259
Epitaphs, 137 n., 594
Evangeline, 265

Fairies, 316, 343
Fairs, 432
Falley, Richard, 39
Felt, Joseph, 407
Field, Darby, 241
Fish and fishermen, 87-93 *passim*, 100, 101, 152-161, 205, 258, 336, 348, 473, 479, 557, 561, 571, 578
Fisher, Dorothy Canfield, 357
Fisk, James, Jr., 550
Fiske, John, 264
Fitch, Elizabeth and Thomas, 273
Flounder, 336
Flowers and weather prognostics, 331, 348
Folk etymology, 234, 248-250, 454
Folk metaphor, 493
Folk speech, 451-522
Forefathers' Day, 476
Fourth of July, 423
Franklin, Benjamin, 75, 263, 266
Freestone State, 240
French and Indian War, 270, 273

ench Canadians, 54, 99, 111, 116, 146, 157, 161, 170, 221, 222, 224, 326, 478, 494
ogs, 183, 193, 349, 571
ost, Mrs. Robert, 403
ller, Margaret, 59
ller, R. H., 550 n.

am, 435, 500
ames, 436-449, singing, 585-588
eorges Bank, 205
eorgia, 76
hosts. *See* Supernatural phenomena.
iant, Indian, 252
oddams, the, 494
offe, 268
oodrich, Samuel G., 358, 408
orbeys, 326
osnold, Captain, 233, 241
ranite State, 240
rant, Ed., 152
raveyard humor, 61, 85, 92, 124
reen Mountain State, 240
uy Fawkes' Day (Pope's Day), 425

aliburton, Thomas Chandler, 5
all, James A., 384
allowe'en, 62, 423
andicrafts, 390, 393, 401
anson, Susan, 553
arris, Israel, 297
arvard University, 253, 522, 581
atch, Thomas, 109
azard, Geoffrey, 137
azard, Jonathan N., 116
azard, Rowland, 137
azard, Sylvester, 119
azard, Thomas B. ("Nailer Tom"), 41
azard, Thomas B. ("Shepherd Tom"), 132, 455
eckewelder, Rev. John Gottlieb, 13, 482
enry, J. E. ("Ave"), 302
eroes, 265-267, 280-313
erring, 83, 369, 473, 578, 593
ewes, Sam, 140
iawatha, 213, 265
ill, George Handel ("Yankee"), 3, 7 n.
ingston, E. P., 60 n.
odskins, Grandma, 262
olbrook, Stewart H., 60 n., 140 n.
olmes, Oliver Wendell, 467, 518
olmes brothers, 590
oosic, 248
oover, Ike, 308
orses and horse trading, 14, 22-29, 52, 103, 282, 295, 304, 305, 306, 346, 433
otten, John Camden, 61
oward, John Tasker, 529
owells, William Dean, 213
owland, Frank, 290
uckleberries, 593
umphrey, Colonel Ebenezer, 43
unters, hunting and trapping, 131-132, 135, 141-152, 297
utchinson Family, 527
yde, Sam, 286
ymns, 237, 526, 536
yperbole, 129-130, 493, 506-511

diom, New England, 459-465, 492-522
ndians, 104-107, 172, 180, 184, 192, 213, 234, 241, 252, 269, 286, 471, 481, 482
nsects, 164, 346-349 *passim*, 434, 598-599 *passim*
ntervale, 455, 472
rish, 46, 202, 343
rving, Washington, 482
ves, Edward, 326 n.

ackson, Andrew, 4
ackson, George Pullen, 526 n.
ackson, George Stuyvesant, 539 n.
efferay, William, 131 n.

Johnson, Burges, 452 n.
Johnson, Edward, 131, 176
Johnson, Jigger, 138
Johnson, Melville, 592 n.
Johnson, Mrs. Clifton, 110, 593 n.
Jonathan. *See* Brother Jonathan.
Jonathanisms, 130 n.
Jonny-cake, 103, 359, 455, 473
Jonny-Cake Papers, The, 132, 357
Josselyn, John, 131, 242
Kemp, "Father" Robert, 527
Kendall, Edward Augustus, 213
Kendall, Richard G., 172
Kidd, Capt., 280-281, 421, 527
Killcow, 455, 474
King, Joe, 259
King Philip's War, 176
Kittredge, George Lyman, 213 n.
Kittredge, Henry G., 489 n.
Krappe, A. H., 264
Krapp, George Philip, 60

Labrador, 170, 399
Lamberton, Captain, 179
Land records, 379
Larcom, Lucy, 393
Lawson, Sam, 59, 129
Ledyard, John, 266
Legends, 175-313 *passim*
Liars, 129-173, 577
"Lining out," 406 n., 526
Lincoln, Joseph C., 60, 61, 92
Liquor, 33, 42, 68, 158, 302
Little Rhody, 240
Livermore, Reverend S. T., 177, 233
Lobster stew, 370, 527
Local characters, 57-129, 233-234
Longfellow, Henry Wadsworth, 213, 265, 518 n.
Lord, Jonas, 137
Loomis, C. Grant, 130 n.
Loups-garous, 215, 221, 222
Lovers' leap, 234
Lowell, James Russell, 5, 59, 61, 129, 518 n., 582, 583
Lumbering and lumbermen, 21, 49-53, 138, 169, 171, 302, 481, 494, 528, 564-570
Lumber State, 240
"Lynn Shoe Worker, The," 468
Maple sugar, 125, 385
Marriage, 74, 107-112, 331-333, 416, 575
Mass delusion and hysteria, 176
Mather, Cotton, 1, 92, 526
Mather, Increase, 131
Maushope, 213, 252
Melville, Herman, 59, 178
Millers, 528, 531, 546
Militia, 427
Mink, 159
Moby Dick, 178
Mooncussers, 455, 474
Morton, Nathaniel, 476
Mosely, Captain, 106
Mother Goose, 592
Moulton, Jonathan, 214, 216
Mount Holyoke College, 474
Mullins, Priscilla, 264, 267, 419
Munching drawer, 476
Mythical animals and birds, 132, 169-173, 190-202
Myths and mythology, 175-253, 265-266, 493-494

Names, apple, 490; personal, 484-488; place, 235-253; ships', 334, 488, 489
Nash, Hon. Lonson, 194
Natives and strangers, 74-85
New Brunswick, 40, 171, 494
New Hampshire Historical Society, 391, 395
Nicknames, 240, 487, 494
Noble, Reverend Seth, 237
Nocake, 363

Norton, Charles Eliot, 582
Nova Scotia, 5, 319, 477 n., 494
Nutmeg State, 240, 494

Old Farmer's Almanack, 317
Old Hundred, 527
Old Put. See Putnam, General Israel.
"Oldtown." See Natick, Mass. Geographical
  Index.
Oxen, 64
Oysters, 593

Paddock, Captain Ichabod, 142
Page, Sewall, 591
Panthers, 146
Patch, Sam, 3
Paul Revere's Ride, 265, 518
Pearson, Edmund Lester, 266 n.
Peavies, 51
Peddlers, 2, 4-5, 16-20, 124, 528
Peters, Rev. Samuel, 131
Peters, Hugh, 244
Phillis, 359, 361
Pigs, 62, 63, 574
Pilchard (pelcher), 493
Pilgrims, 290, 418, 476, 517
Pine-Tree State, 240
Pirates, 280
Place-name stories, 232-253, 491-492, 494
Plattsburg, Battle of, 140
Plum pudding voyage, 88
Pocahontas, 234
Poodic, 495
Portland & Oxford Central Railroad, 491
Portuguese, 207, 422, 487, 493
Pot luck, 478
Powder, 104, 140, 142, 295
Practical jokers, 6, 69
Prince, Reverend Thomas, 181, 477
Pronunciation, Yankee, 455-459
Proverbs and sayings, 357, 494-495, 515-522
Providences and prodigies, 176-189
Pumpkin, 478, 493
Puritans, 57, 59, 61, 176, 236, 266, 418, 421,
  483
Putnam, General Israel ("Old Put"), 270, 271

Quahogs, 227, 365
Quakers, 358, 497
Quarterboards, 488 n.
Quilting, 358, 393

Races, fishermen's, 258
Raccoons, 143
Railroads, 45, 491, 494
Raisings, 358, 382
Rats, 230, 339, 346, 493
Recollections of Olden Times, 358
Regicides, the, 268
Regionalism in Yankee Speech, 452
Reluctant eloquence, 129
Remarkable animal behavior, 158-163
Revere, Paul, 266
Revolutionary War, 3, 143, 185, 204, 273-276,
  393, 536-544
Rhymes and jingles, 591-604
Rich, Captain Richard, 198
Rinehart, 522
Road work, 49, 78, 79
Robinson, Andrew, 479
Robinson, Moses, 301
Robinson, Rowland, 188
Rodman, Tom, 158
Rogers, Will, 312
Royal Society, 178, 193

Sacred cod, 479
St. Christopher, 336
St. Denis, Canada, 222
St. Elmo's fire, 318, 319
St. Ours, Canada, 224
St. Peter, 224

Salt horse, 374, 603
Samplers, 390
Saunders, Sock, 523
Scarborough, Dorothy, 592 n.
Schoolcraft, Henry Rowe, 213, 242
Scott, Captain Martin, 143
Scrimshaw, 401, 502
Sea and sailors, 87-96, 142, 164, 176, 179, 188,
  194, 202, 225, 252, 256-259, 280, 317, 318-326,
  333-337, 350, 369, 374, 396, 399, 401, 434-436,
  459, 470, 473, 474, 476, 479, 480, 481, 488-
  490, 492, 493-494, 496-505, 511, 513, 528-529,
  544, 557-563, 578, 602
Sea's rote, 350
Sea serpents, 132, 177-178, 194
Sewall, Samuel, 420
Shaw, Nathaniel, 43
Shay's Rebellion, 277
Sheep and sheep shearing, 134, 346, 425, 577
Sherman, Jonathan, 238
Ship figureheads, 335
Ships' names, 90, 334, 488, 489
Ships, phantom, 176-177, 179, 188
Shoal Hope, 233, 241
Shoemakers, 134, 526
Shooting, 141-152
Short, Mercy, 214
Shuckburgh, Dr., 273
Signs and Warnings, 318-330
Singing masters, 526
Sisyphean labor, 178, 215
Skimmerton, 415
Skully-jo, 373
Sleigh ride, 430, Nantucket, 135
Slick, Sam, 5, 86
Smith, Captain John, 239 n.
Smith, Seba, 4
Snakes, 178, 192, 193, 196, 296, 337, 355, 554
Soap, 38, 342
Song of Hiawatha, The, 265
Spalding, Jacob, 105
Springfield Mountain, 527
S.S. Pierce, 255
Stackhouse, Archie, 326 n.
Stage-coaches, 53
Standish, Captain Miles, 265, 267
Stark, Molly, 518
Steers, 64
Stoddard, Athanasius, 43
Stone walls, 82, 389
Storekeepers, 5-6, 23, 29-41, 54, 55, 113, 163
Stowe, Harriet Beecher, 59
Stranger's fire, 399
Strong, John, 131, 135
Strong men, 132, 135-141
Stuart, Jeb, 591
Supernatural phenomena, 175-212, 315-356;
  devils, 212-232, 252, 255, 415, 588; haunts and
  haunted houses, 61, 320-330, 343; storm-rais-
  ing witches, 225, 231; witches, 214-215, 225-
  232, 342; witch-weavers, 227; wizards, 230,
  231. See also Ships, Phantom.
Superstitions, 316-356
Surveying, 237, 379
Symptom books, 90

Tall talk, 130
Tall tales, 129-173
Tandy, Jeannette, 60 n.
Tarrying, 413
Tautog, 158
Taverns, 5-6, 75, 301
Taylor, Father, 511, 525
Temple, Sam, 29
Tennessee, 18
Thanksgiving, 418
Thomas, Seth, 469
Thompson, Harold W., 501 n.
Thompson, Zadock, 295
Thomson, Captain Joseph, 238
Thoreau, Henry D., 59, 132
Toads, 354

Tonics, 352
Towner, 480
Town meetings, 427
Trade. *See* Peddlers, Storekeepers.
Traditions, historical, 264
Travelers. *See* Natives and strangers.
Travelers' tales, 131
Trumbull, Jonathan, 274, 455
Twain, Mark, 60, 518
Tyler, Royall, 3

Uncle Sam, 4
Underhill, Abraham, 107

Van Dyke, George, 50, 51, 99
Veazie, Ola G., 452 n.
Vergoose, Elizabeth, 592
Verrill, A. Hyatt, 401 n.
Very poor man's dinner, 372
Vorse, Mary Heaton, 317

Waban, Thomas, 107
Walker, Tom, 214
Wall, Fanny, 300
Ward, Artemus (Charles Farrar Browne), 60
Warner, Seth, 295
Warnings. *See* Signs and warnings.
War of 1812, 140, 529, 544
Washington, George, 7, 274
Weather, 81, 131, 132, 205, 344-351, 495, 499;
    fog, 87, 168, 169, 323; predictions, 344-351;
    rain, 65, 97; rhymes, 599, 600, 602; snow, 81;
    storms, 126, 226; thunder, 133; wind, 99,
    499, 600, 602, 603
Weaving, 228
Webster, Daniel, 266, 368, 454
Webster, Noah, 482

Weed, Abigail, 340
Whales, whaling, and whalemen, 88-90, 91, 135,
    142, 178, 199, 285, 375, 480, 496-503, 519, 557
Whalley, 268
Wheeler, William A., 592
White, George, 282
Whitman, Walt, 453
Whittier, John G., 177, 219, 265, 316
Wildcats, 139
Willey Slide, the, 20
Williams, Abiel, 103
Williams, Roger, 239, 247
Winslow, Gov. Edward, 105
Winthrop, Governor John, of Connecticut, 250;
    of Massachusetts, 420
Witches. *See* Supernatural phenomena.
Wolves, 271
Wood, 30, 86
Woodchuck, 134
Wooden nutmegs, 1, 16, 240, 495
Wooden oats, 18
Wreckers, 94, 100, 474
Wright, Ephraim, 261

Yankee, 482
Yankees, and Englishmen, 7-15; and Indians,
    104-107; and strangers, 74-85; as heroes, 265-
    267; clever and foolish, 113-129; comic, 3, 59;
    curious, 75, 82; diligent, 59, 112; droll, 59;
    eloquent, 60, 129; fabulous, 1-173; sharp, 4-5,
    16-57; stubborn, 74-87; tricky, 16-57; witty,
    59-61
Yankee Doodle, 3, 7, 273, 529
Yankeeisms, 152-192
Yarns. *See* Tall tales.
Yorkshiremen 3, 13-15

GEOGRAPHICAL INDEX

STATES, CITIES, AND COUNTIES
    CONNECTICUT
Bozrah, 237
Brooklyn, 433
Canaan, 109
Centerbrook, 287
Clinton, 287
Colchester, 102, 421
East Canaan, 109
East Haddam, 180
Groton, 279
Haddam, 247
Hartford, 182, 271, 409, 441
Litchfield, 409
Lyme, 108
Millington, 214
Moodus, 180
New Haven, 176, 179, 240
Newington, 108
New London, 108, 182, 250,
    290
Norwalk, 273
Pomfret, 271
Salem, 271
Suffield, 403
Thomaston, 405, 469, 517
Windham, 177, 183
Windham County, 288

    MAINE
Aroostook County, 104, 169,
    438
Bangor, 104, 170, 237
Blue Hill, 396
Brunswick, 410
Cobbossee, 231
Enfield, 594

Georgetown, 594
Greenville, 160
Hallowell, 231
Kittery, 215, 225
Loudon Hill, 231
Milford, 146
Minot, 491
Monhegan, 418
Naples, 259
Old Town, 104, 145, 171
Penobscot, 284
Penobscot County, 169
Piscataquis County, 169
Poland, 115
Portland, 4, 34, 277
Pownalboro, 231
Searsport, 33
Taniscot, 260
Wayne, 137, 138
York, 225, 410
York Beach, 439

    MASSACHUSETTS
Alford, 98
Andover, 410
Ashfield, 115
Auburn, 245
Barnstable, 109, 257, 466, 489
Barnstable County, 100
Barre, 238
Bedford, 495
Beverly, 185, 251
Billerica, 495, 521
Boston, 10, 11, 17, 33, 57, 75,
    95, 114, 101, 198, 237, 253-
    256, 258, 273, 275, 280, 303,
    339, 345, 391, 407, 420, 423,

429, 443, 454, 491, 495, 511,
    519, 592
Brimfield, 408
Cambridge, 185
Canton, 238
Chappaquiddick, 252
Chatham, 84, 88, 256, 494
Chicopee, 47
Cohasset, 1
Dedham, 29
Digby, 256
Dover, 247
Dudley, 32, 112, 423, 449
Eastham, 88, 257
Egremont, 98
Essex, 205
Falmouth, 84
Farmington, 554 n.
Framingham, 247
Gloucester, 177, 194, 206, 258,
    319, 479, 593
Goshen, 97
Great Barrington, 275
Hadley, 268, 407, 415
Hancock, 274
Harwich, 256
Haverhill, 186
Holden, 238
Ipswich, 177, 185
Lexington, 185
Longmeadow, 407
Ludlow, 62
Lynn, 468
Malden, 281
Manchester, 251
Marblehead, 278
Marlborough, 108

Marshfield, 32
Medfield, 247
Medford, 406, 407
Middleboro, 228
Middlesex County, 406
Mingo Beach, 251
Nantasket Beach, 471
Natick, 59, 428
New Bedford, 88, 91
Newbury, 185, 410
Newburyport, 41, 187, 284, 425
Northampton, 43, 269, 311, 494
Northfield, 281
North Weymouth, 43
"Oldtown." *See* Natick.
Orleans, 256, 257
Osterville, 466
Plymouth, 105, 227, 390 n., 418, 476, 595
Provincetown, 88, 89, 256, 258, 259, 336, 344, 373, 422, 487, 489, 593
Quabbin, 456, 480, 485
Rochester, 228
Salem, 95, 212, 335
Salisbury, 186
Saugus, 62
Siasconset 489, 513
Southampton, 355
South Hadley, 414, 593
Springfield, 275
Taunton, 83
Turner's Falls, 51
Truro, 87, 99, 100, 132, 256, 399, 470, 480, 486, 593
Tyringham, 275
Walpole, 10
Ward, 245
Wareham, 228
Washington, 103
Watertown, 246
Wellfleet, 492, 522, 527, 593
Westborough, 281
Westfield, 233
West Pittsfield, 45
Weymouth, 42, 593
Wilbraham, 44, 54, 554 n.
Wilmington, 465
Woburn, 31
Worcester, 245
Yarmouth, 101

NEW HAMPSHIRE
Alstead, 44, 62, 71, 72, 73, 85, 262, 355, 379, 384
Alton, 68
Berlin, 139
Boscawen, 382, 383
Bow, 395
Brookfield, 552
Cheshire County, 29, 379, 474
Concord, 383
Dublin, 467
East Sandwich, 340
Exeter, 187
Francestown, 391
Gilsum, 30
Gorham, 173, 243
Hancock, 25
Henniker, 203
Johnson Village, 306
Keene, 14, 72
Lancaster, 82, 243
Langdon, 61, 62, 64, 65, 66, 76
Littleton, 43, 116, 123, 237
Manchester, 391, 479
Mascoma, 33
Mont Vernon, 382

Newcastle, 425
North Walpole, 63, 67, 68, 69, 70
Pittsburg, 382
Portsmouth, 38, 39, 55, 57, 217, 318, 425, 442, 460
Sandown, 382
Shelburne, 394
Somersworth, 395
South Ackworth, 53, 61, 64, 71, 73, 74, 142
Stoddard, 590
Tioga, 147
Walpole, 11, 12, 13
Washington, 103, 269
West Concord, 383
Whitefield, 30
Wilton, 382
Zealand, 303

RHODE ISLAND
Exeter, 416 n.
Four Corners, 119
Hopkinton, 417
Kingston, 127
Middletown, 213
Narragansett, 41, 119, 127, 154, 158, 188, 357, 359, 361, 364, 416, 473, 527
Newport, 189, 593
North Kingston, 416
Peace Dale, 137
Providence, 11, 359, 399
Rehoboth, 399
South Kingston, 416
Westerly, 110, 276, 417
Woonsocket, 222, 224

VERMONT
Addison, 135
Arlington, 297
Barre, 238
Bellows Falls, 47, 49, 69
Bennington, 274, 297, 543
Brattleboro, 22
Charlotte, 296
Enosburgh, 35
Fairlee, 140
Fayetteville, 261
Hardwick, 291
Middebury, 117
Monkton, 83
Montpelier, 164
Newfane, 261
Northfield, 155
Rutland, 295
South Fairlee, 140
Springfield, 261
Sunderland, 297, 520
Wildersburgh, 238
Williston, 295, 563
Windham County, 29, 261, 379

MOUNTAINS, HILLS, ROCKS, AND CLIFFS
Becky's Ridge, 251
Berkshires, The, 97, 103, 274, 277, 478
Carter Dome, 139
Crawford Notch, 20
Franconia Notch, 243
Green Mountains, 35, 242, 243, 453
Lovel Mountain, 269
McSparran Hill, 188
Mill Rock, 232
Monument Mountain, 110
Mt. Chocorua, 139
Mt. Madison, 140
Mt. Tom, 51

Mt. Washington, 241 n., 243
Pinkham Notch, 139
Purgatory, 213
Sampson's Hill, 252
White Mountains, 173, 241, 242

ISLANDS
Block Island, 94, 188
Clark's Island, 281
Grand Manan Island, 251
Isle of Shoals, 96, 318, 414
Martha's Vineyard, 89, 122, 213, 252, 371
Nantucket, 40, 90, 113, 127, 135, 142, 365, 401, 425, 447, 459, 489, 496, 499, 503, 513, 571
Plum Island, 186
Ram Island, 186
Thatcher's Island, 211
Vinalhaven, 57

RIVERS, BROOKS, LAKES, AND PONDS
Allegash Lake, 171
Androscoggin River, 139, 394
Blackberry River, 109
Bride Brook, 108, 250
Chapman Falls, 214
Chauncey's Creek, 226
Cold Pond, 147
Connecticut Lake, 51
Connecticut River, 129, 141, 246, 415, 454, 472
Elbow Lake, 306
Grand Lake, 160
Grand Lake Stream, 159
Israel's River, 243
Kennebec River, 172, 231
Lake Champlain, 295
Lake Charcogg-Etc.-Maugg, 247
Lemon Fair River, 250
Merrimac River, 186
Middlesex Canal, 465
Moodus River, 182
Moosehead Lake, 170
Mopang Stream, 236
Penobscot River, 242, 564 n.
Quonectacut River, 239
Rangely Lakes, 171
River of Pines, 239
Saco River, 243
Salmon River, 182
Webster Lake, 247

BAYS AND HARBORS
Bay of Fundy, 324
Block Island Sound, 177
Buzzard's Bay, 100, 227
Loblolly Cove, 196
Long Island Sound, 195
Massachusetts Bay, 199
Pamet Harbor, 87
York Harbor, 226

HEADLANDS, CAPES, AND POINTS
Boston Neck, 137
Cape Ann, 194 n., 529
Cape Cod, 75, 84, 87, 90, 92, 93, 99, 100, 233, 241, 256, 258, 277, 290, 323, 324, 369, 437, 454, 455, 466, 468, 470, 474, 479, 484, 488, 492, 493, 494, 578, 594. *See also* individual towns.
Point Judith, 189, 249
Skull Head, 471